Aspen's Fundraising Series for the

Strategic Fund Development

Building Profitable Relationships That Last

Second Edition

Aspen's Fundraising Series for the 21st Century

Aspen's Fundraising Series for the 21st Century

Strategic Fund Development

Building Profitable Relationships That Last

Second Edition

Simone P. Joyaux, ACFRE
Principal
Joyaux Associates
Foster, Rhode Island

AN ASPEN PUBLICATION®
Aspen Publishers, Inc.
Gaithersburg, Maryland
2001

Library of Congress Cataloging-in-Publication Data

Joyaux, Simone P.
Strategic fund development: building profitable relationships that last / Simone P. Joyaux.—2nd ed.
p. cm.—(Aspen's fundraising series for the 21st century)
Includes bibliographical references and index.
ISBN 0-8342-1898-4
1. Fundraising. I. Title. II. Series.
HG177 .J69 2001
658.15′224—dc21
00-068263

Orders: (800) 638-8437
Customer Service: (800) 234-1660

About Aspen Publishers • For more than 40 years, Aspen has been a leading professional publisher in a variety of disciplines. Aspen's vast information resources are available in both print and electronic formats. We are committed to providing the highest quality information available in the most appropriate format for our customers. Visit Aspen's Internet site for more information resources, directories, articles, and a searchable version of Aspen's full catalog, including the most recent publications: **www.aspenpublishers.com**
  Aspen Publishers, Inc. • The hallmark of quality in publishing
  Member of the worldwide Wolters Kluwer group

Editorial Services: Nora McElfish
Library of Congress Catalog Card Number: 00-068263
ISBN: 0-8342-1898-4

Printed in the United States of America

1 2 3 4 5

Table of Contents

Foreword

In this second edition of her cogent and popular *Strategic Fund Development*, Simone P. Joyaux, ACFRE, writes that "visioning is a lively process of sharing what people most care about in a way that creates enthusiasm and shared commitment, a collective sense of what matters to the organization and its participants. . . . Your organization's vision is a snapshot of your desired future." Another contemporary observer of organizational planning and leadership, Joel Barker, author and futurist, offers a prescription for organizations of all kinds, from governments to multinationals, and from highly endowed universities to grassroots not-for-profit agencies:

- Organizations with vision are powerfully enabled.
- Organizations without vision are at risk.

Simone Joyaux provides those of us who labor in the vineyards of the philanthropic sector with invaluable tools and concepts for translating organizational vision into reality. As one who has enjoyed the privilege of being a colleague of Simone's in various venues, I view this volume as but one more component of the innumerable contributions she has made to not-for-profit organizations and their stakeholders over the past quarter century.

A foreword is probably not the place to summarize the key points of a book. But three of the central messages in this volume are so critical to a proper perspective of the philanthropic sector that they warrant highlighting:

1. Success in securing philanthropic gifts is not the result of mastering techniques, deploying the latest technology, or enjoying the most hallowed tradition. Simply stated, successful philanthropic fundraising is the product of the intentional, strategic, and consistent building and nurturing of relationships with an ever-expanding pool of stakeholders.
2. "No organization can survive on mission and vision alone."
3. Even as the practice of fundraising is emerging as a true and recognized profession, volunteers remain critical to the fundraising process and to the validation of the legitimacy of not-for-profit organizations.

Too much of the literature available in the field today gives scant attention to those three essential paradigms. Yet they constitute the very heart and soul of Simone Joyaux's writing.

It has been my privilege to work closely with Simone Joyaux in recent years: as fellow members of two boards of directors—the Association of Fundraising Professionals (AFP), formerly the National Society of Fund Raising Executives (NSFRE), and the CFRE Professional Certification Board—and as fellow faculty members in the Saint Mary's University of Minnesota M.A. in Philanthropy & Development program. In every venue—as well as in this book—she gives evidence of her limitless commitment to advancing the field of philanthropy. She is a true steward of philanthropy.

Tim J. Burchill, CFRE
President, The Metanoia Group
Executive Director, Hendrickson Institute for
Ethical Leadership
Founder and Senior Faculty, Saint Mary's University of
Minnesota M.A. in Philanthropy & Development
Winona, Minnesota

Preface

Welcome to the second edition of this book. It's been a rewarding experience: hearing your comments about the first edition, exploring new readings myself, and once again putting thought to paper.

Because so many of you asked for it, I've included a new chapter on creating a fund development plan. Several clients kindly agreed to share their plans here.

There's more information about leadership and more writing tips. There's a new section on building a culture of philanthropy in your organization. I've also added more examples in each chapter, including resources that you can use and modify for your own organization.

In the preface to the first edition, I said this was a book about fund development. I'm not so sure now. In the end, I think this is a book about organizations and their cultures. And that means that this is a book about organizational development, too.

I'd like to share a story with you. It moved me deeply. It's from *Clicks and Mortar*, by David S. Pottruck and Terry Pearce. This story—as well as their book—is all about organizations and their cultures.

Let your imagination put you in a grandstand at the Seattle version of the Special Olympics. There are nine contestants, all physically or mentally disabled, assembled at the starting line for the 100-yard dash. At the gun, they all start out, not exactly in a dash, but with a relish to run the race to the finish and win. All, that is, except one boy who stumbles on the asphalt, tumbles over a couple of times, and begins to cry. The other eight hear the boy cry. They slow down and look back. They all turn around and go back…every one of them. As you watch, one girl with Down's syndrome bends down and kisses him. You hear her say, "This will make it better." All nine link arms and walk across the finish line together. Everyone in the stadium, including you, stands up, and the cheering goes on for several minutes.

People who were actually there are still telling the story, four years later. Why? Because, deep down, we know this one thing: What matters in this life is more than winning for ourselves. What truly matters in this life is helping others win, even if it means changing our own course (Pottruck and Pearce 2000, 245).

When I read this story, I didn't think about philanthropy and the valuable work that Special Olympics and the millions of not-for-profit organizations do every day. I didn't think about the wonder of a great development officer finding the right donor for a cause.

Yes, all that is true. But what I thought about was the group culture among those contestants. I thought about the values that they share. I thought: "I want to work in a place where people treat each other like that, where people go back for each other and cross the line together."

Strategic Fund Development is, finally, a book about organizations and their cultures. This is a book about the values we have and the choices we make as individuals and organizations. And it's a book about our willingness and capacity as professionals to adopt an organizational development approach to our work.

My values generated the four relationships that I describe here. My experience produced my perspective on fundraisers as technicians and organizational development specialists. Each day, I must reaffirm my values—and I hope that I nurture these four relationships. Every day, I contribute to some organization and its culture—and I can only hope that my contribution is positive.

And for those of you who want a book about fund development, I think this will work for you, too. This book isn't about fundraising, the tactics of constructing campaigns and asking for gifts. Instead, this book talks about fund development as the process that allows not-for-profit philanthropic organizations to effectively seek charitable gifts and continuously engage loyal supporters. The process of fund development provides the opportunity to bring people together and "build community," in John Gardner's sense of the phrase.

Bob Payton defines philanthropy as "voluntary action for the common good." I heard Mexican philanthropist

Don Manuel Arango Arias talk about philanthropy as "freeing the talent of the citizenry." Hank Rosso described fundraising as the servant of philanthropy.

I'll combine them all. Philanthropy is voluntary action for the common good. The not-for-profit philanthropic structure is the mechanism that frees the talent of people by organizing their caring acts. And fund development serves philanthropy by providing a process to generate gifts to support the common good.

Fund development is about much more than asking for money. Sure, fund development includes solicitation strategies, response rates, case statements, volunteer management, and asking for money. But fund development is about everything else in the organization first. And it's the rest of the stuff that's so challenging and often messy.

Just think about it. Is your organization sufficiently relevant to the community to justify asking for gifts? How effective is your organization at fostering relationships with diverse constituencies? How well does your staff empower volunteers to do the best they can? What about the values and leadership within your organization? How about your organization's decision making?

This is all organizational development work. It's complex and complicated. It involves conversation and disagreement and process, process, process. Organizational development involves people and their relationships. And all this can get darned messy!

Quite simply, we cannot raise charitable contributions unless we focus on organizational development, too. And I don't think fund development or fundraisers focus on organizational development enough.

I worry, and I'm frustrated. But I'm also optimistic. I admire and respect fundraising volunteers and professionals. I hope that, together, we can strengthen fund development.

Throughout this book—both the first and second editions—I refer mostly to authors outside the fund development field. I learn more and more about fund development by looking beyond it.

So back to the beginning. This book is about organizations, their cultures, and their development. I think we need to change the way we do fund development within our organizations. I think we need to change the way we build our organizations, paying more attention to the four relationships that I define in this book.

Why bother? Because the reward is an organization and constituents who react like the contestants in the Seattle stadium. Because the reward is organizational survival. And, finally, because the reward is strong philanthropic organizations that make a difference in their communities.

REFERENCE

Pottruck, D.S. and T. Pearce. 2000. *Clicks and Mortar: Passion Driven Growth in an Internet World.* San Francisco: Jossey-Bass, Publishers.

Acknowledgments

Just like we say when recognizing donors, "This book was made possible by the generous contributions of many."

Thanks to my clients, from whom I have learned and continue to learn so much.

And a special thanks to the individuals who reviewed and, in some cases, offered detailed edits to parts of this book, either the first or second editions.

Tom Ahern, ABC, Ahern Communications, Ink., Rhode Island (As my business associate—and life partner—Tom read the entire manuscript for the first edition, then read all the revised sections and additions for this second edition.)

Judith Beckman, Rhode Island

Sarah C. Coviello, CFRE, Coviello and Associates, Washington, D.C.

Doris Stearn Donovan, Consultant on organizational matters, Rhode Island

Susan Davies Goepp, CFRE, Vice President of University Relations, Oakland University, Michigan

Carol Karsch, Executive Director, Jewish Community Foundation of Southern Arizona

Andrea Kihlstedt, The Kihlstedt Group, Pennsylvania

Ellen L. Livingston, Missouri

Dr. Elizabeth A. McAuliffe, R.S.M., President, St. Mary Academy—Bay View, Rhode Island

J. Russell Raker III, ACFRE, California

Joan Ress Reeves, Rhode Island

Jennifer Stavrou Rodine, Massachusetts

Susan Rittscher, President and CEO, YMCA of Greater Providence, Rhode Island

Dennis Stefanacci, ACFRE, Senior Vice President for Philanthropy, Intracoastal Health Systems, Inc., Florida

Chapter 1

Positioning Your Organization To Survive— The Four Relationships That Are Critical to Effective and Productive Fund Development

ARE YOU SLOWLY GOING OUT OF BUSINESS?

Traditional organizations have lost their way. They no longer hear the 'voices' of their various constituents and markets. They are unable to accumulate the kinds of knowledge and information they need in order to perform effectively. They are no longer in touch with their members' emotional needs. They no longer channel their organizational resources and energy toward their operations in an optimal way. And, for the most part, they no longer have a vision of their place in society and the larger world. As a result, many modern organizations are adrift in a sea of complexity, frustration, and change.

Ian I. Mitroff, Richard O. Mason, and
Christine M. Pearson

What are the questions that effective not-for-profit organizations ask themselves?

- Do we have a vision, and is it shared by staff, board, and volunteers?
- Are we unique enough to make a difference and attract dollars?
- If contributions are slowing down, what is it about our organization that is failing to find an audience?
- What could we do to attract more volunteers?
- Do community leaders see how my organization is different from others?
- Does my agency focus only on the bottom-line financial goal or do we see the bigger picture?
- Is collaboration frustrating and merger or acquisition threatening?

- Does my board regularly discuss the implications of trends and the consequences of possible choices?
- Are we constantly ensuring that our organization is relevant?
- Does our fundraising leadership (staff and/or consultant) insist that we address organizational development issues as part of improving fund development?

What are the questions that effective fundraisers ask?

- Do I help my organization ask the right questions?
- Do I know enough about organizational development and the marketplace to help in areas that are not fundraising-specific? For example, do I know the newest strategies for recruiting, training, and enabling board members? Can I facilitate consensus decision making and negotiate conflict? Can I develop community collaborations?
- When I meet with my fundraising colleagues, do we discuss what can be learned from new business theory? Do we discuss community needs and collaborative ways to respond? Do we talk about managing change?

Answering questions like these honestly is only part of the challenge. Just as important is learning to ask the right questions, teasing out all the implications of each question, and nurturing a culture of learning throughout the organization.

Changing the Way We Do Fund Development

Modern fund development is more than a set of strategies and techniques designed to get quick gifts. Yet most organizations value short-term, bottom-line contributions over the long-term returns made possible by building relationships. Boards focus on the cost to raise the charitable dollar. Development professionals spend lots of time pursuing the best direct mail letter, the right special event, and the newest phonathon tactic.

> *Your organization will survive if it develops the four key relationships.*

This short-term approach is necessary but not sufficient to ensure your organization's continued health. An organization moving full speed ahead into the next millennium will need to develop four relationships.

1. Its relationship with itself. The task: creating the holistic infrastructure (culture and systems) that produces a healthy enterprise.
2. Its relationship with the community. The task: using strategic planning to ensure relevance and define marketplace position.
3. Its relations with its constituents. The task: developing and strengthening relationships with individuals and groups so they are ready to be asked and asked for more.
4. Its relationship with its volunteers. The task: carrying out the functions that enable volunteers to take meaningful action on behalf of the organization.

Finding Our Way in the Twenty-First Century

Too many not-for-profits trade upon the presumed value of their missions and the bold implicit statement that "we do good." Indeed, most not-for-profit organizations *do* do good work for their communities.

But to continue and flourish, not-for-profits need to understand their constituents better and create lasting value for them. In a sense, your constituents—your community, your donors and volunteers, the people (or animals or places) you serve—are your shareholders.

Look at your own organization. Begin by asking the questions presented throughout this book. Identify other questions that will challenge your organization to think.

Make sure you develop the four relationships essential to create a healthy institution (Exhibit 1–1): internal, community, constituents, and volunteers. Together, these relationships will produce more philanthropic dollars and long-term organizational health.

PHILANTHROPY BUILDS COMMUNITIES

Since the beginning of time, in every society and in all cultures, human beings have cared for each other. People, as individuals or gathered together in groups,

Exhibit 1–1 The Four Relationships That Ensure Organizational Survival and Health

1. **Your internal relationship** creates the holistic infrastructure that produces a healthy enterprise.

   Your internal relations provide the foundation for all your work, allowing you to develop the other three relationships. Steps include: agreeing on shared values and creating both a corporate culture and systems that reflect those values, ensuring individual and team learning, encouraging dialogue and shared decision making, rewarding critical thinking, welcoming pluralism, and accepting uncertainty and complexity.

2. **Your relationship with the community** ensures your organization's continued relevance and clarifies its marketplace position.

   This relationship is developed through ongoing strategic planning and its implementation. It rewards learning while doing. Steps include: identifying and responding to a community need, finding the most appropriate and effective ways to work with your community to meet its needs and wants, eliminating redundant services and organizations, and regularly testing your mission.

3. **Your relationship with constituents** develops and strengthens connections with individuals and groups so that when you ask, they are ready to respond and respond again.

   It is difficult to overestimate the importance of constituency development. Steps include: identifying and getting to know the interests and needs of your constituents, finding the most appropriate and effective ways to communicate with and to cultivate them, engaging constituents more fully with your organization, evaluating their capacity to participate, determining their readiness to be asked, selecting the appropriate asker, designing the appropriate request, and asking and asking again for more.

4. **Your relationship with volunteers** enables them to take meaningful action on behalf of your organization.

   Volunteers expect to be adequately supported and involved. Steps include: understanding and valuing the concept of enabling; recognizing the functions that are essential to support volunteers; recruiting staff who possess the skills, attitude, and knowledge to enable others to work effectively; and evaluating staff performance accordingly.

voluntarily reach out to help others. This is philanthropy, described by Robert L. Payton, former executive director of the Indiana University Center on Philanthropy, as "voluntary action for the common good."

Philanthropic Organizations Help Build Communities

John Gardner (1991) writes eloquently about the human need for community and the individual role in building community. One way the individual gains a sense of self is through continuous relationships with others.

Community can confer a sense of belonging, and your organization can tap into this fundamental need. Belonging includes a recognition of mutual responsibility for the community and to its members. The individual supports the community through allegiance, commitment, and action. The healthy community (Exhibit 1–2) nurtures its members and provides a secure environment for growing. This community establishes expectations and standards wherein great things can happen.

However, this mutual responsibility often wavers. Many people feel alienated, disenfranchised, and contemptuous of society's failures. These individuals reject the community's attempts to strengthen itself and isolate themselves, accepting no responsibility for the community's health. As Gardner observes, "no society can survive such abandonment by its members" (Gardner 1991, 10). Instead, what is needed is an "active nurturing and rebuilding of community—in a spirit that honors both continuity and renewal" (page 9).

Communities have both needs and wants. Needs include the daily basics: food and shelter, education and employment, safety and health. Wants reflect the person's values and are often expressed through art, faith, and other means, such as a commitment to the environment.

Exhibit 1–2 Gardner's 10 Attributes That Define Community

1. Wholeness which incorporates diversity: sharing a common purpose while welcoming different ideas and interests
2. Reasonable base of shared values: sharing some core values and actively defending this common ground (possibly the most important attribute of community)
3. Caring, trust and teamwork: creating a humane and respectful climate that accepts all individuals so together we can accomplish group purpose
4. Effective internal communication: communicating freely and honestly with one another
5. Participation: ensuring that there are leaders at every level and in every segment of the community; welcoming individuals and making sure they have a role to play
6. Affirmation: building the community's morale through continuous reaffirmation
7. Links beyond the community: reaching out to other communities, maintaining open, constructive and extensive relations with the world beyond
8. Development of young people: enabling one's young people to develop fully, preparing them for future roles, instilling shared values, fostering commitment to shared purpose, and teaching them to preserve and renew the community's heritage
9. Forward view: identifying where uncertainty, complexity and change will take the community
10. Institutional arrangements for community maintenance: developing the formal and informal infrastructures which maintain community

NOTE: Use Gardner's attributes as a checklist to help write your next case statement or fundraising letter. Focus on these points and you will have a strong case.

Source: Reprinted with permission from J.W. Gardner, *Building Community*, © 1991, Independent Sector.

Taking Action

Where people recognize and are moved by wants and needs, not-for-profit organizations (also called non-governmental organizations) are often created to help. What makes these organizations different from for-profit and government agencies is not only legal and regulatory restrictions and governance requirements, but the institution's real sense of mission in responding to the community.

And—at least superficially—what really makes them different is that they seek contributions. The process of seeking charitable contributions is called *philanthropic fund development*, only one component of which is fundraising, the art of asking. See Appendix A for components of fund development.

The truth is, philanthropy is similar in many respects to other kinds of marketing, as discussed later in this book. Philanthropic organizations are the link to fulfill donor interest and aspiration and the bridge to address community needs and wants. This is the mutually beneficial exchange.

Challenging Philanthropy

It's a simple formula that governs philanthropy: As community needs and wants increase and as the cost of providing services grows, more charitable giving is required. Yet studies show that current giving may not be able to keep up with the demand, and uncompetitive organizations will fail.

Organizations and their fundraisers are right to wonder:

- Is there really an ever-increasing number of donors from which we can expect ever-increasing dollars?
- Can we secure more volunteers to reach out to more prospects?
- Can we retain the loyalty of our donors?
- How do we make fund development decisions that best use the strengths and talents of our staff and volunteers?

> To make [healthy communities] possible, we shall first have to rehabilitate the idea of commitments beyond the self. . . . Passive allegiance isn't enough today. The forces of disintegration have gained steadily and will prevail unless individuals see themselves as having a positive duty to nurture their community.
>
> *John Gardner*

Organizations also worry about the political climate and the actions of governments on the local, national, and global levels. Charitable contributions cannot compensate for the dramatic reduction in government financing of community services.

Research and experience clearly indicate that there are more prospective donors out there, in every community. Studies report that the reason many people do not give is because they have never been asked. More good news, reports also say that some people would give more if they were asked to do so.

To reach these prospective donors, organizations need the relationships described in this book. Moreover, organizations (both staff and volunteers) must reflect the diversity in their communities, especially gender and ethnicity. Many don't. This mismatch with changing demographics isolates an organization from its community.

Effective organizations and fundraisers can generate more charitable contributions. The audience of donors is not decreasing. Develop the four relationships, and you can build an organization that reaches a diverse community and continues to earn support.

NO MORE ENTITLEMENT

The halcyon days of unquestioning respect for not-for-profit organizations are past. For decades, communities viewed not-for-profit organizations with awe. Here were grouped all the kind and caring, the wise and far-seeing. Philanthropic missions and values were held higher than other community activities. Operations and activities were above reproach.

Much good was accomplished, and most not-for-profits earned respect and deserved awe. But we may be losing the edge we worked so hard to gain.

It turns out that not-for-profits, just like for-profits and government, can all too easily have feet of clay. Some not-for-profits follow unworthy missions, manage inadequately, and fight change. Others disregard general community needs and abuse power. Myopia stops many organizations from identifying ways to collaborate, merge, or close because of duplicated services or limited relevance. Too many organizations perpetuate weak boards and executive directors who don't have the right skills and knowledge. A handful of organizations actually act improperly and illegally, although some probably don't realize they are doing so. The volunteer and financial needs of all these organizations drain the community of energy, focus, time, and money.

Increased Scrutiny

The world has changed and will continue to change. People grow increasingly skeptical as they are bombarded by message after message—each sincere, each importuning. People no longer assume that all not-for-profits are necessary and do good. Consider the following shifts in attitude.

> To believe that whatever we do is a moral cause, and should be pursued whether there are results or not, is a perennial temptation for non-profit executives—and even more for their boards. But even if the cause itself is a moral cause, the specific way it is pursued better have results.
>
> *Peter Drucker*

Your Donors

Your donors receive more requests for support than ever before. Now they are more discerning. They expect more from you, and you need to understand what their expectations are. Communications must be stronger (not necessarily louder) so that your request can be distinguished from others. Beware: Strong relationships with major donors alone will not be enough. The level of intimacy between your organization and all your donors will be the key to success.

It's harder to secure a gift of time or money. Even donors of the smallest gifts can ask a lot of questions about your organization and their involvement.

- Do I know this organization well enough to give, to give again, to give more?

- Does the organization know me well enough to have asked me for the right thing?
- How does this cause compare to my other interests?
- Does this organization meet my priorities?
- Is this request appropriate to my level of interest, readiness, and capacity to give?
- How well would giving to this organization meet my personal needs?
- Is this organization relevant and well managed?

Your Operations

Constituents are increasingly intolerant of mediocrity in any area of operation, be it your service or the way you manage and govern. Quality service and effective management and governance are expected.

Effective not-for-profit organizations innovate. They seek out and apply appropriate new business theories to their operations. And they design and maintain an infrastructure—corporate culture and systems—that provides for ongoing renewal.

Although they sometimes lead in the development of products and services, not-for-profits often lag behind in business management. Some not-for-profits reject management theory as suspicious or compromising, unfit for philanthropic organizations. Others embrace new theories wholeheartedly, then abandon them too quickly in favor of the next fad.

Your Relevance

Organizations must have missions that respond to contemporary community needs and desires, and must clearly communicate relevancy. Effective organizations test their missions regularly. Those institutions with only marginal value to the community will likely close because people will not volunteer or give enough.

Your Volunteers

Good directions and personal follow-up with volunteers are not by themselves enough to produce the level of action required to move an organization forward. Volunteers—certainly those involved in your organization's governance and fund development—expect much more support from staff. These staff must be good enablers.

The Government

All levels of government around the world are scrutinizing the not-for-profit sector. Legislative and regulatory bodies debate public policy and take more action than ever before. Some of this scrutiny is unjustified and the actions inappropriate. Regardless, not-for-profits need to cope with both the scrutiny and the results.

With no more entitlement, life is much more difficult. Now, more than ever, your organization will benefit if you develop the four relationships central to effective and productive fund development.

HOW WE FUNDRAISE TODAY

Most not-for-profits recognize how critical fund development is to the organization. Nonetheless, fund development is often isolated from other operations. Many staff and volunteers do not understand how intertwined fund development is with the overall organizational system.

Isolating Fundraisers and Fund Development

Sometimes, fundraising consultants and development staff choose to stay away from the rest of the institution. Other times, organizations deliberately keep fundraisers at arm's length from other areas of operation. Consider the following.

Fund Development Activities

Traditional fund development practice states that an organization requires three things to produce dollars: case, prospects, and volunteers. Too often, the fundraisers stop here. They focus on case, prospects, and volunteers to meet the short-term financial goal. They don't help the organization develop the four relationships that strengthen fund development.

Specifically:

- Instead of helping the organization define its relationship to the community, development merely prepares the fundraising case by drawing from the organization's mission and program.
- Rather than ensure good relations with all the organization's constituents, fundraisers focus on donor prospects.
- Development identifies, recruits, and provides logistical support to fundraising volunteers rather, than enabling them.
- Rarely does the fundraiser help develop the organization's internal relations because this seems to be the responsibility of the chief executive and board.

Fundraising Problems

When an organization asks "Why isn't fundraising working?" it's generally something else in the institution that isn't working first.

Fundraising problems generally stem from your organization's internal relations and your relationships with the community, your constituents, and volunteers.

For example, you may lack fundraising volunteers because your board has not been properly recruited and trained. Or volunteers may not sell tickets to your special event because the event conflicts with organizational values.

Unfortunately, many organizations and fundraisers do not realize what generally causes fundraising problems. Neither the organization nor the fundraiser understands that, without the four critical relationships, fund development will not work effectively. Furthermore, neither the fundraiser nor the organization acknowledges the role of the fundraising executive in developing these four fundamental relationships.

Without a strong understanding of the four fundamental relationships and their relationships to one another, fundraisers sometimes recommend strategies that, at best, do not promote organizational health. At worst, these strategies are detrimental to the organization. Sometimes, these situations occur because fundraisers are not integrated into the whole organizational system. At other times, the fundraiser may not have sufficient knowledge and competence beyond fundraising tactics.

Perhaps fundraisers (and particularly fundraising consultants) assume that the rest of the organization is doing fine. They restrict themselves—or are restricted by the organization—to that narrow view, the financial bottom line.

> *Probably 75 percent of the fundraising issues that stymie agencies are actually organizational development issues. This holds true even in major institutions with sophisticated development staff.*

Many fundraisers expect that chief executives will solve problems in the system, because they are responsible for institutional health. But that's an easy way out. This perspective relegates the fundraiser (and other organizational leaders, as well) to the position of a specialist stuck in a private corner of a very complex, interrelated system.

Some Fundraisers Don't Lead

Even when organizations and fundraisers recognize the importance of the four relationships, the fundraiser may not be expected to help develop all these relationships. Many organizations separate the relationships and direct the work to independent specialists. For example, the marketing and public relations staff deal with most constituents and communications. The chief executive addresses internal relations and strategic planning. The fundraiser focuses on donors and prospects only.

Even when organizations do expect the fundraiser to lead the institution, the fundraiser may not be able to. The truth is, fundraising executives who are only technicians cannot solve organizational development problems. These professionals do not have the knowledge, skills, or experience to discern the issues. Typically, these fundraisers identify the symptom as a fundraising problem and try to solve it as such. Frequently, the fundraising solution temporarily conflicts with the appropriate organizational development solution. Usually, the fundraising solution does not address the problem. Ultimately, inadequate or no progress is made.

> *Today, we measure and reward success by the bottom line. We don't reward fundraisers as organizational development specialists, responsible for building the four relationships critical to philanthropy. With this attitude, we promote slowly going out of business.*

Other fundraisers fully understand the problems. However, they are not allowed access to the organization to help resolve the problem. Again, inadequate or no progress is made.

WHAT WE CAN DO NOW

What is your best insurance against obsolescence? Change the way you do business. Forget the quick fix and pay attention to the fundamentals. Strengthen your relationships within your own organization and with your community, constituents, and volunteers.

Are you afraid your organization isn't ready for change? The need for charitable contributions can be a powerful motivator.

Clearly, the major motivation for institutional change should be meeting community need. But if this is too threatening, use the need for increased contributions to get your organization to evaluate itself. Start by evaluating your fund development. If you do this evaluation well, you will examine the four relationships that are essential to effective fund development.

Because charitable gifts are a powerful motivator, the fundraising executive is in a powerful position. There is no better position from which to encourage self-examination and challenge complacency. There is no position with more need to address organizational health than that of the fundraiser.

The fundraiser in your organization must be the individual in your organization most knowledgeable about the institution's program and the community's need. No individual should be better able to develop and foster the four relationships essential to institutional health and fund development. (Indeed, the best fundraising executive is an individual well positioned to become a chief executive. Conversely, service first as an executive director can make a great fundraiser.)

Make Fund Development Part of the Larger System

Too often, fund development and the fundraiser remain somewhat tangential to the rest of the system. Don't let this happen.

Fully integrate fund development and the fundraiser into the organizational system. Then you have a better chance of raising more money.

The more parts your system has, the greater will be its complexity and uncertainty. What affects one function will affect another. A problem in one part of the system is usually stimulated or reinforced by a situation elsewhere. Certainly, an action in one area will affect other areas. Partial solutions are rarely more than temporary.

> In a complex world, there are no simple, bounded problems. Problems continually expand and spill over to involve every aspect of business. . . . The most basic assumption is that all organizations are complex systems that interact constantly and significantly with a host of other equally complex systems. The most important property of these systems is that they cannot be broken down into parts that have separate lives of their own. Thus, in an organization, no basic functions, departments, or objectives exist independently of one another...one obtains a highly distorted and seriously misleading picture of any part of a system if one attempts to study and manage it apart from the larger system in which it exists (Mitroff, Mason, and Pearson 1994, 20).

What can you do? Look at your own institution. As chief executive,

- help board and staff to see the links between fund development and other institutional functions, to identify and resolve systemic issues at various points;
- make sure the fundraising staff understand the program and relate well with the program staff;
- involve your fundraiser in board selection, recruitment, and development;
- insist that fundraising staff work with all other staff, including program and marketing, to identify the agency's constituents, find out their interests

and needs, and brainstorm how the agency can respond;
- show your staff—the janitor, the receptionist, direct service personnel, trustees, chief executive, bookkeeper—the role they play in fund development;
- listen to your fundraiser's thoughts about program quality and community perception;
- expect your fundraiser to be actively involved in the community, serving on boards and exploring community issues, trends, and solutions.

Strengthen the Professional

During the past decades, fund development has been professionalized. There is a body of knowledge, and we are recording it. Education and training proliferate, teaching the history and philosophy of philanthropy, as well as fundraising practice. Academics and practitioners conduct research. Our ethical codes, standards of practice, and certification programs enhance credibility.

As a result, the profession produces effective fundraising executives who are consummate managers and proficient technicians. They believe in their causes and the philosophy of philanthropy. They know how to create infrastructure, document activities, and delineate roles. These professionals mathematically project goals and analyze response rates. Using sophisticated solicitation strategies, fundraisers negotiate major gifts and write effective direct mail. Generally, these competent professionals support volunteers well with strategies that work today.

But what about tomorrow? Entitlement is over, and there is increasing congestion when seeking gifts. Donors are more demanding, and communities look more closely at not-for-profits.

Organizations that focus only on the fundraising bottom line will not increase charitable contributions. Fundraisers who seek a quick fix and pursue short-term techniques will not produce more money for the long term.

No matter who leads your fund development effort (development staff, executive director, consultant, or volunteer), this person must be more than a manager and fundraising strategist. Your fund development leader helps the organization develop its four critical relationships. This leader understands how these relationships affect fund development and possesses the right knowledge, attitude, and competencies.

Your chief development officer is responsible for fostering a culture of philanthropy within the organization. With the chief executive officer, your chief development officer ensures that the organization's corporate culture and operations support fund development, and vice versa. This leader ensures that philanthropy and fund development are institutionalized throughout he organization. See Exhibit 1–3 for a sample job description.

So, as a profession, we have more work to do. We can give equal attention to, or better yet, more attention to the knowledge and competencies required to develop the four relationships critical to institutional health and, therefore, essential to fund development effectiveness and productivity.

What must the fundraiser know? Not only what we will do tomorrow, but how we will think about tomorrow. What makes systems and people work, how, and why? Concepts. Context. Process.

What knowledge and competencies do effective fundraisers need? They demonstrate critical competencies identical to any other executive within an institution. These competencies can be summarized into broad categories adapted from William R. Bryan, PhD, of Bryan Associates, Rhode Island. These are: commitment to results, business savvy, leading change, and motivating.

Commitment to Results

The competent executive builds the four relationships critical to organizational health. She or he is a systems thinker who is customer focused and goal driven. This individual identifies relevant information and helps transform this information into individual and organizational knowledge and learning. The executive is action oriented and innovative. She or he anticipates and solves problems and takes advantage of opportunities.

Business Savvy

The executive possesses comprehensive management knowledge, as well as knowledge about the particular business and operations of his or her agency. Comprehensive management knowledge includes: not-for-profit governance; values clarification and assessment; fiscal planning and management; strategic and program planning and evaluation; volunteer and staff development, role delineation, performance expectations and assessment, recruitment and training, and enabling; marketing and communications; and general management theory.

This competent executive is both a critical and strategic thinker and decision maker. She or he manages and facilitates group behavior and decision making, and helps delineate responsibilities. The capable executive values pluralism and seeks diversity in all its forms, including those of culture, gender, and opinion.

Leading Change

The executive is a flexible leader, possessing the skills and implementing the leadership functions presented in Chapter 2. She or he shares the values and vision of the organization and consistently displays integrity. She or he models behavior, develops people, and builds teams.

Motivating

The competent executive manages continuity, change, and transition. This individual knows how to influence and enable others. She or he is concerned about the impact of attitude and action on the organization and its participants.

Assess yourself, your organization, and your staff. If you are a fundraising executive, compare your own skills and knowledge to the executive competency model presented here. How well do you perform? If you are hiring a staff person or fundraising consultant, assess your candidate against these competencies. If you are a volunteer, ask yourself whether your agency and its staff perform in this manner.

To be successful, organizations and fundraisers must change. Without these competencies, we cannot raise funds well. Nothing less than effective change will suffice if our organizations are to survive.

DEVELOP THE FOUR CRITICAL RELATIONSHIPS

The four relationships critical to effective and productive fund development and institutional health are:

- internal relations
- relationship to community
- relationship to constituents
- relationship to volunteers

Without these four relationships, fund development will be neither effective nor productive over the long term. In this author's opinion, your organization will go slowly out of business.

Developing good relationships requires seven personal and organizational attributes. These are:

1. organizational values that support these relationships
2. actions that reflect the values
3. a focus on the long term as, well as the short term
4. investment of volunteer and staff time, energy, and financial resources
5. adequate management systems and procedures to carry out specific tasks
6. capacity and capability to change individual, group, and organizational attitude and behavior
7. knowledge and competencies presented in this chapter, under "Strengthen the Professional"

Exhibit 1–3 Sample Job Description of a Chief Development Officer

Position Title: Chief Development Officer
Reports To: Chief Executive Officer

JOB SUMMARY

Fosters a culture of philanthropy within the organization. Ensures that the organization's corporate culture, systems, and procedures support fund development and vice versa. Leads staff and volunteers to institutionalize philanthropy and fund development within the organization.

Plans, coordinates, and ensures implementation of strategies to develop donors and contributions to support the organization. Ensures development and maintenance of appropriate systems to fund development, including but not limited to volunteer and donor management, research and cultivation, gift processing, and recognition. Maintains accountability and compliance standards for donors and funding sources.

NATURE AND SCOPE OF POSITION

1. Participates with the chief executive officer (CEO), staff, and board in defining the organization's mission and direction.
   a) Provides vital input in short- and long-term strategic and operational planning and positioning within the organization.
   b) Helps leadership identify and address organizational development issues that challenge and support health and effectiveness.
   c) Ensures that philanthropy and fund development are carried out in keeping with the organization's values, mission, vision, and plans.
   d) Participates with the CEO, staff, and board in charting the organization's course in fund development.
   e) Evaluates the effect of internal and external forces on the organization and its fund development and recommends short- and long-range fund development plans and programs that support the organization's values, mission, and general objectives.
   f) Keeps informed of developments in philanthropy and fund development, as well as the general fields of management and the not-for-profit sector; informs the CEO, development committee(s), and board on current trends, issues, problems, and activities in order to facilitate policy making. Recommends policy positions concerning fund development.
   g) Helps develop a balanced funding mix of donor sources and solicitation programs tailored to the needs of the organization that will enable it to attract, retain, and motivate donors and fundraising volunteers.
2. Helps establish performance measures for fund development, monitors results, and helps the CEO, development committee(s), and board evaluate the effectiveness of the organization's fund development program.

3. Provides general oversight of all of the organization's fund development activities, manages the day-to-day operations of the development function, and monitors adequacy of activities through coordination with board, staff, and volunteers.
   a) Ensures compliance with all relevant regulations and laws, maintains accountability standards to donors, and ensures compliance with code of ethical principles and standards of professional conduct for fundraising executives.
   b) Ensures establishment of and compliance with the organization's own fund development and philanthropic principles, policies, and procedures.
   c) Ensures stability by creating a working environment that is rewarding to staff and volunteers.
   d) Appropriately represents the institution, its board, and executive director to donors, prospects, regulators, development committee(s), and fundraising volunteers.
   e) Fosters a smoothly operating development function through timely and effective resolution of disruptions.
4. Ensures attainment of the organization's fund development goals through the selection, development, motivation, and evaluation of human resources, both professional and volunteer.
   a) Helps the board and development committee(s) determine accountabilities for board members and fundraising volunteers, and helps evaluate performance regularly.
   b) Helps identify, cultivate, recruit, and develop fundraising volunteers and leadership. Trains, places, coordinates, and supervises fundraising volunteers.
   c) Establishes personnel accountabilities for development staff and evaluates performance regularly.
   d) Designs educational programs in fund development for staff and volunteers; participates as teacher and facilitator. Pursues formal and informal education for self and others.
5. Works with the CEO, development committee(s) chair(s), and board president to enable the board to fulfill its fund development role and facilitate the optimum interaction between management and volunteers.
   a) Engages people in process, encourages questioning, and promotes participatory decision making.
   b) With the development committee(s) chair(s), develops agendas for meetings so that the committees can fulfill their responsibilities effectively; develops an annual calendar to cover all crucial development issues in a timely fashion.
   c) Informs the chief executive and volunteer leadership on the condition of the organization's fund development program and on all important factors influencing it.

continues

Exhibit 1–3 continued

d) Gets the best thinking and involvement of each board member and each fundraising volunteer; and, stimulates each one to give his/her best.

e) Works with the chief executive and volunteer leadership to help development committee(s) and the board function effectively in fund development.

f) Annually evaluates the performance of fundraising volunteers and reports to the executive director with recommendations for board candidacy.

6. Designs and ensures implementation of cost-effective fund development programs, employing economy while maintaining an acceptable level of quality and solid return on investment.

a) Ensures proper planning, including goal setting, strategy identification, benchmarking, and evaluation to support fund development.

b) Ensures sound fiscal operation of development function, including timely, accurate, and comprehensive development of charitable contributions income and expense budgets, reporting, monitoring, and implementation.

c) Combines development resources in such a way as to maximize quantity and quality to obtain a set of results. Ensures appropriate market testing to reduce risk and ensure success.

d) Helps board members, chief executive, other fundraising volunteers and staff identify, cultivate, and solicit charitable gifts.

e) Solicits contributions on behalf of the organization, generally by accompanying volunteers.

f) Ensures development and writing of foundation, corporate, and government proposals and solicitation materials.

g) Ensures design and maintenance of donor and prospect records, gift management systems, and informational reports.

h) Ensures appropriate prospect research.

i) Ensures design and implementation of cultivation, acknowledgment, and recognition programs.

PRIMARY RELATIONSHIPS

This position reports to the CEO and serves as a part of the senior management team. The position supervises the following positions: [organization should insert this information].

Within the agency, the position has primary relationships with the financial operation, senior management staff, and program staff. Outside the agency, the position coordinates with the board of directors, fundraising volunteers, donors, and funding sources.

PERFORMANCE EXPECTATIONS

As a member of the senior management team, this is a high-stress position that helps set the direction and ensures the health of the institution. The individual is expected to be a competent fundraising technician and an excellent organizational development specialist.

The individual is expected to: translate broad goals into achievable steps; help set and manage appropriate expectations; handle detailed, complex concepts and problems and make rapid decisions regarding management and development issues; plan and implement programs; establish strong and appropriate relationships with CEO, staff, board, volunteers, donors, and the general community; and develop smooth and constructive relationships with people from all segments of the community.

The individual is expected to: plan and meet deadlines; maintain a flexible work schedule to meet the demands of executive management; demonstrate initiative; and work as a team player.

The individual is expected to: adhere to the highest ethical standards in management, governance, and fund development; convey a professional and positive image and attitude regarding the organization and the not-for-profit sector; demonstrate commitment to continued professional growth and development.

QUALIFICATIONS

Comprehensive management skills and experience are required, including but not limited to short- and long-term planning, evaluation, directing and motivating staff, oral and written communication skills, marketing and financial management, values clarification, organizational behavior and development, and board development and governance.

The position requires demonstrated experience in managing and implementing a comprehensive fund development program and producing charitable contributions. The individual is expected to be a highly competent enabler of volunteers and staff.

Knowledge and experience in the following areas is required: the nature and dimensions of philanthropy; ethics; motivations for giving and volunteering; research and cultivation practices; standard fundraising techniques, including face-to-face solicitation, proposal writing, special events, telephone solicitation, and direct mail; and development office functions, including gift processing, prospect and donor histories, and fundraising reporting. The individual is also expected to have demonstrated experience and confidence in asking people to contribute time and money. Familiarity with computer systems is necessary.

The amount of knowledge required would typically be acquired in a bachelors degree and a minimum of seven years fundraising experience in a professional position. Membership in a professional fundraising association is expected of a professional. Baseline certification in fund raising, the CFRE (Certified Fund Raising Professional), is preferred.

Meet the Needs of Your Constituents

There are two marketing maxims that are well worth keeping in mind as you work to build the four critical relationships.

- "It's not what you are selling that matters. It's what I am buying that counts."
- "Do not tell me what I want. Show me you have what I need."

These hold true no matter what you're doing: whether you are building a relationship with your community through strategic planning, strengthening your relationship with a candidate for trusteeship, enabling a volunteer to carry out fundraising activities, or strengthening the group dynamics among your staff colleagues.

What does this actually mean? If your organization wants my help as a volunteer or donor, you must interest me. Simply put, it doesn't matter that you do good work. It doesn't matter that you respond to a community need. If you do not meet my need—whatever it is—I won't participate in any significant way. I may give you a token gift for some reason, but don't count on more.

Marketing is a highly ethical concept that fosters relationships that share meaningful benefits between parties. There is a mutually beneficial exchange that—to

---

Exhibit 1–4 A Personal Story. It's Not What You're Selling, It's What I'm Buying.

In 1990, my father died suddenly of cancer. We discovered he was sick, then he was dead six weeks later. He died in Michigan, before I could get there.

I arrived in East Lansing a few hours after his death. That afternoon, I called Michigan State University (MSU) and set up a scholarship fund for travel in a French-speaking country. The fund was named for my father, Georges Jules Joyaux. He had not yet been dead ten hours.

Within a few weeks of my father's death, I received solicitation letters from the national and local cancer societies. Timely and appropriate letters. Good philanthropic fundraising.

I threw each of these letters away.

Why?

Too soon? No. Too impersonal? No. (Although a personal call probably would have generated a nominal, one-time gift.)

What was the cancer society selling?

Many things. Freedom from pain. Health. A cure for cancer so others would not suffer as had my father and my family. Protection so I might not die from this dreaded disease. Protection for my husband, mother, my brothers and sisters, and my friends.

But what was I buying?

Not health. I rarely give to health organizations. Certainly, I want everyone to be healthy, myself and loved ones included. But I'm not buying health.

Not freedom from cancer. I am sorry my father died from cancer. It was ugly, as so much of death is. But I'm not buying an end to cancer.

What did I buy that afternoon when I called MSU from the living room of my parents' home?

My French heritage. Love and respect for different cultures, taught by my father. Joy of travel to other countries. Commitment to education as I look at all the teachers in our family.

A warmth toward MSU. My father came to the university as a young man from war-torn France. There, he met my mother and taught for 41 years. All six of us kids went to school there.

Love and admiration for my father, his vision of a world where pluralism is honored, his wit and sarcasm, his intelligence and eloquence, his strengths and weaknesses, his love for teaching and his students.

So, my mother and the six Joyaux kids set up a scholarship fund in Georges's name. Each year, an MSU student receives funds to study in a French-speaking country. The country doesn't have to be France, only French-speaking. An academic curriculum isn't necessary. Traveling and experiencing are what count. My father always reminded everyone: "The most important thing is to step out of your linguistic ghetto and become aware that there are people who live, eat, learn, and make love in a medium which is not English."

It amuses me to think of Georges's reaction to his fund. He would laugh and make a smart remark. But he would remember the students. I think he would be pleased.

With the scholarship, the students receive a description of my father and what he accomplished in his lifetime. I trust they read it.

I tell this story around the country when I teach and consult. I ask people what they think the cancer society is selling. People are so gracious. They use polite words and euphemisms. It takes a while before anyone gets to the nitty gritty—protection from death. Better yet, protecting me personally from dying and protecting others that I care about.

People are just as gracious when they talk about what I'm buying. They always emphasize the honoring of my heritage, my father, and his beliefs. Sure, that's a part of it. But then I laugh. Irreverently, I proclaim: "Just honoring my father and my heritage? I bought a house in France, and that's sure not for my dead father! This gift is about me and my interests. I love France, and I'm committed to pluralism."

You have to look deep. Get down to the essential, not just the surface.

be successful—requires understanding of and respect for personal interests and needs.

On the surface, this is not a hard principle to grasp. Some organizations assume they know what their constituents seek. (Organizations seem to assume that donors and volunteers want to help the cause.) But, in fact, many organizations do not understand the principle well. Most organizations do not behave as though they understand.

Many charities refuse to acknowledge the basic marketing exchange in philanthropy. They assume their good cause justifies the request and motivates the gift. As a result, these organizations are not tapping the full philanthropic potential in their communities. These charities are losing donors.

The statements—It's not what you're selling, it's what I'm buying that counts, Do not tell me what I want, and Show me you have what I need—are rather straightforward. But they offend many organizations, their volunteers, and staff. To some, these maxims seem to suggest that prosperous donors and supporters are selfish. These maxims call to mind an individualistic culture, excessive competitiveness, and alienation from community.

But self-interest need not be interpreted negatively. Psychiatrist Robert Coles explains: "There is an element of self-interest in serving others." Coles observes that this is both morally and psychologically acceptable; "unless individuals can really believe in something and immerse themselves in an activity, they won't have much to offer" (Coles 1994, 14).

> *Fund development is about "making a sale," and "it's what they're buying that counts" is a fundamental law. We cannot ignore it or pretend it doesn't apply. It is not a discussion point. It's a law of human nature.*

With this notion of personal engagement in mind, the thought process of a community member is more easily understood. Each individual has her or his own interests and needs. Each individual defines his or her own relationship with the world. There may be hundreds of charities doing good work for important causes. Community need and your organization's good work are secondary to the individual's interests (Exhibit 1–4).

To be successful at fund development, you identify the constituent's interests and determine whether you can fulfill them. You understand the constituent's needs and decide whether you can benefit him or her.

Your organization is not compromising its mission and values by considering the constituent. Do not change your program to raise funds. Do not invent a new service because someone will fund it. However, within your values, vision, and mission, decide whether you can meet the constituent's needs and interests. If the answer is yes, show the individual you have what she or he needs. If you cannot, leave the constituent alone. Do not waste your time or theirs. Move on.

REFERENCES

Coles, R. 1994. Doing Well by Doing Good: Why We Volunteer. *Advancing Philanthropy*, 2(1):14–16.

Drucker, P.F. 1990. *Managing the Nonprofit Organization: Principles and Practices*. New York: HarperCollins Publishers.

Gardner, J. September 1991. *Building Community*. Washington, DC: Independent Sector.

Mitroff, I., R. Mason, and C. Pearson. 1994. *Framebreak, the Radical Redesign of American Business*. San Francisco: Jossey-Bass, Publishers.

Chapter 2

The First Relationship—
Within Your Organization

Creating the Infrastructure That Produces a Healthy Organization

In every move, in every decision, in every policy, the non-profit institution needs to start out by asking, Will this advance our capacity to carry out our mission? It should start with the end result, should focus outside-in rather than inside-out.

The non-profits are human-change agents. And their results are therefore always a change in people—in their behavior, in their circumstances, in their vision, in their health, in their hopes, above all, in their competence and capacity. In the last analysis, the non-profit institution . . . has to judge itself by its performance in creating vision, creating standards, creating values and commitment, and in creating human competence. The non-profit institution therefore needs to set specific goals in terms of its service to people. And it needs constantly to raise these goals—or its performance will go down.

Peter Drucker

TOPICS DISCUSSED IN THIS SECTION

- what effective internal relations do for your organization and your fund development function
- what infrastructure means
- how group behavior reflects corporate culture
- asking the right questions
- components of an effective infrastructure
  –shared values

  –art of leadership
  –learning organization
  –ongoing conversation
  –participatory decision making
  –well-managed change
  –culture of philanthropy
- how shared values affect your organization and your fund development process
- what leaders do and the attributes and skills leaders possess
- creating your own learning organization
- why a learning organization is prepared for survival
- using conversation to build internal relations and strengthen your organization
- encouraging participatory decision making
- managing change

MAKING YOUR ORGANIZATION EFFECTIVE

Without good internal relationships—between board and staff, among staff, between departments and functions—your organization will most likely falter. And when your organization falters, your fund development program will likely falter, as well.

> *Development professionals cannot succeed by simply changing tactics; they must help cure the institution's ailments. As James Carville might say, "It's the organization, stupid."*
>
> *James Lewis*

No organization can survive on mission and vision alone. Infrastructure provides the supporting systems and framework that allow your organization to pursue its vision and achieve its mission.

Infrastructure defines how your organization conducts its work and is both formal and informal, documented and casual. Infrastructure includes such activities as financial and personnel management, marketing and planning, and the behaviors and attitudes of staff and volunteers. Infrastructure, in short, amounts to your corporate culture plus your organization's systems.

Fund development is part of the infrastructure and, at the same time, depends on infrastructure for support. If the rest of your organization has problems, fund development will, too. For example:

- Poor quality in your services affects your ability to raise charitable gifts.
- Without good decision making, your organization establishes an unrealistic fundraising goal.
- Board members are reluctant to identify prospects or solicit gifts because the board recruitment process doesn't talk about the board member's fundraising role.

The Fundraiser as an Organizational Development Specialist

Most fundraisers know that effective infrastructure is essential to effective fund development. How does this play out?

First, donors prefer to give to well-managed and well-governed institutions. Donors expect organizations to manage money properly, comply with legal and regulatory requirements, make decisions effectively, and continuously improve services. All of this is accomplished through infrastructure.

Second, fundraisers use components of infrastructure to carry out development activities. For example, fund development uses planning to design solicitation activities. Fund development employs marketing strategy to develop relationships with prospects and donors. Personnel practices are used to manage fundraising volunteers.

The best fundraisers know more than just the basics of infrastructure. The best fundraisers are organizational development specialists. These fundraisers understand how and why an organization's infrastructure affects all of its activities, fund development included. The most effective fundraisers pay attention to corporate culture, respect systems, and learn about group behavior. They identify and fix infrastructure problems and stay current with evolving management theory.

These individuals are change agents. They facilitate individual and organizationwide learning, and these individuals build capacity for change. As organizational development specialists, they serve as scouts, identifying challenges and opportunities, and getting them on the table within the organization.

Operating as an organizational development specialist, these fundraisers go back and forth between fund development, the institution, and its other parts. These fundraisers assess fund development by looking at infrastructure first. Consider the sample development audit Appendix B. Note that the first questions focus on overall institutional health. Only at the end of the audit do questions address fund development specifics.

Take a look at the governance assessment included in Chapter 3, Appendix 3–B. This survey approaches institutional health from the board's perspective. Questions are far ranging but always focused through the prism of governance.

Role of Corporate Culture and Systems

Corporate culture refers to the personality of an organization and the way its members interact and behave. Corporate culture is not written. Although it is rarely discussed, it pervades an organization and is transmitted from one individual to another.

> *Fund development is, first, organizational development.*

The authors of *Framebreak: The Radical Redesign of American Business* describe corporate culture as "the set of rarely articulated, largely unconscious, taken-for-granted beliefs, values, norms, and fundamental assumptions the organization makes about itself, the nature of people in general, and its environment. . . . Organizational culture consists of the set of unwritten rules that govern acceptable behavior within and even outside of the organization" (Mitroff, Mason, and Pearson 1994, 65). In *Clicks and Mortar: Passion Driven Growth in an Internet World*, Pottruck and Pearce (2000) comment that cultures are formed in any group, whether small or large. Some of these cultures are explicit but "most are implicit, understood but not spoken, residing in the language and habits of interaction between the people" (page 26).

If the term *corporate culture* refers to the behaviors that underlie group behavior, the term *systems*, on the other hand, refers to the permanent structures in your organization. Systems direct the flow of what happens. Systems include core processes, management and governance hierarchy, and informal networks. Many systems are formal and documented. Others are informal but just as strong.

- Core processes are those that you cannot do without. They include such things as continuous quality improvement, performance measurement and control, financial and personnel management, and board recruitment and development.
- Hierarchy defines the relationships of individuals and groups, one to the other. Hierarchy assigns authority and accountability.
- Informal networks refer to an organization's practices. These networks are not codified or written down, but they do reflect your corporate culture. They describe what "everyone knows is the way we really do business."

> *Everything else can fall away; the industry and products and circumstances may change; but an abiding culture can serve as the custodian of dreams for your company team, and for the customers on whose faith you build your house of business. It is an unchanging constant in the midst of a tornado of change, and it is something people want badly. It allows us to offer choice to those who work here and for those we want to work here…to live and work by their values, and who will toil together toward something larger than themselves. …The company, at its best, can be a vehicle for everyone to make a difference.*
>
> *Pottruck and Pearce*

Together, corporate culture and systems can produce either dysfunctional or healthy organizations. When both corporate culture and systems are effective, the organization flourishes. If corporate culture is dysfunctional, even well-designed systems won't operate too well. However, a healthy corporate culture can compensate, to a large degree, for inadequate systems.

CONCEPT OF A GROUP

To be part of a group, you have to come to the meetings and talk. A group exists only when it comes together.

Too often, group members think it is okay not to attend and not to talk within the group. Is this acceptable? Can members of the group avoid interaction within the group? Is it okay to avoid discussion within the group but talk outside the group about group issues?

The answer is a resounding "no." To be part of a group requires interaction—and within the group. And never more so than within an organization.

Organizations consist of many groups. There are teams of employees addressing selected topics and departments carrying out specific functions. Boards and committees focus on particular issues. These groups are brought together for some unifying purpose. At their most basic, these groups exist to talk and, typically, to decide or do something. Thus, participation—through attendance and talking—is critical.

However, consider this: There are introverts and extroverts. There are differences in culture, position, and perception of power.

Some people are more introverted than others. These individuals may be uncomfortable speaking within the group and may choose not to participate in discussion. Instead, they may share their thoughts with colleagues after the group meetings. In this scenario, great insights and useful information are shared one-on-one, without the advantage of comment and reaction within the full group. The value of the group, the synergy of more than one, is lost.

People from different cultures or positions may approach groups in different ways. Some people may feel overpowered or threatened about active participation, so they remain silent. Sadly, the value of their perspective and experience is not added to the mix, to enhance group learning.

Still others join a group but do not attend its gatherings. The individuals are too busy or focused on other things. However, attendance is critical within a group because a group is defined by its moments of coming together.

It's not negotiable. Effective groups depend on the participation of their members. Silence is not acceptable, nor is absence. Certainly, absence occurs periodically. Naturally, some members will speak more than others. But all members must attend regularly and must speak often.

The challenge, then, is to create an effective group. It is helpful to understand group dynamics and the role of group behavior. It is useful to clarify roles, expectations, and relationships. It is essential to understand diversity—whether cultural, personality, or any other type.

Role of Group Behavior

Group behavior affects the way your organization makes decisions, how well you identify and resolve issues, and how you negotiate conflict. Group behavior affects the willingness of employees and volunteers to stay with your organization and your ability to recruit new employees and volunteers.

Effective fundraisers use group behavior to get the job done well. They understand enough theory to encourage positive behaviors and to control negative ones.

Consider these potentially harmful group behaviors.

- Your development committee is too fragmented to discuss really challenging issues.
- Your board is so cohesive that members rarely question or disagree on anything, thus compromising the quality of your decisions.
- Program staff don't honestly express their concerns about how money is raised, so your organization cannot create a united philanthropic case for the community.
- Group interactions are full of conflict and game playing, so fundraising volunteers leave.
- Almost everyone is concerned about a new program, but no one says so aloud in the group, so you launch a program that no one thinks should be done.
- Your board members have not learned to speak candidly with each other. This avoidance stops discussion about the giving and fundraising expectations of board members.

> *Group behavior can only be altered by changing corporate culture.*

Keep in mind that group behavior reflects corporate culture, just as individual behavior does. Although group behavior can be explained by theory, group behavior can be altered only by changing corporate culture.

Much is published about group behavior. Three theories—group dynamics, groupthink, and managing agreement—may be particularly important for your organization to understand.

Group Dynamics

In groups that function effectively, members feel some linkage, one to the other and to the group as a whole. This linkage produces the cohesion that is necessary for the group to operate successfully. In fact, the degree to which group members are linked defines the level of group health.

The theory of group dynamics (Kurt Lewin, American psychologist, 1896–1947; Harrison 1987, 141–153) describes linking forces as:

- member satisfaction from participating in the group
- degree of closeness and warmth felt between members of the group
- pride of membership in the group

- ability of members to address the crises that face the group
- degree to which members of the group express their ideas and feelings honestly

Take a look at the groups in your organization. How do these dynamics operate within your board, among your staff, within the development committee, or between the development committee and the board? To what degree are your group members linked?

Groupthink

Some cohesion is necessary for a group to operate. Consider what might happen when a group is too cohesive. Members abdicate their independence and objectivity, and support group norms without question. Other group members may mask their real feelings in deference to the consensus.

This is groupthink, "a mode of thinking that people engage in when they are deeply involved in a cohesive ingroup, when the members' strivings for unanimity override their motivation to realistically appraise alternative courses of action. . . . Groupthink refers to a deterioration of mental efficiency, reality, testing, and moral judgment that results from ingroup pressures" (Janis 1982, 9).

Groupthink produces a number of unfavorable results.

- Group members are pressured to avoid expressing arguments against group positions for fear of being considered disloyal.
- Members censor themselves, suppressing their own doubts about the wisdom of group consensus.
- Certain members make sure the group doesn't get information that could interfere with the group's cohesion.
- Group members see only unanimity and assume that silence signifies agreement.
- Members rationalize the group's judgments, ignore warnings, and disregard assumptions.
- Members believe in the group's own morality and disregard the ethical consequences of decisions.
- The group endorses stereotypes, seeing outsiders as adversaries or competitors who are weak and stupid.
- The group sees itself as invulnerable, encouraging excessive optimism and risk taking (Harrison 1987, 271).

Now look at your groups. Do you ever see examples of excessive cohesion?

Managing Agreement

A particularly interesting theory of group behavior is called *managing agreement*. Most people know something about its opposite, managing conflict. Fewer understand managing agreement—and it is just as difficult.

Jerry Harvey calls this the *Abilene Paradox*, based on an unwanted family trip to Abilene. Harvey summarizes the trip this way: "Here we were, four reasonably sensible people who, of our own volition, had just taken a 106-mile trip across a godforsaken desert in a furnace-like temperature through a cloud-like dust storm to eat unpalatable food at a hole-in-the-wall cafeteria in Abilene, when none of us had really wanted to go. In fact, to be more accurate, we'd done just the opposite of what we wanted to do" (Harvey 1988, 18).

> *[Organizations] frequently take actions in contradiction to what they really want to do and therefore defeat the very purposes they are trying to achieve . . . a major corollary of the paradox . . . is that the inability to manage agreement is a major source of organization dysfunction . . . Organization change and effectiveness may be facilitated as much by confronting the organization with what it knows and agrees upon as by confronting it with what it doesn't know or disagrees about.*
>
> *Jerry Harvey*

What a horrible story. But groups and organizations do end up in Abilene regularly. Maybe it's the fundraising event no one wanted but thought everyone else did. Or the fundraising brochure donated by a great copywriter and designer that everyone knows (but doesn't say) is too slick and polished for the organization's values and desired image (Exhibit 2–1).

Components of an Effective Infrastructure

Effective organizations regularly evaluate their infrastructure to determine whether a particular component operates well and contributes to institutional health. Organizations examine infrastructure by conducting self-assessments or by commissioning independent audits. You can incorporate ongoing assessment as part of annual operations. Also, a long-range strategic planning process will always evaluate infrastructure, as well as program (see Chapter 3 of this book).

Generally, effective infrastructure includes the following components:

Exhibit 2–1 Six Elements That Express the Inability To Manage Agreement

- Individual members of the organization agree, privately, about the situation or problem.
- Individuals agree, privately, about the steps necessary to cope with the situation or problem.
- Organization members don't clearly communicate their desires and/or beliefs to each other. They communicate the opposite, causing the group to misperceive what everyone actually believes.
- Based on the inaccurate and invalid information they have transmitted to each other, these individuals make group decisions that are contrary to what they really want to do. Consequently, the group produces results that conflict with the organization's purposes and desires.
- By taking these counterproductive actions, organization members are frustrated, angry, irritated, and dissatisfied with their group or organization. These individuals then form subgroups with those they trust and blame others for the organization's dysfunction.
- The cycle repeats itself with greater intensity if people don't deal with their inability to manage agreement.

Source: Reprinted from *Organizational Management, The Abilene Paradox: The Management Agreement.* J.B. Harvey, Copyright 1988, with permission from Elsevier Science.

- planning and assessment (strategic planning is the method to create the first relationship, relationship with community)
- marketing and communications
- human resource development (staff and volunteer)
- general management
- governance
- financing (both revenue and charitable contributions)
- quality assurance and continuous quality improvement

As you develop your organization for the next millennium, think about the new functions you might add. Decide how you will design your infrastructure—including corporate culture and core systems—to meet complex, changing needs.

Consider the following six components.

1. shared values
2. the art of leadership
3. the learning organization (personal mastery, mental models, shared vision, team learning, and systems thinking)

4. ongoing conversation
5. participatory decision making
6. well-managed change

All organizations—no matter the type or size, whether for-profit or non-governmental organization (NGO)—need these six attributes, and an NGO needs one more: a strong culture of philanthropy.

> *Values precede the birth of an organization and certainly precede mission.*

Together, the seven components, described in this section, will help you develop your organization's relationship within itself. This is the first relationship that will strengthen your fund development.

SHARED VALUES

The first component of effective infrastructure is shared values. Shared values are the foundation for your organization's internal and external relations. Shared values are the most critical element for building any type of community—and your organization is a community.

> *Your organization's life begins with shared values. So does fund development.*

A value is an enduring belief that a specific mode of conduct is personally or socially preferable to another. A value possesses intrinsic worth, desirability, and utility to the individual or group.

In her article, "Decision making in ethics," Barbara H. Marion, CFRE (1994), presents the theory of tiered values. Each of the tiers is built on the preceding one.

Moral values, says Marion (1994, 50–51), are the first tier. These values are the "primary, unvarying bedrock rules of individual conduct that result from culture, experience, and training." These individual values are "unconditional, forming the life philosophy of the individual." Second-tier values are "consciously and deliberately [taken] to form our personal code of honor based on principles such as truth-telling, love of country, respect for others, protection of the weak, and tolerance." The third tier of values reflects the professional's standards of practice.

Psychologist Louis Edward Raths (1966) formulated a seven-step process to determine values. A true value subscribes to each of these seven elements.

1. Prized and cherished. A value is something that the individual or group prizes and cherishes.

2. Publicly affirmed. The individual or group must be willing to publicly affirm the value.
3. Available alternatives. A value is not mandated. One must be free to choose other alternatives.
4. Chosen intelligently. A true value is chosen after intelligently considering the consequences.
5. Chosen freely. Individuals and groups choose values freely after considering consequences.
6. Action. A true value means acting on one's belief. The final test of a value is action.
7. Repeated action. A true value demands repeated action in a consistent pattern.

Individuals have values. These values guide our actions and judgments. Our values are the standards that influence us as we make choices among alternative courses of action. Our values are relatively permanent frameworks that shape and influence our behavior.

Groups, too, have values. Groups are formed when individuals congregate through common interests or a shared purpose. First and foremost, however, individuals congregate because of shared values, those fundamental beliefs that are not negotiable.

Groups operate best through consensus and unity of purpose and action. However, even with unity of purpose and action, groups can still flounder if the individuals do not share values. Shared values are the essential glue, and this means that the individual's values must match those of the collective entity.

A group's values have two parts. First, some of the values reflect the group's purpose or mission. Second, other values describe how group members relate to each other, how members behave and act, and how the organization conducts its business.

Because groups are comprised of individuals, the group must articulate its values to ensure some commonality. Don't assume that everyone shares the same values. Group articulation allows the individual to be assured that her or his values fit well enough with those of the collective entity. These values then provide a framework that guides the actions and judgments of the group.

> *Values, the nonnegotiable tenets against which we measure the worthiness of our choices.*
> *Pottruck and Pearce*

The values of an organization are, generally, articulated as second- and third-tier beliefs. The group deliberately defines its shared code for behaving and operating. These articulated shared values help the group decide its actions, interact among its members and constituents, and choose its consequences.

Operating with Values

Effective organizations possess clearly articulated values and behave in accordance with these values. Values form the foundation for all organizational activities, choices and decisions, and actions. Values are management and governance tools that:

- help test mission and determine vision and program
- serve as a screen to determine the worthiness, appropriateness, and robustness of all operations
- provide the framework for policies and procedures, program delivery system, communications, and fund development strategies

In their study of visionary companies, Collins and Porras (1994) observe that companies last specifically because they have clearly articulated values. These values remain fixed, even while business goals and products, strategies, and practices change in response to the changing world. The authors quote Ralph Larsen, then chief executive officer (CEO) of Johnson & Johnson, who states: "The core values embodied in [Johnson & Johnson's] credo might be a competitive advantage, but that is not *why* we have them. We have them because they define for us what we stand for, and we would hold them even if they became a competitive *dis*advantage in certain situations" (page 222, February 1995 author interview). These most effective organizations continually distinguish between that which is core—unchanging and constant—and that which can and often should change.

Effective organizations discuss how a value affects a particular decision. They identify value conflicts and have a process to make ethical decisions. These organizations regularly assess whether behavior is aligned with values. Also, these organizations ask individuals who do not publicly affirm and act on the group's values to leave.

As groups grow and change—when some people leave and new people join—the values still form the foundation for existence. But be wary. Sometimes the values lose their position in the forefront of the group. Perhaps the new people and incumbents did not discuss the values, so the values did not provide that critical screening for invitation or not or for opting in or out. Groups must keep their values alive, practiced, and promoted.

Articulating Organizational Values

Many groups do not identify their values. When a group's values are not articulated, individuals may behave at cross purposes. Individuals may join the group without sharing the group's values. Conflict arises, and decision making falters. Rather than too much cohesion, as in groupthink, there isn't enough to move the group forward.

However, other organizations do articulate their values. These value statements are distributed to all employees, printed in brochures and annual reports, posted on walls, and given to customers and vendors.

The problem is that, often, the value statement is forgotten. It's just a piece of paper, rather than an active part of organizational infrastructure. In this situation, the organization still follows some of its articulated values but not consciously.

Usually, there are two reasons why organizations don't use their values.

- First, the process of articulating values involves only a small group of people. Perhaps senior management, a special task force, or the board of directors alone determine values. There is little or no ownership because those affected by the results do not participate. Keep in mind: A group's values belong to the group. That means that all members of the group participate in the deliberation. Only then can the group choose intelligently and freely. Then choosing happens over and over throughout the organization's decision making and actions.
- Second, there is no mechanism to use the values as part of operations. Values don't work unless they are institutionalized. For example, the values statement can be used to shape discussion at meetings. The values statement helps you evaluate how you deliberate, make choices, and take action. Then, Raths' (1996) "action" and "repeated action" are not lost.

To articulate your shared values, bring group members together and talk. Through conversation, the group identifies its shared values. Together, the group examines how the values might affect all activities. Sometimes, an objective facilitator encourages the group to question itself more readily. The results are summarized, and a values statement is drafted. The entire group reviews the draft before the values are adopted as institutional policy.

Sometimes, because of geography or organization size, not all group members can get together. In this case, alternative methods must be developed to engage all group members in the process. For example, the YMCA of Greater Providence used a survey directed to all 400 employees and volunteers. Survey statements were generated through meetings with volunteers and staff. Then

Exhibit 2–2 YMCA of Greater Providence Values Statement

We have five core values. Everything we do will be guided by the values we share. We practice these values through our programs and actions.

Respect—All people have worth and value.
As individuals and as an organization, we

- believe that people are basically good, want to do their best, and can learn, change, and grow
- reach out and embrace the full diversity of individuals and families, regardless of ability, age, income, faith, lifestyle, physical challenge, race, or ethnicity
- create opportunities for people to be meaningfully involved through challenging responsibilities and individual and team participation

Caring—We are sensitive and nurturing.
As individuals and as an organization, we

- guard the safety and well-being of youth and adults
- promote self-fulfillment and hope in an atmosphere of optimism, fun, and tolerance
- resolve conflict with honesty, respect, and compassion
- encourage self-sufficiency

Honesty—We trust and earn the trust of others.
As individuals and an organization, we

- behave with integrity, sincerity, and consistency
- keep the lines of communication open
- assess ourselves
- seek consensus

Responsibility—We use our resources to serve the diverse community.
As individuals and an organization, we

- ask those we serve to help define needs, design responsive programs, evaluate quality, and support activities
- collaborate with others for the common good
- operate in a fiscally sound manner

Change—We are future oriented and inspired by change.
As individuals and an organization, we

- honor our traditions and explore new opportunities
- strive for excellence
- make a difference by generating ideas, contributing knowledge, and offering solutions

Courtesy of the YMCA of Greater Providence, RI.

the survey asked which statements should be a value of the YMCA.

Survey results produced 21 values statements that were shared by the majority of employees and volunteers. The CEO and planning consultant used these independent statements to write a narrative that described the YMCA's values (Exhibit 2–2).

The Women's Foundation of Southern Arizona brought together its full board and staff to articulate shared values. Individuals took the risk to speak honestly and share opinions. The resulting values statement helped board and staff members decide whether they wanted to remain within the organization (Exhibit 2–3). Subsequent discussion focused on the degree to which the organization behaved in accordance with these values and what strategies would help enhance alignment with values.

Managing Value Conflicts

Value conflicts are inevitable in the life of an organization. Sometimes, participants in the organization find that their values conflict with those of the group. Sometimes, an organization realizes that its own values conflict.

Participation in an organization may constrain an individual's values. To avoid possible conflicts between the individual's values and those of the organization, communicate your organization's values before confirming an individual's participation. By joining, the individual agrees to subscribe to and support the organization's values.

Even long-time participants may suddenly find themselves in conflict with the organization's values. If the individual is unable to change the group—in a reasonable period of time and in a reasonable manner—the individual must leave the group. The individual cannot stay and agitate and disrupt the group. If necessary, the group must ask the individual to leave.

Sometimes, there may be a conflict between the values of an organization. Now the decision is tough. A particular choice or situation forces a conflict between the organization's articulated values. For example, a bank offers your organization a contribution that will fund much-needed services for youth. You won't have to charge the youth at all, thus supporting your value of being financially accessible. However, the bank's hiring and lending practices penalize the poor and people of color. This conflicts with your values of diversity and respect for others. What will you do?

As Marion (1994) observes, "Questions of right and wrong are easy: do not kill; do not steal; do not cheat. So are ethical questions until the choice is between competing values and one must choose which course of action is more righteous" (page 56).

Exhibit 2–3 Women's Foundation of Southern Arizona Values Statement

We at the Women's Foundation of Southern Arizona share certain fundamental values. These values guide our judgments and actions as we work together to carry out our mission and achieve our vision. We are committed to transforming these values into action.

- Each woman and girl deserves
  - a life of full dignity;
  - an environment safe from physical violence and violence to the spirit;
  - to be given respect, regardless of her circumstances;
  - to make choices, including a woman's right to choose regarding birth;
  - to be empowered as a full participant in her communities, having access and voice and enjoying equality and equity;
  - to be recognized for her unique strengths and talents;
- We believe in **equality**—that all people have the same rights—and **equity**—that all people deserve fairness, impartiality, and justness. We believe that the good of the individual is contained in the common good.
- We believe in **truth**, seeing things as they really are.
  - We value honesty and candor.
  - Each of us is responsible and encouraged to speak up.
  - Although we respect each person's right to disagree, we expect support once a decision is made.
- We reach out and embrace **diversity**, including sexual orientation, economics, race, physical challenge, age and gender, and geographic location. We celebrate this richness as we build community.
- We value **change** and see ourselves as change agents. We are open-minded and creative. We encourage thoughtful risk taking.

- We value women as **leaders**. We strive to empower women and girls and model them as leaders throughout the community. Within our own organization, we create an environment that encourages women and girls to become leaders.
- We believe that a thriving community is built upon **personal responsibility and collective contributions.**
  - Together, we are accountable, both legally and morally, for the mission and vision of the Women's Foundation, and the health of our operations.
  - Individually, each of us honors her commitment and carries out her responsibilities.
  - We operate in a fiscally sound manner, recognizing that we can do only as much good as we can afford, so we aggressively seek the dollars to do our work.
  - We ask the community to help define needs, design responsive programs, and participate in ways that are personally meaningful and fulfilling.
  - We seek collaboration with other organizations to ensure the greatest advantages for the women and girls we serve, for our resources, and for the community at large.
- We believe that an **effective organization** continually examines and improves its practice. This spirit of learning is at the heart of any successful group.
- We believe that people work most creatively and enthusiastically when there is an understanding of **how decisions are made** and each person has the **opportunity to contribute her opinions.**
- We recognize that the **needs of women and girls** are distinct from the needs of the general population.
- We don't exclude men; we support women and girls.

Courtesy of Women's Foundation of Southern Arizona, Tucson, AZ.

The group decides which is the best choice, given competing values. To choose, the group talks together. Decision-making guidelines are also helpful. Marion (1994) proposes an ethical decision-making process that incorporates the following steps.

1. Clarify the problem.
2. Identify the key competing values at stake.
3. Identify the players and stakeholders.
4. Identify the most plausible alternatives.
5. Imagine the potential outcomes.
6. Evaluate the potential outcomes.
7. Decide on a course of action.
8. Test the decision.
9. Implement the decision.
10. Evaluate the results or consequences.
11. Modify policies and procedures.

Marion has an additional step: Share the decision with someone else—located between steps 8 and 9, above. This step is automatic in a group decision-making situation.

Aligning Behavior with Values

Articulating shared values is relatively easy. Finding consensus, particularly around this core, is not too difficult. The challenge is aligning behavior with values. To use the oft-repeated cliché, we have to "walk the talk."

Once the organization has articulated its values, make the values part of the corporate culture. Keep the values alive through behavior; formal and informal discussion; and organizational policy, procedure, and systems.

Your organization can use several strategies to help people understand and behave according to group values.

- When you interview candidates for board and staff positions, you share the values statement and describe how these values are displayed in the actions of the organization and its individuals. You emphasize that all staff and board members must adhere to these values when working with your organization.
- Include the criteria "adheres to our stated values" as part of the performance appraisal for staff and board members.
- Help each person within the organization to hold him- or herself accountable and extend that accountability to his and her colleagues. People provide feedback to each other when behavior does not appear to support the organization's values.
- Begin meetings by asking attendees to pull out the values statement and read it silently.
- When a difficult situation arises, review the values statement to set the stage for deliberation.
- Annually assess the degree to which behavior is aligned with values. Use a survey to compare individual and group behavior with each value. The survey asks respondents to rate their own individual performances and the performances of various teams or groups within the organization.
- Every three to five years, use the strategic planning process to reevaluate values and assess how well the organization is behaving. Convene group discussions and circulate surveys.
- Examine organizational policies and procedures to ensure that they reflect values. As necessary, develop new policies and procedures to support values.
- Compare performance with values when you appraise the performance of staff and volunteers.
- Periodically, start a board meeting with a quick review of values. At the end of the meeting, discuss how the group's behavior and actions reflected the organization's values.
- When you face a particularly difficult decision, talk about your values first. This discussion will offer you insights into decision making.

Defining Core Values

There are values that make groups and organizations function better. These values include such things as respect, honesty, and responsibility.

There are values that are essential to groups but may appear to conflict one with the other, for example, a commitment to the group agenda, rather than to a personal agenda, while respecting different opinions and agreeing to disagree.

Finally, there are the values that are reflective of your organization and its founders. Some differ from organization to organization; others may be similar but expressed differently.

Challenging Values

Group effectiveness depends on some form of common bond and an alignment of some shared views and values. Yet, this may suggest groupthink, exclusion, or totalitarianism to some.

If a group articulates its shared values and uses these as a foundation for the organization, does this produce homogeneity? Will the group seek out only clones of its existing members?

Clearly, this would not be advantageous. To survive in the next millennium, organizations must respond to a complex, changing, and uncertain world. Exclusionary practices and homogeneity threaten survival.

Avoid homogeneity and conformity by taking the following steps:

- First, the process to produce shared values must involve everyone. The collective, collaborative process cocreates values.
- Second, encourage group members to speak honestly.
- Third, include pluralism, diversity, and individual creativity as organizational values. Make sure your values speak to developing the individual's full potential. It is helpful for the group to establish values that support inclusiveness in ethnicity, gender, age, and experience.

> *A group can share values and still avoid conformity.*

Using Values in Fund Development

Naturally, your fund development program must operate in accordance with your organization's values. The need for a dollar cannot compromise your organization's values. For example:

- You are a theatre company with a resident corps of actors. You believe that these actors are the best in the business. You do not endorse the concept of stars. For a fundraising event, your theatre company would not host a national touring production with famous actors.
- You are a youth organization that develops self-esteem and life skills for teens. You offer teens alternatives to street activities and substance abuse. You

would not solicit gifts from alcohol manufacturers or distributors.

- Your organization values diversity. You believe in gender, generation, and ethnic diversity. You would be uncomfortable if all your fundraising activities were chaired by men.
- You are a homeless shelter. Hundreds of your donors give gifts of $50 or less. You also have affluent donors who represent the corporate and social sector of your community. If you plan a fundraising event with a ticket price of $100, you also plan a fundraising event with a more accessible ticket price.

These are fairly straightforward decisions regarding values. But consider those below. Initiate a conversation with your own board and colleagues—and get ready for some emotional discussion.

- Would your organization—no matter your cause— accept a gift from a tobacco company? The U.S. courts have found the tobacco industry guilty of conspiracy to harm people and guilty of falsifying information distributed to the public. But the gift would allow you to do good work. What is your values-based decision?
- If you were an environmental organization, would you accept a gift from Exxon after the Valdez oil spill? The spill was not intentional, although there was some question about negligence. The money would allow you to do good work, including lobbying for stronger regulation to fight future spills of this nature. What is your values-based decision?
- As a fundraising executive, would you accept a bequest made to you and your family from a donor to your agency? Over the years, the agency donor had become a dear friend to you personally. What is your values-based decision?

In addition to complying with the organization's values, you should articulate specific values for fund development. Why? Because fund development is susceptible to the appearance (and sometimes the reality) of inappropriate behavior. Increasingly, people are suspicious of fundraising practice. Respond by articulating values for your fund development program.

The fundraising profession has already defined some values by establishing codes of ethics, standards of professional practice, and donors' rights. Your organization can use these. For example, hire only a fundraiser who belongs to a professional association and subscribes to an ethical code. Communicate the code, standards, and

donors' rights to your various constituents, not just your donors.

Talk with your volunteers and staff about their values for fund development. Involve the development committee, board, and staff. Discuss how your fund development values could affect fundraising activities and decisions. Then adopt the values as organizational policy. See Exhibit 2–4 for examples of how fund development can falter when organizational values are not clarified.

Use the National Society of Fund Raising Executives Code of Ethical Principles (renamed the Association of Fundraising Professionals) and Standards of Professional Practice and the Donor Bill of Rights as a starting point for your organization's conversation. Also take a look at Accountable Not-for-Profit Organizations. Discuss these, then articulate your organization's fund development values. Or adopt these statements as your organization's values for fund development. See Appendixes C, D, and E for copies.

THE ART OF LEADERSHIP

Leadership is the second component of effective infrastructure. Effective fundraisers are good leaders. They lead the fund development function, and they lead organizational development.

Leadership guarantees that your institution develops the four relationships central to an effective organization and critical to productive fund development. Leaders facilitate the ongoing process to develop, sustain, and renew these relationships.

> *What is the leadership issue of our time? How can we create sustained solutions for complex systemic issues whose solutions cannot be mandated from the top? Asked another way: How can human communities productively confront complex issues where hierarchical authority is inadequate to bring about change?*
>
> *Peter M. Senge*

What Is Leadership?

Leadership means the willingness and ability to lead and influence others. A good organization should be rich in leaders. This network of individuals linking together creates a web to support your organization. Leadership acts as the glue that holds your organization's infrastructure together.

The independent school's board of directors was discussing the projected budget for the new year. Staff proposed an increase in gifts, so the fund development plan reflected more volunteer solicitations to meet this goal.

Board members suggested raising tuition instead. "We can reduce the need for more gifts if we increase tuition modestly," they said. Happily, the tuition increase likely would not cause a decrease in enrollment.

But staff countered, "We will appear too expensive for many families. They'll feel excluded."

Staff believed that pricing was a barrier to many of those who wanted to attend the school. Staff recommended retaining current tuition rates in order to encourage enrollment from a more diverse population. More fundraising would subsidize reasonable tuition.

The staff was expressing their shared value. But board and staff had never discussed values. The budget discussion could have been different if the school's values already had been articulated.

A marketing firm agreed to donate copywriting and design services to my small grassroots organization. Staff and volunteers were thrilled!

My organization serves some of the community's poorest people. We provide food and shelter, and some employment and life skills training.

We are known for being well managed, and our volunteers are well respected in the community. Our building is old but serves us well. Our newsletter and agency brochure are attractive but modest.

Funds come from government contracts, business and foundation grants, and thousands of gifts, both small and large, from individuals. We're kind of low-key when we solicit gifts. We use direct mail and face-to-face solicitation. Our special events are carefully designed to avoid the appearance of affluence. That would be uncomfortable for our volunteers, those we serve, and those who give to us.

So now the marketing firm was creating our first-ever fundraising brochure. The draft was gorgeous. Full of photographs, four colors printed on glossy paper. (Thank heavens, the firm agreed to help us get wholesale paper and reduced-cost printing.) The brochure's size was unique so it would stand out in a crowded mail box.

Naturally, the marketing firm and printer would be recognized on the back of the brochure. Everyone would know that we had received donated services.

Strangely, I was increasingly uncomfortable. The brochure was so glitzy, so high-end corporate. We would have to buy specialty envelopes to accommodate the unique size. Even though design and some printing were donated, I wondered how donors and prospects would react. Would they think we had used our donations well? For the donated time and money spent on one brochure, several print pieces could have been produced for our organization.

But even worse, the brochure didn't seem to reflect the feelings or philosophy of our organization. Sure, we deserve good design and copywriting. But we aren't the glitzy or glossy type.

I realized that the brochure was great for some other organization, but not for mine. By the time I figured this out, the brochure was almost finished. It was too late.

How did we arrive at this point? Eventually, I figured it out. I hadn't explained our values to the marketing firm before work began on our behalf. I didn't talk with them about how we wanted to be perceived as an organization and the values we believed in.

And what about the brochure? We used it, minimally and with discomfort.

Leadership should be born out of the understanding of the needs of those who would be affected by it.
Marian Anderson

Because leadership exists to help accomplish group purpose, leaders are accountable to the group. Leadership depends on the shared values and vision of the group, rather than on an independent belief system and personal agenda of the leader. Robert K. Greenleaf (1991) describes this as the servant-leader concept in his work, *Servant Leadership: A Journey into the Nature of Legitimate Power and Greatness.*

Contrast this to an abusive concept of leadership where an individual ensures the outcomes he wants and prevents those he doesn't want. This person diminishes other people, enforcing power to bring about intended consequences in the behavior of others. This is done without concern for the rights and initiative of the others.

Another negative view of leadership is the vision of a parent figure who puts all things right. As Gardner observes, "To some extent the conventional views of leadership are shallow, and set us up for endless disappointment. There is an element of wanting to be rescued, of wanting a parental figure who will set all things right" (Gardner 1990, xi).

Peter Block (1993), author of *Stewardship: Choosing Service over Self-Interest,* uses the concept of stewardship to alter the conventional theory of leadership. Block's stewardship incorporates accountability, partnership, empowerment, and service. He notes that leadership means initiative and responsibility, without taking control and disempowering others. Leaders are partners. They retain initiative and accountability but avoid dominance and parental guidance.

In systems thinking theory, the leader helps create a learning organization and leads the organization's learning. Traditionally, observes Daniel H. Kim (1993), leaders are perceived to be out in front of everyone else, knowing all the answers. However, this conflicts with the concept of a learning organization. Experience shows that people learn by doing and learn by taking risks. When taking risks, people often make mistakes, and that is part of learning. In the new world, Kim remarks, leaders are still out in front. However, these leaders are taking risks, making mistakes, and learning faster than others are.

The leader helps others to learn. The leader of today and tomorrow develops a community of learners by reaching the learner inside each individual. This leader helps others to question and overcome their limitations.

Kim goes on to say that, in addition to leading the learning process and being open to making mistakes, the leader seeks the truth. The leader lets everyone know that the truth is what she or he wants and expects to hear.

The leader also ensures safety. An organization committed to learning is a safe place. These organizations recognize that, without a sense of safety, people will not take risks and will not tell the truth. In a safe environment where trust, commitment, and responsibility are shared, people will raise the tough issues and help the organization change.

Leaders are made, not born. Sure, circumstance and situations often produce leaders. But more importantly, leadership can be developed. Individuals can develop leadership skills and learn leadership tasks.

Just as leaders are obliged to develop new leaders, so are organizations. Effective organizations create an infrastructure that produces new leaders regularly.

> *As a leader, you can influence only three things. You can influence people, you can influence your strategy, and you can influence operations.*
> *Lawrence A. Bossidy*

Ideally, there is a leadership partnership between volunteers and staff. Unfortunately, despite the best recruitment process, securing volunteer leaders cannot be guaranteed. However, organizations can ensure that they hire leaders. The board hires a chief executive who possesses leadership attributes and skills and demonstrates the ability to carry out leadership functions and tasks. The board then expects that the chief executive will hire other leaders at all levels within the organization.

Your organization needs a leader as your chief fundraising executive. She or he leads the development operation and serves as a key leader within the institution itself.

What Do Leaders Do?

Leaders carry out key functions and specific tasks. Effective leaders know leadership is an art, as well as a developed skill. Committed leaders actually study leadership to improve their own performance.

> *Leadership should be more participative than directive, more enabling than performing.*
> *Mary P. Poole*

The leadership functions and tasks presented here are a synthesis of the author's opinion and a wealth of writings available about leadership and leadership development. Sources used in this section include Drucker (1990), Gardner (1990), DePree (1989), Pottruck and Pearce (2000), Collins and Porras (1994), and Chatterjee (1998). Other sources include *Leader to Leader*, a publication of the Drucker Foundation and Jossey-Bass Publishers, *Harvard Business Review*, and *Perdido: Leadership with a Conscience* (Trinity Foundation, IL).

Each of the functions and tasks described here is essential to help build the four relationships critical to effective fund development. More important, these functions and tasks are essential to developing a healthy organization.

The tasks are grouped into four function areas: people, organizational, personal, and community.

- The people function presents tasks that relate to the individuals within the organization.
- The organizational function focuses on tasks that bring people together as one entity, moving them forward to achieve the organization's mission and vision.
- The personal function entails tasks that describe how the leader relates to him- or herself.
- The community function highlights tasks that connect the organization to the external community.

As you review this list, ask yourself

- Do I carry out these leadership functions as part of my life's work, no matter in which organization I operate?
- Have I developed the skills necessary to carry out these functions?
- Do I evaluate my own performance regularly, improving as necessary?
- Does my organization know that these tasks are the responsibility of our leaders, and do we regularly evaluate the performance of our leaders?

- Does my organization discuss leadership regularly at the governance and management levels? Have we articulated together what we mean by leadership, how we will develop leaders, and how we will evaluate them?
- Does my organization have a plan to foster continuity within its leadership and to ensure succession?
- Does my organization have a plan to identify, cultivate, and develop leaders, and do we implement it effectively?

People Functions

1. Value each individual.

   Recognize the importance of each individual compared to her or his tasks or functions. Encourage personal mastery and self-fulfillment. Encourage diversity and pluralism. Welcome the unusual person and different idea. Consistently advocate for equity.

2. Gather and develop leaders.

   Recruit leaders to join the organization. Help others within the organization to exercise leadership. Choose the best and brightest to replace existing leaders. Seek competence in others and in self.

3. Motivate others.

   Encourage commitment, not just compliance, by engaging the collective beliefs of people in your organization. Align group and individual beliefs and actions.

4. Exercise political judgment.

   Cope with the conflicting needs and desires of diverse constituencies, both internal and external.

5. Remove obstacles.

   Eliminate barriers that prevent others from doing their jobs. Enable others to realize their full potential and aspirations. Anticipate problems, identify solutions, and redirect energies of self and others.

6. Engage constituents.

   Enlist constituents in conversation, ensure participative management, and develop consensus. Ensure that everyone influences decision making and understands the results.

7. Teach and promote the skills and art of the specific job, as well as the organization's work.

8. Enable others.

   Specific functions of enabling volunteers (also applicable to staff) are described in Chapter 5. In summary, they are:

   –transmitting organizational values

   –engaging people in the meaning of your organization

   –respecting and using the skills, expertise, experience, and insights of people

   –providing direction and resources, removing barriers, and helping develop skills

   –articulating expectations and clarifying roles and relationships

   –communicating (which includes helping people transform information into knowledge and learning)

   –encouraging people to question organizational assumptions and to ask strategic questions

   –ensuring quality decision making

   –anticipating conflicts and facilitating resolution

   –engaging people in process, as well as tasks

   –encouraging people to use their power, practice their authority, and accept their responsibility

   –modeling behavior

   –coaching people to succeed

   –managing

   –enhancing attrition

   –monitoring, evaluating, and enhancing enabling

Organizational Functions

1. See the entire system, the big picture, as well as its interrelated parts. Think long term, as well as short term.

2. Affirm values and set the highest ethical standards.

   Ensure that the organization articulates its shared values and communicates these values. Help the organization to act in accordance with its values.

3. Envision direction and goals.

   Create vision through a process that engages people throughout the organization. Sometimes, the leader has a vision and uses group process to test, refine, and build ownership for his or her vision. Sometimes, the leader intentionally does not envision a future but rather engages the organization in a process to generate vision together.

4. Institutionalize leadership.

   Create an infrastructure (corporate culture and systems) that supports leadership development. Ensure that the organization designs and implements specific programs and activities so that others can develop and practice leadership.

5. Ensure that the questions worth asking are asked.

   Encourage intellectual curiosity. Encourage others to ask strategic questions. Identify issues and focus the organization's attention.

6. Have ideas and point the organization toward opportunities and solutions.

   Articulate reality and anticipate multiple futures.

7. Manage.

   Set priorities and devise plans. Allocate resources. Organize and build the institution. Keep the system functioning, and make decisions.

8. Build community.

   Unify the group and preserve trust within the organization. Use dissonance but diminish dysfunctional conflict.

9. Listen and communicate.

   Find out what others think. Bring everyone to the table and make sure they have a voice. Inform, explain, and teach. Communicate why, not just what or how.

10. Serve as a symbol within and outside the organization.

    Serve as the organization's chief spokesperson and diplomat. Promote the organization's unique character. Tell the organization's stories.

11. Represent the group.

    Cross boundaries and build relationships between groups, organizations, and communities.

12. Renew, change, and build a learning organization.

    Foster the process of individual and team learning, renewal, and change. Create a safe, risk-free environment.

13. Keep it all going—and that includes implementation!

    Provide momentum and facilitate transformation. Balance continuity, transition, and change. Make sure that things are implemented. Remember: "Implementation is the real source of competitive advantage! Even the best idea is only as valuable as your ability to execute it!" (Roberts 2000, 147).

14. Create a legacy for the future.

    Leave behind such things as financial health, strong relationships, effective leadership, and a solid reputation for the organization.

Personal Functions

1. Delegate but do not abdicate.
2. Be prepared to do anything you would ask of others.
3. Take risks and make mistakes.
4. Recognize and, as appropriate, change your own assumptions or paradigms (called *mental models* in learning organizations), and help others to identify and change theirs.
5. Set high standards for yourself and others. Evaluate your own performance and change.
6. Welcome criticism. Learn from it.

As Dee Hock observes, "Active critics are a great asset. Without the slightest expenditure of time or effort, we have our weakness and error made apparent and alternatives proposed. We need only listen carefully, dismiss that which arises from ignorance, ignore that which arises from envy or malice, and embrace that which has merit" (Hock 2000, 25).

Community Functions

1. Ensure that the organization is relevant to the external community.

   See Chapter 3 on strategic planning.

2. Perpetually connect the organization to the external community.

   Use the ongoing strategic planning process. Build knowledge alliances with organizations and community leaders to ensure ongoing, two-way conversation, information sharing, and learning. Collaborate with other organizations to meet community needs. Leaders also participate as volunteers in the community, encouraging the organization's employees to do the same.

3. Build civic capacity.

   Civic capacity refers to the ability of a community to identify the challenges and opportunities it faces and to bring together the diversity of the community to address these issues effectively. Civic capacity is about empowering individuals and organizations across the three sectors to work together for the good of the whole. When a community is strong in civic capacity, the community welcomes traditional and non-traditional organizations and individuals to the table to share power. Effective leaders work to build civic capacity, for the good of the community, regardless of their own organization's role or position.

4. Ensure environmental accountability.

   Environmental issues are of grave concern in the world of today and tomorrow. As leaders connect their organizations to the external community, these leaders promote accountability to the environment.

> *The kind of leadership most effective today is similar to the kind of service that the best consultant gives a client: collaborative assistance that is both problem solving and developmental. Its target is both the situation and the professional capability of the person.*
>
> *Bridges and Mitchell*

Attributes and Skills of Leaders

Effective leaders possess certain attributes or attitudes. Leaders master learnable skills and behave in certain ways. The ideas presented here incorporate the author's opinion with the various sources noted previously in this section.

- Leaders are willing and eager to accept and share responsibility. Believing in Block's stewardship, they empower others by distributing responsibility and authority, even while retaining responsibility for the whole.
- Leaders possess emotional, intellectual, and physical vitality and stamina. They are dependable, confident, assertive, adaptable, highly tolerant, and flexible. They are courageous, resolute, patient, and steadfast.
- Both visionary and practical, leaders lead through serving. They neither coerce others nor depend on official status or authority.
- Leaders balance being out in front with following and supporting. They balance their own egos with the egos of others. Leaders acknowledge responsibility for failure and share responsibility for success.
- Competent and knowledgeable in key fields, leaders know the organization and its work. DePree (1989) refers to this as *task competence*. For him, this includes personal performance and achievement plus the potential for continuing growth and accountability. Self-aware leaders evaluate their own strengths and weaknesses and work toward personal mastery.
- Leaders seek diversity and nurture pluralism. They are comfortable with complexity, ambiguity, and uncertainty. They welcome and learn from the skills and experience of others. Leaders encourage contrary opinion, are comfortable with disagreement, and accept conflict. Leaders recognize that creativity and innovation result from new opinions, conflicting ideas, and stimulating questions.

> *The art of leadership is liberating people to do what is required of them in the most effective and humane way possible.*
>
> Max DePree

- Even while they are achievement-oriented, leaders are committed to process and demand outcomes from process. Whether choosing "ready, aim, fire" or "ready, fire, aim," leaders make sure that their colleagues understand and own decisions.
- Leaders are intelligent and able to judge and act. They exercise good management and decision-making skills.
- Leaders know that their individual behavior engenders the behavior of others.
- Leaders deal well with people and motivate themselves as well as others. Leaders are sensitive to others and respect and understand the wants and needs of their diverse constituents. Leaders understand group behavior, as well.
- Leaders communicate easily at all levels and with diverse constituents. They listen and hear. They tell stories and use symbols well.
- Leaders are ethical and honest. They are clear about their own beliefs and values regarding human nature, the role of the organization, measurement of performance, and so forth. Leaders are consistent in belief and practice, at work and in their personal lives. Leaders are disciplined and persevering.
- Leaders are excellent organizational development specialists and good managers.
- Leaders possess emotional intelligence, which they have translated into a high level of emotional competence (see overview in the section below).

In *Clicks and Mortar*, Pottruck and Pearce (2000) summarize the core competencies that Schwab identified for its future leadership. Most of these competencies are similar to those described in this text. However, some offer a new perspective or emphasis, and some are new (pages 191 and 192).

- Has passion for service
- Inspires trust
- Communicates effectively
- Seeks self-development
- Drives execution, demonstrates results orientation
- Builds organizational relationships
- Leads change and innovation
- Inspires and develops others
- Creates vision, thinks through strategy, correctly judges tactics
- Encourages and manages differences in hiring, dialogue, and development
- Manages resources effectively
- Manages technology

Are leaders all of this all of the time? Of course not. Leaders try and fail in small and large ways. Leaders know this. But they continue to strive.

Issues in Leadership

Roots of Excellence

Excellent performers at work possess three domains of competence. These are IQ, expertise, and emotional intelligence. But emotional intelligence is the most critical performance factor (Research, David McClelland, Harvard University psychologist, and Goleman, 2000).

Leaders possess a high degree of emotional competence. See Exhibit 2–5; it reads like a litany of leadership qualities.

According to the research on high performance, IQ is of limited importance; expertise is important; and emotional intelligence is most important. Emotional intelligence is what affects an individual's ability to learn emotional competence. This competence is a learned capability and results in outstanding work performance.

An individual's emotional competence shows the degree to which that emotional intelligence has been translated into on-the-job capabilities. Emotional competence depends on four elements of emotional intelligence: self-awareness, self-management, social awareness, and social skill. As Goleman notes (2000), good customer service is an emotional competence based on empathy, whereas the competence of trustworthiness depends on self-regulation.

Just because someone is high in emotional intelligence does not mean that she or he will learn the emotional competencies required for high performance at work. However, possessing high emotional intelligence does indicate the potential to learn the emotional competencies.

Just because you are high in emotional intelligence does not mean that you have translated that into emo-

---

Exhibit 2–5 Framework for Emotional Competence—The Relationship between Emotional Intelligence and Emotional Competencies

Emotional intelligence—the ability to manage our relationships and ourselves effectively—consists of four fundamental capabilities: self-awareness, self-management, social awareness, and social skill. Each capability, in turn, is composed of specific sets of competencies. Below is a list of the capabilities and their corresponding traits.

SELF-AWARENESS

- Emotional self-awareness: the ability to read and understand your emotions, as well as to recognize their impact on work performance, relationships, and the like.
- Accurate self-assessment: a realistic evaluation of your strengths and limitations.
- Self-confidence: a strong and positive sense of one's self-worth.

SELF-MANAGEMENT

- Self-Control: the ability to keep disruptive emotions and impulses under control.
- Trustworthiness: a consistent display of honesty and integrity.
- Conscientiousness: the ability to manage yourself and your responsibilities.
- Adaptability: skill at adjusting to changing situations and overcoming obstacles.
- Achievement orientation: the drive to meet an internal standard of excellence.
- Initiative: a readiness to seize opportunities.

SOCIAL AWARENESS

- Empathy: skill at sensing other people's emotions, understanding their perspective, and taking an active interest in their concerns.
- Organizational awareness: the ability to read the currents of organizational life, build decision networks, and navigate politics.
- Service orientation: the ability to recognize and meet customers' needs.

SOCIAL SKILL

- Visionary leadership: the ability to take charge and inspire with a compelling vision.
- Influence: the ability to wield a range of persuasive tactics.
- Developing others: the propensity to bolster the abilities of others through feedback and guidance.
- Communication: skill at listening and at sending clear, convincing, and well-tuned messages.
- Change catalyst: proficiency in initiating new ideas and leading people in a new direction.
- Conflict management: the ability to de-escalate disagreements and orchestrate resolutions.
- Building bonds: proficiency at cultivating and maintaining a web of relationships.
- Teamwork and collaboration: competence at promoting cooperation and building teams.

Source: Reprinted with permission from D. Goleman, Leadership That Gets Results, *Harvard Business Review*, March–April 2000, p. 80, © 2000, Harvard Business School Publishing.

tional competence on the job. But leaders certainly have. Leaders display emotional competence and continually enhance it within themselves.

With information in hand about emotional intelligence and competence, leaders develop this understanding within colleagues in the organization. The best leaders develop ways to enhance emotional competence within workers.

Six Styles of Leadership

Through further research, Goleman (2000) describes six styles of leadership resulting from the different components of emotional intelligence. Different styles of leadership clearly affect performance and results, and the research provides guidance about which style is most effective when.

To paraphrase Goleman, the six styles of leadership are:

1. Coercive leaders: These individuals demand immediate compliance.
2. Authoritative leaders: These leaders mobilize people toward a vision.
3. Affiliative leaders: These individuals create emotional bonds and harmony within the organization.
4. Democratic leaders: These leaders build consensus through conversation and participation.
5. Pacesetting leaders: These individuals expect excellence and self-direction from those they lead.
6. Coaching leaders: These leaders develop their people for the future.

The research "strongly suggests" that leaders should be flexible, changing styles as the situation demands. Moreover, the research clarified links between leadership, emotional intelligence, organizational climate, and performance. According to the research data, the authoritative leadership style affects climate most positively. However, affiliative, democratic, and coaching leadership styles follow closely (Exhibit 2–6). Nonetheless, Goleman stresses that no leadership style should be used exclusively and that "all have at least short-term uses."

> *All six leadership styles have a measurable effect on organizational climate and on performance.*
> *Danial Goleman*

Organizational climate—or working environment— has long been known to affect performance, and six factors influence climate.

To paraphrase Goleman, these factors are:

1. Flexibility: how free employees feel to innovate without red tape
2. Responsibility: employee sense of responsibility to the organization
3. Standards: the level of standards that people set within the organization
4. Rewards: the sense of accuracy about performance feedback and the appropriateness of rewards for performance
5. Clarity: how clear mission and values are to the people within the organization
6. Commitment: the level of commitment to a common purpose shared by those within the organization

Can Leaders Be Managers, Too?

At some time, someone started the myth that those who are good leaders typically are not good managers. In this myth, leaders see the forest but cannot see the trees. Leaders lead but they are not good at implementation and follow-through.

Nonsense. The most effective leaders see the forest *and* the trees. Maintaining perspective on the big picture, as well as the small details, is essential to get where you are going.

Leaders must help themselves and others translate vision into the small steps to get there. Leaders must acknowledge the challenges inherent within the detail and help manage process to accomplishment.

Is Charisma Essential to Leadership?

Absolutely not. Just read *Built to Last* (Collins and Porras, 1994) if you want documented proof.

The dictionary defines *charisma* as "a personal magic of leadership arousing special popular loyalty or enthusiasm for a public figure; a specific magnetic charm or appeal." But charisma does not guarantee substance, and leaders have substance. Take a look at those you would describe as charismatic. Are they necessarily good leaders, or are they simply engaging and somehow magical?

Now take a look at the individuals you respect as leaders. Is it charisma that encourages you to follow these leaders, or is it their ability to influence you with meaningful information? Is it charisma that inspires you, or is it the leader's ability to communicate values and involve you in dialogue?

Consider this definition for leadership, modified from the *U.S. Marine Corps Manual.* Note there is no reference to charisma: "Leadership is the art of influencing and directing people in such a way as to obtain their willing support, confidence, respect, and loyal cooperation to accomplish a mission."

Exhibit 2–6 Six Leadership Styles, Their Origin within Emotional Intelligence, When They Work Best, and Their Impact on Climate and Performance

	Coercive	*Authoritative*	*Affiliative*	*Democratic*	*Pacesetting*	*Coaching*
The leader's modus operandi	Demands immediate compliance	Mobilizes people toward a vision	Creates harmony and builds emotional bonds	Forges consensus through participation	Sets high standards for performance	Develops people for the future
The style in phrase	"Do what I tell you."	"Come with me."	"People come first."	"What do you think?"	"Do as I do, now."	"Try this."
Underlying emotional intelligence competencies	Drive to achieve, initiative, self-control	Self-confidence, empathy, change catalyst	Empathy, building relationships, communication	Collaboration, team leadership, communication	Conscientiousness, drive to achieve, initiative	Developing others, empathy, self-awareness
When the style works best	In a crisis, kick-start a turnaround, or with problem employees	When changes require a new vision or when a clear direction is needed	To heal rifts in a team or to motivate people during stressful circumstances	To build buy-in or consensus, or to get input from valuable employees	To get quick results from a highly motivated and competent team	To help an employee improve performance or develop long-term strengths
Overall impact on climate	Negative	Most strongly positive	Positive	Positive	Negative	Positive

Source: Reprinted with permission from D. Goleman, Leadership That Gets Results, *Harvard Business Review*, March–April 2000, p. 80, © 2000, Harvard Business School Publishing.

Leaders as Reflective Practitioners

Leaders are reflective practitioners. Leaders create an organizational climate that encourages individual and group reflection. Also, leaders help others to develop their capacity for reflection.

"Reflection is the art of listening to our inner voice for insights about a question and accessing intelligence that may go beyond our personal knowledge or experience." So says Robert Gunn in his article, "Leading from Within: Strategies for and Reflections on Becoming a Leader of Leaders," (2000, 11).

Paul Pribbenow, PhD, CFRE, speaks and writes about professionals as reflective practitioners. He encourages each of us to reflect on the work that we do, to understand better the why, not just the how. Paul challenges us to find ways in which we can become reflective practitioners, committing the time and focus to this important endeavor. Finally, Paul invites us to speak reflectively with each other, with colleagues across the diverse sectors, sharing with and learning from each other.

Gunn reminds us that our thinking creates our reality. He also notes that, as humans, we have a unique gift: the power to change our thoughts. As we change our thoughts, so our reality will change. Surely, Pribbenow would echo the same. To reflect upon one's history, experience, actions, and their implications helps us understand, then allows us to create a new future. Reflection can help us create our reality.

As reflective practitioners, leaders have a deep understanding of themselves and strive to understand those around them. These leaders strive to create communities of reflection, thus expanding understanding and learning. As Gunn notes, these leaders serve others, as well as themselves.

Gunn proposes a set of questions to help the reflective practitioner become aware of his or thinking habits: (page 17)

- Am I responding to my own ego?
- Do I allow myself some quiet time to reflect (or am I booking my schedule fully, going from one project or meeting to the next without break)?

- Am I asking questions of others to elicit a full understanding of their thoughts or statements?
- Am I thinking in terms of puzzles, rather than crises?
- Do I look for blame or innocence in what others tell me?
- Do I spend time thinking about issues or jump to conclusions as rapidly as possible?
- Am I comfortable admitting that I do not know the answer?

Leaders as Communicators

Read any business book. The job of leaders is to make information "useful and meaningful to others, as a way of moving them toward committed engagement in [the organization]" (Pottruck and Pearce 2000, 110). That's not much different than the theory that communication is two-way and begins with listening.

> *Conscious leaders have the ability to listen simultaneously to three dimensions of language—the factual, the intentional, and the transformational. They pick up factual details with the precision of the scientist; gain insight into the intention of the speaker with the imagination of a poet, and are willing to be transformed by what they hear with the zeal of a pilgrim.*
> *Debashis Chatterjee*

Pottruck and Pearce go on to say, "As a leader, every day I try to remember that others will tolerate my point of view, but they will act only on their own. Accordingly, part of my job is to reconcile those points of view, to try to help everyone, including myself, gain a more insightful view of reality. In this work, listening is every bit as critical as speaking. Two-way communication is vital" (page 112).

Too often, people may confuse listening as the precursor to answering, rather than listening as a way of learning. How many times have you watched someone prepare an answer while listening to another, rather than truly listening to hear and learn? How often have you done that yourself?

Pottruck and Pearce (2000) talk about listening as an "attitude with a single focus: The more I *am known* by those I want to follow me, and the more I *can know* them, the greater will be our ability to do great things together" (page 116). Approaching listening with this attitude allows the leader to reaffirm that others are "real partners in the enterprise," being heard *and* sharing accountability.

In *Clicks and Mortar*, Pottruck and Pearce (2000) note that effective leadership communication incorporates three separate elements: speaking, listening, and engagement. Although speaking and listening are skills that can be learned, Pottruck and Pearce observe that engagement requires a genuine interest in others, a respect for their diversity, and a desire to hear what they feel and believe.

Engaging others does not take away the authority of the leader, nor does engagement compromise the leader's ability to make quick decisions. Leadership is about ongoing conversation and participatory decision making. Leadership is also about making decisions that are best for the entire organization, regardless of any single individual's opinion. As Pottruck says, "Even as I encourage dialogue and listen carefully to everyone who contributes, my responsibility is to make decisions that are best for the whole...and to continue to have the participation of those who disagree with me. It requires that I understand other people's points of view—and that I can acknowledge our differences" (page 115).

People make a commitment to their leader. Indeed, there are no leaders without followers, and, to be a follower, one commits to a leader. Pottruck and Pearce wrestle with the relationship between the leader and his or her colleagues. They turn to business coach and author Noel Tichy, who claims that people seeking to commit need basic information to make their decisions and constantly seek reinforcement of that basic information throughout their lives in the organization. And what is this basic information? People want to know who the leader is and where the organization is going. They expect the leader to answer these questions well and to answer them again and again. Pottruck and Pearce add another element of basic information: why the organization is going there.

So leaders communicate who they are personally, where the organization is going, and why it is going there. And leaders do this over and over, in ways that can be heard and understood by their colleagues.

> *The day [people] stop bringing you their problems is the day you have stopped leading them. They have either lost confidence that you can help them or concluded that you do not care.*
> *Colin Powell*

Leadership and Diversity

Leadership is all about diversity—welcoming it, respecting it, and reveling in it. Diversity is more than racial or cultural, gender or age. Diversity refers to differing opinions and varying approaches. Diversity makes for a rich and complex world.

As Pottruck and Pearce (2000) note, diversity is more than affirmative action, and its rationale is more than moral fairness. Diversity is "the practical ground of good business" (page 57). Significant diversity in the people of your organization brings significant diversity in the perspectives offered within your organization. Significant is what is important. Effective organizations bring together people who may disagree on matters of substance. That's what adds value to the organization: enough diversity to ask questions, question assumptions, and question answers, to stimulate breakthroughs and encourage change, to facilitate learning and reaffirm values.

Leaders know that their organizations must be innovative and cutting-edge to respond to this rich and complex world. So leaders encourage diversity. Leaders figure out "what it will take to make *sustainable, long-term* progress in gaining and keeping a diverse group of people" (page 62).

When Dee Hock, founder and CEO emeritus of Visa USA and Visa International, talks about hiring, he is certainly mindful of diversity: "Never hire or promote in your own image. It is foolish to replicate your strength. It is stupid to replicate your weakness. Employ, trust, and reward those whose perspective, ability, and judgment are radically different from your own and recognize that it requires uncommon humility, tolerance, and wisdom" (Hock 2000, 25).

Leaders know, too, that diversity increases complexity, and complexity produces ambiguity. Leaders know that people are often frustrated by complexity and threatened by ambiguity. So leaders help their organizations develop tolerance for both.

Encouraging diversity and tolerating complexity stand in direct opposition to complacence. Leaders fight complacence. They work against the status quo, or what Pottruck and Pearce call "incumbency." In this vein, Collins and Porras (1994) urge leaders to consider the following questions (page 190):

- What "mechanisms of discontent" can you create that would obliterate complacence and bring about change and improvement from within, yet are consistent with your core ideology? How can you give these mechanisms sharp teeth?
- What are you doing to invest for the future *while* doing well today?
- Do people in your company understand that *comfort is not the objective*—that life in a visionary company is not supposed to be easy? Does your company reject doing well as an end goal, replacing

it with the never-ending discipline of working to do better tomorrow than it did today?

Chaordic Leadership

Understanding Complexity

Some say that understanding is the principal science of the future. And just what is complexity? It's "autocatalytic, nonlinear, complex adaptive systems" (Hock 2000, 21). Many believe that these systems—even life itself (remember *Jurassic Park* and chaos theory?)—"arise and thrive on the edge of chaos with just enough order to give them pattern" (page 21).

Hock has coined the term *chaord* to describe what he means by "any self-organizing, self-governing, adaptive, nonlinear, complex organism, organization, community or system, whether physical, biological, or social, the behavior of which harmoniously blends characteristics of both chaos and order." His new term combines portions of the words *chaos* and *order*.

For Hock, organizations are chaordic and, thus, require a new form of leadership. He observes that an organization harmoniously blends conflicting characteristics such as competition and cooperation or theoretical and experiential learning.

In some ways, this complex or chaordic blending is reminiscent of the intentional choice fostered in *Built to Last*: "No 'tyranny of the or' rather embrace the genius of the and." Collins and Porras (1994) stress that visionary companies avoid choosing between two apparent paradoxes, e.g., change OR stability, low cost OR high quality, and so forth. Instead, organizations that are built to last welcome two "seemingly contradictory forces or ideas at the same time." In other words, these organizations accept and tolerate Hock's theory of the chaord.

Chaordic organizations require chaordic leadership. For Hock, this means a different understanding of the relationship between the leader and follower, yet another dichotomy.

Leaders and followers require each other to exist, and both presume choice. Any coercion is merely a form of manipulation. If a follower is coerced—even following willingly the dominance of the leader—then she or he is no longer a follower. Neither the follower nor the leader can be "bound" one to the other. Hock observes that "where behavior is compelled, there you will find tyranny, however benign" (page 21). For Hock, the leader/follower relationship reflects, instead, induced behavior.

Everyone agrees that leadership is not always ethical, open, and constructive. Everyone seems to know a leader who induces destructive behavior and does so through unethical and even corrupt ways. If you cannot find one such leader close to home today, just look at history. There you will find any number of examples of leaders and followers—choosing to work together—in ways harmful to others.

But surely when we think of leadership, we aspire to an ethical, constructive, open behavior that generates positive results for the good of many. This leadership requires leaders who are ethical and honest, trustworthy and open.

Hock challenges us with the question, How do we make sure that our leaders are ethical, honest, trustworthy, and open? His answer is simple. Follow only those who are! He observes: "True leaders are those who epitomize the general sense of the community—who symbolize, legitimize, and strengthen behavior in accordance with the sense of the community—who enable its shared purpose, values and beliefs to emerge and be transmitted.

> *In the deepest sense, distinction between leaders and followers is meaningless. In every moment of life, we are simultaneously leading and following. There is never a time when our knowledge, judgment, and wisdom are not more useful and applicable than that of another. There is never a time when the knowledge, judgment, and wisdom of another are not more useful and applicable than ours. At any time that "other" may be superior, subordinate, or peer.*
>
> *Dee Hock*

A true leader's behavior is induced by the behavior of every individual choosing where to be led. The important thing to remember is that true leadership and induced behavior have an inherent tendency to the good, while tyranny (dominator management) and compelled behavior have an inherent tendency to evil" (page 22).

Hock brings us back to the inextricable link between leader and follower—the partnership of the individual and the collective. Leadership is about our shared sense—shared between leader and follower—of our values and mission, vision and direction. As Hock says, followers lead by choosing whom to follow. Leaders lead with an understanding of and commitment to their followers.

So what do chaordic leaders do? Hock proposes four things.

- First and most important, manage yourself. By this he means your own integrity, character, ethics, knowledge and wisdom, temperament, words, and acts.
- Second, manage those who have authority over you. Manage your own boss, supervisor, director, or regulator—whomever—to ensure their consent and support. Without their consent and support, no leader can exercise his or her own judgment, follow his or her own conviction, innovate and enable others, or achieve results.
- Third, manage your peers. That's right, manage those over whom you have no authority and who have no authority over you. Manage these relationships well so that your associates—whether inside or outside the organization—respect and have confidence in you, your behavior, words, and deeds.
- Fourth, manage those who report to you. But Hock claims, if you manage yourself, your superiors and your peers, there won't be enough time to manage your subordinates—and that's great! Hock summarizes in this way: "One need only select decent people, introduce them to the concept, induce them to practice it, and enjoy the process. If those over whom we have authority properly manage themselves, manage us, manage their peers, and replicate the process with those they employ, what is there to do but see they are properly recognized and rewarded—and stay out of their way?" (page 23).

Hock acknowledges the obvious question in his litany of whom leaders manage: How is it that we manage our superiors and peers? His answer? You cannot. It is simply not possible to manage your superiors and peers. But you can understand them and persuade them. You can motivate them and cause them to question. You can influence them and set an example. Hock even suggests that you can forgive them. And for Dee Hock, all of this is, indeed, leading them.

And what about managing yourself? That is, perhaps, the easiest and hardest leadership task of all. But this is where each of us has the greatest power. Think about it. What prevents each of us from managing the self? To paraphrase Hock, surely there are no rules or regulations that can stop us. There is no hierarchy and there are no bosses that can prevent us from behaving in the way that we choose. Sure, others can make it difficult sometimes. But finally, each of us has the power.

> *No individual and no organization, short of killing us, can prevent such use of our energy, ability, and ingenuity. They may make it more difficult, but they can't prevent it. The real power is ours, not theirs, provided only that we can work our way around the killing.*
>
> *Dee Hock*

Connective Leadership

Lots of business leaders are talking about the increased interdependence inherent in today (and tomorrow's) world. This interdependence is driven largely by technology, once television and certainly now the Internet.

Everyone is connected to everything everywhere. This makes much of our work transparent, demanding an alignment of what we say with what we do. Now it's much easier for our constituents—whether employees, clients, donors, board members, or other volunteers—to watch what we say, what we actually do, and how well the two match. It's all about access and alignment.

Pottruck and Pearce (2000) note the following:

> The Web is merely a symbolic depiction of that interdependence, and of course that symbol makes the universal impact of our action or messages obvious. The Web also allows and encourages a free flow information, so it is impossible for one person to operate in a vacuum. It makes information available to everyone, and is, therefore, the single most important tool for collaboration that has ever been invented. No longer can a single individual operate independently by hoarding and monopolizing information.

These two aspects of the Internet—the free flow of information and its symbol of interconnectedness—make conscious teamwork eminently possible. Organizations that are aligned behind common purpose will find it a powerful tool. Those still operating with rules of independence and control will find it a formidable obstacle.

Interdependence then drives organizations into the continuum of collaboration—from communication and knowledge alliances to networking and coalitions, from collaboration and joint ventures to merger.

But diversity remains even with interdependence. The best organizations foster both. As Jean Lipman-Blumen notes (2000), diversity refers to the different characteristics of individuals, groups and organizations. "Reflecting the human need for identity, diversity highlights everyone's uniqueness, underscoring differences and emphasizing independence and individualism. It is a force for social, economic, and cultural differentiation" (page 39).

These two—interdependence and diversity—distinguish what Lipman-Blumen calls the "connective era." She notes that "the importance of diversity and the inevitability of interdependence require a more fully developed leadership repertoire" (page 40).

Connective leaders discern and understand the connections between diverse people, experiences, ideas, and organizations. These leaders perceive the overlap, reinforce the commonalties, and expand the common ground.

Lipman-Blumen notes that connective leaders "negotiate, persuade, and integrate antagonistic groups. They reach out to longstanding adversaries in order to accomplish mutual goals. ...They construct and call upon social networks and multiple, shifting coalitions. They open these networks to colleagues. They seek active constituents, unshackled by orthodoxy, who can share the burdens of leadership but feel free not to support the leader's every issue" (page 40).

In this connective era—balancing interdependence and diversity—Lipman-Blumen describes six important leadership strengths.

1. Ethical political savvy

    Connective leaders possess lots of savvy to "use themselves, others, and all the resources they can garner as instruments for accomplishing their goals" (page 40). To paraphrase Lipman-Blumen, connective leaders use this political savvy in an ethical, altruistic, and overt manner. This is their strategy to link interdependence and diversity.

2. Authenticity and accountability

    Authenticity refers to the leader's dedication to the group and the purposes of the group. Authenticity establishes the leader's credibility and reinforces the followers' faith. For Lipman-Blumen, authenticity helps the leader's constituents to discern whether changes in behavior are due to waffling or due to an increased understanding of a situation.

    Accountability is authenticity's "twin imperative." To be accountable to others means that we explain our decisions and actions, and accept our obligation to the others. Leaders accept their accountability, subjecting themselves to examination by their constituents.

    In the connective era—where everything is known and seen—connective leaders operate transparently, with maximum disclosure.

3. Politics of commonalties

    In other words, the connective leader builds community. Strong community allows for the simultaneous flourishing of interdependence and diversity.

4. Thinking long term, acting short term

    Building community is about keeping it all going. Regardless of today's issues and performance measures, leaders keep an eye on the future. Leaders make decisions that are best for the future, even when it means choosing against current demands.

    Building community is also about ensuring a legacy for the future. That's why leaders put aside their own egos and find the best people to replace them.

5. Leadership through expectation

    Connective leaders enable others. Lipman-Blumen notes that these leaders "stand back and rely upon the principle of reciprocation, whereby the gift of the leader's confidence is usually repaid by the constituent's outstanding performance" (page 43). Connective leaders encourage creativity and questioning, requiring only that their colleagues "act ethically and legally."

6. A quest for meaning

As a leader, you are measured by your ability to influence others, your ability to help others make a difference. Finally, that is your legacy. "In reconciling the forces of interdependence and diversity, [connective leaders] invite those around them to join their quest for greater meaning. By calling supporters to change the world for the better, connective leaders present constituents with elevating opportunities. They also stand as shining examples" (Lipman-Blumen 2000, 43).

Lipman-Blumen describes the behavioral foundations of connective leadership as three major sets of achieving styles: direct, relational, and instrumental. Each set has three broad strategies whereby an individual can accomplish her or his goals. The best connective leaders choose between the various styles, personalized to the situation or circumstance (pages 44,45).

1. Achieving style: direct (closely linked to diversity, the force of the individual)
   - Intrinsic: Individual derives satisfaction from mastering own tasks compared with internal standards of excellence
   - Competitive: Individual derives satisfaction from outdoing others, comparing performance with external standards
   - Power: Individual takes charge, delegates to and coordinates others
2. Achieving style: relational (closely linked to interdependence, working together)
   - Collaborative: Individual works with others, sharing responsibility for action and results
   - Contributory: Individual works behind the scenes, helping others to complete activities
   - Vicarious: Individual derives satisfaction from facilitating, coaching, and observing the accomplishments of others
3. Achieving style: instrumental (linked to political savvy)
   - Personal: Individual uses all her or his personal assets—intelligence, wit, personal background, etc.—to attract supporters
   - Social: Individual creates social networks and uses these and others to accomplish shared goals

- Entrusting: Individual relies on others to enhance shared vision, doing so without supervision but with strong expectations for success

Connective leaders understand and support this new era. They develop their leadership strengths and carefully use the achieving styles and strategies.

THE LEARNING ORGANIZATION

The learning organization is the third component of your organization's internal relations. Effective organizations are always learning, and the best fundraisers lead the crusade for learning. They know that organizational health and fund development depend on how well (and how quickly) the organization learns.

A learning organization is a way of operating. Learning means enhancing one's capability—as an individual and as an organization—to achieve desired results. Peter Senge (1990) notes that, for organizations to excel in the future, they must tap people's willingness and ability to learn. Through learning, we continually recreate ourselves.

There are two types of learning, adaptive and generative. Effective organizations use both.

- Adaptive learning means you modify existing operations, thereby producing an altered concept.
- Generative learning means you create something previously unknown from current experience and information. Generative learning is the most stressful for an organization because it is unfamiliar.

Creating a learning organization is no easy task. To do so, Senge says, build an infrastructure that includes five specific disciplines: personal mastery, mental models, shared vision, team learning, and systems thinking (Exhibit 2–7). Woven together, these disciplines create the learning organization.

> *Consider this: Every second, the Web grows by 17 pages and, according to some sources, the world has generated more data in the past 30 years than it did in the preceding 5,000 years. The challenge then is not only to learn what you need to know but also to unlearn what you no longer need. That means eliminating the habits, practices, and assumptions that once worked—even those that may have accounted for past successes—to make room for new methods that better fit your new circumstances.*
>
> *Anna Muoio*

Exhibit 2-7 Five Disciplines of a Learning Organization

1. Personal mastery—personal development of the individuals in the organization.

   An organization will only learn if the individuals within it learn too. Each individual must commit to lifelong learning. Personal mastery means we each commit to self-examination, patience, and an objective view of reality. Every individual can achieve a special level of proficiency in her or his personal and professional life.

2. Mental models—deeply held paradigms that affect choices and action.

   Individuals and groups hold assumptions and generalizations that influence their view of the world, shape their decisions and actions, and affect their interpretation of what is possible. Often, we fail to use new insights because they conflict with our fundamental images of the world. Effective individuals and groups learn to discern their own mental models, examine them, and encourage others to examine and influence these models.

3. Shared vision—common aspiration held by the group.

   Together, an organization's stakeholders create their shared vision, thereby building a sense of commitment. These stakeholders are bound together through their shared values, common vision, and a sense of identity.

4. Team learning—working together for action.

   Teams develop intelligence and ability that is greater than the sum of the team members' individual abilities. Team learning starts with dialogue where members suspend their assumptions so that the group discovers insights not available individually. Dialogue also helps the team identify its own behaviors that may undermine learning.

5. Systems thinking—process for seeing the whole.

   Systems thinking focuses on the whole and how its parts relate one to the other. Systems thinking helps us reflect upon, talk about, and understand the forces and interrelationships that affect the behavior of various systems. This discipline helps organizations see how to change systems more effectively.

Source: Data from Peter M. Senge.

Senge observes that the individuals who contribute most to your organization are those who practice these disciplines. Through practice, individuals enhance their own ability "to hold and seek a vision, to reflect and inquire, to build collective capabilities, and to understand systems" (Senge et al., 1994).

As the practitioner becomes more proficient with the discipline, she or he finds new ways of seeing and doing.

Systems Thinking Is the Cornerstone

Systems thinking means seeing interrelationships rather than linear chains. You see a whole whose parts relate and operate for a common purpose. You see processes of change, rather than snapshots of activity.

Systems thinking helps your organization understand how its actions have created current reality. Then, as a learning organization, you create your future vision and design the infrastructure that will move you from your current reality to your future vision.

Systems include both detail and dynamic complexity.

- Detail complexity refers to many individual variables that seem not to be related.
- Dynamic complexity focuses on the whole system and its interrelated parts. Dynamic complexity exists when the same action has dramatically different effects in the short and long run, when an action has different consequences in different parts of the system, or when obvious interventions produce nonobvious consequences.

Fund development includes both detail and dynamic complexity.

Fundraising technicians tend to focus more on detail complexity. They can be overwhelmed by the many variables of fund development, losing the big picture.

Effective fundraisers recognize the importance of dynamic complexity. They see the whole system—fund development and organizational development—and its interrelated parts. They act as systems thinkers, seeing when and how a change in action or structure can generate significant and enduring improvement.

Systems thinkers know that each action produces a reaction. Action in one area will likely affect another area, producing both intended and unintended consequences. For this reason, systems thinkers learn to anticipate the reactions and trade-offs of a chosen action. These leaders identify high and low leverage points within a system and evaluate the potential impact before deciding how to act.

Organizations are complex systems that interact constantly and significantly with a host of other equally complex systems. The most important property of these systems is that they cannot be broken down into parts that have separate lives of their own. Thus, in an organization, no basic functions, departments, or objectives exist independently of one another.

Ian I. Mitroff, Richard O. Mason,
and Christine M. Pearson

Systems thinking benefits organizations by helping them figure out the best leverage in complex situations. By approaching situations in a systemic way, people see what causes the problem and how it can be fixed. Senge (1990) states that the bottom line of systems thinking is leverage. He goes on to observe that, although people often think they need more information to address issues today, the opposite may be true. People may actually have so much information they have trouble deciding what is most important. And systems thinking helps to distinguish what is most important.

Senge views systems thinking as the cornerstone of the learning organization. Systems thinking relates and integrates the other four disciplines—personal mastery, mental models, shared vision, and team learning—into the whole organization.

Now look at your organization. Consider how an action in one part of the system will affect another area, whether sooner or later.

- How might the diverse, sometimes conflicting or competing relationships between clients, donors, trustees, staff, and other volunteers affect budgeting?
- What might be the effect of a new service on current services and their delivery?
- What would be the short- and long-term effects of discontinuing a service on your fund development?
- How might changing community demographics affect your board composition?
- How could your marketing strategy for a particular service affect donor perception and public image?
- How will the actions of your maintenance staff affect your ability to solicit funds from donors?

Create Your Learning Organization

Practitioners say there are five major benefits when you function as a learning organization.

1. Your organization adapts more readily and rapidly to the changing environment.
2. People are recognized as the organization's top assets, creating intellectual resources and producing innovation.
3. Your organization becomes its own "community brain," which generates, integrates, and organizes information, knowledge, and wisdom.
4. Your organization creates its own conversations that, by linking the organization's knowledge, produce learning.

5. The parts of your organization cooperate to help the larger whole survive and grow. Together, the organization enhances its capacity to achieve desired results.

To create your own learning organization, use the five disciplines of personal mastery, mental models, shared vision, team learning, and systems thinking. Review the earlier information in this section. Then design an infrastructure that incorporates the attributes of a learning organization, described in Exhibit 2–8.

ONGOING CONVERSATION

Pay attention to conversation because it can change your organization! Conversation helps you develop and renew the four relationships fundamental to effective organizations and effective fund development.

Conversation means an interchange of ideas in which two or more participate. But conversation is more. Consider this thought: "It is in how we speak with one another that we experience respect from others and whether we are being heard" (Ellinor and Gerard 1998, 12).

In this book, conversation is more than talking. Conversation

- is carried out face to face, in writing, and through technology
- includes casual, informal chatter and more formal discussion and dialogue
- uses discussion and dialogue as specific techniques to accomplish particular goals.

Humans are social beings. We connect through conversation. That's how we learn. Through conversations, we build shared knowledge and generate new insights. We make commitments and organize for action.

> *Conversation produces community, and a sense of community generates commitment.*

Conversation happens between individuals and among groups within your organization and between your organization and its community. Your conversation can be formal and structured or casual and unstructured. Either way, conversation—even chance encounters—requires both intent and an initiator. Sometimes, there is a

Exhibit 2–8 Attributes of a Learning Organization's Infrastructure

- Involves all stakeholders. People are free to choose within recognized boundaries. (Peter Block notes in *Stewardship* that even in the most empowered organizations, there are still bosses who set the boundaries.)
- Uses learning (and its five disciplines) as a major strategy for organizational success. Devises ways for the organization to practice and learn from its mistakes. This process of practice and learning happens while you carry out daily operations, but it is separate from operations.
- Stakeholders share an overall view of the system and see their own places in it.
- Clearly articulates values, vision, and mission. These are developed through an ongoing, honest participatory process.
- Corporate culture and core systems are based on stewardship. Responsibility and authority are shared throughout the organization.
- A critical mass of organization members commit to redesign the infrastructure into a healthy system. Enough individuals share new insights and skills, thus passing on learning through the whole organization. This new learning belongs to the system and everyone in it, not to any single individual or small group of individuals.
- New concepts of leadership engage people throughout the organization. Leaders work toward personal mastery and participate in and facilitate learning.
- Personal mastery and team learning are key accountabilities for employee and volunteer selection and orientation. The reward and recognition system reinforces both accountabilities.
- People work together in learning situations, developing new strategies and techniques to address issues.
- The communications system, ongoing conversation, and participatory decision making provide all constituents with a systemic view of the organization, helping everyone to understand individual and group contributions.
- People create ways to identify, share, and celebrate learning and results.

Source: Data from Phillip J. Carroll, "Infrastructure for Organizational Transformation at Shell Oil," *Collective Intelligence*, vol. 1, no. 1, MIT Center for Organizational Learning, and from Carolyn J.C. Thompson, presentation at Systems Thinking in Action Conference, Boston, 1995.

versation is the chief management tool that makes learning happen. Through conversation, organizations learn and can then stimulate change (Exhibit 2–9).

Conversation is critical to organizational health and learning because it

- gathers information
- shares knowledge
- questions assumptions
- identifies implications and consequences
- generates answers
- builds understanding and linkages
- creates camaraderie

Talking in Your Organization

Look at your own organization. Do you have lots of conversations? Is conversation encouraged, whether

Exhibit 2–9 Conversation among the Titmice and Robins

Years ago, bottles of milk were delivered to porch steps in rural England. The glass bottles had no caps, so the robins and titmice perched on the bottle lips and drank the cream. Generation after generation of robins and titmice enjoyed the cream.

One day, the bottles began arriving with cardboard caps. The robins and titmice perched again on the bottle lips, only to encounter a barrier to their enjoyment.

The robins finally flew away, never to return to the bottles. But the titmice learned to break through the cardboard cap with their beaks and continued to enjoy the cream.

The robins didn't learn to break through the milk cap, but the titmice did. Why?

Robins are territorial birds. It's safe to assume that one robin figured out how to break through the cap on the bottle. But she stayed in her own territory and didn't share the information with her fellow robins.

Titmice are flocking birds. They hang out together. Somehow, they communicate and share information. The titmouse who learned to break through the cap shared it with the other titmice. And generation after generation of titmice continued to enjoy the cream.

Effective organizations are comprised of titmice, nonterritorial flockers, who regularly communicate and learn together. All those wonderful conversations help them organize for action.

Source: From a story told by Arie de Geus at the 1994 Systems Thinking in Action™ Conference.

purpose and desired result for the conversation. At other times, there may be no purpose but casual contact.

Systems thinker Alan Webber (1994, 7) says that the most important work in the new economy is creating conversations. Systems thinking theory states that conformal or informal? Is participation inclusive, extended to bring in more people and perspective? Does conversation encourage questioning and innovation? Do individuals and groups learn through conversation?

Consider the following:

- How often have you watched one individual or a small group dominate discussion and control the decision?
- Have you seen groups make poor choices because participants did not talk enough about consequences?
- Have you ever gone along with a decision without asking enough questions because you assumed some other group had discussed the issue adequately?
- Do your board and staff talk about the tough issues, such as eliminating programs or overcoming gender and ethnic bias?
- Are your trustees and staff uncomfortable with disagreement?
- Do any of your staff or volunteers withhold information from others, seeking to control decision making?
- Do some individuals push their own personal agendas, ignoring the will of the group?
- Does your organization isolate discussion to a handful of people, thinking that this is efficient and protects confidentiality?

> *If your organization dialogues well, your decision making will likely improve.*

Look at the design of your board meetings. Do you structure them for brevity, avoiding extensive conversation? In their haste to run "good meetings," do your committees do most of the talking, and then recommend action to the board, which reacts without much talking? The result may be efficient meetings. However, this also produces uninformed, disengaged, and bored boards.

The theory of "committees do the work and the board acts on committee recommendations" is fine for routine or straightforward decision making. But when your organization makes challenging judgments about uncertain and complex issues, you are best served if the board is fully engaged. As the legal and moral corporate entity, the board must fully understand its choices. Committees may research and talk, but they must then come to the board for extensive conversation, which helps produce good decision making.

Consider how people gather together in your organization. Do they get together only at formal, scheduled meetings? Do they encounter each other casually and

talk informally about issues that matter? Do people hang out with their department colleagues only or do they mingle across the boundaries of the organization?

Examine the physical layout of your organization. How does this layout affect conversation? Are people isolated in cubicles and are departments separated one from the other, even in different buildings?

Think about the grapevine and gossip in your organization. Oh, how fast information travels through the grapevine! Use it. Use the grapevine and the power of positive gossip to share information and encourage conversation. Sure, formal communication is important, but don't discount the parking lot conversations and the lunchroom chatter. Reinforce these conversations for the good of the organization. Pass on the news and share the questions. Encourage the exploration and value the insights.

In their article, "Conversation as a Core Business Practice," Brown and Isaacs (December 1996–January 1997) note that "thoughtful conversations around questions that matter might be *the* core process in any company— the source of organizational intelligence that enables the other business processes to create positive results." Brown and Isaacs (December 1996–January 1997, 2) quote Fernando Flores, who states "an organization's results are determined through webs of human commitments, born in webs of human conversations."

The irony is that, if conversation is a core business practice, why do so many organizations focus on "stop talking and get back to work!"

Effective organizations work hard to encourage conversation. These organizations know that people (and the organization itself) learn and make better decisions because of conversation. Indeed, these organizations continually explore how to develop the attitude, systems, and processes to foster meaningful conversations.

Fundraising leaders also understand the value of conversation. They create opportunities for people to talk about strategic issues and bring up controversial topics.

Discussion and Dialogue Are Different

Formal conversation uses two techniques, discussion and dialogue, to help accomplish activities. Although both are important to organizational health and learning, dialogue is the more critical and the less familiar.

There's a fair amount of discussion in most organizations. People pass information and opinions back and forth, hoping to convince each other of a particular perspective. By trying to convince each other to accept an opinion, discussion does not seek "coherence and truth," says physicist David Bohm (Senge, 1990).

Dialogue, on the other hand, sees the larger picture and seeks Bohm's "pool of common meaning." The purpose of dialogue is to move beyond the understanding of any individual and to explore the complex issues. To this end, dialogue is collaborative conversation (Exhibit 2–10). People pool their information and experience, suspend personal assumptions, and avoid the need to persuade others.

During dialogue, people observe their own thinking process and mental models. As each person reflects on and shares his or her views, group understanding deepens. People notice inconsistencies and fragmentation, incoherence, and polarities. People seek the patterns and missing pieces.

Then shift happens. Participants integrate their diverse perspectives into a new collective view. Together, people are transformed so that they can make decisions that transform the organization.

Effective dialogue, contrasted to discussion, requires the intent and support of the group. Your organization engages the right people, erring on the side of inclusiveness, rather than exclusiveness. Dialogue accepts everyone as equal, without any power structure. Dialogue uses face-to-face interaction to enhance perception and build teams.

In their book, *Dialogue: Rediscovering the Transforming Power of Conversation*, Ellinor and Gerard (1998) present a continuum for conservation (page 21).

Dialogue	Discussion/Debate
Seeing the *whole* among the parts	Breaking issues/ problems into *parts*
Seeing the *connections* between the parts	Seeing *distinctions* between the parts
Inquiring into assumptions	*Justifying/defending* assumptions
Learning through inquiry and disclosure	*Persuading, selling, telling*
Creating *shared* meaning among many	Gaining agreement on *one* meaning

Ellinor and Gerard (1998) observe that interconnectedness and diversity are the basis for dialogue. "Dialogue rests on the idea that we live in a world that is collective in nature with interconnected parts" (page 51). First, dialogue helps people see the interconnections. Then dialogue helps people build the capacity to "leverage the team's inherent diversity" (page 52).

Good dialogue leads with uncertainty. Critical strategic questions are asked, and people identify the unspoken questions and issues. Dialogue embraces pluralism and accepts diversity and its resulting paradoxes.

Exhibit 2–10 What Does Dialogue Mean?

In learning organization theory, dialogue is a group process that helps produce organizational change. What do people do when they dialogue?

- Treat everyone as equals.
- Share information and experience without advocating one position or another.
- Suspend personal assumptions and really listen to what others say.
- Identify hidden questions and issues.
- Determine what lies behind opinions so that deeper understanding is possible.
- Integrate diverse perspectives into a new collective view.
- Learn together.

Dialogue is progressive. It moves throughout the organization, stimulating learning and producing change. Dialogue flows from a person's internal conversation to small groups. From small groups, dialogue moves to multiple groups. Finally, multiple group dialogues produce large-scale impact. You make dialogue practical by discussing the implications for your organization. This is learning.

Whether you use discussion or dialogue may seem a fine distinction, but effective organizations use dialogue to focus and deepen the ongoing conversations that Webber (1994) describes as critical for organizational success in the growing knowledge economy.

Conversation Supports Strategic Thinking

As an aside, organizations that survive think strategically. Conversation, especially the dialogue form, stimulates strategic thinking.

Strategic thinking is a group process, dependent on the highest quality of collective thought. That's why leaders bring people together and encourage them to ask questions. Strategic thinking depends on this ongoing conversation to support organizational continuity, promote creativity, facilitate transition, produce learning, and generate change.

Thinking strategically means understanding why, not just what and how. When you think strategically, you consider the whole system, its various parts, and their interconnectedness. You see dynamic complexity, rather than focus on details. You consider the implications of information and the consequences of choices. You transform information into knowledge, then knowledge into learning.

Thinking strategically allows individuals and organizations to identify and resolve dilemmas by shifting the context in which they are understood. Organizational members explore long-term, complex issues that are important to the organization's survival. This exploration helps people examine their assumptions (Senge's mental models) about what drives the organization and its various stakeholders and how the dynamics of the larger community affect the institution.

Strategic thinking means asking the right questions. Clear, challenging, and penetrating questions elicit creative thinking. By questioning current assumptions, an organization can change the assumptions. Shifts in assumptions then produce innovation.

Use dialogue to stimulate strategic thinking in your organization. Dialogue helps improve the quality of thinking together because individuals shift awareness and notice more. Through dialogue—not discussion—organizational members identify patterns, recognize barriers, distinguish issues, and find new opportunities. Dialogue helps people explore the connections between ideas, not just the ideas themselves. Participants observe differences, rather than conflicting views, thereby bringing new insight to the whole.

A reminder: Decide whether dialogue is or is not necessary. Many times, a decision belongs to a single individual or small group; no dialogue is needed. Be vigilant, though, because there are many more situations when good dialogue is beneficial.

Create Conversation in Your Organization

Effective organizations develop and sustain an infrastructure that allows conversation to happen. Here are a few ideas to help your organization create conversations.

1. Identify the essential qualities that make conversation good and promote these qualities in your organization.
2. Identify the one question that, if you all answered it together, would help your organization create conversations.
3. Create a spirit of inquiry before you begin conversations.
4. Make sure the environment is safe so it's risk-free to ask questions and question assumptions.
5. Differentiate between dialogue and discussion, and make sure both happen.
6. Know when conversation is unnecessary because decisions are routine.
7. Involve as many persons as possible, making sure that conversation happens between various individuals and groups within your organization.

> *Questions are catalysts for change. Questions bring people together. Questions attract people and resources to your organization.*

Start by asking the individuals in your organization to identify the qualities necessary for conversation. Compare your organization's list with Exhibit 2–11, qualities commonly identified by people in different settings.

Once your organization has identified the essential qualities, ask people: "Do we create conversations that reflect the qualities we desire?" Together, figure out why and why not. Talk about how you can promote the essential qualities within your organization. For example:

- Ask yourselves whether it is a lack of faith and trust that stops your organization from creating conversations that reflect these qualities. Perhaps individuals worry that, although they seek good conversation, others in the group do not. Ironically, experience shows that most people seek the same qualities in conversation, and certainly the majority in any group does. It appears, then, that people must make a leap of faith and behave in keeping with these qualities. Because most people want these same qualities, someone must take the risk and act accordingly.
- Together, examine your organization. What core question, if answered, would allow real learning conversations to become the norm, rather than the exception? Remember, the question might not have anything to do with conversation itself. The ques-

Exhibit 2–11 Qualities Essential to Good Conversation

- safe to speak honestly
- mutual risk taking
- respect for everyone in the room
- participant perceptions change
- empathy with one another
- sense of exploration
- climate of discovery
- common language
- pluralism and diversity among participants and opinions
- when conversation ends, participants want to talk more
- conversation challenges the way participants think
- energy and synergy within the group
- feeling of intimacy and shared values
- topic really matters to the participant individually
- no one judges
- build on each other's remarks

tion simply stimulates your organization to identify and eliminate the barrier to good conversation.

Consider these:

1. How do we create a safe space for conversation that produces individual and organizational learning and results in good decision making?
2. What do I have to lose by creating good conversation myself?
3. How can I better convey who I am without fear?
4. How do the parts of our organization relate to the whole?
   - Create a spirit of inquiry among the members in your organization. Begin by talking with the group. Ask yourselves, "How can we create a spirit of inquiry here and now?" Together, define the traits that characterize this spirit. Establish general guidelines to use as you create conversations.
1. Meet in a place with no distractions.
2. Make sure that people feel relaxed and comfortable.
3. Give everyone a chance to talk. Help people find out what they share in common.
4. Respect people's experience and expertise.
5. Ask questions that stimulate thinking and help people look deeply into the situation.
6. Make sure everyone recognizes that the dialogue might produce some discomfort. And that's okay.

Use diagrams, tape recordings, and other tools to help people understand the connections between the various thoughts presented (Bennett and Brown 1995, 173).

Asking the Right Questions

Good conversation depends on good questions. The questions we ask are as important as, and sometimes more important than, finding the right answers. Questions open minds and stimulate change. Questions bring people together with the hope of decision making and action.

Asking questions means that we must suspend our own assumptions about "what is right" and "what is best." We need to listen to others and question our own assumptions, rather than advocate for our own opinion. Consider what our colleague, Karla A. Williams, ACFRE, Charlotte, NC, says: "Pursuit of knowledge is based on asking questions and questioning the answers." And I would add, "asking the questions that matter in the first place."

Too often, we only probe the surface when asking questions. We don't question our own assumptions. We ask the obvious questions. The challenge is to ask the

deeper questions and to question those questions to learn more (see the example in Exhibit 2–12).

Skill is required to identify and ask the questions that matter. Skill is required to explore the questions, question the inherent assumptions, and discover new questions of meaning. People develop these skills by talking together and practicing more.

Brown and Isaacs (December 1996–January 1997) note that "the quality of our learning process depends on the quality of questions we ask" (page 4). In learning organizational theory, learning is both an individual and a group process. Group learning is where the added value is most critical because the organization learns and can then change. Brown and Isaacs go on to say "Clear, bold, and penetrating questions that elicit a full range of responses tend to open the social context for learning. People engaged in the conversation develop a common concern for deeper levels of shared meaning" (page 4).

> *Strategic questions create dissonance between current experiences and beliefs while evoking new possibilities for collective discovery. But they also serve as the glue that holds together overlapping webs of conversations in which diverse resources combine and recombine to create innovative solutions and business value.*
>
> *Brown and Isaacs*

As you enhance your own capacity and willingness to ask the right questions, consider the questions below, generated during the class on volunteerism and boards by Cohort 9 from the Masters Program in Philanthropy and Fund Development, St. Mary's University of Minnesota.

1. Do you possess enough experience and knowledge in key areas to ask the right questions?
   - Do you know enough about fund development, organizational development, business management, and governance? What else might you need to know?
2. Can you judge the optimum time to ask which questions within which group?
3. Do you possess sufficient experience and knowledge to help answer the questions?
4. Can you help personalize the answer to the particular situation or organization?
5. Are you comfortable pushing around multiple questions and diverse answers?
6. Are you comfortable creating new answers?
7. Do you value the fact that the questions and answers keep changing?
8. Do you question your own assumptions and do you welcome that questioning by others?

Exhibit 2–12 Asking the Right Questions: A Personal Example

I was presenting a seminar to advanced executives about how to build effective boards. I had developed an entire set of questions about building effective boards. (I was mighty proud of those questions!)

One of the participants, Henry Goldstein, CFRE, observed: "I think you are missing a question, the question that precedes all your other questions. That is: Do we want effective boards? Does an effective board add any value other than that of fundraising?"

He questioned my assumption. Yes, I had made an assumption: that we all wanted effective boards. Certainly, I was willing to accept that we might define effective boards differently. And then I had lots and lots of questions following that. But I had not considered the first question: Do we want effective boards?

Now here are the questions I've generated—with the input from various seminars—directed at how to build an effective board. How would you change these? How can you use questioning to stimulate strategic dialogue and strengthen your board? How will you get your board to ask these questions of itself and to work regularly toward answering them?

1. What value is added to an organization by having a board? Is the only value added for fund development?
2. Who defines what is an effective board?
   a) What is the process for creating a shared vision of the effective board for an organization and the value added by the board to the organization?
   b) What (and who) is the critical mass necessary for sharing the vision and transforming the board?
   c) What is the difference between the board and the individual as a board member? How do we communicate this and manage this?
   d) How do we develop standards of board and board member effectiveness? How do we appraise performance for each and design and manage an improvement process as necessary?
3. In general, are not-for-profit boards less than effective? If yes, do we really need effective boards or are weak boards adequate for some organizations? Why? Why not?
4. If boards are ineffective, what is our responsibility as leaders for the lack of effectiveness and developing that effectiveness?
   a) Who determines and how is it determined that the board is ineffective?
5. Groups develop their own cultures, the way they do things. The way they treat each other. How do we work together to create the optimum group culture for a board?
   a) How do we address cultural issues within diverse organizations? How do we put them on the table for discussion and resolution?
   b) How do we address issues of diversity with a board as we seek to build capacity?

6. What is the role of staff in the process of enabling and developing the board?
   a) What happens if the chief executive and chief development officers do not share a vision?
   b) If the chief executive and chief development officer are ineffective, can the board be effective?
   c) Who can destroy an organization faster, the chief executive or the board? Why and how?
7. What does governance really mean? How is it different than and/or similar to management?
   a) What does a board do and how do we help members learn to do it and then help them do it?
   b) How does a board ensure its accountability—carry out due diligence—without crossing into management?
   c) How do we design and facilitate board meetings to carry out due diligence best and to ensure institutional effectiveness?
   d) What kind of information does the board need to carry out its due diligence function?
   e) How do we take the experiences, qualifications, and skills of individual board members and build a cohesive organization?
8. How will the future see any change in the role of board and the relevance of the questions asked? Should there be a new governance model?
   a) The National Center for Nonprofit Boards and the Hauser Center for Nonprofit Organizations at Harvard University are jointly inquiring into this very issue. Their inquiry assumes that, although traditional governance may work well for some organizations, it doesn't for others.
      • What do you think about their assumption? What are the questions they should be asking during their inquiry?
   b) What's driving the lack of faith/questioning of existing governance "models"?
9. What makes a board effective?
   a) What activities and behaviors contribute to group effectiveness, e.g., values clarification, group process, etc.?
   b) To what degree does a board need to understand theory and philosophy—or at least value the key concepts—in order to perform well and carry out strategies and tactics?
   c) How do we transmit the theory of the collective and governance?
   d) How do we change and/or model behavior?
   e) How do we strengthen best practice?
   f) How do we ensure continuity as board members change?
   g) How do we address issues of leadership succession and ensure that those we select focus on the organization's agenda and vision, not a personal agenda?

continues

Exhibit 2–12 *continued*

h) How does a board avoid complacency when the organization is sufficiently well managed to avoid crises?

10. Does the vision of the "best board" change through the organization's lifecycle? If yes, how? How, then, does the organization define and transform the board as the organization changes?

11. What is the optimum process to identify and recruit the best individuals to serve as board members? How can we enable our boards to see that, if they do not take a proactive approach in this arena, the organization will have to live with the consequences, thus impeding its ability to achieve its mission?
   a) What is the composite of skills required within the board, given its role and accountabilities?
   b) What are the personal qualifications expected of each board member?
   c) What are the considerations regarding diversity that will strengthen the board?
   d) What is the process for articulating and facilitating performance expectations common to each board member, assessing performance, and thanking and releasing?

12. When management is highly successful and effective, does the board become impotent? How, why? How not and why not?
   a) How do we keep a board engaged and prepared for crisis, rather than complacent and ill-prepared for challenges and transformation?
   b) How do we discuss issues of board effectiveness with the board?

13. What is the process for transforming a board?
   a) Who has to participate in defining the current reality and desired future?
   b) Who has to participate in the transformation process?
   c) What (and who) are agents of change? How do we notice and develop them?

14. If fund development is important to an organization, how do we ensure that fund development recommendations are in concert with what is best for the organization as a whole?
   a) How do we ensure that strategies and tactics to build a board that is effective at fund development do not negatively affect the development of a healthy board?

15. How do we create a level of security for risk taking within a board?
   a) How do we encourage questioning both the questions and the answers?
   b) How do we learn to suspend judgment and question our own assumptions?
   c) What levels of personal and professional risk (e.g., asking questions and disagreeing) can staff and volunteers sustain?
   d) What is the appropriate level of spontaneity and risk taking within board work?

e) How do we develop an acceptable risk-taking mentality within staff and volunteers?
   f) How do we discern and clarify the difference between appropriate questioning and disagreement versus dysfunctional behavior?
   g) What happens to those who ask questions? Have they been enabled to ask these questions and provided with a safe environment in which to do so?

16. When should questions get raised? Is there an appropriate time or setting? Are there situations where questions might be inappropriate? To what degree is it essential that questions be asked "formally" and in the "appropriate" group?
   a) How do we learn to figure out what is behind the question so that we can restate the question and answer the appropriate question?
   b) Who initiates questions and who answers them?
   c) Who says our board members aren't asking questions? Are we, as staff, listening and hearing what they ask?

17. How do we engage boards in the process of deliberating and deciding?
   a) What is the appropriate information—translated into trends and implications—necessary to facilitate discussion?
   b) When is the moment of decision making and how do we decide who has the authority to make a decision?
   c) How do we prepare for the moment of decision making or evaluate whether we are ready for that moment?

18. When is informal and ongoing conversation between board members value-added versus inappropriate behind-the-scenes, exclusionary discussion?
   a) How do we design and facilitate disciplined group discussion, discourage inappropriate and exclusionary discussion, and encourage ongoing and informal conversation?

19. How do we foster a deep commitment to change within the board and staff?

20. What is the optimum way to organize the board to do its work?
   a) What is the difference between the board and its committees or task forces?
   b) Is there a way for leaders to participate in strategic decision making without serving on the board itself? How would these individuals or bodies (e.g., task forces) link to the board?
   c) How do we make both experiences meaningful and useful?
   d) How do we avoid doing committee or task force work at board meetings while informing and engaging the board adequately in strategic dialogue and decision making?
   e) What are the questions to be asked regarding functional silos within board operations? For example,

continues

Exhibit 2–12 continued

the development committee members talk only about development, etc.

f) How do we establish ground rules and the operating behavior of the group, e.g., maintain, modify, facilitate, evaluate adherence to, sanction, thank, and release?

21. What do we mean by "leadership" and how does it add value to our board and our organization's work?

a) How do we develop leaders, diversify the nature of leadership, and share power?

22. How are these questions relevant to all organizations, whether grassroots or major?

a) How can the questions be asked, managed, and answered, regardless of an organization's type, size, or capabilities?

To a large degree, the process of asking questions is about sharing power and tolerating complexity. Can you do it?

PARTICIPATORY DECISION MAKING

This is the fifth component of the organization's internal relationship. Decision making means choosing. An individual or group selects one among several possibilities.

Effective organizations choose well. Their decision making combines the four components of the organization's internal relationships: shared values, leadership, learning organization, and ongoing conversation.

When appropriate (and this is more often than not), effective organizations involve multiple people in the decision-making process. These organizations know that certain decisions require group decision making, for example, those choices that belong to the board.

Effective organizations also recognize the distinct advantages of participatory decision making, even if it is not required. These organizations know that group decision making brings together diverse opinions and expertise. Together, the result can be greater than the sum of the individual parts. These organizations recognize that participatory decision making builds group understanding and develops support for and ownership of the choice. Also, the process of group decision making contributes to individual, group, and organizational learning.

In their book, *Clicks and Mortar: Passion Driven Growth in an Internet World*, Pottruck and Pearce (2000) talk about listening to learn, rather than to answer. The process of asking and listening helps us know each other better and allows us to work together to create better solutions. The process of engagement and participatory decision making most often produces better solutions than does "lone ranger" behavior.

Pottruck and Pearce (2000) observe:

I want the engagement of everyone in the company...but the business requires that I also have the ability to move fast, to make decisions quickly when I need to...leadership is not only about facilitation or consensus, it is about ultimate responsibility. Even as I encourage dialogue and listen carefully to everyone who contributes, my responsibility is to make decisions that are the best for the whole of the business, and to continue to have the participation of those who disagree with me.

It requires that I understand other people's points of view—and that I can acknowledge our differences. ...Acknowledging resistance does not mean giving up your own point of view. It doesn't mean that other people have to have their way. It merely means that they know they have been genuinely heard and considered, even if the hearing and considering do not change your decision (page 115).

Strategic Decision Making

For the purposes of this text, decision making refers to those choices that are not routine and repetitive. Instead, these decisions are characterized by uncertainty and risk. Strategic decisions are most important to your organization and, according to decision-making theory, possess certain attributes.

- Strategic decisions are critically important to your organization's success and its future.
- These decisions commit major resources, thus directing and limiting activities throughout the organization.

- Strategic decisions have a dual orientation, involving both the worlds inside and outside of your organization and may take you into a new area of work.
- Strategic decisions affect the entire organizational system, not just one part.
- The results of the decision—whether good or bad, intended or not—will likely not be known for some time.

> *The decisions that affect the future of our civilization and of the human race are, increasingly, made in a group context . . . when people convene in groups, a new entity is created, with its own dynamics and complexity, and "its" decisions cannot be predicted even from a thorough knowledge of its constituent members.*
> *Walter Swap*

Exhibit 2–13 compares strategic and routine decisions. This descriptive list can help you decide which decisions would benefit from whose participation.

The Process of Decision Making

There is much more to decision making than the outcome. Generally, the decision-making process includes the following components:

- identifying who needs to participate in the decision-making process and why
- designing the decision-making process
- determining who will facilitate the decision-making process
- articulating the issue, its scope, and the context for decision making
- identifying alternatives and their implications and consequences
- discussing implementation strategies, time frames, and accountability
- deciding
- informing people of the decision and its impact on them
- monitoring progress of action
- if necessary, modifying action
- evaluating action and discussing learning for next decision

The process produces a choice. Because each choice has its own consequences, decisions involve risk. The more important or larger the scope of the decision, the greater will be the risk. When you decide, you choose your preferred consequences. As Drucker (1990) observes, "Every decision is a commitment of present resources to the uncertainties of the future . . . [the laws of probability mean] that decisions will turn out to be wrong more often than right. At the least, they will have to be adjusted" (page 129).

Exhibit 2–13 A Categorization of Decision Characteristics

	Category I Decisions	*Category II Decisions*
Classifications	Programmable, routine, generic, computational, negotiated, compromise	Nonprogrammable, unique, judgmental, creative, adaptive, innovative, inspirational
Structure	Procedural, predictable, certainty regarding cause/effect relationships, recurring, within existing technologies, well-defined information channels, definite decision criteria, outcome preferences may be certain or uncertain	Novel, unstructured, consequential, elusive, and complex; uncertain cause/effect relationships; nonrecurring; information channels undefined; incomplete information; decision criteria may be unknown; outcome preferences may be certain or uncertain
Strategy	Reliance upon rules and principles, habitual reactions, prefabricated response, uniform processing, computational techniques, accepted methods for handling	Reliance on judgment, intuition, and creativity; individual processing; heuristic problem-solving techniques; rules of thumb; general problem-solving processes

Source: Harrison, E. Frank, *The Managerial Decision-Making Process*, Third Edition. Copyright © 1987 by Houghton Mifflin Company.

Without action, there is no decision making. Someone must be designated to implement the decision, and action must be taken.

Effective decision making relies on effective group behavior, described earlier in this section. Effective decision making also depends on trust. Groups, whether small teams or large organizations, function because there is trust. When you trust, you are confident in the reliability of persons or things without making careful investigation. You believe the person or thing will not fail in its duty. Drucker (1990) describes trust as predictability, knowing what to expect of someone. For Drucker, this is mutual understanding but does not require either mutual love or respect.

Dissent and Decision Making

Conflict is inevitable. It's part of all human interaction and certainly part of group decision making. Individual experiences, perception, and expertise make people see things differently. Conflict is also healthy. It helps to keep a group lively and alive.

But how organizations struggle to avoid conflict! Many staff see dissent as a challenge to management's authority. Too many volunteers avoid disagreement as though it were an affront to politeness.

This is the wrong way to do business. Good decision making rarely happens without conversation, and good conversation often produces differing opinions and disagreement. If it's real easy to decide something important, you'd probably be best to hold off. The more important the decision, the greater will be the risk. And risky decisions should cause lots of questions and disagreement. Then people understand better the choices and consequences. Keep in mind: Dissent helps your organization explore issues, create understanding, develop mutual respect, and learn.

Mary Parker Follett (1868–1933), pioneer in analyzing the human interaction of effective organizations, observed that dissent within an organization does not beg the question of who is right or what is right. Rather, each participant is giving his or her best answer to the question that she or he perceives. What the group needs to ask is, Which question are we trying to answer? Drucker (1990) reinforces this when he observes that the most important part of effective decision making is asking what the decision is really about.

That's why organizational members are responsible to ask the questions worth asking. By asking the right questions and exploring the possible answers, each individual gains understanding. Through understanding, the group learns. By pulling together different pieces of various responses, the group produces the best decision.

Conflict isn't resolved by keeping it quiet. Conversation (both discussion and dialogue) addresses conflict and helps groups make good decisions. If the decision that needs to be made is important enough, the decision-making process will benefit from multiple people talking. Through conversation, people and groups share diverse information, opinions, and experience.

> *Dialogue should involve considerable conflict and disagreement. It is precisely such conflict that pushes [people] to question existing premises and make sense of their experience in a new way.*
>
> *Ikujiro Nonaka*

Resolving conflict by creating shared understanding (not necessarily agreement) generates unity and commitment. Organizational health also depends on the group's ability to work through the mess of disagreement and conflict. The challenge, then, is to use the benefits of conflict and to minimize the negative effects.

Effective groups differentiate between acceptable and dysfunctional conflict. They use acceptable conflict to help make the best decisions and minimize dysfunctional conflict. Dysfunctional group conflict usually arises from one or a combination of the factors below.

- attempt of one individual or subgroup to hold power over another
- lack of consensus about organizational values, vision, and direction
- low tolerance for diversity
- feelings of competition for resources and rewards
- different goals

Securing Consensus

After all the conversations, a decision is made. The best group decisions result from consensus. Contrary to popular perception, consensus does not mean unanimity, nor should consensus produce the lowest common denominator.

Consensus decision making is a highly effective, win-win negotiating process. Although consensus decision making is more time-consuming, it generally produces a longer-lasting result. Decisions are made through high-quality conversation, communication, equal access to influence, and exploration of alternatives and implications thereof, and are supported by a series of agreements.

First, the group clearly identifies what is being decided. Second, the group agrees to the process for decision making. Then, the group proceeds with the content of actual decisions.

Often, voting is required to make the decision. But sufficient dialogue has happened in advance so that everyone is heard, information is transformed into knowledge, and individuals and the organization have learned.

Naturally, the resulting decision may not be the first choice for every group member. However, each participant has been heard and has had the chance to influence others and to learn together. Participants recognize that the process has been fair and open and that the resulting decision reflects the best thinking by those involved.

Ultimately, the quality of decision making is judged on the success of implementation. And, successful implementation depends on the group's shared sense of ownership for both the decision-making process and the resulting decision.

WELL-MANAGED CHANGE

Managing change is the sixth component of your organization's internal relationship for the new millennium. To survive well, effective organizations manage continuity, change, and the transition between the two. The intersection of these three management functions is the point of highest organizational vitality.

In this book, change refers to the external trappings, as well as to the internal transition that people go through to live with the change. As William Bridges observes, "unless transition occurs, change will not happen" (Bridges 1991, 4). For change to work, people have to let go of the current reality and accept a new vision. They have to envision the way things are supposed to be in the changed organization.

Usually, change is either adaptive or innovative, just like learning is either adaptive or generative (see "The Learning Organization" earlier in this chapter). Adaptive change is the most conservative, reflecting only a modest alteration in the status quo. This type of change is relatively easy to accomplish. Contrarily, innovation signals a high degree of change. This is the most challenging to execute and the most worthwhile and useful to organizational health and survival.

Most often, organizational change includes changing corporate culture and core systems. Changing corporate culture is harder because it requires adjusting individual and group attitudes, then modifying individual and organizational behavior. Changing core systems (i.e., policies, procedures, and structure) is easy by comparison.

Change Is Constituent Action

No matter the official policy or the leadership mandate, change requires grassroots activist support. Change depends on engaging your organization's diverse constituents. Change results from the melding of constituent understanding and commitment, influence, and action.

Accepting Change

Effective organizations accept change as a vital and essential part of individual and organizational life. These organizations accept change and develop their infrastructure to support change.

The most effective organizations seek leaders who are comfortable with change and can manage it well. Actually, these leaders welcome change, as long as it is stimulated by organizational learning.

> *People decide that change is difficult and threatening. Despite the reality of a complex and uncertain world (and that means ongoing change!), many act as if change is unexpected and unwelcome.*

In the same way, effective fundraisers know that change is part of fund development. These fundraisers are comfortable and prepared—whether or not donors change interests or community needs shift and whether or not volunteers alter their priorities or need different kinds of support, and so forth.

Reacting to Change

Certainly, hesitancy and anxiety are part of every change process. Suspicion may also be a part. And, in some situations or in certain organizations, mistrust may rear its ugly head.

Recognize this. Identify which is happening, even if it's all three. Respect the reality, then you can manage it.

Generally, individuals and groups react to change in three ways. Some passively resist. Others aggressively undermine. Still others sincerely embrace the change.

> *As human begins we accept change that enhances our sense of well-being—our identity. Any change that threatens our basic identity is resisted. That is the law of human nature.*
> *Debashis Chatterjee*

Just remember, change happens more easily when people are predisposed to it. So your organization may need to change its corporate culture about how people react to change.

For example: In learning organizations, people recognize the world's ambiguity and uncertainty, and expect the same in the organization. They know that the organization's ongoing learning will likely generate change. If you are not yet a learning organization, you might find support for change because people are dissatisfied with the status quo or because they recognize potential alternatives.

But what about those who resist? Kotter and Schlesinger (1979) have identified four primary reasons. First, the resister fears losing something of value. Second, she or he misunderstands the change and its implications. Third, the resister does not believe that the change makes sense for the organization. Fourth, the resister has a low tolerance for change.

You'll have to face the resisters if you want change to happen. You can't ignore them.

Building Support for Change

Effective organizational leaders build commitment to the change process. Once the attitude for change is in place, behavior can change.

The first behavioral adjustment comes from the top. This means your management and your organization's trustees. According to Duck (1993), these leaders must ask themselves, "If we were managing the way we say we want to manage, how would we act? How would we attack our problems? What kind of meetings and conversations would we have? Who would be involved? How would we define, recognize, compensate, and reward appropriate behavior?" (page 112).

Successful change involves stakeholders throughout the process. Use the strategies of learning organizations, ongoing conversation, and participatory decision making. Include stakeholders in deliberations. Seek their opinions. Listen to their perspective. Use their input. Make sure they understand the resistance to change. Encourage them to identify strategies to overcome the resistance. Ensure that stakeholders help implement and evaluate the change strategies.

> *Managing change means managing courage.*

Communicate change with stakeholders directly and frequently. Provide updates on progress and challenges. As often as possible, communicate face to face. Talk about the need for change. Explain the process for change. Describe the plan for change. Remind people that change is normal and part of business as usual.

Create the opportunity for questions and encourage feedback. Discuss how the current processes are affecting mission, vision, and program. Describe how the proposed changes will improve program and achieve vision.

Effective leaders remember that change is intensely personal. Change relates to each individual, as well as to the group together. Change is successful when each individual understands and accepts his or her role in change and acts accordingly. Individuals and groups within the organization must understand their connection to the overall system. People need to know about any new roles, relationships, processes, expectations, and required skills.

Although change is a standard part of organizational life, change does require patience. Leaders provide both support and consistent pressure. Duck (1993, 114) allows that "once a week, people could visit Pity City. But they weren't allowed to move there." With this same balance of support and pressure, another change agent notes, "we carry the wounded and we shoot the resisters."

Managing the Change Process

Duck (1993, 112) outlines eight steps for managing change:

1. Establish context for change and provide guidance.
2. Stimulate conversation.
3. Provide appropriate resources.
4. Coordinate and align projects.
5. Ensure congruence of messages, activities, policies, and behaviors.
6. Provide opportunities for joint creation.
7. Anticipate, identify, and address people problems.
8. Prepare the critical mass.

Consider how this plays out. Well-managed change requires that everyone understands the meaning and reason for change. Leaders explain why, from their viewpoint. Through conversation, everyone in the organization talks about why the change is necessary. People get together and ask questions, talking about what will happen if the organization does and doesn't change.

Well-managed change demands appropriate resources. If your organization needs more staff, different systems, or new rules to support change, provide them.

Make sure that activities are coordinated and carefully integrated to complement each other and the change process. Along with this, make your messages, policies, and behaviors congruent with the change.

Get ahead by anticipating people's needs, concerns, and problems. Figure out ways to address these issues immediately.

Throughout the change process, gain people's commitment to change by involving them in the diagnosis of situations and identification of solutions. Give people the chance to work together and create new ways of doing things. Make sure you build a sufficient number of people who are committed to the change process.

See Exhibit 2–14 to try an even more no-nonsense approach, proposed by Pritchett and Pound (1993) in their work, *High-Velocity Culture Change: A Handbook for Managers*. This may provide the extra push that your organization and your development function need.

Understanding Transition

Sometimes, it actually seems easy to move forward with change. The vision is in hand. The organization has outlined strategies to move from current reality to the new vision for the future. Everyone is committed. "It's a go. Let's push the button!"

But don't forget transition. As noted earlier, transition is essential for change to result. In their article "Leading Transition: A New Model for Change," Bridges and Mitchell (2000) define transition as internal, "a psychological reorientation that people have to go through before the change can work" (page 31).

Transition isn't automatic. People have to get through the transition before the change is actually accomplished. The authors note that transition includes three distinct processes or phases—and each is distressing to people.

First, people need to say goodbye to the old ways. Sometimes, letting go may be relatively easy because the old ways are seen as less than satisfactory. At other times, letting go is troublesome because those old ways are familiar. Leaders can help people through this phase by "marking the ending" with a symbolic event or activities.

After letting go, people "shift into neutral." They've let go of the old but have not yet started anew. This "neutral zone" is confusing and worrisome. During this time, leaders must be particularly visible, accessible, and communicative.

Don't rush through the neutral zone. It is a time for thinking, learning, and clarifying the reasons for change.

Finally, it's time to move forward and start anew. People have let go and come to closure about the old ways. These individuals have survived the neutral zone, developing energy and finding the creativity to move forward. They hit the third phase in strong stride.

Starting anew is risky. People have to behave differently, risking false starts and even mistakes. The organization has to facilitate and support all three phases of

Exhibit 2–14 No-Nonsense Approach to Change

1. Promote the vision and focus on the future. Don't waste precious time and resources looking backward.
2. Demonstrate unwavering commitment, and practice what you preach. You don't road test culture change; you just do it. The world is uncertain and complex. If your culture doesn't adapt rapidly, everyone loses.
3. Shake the group up. Show everyone that the old culture is incompatible with what is to come.
4. Involve everyone but expect casualties. Engage stakeholders in identifying, designing, implementing, and evaluating change. Make them responsible for changing group culture. Show that you care. But remember you can't make everyone happy. Old behaviors that conflict with the new culture have to go. Let go of the people whose attitude and behavior could sabotage the change your organization needs. Better to lose them than risk your organization's health.
5. Don't let the existing culture control your new approach. Honor history when it helps. Otherwise, get rid of any traditions that stop change.
6. Change infrastructure. Eliminate out-of-date or unnecessary policies and procedures. Create new practices.
7. Bring in new people. Don't hesitate to remove those who fight change. It's harder to convert resisters than it is to bring in new people who will embrace the changing culture.
8. Encourage eccentricity. Reward questions and unconventional acts. Reward those who welcome pluralism.
9. Create a critical mass of like-minded people so you can carry out big changes. Give your best people the big jobs.
10. Honor loyalty to the organization when the loyalty is demonstrated appropriately. Stop loyalty to the past culture. People who feel threatened don't mind fighting dirty to keep things the way they are.
11. Communicate more and more. People need to hear the logic and rationale behind the decision to change. Tell them what is coming and how they will be affected. Cheerlead!
12. Make things happen fast. You cannot afford months or years for staff and volunteers to catch the spirit and change their behavior.

Source: Reprinted from Price Pritchett and Ron Pound, *High Velocity Culture Change: A Handbook for Managers*, Pritchett Publishing Company, Dallas, 1993. Reprint used with full permission of Pritchett & Associates. All rights are reserved.

transition. The organization must operate in accordance with its values and must provide guidance and a risk-free environment.

Always remember, some people will not make it through the transition. They will be unable to let go of the past. Still others will be so anxious that they will never get out of the neutral zone and move forward. Those individuals who do not make it through the transition should not stay in the organization.

Changing through Dynamic Stability

In his article "Change Without Pain," Abrahamson (2000) urges organizations to avoid the disruptive change that can tear them apart. Instead, Abrahamson recommends interspersing dramatic change with smaller initiatives, what he calls *dynamic stability*. This change process reduces organizational overload and chaos, thus reducing resistance.

> **Try tinkering and kludging to make changes in your organization.**

Dynamic stability is defined as "a process of continual but relatively small change efforts that involve the reconfiguration of existing practices and business models rather than the creation of new ones" (page 76).

First, try tinkering. Take a look at what you are already doing. Examine your existing programs, services, structures, and processes. Then modify here and there. Adapt. Abrahamson observes that this tinkering doesn't guarantee successful change. However, tinkering is less costly, less stressful, capitalizes on existing resources, and typically produces results more quickly.

Then there is kludging. Kludging is like tinkering but on a larger scale with more parts. Organizations capitalize on their internal resources but also go outside their own boundaries, adapting from other organizations and external observation.

Pacing is another critical factor in dynamic stability. Instead of changing as much as you can as quickly as possible, consider pacing. The pace of change should be personalized to your organization, some changes more quickly and some more slowly. Learn when to rest and when to push forward quickly.

Abrahamson offers four guidelines for dynamic stability.

1. Reward shameless borrowing.
   First play around with what already exists within your organization. Only as a final resort should you invent from scratch.
2. Appoint a chief memory officer.
   Change is great but only if you learn from the past. Your chief memory officer remembers the

past so that you avoid repeating mistakes while tinkering and kludging.
3. Tinker and kludge internally first.
   It's easier and more stable if you tinker and kludge inside first. Then, with experience, you can venture outside your own boundaries.
4. Hire generalists.
   Generalists possess a wide range of skills, and this diversity promotes open-mindedness, innovation, collaboration, and a combining of experience and information that is critical. Abrahamson calls generalists "boundary spanners."

Appreciative Inquiry

Dr. David L. Cooperrider (Department of Organizational Behavior, Weatherhead School of Management, Case Western Reserve University, Cleveland, OH) proposes "appreciative inquiry" as an organizationwide context for innovation and change.

Much of organizational theory—including change—examines the challenges and threats and outlines how to address these. Contrarily, appreciative inquiry focuses on positive affect, cognition, and interaction. Through this process, organizations discover and understand what works well, then foster innovation.

Cooperrider articulates four principles for appreciative inquiry.

1. Inquiry into "the art of the possible" in organizational life should begin with appreciation.
   Begin first with what works. Discover, describe and explain the "exceptional moments" in your organization. These moments give life to the functioning system and activate the competencies and energies of the workers.
2. Inquiry into what's possible should be applicable.
   Use the results of your appreciative inquiry to generate knowledge within the organization and to build shared learning.
3. Inquiry into what's possible should be provocative.
   An organization can be anything its members want it to be. Also, an organization can learn to guide its own evolution. Cooperrider notes that appreciative inquiry becomes provocative "to the extent that the learning takes on a normative value for members. In this way, appreciative inquiry allows us to use systematic management analysis to help the organization's members shape an effective future according to their own imaginative and moral purposes" (page 4).

4. Inquiry into the human potential of organizational life should be collaborative.

   Work together. Remember the internal relationship, the supportive infrastructure, the process of conversation, and participatory decision making.

> *Appreciative inquiry seeks out the very best of "what is" to help ignite the collective imagination of "what might be."*
>
> *David L. Cooperrider*

Typical management inquiry organizes around the problem to be solved while appreciative inquiry organizes around the "solution to be embraced" (Cooperrider 1993, 5). Appreciative inquiry seeks to generate new knowledge, thus allowing the organization to learn, to envision a new future, and to change into that future. Appreciative inquiry focuses on two basic questions:

1. What in this particular setting and context makes organizing possible?
2. What are the possibilities, expressed and latent, that provide opportunities for more effective (value-congruent) forms of organizing?

Four steps in appreciative inquiry

1. Discover and value what makes your organization work. Think about when commitment was at its highest, examine those factors, and determine why.
2. Envision your future. Once you have discovered what was best, your mind begins to look at future possibilities. Think about what might be. Create a positive image of your desired future.
3. Engage in dialogue. Only through this conversation can you ask the right questions, question assumptions, discover shared meanings, and learn together. Through dialogue you create consensus.
4. Construct the future through innovation and action. Cooperrider notes that appreciative inquiry "creates a momentum of its own." The desired future is grounded in the realities of what worked. This grounding produces the confidence to "try to make things happen."

For more information about appreciative inquiry, see "Appreciative Inquiry in Organizational Life," by D.L. Cooperrider and S. Srivastva, *Research on Organizational Change and Development*, Volume 1, JAI Press, 1987, Woodman and Pasmore, editors.

A CULTURE OF PHILANTHROPY

The seventh component of your organization's internal relationship is a culture of philanthropy. A "culture of philanthropy" refers to your organization's attitude toward philanthropy and fund development.

Why is a culture of philanthropy so important? Because philanthropy is not just about raising money; it's not just another management function. Philanthropy is part of the mission of the for-for-profit organization. You're not just a zoo; you're a zoo and a philanthropic organization. Indeed, it might be said that successful not-for-profits pursue two missions: program and philanthropy.

Organizations that operate with a culture of philanthropy understand three things: the value of organizational culture; the importance of philanthropy; and the inextricable link between philanthropy and fund development.

Keep in mind: Without philanthropy, not-for-profits cannot survive. Whether it is the volunteer board of directors, other volunteers, or charitable gifts, not-for-profits depend on some form of philanthropy. But philanthropy does not last long without fund development because fund development is the process to encourage philanthropy. Together, philanthropy and fund development form a perpetual circle.

Effective organizations incorporate a culture of philanthropy as part of organizational culture. Each volunteer and every employee feels it. Clients and donors recognize it whenever they connect with the organization.

But too often, there is no culture of philanthropy. The program staff is too busy to share client stories with the development officer. Board members are happy to delegate fund development to someone else, whether a committee or staff. Some staff and volunteers view development with distaste. Still others think that philanthropists are only the wealthy.

These organizations have not yet developed a culture of philanthropy. As a result, their success is compromised. Within a culture of philanthropy, everyone in the organization—from the janitor to the president of the board—understands that philanthropy and fund development are critical. Furthermore, each individual understands that she or he has a role in the process.

First and foremost, everyone is an ambassador. As an ambassador for the organization, everyone does his own job well. Everyone understands how all the various jobs in the organization create one integrated system. Everyone talks positively about the organization within the community. Most especially, everyone treats all of the organization's customers (clients, donors, volunteers, community people, etc.) with care and respect.

In a culture of philanthropy, everyone understands that if the organization's programs are weak, it doesn't matter what the fundraiser does. Everyone knows that if board members don't talk about the organization with their friends and colleagues, it doesn't matter how hard the executive director tries to raise funds. Each person knows that if the receptionist isn't sufficiently helpful, the best direct mail solicitation will not be as effective as it can be.

How You Can Build the Culture of Philanthropy in Your Organization

Consider, first, the questions that you might ask yourself about building a culture of philanthropy. For example:

1. How do the people in my organization define philanthropy? How do they define fund development? What are the differences in thought and attitude when describing these two functions?
2. What is organizational culture and how would the people in my organization define our culture?
3. What effect does organizational culture have on our organization's operations and effectiveness?
4. What effect does our organizational culture have on philanthropy and fund development?
5. What are our values regarding philanthropy and fund development, and how do we develop systems and processes to reinforce these values?
6. How can we enhance our organizational culture to best reflect our values?
7. How can we engage staff and volunteers in meaningful conversations to foster a culture of philanthropy?
8. How can we modify these questions and add more questions?

Review this chapter and make sure that you have the skills and knowledge to build the necessary infrastructure. Take a look at your colleagues within the organization. Which of them has the skills and knowledge to do this work? How can you enhance your skills and knowledge together?

Think long and hard about how you will initiate conversations about organizational culture and the culture of philanthropy. Consider formal and informal conversations. Think about extending the conversations and engaging more people.

When the time is right, bring together some of your organization's leadership to initiate the conversation. Evaluate the effectiveness of the conversation and outline your next steps.

Think about formal training opportunities and informal chats about the meaning of philanthropy and fund development.

Engage staff in storytelling about clients and organizational accomplishments.

Encourage the honest sharing of concerns and discomfort about fund development. Host a "complain and whine" session about fund development with staff and volunteers. You'll find that much of what they say is justified—and you'll want to make sure that your fund development program avoids those inappropriate behaviors. Some of what they say reflects a lack of understanding about best practice—so you can inform them. A small part of what they express describes their own fears—and you can help overcome these.

A LAST WORD ON HOW TO BUILD AN ORGANIZATION THAT WILL LAST

In a 1990 interview (Collins and Porras, 1994), the cofounder of the Hewlett-Packard Company, William R. Hewlett, talked about his life's work. "I'm probably most proud of having helped to create a company that by virtue of its values, practices, and success has had a tremendous impact on the way companies are managed around the world. And I'm particularly proud that I'm leaving behind an ongoing organization that can live on as a role model long after I'm gone" (page 1).

Hewlett is talking about organizational development—and so did the other 18 companies in a 6-year study of timeless management principles, conducted by Collins and Porras (1994). The authors identified the differences between extraordinary companies and highly successful ones.

And what did they discover? Timeless principles that distinguish the extraordinary company from the merely highly successful company. These principles shatter myths and reinforce the critical importance of organizational development.

Here are a few of the 12 shattered myths:

1. It takes a great idea to start a great company.
   Wrong. Some of the visionary companies began without any idea, and others failed with their original ideas. And, as Collins and Porras note, "all great ideas eventually become obsolete."
2. Visionary companies require great and charismatic visionary leaders.
   Wrong again. Indeed, high-profile charismatic leaders often hindered the company's development. CEOs of the visionary companies focused on building a strong company. The study showed that "the continuity of superb individuals atop

visionary companies stems from the companies being outstanding organizations, not the other way around."

3. The only constant is change.

On the contrary. Visionary companies protect their core values pretty much forever, creating a stable foundation. But they change and adapt their products and services, ensuring their relevance. Collins and Porras call this "preserving the core and stimulating progress."

4. Visionary companies are great places to work, for everyone.

Not at all. These companies are great for only those who fit well with the company's core ideology and its demanding standards. "Visionary companies are so clear about what they stand for and what they're trying to achieve that they simply don't have room for those unwilling or unable to fit their exacting standards."

5. Visionary companies make their best moves by brilliant and complex strategic planning.

Sometimes. But then these companies also experiment, take advantage of opportunities, and work by trial and error. The authors comment that visionary companies "mimic the biological evolution of species," trying lots of stuff and keeping what works.

6. The most successful companies focus primarily on beating the competition.

Nope. Instead visionary companies continually pursue the question, How can we improve ourselves to do better tomorrow than we did today?

7. You can't have your cake and eat it, too.

Oh yes you can. Visionary companies avoid the "the tyranny of the OR" and choose the "and." Visionary companies refuse to choose between A or B but try for A *and* B.

> *A group of people get together and exist as an institution that we call a company so they are able to accomplish something collectively that they could not accomplish separately—they make a contribution to society."*
> *David Packard, speech given to Hewlett-Packard's training group on March 8, 1960, quoted in Collins and Porras*

Built to Last notes that the company itself is the ultimate creation. It isn't the product or service. These are merely the vehicles for the company. This is about designing an organization—and visionary companies spend more time designing the organization than they do

designing the product and services. And what about the stream of quality products and services? They come to fruition because of the outstanding organization.

To summarize, "The essence of a visionary company comes in the translation of its core ideology [core values and purpose] and its own unique drive for progress into the very fabric of the organization—into goals, strategies, tactics, policies, processes, cultural practices, management behaviors, building layouts, pay systems, accounting systems, job design—into *everything* that the company does. A visionary company creates a total environment that envelops employees, bombarding them with a set of signals so consistent and mutually reinforcing that it's virtually impossible to misunderstand the company's ideology and ambitions" (Collins and Porras 1994, 202). Surely that's organizational development.

SUMMARY

If you want to raise more money for your organization, first strengthen your organization's internal relationship. This relationship relies on an effective infrastructure that produces a healthy corporate culture and sound systems.

Traditionally, organizations develop an infrastructure with such components as:

- planning and assessment
- marketing and communications
- human resources, both staff and volunteers
- general management
- governance
- financing
- quality assurance and continuous quality improvement

Effective organizations add seven more components to develop their internal relationship and move strongly into the next millennium.

1. shared values
2. art of leadership
3. learning organization
4. ongoing conversation
5. participatory decision making
6. well-managed change
7. culture of philanthropy

First, these organizations articulate shared values and operate accordingly. Second, these effective organizations recruit and develop leaders who possess specific attitudes and skills and perform certain functions. Third, the most effective organizations turn themselves into learning organizations. They know that this may well be the most critical attribute for survival. Fourth and fifth, these organizations stimulate ongoing conversation and participatory decision making, both essential to learning organizations. Managing change is the sixth and final component that effective organizations use to strengthen their internal relations.

REFERENCES

Abrahamson, E. 2000. Change without Pain. *Harvard Business Review*. Boston: Harvard Business School.

Anderson, M. 1993. *Words of Wisdom*. Silver Spring, MD: Philanthropic Service for Institutions.

Bennett, S. and J. Brown. 1995. Mindshift: Strategic Dialogue for Breakthrough Thinking. *Learning Organizations, Developing Cultures for Tomorrow's Workplace*, ed. S. Chawla and J. Renesch. Portland, OR: Productivity Press.

Block, P. 1993. *Stewardship: Choosing Service Over Self-Interest*. San Francisco: Berrett-Koehler Publishers.

Bridges, W. 1991. *Managing Transitions: Making the Most of Change*. New York: Addison-Wesley Publishing Co.

Bridges, W. and S. Mitchell. 2000. Leading Transition: A New Model for Change. *Leader to Leader*. New York: Peter F. Drucker Foundation for Nonprofit Management; San Francisco: Jossey-Bass, Publishers.

Brown, J. and D. Isaacs. December 1996–January 1997. *The Systems Thinker*, 7(10).

Chatterjee, Debashis. 1998. *Leading Consciously: A Pilgrimage Toward Self-Mastery*. Newton, MA: Butterworth-Heinemann.

Collins, J.C. and J.I. Porras. 1994. *Built to Last*. New York: HarperCollins Publishers.

Cooperrider, D.L. 1993. *Appreciative Inquiry: A Constructive Approach to Organization Development*. Cleveland, OH: Department of Organizational Behavior, Weatherhead School of Management, Case Western Reserve University.

Cooperrider, D.L. and S. Srivastva. 1987. Appreciative Inquiry in Organizational Life. In Woodman and Pasmore (Eds.), *Research on Organizational Change and Development* (Vol. 1). PAI Press.

DePree, M. 1989. *Leadership Is an Art*. New York: Dell Publishing.

Drucker, P. 1990. *Managing the Nonprofit Organization: Principles and Practices*. New York: HarperCollins Publishers.

Duck, J. November–December 1993. Managing Change: The Art of Balancing. *Harvard Business Review*. Boston: Harvard Business School.

Ellinor, L. and G. Gerard. 1998. *Dialogue: Rediscovering the Transforming Power of Conversation*. New York: John Wiley & Sons, Inc.

Gardner, J. 1990. *On Leadership*. New York: The Free Press/Macmillan, Inc.

Goleman, D. 2000. *Working with Emotional Intelligence*. New York: Bantam Books.

Greenleaf, R. 1991. *Servant Leadership: A Journey into the Nature of Legitimate Power and Greatness*. New York: Paulist Press.

Gunn, R. 2000. Leading from Within: Strategies for and Reflections on Becoming a Leader of Leaders. *Perdido*, Winter, 11.

Harrison, E. 1987. *The Managerial Decision-Making Process*, 3rd ed. Boston: Houghton Mifflin Company.

Harvey, J. 1988. *Organizational Dynamics, The Abilene Paradox: The Management of Agreement*. American Management Association.

Hock, D. 2000. The Art of Chaordic Leadership. *Leader to Leader*. New York: Peter F. Drucker Foundation for Nonprofit Management; San Francisco: Jossey-Bass, Publishers.

Janis, I. 1982. *Groupthink*. 2nd ed. Boston: Houghton Mifflin.

Kim, D. July/August 1993. The Leader with the "Beginner's" Mind. *Healthcare Forum Journal*.

Kotter, J. and L. Schlesinger. March–April 1979. Choosing Strategies for Change. *Harvard Business Review*. Boston: Harvard Business School.

Lewis, J.H. 1997. *Advancing Philanthropy*. Alexandria, VA: National Society of Fund Raising Executives.

Lipman-Blumen, J. 2000. The Age of Connective Leadership. *Leader to Leader*. New York: Peter F. Drucker Foundation for Nonprofit Management; San Francisco: Jossey-Bass, Publishers.

Marion, B. 1994. Decision Making in Ethics. *Ethics in Fundraising: Putting Values into Practice*, ed. M. Briscoe. New Directions for Philanthropic Fundraising, No. 6. San Francisco: Jossey-Bass, Publishers.

Mitroff, I., R. Mason, and C. Pearson. 1994. *Framebreak, the Radical Redesign of American Business*. San Francisco: Jossey-Bass, Publishers.

Muoio, A. July–August 1999. The art of Smart. *The Fast Company*.

Nonaka, I. November–December 1991. The Knowledge Creating Company. *Harvard Business Review*. Boston: Harvard Business School.

Poole, M.P. 1993. *Words of Wisdom*. Silver Spring, MD: Philanthropic Service for Institutions.

Pottruck, D.S. and T. Pearce. 2000. *Clicks and Mortar: Passion Driven Growth in an Internet World*. San Francisco: Jossey-Bass, Publishers.

Powell, C. 1995. *Retired Army General, My American Journey*. New York: Random House.

Pritchett, P. and R. Pound. 1993. *High Velocity Culture Change: A Handbook for Managers*. Dallas: Pritchett Publishing Company.

Raths, L. 1966. *Values and Teaching*. Columbus, OH: Merrill.

Roberts, P. 2000. *Fast Company*. Boston, MA.

Senge, P., A. Kleiner, C. Roberts, R. Ross, and B. Smith, 1994. *The Fifth Discipline Fieldbook: Strategies and Tools for Building a Learning Organization*. New York: Doubleday.

Senge, P. 1990. *The Fifth Discipline: The Art and Practice of the Learning Organization*. New York: Doubleday.

Swap, W.C. and Associates. 1994. *Group Decision Making*. Newbury Park, CA: Sage Publications.

Webber, A.M. September–October 1994. Surviving in the New Economy. *Harvard Business Review*. Boston: Harvard Business School.

Chapter 3

The Second Relationship—With Your Community

Ensuring Your Organization's Relevance through Strategic Planning

A company is not a machine but a living organism. Much like an individual, it can have a collective sense of identity and fundamental purpose. This is the organizational equivalent of self-knowledge—a shared understanding of what the company stands for, where it's going, what kind of world it wants to live in, and most importantly, how it intends to make that world a reality.

Ikujiro Nonaka

For a football team to function as an intelligent organism rather than as a group of individuals, the players need to take advantage of not only the fact that they have a stronger potential together than one by one, but also that they have different competencies and skills as individuals. This, in turn, requires that the players create shared mental models about football. To merge the different skills of all the players into an effective whole, they need to have exactly the same overall perception of what the game is all about—the non-negotiable set of rules for football.

Karl-Henrik Robèrt

You and I are constantly called upon to make assumptions about what the world will be like in five or ten years—and we guide our programs on the basis of these assumptions. The degree to which we are successfully clairvoyant will vary. But we all know what it is like not to be able to see ahead. And we all have had that queasy feeling that comes when we are surprised by something we should have known was coming all along.

Samuel Beckett caught that insight best. He penned one of the great, instructive thoughts of our time: "Everything will turn out all right—unless something foreseen crops up."

That thought of Beckett's haunts me. If we remain . . . trapped in political gridlock, paralyzed in the face of challenge, it will not be because there were too many surprises. It will be because of what we can foresee but choose to ignore.

Peter C. Goldmark

TOPICS DISCUSSED IN THIS SECTION

- what strategic planning really means and how it benefits your organization
- how organizations avoid or compromise strategic planning
- planning for the future while you operate today
- what to include in your written plan
- roles in the planning process
- principal components of an effective strategic planning process and implementation steps
- using market research to secure the information you need to make decisions
- crafting your vision and outlining your goals
- keeping the plan alive
- challenges facing strategic planning

MAKING SURE YOUR ORGANIZATION IS RELEVANT TO THE COMMUNITY

Your organization's relevance to the community significantly affects your ability to fundraise. Your relevance is defined and renewed through the process of strategic planning. If your organization's internal relations provide the foundation for good fund development, then let's say that strategic planning provides the framework.

Strategic planning defines your relationship with the community and provides the framework for all other organizational activities. Just ask yourself, how can we raise money without knowing

- where we are going?
- how we will get there by doing what?
- how much it will cost?
- how all this fits in with community needs and priorities?
- how our organization fits in with other groups in the community?
- who might be interested in the needs we meet?

Your Organization and Strategic Planning

Clearly, an organization's strategic plan establishes direction. The written plan clarifies where the organization is going, how it will get there, and why money is needed. The plan generally describes a vision for the future and a blueprint for action. With this delineation of vision, direction, and action, the fundraiser can seek charitable contributions.

But strategic planning is more than a written document and a road map. Effective strategic planning is a process that brings about organizational commitment and produces organizational learning and change. The planning process is a way of thinking and acting. An organization that thinks strategically and acts accordingly is better positioned for everything, including fund development.

Effective strategic planning is designed to answer the following "big picture" questions.

- What are we doing now? Who are our customers? What do they value? What has been the outcome of our work?
- What is happening in the outside world? What needs are being met and who is meeting these needs? How do we cooperate and collaborate with these organizations? What is our unique contribution to the community? What needs are not being met? Might we have the capability and wish to respond to any of these needs? Could we build alliances and collaborate to meet the needs?
- What is our vision for the future? Will we change who we are? What is our business? Who will be our customers? What do they value? Who are our collaborators? What knowledge alliances will we need?

- Now, what will be the outcome of our work? How will we achieve this?
- What is our plan? Who will do what in which time frame? How will we measure success?
- How much will all this cost and how will we finance our endeavors?
- How will we ensure that we are accountable?

> *A key responsibility of [organization leadership] is to define where the organization is going, or where it is supposed to go. The strategic planning process starts with the development of a macro view. It proceeds with various steps to smaller, more narrowly defined issues and, subsequently, to explicit objectives that can be monitored and measured.*
>
> *David B. Luther*

Strategic planning should also strengthen your fund development by

- assessing the productivity and effectiveness of fundraising activities
- evaluating board, staff, and volunteer understanding of and performance in fundraising
- developing and enhancing relationships with donor constituents
- targeting areas of constituent interest
- identifying fundraising themes
- increasing the organization's visibility
- building board and staff understanding of how the organization fits within the community and the fundraising and volunteer marketplace

Avoiding or Compromising Strategic Planning

Strategic planning—which includes strategic thinking and acting—is part of doing business. Actually, planning is the central business function from which all other functions evolve.

Despite its obvious benefits, the process is not always embraced. Some organizations avoid planning altogether. They claim

- "There isn't enough time."
- "We are so busy (and threatened) that we must focus on the here and now."
- "We know who we are and our mission is clear. We don't need to do strategic planning."
- "We are a strong organization. Nothing is wrong. Not much has changed. We're headed in the right direction."

Many organizations try the quick version of planning. These groups acknowledge some need for a plan but deny the value of a planning process. They

- conduct a one-day retreat with the board and bang out a plan
- get together a small group of key leaders and let them recommend direction and action to the board
- expect staff to develop the plan for board review

Other organizations focus on programs only when planning. These organizations address mission but ignore the infrastructure, those critical supporting systems such as management and governance, fund development, marketing and communications, physical plant, and information systems.

Some people say that organizations should not do strategic planning. These individuals say that planning is too binding and inhibits thinking and acting. Instead, perpetual motion and quick change are best.

Certainly perpetual motion and well-thought-out change are essential in today's world. But how do organizations develop this capacity and know which change to embrace? Organizations learn through ongoing and continual planning. This is a leadership attitude, a corporate culture, and a key component of your organization's internal systems and processes.

Don't kid yourself. Strategic planning is all about motion and change. Indeed, the best strategic planning teaches organizations and people to think and move continually.

Planning for the Future While You Operate Today

Strategic planning is so important that every organization, no matter its size, experience, or longevity, can benefit. However, planning for the future occurs in tandem with current operations. While you plan, you also carry out your business. Because planning is an ongoing process, your organization implements a plan and evaluates its progress while you prepare the plan for the next interval.

Expect that a comprehensive strategic planning process will require at least six months of concentrated effort. From the moment your organization launches the process to the time you adopt the plan, as much as a year could pass. The board, chief executive officer (CEO), and key staff will be closely involved. Other staff and key constituents play a role.

Here are some cautions as you plan and operate simultaneously.

- Do not launch major new initiatives while you are planning. Instead, consider these initiatives as possible choices within the strategic planning process.
- If a unique opportunity arises and a decision cannot wait until the planning process is completed, assess the opportunity very carefully. While you may need to launch this new activity before the planning process is finished, use the information you have already learned in the planning process.
- During the planning process, you may identify infrastructure issues that demand immediate attention. Often, these issues relate to customer satisfaction or management activities. If immediate attention is necessary, refer these issues to the appropriate group (e.g., management or board) for action.

> *Planning is the creative act of synthesizing experiences into a novel strategy.*
>
> *Henry Mintzberg*

WHAT IS STRATEGIC PLANNING AND HOW WILL IT BENEFIT YOUR ORGANIZATION?

Planning determines your direction and devises strategies to move you forward. Through planning, you create a mission, vision, and values powerful enough to engage the hearts and minds of all people within your organization. The process itself produces valuable dissonance that forces individuals and groups to look into themselves.

The best strategic planning means systems thinking, individual and organization learning, and strategic action. To plan well, you see the whole and the interconnections of its parts. To survive, effective organizations learn. To progress, you act strategically. Look back at Chapter 2 for further discussion of systems thinking and learning organizations.

Good planning is both a process and a product, both an attitude and behavior. The planning process is as important as the resulting plan, perhaps more important. The process informs the organization, builds investment, mobilizes participants, and leads change. The planning process must be sufficiently comprehensive while maintaining momentum to reach completion.

In this book, strategic, long-range, and business planning are synonymous. "Strategic" suggests the big picture and a flexibility and responsiveness to the environment. "Long-range" connotes a time frame of multiple years. "Business" outlines how the work will be implemented, financed, and evaluated.

Planning demands honest dialogue and difficult decision making. The process identifies and challenges the most critical and sacred assumptions of the organization and its members, including the relevance of your mission. This is tough stuff.

Rules are suspended and assumptions are questioned. Good planning actually rewards individuals for raising difficult issues and asking tough questions.

> *Planning means choosing—choosing between various consequences.*

Decision making relies on data produced by market research, insights provided from experience, and critical self-assessment. The organization explores different strategies and examines the system consequences of possible choices.

Strategic planning always involves those who will be affected by the plan. Whether they are clients, staff, volunteers, donors, or community leaders, these constituents have a stake in the decisions of the organization.

Strategic planning does not forecast the future. The world is too complex and uncertain for forecasting. Instead, strategic planning tries first to understand multiple possible futures. Second, through planning, the organization learns how to respond robustly to different alternative futures.

In summary, strategic planning makes sure that your organization clearly knows its shared purpose and destiny. The *Fifth Discipline Fieldbook* (Senge et al., 1994) notes that shared purpose and destiny include vision, values, mission, and goals.

- Vision is an image of an organization's desired future. Vision describes where an organization wants to go and what it will look like when it arrives. Vision is tangible. Its sense of immediacy helps direct your organization and its members.
- Values indicate how an organization expects to get where it is going. Values describe how the organization intends to operate and behave. The *Fieldbook* describes values as: "If we act as we should, what would an observer see us doing? How would we be thinking?" (Senge et al. 1994, 302).
- Mission or purpose describes what your organization is here to do. It is rare that an organization ever achieves its purpose.
- Goals are "the milestones we expect to reach before too long" (Senge et al. 1994, 302). They should be challenging, but at the same time realistic and achievable.

Is Your Organization Relevant?

First and foremost, effective strategic planning ensures your organization's relevance. Planning justifies your existence by defining your relationship with the community and defining your position in the marketplace.

Too often, organization leaders focus on their own opinions, experience, and desires. Instead, these leaders should be executing an objective planning process that turns to the community.

Organization leaders are stewards, caretakers of the public trust. These leaders are expected to ensure the organization's relevance, rather than to focus on the organization's desires, needs, and turf.

Through effective planning, your organization reaches out to the community, ensuring relevance. Organization leaders forgo their own opinion and desires, turning first to the community.

The process of planning makes your organization more effective and helps ensure your survival. And, for those concerned about money, the resulting long-range strategic plan provides the framework for your fund development.

A wonderful example of effective strategic planning was done by Royal Dutch/Shell in the early 1980s. Because of this planning process, the company moved from the bottom of the seven major oil companies to one of the top two. Arie de Geus (1995), then head of Shell's planning, explained what happened.

The planning team looked for businesses around the world that had survived over the long term. Only a few had survived more than the average of 30–50 years. Those companies that lasted longer possessed four common attributes.

- First, the companies were sensitive to the world around them. Their leaders were aware and active in the world in which they lived. They were out looking. Author's note: Drucker (1990) calls this one of the basic rules. "Focus your people, and especially your executives, to be on the outside often enough to know what the institution exists for. There are no results inside an institution. There are only costs. Yet it is easy to become absorbed in the inside and to become insulated from reality. Effective [organizations] make sure that their people get out in the field and actually work there again and again" (Drucker, 1990, 120).
- Second, there was a sense of cohesion and company identity. Employees and management had a good understanding of what the company stood for and what it did. People willingly committed to the company values.

- Third, these companies changed successfully by fully using decentralized systems and structures. Slowly, carefully, and incrementally, these companies diversified. They developed new portfolios of service and product in response to the changing world. The enduring companies had a high tolerance for pluralism and diversity, both inside and outside the company. According to de Geus (1995), the surviving companies "accepted activities in the margin" and took risks.
- Fourth, the handful of companies that survived longer than average were conservative in their financing. They knew the value of dollars in hand: allowing flexibility and options. De Geus commented that a surviving company is in any business that allows it to survive. If an organization changes its portfolio, it scuttles assets, and that's okay. Assets are expendable capital, and profits are not a top priority (de Geus 1995).

Through strategic planning, Royal Dutch/Shell learned what all organizations must learn, even not-for-profits.

- First, the world is complex, impermanent, and pluralistic. Because this is an unstable, uncertain, and uncontrollable environment, organizations must have high tolerance for openness and diversity to survive. Organizations that are centralized, controlled from the top, ignorant of the environment, and intolerant of diversity will not survive. They haven't in the past, they aren't now, and they certainly won't survive in the future.
- Second, successful organizations understand that the purpose of any planning or plan is to achieve constructive change. Change is a prerequisite for success. The process of planning is the catalyst for change, altering the way an organization thinks about itself, its community, and the larger world.

> *The ability to learn faster than your competitors may be the only sustainable competitive advantage.*
>
> *Arie P. de Geus*

Strategic Planning Produces Learning, and Learning Produces Change

Change requires information, learning, and innovation. Innovation involves intuition, information, and creativity. Drucker notes that successful innovation depends on seeing change as an opportunity, rather than a threat. He goes on to observe that, when faced with change, one of the common mistakes is repairing the old, rather than seeking the new.

It has been said that there is no such thing as a new idea. There are only old ideas that can be used in new contexts or configurations. Perhaps, then, organizational creativity identifies new contexts and configurations for the old ideas that add value to your organization.

High-level, effective, and continuous institutional learning produces organizational change. Philip J. Carroll, president and CEO of Shell Oil Company, calls learning "the fulcrum for change" (1995). Arie de Geus (1988) notes that organizations learn as they make decisions because "people change their own mental models and build up a joint model as they talk" (page 71). The problem, observes de Geus, is how slowly organizations learn—too slow, he claims, for a world where learning faster is likely an advantage. An organization's most relevant learning is done by those people with the power to act. Following this, de Geus observes that the purpose of planning is to change the mental models of decision makers, not to make plans.

Effective organizations produce change when they understand the environment and themselves. These organizations recognize and react to environmental change before they are in crisis. Unfortunately, according to de Geus (1988), it typically takes 12–18 months for an organization to act on information received. The organization has learned, but with such delay that the learning may be useless. The thought arises, is the organization slowly going out of business?

The challenge, then, is to accelerate learning by organizations. Strategic planning can help. Effective planning enhances organizational learning. Conversely, learning organizations do more effective strategic planning.

De Geus (1988) observes that the learning of the group is much harder to accomplish than that of its individual members. "The level of thinking that goes on in the management teams of most companies is considerably below the individual managers' capacities. In institutional learning situations, the learning level of the team is often the lowest common denominator..." (page 70).

The process of planning produces commitment. Commitment is a personal choice, and no one can demand it from another. Once made, commitment can be a powerful catalyst for change. Planning mobilizes the enthusiasm, investment, and action of your board, staff, volunteers, clients, and the community. When invited to participate in creating something one truly cares about, people are usually willing to change. It is said that, to make change, 17 percent of your staff must support the change effort and direction. Further, for every 100 employees, studies show that it requires 10 months for change to happen. The results of effective planning are outlined in Exhibit 3–1.

PLANNING COMPONENTS

Components of the Written Plan

The process of planning produces a written document for use by staff, board, and committees as they lead the organization. Each plan has its own personality and format relevant to the particular organization.

Your plan provides the blueprint for organization direction and action. The plan serves as the guide to assess institutional health and your relationship with the community. The plan helps you evaluate board and staff performance. Progress of the strategic plan is the single most critical factor to evaluate the CEO's effectiveness.

The strategic plan also helps to define the performance goals and assessment of other staff.

The strategic plan is used to create all other plans within the organization, including the fund development plan. The budget, as well as annual work plans for board, staff, and committees, are prescribed by the strategic plan.

Key components of the written strategic plan are

- statement of values and mission
- description of future vision
- goals (program and infrastructure) for the multiyear period (duration of plan)
- indicators of success (sometimes called *benchmarks* or *critical success factors*)
- strategies or action steps to achieve the goals
- general time frames and key assignments of responsibility

Exhibit 3–1 Eight Key Results Produced by an Effective Strategic Planning Process

1. Determine shared vision and direction of your organization and define how to get there.
   - Test validity of your mission and perhaps recommend adjustments or major change.
   - Define your direction.
   - Determine priorities and set limits.
2. Justify your organization's existence in the community and clarify your organization's position in the marketplace.
   - Assess community needs.
   - Identify responses to meet those needs and gaps in meeting those needs so that your organization can choose what it will be and do.
   - Examine institutional capacity and capability to meet the needs.
3. Identify constituents and build stronger relationships with them.
   - Identify new constituents.
   - Bring current constituents closer to the organization.
   - Build constituent understanding of community needs and your organization's response.
4. Build an aligned, cohesive organization.
   - Engage the hearts and minds of those closest to the organization.
   - Produce positive experiences for participants.
   - Foster shared vision, ownership, and teamwork.
   - Bring key constituents closer together and give permission for others to move on.
   - Mobilize people for investment of time, money, and action.
   - Clarify roles and relationships and distribute workload.
   - Build cross-functional bridges.
5. Build a learning organization.
   - Encourage pluralism and diversity.
   - Develop individual and team skills.
   - Foster flexibility within a general direction.
   - Encourage critical thinking and creativity.
   - Enable the organization to use its strengths for comparative advantage and to mobilize against threats.
   - Develop capacity to detect and respond to changes in the internal and external environments.
   - Create a forum for conversation, dialogue, and improved consensus decision making.
6. Identify cost of doing business and income sources.
   - Justify fund development.
   - Create case for support.
7. Set benchmarks for success.
   - Define accountability.
   - Outline criteria for success and evaluation process.
   - Establish general time frames.
8. Produce the best planning process and written plan.
   - Create visionary guide and practical governance and management tool.
   - Guide annual work plans and budgeting for staff, board, and volunteers.
   - Assign responsibility.
   - Support staff and board performance assessment.

- multiyear financial projections and guidelines for income and expense
- process to monitor progress, evaluate performance, and extend the plan
- overview of planning process

> *Your institution's strategic plan is critical to fund development success. Moreover, your strategic planning process is fundamental to fundraising effectiveness.*

Principal Components of an Effective Strategic Planning Process

Six components are essential to effective strategic planning: values clarification, situation analysis, market research, decision making, writing the plan, and implementing and monitoring the plan.

Use these components to design a strategic planning process that is relevant for your organization. Tailor the process to your organization by considering such things as

- your organization's age, size, and complexity
- resources (staff, volunteers, consultants) available to devote to planning
- your marketplace
- the internal and external environments

Values are the standards that influence us as we make choices among alternative courses of action. Values are the manners by which we operate as an organization. They guide our actions and judgments. When we state our values, others can decide whether they wish to affiliate with us, living with us in the way we want to live. Chapter 2 discusses values in detail.

The situation analysis, also called an environmental scan or SWOT analysis, examines where your organization is now. Look at your internal strengths and weaknesses (SW) and external opportunities and threats (OT). At the start of the planning process, conduct the situation analysis through group dialogue with your agency's key leadership, both staff and board. The information gleaned is used to outline the market research for the planning process. For details, see step 4, "Launch the process with board, staff, and planning committee," under "General Steps for the Strategic Planning Process," later in this chapter.

Market research provides you with qualitative and quantitative information upon which to base your decisions about the future. Through market research, you examine current and future trends in the marketplace. You

also examine your program and infrastructure. There are four major components to market research: community needs assessment; analysis of competitors, collaborators, and knowledge alliances; customer satisfaction review; and assessment of institutional capacity. See step 5 under "General Steps," to follow.

With the results of your situation analysis and market research in hand, your organization must make key decisions. You create your vision for the future and outline key corporate goals to achieve the vision. You establish benchmarks for success and align your mission with vision.

Often, these decisions are made at a planning retreat, discussed more fully in steps 7–12 of the planning process. Your organization's leaders gather together, including the planning committee, board, and key staff. You review the results of the situation analysis and market research, and discuss the implications for your organization. Then you choose your organization's direction. With these key decisions made, the organization's staff identify strategies to achieve the goals. Staff members project time frames and financing for review by the planning committee.

The planning process manager usually writes the plan, incorporating the general components outlined previously. Once the planning committee has reviewed the draft plan, it is presented to the board for review and action.

The planning process does not stop once the plan is written. Implementing the plan involves both staff and board members. Implementation also includes monitoring the plan's progress, adjusting when necessary, evaluating overall performance, and launching the next planning process. See a diagram of the planning process in Figure 3–1.

General Steps for the Strategic Planning Process

The six principal components of strategic planning can be detailed as 19 steps. Although these steps are presented in sequential order, remember that planning is not necessarily linear. You may conduct some steps simultaneously, modify the order, or merge some steps. However, be cautious about eliminating any steps.

The general steps for planning are as follows:

1. Formally agree to do planning.
2. Engage key constituents in the planning process.
3. Get ready to plan.
4. Launch the process with board, staff, and planning committee.
5. Design the planning process, develop the market research outline, and conduct the research.

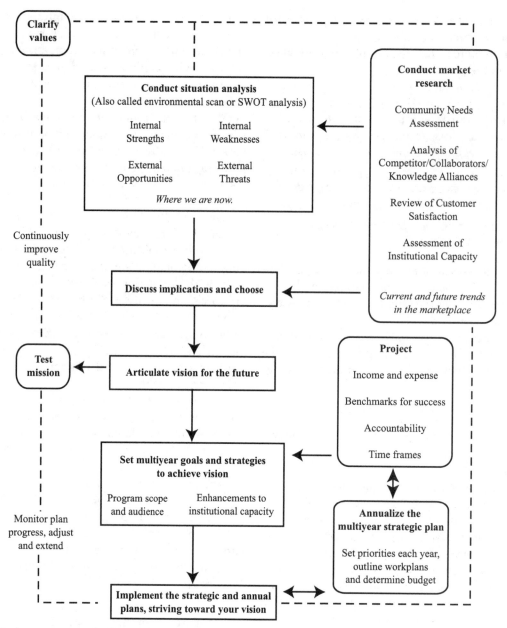

The dotted line represents the feedback loop and operates in all directions between elements.

Figure 3–1 The Strategic Planning Process

6. Articulate (or review) values.
7. Tabulate research results, analyze findings, and prepare the information report.
8. Design the decision-making process.
9. Discuss findings and determine implications.
10. Determine direction or vision.
11. Review (and possibly adjust) mission.
12. Determine goals and strategies.
13. Identify core competencies and supporting structure.
14. Establish benchmarks for success.
15. Assign time frames and entities responsible for strategies or action steps.

16. Project costs and income sources.
17. Outline process to monitor progress of plan, evaluate performance, and extend plan for subsequent years.
18. Write the strategic plan, review, and adopt.
19. Translate the plan into personal commitment.

What Makes Planning Work

There are many different versions of strategic long-range planning: standard tactics and cutting-edge techniques, bells and whistles, and assorted models with various components. The key is to tailor the process to meet your organization's needs and resources.

Factors that contribute to a viable planning process and meaningful plan are:

1. the right planning process tailor-made to your organization
2. involvement of those who will be affected by the plan
3. critical mass of leaders who support the planning process and will guide the resulting plan
4. accomplished manager for the planning process
5. commitment of time to carry out the process, balanced with adequate pace to maintain forward momentum
6. receptivity to new information and willingness to change
7. adequate and appropriate information upon which to make decisions
8. ongoing critical thinking and behavior
9. ability of your organization to engage in dialogue, argue, and decide

ROLES IN THE PLANNING PROCESS

There are four groups or individuals who are critical to produce an effective planning process.

1. planning committee: committee of the board that oversees the process and leads the board through planning
2. board: decision makers regarding the organization's future and plan to achieve that future
3. staff: leaders in the planning process
4. planning process manager: staff person or consultant responsible for designing and coordinating the planning process

Planning Committee

The planning committee oversees the planning process on behalf of the board. Key responsibilities are:

- Engage the board in the process of planning.
- Work with the organization's CEO and planning process manager to design the overall process, most particularly, the research and decision-making components.
- Identify strategic issues facing the organization.
- Identify areas of challenge and opportunity for the board.
- Identify and recruit volunteers to help conduct the market research.
- Review research results.

- With the board, participate in the decision-making process.
- Help outline goals, action steps, indicators of success, and assignments of responsibility.

Put together the best planning committee by combining the right skills and behavior, experience, and diversity. All candidates should possess the requisite skills and behavior. Experience and diversity should be considered in overall composition of the committee.

- Skills and behavior: Choose critical thinkers. They must see the big picture, ask the difficult questions, challenge the status quo, dialogue well, argue, create consensus, and seek change. Good committee members set aside their personal agendas and work to benefit the organization and the community.
- Diversity: Standard considerations are gender, generation, and ethnicity. Undoubtedly, your organization will need additional diversity. Depending on your mission and scope of service, you may need to be sensitive to geography, socioeconomics, and other factors.
- Experience: Recruit individuals both inside and outside the organization. Consider clients, donors, current and past trustees, key staff, community leaders and philanthropists, and representatives from other organizations.

Your organization's CEO serves as a member of the planning committee. She or he participates in all deliberations, offers insight and perspective, and provides significant leadership to develop future vision and goals.

Some committee members should have extensive experience with your organization, knowing the history, service, and reasons for past decisions. These individuals may be current or past board members, major donors, clients, and so forth. These individuals must know how to balance history and change. Others should be more distanced so that they can challenge your past assumptions and offer new perspective.

> *Planning committee members challenge your organization by asking the tough questions. Don't just recruit board members and other insiders. Seek new perspective and expertise in your community.*

People external to your organization bring particular expertise and insights to your deliberations. Look for experts in your organization's particular field of endeavor, recruit a respected CEO from another not-for-profit organization, and seek people of influence who work in key areas of the community.

A current board member chairs the planning committee. She or he should be well respected within the board, capable of commanding attention for the planning process. If you have a chair- or president-elect, this individual is a good candidate to lead the planning committee because he or she will be motivated to move the plan forward during his or her tenure as chief volunteer officer. Sometimes, the chair of the planning committee and the CEO invite other key staff to serve as members of the planning committee. However, staff should not outnumber volunteers.

Recruit as many people as you need to ensure the appropriate skills, behavior, experience, and diversity. Certainly, 7 or 8 is likely the smallest committee; as many as 12 or 13 members work well, and even 20–30 can work.

Prior to confirming any planning committee member, explain the role of the committee and the performance expectations of the committee member. Make sure that each candidate agrees to carry out this role or select another candidate.

Planning committee members are expected to:

- regularly attend planning committee meetings, estimated at 506 sessions during a 9- to 12-month planning process
- review planning materials in advance and participate actively in discussion
- help design the research component of the planning process
- identify key constituents who might provide useful information for the planning process
- carry out portions of the research, in particular, conduct personal interviews
- make personal contact with board members regarding the planning process
- participate in the decision-making process (generally, a planning retreat)
- for those committee members who also serve on the board, provide leadership to board discussion about planning

Board

The role of the board is particularly critical in planning. The board examines the relevant information, discusses the implications, asks the challenging questions, then determines the organization's direction. The planning committee does not recommend.

Remember, your board is legally and morally responsible for your organization. The board has authority and responsibility only as a group. No single individual has more authority or voice than any other. No officer or committee should take away the board's responsibility to explore, examine, dialogue, argue, and decide.

> *Often committees usurp the board's role. Too much dialogue happens with the committee and too little dialogue happens with the board. The board just acts as a rubber stamp, albeit a careful one.*

As a group, the board is responsible to:

- Decide to launch a comprehensive strategic planning process.
- If desirable, retain consulting services.
- Identify strategic issues facing the organization.
- Identify key constituencies who might provide useful information to the planning process.
- Review and endorse the research outline for the planning process.
- Discuss research findings and their implications.
- Serve as the focus for the decision-making process, determining such things as future direction and vision and key steps to achieve vision.
- Review and adopt a comprehensive written plan.
- Use the plan as a basis for board, committee, and staff work.
- Regularly monitor progress of the plan and evaluate performance.

As a member of the board, the individual trustee is expected to:

- Review planning materials.
- Regularly attend board meetings and participate in planning dialogue.
- Carry out portions of the research; in particular, conduct personal interviews.
- Provide information to the planning process by responding to surveys and other inquiries.
- Participate in the decision-making process (generally, a planning retreat).
- Review the draft plan, discuss, and take action.
- Ensure that the planning process is appropriate and is implemented properly. Ensure that the resulting written plan is monitored regularly.

Staff

The institution's staff is accountable for the success or failure of the planning process and the plan's implementation. Staff advocate for strategic planning and encourage strategic thinking and acting.

The CEO provides overall leadership to the planning process. She or he must be committed to the process and welcome the opportunity for institutional self-assessment and external exploration. The CEO ensures that the most difficult questions are asked and answered, encourages creativity, and welcomes change.

As the institution's leader, the CEO helps determine the organization's future vision, direction, and goals. The most effective CEO actually has a vision for the organization's future and tests the validity of that vision through the planning process.

The CEO ensures that all constituencies participate in the planning process. As a partner to the planning process manager, the CEO:

1. keeps planning on track, moving forward with consistent momentum
2. enables the planning committee, board, and staff to carry out the planning function
3. ensures that adequate and appropriate information is gathered for decision making
4. integrates the planning process with other agency activities
5. ensures the necessary administrative support for the process

Staff help gather information to support the planning process. They provide internal institutional data regarding client service, financing, and so forth. Staff secure relevant printed information from various sources. Staff also provide information to the process when they are asked for their opinion through surveys and conversation.

Planning Process Manager

The planning process manager acts as navigator for the planning process. She or he serves as staff and advisor. Serving as staff means that the planning process manager prepares meeting agendas and communications materials, ensures that advance materials are available, and prepares meeting summaries. Serving as advisor means designing and leading the planning process and providing expert counsel. Your planning process manager anticipates challenges so they can be avoided and has sufficient expertise and experience to solve problems when they arise.

Generally, the planning process manager is one of three people: the CEO, another person on staff who is responsible for planning, or a consultant retained specifically for the planning process. Sometimes, a professional planner volunteers time to act as the process manager.

Watch out. It can be difficult for a staff member to serve as the planning process manager, even if the staff person's position is planning. Staff need to participate in the process, and it is difficult to participate while managing and facilitating. Also, staff members (particularly the CEO) may be seen as driving the process to their own conclusions, rather than maintaining sufficient objectivity.

> *If your planning process is not effective, examine the performance of your CEO and your planning process manager.*

No matter who fulfills the function of planning process manager, the individual must be an experienced strategic planner. Strategic planning—just like financial management, fund development, or your specific service area—requires skills, knowledge, and experience.

Mintzberg (1994) describes planners (in this text, the planning process manager) as strategy finders, analysts, and catalysts. As an analyst, the planner studies both hard and soft data and pursues tangible and intangible information.

- As a strategy finder, the planner can "snoop around places they might not normally visit to find patterns amid the noise of failed experiments, seemingly random activities, and messy learning" (page 113). In this way, the planner may identify new ways of doing business and find new information and strategies that can assist the strategic planning process.
- As a catalyst, the planner makes sure that decision makers pay attention to the information. Planners get the right people involved in planning, including those working on the line and in the field. Planners "encourage managers to think about the future in creative ways . . . [seeing] their job as getting others to question conventional wisdom and especially helping people out of conceptual ruts" (page 114). Planners provoke reaction by asking challenging questions and questioning organization and individual assumptions.

Because effective planning causes temporary dissonance within the group, the process is stressful, and issues may be controversial. Your planning process manager must manage the process to produce positive experiences and best results. Planning expertise is not sufficient. The individual also must understand group dynamics and conflict resolution, organizational development, and the differences and similarities between governance and management.

The best planning process manager for a not-for-profit possesses the following attributes:

- experience designing and managing planning processes for diverse organizations in various stages of evolution
- expertise in strategic planning, organizational development, governance, and fund development
- knowledge about standard and cutting-edge theories and strategies for planning and organizational development
- ability to tailor a process for your organization, given its personality, evolution, and needs
- ability to enable others to participate in the process
- sufficient time to focus on your planning process
- competence as a group facilitator, stimulating creativity, critical thinking, conflict resolution, and consensus

Key responsibilities of the planning process manager are:

1. Provide information, advice, and recommendations about the various planning techniques.
2. Ensure that the organization's planning process produces the eight key results of an effective planning process (see Exhibit 3–1).
3. Engage the institution's leadership and constituents in the planning process.
4. Ensure that your institution is adequately communicating with its key constituencies about the planning process.
5. With your agency's CEO, keep the process moving forward aggressively, while balancing planning with other demands.
6. Anticipate challenges and opportunities that might arise during the planning process and, with your CEO and planning committee, devise solutions.
7. Based on standard principles and cutting-edge developments, tailor a planning process for your organization.
8. Develop the market research outline to secure adequate and appropriate information for your decision making.
9. Write the research instruments (for example, surveys, focus group questions, and key informant questions).
10. Help your organization identify useful reports, studies, articles, and other resources (secondary research).
11. Prepare resource materials for the planning process, for example, a description of the planning process, calendar, interview, and focus group guides.
12. Train volunteers to help conduct research.
13. Facilitate meetings and focus group sessions.
14. Tabulate and analyze research findings.
15. Prepare information reports based on research findings, then help identify implications for your organization.
16. Design the decision-making process for your board and planning committee, then facilitate the process.
17. Help board, planning committee, and staff:
    - Define vision and future direction.
    - Establish corporate goals and indicators of success.
    - Outline strategies and action steps to achieve goals.
    - Project income and expense.
    - Outline steps to monitor progress and evaluate performance.
18. Draft the written plan or serve as editor to a staff-drafted plan.
19. Help the institution craft a communications document, once the strategic plan is completed and adopted.

Using a Consultant as Your Planning Process Manager

Only your organization can decide whether you should hire a consultant. This is a joint decision of the board and CEO. The question is, Can you manage and guide the process on your own? Do you have an individual who can serve as the planning process manager?

To decide, consider these questions.

- Is there an individual available—staff or volunteer—who has sufficient strategic planning expertise and experience?
- Can she or he anticipate problems in the planning process and intervene with solutions?
- Does this individual keep current on the trends and techniques in strategic planning?
- Does she or he have the respect and trust of your organization's leadership?
- Does she or he have the time to manage and guide this process?

Talk to other organizations in your community and industry. Have others done planning? Did they use a consultant? If yes, why? If no, why not? Would they use a consultant for their next planning process?

If you use a consultant, consider the following:

- Hire a consultant at the start of the planning process. If you bring in a consultant later, it's hard to adjust what your organization may have already done (and this is almost always necessary!).

- Anticipate the costs. In addition to consulting fees, expenses include such items as: printing and distributing surveys, photocopying and distributing meeting agendas and summaries, conducting data searches, purchasing relevant publications, hosting meetings and retreats, photocopying and distributing the resulting market research results and trend summaries, and printing and distributing the written plan.

- Depending on the consultant, you may negotiate the scope of service provided. Although all the tasks must be accomplished, you might limit the consultant's responsibilities to certain activities, thereby reducing your cost.

- Use a good process to select your consultant. Seek the expertise, experience, and behaviors described here. Find an individual that you can respect and trust. Involve your board in the selection of a planning consultant, just as you would the selection of a fundraising consultant.

Remember, do not hire a consultant unless you need one. But if you need a consultant, hire one.

CARRYING OUT YOUR STRATEGIC PLANNING PROCESS

Exhibit 3–2 presents the 19 steps to carry out an effective strategic planning process. All steps build one upon the other. Appendix 3–D presents key components of the strategic planning process for the Lucy Robbins Welles Library in Newington, Connecticut.

1. Formally Agree To Do Planning.

The board should formally vote to do planning. Before the vote, make sure the board understands the scope of the planning process, the principal components of the process, the various roles (including its own), the time and resources required, and the possible implications for changing the organization.

2. Engage Key Constituents in the Planning Process.

At the heart of strategic planning is a group of people building a shared vision. For strategic planning to be effective, it must create "ongoing processes in which people at every level of the organization, in every role, can speak from the heart about what really matters to them and be heard—by senior management and by each other. The quality of this process, especially the amount of openness and genuine caring, determines the quality and power of the results" (Senge et al. 1994, 299).

Exhibit 3–2 Nineteen General Steps for Effective Strategic Planning

1. Formally agree to do planning.
2. Engage key constituents in the planning process.
3. Get ready to plan.
4. Launch the process with board, staff, and planning committee.
5. Design the planning process, develop the market research outline, and conduct the research.
6. Articulate (or review) values.
7. Tabulate research results, analyze findings, and prepare findings report.
8. Design the decision-making process.
9. Discuss findings and determine implications.
10. Determine direction or vision.
11. Review (and possibly adjust) mission.
12. Determine goals and strategies.
13. Identify core competencies and supporting structure.
14. Establish benchmarks for success.
15. Assign time frames and entities responsible for strategies.
16. Project costs and income sources.
17. Outline process to monitor progress of plan, evaluate performance, and extend plan for subsequent years.
18. Write the strategic plan, review, and adopt.
19. Translate the plan into personal commitment.

Effective engagement produces one of two results, both of which are valuable and acceptable. Usually, engaging people well generates understanding and ownership, cohesion, and alignment. Sometimes, engaging people shows them that they no longer support the organization's direction. In these cases, an effective engagement process gives people permission to move away without anger or frustration.

Those who will be affected by the plan should participate in the planning process. That means just about everyone in your organization in some way! Engage them in the process so they will be invested in the outcome. Through involvement, you build loyalty and acceptance of your vision.

Staff should be involved in the planning process. These individuals are on the front lines, facing the challenges and testing ways to cope. Staff learn while doing, thus providing valuable information and knowledge to the organization.

From a fundraiser's perspective, constituent participation in planning is critical. Donors who understand and support your organization's vision and strategic direction will, at least, maintain their gifts and may well increase them. By helping to plan, other constituents may become donors.

There are two types of constituents, internal and external. Your internal constituents include such groups as your customers (clients, audience members, service users, or whatever you call them), staff, board members, direct service volunteers, administrative volunteers, fundraising volunteers, donors and funding sources, and vendors. These constituents are closest to you.

> *Effective strategic planning may cause some people to leave your organization. That's okay.*

Your external constituents include such groups as elected and regulatory officials, community leaders and people of influence, and collegial organizations (cooperators, collaborators, competitors). These constituents are further removed but do have an affect on your organization.

There are three principal ways to engage your constituents in the planning process. First, seek their opinions and perspective because this information is vital for your decision making. Second, keep your constituents informed about the planning process. Explain why your organization is planning and tell constituents about progress and decisions. Distribute a summary of the final plan to your constituencies and keep communicating, once the plan is put in motion. Third, some of your constituents will be engaged in decision making, for example, your board, planning committee, CEO, and key staff.

Often, it is difficult to engage the board in the planning process. In its governance capacity, the board is legally and morally accountable for your agency. As individuals and a group, the board must understand the market research information, discuss the implications, create shared values and vision, evaluate mission, and determine future direction.

Use these strategies to engage your board in the planning process.

- Discuss the planning process and its progress at every board meeting and at all committee meetings.
- Give board members regular and timely updates about information secured through market research.
- Help the board talk about the implications of the market research information.
- Practice self- and world-examination, critical thinking, and honest, forthright dialogue.
- Practice conflict resolution.
- As necessary, maintain personal contact with individual board members between meetings.

3. Get Ready To Plan.

Recruit your planning process manager. If you decide to hire a consultant, make sure that several board members have an opportunity to participate in the interview process and review the proposals.

Determine the composition of the planning committee and identify candidates. Discuss job responsibilities with all candidates and secure their commitment to carry out the job description before confirming their participation.

4. Launch the Process with Board, Staff, and Planning Committee.

Launching your planning process is as important as any other campaign start. An effective kickoff strategy involves the board, staff, and planning committee in an introductory work session. If your organization is small enough, gather everyone together at a regular board meeting or special meeting. If your organization is too large or geographically diffuse, meet via conference call or conduct separate work sessions.

This introductory work session engages key constituents in the planning process, generates preliminary information so the planning process manager and planning committee can develop the market research outline, and helps key constituents understand the planning process.

At the work session, identify issues and opportunities by describing your organization's current situation. Talk about where your organization is now. Get the group to list internal strengths and weaknesses and external opportunities and threats. This is called *SWOT*, or *situation analysis*. You also might consider it a "heartburn and champagne" discussion.

Internal strengths and weaknesses refer to things that your organization can control. Reflect on what you do well and consider how you might capitalize on this. Expand the discussion by describing when things were at their best and why. Then consider areas that could use improvement, often called your organization's weaknesses. Don't be put off by the word! Discuss how your strengths might help you address your weaknesses.

External opportunities and threats are issues describing the environment in which your organization operates. You cannot control the environment but you must manage it well for your organization to flourish. Look at your community and the larger world. Identify the trends, events, and developments that affect your organization.

Conducting this situation analysis is your first research in the planning process. Prepare a summary of the introductory work session for participants and use the results to create the market research outline.

5. Design the Planning Process, Develop the Market Research Outline, and Conduct the Research.

The planning process manager designs the overall planning process. Initial activities (steps 1–6) are designed at the start. The final steps (7–19) are designed later because they evolve from the research findings and your group dynamics observed during the planning process.

> *Effective strategic planning includes honest self-assessment as well as in-depth examination of the outside world.*

Good planning depends on the scope and quality of information upon which your organization will base its decisions. Too little information compromises the quality of your plan. Too much information overwhelms decision making and demands unnecessary effort.

Keep key constituents informed of progress while you conduct the research. Because the research phase takes a long time, people who are not closely involved may feel that the planning process has lost momentum. Your updates help constituents feel connected to the process. Carefully share limited findings without drawing conclusions or discussing implications. Save extensive conversation until all research is completed.

Market Research

With the right information, good people usually make the optimum decisions. The key is to secure the right information.

Generally, market research for strategic planning requires three to six months. Actual time depends on the scope of your issues and the information necessary for decision making.

Using the earlier SWOT results, the planning process manager drafts the market research plan. This outline describes the data needed and how to obtain them. Once approved by the committee, the research outline is distributed to the board as information. See the sample research outlines in Appendix 3–A and Appendix 3–D.

Research includes both primary and secondary sources. The term *primary data* refers to those data that must be developed for your planning process. *Secondary data* refers to information that already exists for some purpose other than your planning process. These types of research are described below in more detail. For further information, see *Marketing Research: Measurement and Method*, 4th ed., by Tull and Hawkins (1987).

Volunteers help do the research. Planning committee members and board members conduct key informant interviews. Volunteers help identify existing reports and studies that might provide vital information about issues and trends.

The market research process includes four major components, the first two external and the latter two internal.

1. community needs assessment
2. analysis of competitors, collaborators, and knowledge alliances
3. customer satisfaction review
4. assessment of institutional capacity

Assessing community needs and analyzing competitors, collaborators, and knowledge alliances focuses on the external environment. Make sure you investigate such issues as economics, education, public policy, demographics and lifestyles, technology, and societal issues such as employment, health care, crime, and violence.

Then, turn inside to assess institutional capacity and review the satisfaction of your own customers. Institutional capacity refers to how well your organization's infrastructure operates and includes such elements as:

- administration/management (staffing, technology, fiscal and personnel systems, and so forth)
- governance
- program scope and service delivery
- human resources
- corporate culture (alignment of values and action, cultural diversity and sensitivity, group dynamics)
- financing (revenue and charitable contributions)
- marketing and communications and image
- facilities

Community needs assessment. Strategic planning does not begin with who you are and what you want to do. Rather, planning begins with who your community is and what it wants and needs. Your organization operates within a community, and planning clarifies how you fit in and meet the community's wants and needs.

The community needs assessment helps answer the questions posed earlier in this text.

1. What is happening in the outside world?
2. What needs are being met and by which organizations? Are these competitors or collaborators?
3. What needs are not being met?

With this information, you can decide whether or not you want to respond.

Do not ask people what your organization should do or what your role should be to meet community needs. Why? First, the question is premature. You ask this question during your decision-making process, once all the information has been gathered and reviewed.

Second, don't ask what others think you should do because you may not choose to do it. You may focus on another need. The assessment will likely identify conflicting and competing needs. Your organization evaluates all the market research information together and discusses the implications before you make decisions. Furthermore, if you ask others what you should do—and then you choose not to do it—you may alienate them, rather than produce understanding and ownership.

> *The organization that starts out from the inside and then tries to find places to put its resources is going to fritter itself away. Above all, it's going to focus on yesterday. One looks to the outside for opportunity, for a need.*
>
> *Peter F. Drucker*

Once the market research is completed and your organization begins to make decisions, you will answer the question, Might we have the capability and wish to respond to any of the needs identified during our market research? And if yes, what will we do and how?

Analysis of competitors, collaborators, and knowledge alliances. Many organizations spend too little time on this portion of market research. Narrowly focused on their own territory, these organizations are threatened by others in the marketplace.

As you examine the external environment and assess community needs, turn your attention to other organizations, whether for-profit, not-for-profit, or government. You can learn a lot.

Keep in mind: Your organization must move quickly and must be flexible. But your organization doesn't need to do everything on its own or by itself.

As Duarte and Snyder (2000) note, "Leaders are seeing that it is no longer necessary—or desirable—for their organizations to own all the assets required to serve customers" (page 43). Instead, you can share resources and compensate for each other's gaps. Work with other organizations to achieve shared goals and meet community needs. Perhaps, based on your market research, you will decide to withdraw from a particular service and leave it to a competitor.

As you examine the external environment and assess community needs, you encounter other organizations, some competitors and some collaborators. You can learn a lot from these organizations.

Based on your research, you may decide to withdraw from a particular service and leave it to a competitor. If you continue to provide the service, the research results should help you to differentiate yourself better from the competition. Or, you may choose to expand a service area by collaborating with others to create a marketplace niche.

Certainly, you will identify individuals and organizations with whom you should maintain relationships to exchange information. These knowledge alliances help your organization carry out its mission.

Customer satisfaction review. Your organization has many constituents or customers. Find out how satisfied these customers are with your performance. In particular, speak with the clients who use your service and the volunteers and donors who give. Find out what they all value and why they choose to associate with your organization.

Assessment of institutional capacity. You need to know how well your organization does its work and whether you have the skills and resources to take on new endeavors or expand current activities. To assess institutional capacity, examine your organization's infrastructure. Evaluate such things as organizational design, governance and management, role delineation, information flow, allocation of resources, fund development, and marketing and communications.

Get opinions from volunteers and staff, as well as other constituents. Examine your organization's existing information, such as donor and service statistics, trends in income and expense, and so forth. Plot relevant information over a 5- to 10-year period.

> *In today's environment organizations must move fast or die. No enterprise, large or small, private or public, can afford to be slow, inflexible, or insular.*
>
> *Duarte and Snyder*

Market Research Methods

There are lots of research methods. For primary research, use surveys (written, telephone, and intercept), focus groups, and personal interviews. Each is described below.

Construct your research instruments to ensure useful and valid responses. Usually, research instruments include questions about each of the market research components (community needs, customer satisfaction, institutional capacity, and collaborator/competitor/knowledge alliances).

For example, the Norman Bird Sanctuary in Rhode Island mailed self-administered anonymous written surveys to its members and randomly distributed surveys to residents of nearby communities. The Lucy Robbins Welles Library in Newington, Connecticut asked its patrons to complete a written survey. Patrons picked up the survey while visiting the Library. See Appendices 3–B and 3–D for copies of these surveys.

A governance self-assessment survey provides important insight into board performance, a critical component of institutional capacity. See Appendix 3–B for a sample survey that you can copy or modify for use with your own board. Make sure that the key staff who work with the board also complete this survey. Compare the staff and board answers and note commonalties and differences.

In another example, results of a St. Mary Academy–Bay View governance survey indicated that the Board of Trustees operated well in the areas of decision making, financial oversight, organization, and communication. Areas for improvement included trustee recruitment, orientation and evaluation, and role delineation.

Assessment results contributed to a number of goals and activities in Bay View's strategic plan.

1. Create a learning organization/culture within the Bay View community, principally, students, staff, and board, so that we are prepared to meet ever-changing current and future needs.
   - Develop the skills of individual staff, volunteers, and work groups (board of trustees, management team, trustee teams) to carry out the work and vision of a learning organization.
   - Design and implement integrated systems and structures to institutionalize ongoing planning and evaluation throughout Bay View, including such components as: community needs assessment; program evaluation and customer (student and parents) satisfaction; cultural diversity assessment; individual self-assessment for volunteers, students, and staff; governance assessment; values/behavior assessment; and communications audit.
2. Ensure appropriate human resources necessary to meet the changing needs of Bay View.
   - Develop and implement cultivation, recruitment, mentoring, enabling and retention behaviors, policies and procedures, and systems so that the Bay View community of students and staff reflects the multicultural and economic diversity of our extended community and so that Bay View secures individuals with the skills, attitudes, and behaviors we require to work and volunteer here.
   - Develop and implement a performance assessment system for staff and volunteers that sup-

ports individual initiative and growth while supporting the overall vision and goals of Bay View.

Key informant interviews provide in-depth perspective for planning. You conduct personal interviews with external constituents who warrant privacy, due to their position or to the nature of their information, or who are unable to participate in a focus group.

Ask open-ended questions that focus on community needs and trends, as well as your organization's image. Tailor some of the questions to a particular audience, for example, donors.

> *Market research acts as a catalyst to help leadership think strategically.*

Interview questions provided information about community needs, customer satisfaction, and institutional capacity for Kappa Alpha Theta International Fraternity for Women. Questions asked of selected college and university administrators around the nation included:

1. What are the general issues/concerns that you believe face collegians in contemporary society? (community needs assessment)
2. What resources do you believe are currently available to help collegians address these issues? What additional types of resources do you think should be available? (community needs assessment)
3. What role do you think the fraternity movement currently plays in addressing these issues and should play in addressing these issues? (assessment of institutional capacity)
4. What do you think are the biggest challenges facing fraternities today? (assessment of institutional capacity)
5. Given your vision of a fraternity's role in meeting women's needs, how would you describe Theta's performance? (customer satisfaction, competitor/collaborator analysis)

The Greater Providence YMCA conducted more than 75 key informant interviews with state and city elected and departmental officials, corporate leaders, philanthropists, and foundation representatives. Questions asked of all interviewees were:

1. Based on your experience and observations:
   - What are the biggest challenges faced by the citizens of Greater Providence today?
   - What resources are currently available to help individuals and families address these challenges?
   - What resources are missing?

2. When you think of the YMCA of Greater Providence, how would you describe the organization? What key descriptive words or phrases would you use?
3. In your opinion, what will be the most important achievement of the YMCA of Greater Providence in the new century?

Additional questions were tailor-made for funding sources and government agencies.

- For funding sources: Not-for-profit agencies are expected to address more and more of the challenges facing our community. Accordingly, the demand for charitable contributions grows. What role will your organization play in funding? Do you anticipate changes in your giving patterns? What do you expect from a not-for-profit like the YMCA?
- For government agencies: What role do you believe public policy can play to address the challenges facing our citizens? What types of public policy do you think our community needs? To meet community needs, government agencies often negotiate contracts and/or provide grant funds to not-for-profit organizations. How do you think government and the YMCA can work together to meet Greater Providence's challenges?

Volunteers conduct most key informant interviews. By doing so, board members and planning committee members hear from key constituents firsthand. This helps engage volunteers in the planning process and builds their understanding of the issues facing the organization. Second, more interviewers can conduct more interviews.

Focus groups refer to a discussion with 5–15 people, facilitated by an experienced leader. You might conduct focus groups with donors, clients, volunteers, and other community not-for-profit organizations. Sometimes, the planning process manager facilitates the focus groups. In other cases, independent facilitators or volunteers may facilitate.

Like key informant interviews, focus groups provide qualitative, anecdotal information. Often, the synergy of the focus group offers unique insights and ideas for your organization. Interesting collaborations and knowledge alliances can also result from this group process.

Focus group questions are similar to those asked during key informant interviews. The focus group facilitator prepares a summary of the focus group. You might provide this summary to the focus group participants as a benefit for giving you their time.

The YMCA of Greater Providence conducted focus groups with not-for-profit organizations working with families and youth. Invitees included environmental groups, libraries and literacy organizations, agencies providing human services to Southeast Asian and Latino individuals and families, and arts groups. Focus group questions were very similar to the interview questions used by the YMCA.

> *Strategic planning is not like a capital campaign feasibility study. For planning, use volunteers to conduct interviews.*

The Women's Foundation of Southern Arizona (WFSA) also conducted focus groups and personal interviews during its strategic planning process. The questions were directed to donors, community leaders, the Foundation's grant recipients, and other not-for-profit organizations. See Exhibit 3–3.

Secondary research includes reports, studies, articles, and plans from your particular field of endeavor and the not-for-profit sector itself. The planning process manager and staff identify secondary information based on personal experience, industry resources, information searches, and referrals from planning committee and board members.

As an organization committed to health and fitness, the YMCA reviewed the State of Rhode Island's plan to develop healthy Rhode Islanders. In its capacity as a human service provider, the Y examined basic human needs reports prepared by the local United Way. The YMCA reviewed U.S. Census data for demographic information and state and federal sources for statistics of crime and violence, poverty, and families at risk. To assess its own institutional capacity, the YMCA used *Giving USA: The Annual Report on Philanthropy* (American Association of Fund-Raising Counsel [AAFRC], 1995) and *Giving RI* (1995), along with financial and service information from comparable YMCAs nationwide.

The Lucy Robbins Welles Library also gathered secondary research. The Library reviewed the Town Comprehensive Plan, the long-range plans for the Connecticut State Library and the Connecticut Library Association, trend articles from pertinent library publications, and philanthropic information presented by *Giving USA*, the annual publication of the AAFRC Trust for Philanthropy.

6. Articulate (or Review) Values.

Shared values form the foundation for any group or organization. Healthy institutions are well aligned, displaying a cohesion between values and behaviors.

COMMUNITY ISSUES (ASKED OF ALL)

1. What do you think are the major issues facing Southern Arizona now and into the next five years?
2. What do you think are the major issues facing women and children now and into the next five years?

PERCEPTIONS AND AWARENESS OF THE WOMEN'S FOUNDATION (ASKED OF ALL)

1. What comes to mind when you hear the name "Women's Foundation"? (Probes: How would you describe the organization? What adjectives would you use?)
2. What are the greatest strengths of the Women's Foundation?
3. What are the greatest weaknesses of the Women's Foundation?
4. How would you describe donors to the Women's Foundation?

DEVELOPING A RELATIONSHIP WITH THE WOMEN'S FOUNDATION (ASKED OF ALL)

1. How did you first learn about the Women's Foundation?
2. How would you describe your relationship with the Women's Foundation?
   - Has your experience been different than you expected? If yes, how?
   - What motivated you to develop a relationship with the Women's Foundation?
3. Have you recommended the Women's Foundation to a friend or colleague? Why? Why not?
4. How can the Women's Foundation help you feel more connected to its mission and activities? (Probe: What strategies, tools can we use to engage you?)

PUBLIC POLICY AND COLLABORATION (ASKED OF ALL)

1. What are the trends you see regarding public policy and citizen action today and into the next five years?
2. Public policy plays a major role in meeting community needs. What role do you see the Women's Foundation having in the public policy debate?
3. How can community organizations and diverse sectors collaborate to meet community needs better?

ORGANIZATIONAL CAPACITY (FOR FOUNDATION GRANTEES AND APPLICANTS ONLY)

1. What are the major issues affecting your organization's ability to carry out its mission?
2. What kinds of resources does your organization need to carry out its work?
3. Where do you go to find resources to enhance your organization's capacity to do its work?
4. If you could develop or transform your organization in any way you wished, what would heighten its overall effectiveness and vitality?

COMMUNICATIONS (FOR DONORS AND PROSPECTIVE DONORS ONLY)

1. How do you learn about/hear what is happening in the community?
2. What local, state, and national publications do you read on a regular basis? What interests you?
3. Do you get information through the Internet? Which Web sites do you visit most frequently and why?
   - Do you use e-mail and do you like this as a communication strategy?

PHILANTHROPIC GIVING (FOR FOUNDATION DONORS ONLY)

1. What are your major philanthropic interests?
   - Which causes/organizations do you support regularly?
   - Which organizations do you think are the most effective in this community? Why?
   - Which organizations do you consider the most effective in philanthropic fund development and why?
2. What was the primary reason (the critical decision factor) you chose to give a gift to the Women's Foundation?
3. On a scale of 1–5 (with 1 being hard and 5 being easy), rate the process of making a gift to the Women's Foundation.
4. What are the key benefits the Women's Foundation provides to you as a donor?
5. What types of donor events/activities/programs do you like to participate in? Why?
6. What would you say to persuade people that the Women's Foundation is worthy of philanthropic support?
7. In your candid opinion, will major donors accept the Women's Foundation as a high philanthropic priority? If so, why? If not, why not?
8. Do you volunteer? For which issues/organizations?

PHILANTHROPIC GIVING (FOR PROSPECTIVE DONORS ONLY)

1. What are your major philanthropic interests?
   - Which causes/organizations do you support regularly?
   - Which organizations do you think are the most effective in this community? Why?
   - Which organizations do you consider the most effective in philanthropic fund development and why?
2. What types of donor events/activities/programs do you like to participate in? Why?
3. In your candid opinion, will major donors accept the Women's Foundation as a high philanthropic priority? If so, why? If not, why not?
4. Do you volunteer? For which issues/organizations?

Courtesy of the Women's Foundation of Southern Arizona, Tucson, AZ.

Conversation about values helps establish the context for the rest of the planning process. Chapter 2 outlines the process for defining your core values. If your organization has not already done this, do so at the start of the strategic planning process.

If your organization has articulated its shared values at some point in the past, review your values during the planning process. Consider these strategies.

- Develop a survey that evaluates how well aligned your organization's actions and values are. Distribute the survey to all board members and staff. Tabulate the responses and present the results to all those who were invited to participate in the survey. Discuss the results with staff, board, and the planning committee. Identify areas of conflict and outline strategies to align articulated values and action.
- Discuss values in small group sessions with board members, staff, and other key constituents. Use open-ended questions to stimulate dialogue. For example:
  - Reflect on our organization's stated values. Discuss how well our actions reflect our values. Describe why and how our values and actions were particularly well aligned in certain situations. Discuss situations when our values and actions were not well aligned and how we could improve.
  - Think about the operations and activities within our organization. Look also at the outside world. Are there other values we might wish to add or change at this time?

7. Tabulate Research Results, Analyze Findings, and Prepare Findings Report.

Once the research is finished, tabulate your quantitative results. Compile notes from key informant interviews and focus groups, and review the highlights from your secondary research. Then the planning process manager analyzes these results, identifying trends and themes, and prepares the findings report. This report describes all the market research results without censoring or making recommendations.

The findings report is one of the most critical products in the planning process because it is used to make your decisions for the future. Also, the report provides information that staff and volunteers can use to carry out the organization's activities.

Once the findings report is completed, distribute it to everyone who will participate in the decision-making process. These individuals read the findings report, consider the possible implications for the organization, and participate in discussion about the information therein.

For example, the YMCA of Greater Providence spent six months conducting market research for its strategic planning. More than 30 volunteers, as well as consultants and the CEO, helped collect information across the Y's eight operating divisions. The resulting 50-page findings report summarized the findings of the Y's market research, which included the following activities:

- nine introductory SWOT sessions
- fifty key informant interviews and two focus groups examining community needs and the Y's position in the marketplace, and identifying its competitors/collaborators
- thirty-five key informant interviews focusing primarily on institutional capacity
- telephone surveys with approximately 500 members and potential members to evaluate customer satisfaction and desires (conducted by consultants)
- analysis of approximately 15 competitors through visitation and review of printed materials (conducted by consultants)
- secondary research materials included one dozen written reports and articles, including U.S. Census data, local studies of basic human needs and families at risk, and plans of key government agencies

Analysis of the market research results identified numerous themes and issues, which are apparent in the table of contents for the YMCA's information report, presented here.

- Introduction
  - Values Statement of the YMCA
  - Definitions
- Section I: The world in which we live
  - Key trends in organizations at this time
  - A picture of our community
  - Highlights from Healthy Rhode Islanders 2000, the statewide plan for health and wellness
  - Building a nation of learners
- Section II: Community needs
  - Challenges facing our community
  - Resources missing from our community
  - Program ideas—what the YMCA might do to meet community needs
- Section III: Selected community responses to community needs
  - Public-private partnerships
  - General community resources

- Section IV: Institutional capacity
  - Program, audience, delivery system
  - Facilities and location
  - Image, identity, and communications
  - Board and volunteers
  - Management
  - Financing (revenue and fund development)
- Appendix
  - List of interviewees and focus group participants
  - Focus group questions
  - Key informant interview questions

See also Appendix 3–D for the Table of Contents of the *Findings Report*, prepared for the Lucy Robbins Welles Library.

8. Design the Decision-Making Process.

The purpose of the decision-making process is to determine who your organization is (its mission) and what your direction is (vision and goals) for the upcoming years. Based on the research findings and their implications, you discuss your organization's possible choices and the consequences of each choice. Then your organization picks its preferred consequences. Remember, there will always be consequences. You simply must choose the ones you prefer.

There are two levels of decisions that must be made during the decision-making phase of the strategic planning process.

- First, your organization decides its direction and mission. Generally, this includes establishing goals. Sometimes, organizations choose direction by creating a vision of the future. This level of decision making requires full dialogue with the board, planning committee, CEO, and key staff, followed by confirming action by the board.
- Second, the organization decides how it will get where it is going. Generally, the staff, perhaps with help from the planning committee, outline the strategies to achieve goals or create the future vision. The board reviews these strategies and takes action.

The planning process manager designs the decision-making process for review by the planning committee. With the research results in hand, the process manager understands the scope of the issues facing the organization, as well as the opportunities and challenges available within the community. By now, the planning process manager also has a feel for the organization's corporate culture, including its group dynamics.

> *The decision-making process is tailor-made for your organization, based on the market research findings and the group dynamics of your organization.*

Decision making usually happens at a planning retreat. Groups go off together, away from regular interruptions, to deliberate and decide. Actual decisions depend on the market research results, as well as the experience and expertise of your leadership. The board, as legal corporate entity, confirms these decisions by adopting the written strategic plan.

The retreat format depends on the nature of your organization and the issues you face. The planning process manager considers many variables, including:

- How complex are the issues presented in the findings report? How can conversation be structured to bring the decision makers to consensus?
- Which decisions of what scope should be made by which group (e.g., the planning committee, board, or staff?)
- What kind of exercises or group activities will help the decision makers deliberate?
- What kind of facilitation techniques will work best?
- Are there particular group dynamics that must be managed during the decision making?

The effectiveness of the decision-making process depends on a combination of elements, specifically:

- Participation of your institution's key leadership. Those invited to help decide include the board, planning committee, and senior management staff.
- Equity in the decision-making setting. Every invitee has equal voice in the dialogue. No individual, by virtue of position or behavior, has any more power than another. Although the board is the legal corporate entity, at the retreat, everyone talks and everyone votes.
- Adequate time balanced with timely choosing. Sometimes, a single session of four to six hours suffices; sometimes, a two-part retreat—four hours each in consecutive weeks—works. And there are other versions. Whatever your format, allocate sufficient time to accomplish your desired outcomes. The challenge is to ensure that decisions are made and sustained, rather than delayed and revisited.
- Ability to talk, argue, resolve conflict, and come to consensus. Deciding your organization's mission and direction for the future requires critical think-

ing and forthright conversation. This happens well when individuals display respect for one another, know how to listen, understand the difference between discussion and dialogue, and value constructive conflict for the understanding and synergy that it produces. Take a look at Chapter 2 for further information.

Exhibits 3–4, 3–5, and 3–6 present sample retreat formats. See also Appendix 3–D for another retreat format.

9. Discuss Findings and Determine Implications.

Your organization begins the decision-making process by discussing the research findings and their implications. The more you talk, the clearer your choices are. No matter whether you have many or few choices, they are probably challenging and stressful.

Generally, this discussion happens at your retreat. Allocate time at the start to talk about the market research results, clarify the findings, and discuss the implications.

Sometimes, you talk about specific findings and their possible implications before the market research is finished. The planning committee engages the board in conversation to build understanding. However, take care. Don't draw conclusions prior to completing all the market research and integrating the various findings.

Use questions to stimulate conversation and focus choices. Raise the questions worth asking. Many are presented throughout this text, and your organization will have its own. Here are more.

1. What are the changing short- and long-term needs in the community? Which of these needs are of greatest interest to our organization? Consider such things as compatibility with current mission, organizational experience and capability, marketplace competition, and return on investment.
2. Who are the primary and secondary customers seeking services to meet these needs? Which customers do we currently serve? How might we reach new audiences in need? Are there customers we no longer choose to serve?
3. Which internal and external factors, both recent and anticipated, are most important to the health of our organization? Consider such things as: changes in the philanthropic sector and within our industry specifically, changes in our customer base and customer expectations, technology demands, and competitors entering and leaving the service arena.
4. What are the major relationships our organization needs to operate well? Which collaborations should we develop to provide services, to fundraise, to

Exhibit 3–4 Retreat Format #1

The board, planning committee, and senior staff gather together at a daylong retreat. Everyone has read the market research findings report, and volunteers briefly present highlights. Retreat attendees ask questions and discuss possible implications for the organization.

First, retreat attendees focus on program. The group identifies areas for continued, expanded, and new services. The group also identifies service areas to discontinue. The full group breaks down into small teams, and each team defines the scope and audience for a specific service. After reconvening and discussing small group work, attendees select program focus and priorities by voting.

Next, retreat attendees examine the infrastructure issues that arose in the market research. The full group chooses which issues warrant attention and what the priorities are. Looking back at the program focus, the group adds any other infrastructure issues that must be addressed in order to move the organization forward.

The retreat ends and the summary is distributed to all invitees. The CEO and planning process manager use the results of the decision-making retreat to draft two items for immediate board action.

- A brief description of each program area for the three-year interval of the plan. Attached to this narrative is a paragraph that describes which programs will be discontinued and why.
- Corporate goals, both program and infrastructure, for the three-year plan.

The board reviews and discusses the proposed program descriptions and corporate goals. This material is very familiar because it was derived from the retreat. The board approves the program descriptions and goals, thereby authorizing the planning committee and staff to move forward with their work.

Staff outline strategies to accomplish the corporate goals, and the planning committee reviews, adjusts, and endorses. Then staff estimate income and expense, assignments and time frames for review, adjustment, and endorsement by the planning committee.

Now the planning process manager and CEO write the plan. The already-approved items form the foundation of the document. Other sections of the plan are written and the draft is reviewed and approved by the planning committee. The planning committee then recommends the draft plan to the board for review and action.

train volunteers, to order supplies in bulk? What kind of alliances should we maintain to secure the information and knowledge to do our business better?

Exhibit 3–5 Retreat Format #2

Prior to the retreat, the planning process manager and CEO write statements that describe the organization's current reality. These statements come from the market research findings report and cover such topics as: community trends and issues; organization's program scope, delivery system, and facilities; marketing and communications; fund development; management and governance; and human resources.

The decision-making retreat is designed as a visioning experience. Working in preassigned teams, participants use the descriptions of current reality to create their desired vision of the future. By the end of the retreat, participants have produced a cultural shifts document: descriptions of current reality juxtaposed against descriptions of the desired future. The gap between now and the future represents the cultural shifts that your organization must make to achieve its vision.

The planning process manager and CEO use the cultural shifts document to draft three pieces for review by the planning committee and then review and action by the board.

- First, a brief vision statement for the organization. No more than one page in length, this inspirational statement captures the spirit of the multiple visionary statements produced at the retreat.
- Second, the organization's corporate goals for the new century. These goals clearly state how the organization will move from its current situation to its future vision.
- Third, benchmarks for each goal. These benchmarks help the organization evaluate whether it has moved from the current situation to the desired future.

Once the board approves the vision statement, corporate goals, and benchmarks, the staff projects strategies, financing, time frames, and assignments of accountability. These results are discussed by the planning committee.

At the same time, the planning committee reviews the organization's mission statement to determine if it is aligned with the vision of the future. Based on committee discussion, the CEO drafts a revised mission statement for review by the planning committee and then action by the board.

The planning process manager and CEO recommend that detailed action steps be developed as annual work plans, in conjunction with the annual budgeting process. The planning committee agrees. The draft strategic plan recommended to the board includes vision, values, and mission; corporate goals and benchmarks with strategies, time frames, and assignments.

Exhibit 3–6 Retreat Format #3

The board, planning committee, and senior staff gather together at a daylong retreat. Prior to the retreat, everyone has read the market research findings report and is prepared to discuss the implications of this information.

At the start of the retreat, attendees review the values statement and discuss how their organization's values will affect retreat dialogue and decisions. If the group is still developing its ability to talk together candidly, the planning process manager may use a group activity or exercise to strengthen relations.

Time is allocated for attendees to share their observations and ask questions about the findings report. This brief discussion helps energize retreat participants and highlights issues raised in the findings report.

Next, attendees describe what the world will look like in the next decade. The description focuses on the world that the organization must operate in and manage. This description is posted on the wall so attendees are mindful throughout the retreat.

In small groups, attendees write narrative statements describing the current reality of the organization. Typically, the small group topics include such areas as program, governance and management, marketing and communications, philanthropy and fund development, planning, and decisionmaking. The small groups present their descriptions to the full group for review and comment.

The small groups reconvene to write narrative statements describing their vision of the future for the assigned topic. The small groups present their vision descriptions to the full group for review, adjustment and adoption.

Following the retreat, the planning process manager prepares a lengthy narrative vision for the future. (See Exhibit 3–8 for the vision statement drafted as a result of the retreat for the Women's Foundation of Southern Arizona.)

5. How must we change our services to meet the changing needs of current and future customers? How can we alter our service scope and delivery

without harming the customer? How do we differentiate our programs and services from those of other organizations?

Linkage analysis is another way to structure conversation. This planning tool helps organizations recognize the various interrelationships that exist in current operations and identifies the interrelationships necessary to implement a new vision (Primozic, Primozic, and Leben 1991).

You create diagrams that describe your organization's internal and external relationships. Start with a question you want to answer or a goal you wish to achieve. The linkage diagrams document the factors that answer your questions or affect your goal. Discussion continues by constructing multiple levels of diagrams that pursue factors in greater depth.

Linkage analysis makes no assumptions. Participants put aside any preconceived notions. Whatever is important goes on the linkage chart. As dialogue proceeds, participants continually ask, "How will this item I add to the chart help us achieve 'substantial and sustainable strategic advantage?'" (Primozic, Primozic, and Leben 1991, 158).

Scenario planning is another tool to stimulate your thinking. People work together to create pictures (scenarios) of possible futures. The pictures are bound by predetermined forces—those things that are reasonably predictable—identified by the group. The group then introduces uncertainties into the pictures.

Scenarios are not predictions but "posit several potential futures, none of which will probably come to pass, but all of which make you more keenly aware of the forces acting on you in the present" (Senge et al. 1994, 275). By creating these alternate futures, your organization examines its assumptions and the uncertainties of the environment. Scenario planning forces your organization to consider how it might respond to different futures. Then you test various strategy options against the scenarios of possible futures.

The planning process manager facilitates the group so that questions are asked and the status quo is questioned. The process manager keeps dialogue focused and moving. She or he summarizes key points, brings conversation to closure, helps the group reach consensus, and moves the group toward its final decisions.

10. Determine Direction or Vision.

Conversation is finished and now your organization must choose. It doesn't matter whether or not you define your direction (where you are going) or determine your vision (what you will look like). This shared vision or direction is the major outcome of the decision-making retreat.

The concept of shared vision or direction brings to mind the same concern as shared values: Does "shared" encourage homogeneity and discourage pluralism and diversity? No.

Nonaka (1991) observes that "umbrella concepts and qualitative criteria" are critical to produce a unified direction within all the group's individuals. Karl-Henrik Robèrt (1994) describes these as a set of non-negotiable agreements that allow teams to function. Nonaka goes on to say that "a company's vision needs also to be open-ended, susceptible to a variety of different and even conflicting interpretations. . . . If a vision is too unambiguous . . . it becomes more akin to an order or an instruction. . . . A more equivocal vision gives [people] the freedom and autonomy to set their own goals" (Nonaka 1991, 104).

You can determine direction or vision in different ways. Look back at the sample formats presented in Exhibits 3–4, 3–5, and 3–6. Combine elements. Invent your own format, tailored to your organization.

Sometimes, decision-making retreats focus on strengths and weaknesses and opportunities and threats of program and infrastructure, described in the first retreat format, Exhibit 3–4. The group uses market research results, experience, and wisdom to select program areas for the duration of the strategic plan. Conversation focuses on such issues as:

- what the organization currently does well
- what are the unmet community needs
- which audiences need which programs
- which organizations provide service within the marketplace
- what capabilities the organization currently has or can develop to maintain and expand current programs and start up new programs

Participants define goals to ensure that the programs are developed and carried out during the course of the strategic plan. Next, the group focuses on infrastructure. Market research results clearly state what areas need to be addressed. This may involve adjustments in fund development, management and governance, human resources, marketing and communications, and so forth. The group decides which areas need to be addressed during the course of this strategic plan. Then infrastructure goals are established.

> *Not all visions are equal. Visions, which tap into an organization's deeper sense of purpose, have unique power to engender aspiration and commitment. To be genuinely shared, such visions must emerge from many people reflecting on the organization's purpose.*
>
> *Peter Senge*

Sometimes, organizations use the concept of visioning to make their decisions about the future, described in Exhibits 3–5 and 3–6. Visioning is a lively process of sharing what people most care about in a way that creates enthusiasm and shared commitment, a collective sense of what matters to the organization and its participants.

An organization's vision is different than its mission or purpose. The dictionary defines *vision* as something seen in a dream or trance; an act or power of imagination; unusual discernment, or foresight. Your organization's vision is a snapshot of your desired future. Vision tells "what," not "how." Senge describes vision as a "sense of commonalty that permeates the organization and gives coherence to diverse activities" (Senge 1990, 128). People who share a vision are connected by a common aspiration.

Your organization's vision may not be achievable during the three- to five-year time frame of your strategic plan. Indeed, your vision should be a stretch. Your organization moves toward its vision by bridging the gap between current reality and desired future. Each subsequent multiyear strategic plan moves you closer to your vision of the future until you finally reach it and must create a new vision.

Bryan Smith, in *The Fifth Discipline Fieldbook* (Senge et al., 1994), describes five ways for building shared vision. These are telling, selling, testing, consulting, and cocreating.

- Telling: Leadership decides the vision and informs the organization.
- Selling: Leadership decides the vision but seeks organizational support before moving forward.
- Testing: Leadership has an idea or two about the future and seeks the organization's reaction before making a decision.
- Consulting: Leadership seeks creative input from various groups within the organization before determining vision.
- Cocreating: Together, leadership and the various constituencies of the organization build a shared vision.

Although the strategic planning process described here uses the cocreating method, your organization may be at a different stage of development. Attempting to use this method may stymie your planning process. If this is the case, use one of the other methods for determining vision. Then, during the implementation of your strategic plan, you can build organizational capacity to use cocreating in your next planning interval. See *The Fifth Discipline Fieldbook* (Senge, 1994) for tips about developing your vision through telling, selling, testing, and consulting.

St. Mary Academy–Bay View used visioning for its decision making. The first of two evening sessions began with the full group discussing the findings report. With this information, attendees created a description of the community. Then, in small teams, attendees described the current reality of the school. Each team focused on one area, such as program, physical plant, management, governance, marketing, or fund development. Descriptions of current reality were recorded and distributed prior to the next decision-making session.

At the second session, teams reviewed current reality and created their visions for the desired future. The full group discussed the team visions, made adjustments, and confirmed a shared vision for each area. Using these narrative descriptions, the president wrote a brief vision statement for the school. This vision statement serves as the introduction to the strategic plan and inspires the school's constituents. The detailed descriptions still guide the school's work. Excerpts from the narrative descriptions as well as the final vision statement are presented in Exhibit 3–7.

The WFSA defined its vision in a day-long retreat, described in Exhibit 3–6. Exhibit 3–8 presents the Foundation's vision. Notice the length of this vision statement. Compare this long vision to the brief vision statements of the YMCA and St. Mary Academy–Bay View. Consider this: Is a vision statement only a few sentences or brief paragraphs in length?

Forget any rules you've heard. What will best serve your organization?

Distinguish between the brief inspirational summary that describes your vision. You post this on the wall and publish it in newsletters and annual reports. But rarely do these brief paragraphs provide the richness and detail required to describe your desired future clearly. Call it vision or direction—or something else entirely—your organization needs a description of sufficient detail that it is no subject to interpretation.

Remember: This lengthy and comprehensive description provides the foundation for the strategic plan and serves as the basis for your future decision making. Make sure you have the detail that you need.

11. Review (and Possibly Adjust) Mission.

Mission describes your organization's purpose, the reason you exist. Here, you define what specific role your organization takes to achieve the result you desire.

Effective strategic planning tests mission. You do not create a plan to meet your mission. Instead, a healthy organization continually evaluates whether its mission best serves changing community needs and reflects the organization's vision of the future.

Once your organization has determined its direction for the future, review your mission. Ask yourselves, "Does our current mission statement reflect our direction and vision for the future that we decided during our planning process?"

To evaluate your mission statement, use the decisions made about vision and direction to answer these questions.

- What is your geographic catchment area?

Exhibit 3–7 St. Mary Academy–Bay View: Vision

EXCERPTS FROM NARRATIVE DESCRIPTIONS OF THE DESIRED FUTURE

In the year 2005, our *program* has

- holistic, individualized, integrated, interdisciplinary, multicultural, intergenerational curriculum
- innovative educational programs for students pre-K through grade 12, which meet the needs of students so that they can face tomorrow's challenges
- an excellent library/media center that supports our innovative educational programs
- a student body and staff that reflect the diversity that exists in our world

In the year 2005, our *management and operations* includes

- a structure that facilitates communication, cooperation and collaboration, and empowers staff and students
- diverse staff, faculty, and student body
- professional development opportunities for all staff

In the year 2005, *financial aid* and scholarships are consistently used at all levels, in conjunction with marketing, to maximize student enrollment. Our marketing efforts have ensured a student waiting list. Finances are not a barrier to qualified applicants because sufficient financial aid is available. We are not dependent upon the annual appeal to bridge the annual operating expense gap. Instead, our fundraising income is used for capital and special projects.

FINAL VISION STATEMENT

Our vision for the 21st century
"The greatest work of charity is the education of women."
Motivated by these words of Catherine McAuley, foundress of the Sisters of Mercy, and energized by the rich tradition of our past . . .
We are compelled to create a learning community that promotes academic excellence and empowers young women toward a holistic approach to living that culminates in compassionate service to others. We commit ourselves to create structures at all levels that are collaborative and foster participatory decision making. We strive to ensure quality planning time for all within Bay View because we believe planning is central to responsible management and governance.
We ensure diversity among us by means of admissions and hiring practices. We seek to be responsible stewards of all of our resources by developing a solid financial base that ensures our vision and allows flexibility for future planning.

Courtesy of St. Mary Academy–Bay View, RI.

- Who is your audience? To whom do you provide your activities and services?
- What is your desired outcome? That is, what do you want to achieve by investing resources to carry out your activities?
- What are the basic means to achieve your desired outcome? That is, what activities/services will you do to achieve your vision?

Compare your answers with your current mission statement. Are all these answers reflected in your mission statement? If there is alignment, your mission statement is still relevant. If not, adjust it.

You can evaluate your mission statement in a number of ways. For example:

- Test mission at the decision-making retreat. Once retreat attendees have chosen your organization's direction, evaluate your mission. As a full group, answer the mission questions. Compare the group's responses with the current mission statement. If the group decides that adjustments must be made, assign the rewriting to staff. Staff present the revision to the planning committee and then to the board. Or, have retreat attendees work in small groups to answer the mission questions and compare their team's answers with the current mission statement. Reconvene the full group and discuss findings. Then, if the full group decides that adjustments must be made, proceed as described above.
- Test mission with the planning committee. Following the retreat decisions, the planning committee evaluates the mission statement. The committee answers the mission questions and compares results to the current mission statement. If necessary, staff draft an adjusted mission for review and action by the board.

12. Determine Goals and Strategies.

Once your organization has determined its direction or vision, establish goals for the time frame of the plan. Goals must address both program and infrastructure and must describe how you will pursue your direction and achieve your vision.

> *Look at the mission again and again to think through whether it needs to be refocused because demographics change, because we should abandon something that produces no results and eats up resources, because we have accomplished an objective.*
>
> *Peter F. Drucker*

Exhibit 3–8 Women's Foundation of Southern Arizona: Vision

OUR DREAM OF THE WORLD

The Women's Foundation of Southern Arizona (WFSA) envisions a world where women occupy positions of strength, power, and leadership, and are active philanthropists. Women and girls have equal opportunities in society, economically, socially, culturally, and politically. In this world, women and girls are healthy and safe and are celebrated for their unique roles in society. All human beings value each other, treating each other with respect and decency.

In our dream for the future, the community works effectively together to identify and address both problems and opportunities, making Southern Arizona a great place to live for all. Effective not-for-profit organizations contribute to the strength of the community and add value to the lives of women and girls.

TODAY'S REALITY

Unfortunately, today's reality is different than our dream for the world. It will take decades for change to happen, and the Women's Foundation of Southern Arizona is part of that change process.

In order to help change the world for women and girls, WFSA must be a strong, effective, and innovative organization. So we have created a vision—attainable within a decade or less—of the best women's foundation.

OUR VISION OF THE WOMEN'S FOUNDATION OF SOUTHERN ARIZONA: IN 10 YEARS OR LESS, THE BEST WE CAN BE

The Women's Foundation of Southern Arizona is part of a strong movement of women's funds across the world. This movement focuses educational and grantmaking efforts explicitly on the needs of women and girls. Together, we promote philanthropy by, about, and for women. We involve women in all parts of our work. We also involve men as allies in achieving our vision.

In Southern Arizona, the Women's Foundation makes significant contributions to the quality of life in this community by acting in accordance with its values, striving for its vision, and vigorously pursuing its mission. WFSA creates synergy and strengthens the ability of the community to work together. We do not duplicate the efforts of others, but rather reinforce, convene, leverage, and collaborate.

We know that diversity is strength, so we are welcoming and comfortable to a diverse community. We reach out and cross traditional boundaries, achieving inclusion. We are open and communicative, and diversity friendly.

The Women's Foundation of Southern Arizona is known for its high-profile, quality programs that promote the empowerment, advancement, and full participation in society of women and girls. Our programs change the world for women and girls through grantmaking, advocacy, develop-ment of leaders and philanthropists, convening, research and information, and strengthening organizations.

OUR PROGRAMS

Grantmaking

In our vision, the Women's Foundation is admired as a major funder in Southern Arizona. The Foundation values and fosters the growth of organizations that may not have access to traditional funding sources.

The Foundation makes meaningful grants to an ever-growing diversity of organizations and projects that have a direct impact on women and girls. Careful review by the Foundation guarantees that grants are awarded to the most effective, creative and innovative programs serving the unique and distinct needs of women and girls in Southern Arizona.

The Foundation's expanding, unrestricted endowment fund allows it to change direction based on changing community needs. The special interest endowment funds allow donors to pursue their own interests in grantmaking.

Leadership Development

The Women's Foundation effectively develops leaders through training and practical experience. Within WFSA, our ongoing process identifies, cultivates, and develops leadership skills. This process ensures succession planning within WFSA. Our leadership development activities also support the growth of female leaders within the larger community.

Convening

The Women's Foundation leverages its many connections to address the issues facing women and girls. The Foundation brings together individuals and organizations from the three sectors of our community: for-profit, not-for-profit, and government. WFSA facilitates discussions about issues of mutual interest and encourages communication, cooperation, and collaboration that produce results.

Public Policy

The Women's Foundation of Southern Arizona is a leading advocate for public policy that supports women and girls. Through our advocacy program, WFSA keeps informed about critical issues, articulates public positions, educates constituents, brings together advocates to take action, and lobbies with elected and regulatory officials.

As effective advocates, we think globally and act locally. We educate our constituents, including donors and volunteers, grantees, and strategic partners. We explain how individuals can affect public policy and encourage our constituents to take action, contributing to the community's civic capacity. We build strong relationships with elected

continues

Exhibit 3–8 continued

officials and others affecting public policy, educating and engaging them in dialogue.

Women in Philanthropy

In our vision, WFSA is esteemed throughout the United States for its creative strategies that empower diverse women and girls to be active philanthropists. We know that all women can be philanthropists. Each woman can give a gift of time or money, no matter the amount.

Research and Information

Understanding the status of women and girls is central to doing our work. The Women's Foundation is the recognized resource for information and referral regarding issues related to women and girls. With our strategic partners, the Women's Foundation identifies useful information and ensures its availability for use by the community.

Strengthening Organizations

Just as the Women's Foundation strengthens its own organizational capacity, the Foundation helps strengthen other organizations. We call this *capacity building*. The Foundation's capacity building program sets a new standard statewide, providing grants, training, and information to help strengthen organizations that serve women and girls.

OUR IMPROVED WAY OF DOING BUSINESS

Philanthropy and Fund Development

For the Women's Foundation of Southern Arizona, philanthropy and fund development are both a means to achieve our vision and an end, in and of itself. First, a broad base of donors invests significant resources so that WFSA can help create a more desirable world for women and girls. Second, significant endowment assets ensure that WFSA will be available in perpetuity to change the world for women and girls.

Giving through the Women's Foundation is recognized as adding value to the donor and to the community. Collective gifts are leveraged for maximum impact.

Our donors represent the diversity and interests of our community, and these donors understand our mission, vision, values, and the benefits of their giving. Our fundraising volunteers and donors, both women and men, are diverse economically and culturally.

Our comprehensive, integrated fund development program incorporates annual fundraising, endowment expansion, and planned giving. Diverse solicitation strategies are targeted to specific audiences. Our stewardship and cultivation program serves as a model for relationship building and accountability. Our outstanding donor services program provides useful advice and meaningful support.

As with our other planning, our fund development plan establishes short- and long-range goals, benchmarks to measure success and diverse strategies to reach the benchmarks.

Our comprehensive fundraising reports help us monitor progress, measure cost-effectiveness, and evaluate performance.

In our vision, our Board members are excellent fundraisers, sharing meaningful stories with people and generating a giving response. Personal solicitation is our most effective strategy. Our fundraising events are well known, highly visible, oversubscribed, and used well for cultivation.

Strategic Discussion, Planning and Evaluation, Decision Making

We spend our time talking about the important things and handle routine matters quickly and efficiently. Decision making takes place in a respectful, diversity-friendly environment, always mindful of our mission, vision, and values.

We know that information is power. We have a process and systems to decide what information is necessary, to collect it, and to use it appropriately. This quality information—interpreted for trends and implications—helps us ask the right questions and make the best decisions. We question, we argue, we learn and decide. We constantly evaluate emerging trends in women's foundations, customer service, not-for-profit management and governance, marketing and communications, philanthropy and fund development, and other areas relevant to achieving our vision.

Ongoing planning brings us together to dream, research and conceptualize, secure financing, implement, and continuously evaluate. We regularly establish standards and benchmarks by which we measure our performance, cost-effectiveness, return on investment, and accountability. We regularly evaluate performance, provide feedback, and introduce improvements.

The Women's Foundation continually acquires knowledge, learns, and changes in a timely and well-managed manner. We encourage learning as individuals and within the group.

Continuous feedback from the community, coupled with our own enhanced capacity, allows us to respond in a timely and innovative fashion to meet changing needs and interests. Today's programs and services may well be delivered in a different way tomorrow, we may change or discontinue some, and we may develop others. Effective mechanisms exist to implement needed change.

Operations

The Women's Foundation is admired as a model organization in all areas of operations and interaction. We are known for our excellence, creativity, and innovation. Our high standards set the benchmarks for other organizations.

We continually assess and enhance our own capacity to do our work and achieve our vision. We improve current competencies, develop new competencies, and hold ourselves accountable for optimum performance.

A diversified funding base ensures the stability and vitality of the Women's Foundation of Southern Arizona. Balanced

continues

Exhibit 3–8 continued

annual operations and strong reserves limit risk. Endowment assets produce sufficient interest to finance meaningful, unrestricted grantmaking, high-quality programming and services, and adequate management resources, including staff and technology.

Comprehensive plans, policies, and systems are in place throughout WFSA and are communicated well to our constituents. Superior fiscal management generates confidence in the Women's Foundation. Financial reports are in perfect order, exceed industry standards, and provide quality information for decision making.

We recognize that technology enhances communications, may increase access, and provides invaluable management support. We keep abreast of technological trends and barriers, and use this resource to best serve our constituents and our own operations.

Collaboration

The Women's Foundation of Southern Arizona does more than communicate and cooperate with other groups. In our vision, WFSA is a recognized leader in collaborative efforts, locally and regionally. Organizations seek WFSA as a strategic partner and we serve as a model to others.

As we collaborate, we emphasize inclusion and access, rather than ownership. WFSA can neither own nor specialize in all areas, so we convene, leverage, and collaborate extensively.

Human Resources

The WFSA is the best place to work and volunteer. We offer challenging opportunities, encourage teamwork, and support learning. We use the diverse talents and expertise of our staff and volunteers effectively, respectfully, and judiciously. We provide opportunities for personal and professional development. We anticipate new skill needs and ensure training in a timely fashion.

Everyone who works and volunteers with the Foundation supports its values, mission, and vision. Roles and responsibilities of staff and volunteers are clearly articulated, candidly communicated, regularly reinforced, and people are held accountable. Individuals understand their roles and responsibilities and exceed performance expectations.

Volunteers and staff in all positions are formally developed, enabled, evaluated, and recognized, thus resulting in their own satisfaction and high retention. WFSA has a comprehensive human resources program to seek out, recruit and appoint, orient and train, evaluate, reward, recognize, and release its volunteers and staff. This program helps recruit and retain the best people. Our performance expectations and appraisal processes provide meaningful feedback and learning for all involved.

As partners, volunteers and staff work together to achieve the WFSA vision. Staff, Board, and committees operate as a value-based, flexible, decisive, and cross-functional team.

Our diverse, innovative, and dynamic staff are learning oriented, flexible and adaptable, and stimulated by change. Our staff demonstrate relationship, conceptual, and leadership skills.

Our dedicated, diverse, and dynamic Board is results-driven and is respected as a model of inclusion and creativity. Our Board, committees, and task forces link, influence, and leverage resources for WFSA.

As a group, our Board carries out its due diligence function, ensuring its legal and moral accountability for the health and effectiveness of WFSA. As individuals, Board members exceed their performance expectations through extraordinary commitment.

Marketing and Communications

In our vision, the Women's Foundation of Southern Arizona is well recognized and highly visible in the community. The community is well aware of the mission, vision, and accomplishments of the Women's Foundation. WFSA is well positioned and highly visible within our targeted audiences. Our image in the community reflects our own identity and vision.

Our integrated internal and external marketing and communications program helps us maintain this strong marketplace position. Our annual marketing and communications plan includes goals, benchmarks to measure success, and diverse strategies, such as electronic and print media, public relations, a great Web site, and quality collateral materials. We use multilingual and collaborative strategies when appropriate. As with all our work, we regularly monitor progress of the plan, evaluate performance, and change as necessary.

We are clear about the key messages we wish to communicate, and we effectively communicate these to targeted audiences, using appropriate strategies with adequate frequency. Our audiences understand the vision and mission of WFSA, its services and benefits, and seek us out.

Courtesy of Women's Foundation of Southern Arizona, Tucson, AZ.

Robèrt (1994) describes this process as forecasting and back casting. The group forecasts its vision and back casts how to achieve the vision. Then the organization's various parts draw conclusions specific to their areas of operation.

Develop goals that are both realistic and challenging. Make sure the goals are measurable or observable. Achieving them propels you in your desired direction, toward your vision.

Outline the general strategies (also called *action steps* or *activities*) you will use to achieve your goals. Strategy, as postulated by Andrews in his classic book, *The Concept of Corporate Strategy* (1971), reflects "the match between what a company can do (organizational strengths and weaknesses) within the universe of what it might do (environmental opportunities and threats)."

> *When you know what to do when there is something to be done—that's tactics. When you know what to do when there is nothing to be done—that is strategy.*
>
> *Melanie Rawn*

There is no best format for presenting your organization's goals for the strategic plan. There are no rules that demand that you include objectives for each goal and strategies to accomplish each objective. You may find objectives useful or you may not. You may or may not choose to establish benchmarks (see step 14, below). You may use the terms *strategies* and *action steps* interchangeably, or you may decide that action steps are more detailed and will be done annually in work plans.

Whichever you choose, at least include measurable or observable goals accompanied by strategic activities to achieve the goals. Whatever you choose, don't be too specific. Don't get caught with detailed objectives, too many strategies, lots of activities, or action steps. A certain vagueness maintains your flexibility. As the plan proceeds, you develop annual activities that reflect the constantly changing environment.

Also, remember that action is short term. Drucker (1990) tells organizations to always ask: "Is this action step leading us toward our basic long-range goal, or is it going to sidetrack us, going to divert us, going to make us lose sight of what we are here to do?" (page 46). Your organization needs to be results-driven as you outline your activities. Ask yourself whether you are getting sufficient return on your investment of time, money, and other resources. Ask yourself whether you are allocating resources in the best way possible, using your organization's strengths, to meet your benchmarks and achieve your goals.

> *The test of a vision is not the statement, but in the directional force it gives the organization.*
>
> *Peter Senge*

Everyone should recognize the goals because they are a natural outgrowth of the market research results and the chosen direction or vision. The board approves the goals before the plan is actually written. With this approval, the board authorizes the planning committee and staff to move forward with the next steps in the planning process. These incremental approvals help build understanding and ownership.

Goals for St. Mary Academy–Bay View are given in Exhibit 3–9. Exhibit 3–10 presents the goals for the WFSA.

Exhibit 3–9 St. Mary Academy–Bay View: Goals for the Period 1996–2000

1. Design and launch an innovative educational program (curriculum and delivery system) that meets the needs of students pre-kindergarten through grade 12, so that our young women can face the future's challenges.
2. Develop state-of-the art buildings and grounds to support innovative teaching and learning (our program) and cutting-edge management, governance, and operations (supporting systems).
3. Create a learning organization/culture within the Bay View community, principally students, staff, and Board, so that we are prepared to meet ever-changing current and future needs.
4. Ensure that we have the appropriate human resources necessary to meet the changing needs of Bay View.
5. Improve the systems and structure required to support the new Bay View.

Sample activities to achieve goal #1

- Research educational programs that reflect Bay View values and can achieve our vision.
- Define the core components of our innovative educational program, including such elements as multiculturalism, feminism, faith, curriculum content, teaching methodology and delivery systems, educational standards, and faculty configuration, skills, behaviors, and development.
- Develop a workplan to launch the new educational program, including such elements as financing, curriculum development, faculty development, implementation schedule, evaluation, communications, and marketing.

Methodology and time frame to carry out activities

Establish a Program Vision Task Force, responsible to the Board of Trustees, which carries out the activities. The task force will be composed of trustees, Bay View staff (faculty and other staff), students, parents, and educators who do not serve as Bay View staff. Begin work in fall 1995. Present implementation plan to the Board in the fourth quarter of 1996. Implementation may be proposed in phases and will be incorporated in the spring 1997 budget process for initial phase launch in the academic year 1997–1998.

Courtesy of St. Mary Academy–Bay View, RI.

13. Identify Core Competencies and Supporting Structure.

With your vision, goals, and strategies in hand, identify the core competencies that your organization will need to move forward. Consider the competencies required of staff, as well as of board and committees. Your

Exhibit 3–10 Women's Foundation of Southern Arizona: Goals for the Period 2000–2004

1. Increased endowment—achieved through relevance and enhanced philanthropy and fund development
2. Adherence to WFSA values
3. High-profile quality programming
4. Recognized leader in collaboration
5. Best place to work and volunteer
6. Sound planning, decision making, and operations
7. Well recognized and highly visible in the community
8. Active part of women's funding movement

Courtesy of Women's Foundation of Southern Arizona, Tucson, AZ.

Exhibit 3–11 YMCA of Greater Providence: Excerpt from Goals and Benchmarks

Family Focus Goal: Through imagination and innovation, develop programs and facilities that answer the learning, living, spiritual, and recreation needs of today's family or individual family members.

Sample benchmarks to measure accomplishment of goal:

- Developing models for active family centers that are accessible, affordable, and convenient, as well as consistent with our mission.
- Expanding our delivery of child care services through innovative partnerships with schools, businesses, and communities, and upgrading our quality through accreditation.
- Integrating our camping programs into year-round, family-centered programs that are adventure-based and environmentally sensitive.

Courtesy of YMCA of Greater Providence, RI.

organization may need to develop new competencies and strengthen others.

As the old saying goes, form follows function. Now that you know your direction (or function), determine what is the best structure to support your forward movement. It is likely that your organization may need to restructure itself. Perhaps your organization should abandon certain committees and institute new ones. Maybe you need to redefine committee and officer roles. Certainly, the CEO will have to examine the staff structure and may initiate changes.

Think about how you will make these changes. Does your organization need a comprehensive training program to develop the competencies required of board and staff? How will you introduce and manage the change?

14. Establish Benchmarks for Success.

Hold your organization accountable for achieving its goals by defining benchmarks that are quantifiable or, at least, observable. Benchmarks describe how you will know whether you have accomplished your goals. These measures should be both short and long term, both qualitative and quantitative. Often, it is easier to project quantitative targets over the shorter term.

Although general parameters for success may be defined at the retreat, staff usually develop benchmarks later. Staff may involve the planning committee in preliminary discussion or staff may present a draft for committee discussion and review.

You might find it useful to present the benchmarks, along with their relevant goals, to the board for discussion. Do this as an incremental step in the strategic planning process. Once the board has reviewed and adjusted the benchmarks, include these measurements in the strategic plan.

To set its benchmarks for success (Exhibit 3–11), the Greater Providence YMCA used its cultural shifts document. The CEO compared current reality to future vision. She examined the gaps that had to be bridged to move from reality to vision. She examined the strengths and weaknesses in infrastructure. Then she described, in measurable terms, the YMCA's future vision and direction.

15. Assign Time Frames and Entities Responsible for Strategies.

Accountability is more than just achieving benchmarks. Accountability demands a time frame and requires assignments of responsibility.

An effective strategic plan includes an implementation calendar and a general description of which entity is responsible for which activity. In St. Mary Academy–Bay View's plan, time frames and assignments were addressed in two ways. First, each goal statement was accompanied by a narrative projecting time frames and responsibilities. Then, an integrated calendar, by quarter, was included at the end of the plan.

The Lucy Robbins Welles plan in Appendix 3–D shows a detailed timetable and assignments of responsibility. This plan also presents a new board structure.

16. Project Costs and Income Sources.

Some organizations included financial projections as part of the strategic plan itself. With financial projections, your organization can establish goals that will be carried out during the multiyear plan.

The financial section of your strategic plan does not replace your annual budgeting process. Neither does the financial section guarantee income and expenses. The financial section does, however, establish parameters and demonstrate the viability of your goals.

Although it is not possible to estimate the cost or identify the income for all the activities in your plan, you can present general financial considerations. You can outline the process you will use to secure funding for a specific activity. Often, the strategic planning process establishes a new or extended set of guidelines for financial decision making and planning.

> *It is irresponsible for a board to adopt a strategic plan without financial considerations included.*

Staff prepare the financial section of the strategic plan. The board's finance and fund development committees provide useful insights. Further, their understanding and support helps build full board ownership.

Other organizations do not include financial projections in the strategic plan. Instead, these organizations articulate a financial planning process, typically annualized.

Using the multiyear strategic plan, the organization establishes annual priorities. These priorities provide the framework for the annual budgeting process.

At the YMCA of Greater Providence, the strategic planning process segued into the annual budgeting process. Staff and the Finance Committee used the strategic plan and its priorities to project income and expense for the first fiscal year of the strategic plan.

In each subsequent year of the strategic plan, an annual retreat prepared the staff and Finance Committee for the new budget process by reviewing progress on the strategic plan and determining priorities for the new fiscal year. Then staff and the Finance Committee drafted the annual budget for board approval.

The strategic plan for the Lucy Robbins Welles Library (see Appendix 3–D) addresses financing in two ways. First, financing is noted for each strategy in the plan. Second, one section of the plan describes the parameters and calendar for financial planning.

17. Outline Process To Monitor Progress of Plan, Evaluate Performance, and Extend Plan for Subsequent Years.

A viable plan requires a process for monitoring progress, evaluating overall performance, and extending the plan in subsequent years. This section of the plan describes the steps by which staff and volunteers gauge progress and performance. Here, too, target dates or time frames are noted.

Exhibit 3–12 St. Mary Academy—Bay View: Process to Monitor Progress and Evaluate and Extend the Plan

At Bay View, we recognize that monitoring progress of the plan is as important as developing the plan. Monitoring progress is a partnership between Board and staff. The key leader in monitoring progress of the plan—and ensuring its implementation—is the President of Bay View.

Specific steps we will take to move the plan forward are:

1. Build staff and trustee understanding of the value of planning, their roles in planning, and the activities essential to ongoing planning (ongoing evaluation in all areas of operation).
2. Build parent, donor, alumna, and student understanding of the value of planning, their roles in planning, and the activities essential to ongoing planning (e.g., ongoing evaluation in all areas of operation).
3. Use the strategic plan as the basis for annual workplans for staff, Board, and committees.
4. Engage management staff and Board of Trustees in strategic dialogue about vision, the plan, and its progress. Design management and trustee meetings to focus on these three elements.
5. Tie staff performance criteria and appraisal process to Bay View's vision and the plan to achieve this vision.
6. Tie the annual budget process to the activities in the strategic plan.
7. At least twice during the course of this plan, assess the following:
   • Is our behavior aligned with our articulated values?
   • Are our customers (students and parents) satisfied with the quality and scope of our program?
   • How well are we governing?
   • How well are we managing?
   • Has our fund raising and marketing grown stronger?
8. Provide regular updates on the plan's progress to the entire Bay View community. Secure their ongoing feedback.
9. Conduct an annual Board of Trustees/management staff planning retreat to formally review the plan's progress and project the activities for the next year.
10. In the fall of 1999, design the planning process to develop the subsequent strategic plan. As necessary, conduct research to support decision making. Update vision and review mission. Outline activities to move Bay View from reality in 1999 to desired future vision.

Courtesy of St. Mary Academy–Bay View, RI.

Your strategic plan has a time limit, generally three to five years. Toward the end of the current plan, you start the process of strategic planning for the next interval. Your current plan may briefly describe how you propose to extend the plan or launch another strategic planning process. Exhibit 3–12 shows the process for St. Mary Academy–Bay View.

18. Write the Strategic Plan, Review, and Adopt.

Now put all the pieces together. A viable strategic plan is a living resource for your organization. It guides your organization's activities and decisions. Well-used, smudged, and dog-eared, the plan accompanies board, committee members, and staff to meetings, sets the context for fund development, defines annual budgeting, and helps evaluate staff and volunteer performance.

To be this useful, make sure your plan is user-friendly. Write clearly and organize well. Provide enough detail but not too much. See Appendix 3–C and Appendix 3–D for the strategic plans of the YMCA of Greater Providence and the Lucy Robbins Welles Library in Newington, Connecticut.

Often, the planning process manager writes the strategic plan, bringing together the various components in an organized fashion. The CEO reviews and edits the draft. Sometimes, the organization writes the plan, and the planning process manager serves as guide and editor. This is a good way to save money if you're using a consultant as your process manager.

Key staff, the planning committee chair, and chief volunteer officer review the draft plan before it goes to the planning committee for review and approval. The planning committee recommends the plan to the board. Board discussion will likely be quite brief if they have been engaged throughout the process and if you have done incremental approvals along the way.

19. Translate the Plan into Personal Commitment.

The planning process began by securing the opinions and perspective of individuals and organizations. Individuals worked together to produce shared vision and strategies for your organization.

Now return to the individual. How will each individual in your organization translate this shared plan into her or his personal commitment? What tasks are appropriate for each person? What kind of short- and long-term financial commitment will be forthcoming? How will each individual use the learning acquired during the planning process to strengthen personal performance?

For example, use a number of activities to translate the plan into personal commitment for board members.

- First, return to the beginning, before board members become board members. Many of your constituents are potential board members. Develop their understanding and commitment, for example, through the strategic planning process. Then, if these constituents are recruited, they already understand how your organization plans and what the vision is.

- Second, based on the new vision and strategic plan, examine the roles and responsibilities and performance expectations of board members. Make changes as necessary. When you interview candidates for board membership, discuss your values, current vision, and the strategic plan that takes you there. Explain how your organization uses planning to help produce learning. Evaluate the candidate's commitment to your vision and strategic plan before offering her or him a position on the board.

- Third, make sure each incumbent participates in the planning process. Ensure that each one supports the shared values, vision, and strategic plan. If a board member is not comfortable with the results of planning, encourage him or her to resign from the board. If possible, keep the individual involved on a committee or in some manner.

- Fourth, meet personally with each board member and negotiate his or her individual commitment to the vision and plan. Naturally, this commitment includes task assignments, committee or team participation, financial investment, and assistance with fund development. Many organizations create a written contract, which is signed by each board member. Share the commitments with the entire board, except for the confidentiality of gift amounts. The full board should know what each of its members commits to the organization and, thus, to each other.

KEEPING THE PLAN ALIVE

The planning process is finished, and your organization has its plan. Let's assume your planning process was effective. Your constituents participated actively, and they own the resulting plan. Your organization is more cohesive than it has ever been, sharing a vision and excitement for the future.

Now you must implement the plan, keeping the vision alive and moving forward. This may be the hardest process you face.

For many organizations, the strategic plan generates significant change. In this situation, the organization must focus on the transition and change process. Don't just assume that change will happen. Look back at Chapter 2, the section on well-managed change.

Bring together organization leadership to discuss transition and change. In the context of the vision and strategic plan, outline what will have to be done. Consider the barriers to change. Consider the resources that can overcome the barriers.

> *Once a shared vision has been developed, it is critical that all components of the [organization] be aligned to achieve the goals and objectives laid out in the plan.*
>
> *John F. Schlegal*

Remember. You will not achieve your vision of the future if you end the process with the strategic plan. Your plan now serves as the starting point for the next process, that of transition and change. Plan this next process well, execute with care, and you will realize your vision.

As you implement your plan, focus first on your CEO. Your organization's CEO is responsible for ensuring institutional health, which includes achieving the organization's vision. In operational terms, this means that the CEO is principally responsible to ensure progress of the plan. The CEO enables staff and volunteers to work together, moving the organization forward. Achievement of vision and progress of the plan is the focus of the CEO's annual performance appraisal.

There are a number of strategies that can help your organization keep its plan alive.

- Follow the plan. Carry out activities to reach your benchmarks and achieve your goals. Adhere to the time frames.
- Create integrated subplans. Use the strategic plan to develop other plans, such as marketing and fund development. Construct the plans as a coordinated, integrated whole.
- Annualize your strategic plan. Translate your multiyear strategic plan into detailed annual work plans for board, committees, and staff. Use the strategic plan as the framework for annual budgeting.
- Annually, conduct a planning retreat. Review progress to date and make adjustments for the next year of the plan.
- Hold each individual and all groups accountable. Make sure that each committee, department and team, and individual regularly explores his, her, or its role and progress in achieving your organization's vision.
- Use the plan to set the context for deliberations, decision making, and action. Make sure that leadership communicates the linkages between the plan-

ning process, plan, and current activities. Use the plan as a guideline for decisions.
- Link staff, board, team, and committee performance to the strategic plan. Translate the goals and benchmarks of the strategic plan into goals and responsibilities for departments, work teams, and individuals. Define key performance criteria in terms of progress of the plan.
- Reshape board and staff meeting agendas. Use the goals of the plan as the key elements for each agenda. Use the plan's benchmarks as the focus for leadership's dialogue.
- Regularly review and discuss progress of the plan. Provide written and oral updates. Discuss challenges and opportunities.
- Institutionalize internal and external assessment as part of operations. Alternate the assessment process yearly. One year, evaluate program and institutional capacity; the next year, assess community needs. Use the information for continuous quality improvement for your institution's operations. Also, use the information to make adjustments to the strategic plan. When it is time to update the strategic plan, your organization will have much of its market research completed.
- Maintain a planning committee or team that reports to the board. This group carries out many of the strategies suggested here.
- Remember that planning is learning. Create a learning organization.

Most important, the right attitude keeps the plan alive. Every choice, each decision, and all actions evolve from organizational vision and the strategic plan. Because planning is learning, organization leaders consistently and continually use the plan to frame all activities. These leaders keep the plan alive by asking the questions worth asking. A useful mantra for the individual and his or her group might be:

- How does what I am/we are doing relate to the vision and strategic plan?
- Are these activities the best use of my/our resources?
- What should I/we not do?
- What should I/we do next to make progress on the plan and move toward our vision?

Recognizing the challenge to implementing its plan, the WFSA established a Change Team. The team began its work, once the plan was adopted by the Board of Trustees. According to plan, the Change Team would likely exist for 18 months. The Board would evaluate the effectiveness of the Team and later make a decision about permanence. It might be advantageous to establish a permanent Change Team, thus focusing attention on this ongoing process.

The Change Team was comprised of 7–10 people, including the CEO and Board President. Other Team members included trustees and the Chair of the Advisory Council. The Change Team elected its own chair.

Responsibilities of the Change Team are:

Overall responsibility

- Institutionalize the vision, values, planning, and the current strategic plan throughout WFSA.
- Ensure progress on the strategic plan.
- Facilitate the change process.

Activities, working with staff and consultant

- Ensure that WFSA does benchmarking to measure progress and performance against goals.
- Monitor progress of the strategic plan—including organizational structure and internal capacity—and report regularly to the Board.
- Engage the Board in strategic discussion regarding change and the plan.
- Serve as a think tank to support the change process and to identify and facilitate interventions as necessary.
- Monitor the health and effectiveness of Board meetings, recommending agenda and process enhancements.
- Design annual planning process and planning retreat.

Documenting and Communicating Your Planning Process and Plan

Documenting and communicating are essential to keep the planning process and plan alive.

First, documenting both the process and plan provides multiple benefits to your organization and its constituents. Use the wealth of information produced during the planning process to develop programs and other activities.

Documentation serves as an important part of individual and organization learning. By documenting the process of planning (and organization learning), you can evaluate your processes and make improvements for the future.

Second, communication enables your organization to build understanding and support for its processes, decisions, and direction. Throughout the planning process

and the plan's implementation, communicate with your constituents. For example, tell them:

- why your organization is planning and how planning will strengthen your service to the community
- what the planning process looks like and why the process itself is so important
- why the constituents' participation in planning is critical
- general findings and implications of the planning process
- key decisions of the planning process
- how the organization will change
- progress of implementing the plan

EVALUATING YOUR STRATEGIC PLANNING PROCESS

Effective organizations regularly evaluate management and governance functions, including the process of strategic planning. Debrief when the planning process ends and use the evaluation results to improve the design of your next strategic planning process.

The planning committee can lead this assessment. Conduct formal and informal conversations with constituencies who participated in the planning process. You could even conduct focus groups and surveys to help evaluate the planning process.

Consider the following issues as you evaluate the effectiveness of your planning process.

- Which constituents were involved in what components of the planning process? How many, how often, and to what extent? What might you change in the next planning process?
- Was the market research—both internal and external—sufficient to help you ask the right questions and make the best decisions? What would you do differently in the next planning process?
- Were all parts of the organization—all functions and systems—involved in the planning process? How well did the process reach throughout the system?
- Were the critical questions asked? Were the questions sufficiently broad and deep?
- How involved were various constituents in the asking process? How might you engage people differently in the next planning process?
- How well did you address issues of program and infrastructure?
- How engaged were your trustees and staff in the planning process? What was the level of understanding and enthusiasm for the process? What might you do in the future to enhance understanding and participation?

- How well did you maintain the momentum of planning while maintaining normal operations? Are there other strategies that would help you balance future planning and current implementation?
- How well did you inform constituents of the progress of planning? Was communication adequate? How might it be improved?
- Throughout the process, was there extensive formal and informal conversation about planning? How might you encourage even more conversation?
- How well did your decision makers engage in dialogue? How comfortable were they with disagreement and conflict resolution? How can you enhance this capability?
- Overall, how well did your organization and its individuals learn? Did planning produce learning? How can you enhance your organization's learning capacity?
- How excited are people about the resulting plan? To what extent are individuals, teams, departments, and committees using the plan? How well is your strategic plan integrated into the organization?

CHALLENGES TO STRATEGIC PLANNING

Healthier communities would be the result if all not-for-profit organizations did effective strategic planning processes regularly. Why? Because community needs assessments encourage organizations to be more responsive. Analysis of competitors, collaborators, and knowledge alliances can create integrated systems that provide better service by reducing duplication and producing areas of excellence. Examination of institutional capacity builds stronger, more stable organizations.

There are many challenges to effective strategic planning. Effective organizations anticipate and accommodate the challenges, thus benefiting from the planning process.

Committing Time

Often, staff and board members are reluctant to commit sufficient time. Current demands are so overwhelming that considering the future is not possible.

This excuse reminds me of a colleague who could not attend a time management seminar—offered in our own facility at no charge—because she did not have the time. There is no response to this attitude. Either the individual or organization eventually recognizes their own folly or they do not.

Maintaining Momentum

Once embarked upon planning, some organizations cannot maintain sufficient momentum. Current reality interrupts so frequently that the planning process lingers, limping along beyond anyone's interest and out of step with the changing environment.

Often, this happens because a staff person with too many other responsibilities acts as the planning process manager. Anticipate this problem in advance. It's easier to succeed if you take responsibilities away from the staff person until the planning process is finished or hire a consultant.

Narrowing the Scope of Planning

You compromise the planning process by narrowing its scope. Be inclusive, rather than exclusive. For example, make sure you focus on program and infrastructure, project income and expense, and include your key constituents.

Succumbing to the Marketplace

Organizations are relevant when they are meaningful to the community. Fund development works when the organization meets the need of the donor and volunteer. But organizations can be too responsive, thereby compromising their values and vision.

For example:

- A donor offers a significant gift if your organization agrees to develop a specific program. The proposed program does not reflect your organization's vision and priorities at this time. Should your organization respond to the donor? No.

Within your values, vision, mission, and priorities, you seek donors. You learn their interests and meet their needs if possible. Seeking funds happens within the framework of your values, vision, and mission.

- Although most organizations should alter their mission if so indicated by an effective strategic planning process, this is not appropriate for arts groups. An arts organization possesses an artistic vision. A theatre's vision might be to produce contemporary and avant-garde work. Market research indicates that the community prefers light-hearted, classic comedy. Should the artist change his or her artistic vision? No. But the theatre must either find an audience for the vision or choose to close. "Marketing does not tell an artist how to create a work of art; rather, the role of marketing is to match the artist's creations and interpretations with an appropriate audience. . . . The belief that the consumer is [king or queen] . . . would be harmful if applied to the arts world. The artist, not the consumer, should have the final deciding vote" (Mokwa et al. 1980, 68, 69).

Issues Conspiracy

A group can compromise its own planning process through issues conspiracy. In this situation, group members recognize that the organization faces significant issues. The issues are stressful and controversial, and may demand dramatic changes for the organization. Anxious about conflict and threatened by possible change, the group colludes to avoid discussion.

Whereas issues conspiracy is dangerous to institutional health, planned delay can be appropriate. Some organizations are simply not prepared to discuss challenging issues. Group members may not have enough experience with conversation. They may be unable to share their opinions and concerns, afraid of disagreement, and uncomfortable resolving conflict.

If this is your situation, build in delay. Put the issues on the table but don't expect to resolve them by the end of the planning process. Describe the issues in the plan and outline a process whereby the organization learns to engage in dialogue and address difficult issues. Establish goals that include discussion and resolution of the issues. This intentional delay provides time for the organization to learn how to discuss and resolve difficult issues. The issues do not need to be resolved during the planning process itself.

Routine Instead of Visionary

Some individuals in your organization expect a creative, farseeing, and visionary strategic plan. However, the organization may not yet be ready for this. Your organization may need to address more routine operating issues before moving into a visionary phase. A less visionary plan may be the necessary bridge, preparing the organization for a more creative plan in subsequent years.

False Expectations

Some people expect that all issues will be resolved during the planning process so the resulting written plan has all the answers. This is not possible. The best plans contain some answers but not all. However, the best plans outline how the organization will address any outstanding issues during the course of the plan's implementation.

Balancing Flexibility and Inflexibility

Even though you have a plan, opportunities may arise that you wish to pursue, or new challenges may need to be addressed. The plan is a road map to get to your destination, but there may be detours along the way. Experienced and successful voyagers anticipate and accommodate these detours. Just remember, adding something new requires additional resources, or your organization will have to decide what to eliminate from the current plan.

Be careful. Don't be too flexible because this suggests that you do not value the plan. Sometimes, organizations use flexibility as an excuse to avoid their goals.

Changing Leadership

Some of your leadership will change during the plan's implementation and during the planning process. Yet this change has little effect in effective organizations because a good plan, produced by an effective planning process, belongs to the entire institution and all its constituents. When changes in position occur, they are of little consequence. The new players helped design the plan and/or have been adequately oriented to understand and support the plan and its process.

Planning While Implementing

Mintzberg (1994) postulates that traditional strategic planning behaves as though the world holds still while we plan. Then the world stays on the course we predicted while we implement the plan.

Naturally, as Mintzberg observes, this is absurd. Locally and globally, change is constant. True strategic planning does not rely on predictability. Rather, strategic thinking and action are part of strategic planning. Effective organizations balance planning while implementing another plan. These organizations embrace uncertainty and ambiguity, and effective strategic planning helps them do so.

SUMMARY

Strategic planning ensures your relevance by defining and renewing your relationship with the community. And your relationship with the community is the second of four relationships that are essential to effective fund development.

Planning is a well-devised campaign, on a broad scale, conducted to achieve an end. Effective planning is, first, a process whereby an organization or group decides where it wishes to be in the future and how to reach that future. You map out modes of related action and invest and mobilize resources to attain your goals.

Strategic planning helps your organization accept ambiguity and uncertainty, and develop a high tolerance for complexity, learning, and change. Planning focuses your organization's activities, determines priorities, and sets limits.

Strategic planning takes the long view. Your organization will likely decide things today whose effect will not be felt for five or even ten years. The plan's time frame is generally three to five years—no longer, because we live in such a swiftly changing world.

Your written plan answers the following questions:

The questions	Answers articulated as . . .
Where is our organization going?	Vision and mission
How will we get there?	Program and infrastructure goals and strategies
What is our blueprint for action?	Budget and time frames
How will we know if we are on track?	Accountability and control (benchmarks for success, assignments, process for monitoring progress)

REFERENCES

Andrews, K. 1971. *The Concept of Corporate Strategy.* Homewood, IL: Richard D. Irwin.

Carroll, P.J. 1995. Infrastructure for Organizational Transformation at Shell Oil. *Collective Intelligence* 1, No. 1.

de Geus, A. March–April 1988. Planning as Learning. *Harvard Business Review.* Boston: Harvard Business School.

de Geus, A. September 1995. *Systems Thinking in Action Conference.* Sponsored by Pegasus Communications, Boston.

Drucker, P. 1990. *Managing the Nonprofit Organization: Principles and Practices.* New York: HarperCollins Publishers.

Drucker, P. 1993. *The Five Most Important Questions You Will Ever Ask About Your Nonprofit Organization.* San Francisco: Jossey-Bass, Publishers.

Duarte, D.L. and N.T. Snyder. 2000. Leadership in a Virtual World. *Leader to Leader,* Spring 2000. New York: The Peter F. Drucker Foundation for Nonprofit Management; San Francisco: Jossey-Bass, Publishers.

Giving RI. 1995. Foster, RI: Joyaux Associates.

Giving USA: The Annual Report on Philanthropy. 1995. New York: American Association of Fund-Raising Counsel Trust for Philanthropy.

Goldmark, P. 1991. Toward a New Social Contract. 1991 Independent Sector Annual Meeting, Atlanta, Georgia.

Luther, D. 1995. *Leadership 1995.* Washington, DC: American Society of Association Executives.

Mintzberg, H. January–February 1994. The Rise and Fall of Strategic Planning. *Harvard Business Review.* Boston: Harvard Business School.

Mokwa, M., W.M. Dawson, and E.A. Prieve. 1980. *Marketing the Arts.* New York: Praeger Publishers.

Nonaka, I. November–December 1991. The Knowledge Creating Company. *Harvard Business Review.* Boston: Harvard Business School.

Primozic, K., E. Primozic, and J. Leben. 1991. *Strategic Choices: Supremacy, Survival or Sayonara.* New York: McGraw-Hill.

Rawn, M. 1994. *The Ruins of Ambrai.* New York: Daw Books.

Robèrt K. 1994. *The Natural Step: Simplicity without Reductionism.* Stockholm: The Natural Step Environmental Institute.

Schlegal, J.F. 1995. The Power of Plan. *Association Management.* Washington, DC: American Society of Association Executives.

Senge, P. 1990. *The Fifth Discipline: The Art and Practice of the Learning Organization.* New York: Doubleday.

Senge, P., A. Kleiner, C. Roberts, R. Ross, B. Smith, 1994. *The Fifth Discipline Fieldbook: Strategies and Tools for Building a Learning Organization.* New York: Doubleday.

Tull, D., and D. Hawkins. 1987. *Marketing Research: Measurement and Method,* 4th ed. New York: Macmillan Publishing.

Appendix 3–A

Kappa Alpha Theta Fraternity: Research Outline for the Strategic Planning Process

1. WHY PLAN?

The world continually evolves and changes, as does the Kappa Alpha Theta community. Sometimes the changes are great; sometimes only small. To be an effective organization, we must plan for these changes. That is, we must integrate strategic planning into our day-to-day operations.

Strategic planning is the process of determining where we want to go over a multiyear period and how we intend to get there. While the resulting strategic plan provides a framework or blueprint for direction and activities, the plan must also remain flexible.

In January 1994, Kappa Alpha Theta Fraternity embarked on a strategic planning process. The process will produce a written plan for the three-year period, 1994–1996. Recognizing that the process of planning is as important as the resulting written plan, Kappa Alpha Theta will reach out to its constituents and involve them in the process. The fraternity will examine industry trends and will examine the infrastructure necessary to support its desired direction.

The Grand Council, supported by staff, will serve as the decision-making body for the strategic planning process. A Steering Committee—comprised of representatives from the Council, Foundation, general membership, and staff—will provide leadership to the process. Consulting services have been retained to manage the process.

Courtesy of Kappa Alpha Theta International Fraternity for Women.

2. WHAT DO WE WANT TO ACCOMPLISH BY THIS PLANNING PROCESS?

The Steering Committee has identified a number of items that are to be accomplished during the planning process. Specifically:

- Ensure that our direction and activities are relevant and meaningful to the changing needs of our current constituents, as well as germane to the changing constituencies in our communities.
- Make our decisions based on quality information from our constituents and mindful of industry trends.
- Clarify our philosophy regarding programming for collegians and alumnae.
- Allocate resources (time, staff, and volunteer resources, dollars, etc.) based on priorities established in the plan.
- Institutionalize the process of planning into our organizational behavior and operations. Make sure that strategic planning is not a special biennial event but rather an essential part of the way we do business.

3. WHAT ARE THE CRITICAL ELEMENTS OF THE PROCESS AND THE PLAN?

To ensure that the organization is relevant, a strategic planning process gathers information both externally and internally. It is important to think in terms of marketing and market research. Externally, Kappa Alpha Theta will want to consider:

- What are the trends in the industry and the market-place?
- How satisfied are our customers now, and what kinds of products and services do they want in the future?
- Who is the competition and how do we compare?

Internally, Kappa Alpha Theta will want to consider things such as:

- Do we have the appropriate volunteer and staff infrastructure to do our job?
- Are we able to generate sufficient funds?

The planning process should produce a plan that functions as a useful tool during the multiyear period. The Council-adopted strategic plan forms the basis for staff and committee operating plans and activities. The strategic plan establishes the parameters for budgeting and defines the general timetable for the institution. Also, the plan actually assigns general areas of responsibility. Key elements of the plan are

- clear statement of organizational values
- vision of constituents and program
- program goals and strategies to achieve the goals
- any adjustments to infrastructure to support the program
- time frames, entities responsible, and projections of income and expense

4. WHAT ARE THE ISSUES THAT THE PROCESS MUST ADDRESS?

In preliminary discussions, members of the Steering Committee and consultants identified a number of issues that must be addressed during the strategic planning process. These are:

Membership Issues

- Who are our future members and where will we find them? Membership is declining on college and-university campuses; women are going to school in different ways. Should we have an alumnae initiation program?
- How can we embrace the diversity of American society? How might we encourage participation?
- We seem to be losing touch with our alumnae. Is it reasonable to expect that we can maintain close ties? If yes, how?
- What kinds of programs do our members and alumnae want? What is relevant to their lives?

- Are we competing with sororities for membership on college and university campuses? If yes, what is our unique marketplace niche?
- What is the image Greeks have on college and university campuses—particularly among administration and faculty? How does this affect our work?

Housing

- As our membership changes, what role will collegian housing play in our future?
- How will we maintain and/or divest ourselves of our real estate?

Relationship with Men's Groups

- Will we survive, with or without men? Should we cooperate or collaborate more? Should we become coeducational?

Communications

- How effective are we at communicating with members, boards, volunteers, and staff? Are changes necessary?

Funding

- Does our membership clearly understand the difference between supporting the Foundation and joining the fraternity? How can we enhance the case to support the Foundation?

5. HOW WILL WE GATHER THE NECESSARY INFORMATION FOR DECISION MAKING?

The information-gathering phase is the most time-consuming process in strategic planning. The consultants recommend:

1. Survey directed at each individual member— alumnae and collegian

- Alumnae survey printed as part of the Kappa Alpha Theta magazine, scheduled for mailing in mid-March; banner across the magazine front to encourage readers and non-readers to respond quickly.
- Collegian survey distributed through chapters, scheduled for distribution in mid-March.
- The survey will be written by Joyaux Associates and collated by Kappa Alpha Theta. Joyaux Associates will provide collating guidelines and a form.

Issues in the surveys: satisfaction, program interests, housing desires, communications.

2. Chapter and club focus groups

- Request that chapters and clubs conduct a focus group with members.
- Joyaux Associates will write questions and guidelines. Kappa Alpha Theta will distribute, make reminder telephone calls, and collate.
- Issues: satisfaction, program interests, more in-depth housing desires, communications, met and unmet needs of collegians, competition for members, donor/case perspective.

3. Key informant interviews

The Steering Committee is identifying individuals, inside of and external to Kappa Alpha Theta, who might provide important information to the strategic planning process, for example, donors to the Foundation, national interfraternity organizations, national association of student personnel administrators, Junior League, American Association of University Women, etc.

Joyaux Associates will write interview questions and guidelines. Volunteers from Kappa Alpha Theta will be identified and recruited by the Steering Committee to conduct interviews. Kappa Alpha Theta will send out an invitation letter to the interviewee. The interviewer will actually schedule and conduct the interview and provide the notes directly to Joyaux Associates.

4. Non-member focus groups on targeted college campuses

The Steering Committee will identify four to five sites where Kappa Alpha Theta volunteers can facilitate focus groups with collegians who did not join a fraternity. Sites will include campuses that include large and small Greek populations.

5. Review of printed information

Joyaux Associates will review both internal and external information. Externally, we will examine relevant reports and information within the Greek system, as well as demographic trends available for collegians and society as a whole.

Internally, Joyaux Associates will work with Kappa Alpha Theta staff to identify corporate information such as:

- five-year (or if available, 10-year) acquisition, renewal, and attrition rates of collegians and alumnae (cumulative and by district)

- five-year contribution history, including acquisition, renewal, and attrition rates of collegians, alumnae, chapters, and clubs (cumulative and by district)
- attendance rates at specific programs (is this possible or relevant, based on the way you do programming?)
- outline of current communication strategies (item, frequency, audience, etc.)
- reports from chapter/club consultants

6. USING THE APRIL 8–10 GRAND COUNCIL MEETING AND THE JUNE GRAND CONVENTION

Both of these meetings offer an opportunity to provide a planning update and build ownership in the planning process.

The April Grand Council meeting will be a work session to address institutional infrastructure and volunteer and staff roles. A self-assessment will be provided to Grand Council members, Foundation trustees, and senior staff prior to the April meeting. The self-assessment, an anonymous written survey, will examine such items as: role and responsibilities of staff and volunteers; operations and management of boards and committees; perceived mission and values; and recruitment, evaluation, and management of volunteers. Joyaux Associates will collate and analyze the self-assessment results so that this information can be used at the April meeting.

The work session in April will address such issues as:

- findings of the self-assessment
- organizational values
- internal strengths and weaknesses

For the Grand Convention, a formal update will be provided orally and in writing to the delegates. This would be, essentially, a public relations strategy because no decisions would have been made by this time. Further, there is no proposal to gather information from delegates at the Convention because members are being contacted directly and through alumnae and collegian local chapter/club focus groups.

7. THE PLANNING RETREAT

Once the information is gathered, compiled, reviewed, and analyzed, leadership gathers together in a planning retreat. The Kappa Alpha Theta strategic planning retreat is scheduled for August 5–7. The retreat will be designed to accomplish the following:

- Review the information (mailed in advance) and discuss the implications.

- Make decisions about future direction, targeted constituents, and specific program focus.
- Determine infrastructure needs to support direction. A work session on infrastructure would address such issues as: fund development and the Foundation, volunteer and staff roles, marketing and communications.

8. COMMUNICATING WITH OUR CONSTITUENTS

Throughout the strategic planning process, it is important that Kappa Alpha Theta communicate with its constituents. The following is suggested:

- Letter to Fraternity Grand Council and Foundation Board of Trustees. Explain purpose, process, and their role. *(February 15)*
- Letter to chapters and clubs. Explain purpose, process, and their role, and ask them to schedule a focus group. *(February 15)*
- Exciting, catchy "letter from the president" in every issue of magazine and any newsletter, beginning in March (i.e., *the Bulletin*).
- Letter to chapters and clubs. Update. *(March 15, April 15)*
- Present update at June Grand Convention. (June)
- Mail formal plan to chapters and clubs. *(September 15)*
- Publish executive summary of adopted plan as feature in magazine.

9. PROPOSED TIMETABLE

Date	Entity	Activity
By February 4	Joyaux Associates	Draft membership survey(s) to Marcia.
By February 11	Joyaux Associates	Draft chapter/club focus group process and questions to office.
February 15	Kappa Alpha Theta	Special mailing to alumnae and collegian chapters/clubs regarding planning process and focus groups.
February 18	Steering Committee	Meeting to adopt research plan, confirm interviewees and interviewers, present any materials.
By February 28	Steering Committee	Recruit all interviewers.
By February 28	Joyaux Associates	Key informant questions, interview guidelines, and introductory letter to office.
By March 1	Joyaux Associates	Self-assessment to office.
By March 7	Kappa Alpha Theta	Mail self-assessment to volunteers.
March/April	Members	Complete individual survey.
March/April	Alumnae and college chapters and clubs	Conduct focus groups.
March/April	Volunteers	Conduct key informant interviews.
By March 4	Kappa Alpha Theta office	Mail introductory letter to interviewees and interviewers.
March 21, 8:30	Steering Committee/Joyaux	Meeting
March 21	Kappa Alpha Theta staff and volunteers	Self-assessment survey due to Joyaux Associates.
By March 25	Joyaux Associates	Questions for non-Greek campus focus groups to office.
Monday, April 4	Steering Committee/Joyaux	Meeting to discuss April work session.

Date	Entity	Activity
April 8–10	Grand Council	Work session.
April	Volunteers	Conduct non-Greek campus focus groups.
April 21	Steering Committee/Joyaux	Meeting
May 2	Volunteers	Reports from chapter/club focus groups, non-Greek focus groups, and key informant interviews to Joyaux Associates.
By June 6	Kappa Alpha Theta	Collated results of member survey to Joyaux Associates.
June 6	Steering Committee/Joyaux	Meeting
By June 27	Joyaux Associates	Summary of information to office for distribution to steering committee.
July 6	Steering Committee/Joyaux	Meeting to discuss information and implications.
By July 12	Joyaux Associates	Final packet and retreat agenda to office.
By July 15	Office	Mail retreat packet to grand council.
August 5–7	Grand Council/Joyaux	PLANNING RETREAT
By August 10	Joyaux Associates	Retreat summary to office for distribution to grand council and steering committee.
August 15	Steering Committee/Joyaux	Meeting
By August 22	Kappa Alpha Theta staff	Outline strategies and project expense and income. Provide information to Joyaux Associates.
By August 25	Joyaux Associates	Provide draft plan to office.
By August 29	Kappa Alpha Theta	Provide edits to Joyaux Associates.
By August 31	Joyaux Associates	Provide final plan to Kappa Alpha Theta.

Appendix 3–B

Sample Constituency Surveys

CALLING ALL MEMBERS.
WE NEED YOUR OPINION NOW!

Please complete this questionnaire and return it by April 29 to S.P. Joyaux, our planning consultant. An envelope is enclosed for your use. Your response will be very helpful and greatly appreciated. Thank you.

AS YOU LIKE IT

1. **How satisfied are you with the following aspects of the Norman Bird Sanctuary?**

	VERY SATISFIED	SATISFIED	NOT CERTAIN	DISSATISFIED	VERY DISSATISFIED
a. Membership benefits	☐	☐	☐	☐	☐
b. Programs in general	☐	☐	☐	☐	☐
c. Activities and attractions compared to other environmental groups & wildlife sanctuaries	☐	☐	☐	☐	☐
d. Membership cost	☐	☐	☐	☐	☐
e. Program fees	☐	☐	☐	☐	☐
f. Preservation of natural habitats	☐	☐	☐	☐	☐
g. Environmental advocacy	☐	☐	☐	☐	☐
h. Helpfulness and knowledge of staff	☐	☐	☐	☐	☐
i. Accessibility	☐	☐	☐	☐	☐

2. **To what extent are you interested in the following types of programs?**

	VERY INTERESTED	SOMEWHAT INTERESTED	UNCERTAIN	NOT INTERESTED
a. Programs for adults (e.g., natural science, etc.)	☐	☐	☐	☐
b. Programs for teenagers (e.g., camp, nature club, hiking club, etc.)	☐	☐	☐	☐
c. Programs for preteenagers (e.g., camp, nature club, etc.)	☐	☐	☐	☐
d. Programs for preschoolers (e.g., mini-nature walks, nature crafts, etc.)	☐	☐	☐	☐
e. Programs for families	☐	☐	☐	☐

3. **How often do you or a member of your family visit the Norman Bird Sanctuary?**

☐ once or twice a year   ☐ 3 to 4 times a year
☐ 5 to 10 times a year   ☐ more than 10 times a year

Courtesy of the Norman Bird Sanctuary.

4. **What are the most critical environmental issues in Rhode Island?**

		VERY CRITICAL	CRITICAL	NOT CRITICAL	UNCERTAIN
a.	Waste management	☐	☐	☐	☐
b.	Habitat preservation	☐	☐	☐	☐
c.	Clean water	☐	☐	☐	☐
d.	Clean air	☐	☐	☐	☐
e.	Protection of endangered wildlife	☐	☐	☐	☐
f.	Open space/recreation	☐	☐	☐	☐
g.	Other (please specify):				

5. **Do you believe that people need more education about environmental issues?**

   ☐ yes, definitely   ☐ yes, probably   ☐ not certain   ☐ no

6. **How often do you or a member of your family attend Norman Bird Sanctuary programs?**

   ☐ 1 to 3 times a year   ☐ 4 to 6 times a year
   ☐ 7 to 10 times a year   ☐ more than 10 times a year

7. **How interested are you in the following program topics?**

		VERY INTERESTED	SOMEWHAT INTERESTED	NOT INTERESTED	UNCERTAIN
a.	Global issues and how they relate to day-to-day living (e.g., recycling, composting, attracting wildlife, using environmentally friendly household cleaners, etc.)	☐	☐	☐	☐
b.	Natural science (e.g., birds, seashore animals, wildflowers, New England trees, geology, etc.)	☐	☐	☐	☐
c.	Human element and human interest topics (e.g., Native Americans, herbal medicine, edible wild plants, etc.)	☐	☐	☐	☐
d.	Nature arts and crafts (e.g., watercolor instruction, drawing from nature, photography, craft workshops, etc.)	☐	☐	☐	☐
e.	Outdoor recreation (e.g., bird watching, hiking, natural history, walks, outdoor scenery, cross-country skiing, rock climbing, etc.)	☐	☐	☐	☐
f.	Agricultural history (e.g., colonial farm life, historical farm life, etc.)	☐	☐	☐	☐
g.	Land stewardship (e.g., acquisition of open space, ecological habitat management, etc.)	☐	☐	☐	☐
h.	Environmental advocacy (e.g., influencing public policy)	☐	☐	☐	☐
i.	Eco-tourism (e.g., trips to other regions where efforts are underway to protect endangered wildlife)	☐	☐	☐	☐

8. **Have you ever given a contribution to the Norman Bird Sanctuary in addition to purchasing a membership?**

   ☐ yes   ☐ no

9. **If you have given a contribution, would you consider increasing your gift?**

☐ Yes ☐ Yes, but only if properly approached by the right person.
☐ No. I feel my contribution is adequate for my means.
☐ No. Other contributions are more important to me.

10. **To which of the following kinds of organizations are you or your family a regular contributor?**

☐ Arts/culture/history   ☐ Environment/wildlife   ☐ Education
☐ Health   ☐ Human services   ☐ Religion
☐ Youth programs   ☐ Federated appeals (e.g., United Way)
☐ Public/societal benefits (e.g., civil rights, public policy groups, etc.)
☐ International affairs
☐ Other (please specify):

11. **What types of Norman Bird Sanctuary fundraising events would you attend?**

	WOULD DEFINITELY ATTEND	WOULD PROBABLY ATTEND	WOULD PROBABLY NOT ATTEND	WOULD DEFINITELY NOT ATTEND
a. Well-known environmental speaker	☐	☐	☐	☐
b. Social event	☐	☐	☐	☐
c. Recognition gathering for donors and volunteers	☐	☐	☐	☐
d. Sports event (e.g., walk, run, baseball game, etc.)	☐	☐	☐	☐
e. Family-oriented event	☐	☐	☐	☐
f. Dinner with sanctuary board members and staff	☐	☐	☐	☐

12. **Do you volunteer for the Norman Bird Sanctuary?**

☐ Yes, currently.   ☐ Yes, in the past but not currently.   ☐ No

If you do not volunteer, which of the following best describes why not?

☐ I don't have the time.   ☐ I prefer to volunteer for other causes.
☐ I've never been asked.   ☐ I feel no obligation to volunteer.

13. **How important are the following reasons why you support organizations such as the Norman Bird Sanctuary?**

	VERY IMPORTANT	IMPORTANT	OF MINOR IMPORTANCE
a. Have personal positive experience with the organization.	☐	☐	☐
b. Feel good when I donate to the organization. ...	☐	☐	☐
c. Strongly believe in the things the organization stands for and works to achieve.	☐	☐	☐
d. Organization is very effective.	☐	☐	☐
e. Organization spends contributions carefully and wisely.	☐	☐	☐
f. Organization communicated an urgent need. ...	☐	☐	☐

ABOUT YOU

14. Where do you live?

☐ Jamestown ☐ Little Compton/Tiverton ☐ Portsmouth ☐ Newport
☐ Middletown ☐ South County ☐ Nearby Massachusetts ☐ Other (please specify):

15. What is the highest level of education you have completed?

☐ high school ☐ 2-year college degree ☐ 4-year college degree ☐ graduate degree

16. What is your marital status?

☐ married ☐ divorced/separated ☐ widowed
☐ single ☐ unmarried, living with partner

17. How many children, age 13 or younger, live in your household?

☐ none ☐ one ☐ two ☐ three or more

18. What is your age?

☐ 20–29 ☐ 30–39 ☐ 40–49
☐ 50–59 ☐ 60 or older

19. In what range is your total annual household income?

☐ less than $20,000 ☐ $20,000 to $29,999 ☐ $30,000 to $39,999
☐ $40,000 to $49,999 ☐ $50,000 to $59,999 ☐ $60,000 to $69,999
☐ $70,000 to $79,999 ☐ $80,000 to $89,999 ☐ $90,000 or more

20. In what way could the Norman Bird Sanctuary better satisfy the needs of the local community?

21. Please use this space for any comments you wish to make.

22. Optional
Name, Street Address, City, State, Zip

PLEASE RETURN THIS COMPLETED SURVEY NO LATER THAN APRIL 29 TO:

THANK YOU!

Help! Calling all Thetas—What should we do?

Your opinion—here and now—will help decide the future.

Please return your completed survey by <u>April 15</u> to your Vice President of Administration or mail it directly to Paige Thompson at Central Office

1. How important is Kappa Alpha Theta to you? Circle one.

1	2	3	4	5
Extremely important	Very important	Important	Somewhat important	Not important

2. Imagine you are responsible for designing Theta programs. Your decisions provide direction for the Fraternity—such as what programs are expected of the chapters and what types of resource materials and program manuals the Fraternity should develop. What are your choices? Please evaluate each selection by placing an X in the corresponding blank

Ideas . . .	We do now. Great as is.	We do now. Needs improvement.	Don't want to do.	Don't do now but should do.
1. *The Balanced Woman* (member education program)	1._____	1._____	1._____	1._____
2. *Not for Ourselves Alone* (new member program)	2._____	2._____	2._____	2._____
3. *Talking about Alcohol . . . The Greek Consortium*	3._____	3._____	3._____	3._____
4. National Court Appointed Special Advocates for Children (CASA)	4._____	4._____	4._____	4._____
5. Career development (e.g., resume writing, interviewing, and negotiating skills)	5._____	5._____	5._____	5._____
6. Social activities (e.g., gatherings and parties, sports, arts, and cultural activities	6._____	6._____	6._____	6._____
7. Volunteerism (e.g., opportunities to serve the community)	7._____	7._____	7._____	7._____
8. Academic Support (e.g., study techniques, time management, writing workshops)	8._____	8._____	8._____	8._____
9. Other _____	9._____	9._____	9._____	9._____

Now, please select the topics you consider your top two priorities by placing the number in the blanks:

#1 priority _____   #2 priority _____

Courtesy of Kappa Alpha Theta International Fraternity for Women.

3. **Please circle what you think should be the most critical focus of a Fraternity.**

1
Group of people sharing
similar interests, promoting a
sense of belonging and self-worth.

2
Organization that provides
support and networking programs
for issues relevant to members' lives.

3
Socially relevant organization
contributing to the health and
quality of life in our society.

4. **What do you value about your Theta membership? Please number your top three, with 1 being the most important.**

Enhances my social life _____
Enhances my academic performance and career development _____
Camaraderie among women _____
The programs and activities _____
A family tradition _____
Other _____

5. **American Society is changing. More women work. Older women are returning to college. The population is becoming increasingly diverse. Each of us will face these changes more and more in our own personal, social, academic, and work lives.**

Would you find it helpful for your personal development if Kappa Alpha Theta offered programs that address issues of diversity? Please circle your opinion.

1
Great. I would love an opportunity to participate

2
No. I would not participate.

3
I do not care either way.

6. **If you had a choice, would you choose to live in the Theta facility? __ yes __ no If no, please comment below.**

__ not enough privacy   __ too many restrictions   __ prefer coed living   __ would like my own apartment
__ other _____

7. **Are you involved in other types of organizations? Please check all that apply.**

__ political   __ religious   __ academic society   __ sports team   __ theatre/arts
__ organizations serving the community   __ other, please explain _____

8. **Do you expect to continue your involvement with Kappa Alpha Theta beyond college?**

1
Absolutely. I can't imagine
my life without Theta.

2
Perhaps, if I have the time.

3
No. I can't imagine ever being
involved once I graduate.

The following information will help us learn more about our members. Thanks!

Year you will graduate: _____   Your age: _____ Your Theta chapter District: _____
Years as a Theta: _____   Do you plan to pursue a graduate degree __ yes __ no

Please return your completed survey by April 15 to your Vice President of Administration or mail it directly to
Paige Thompson at Central Office
Thanks!

IF YOU'RE A NATURE LOVER,
IT'S IMPORTANT THAT YOU FILL OUT THIS SURVEY.

You could win a free family membership to the Norman Bird Sanctuary. *And this includes free membership to the Mystic Marinelife Aquarium!*

Return the survey by April 29, and your name will be entered in a drawing to win one of five free memberships!

1. **Have you ever heard of, or are you a member/supporter of, the following organizations?**

	HEARD OF			MEMBER/ SUPPORTER		YOUR OPINION		
	FREQUENTLY	OCCASIONALLY	NEVER	YES	NO	EXCELLENT	GOOD	FAIR
a. Audubon Society	☐	☐	☐	☐	☐	☐	☐	☐
b. Coggeshall Farm Museum	☐	☐	☐	☐	☐	☐	☐	☐
c. URI Center for Environmental Education	☐	☐	☐	☐	☐	☐	☐	☐
d. Lloyd Center for the Environment	☐	☐	☐	☐	☐	☐	☐	☐
e. Mystic Marinelife Aquarium	☐	☐	☐	☐	☐	☐	☐	☐
f. Norman Bird Sanctuary	☐	☐	☐	☐	☐	☐	☐	☐
g. Rose Island Lighthouse Foundation	☐	☐	☐	☐	☐	☐	☐	☐
h. RI Fisherman & Whale Museum	☐	☐	☐	☐	☐	☐	☐	☐
i. Save The Bay	☐	☐	☐	☐	☐	☐	☐	☐
j. Roger Williams Park Zoo	☐	☐	☐	☐	☐	☐	☐	☐

2. **Have you ever visited any of the following places?**

	VISITED			YOUR OPINION		
	OFTEN	OCCASIONALLY	NEVER	EXCELLENT	GOOD	FAIR
a. Audubon Society preserves (e.g., Caratunk, Ruecker, etc.)	☐	☐	☐	☐	☐	☐
b. Coggeshall Farm Museum	☐	☐	☐	☐	☐	☐
c. Lloyd Center for the Environment	☐	☐	☐	☐	☐	☐
d. Mystic Marinelife Aquarium	☐	☐	☐	☐	☐	☐
e. Norman Bird Sanctuary	☐	☐	☐	☐	☐	☐
f. Rose Island	☐	☐	☐	☐	☐	☐
g. RI Fisherman & Whale Museum	☐	☐	☐	☐	☐	☐
h. Roger Williams Park Zoo	☐	☐	☐	☐	☐	☐

3. **Have you ever participated in any programs or activities of any of the following organizations?**

	PARTICIPATED IN PROGRAMS		YOUR OPINION		
	YES	NO	EXCELLENT	GOOD	FAIR
a. Audubon Society	☐	☐	☐	☐	☐
b. Coggeshall Farm Museum	☐	☐	☐	☐	☐
c. URI Center for Environmental Education	☐	☐	☐	☐	☐
d. Lloyd Center for the Environment	☐	☐	☐	☐	☐
e. Mystic Marinelife Aquarium	☐	☐	☐	☐	☐
f. Norman Bird Sanctuary	☐	☐	☐	☐	☐
g. Rose Island Lighthouse Foundation	☐	☐	☐	☐	☐
h. RI Fisherman & Whale Museum	☐	☐	☐	☐	☐
i. Save The Bay	☐	☐	☐	☐	☐
j. Roger Williams Park Zoo	☐	☐	☐	☐	☐

Courtesy of the Norman Bird Sanctuary.

4. **Have you visited the Norman Bird Sanctuary during the past year?**

☐ Yes, to go hiking.   ☐ Yes, to attend a program or special event.
☐ Yes, for animal and wildlife interests.
☐ Yes, for other reasons. ☐ No.

5. **How often do you visit places to hike, walk, and enjoy nature and the outdoors?**

☐ once or twice a year   ☐ 3 or more times a year   ☐ very rarely   ☐ never

6. **Do you believe that not-for-profit organizations can successfully influence public policy about the environment?**

☐ yes, definitely   ☐ yes, probably   ☐ not certain   ☐ no

7. **Do you believe that people need more education about environmental issues?**

☐ yes, definitely   ☐ yes, probably   ☐ not certain   ☐ no

8. **What do you think is the relative importance of the following environmental issues in Rhode Island?**

	SINGLE MOST IMPORTANT	SECOND MOST IMPORTANT	THIRD MOST IMPORTANT	ALSO IMPORTANT	NOT IMPORTANT
a. Waste management	☐	☐	☐	☐	☐
b. Habitat preservation	☐	☐	☐	☐	☐
c. Clean water	☐	☐	☐	☐	☐
d. Clean air	☐	☐	☐	☐	☐
e. Protection of endangered wildlife	☐	☐	☐	☐	☐
f. Open space/recreation	☐	☐	☐	☐	☐
g. Other (please specify):	☐	☐	☐	☐	☐

9. **How concerned do you think Rhode Islanders are about the environment?**

☐ very concerned   ☐ somewhat concerned   ☐ not concerned   ☐ uncertain

10. **How interested are you and your family in the following leisure time activities?**

	VERY INTERESTED	INTERESTED	NOT INTERESTED	FOR ADULTS YES NO	FOR TEENS YES NO	FOR CHILDREN YES NO	FOR FAMILIES YES NO
a. Arts/culture (e.g., theatre, museums, music, etc.)	☐	☐	☐	☐ ☐	☐ ☐	☐ ☐	☐ ☐
b. Outdoor recreation (e.g., hiking, bird watching, nature walks, cross-country skiing, etc.)	☐	☐	☐	☐ ☐	☐ ☐	☐ ☐	☐ ☐
c. History and historic preservation	☐	☐	☐	☐ ☐	☐ ☐	☐ ☐	☐ ☐
d. Exercise/fitness	☐	☐	☐	☐ ☐	☐ ☐	☐ ☐	☐ ☐
e. Travel	☐	☐	☐	☐ ☐	☐ ☐	☐ ☐	☐ ☐
f. Sports	☐	☐	☐	☐ ☐	☐ ☐	☐ ☐	☐ ☐

11. **What is your primary source of information about leisure time activities? (Please check only one.)**

☐ *Providence Journal*   ☐ *Newport Daily News*   ☐ Internet or World Wide Web
☐ Radio   ☐ Television   ☐ Other (please specify):
☐ Word-of-mouth   ☐ Posters or flyers

ABOUT YOU

12. Where do you live?

☐ Jamestown   ☐ Little Compton/Tiverton   ☐ Portsmouth   ☐ Newport
☐ Middletown   ☐ South County   ☐ Nearby Massachusetts   ☐ Other (please specify):

13. What is your marital status?

☐ married   ☐ divorced/separated   ☐ widowed
☐ single   ☐ unmarried, living with partner

14. How many children, age 13 or younger, live in your household?

☐ none   ☐ one   ☐ two   ☐ three or more

15. What is your age?

☐ 20–29   ☐ 30–39   ☐ 40–49
☐ 50–59   ☐ 60 or older

16. In what way could the Norman Bird Sanctuary better satisfy the needs of the local community?

17. Please use this space for any comments you wish to make.

18. (Optional)—But fill this out if you want a chance to win your free membership!
Name, Street Address, City, State, Zip

Due no later than April 29.
If you received this survey in the mail: Please complete and
return in the enclosed envelope to S.P. Joyaux.

If you picked up the survey at a local library or other site:
Please complete and return in the collection box.
Thank you!

Your opinion is crucial!

Please tell us what you think about governance at our organization.

Please return your completed survey no later than _____.
Mail to _____ or fax to _____.

Thank you for your participation

This survey asks you to assess the performance of our organization against a set of standards for all areas of operation. These standards have been devised by Joyaux Associates, based on the firm's consulting experience and commonly held perspectives within the not-for-profit sector.

First: How many years have you served on the board? _____

Section I: Your role as a board member

1. When you were asked to serve as a Board member, to what extent were the following presented to you?

	TO A VERY GREAT EXTENT	TO A GREAT EXTENT	TO A LITTLE EXTENT	TO A VERY LITTLE EXTENT	NO OPINION
a. Expectations of the board and you as a board member.	☐	☐	☐	☐	☐
b. Overview of the organization and its challenges.	☐	☐	☐	☐	☐
c. Specific skill(s) and expertise you are expected to use on behalf of the organization.	☐	☐	☐	☐	☐

2. How satisfied are you with the following?

	TO A VERY GREAT EXTENT	TO A GREAT EXTENT	TO A LITTLE EXTENT	TO A VERY LITTLE EXTENT	NO OPINION
a. Level of information, support, and guidance to do your job as a board and board member.	☐	☐	☐	☐	☐
b. Ability of the organization to use your skills and expertise.	☐	☐	☐	☐	☐
c. Ability of the organizaton to engage your interest.	☐	☐	☐	☐	☐

3. What are the three most important things that the board of the organization does?

4. What are the three most important things you do as a board member of the organization?

5. How would you rate the board's overall performance on a scale of 1–5, with 5 being high? Please circle one only.

1 2 3 4 5

6. What are your top three areas of concern regarding board effectiveness?

Section II: Assessing the board of directors

Please respond by checking in the appropriate column. Please answer every question. Thank you.

	YES	YES, BUT NEEDS IMPROVEMENT	NO	DON'T KNOW

1. Composition of the board of directors

    a. The recruitment process considers issues of diversity, e.g., gender, ethnicity, age, skills, etc. when identifying board member candidates. .. ☐ ☐ ☐ ☐
    b. The board is representative of the organization's constituencies. ...... ☐ ☐ ☐ ☐
    c. Bylaws limit tenure and ensure rotation of board members .... ☐ ☐ ☐ ☐
    d. The recruitment process ensures that the board is comprised of experienced individuals to guarantee continuity and new members to encourage new ideas. .... ☐ ☐ ☐ ☐

2. Selection, recruitment, and evaluation of board members

    a. Written recruitment policy and procedures are used and reviewed by the board regularly. .... ☐ ☐ ☐ ☐
    b. The recruitment policy and procedures include:
        • assessment of boardroom expertise and identification of gaps .... ☐ ☐ ☐ ☐
        • process to screen candidates .... ☐ ☐ ☐ ☐
        • performance assessment of incumbents .... ☐ ☐ ☐ ☐
    c. Board member qualifications and performance expectations are clearly articulated, orally and in writing, prior to nomination and regularly thereafter. .... ☐ ☐ ☐ ☐
    d. Candidates are personally interviewed, and their performance commitment is secured before nomination to the board. .... ☐ ☐ ☐ ☐
    e. In addition to general expectations of board membership, each candidate under consideration is asked to use a specific skill/expertise on behalf of the organization. .... ☐ ☐ ☐ ☐
    f. Throughout the year, the recruitment process identifies and cultivates candidates for consideration. .... ☐ ☐ ☐ ☐
    g. The recruitment process solicits candidate suggestions from staff, committees, and board members. .... ☐ ☐ ☐ ☐
    h. The chief executive officer of the organization participates in the board member recruitment process. .... ☐ ☐ ☐ ☐
    i. Performance evaluation of board members distinguishes between those who should be invited to continue service and those who should be thanked and released. .... ☐ ☐ ☐ ☐
    j. There is a process to discuss with board members whether or not it is desirable for them to remain on the board. .... ☐ ☐ ☐ ☐

3. Orientation and development of the board

    a. An annual orientation is conducted for the entire board of directors. .... ☐ ☐ ☐ ☐
    b. Board orientation includes discussion of such items as roles and responsibilities of staff and board, overview of mission and services, and committee operations. .... ☐ ☐ ☐ ☐
    c. Supporting information is provided at the orientation, including such items as board and committee job descriptions, bylaws, financial information, etc. .... ☐ ☐ ☐ ☐
    d. Education and training opportunities are provided to build board member skills and knowledge. .... ☐ ☐ ☐ ☐

4. Board monitoring of organizational health

a. The board has a vision for the organization's future—both program and infrastructure—articulated as a strategic, long-range plan. The plan includes the following: ☐ ☐ ☐ ☐
   - goals and action steps to achieve that vision ☐ ☐ ☐ ☐
   - financial projections ☐ ☐ ☐ ☐
   - process to monitor progress and evaluate performance ☐ ☐ ☐ ☐

b. The vision and mission are understood by all board members. ☐ ☐ ☐ ☐

c. The process to develop vision and plan involves key constituencies. ☐ ☐ ☐ ☐

d. The board spends an appropriate amount of time discussing the long-range future of the organization. ☐ ☐ ☐ ☐

e. The board proposes changes in organizational direction. ☐ ☐ ☐ ☐

f. The board is prepared to deal with unforeseen organizational crises. ☐ ☐ ☐ ☐

g. The board has appropriate structures and processes to help evaluate organizational health, including program, direction, and strategies. ☐ ☐ ☐ ☐

h. The board effectively inquires into major performance deficiencies. ☐ ☐ ☐ ☐

i. There is a healthy balance of power between board and the CEO. ☐ ☐ ☐ ☐

j. The board understands its role and authority as a collective and exercises due diligence—legal and moral—to ensure the organization's health. ☐ ☐ ☐ ☐

k. The board ensures fiscal integrity by:
   - thoroughly examining all budgets before approval; ☐ ☐ ☐ ☐
   - comparing performance with budget and addressing trends and implications; ☐ ☐ ☐ ☐
   - discussing annual audit and management letter. ☐ ☐ ☐ ☐

l. Board ensures that there is:
   - consistency between priorities and financial allocation ☐ ☐ ☐ ☐
   - sufficient resources for the future. ☐ ☐ ☐ ☐
   - sustainability for the organization. ☐ ☐ ☐ ☐

5. Board operations

a. The board's group process fosters candor, rich discussion, and participation by everyone. ☐ ☐ ☐ ☐

b. The board encourages differences of opinion, and board members are encouraged to ask tough questions. ☐ ☐ ☐ ☐

c. There are policies and procedures that address:
   - general functions and responsibilities of the board of directors ☐ ☐ ☐ ☐
   - performance expectations of the individual as a board member ☐ ☐ ☐ ☐
   - role and responsibilities of officers ☐ ☐ ☐ ☐
   - role and responsibilities of committees ☐ ☐ ☐ ☐
   - conflict of interest ☐ ☐ ☐ ☐
   - risk management ☐ ☐ ☐ ☐

d. The board spends its meeting time engaged in substantive discussion and decision making. ☐ ☐ ☐ ☐

e. Board meetings are well organized, focusing on priority issues and handling routine matters quickly. ☐ ☐ ☐ ☐

f. Board meetings occur on a regular schedule, frequently enough to ensure continuity and strategic discussion. ☐ ☐ ☐ ☐

g. Communication regarding board business is appropriately frequent, timely, informative, and useful. ☐ ☐ ☐ ☐

	YES	YES, BUT NEEDS IMPROVEMENT	NO	DON'T KNOW
h. Board receives critical in-depth information for advance review in order to come to meetings prepared to discuss critical issues	☐	☐	☐	☐
i. Concise, accurate minutes are distributed in a timely fashion after each board meeting.	☐	☐	☐	☐
j. Staff appropriately direct and enable board members and committees, clearly differentiating between governance and management.	☐	☐	☐	☐
k. Board distinguishes between management and governance, and discusses and resolves any such conflicts.	☐	☐	☐	☐
l. The board understands that the chief executive serves as official spokesperson for the organization.	☐	☐	☐	☐
m. The board has in place appropriate processes to assess the CEO and does so on a regular basis.	☐	☐	☐	☐
n. The board has sufficient information for CEO evaluation.	☐	☐	☐	☐
o. The board has an appropriate level of involvement in CEO succession.	☐	☐	☐	☐

6. Committee or task force operations

	YES	YES, BUT NEEDS IMPROVEMENT	NO	DON'T KNOW
a. The board has active committees/teams/task forces through which work is channeled.	☐	☐	☐	☐
b. Responsibilities of these small groups are clearly articulated.	☐	☐	☐	☐
c. These small groups develop an annual work plan, based on the strategic plan, with specific assignments and timetables.	☐	☐	☐	☐
d. The small groups include board members and non-Board bembers.	☐	☐	☐	☐
e. These groups engage the board in strategic dialogue, critical thinking, and decision making.	☐	☐	☐	☐
f. Group chairs provide appropriate leadership by:				
• facilitating active participation from all participants.	☐	☐	☐	☐
• monitoring activity through regular contact with participants.	☐	☐	☐	☐
g. Board's presiding officer (chief volunteer) provides appropriate leadership to these small groups by:				
• assigning responsibilities in consultation with the chief executive and board	☐	☐	☐	☐
• monitoring activity through regular contact with group leaders.	☐	☐	☐	☐

7. Evaluation of the board

	YES	YES, BUT NEEDS IMPROVEMENT	NO	DON'T KNOW
a. The board regularly evaluates its own effectiveness.	☐	☐	☐	☐
b. Relationships between board, staff, and committees are clearly articulated and evaluated regularly.	☐	☐	☐	☐
c. There is strong attendance at board meetings.	☐	☐	☐	☐
d. Board members participate in board dialogue by asking tough questions and focusing on strategic issues.	☐	☐	☐	☐
e. Board members complete assigned tasks in a timely, effective way.	☐	☐	☐	☐
f. The presiding officer of the board discusses attendance and performance with board members who are often absent or inactive.	☐	☐	☐	☐
g. Board members are aware of activities and trends relevant to the organization and use this information to inform board deliberations.	☐	☐	☐	☐
h. New leadership regularly emerges from the board and its work groups.	☐	☐	☐	☐
i. The board recognizes when change is necessary and stimulates it.	☐	☐	☐	☐
j. Leadership succession is ensured.	☐	☐	☐	☐

k. The board and its members understand that they are the "owners" of the organization and act and speak accordingly. . . . . ☐ ☐ ☐ ☐

8. Fund development
    a. The organization cultivates relationships well in order to develop future donors, board members, and other volunteers. . . . . ☐ ☐ ☐ ☐
    b. The board understands the organization's fund development strategy. . . ☐ ☐ ☐ ☐
    c. The organization has a clear policy on the individual board member's responsibility in cultivating and soliciting gifts, and non-adherence to this policy is addressed. . . . . ☐ ☐ ☐ ☐
    d. Each board member understands his/her role in:
        • identifying and cultivating donors and prospective donors; . . . . ☐ ☐ ☐ ☐
        • giving an annual financial gift to the best of personal ability; . . . . ☐ ☐ ☐ ☐
        • helping to raise funds on behalf of the organization through diverse means. . . . . ☐ ☐ ☐ ☐
    e. A board committee provides strategic leadership in fund development. . ☐ ☐ ☐ ☐
    f. The board ensures that the organization fulfills its accountability and reporting requirements to regulators and donors. . . . . ☐ ☐ ☐ ☐
    g. The board evaluates fund development by examining fundraising productivity and return on investment and discussing strategic issues. . . ☐ ☐ ☐ ☐

Name (optional) _____

Please return your completed survey to _____

no later than _____, so that your opinions can be included in the summary.

Thank you.

Appendix 3–C

New Century Plan: YMCA of Greater Providence

EXECUTIVE SUMMARY

Reach high, for stars lie hidden in your soul. Dream deep, for every dream precedes the goal.

Pamela Vaull Starr

In 1994, this YMCA's board of directors issued a clarion call for creative, innovative, and responsive change to our organization.

The strategic plan summarized here is a bold and comprehensive answer to this call for change. It is an agenda for adaptation and growth we choose to call The New Century Plan.

As with any good plan, ours begins with a vision of where we want to go as an organization.

Our vision is clear and unwavering—we seek to make this YMCA both a preeminent family resource organization and an effective catalyst for community improvement.

We will pursue and achieve this vision by reinventing our organization. We will become open, accessible, progressive, responsible, and dynamic. And we will integrate with the community around us, guided by our values and inspired by imagination and innovation.

As we pursue our New Century Vision, we will strive to promote stronger families and healthier people, foster meaningful community development, and achieve rigorous standards for organizational quality.

Our Family Focus goal will lead us to development of model active family centers and the creation of a seamless continuum of services to families and the people who belong to them. These services include expanded, high-quality child care, new initiatives for teens, integrated and expanded camping programs, and new health/fitness and aquatic programs.

Our Working With Others goal imagines a future YMCA without walls. We will develop strategic alliances and collaborations; work with underserved and at-risk families and youth; eliminate barriers to participation; become more diverse and culturally sensitive; develop prototype urban resource centers; and learn how to deliver programs in partnership with others.

Our Quality Improvement goal builds on the strength of our internal organization. We will become a learning organization, working as a network of teams and strengthening the skills and competencies of all.

We will launch a major capital and fund development effort to improve and upgrade our facilities and provide resources to fund our commitment to those in need. Our infrastructure will be sustained through a continuous process of planning, implementation, and evaluation.

Our vision must balance its imagination and aspirations with a commitment to be measurable in its results.

In the end, therefore, what do we hope will be said about us as a New Century organization? We expect that those so taking our measure will say that we . . .

Are recognized for developing programs that help strengthen families

Make a significant difference in the lives of young people through building character and providing wholesome recreation

Improve the quality of life of everyone who participates by focusing on developing healthy lifestyles

Enjoy the commitment of volunteers who have the capacity to make a difference in the lives of others

---

Courtesy of YMCA of Greater Providence.

*Have a highly competent and diverse staff who
think and act as a team
Are a prototype of a dynamic new century organization
Participate with other organizations to meet
the social needs of the community*

Join with us now in our
shared journey to these bold
destinations.
For the call has been heard,
our vision is clear,
and our direction is set.
The time to begin is now.

John Bowers   Susan Rittscher
Chairman/New Century Planning   President/CEO

NEW CENTURY PLANNING PROCESS

Overview and Methodology

In September 1994, the Metropolitan Board of the
Greater Providence YMCA charged the president to
develop a strategic plan for the association.

Prior to this time, the YMCA had been operating
under a series of annual objectives. While this had
worked well in the past, the Board determined that the
time had come to develop a new vision for the Association . . . one that was shared by each and all of its
constituencies and one that would propel it into the next
century.

Because a comprehensive, strategically-focused planning process for the Association had never been undertaken, an appropriate foundation for the effort had to
be prepared. Accordingly, a "plan to develop the plan,"
one that would be driven by an inclusive process, the
first expression of our commitment to the New Century
effort. Joyaux Associates was hired to assist in shaping
such a process and to be a resource in developing the
plan.

To guide the project, a flow chart with calendar, activities, and assignments was developed. Two committees
were established to shape and implement the process: A
planning team—designed to be a steering committee of
the effort—was established, while the planning council—
comprised of diverse representation from the Branches—
was established to review components of the plan for
action by the board.

The process began with a comprehensive research and
data-gathering phase. Between November of 1994 and
April of 1995, no stone was left unturned as our Association set out to evaluate itself and the environment in
which it exists today. Areas of consideration included:

*Strength, Weakness, Opportunity, and Threat
Analysis,
State of the YMCA peer review,
Review and renewal evaluation,
Key leader interviews,
Focus groups,
Trend analysis,
Community plan analysis,
External market research by the Winfield Group,
Values survey.*

The vast array of data, perspective, opinion, and evaluation collected in this process was then synthesized
during the second phase of the planning effort. A comprehensive data packet—which summarized and interpreted the assessment phase—was prepared for use at an
Association Vision Retreat in June.

Through an intense, open, and honest group process,
staff and volunteers shared the labor of creating a new
vision for our future. The summary of what we have
come to call the "Fleet Retreat" and subsequently developed "cultural shifts" document became cornerstones
of the strategic plan. This occurred between June 1995
and August 1995.

The third phase of this comprehensive undertaking
consisted of drafting corporate vision, mission, goals,
benchmarks for evaluation, and implications for our delivery system. Here, ad-hoc task forces worked diligently
to identify strategic directions and initiatives suggested
by the first two phases of the planning effort. These tasks
were undertaken in August 1995–November 1995.

From this point, we head—with courage and conviction—toward implementation of the plan. It will be
launched with the development of annual plans and
budget for 1996. Projections for subsequent years will
also be made. This will allow for more precise delineation of quantitative measures for evaluation through the
year 2000.

The planning has been enriched beyond measure by
the tireless and selfless efforts of over 300 volunteers
and staff, as well as 150 community leaders. Through
mutual respect, honesty, and patience, what began as the
untried efforts of a largely unconnected group became
a powerful and cohesive agent for change and renewal
within our Association.

VALUES STATEMENT

*We have five core values. Everything we do
will be guided by the values we share. We practice these values through our programs and
actions.*

Respect

All people have worth and value.
As individuals and an organization, we:

- Believe that people are basically good, want to do their best, and can learn, change, and grow;
- Reach out and embrace the full diversity of individuals and families, regardless of ability, age, income, faith, lifestyle, physical challenge, race, or ethnicity; and,

- Create opportunities for people to be meaningfully involved through challenging responsibilities and individual and team participation.

Caring

We are sensitive and nurturing.
As individuals and an organization, we:

- Guard the safety and well-being of youth and adults;

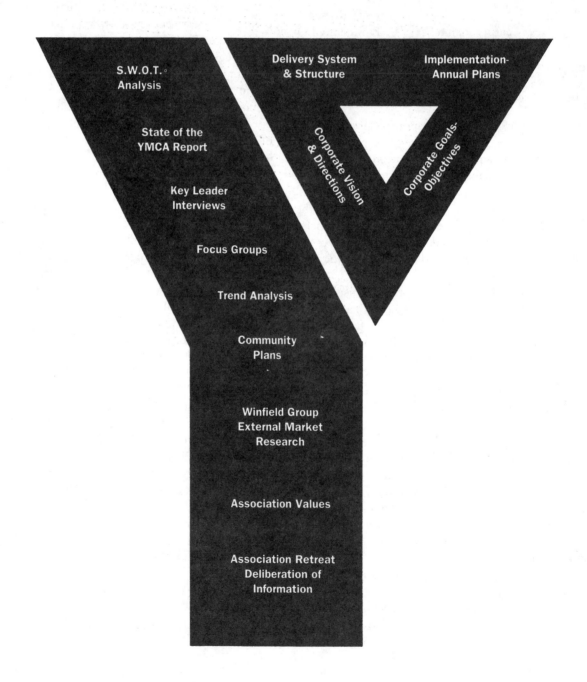

- Promote self-fulfillment and hope in an atmosphere of optimism, fun, and tolerance;
- Resolve conflict with honesty, respect, and compassion; and
- Encourage self-sufficiency.

Honesty

We trust and earn the trust of others.
As individuals and an organization, we:

- Behave with integrity, sincerity, and consistency;
- Keep the lines of communication open;
- Assess ourselves; and
- Seek consensus.

Responsibility

We use our resources to serve the diverse community.
As individuals and an organization, we:

- Ask those we serve to help define needs, design responsive programs, evaluate quality, and support activities;
- Collaborate with others for the common good; and
- Operate in a fiscally sound manner.

Change

We are future oriented and inspired by change.
As individuals and an organization, we:

- Honor our traditions and explore new opportunities;
- Strive for excellence; and
- Make a difference by generating ideas, contributing knowledge, and offering solutions.

MISSION STATEMENT

To put Christian principles into practice through programs that build healthy spirit, mind, and body for all.

NEW CENTURY VISION STATEMENT

*As the YMCA of Greater Providence,
we will make significant and positive contributions
to the quality of life in our service area.
We will do so by becoming an open, progressive and
dynamic organization—one that unites our various
branches and reaches out to the community.
We will be accessible and open as we welcome all who
share our values.*

*We will become our community's premier family resource organization.
We will become fully integrated with the community around us, seeking innovative collaboration with others to promote healthier people, stronger families, and social progress.*

NEW CENTURY GOAL ONE: FAMILY FOCUS

Strategy

Through imagination and innovation, develop programs and facilities that answer the learning, living, spiritual, and recreation needs of today's family or individual family members.

Benchmarks

1. Developing models for active family centers that are accessible, affordable, and convenient, as well as consistent with our mission.
2. Ensuring that each of our services and programs has measurable criteria for improvement of individual health and well-being.
3. Expanding our delivery of child care services through innovative partnerships with schools, businesses, communities, and upgrading our quality through accreditation.
4. Enhancing the personal development of teens through programs that emphasize life skills, leadership, health and fitness, personal responsibility, and interest in and concern for technology, culture, and the environment.
5. Integrating our camping programs into year-round, family-centered programs that are adventure-based and environmentally sensitive.
6. Energizing and expanding our programs through innovative partnerships with allied providers of human services.
7. Building on our core programs through continuous program development in response to community needs and interests.
8. Developing rigorous, measurable quality standards for each endeavor in pursuit of our overall membership growth and retention goals.

NEW CENTURY GOAL TWO: WORKING WITH OTHERS

Strategy

With vision and determination, establish working relationships with other community organizations that share our values, to identify and answer unmet needs in our urban and suburban service areas.

Benchmarks

1. Forging strategic alliances with the education, religious, health, social service, government, and business sectors of our communities.
2. Expanding the service capability we bring to these partnerships through innovative collaboration with other YMCA organizations on a regional, national, and international basis.
3. Improving our service delivery through development of extension service sites.
4. Working with other organizations on behalf of families and children at risk from poverty, illiteracy, inadequate housing, unemployment, violence, and substance abuse.
5. Leading a communitywide effort in multicultural development through education programs and coalition building.
6. Eliminating barriers to membership and/or participation in all our programs through financial assistance, development of culturally relevant programs, and other initiatives.
7. Recruiting partners in Providence so that our InTown facility, Tower, and other facilities may become multifaceted resource centers for urban communities.

NEW CENTURY GOAL THREE: QUALITY IMPROVEMENT

Strategy

With foresight and stewardship, strengthen the governance, management, and financial resources necessary to remain a quality, mission-driven, easy-to-use, and accessible organization.

Benchmarks

1. Promoting efficiency, effectiveness, and synergy of our volunteer and staff efforts through application of leadership teamwork, cross-functional task forces, and the development of a network system.
2. Enhancing well-being and quality of life for our staff and volunteers by evolving as a learning organization that positions our staff for the future by providing new competencies through training and development.

3. Strengthening our fund development efforts to support facility, program, financial assistance, and community outreach efforts.
4. Improving our financial management systems to support balanced operating results, strong reserves, and modest debt.
5. Creating a fully integrated management information system using cutting-edge computer technology to provide quantitative data for measurement.
6. Developing a comprehensive and fully integrated risk management and regulatory compliance program.
7. Creating a master facility plan to support all program and service goals.
8. Sustaining organizational planning based on strategic vision, community integration, and quality outcome measurement.

DIRECTIONS

Membership

The Greater Providence YMCA has achieved rapid growth in membership in recent years, peaking over the last two years to our current high of 16,587 membership units.

Between 1991 and 1995, the average annual growth rate was 8.7 percent, with InTown and South County branches both growing by more than 20 percent. Through the use of a linear statistical projection, 9.2 percent growth can be estimated from 1995–2000, based upon this past experience. Our actual targets will be projected each year during our annual planning process.

The branches likely to experience the greatest growth in population demand during the next ten years are South County and Kent County. The overall population is projected to be stable, with less than 2 percent growth expected in Rhode Island.

It appears that our current market penetration, based on the number of members, is almost 6 percent of the communities we serve. Our current retention rate is 57.5 percent, with slight increases shown in recent years. The national average reflects a 3 percent market penetration and 50 percent retention rate. Our YMCA will continue to exceed the average.

The results of the Winfield research have indicated additional potential market demand in Kent County, South County, Barrington, and Providence that could produce up to 2,900 units of new net growth.

Cranston and Newman branches are not expected to experience new net growth. These branches will focus on retention and niche marketing strategies to continue to remain strong into the New Century.

Developing our membership base—and enhancing it—over the next five years will be contingent upon three key factors.

The first is a major facility development effort. All of the branches need to be upgraded to meet the demands of today's markets. Improved cardiovascular/strength training and aerobic centers, warm-water pools, new walking/running, and child watch areas are needed in many of our branches.

The second factor is an improved retention rate. The overall goal will be to improve membership satisfaction, increasing the retention rate to 62.5 percent across the Association. Kent County, Newman, and Cranston will be required to realize higher rates, due to flat growth projections. This will be achieved through the use of proven retention strategies, including member recognition and incentive programs; membership tracking/feedback programs; fitness testing; and provisions for clean, safe, and well-maintained equipment.

The final factor is the development of discrete strategies to promote both vertical and horizontal growth in market share. These strategies will include extension programs and collaboration with other providers, increased marketing efforts, new health/fitness programs, and alliances with health care providers.

It is our conviction that the YMCA has the potential to realize new market growth, whether through further penetration of existing market segments or through development of new niche markets.

Program

The YMCA has the potential to realize new net growth in program participation. The Winfield market research has identified new demands for program development and growth in all of our core program areas.

Our program emphasis will be on youth, teen, and health/fitness programs.

The values and character development initiative will be interwoven into all of our activities to provide us with unique and compelling points-of-differentiation, when compared with competitors.

Child care is projected to grow, but only if our product is modified to meet changing market conditions. We will improve quality and secure accreditation, while developing new responses to a decreasing preschool population and an increasing home-based work force. New growth is attainable if a concept of service is developed—specifically, fun clubs, middle school programs, enhanced and computer-assisted tutorial care, and preschool/after-school programs.

Growth is expected in youth and teen recreation programs, despite the fact that most of them depend on alternative funding sources such as grants and sponsorships. Market research has indicated a demand for teen nights, computer-assisted programs, sports leagues, karate and self-defense, fitness centers, and gymnastics.

Limited growth and/or reduction in sports and recreation is anticipated as the YMCA focuses on families. Recreational space will be at a premium within our facilities, and we will have to focus on development of new extension facilities as a strategy to address this challenge. New enhancements and development are projected for self-defense/karate, volleyball, basketball, dance programs for adults, and fellowship and social programs for families, such as fun runs and holiday events.

Aquatics will grow when we diversify our offerings, expand facilities to include warm-water pools, and develop expanded offerings in the areas of rehabilitation, water safety lessons, and exercise classes. An increased staff certification effort will be needed to improve the quality and sustain growth.

A high level of demand is indicated in health and fitness programs. Growth will be determined by new facility enhancements and new program development.

Greatest growth will be realized by tapping into the "yet-to-be-fit" audience, estimated to be 70 percent of the population. Staff will be developed to implement new toning/stretching classes; 30-minute circuit training; personalized fitness and beginners programs; step, bench and low-impact aerobics; and running/walking programs, as well as nutrition, diet, and weight-management programs.

The summer resident camping program at Camp Fuller will grow with the addition of new specialty programs in nature and environment with animals: horseback riding, water sports, arts and crafts, outdoor adventure, and camping skills.

High demand also exists for weekend camps for family and friends to be implemented for 30–35 weekends per year and trip programs. Day camps will continue to grow with emphasis on specialty areas, as noted above, and sports.

Market demand does not necessitate the further development of Shepard or Massasoit into more comprehensive program centers.

Community and Teen Development

A major emphasis in the next five years will be to develop programs to meet the needs of the younger, underserved, and at-risk population.

Program development will focus on direct intervention programs and partner with others for intervention programs, particularly in economically disadvantaged areas. The growth potential in this area is unprecedented, and the challenge to our community has never been greater.

The growth of this area will be dependent on the development of funding resources, a network system to support this, and a clear understanding of and commitment to collaboration.

Existing social services in Rhode Island may be reduced in coming years and may impact the YMCA's program development in this area. The stable foundation we have established, coupled with progressive planning, will position us for the expected consolidation of the social services provider segment. We will be attractive to those interested in mergers and alliances of programs and agencies that will surely characterize this consolidation.

We will focus our efforts on increasing the number of staff members who possess demonstrated youth and community development skills. Initiatives will include family and youth development, organized teen group programs, referral, direct intervention services, and provision of safety net services for youth and teens.

Our adult services will also expand, leveraging the success of the Tower to position our Association as a model for urban resource centers that provides resident, neighborhood development, and support services.

Human Resources

The achievement of our New Century vision will require significant and innovative changes in how we allocate, organize, and motivate our human resources.

Our new vision for human resource development will be shaped by four key strategic directions, as follows:

1. We will create a learning organization.
2. We will develop a network system.
3. We will prepare our staff for the future.
4. We will enhance the board and volunteer structure.

Creating a Learning Organization

The YMCA will adopt a learning organization model to prepare the organization for the ever-changing climate of the future.

A learning organization is committed to think in new ways, then to act based on the new knowledge. It is always changing, evolving, and learning, and is based on the following five disciplines:

Shared Vision. Shared vision is important in a learning organization because it builds a sense of commitment by developing shared images of the future of the organization. It is reinforced by the agreed-upon principles and guiding practices by which the organization hopes to get there.

Systems Thinking. Systems thinking involves understanding the forces and interrelationships that shape the behavior of systems within the organization. This allows staff and volunteers to see how to change systems more effectively and integrate them with the bigger picture.

Mental Models. Mental Models mean the organization needs to continually reflect on, clarify, and improve on how it sees the world, and recognize how those perceptions shape our actions and decisions.

Team Learning. Team learning requires the organization to change people's communication and thinking skills so that the efforts of groups far exceed the potential of individual efforts.

Personal Mastery. Personal mastery means "learning to expand capacity to create results that we most desire and creating an organizational environment that encourages all of its members to develop themselves toward the goals and purposes they choose."

A New Creative Network System

Becoming a learning organization requires bringing groups of people and networks together to work on different projects and functions.

By changing to a new network system, the YMCA of Greater Providence will be more effective in achieving our vision and long-range goals.

Networks—in this context—are groups of branches, staff, and volunteers organized around either program delivery or support areas. The YMCA's new network system consists of two different types of networks: Program Networks and Support Networks.

Program Networks. The YMCA of Greater Providence has eight core program areas: aquatics, health/fitness, recreation, membership, community development, teens/older youth, camping, and child care.

The YMCA will deliver these programs through the branches, program centers, and extensions under a new network-oriented delivery system. These networks, described below, will work across the Association to produce synergy and efficiency.

The Active Family Center or Bay Network will focus on providing leadership in premier family and membership services at our branches, including family service, child care, membership retention, and growth of health/fitness, recreation, and aquatics.

The Urban Redevelopment or Central Network will be a catalyst for community building by leading the Association toward creative collaborations with other providers and by managing programs for our teen and older youth and community development activities.

The Program Development Network will provide leadership for imaginative and customer-responsive program development within the Association. This Network will work with the other two Networks leading the Associationwide, integrated extension programs and adventure camping programs. This Network will also develop new program centers, extensions, and alliances with other organizations and will develop specialized technical skills in our staff and volunteers.

Support or Infrastructure Networks

A comprehensive infrastructure is needed to support the delivery of our programs. Our Network system for support has two different networks. These networks would also work laterally across the organization.

Finance Network will provide leadership for the key elements for institutional advancement and development. This includes areas such as management information systems, financial management, legal compliance, property and risk management, and human resources.

Financial Development Network will be responsible for constituency development, annual fundraising, capital and endowment development, special events, and communications.

Utilizing Teams and Decision Making

The key to our success is the increased use of teams, as opposed to individual efforts.

Three types of teams (Focus, Network, and Governance Teams) will each play vital roles developing, monitoring, and executing key areas within the organization. Teams will take on major functions for decision making within the organization. Each team will have a team leader or facilitator and will be assisted by a staff member in the role of coach. All staff will continue to be supervised by their supervisor, but their performance evaluations will be partially based on their team's overall performance. Volunteers utilize the same procedures in the governance of the association.

Focus Teams will consist of a group of employees who share responsibility for a specific part of the organization.

Governance Teams will consist of only board members and other community people and will focus on areas such as Finance, Fund Development, and Planning. These teams report directly to and carry out the governance function of the Board of Directors.

Network Teams will consist of volunteers, staff, and community. These teams will focus on specific purposes or tasks related to New Century Initiatives, such as collaborations/strategic alliances, human resource development, and diversity.

Positioning Our Staff for the Future

A Senior Management team for the Association will be developed to staff Finance, Operations, Program Development, and Financial Development.

Conceptually, the Vice President—Operations is responsible for the vertical or traditional supervision of the branches while the other three Vice Presidents are responsible for the cross-functional or horizontal coordination across branches.

The four Vice Presidents will strengthen pursuit and achievement of the Association's new vision and strategic plan. This will better position the YMCA by providing the President with sufficient staff support to meet her responsibilities more effectively and by promoting the preparation for a major capital effort.

The President will focus on strategic planning, financial development, relationship building, board development, collaborations, visioning, and overall leadership in the staff structure.

The Vice President—Network Operations will have the line, or supervisory authority for branch Executive Directors. A major focus of his or her responsibilities would be on urban branch development while still supervising the suburban branches. The Bay and Central Networks would fall under his or her responsibilities. This person would be in charge of program supervision, facility management, membership retention and growth, and risk management. He or she would have the key role in maintaining strong branch operations and facilities during a time of change and growth.

The Vice President—Network Program Development will be responsible across the Association for working with branches on program development for the Association. He or she would coordinate the program teams, extension programming, new markets and program sites, and collaborations. YMCA Camp Fuller would be expanded into a much broader Camping Services branch responsible for coordinating day camp, trip camping, and outdoor education programming for the Association. The Vice President will have the key role in facilitating the Association's change toward a learning organization and the use of self-directed teams.

The New Century Network Structure

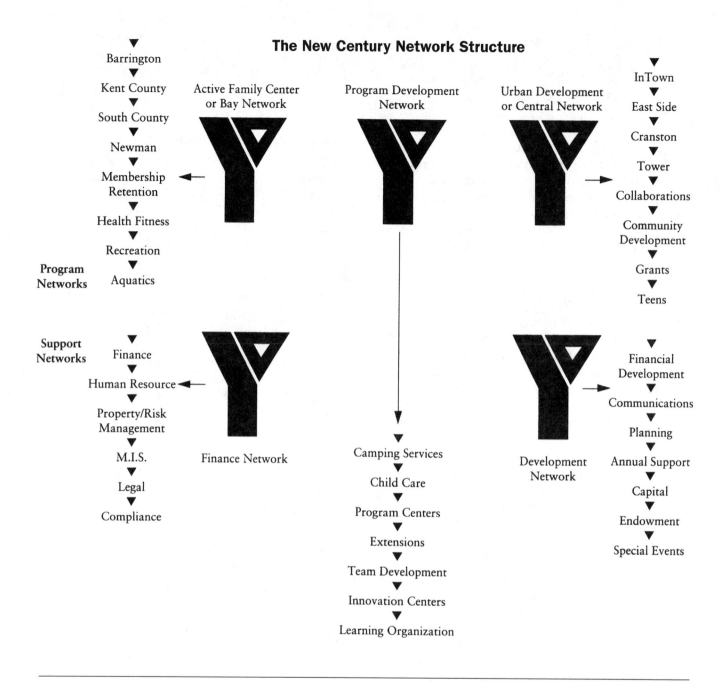

Program Networks

▼ Barrington
▼ Kent County
▼ South County
Newman
▼ Membership Retention
▼ Health Fitness
Recreation
▼ Aquatics

Active Family Center or Bay Network

Program Development Network

Urban Development or Central Network

▼ InTown
East Side
▼ Cranston
▼ Tower
▼ Collaborations
▼ Community Development
▼ Grants
▼ Teens

Support Networks

▼ Finance
▼ Human Resource
▼ Property/Risk Management
▼ M.I.S.
▼ Legal
▼ Compliance

Finance Network

Camping Services
▼ Child Care
▼ Program Centers
▼ Extensions
▼ Team Development
▼ Innovation Centers
▼ Learning Organization

Development Network

Financial Development
▼ Communications
▼ Planning
▼ Annual Support
▼ Capital
▼ Endowment
Special Events

He or she would coordinate training focused on team building, group work, coaching, and organization development.

The **Vice President—Network Financial Development** is a critical position, not just for coordinating the YMCA's ongoing Annual Support and other fundraising efforts, but for beginning to lay the groundwork for future capital and endowment campaigns. He or she would also be responsible for communications and special events and would work across the organization with staff and teams. Critical to this position is developing and maintaining key relationships for the organization.

The **Vice President—Network Finance** provides support to the branch Executive Directors and their staff in the areas of finances, human resources, MIS, property, and risk management through support service and by working with inter-association teams. This position is key in managing and ensuring that all legal, regulatory, and policy considerations are met.

The **Executive Directors** will continue to manage their YMCAs but will assume more involvement in managing and coaching program and network teams. The Executive Directors will increasingly spend more time in the areas of community relations and collaborations, program extensions, financial development, volunteer development, and preparing for future capital efforts.

The **Program Directors** and support staff will assume greater responsibilities in the areas of program development, community collaborations, and extension work. The Association will train all staff in program development and how to respond to both community needs and members' needs, as well as new skills in working in teams.

The Association's commitment and renewed focus on addressing urban issues would be best reflected by a greater emphasis by the Vice President—Operations on supporting and supervising the development of urban branches. The Vice President—Operations could bring other branches together to support the urban work. A significant part of the other Vice Presidents, especially Program Development and Financial Development, will also focus on and support the urban initiatives.

The YMCA of Greater Providence recognizes the need for developing and fostering greater diversity within the staff of the organization. Recognizing, welcoming, and utilizing the variety of skills and experiences that many different people have to offer can only strengthen the Association.

Specific policies and plans aimed at achieving more cultural and personal diversity will be developed.

The Association will need to develop a new performance appraisal and compensation system that supports the use of networks and teams and the movement toward

Proposed Staff Organization Structure

New Volunteer Structure

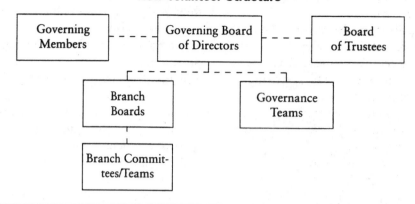

a learning organization. Accountability will shift from individual efforts to group or team efforts. The Association will determine key result areas and benchmarks and develop evaluation processes that are more progressive.

Enhancing the Board and Volunteer Structure

The evolution of governance for not-for-profit agencies is changing dramatically in the 1990s.

Currently, most boards focus their roles on implementation, tactical planning, general roles, and narrow deliverables. In the future, boards will move from this management model to a stewardship/leadership focus.

In the future, as we transition to New Century implementation, our governance focus will shift to vision, follow-up/monitoring, strategic planning, and clear roles with high-level deliverables.

Volunteer Structure

To attain our New Century vision, our current system and volunteer system will need to change.

Training and education on new governance models; a review of our current structure, By-Laws, and Charter; and the integration of learning organization and team principles need to be activities undertaken early in the New Century Plan implementation cycle.

Our future volunteer system forecasts the following teams to fulfill our Mission in a different way. They are:

    Governing Members. A broadly diverse and representative group of key community leaders, donors, and other volunteers who serve as ambassadors for the YMCA.

    Board of Trustees. The team of leaders responsible for asset stewardship and endowment development. This team's membership could increase and become more diverse, possibly governing a separate foundation for the YMCA.

Governing Board of Directors. The team that remains the legal corporate entity responsible for the governance of the Association. Areas of focus include policy, strategic planning, leadership development, financial development, and evaluation. A more broadly representative, smaller, and diverse team would govern the Association. Branches would still have representation on the Board of Directors.

Governance Teams, such as Finance, Fund Development and Planning would report to and carry out the governance function of the Board of Directors. Team members will consist of YMCA Board members and other community people and would also include representatives from the branches.

Branch Boards will focus on delivering high-quality membership services and programs based on local needs, local branch plans, and Association strategic direction. Each branch will continue to recruit and elect community individuals to serve on its board. The Branch Board will also focus more time on constituent development, fund development, and site operations. Branch Boards are responsible for working cooperatively with other Branch Boards on common issues and needs through network teams.

The new infrastructure requires that volunteers bring new competencies to the YMCA. We also develop new measures of effectiveness. The goal is to create an enhanced network and volunteer leadership development system that will serve as a model to fulfill our vision.

Volunteer Development

What has been missing from the volunteer side of many not-for-profit organizations is volunteer development. Through proper orientation, training, recruitment, promotion, and recognition, the YMCA accomplishes two great things at the same time.

First, we develop important leadership skills in many community-minded people whose effect spills over into the community at large. Second, we strengthen the governance and board structure of the YMCA, making it a more viable and dynamic organization.

An organized and purposeful volunteer development program for both policy making and program volunteers will dramatically affect our future.

The YMCA of Greater Providence recognizes the need for developing and fostering greater diversity within the volunteers, as well as the staff of the organization. As indicated before under the staff section, specific policies and plans aimed at achieving more cultural and personal diversity will be developed to reflect the Association's commitment to diversity.

FACILITY DEVELOPMENT

The investment and careful stewardship of the Association over the years has provided our organization with significant capital strength.

With over 250,000 square feet of building space and 353 acres of property, the YMCA of Greater Providence has a very strong portfolio upon which to build for the future.

The New Century plan calls for the strengthening and improving of our facilities. Our facilities are in need of upgrading to meet our members' needs and market demands. Market research indicates that we cannot grow without a major initiative to improve our facilities in this planning cycle.

The Winfield research has identified many new opportunities for the YMCA, based on current trends. Our future branch facilities will include a variety of new facility amenities, such as warm-water pools, cardiovascular fitness centers, aerobics dance studios, water play parks, muscle-strengthening areas, running and walking tracks, and teen centers.

Our camp facilities will be upgraded to improve our summer program and house weekend groups to meet the new market for fellowship and family programs.

A facility development team will coordinate the Association's significant maintenance, capital improvement, and new development projects.

Capital projects will be prioritized, categorized, and financed by assessing the potential risk/safety needs, member impact, return on investment, and consistency with strategic direction.

We will develop a master site and facility plan through the year 2005. Staff will be assigned to ensure that all facility, risk, safety, and maintenance procedures are upgraded and standardized.

New development projects will include new relationships and partnered—or joint venture—facility initiatives. These initiatives will provide for the development of extension sites and new program centers by others.

FINANCIAL DEVELOPMENT

In an era of high competition and shrinking discretionary dollars, the YMCA must respond aggressively.

When coupled with our new vision, there is a heralded call to action for unprecedented effort in financial development.

The first step in answering this call will be the development of a comprehensive, integrated, written financial development plan for capital and annual support, earned income, and endowment. This program will be predicated on our developing clear case statements, cultivating major donors, and focusing on key leadership.

A key strategy will be to strengthen the Association's Board and volunteer system to attract and retain volunteer leadership of influence and affluence. We will cultivate, train, and develop leaders who can help us realize our fund development targets.

The foundation of our fund development effort is a strong annual support campaign.

By the year 2000, we will double our results in the number of volunteers involved, funds raised, and lives touched. Particular emphasis will be placed on personal solicitation and major gift development on an Association basis.

We will focus on new gifts, renewals, and upgrading our current gift levels. Different activities will be undertaken, including the annual campaign, special gift solicitation, direct mail, and phonathon wrap-ups.

The development of foundation and grant money will play an important part in the fund development mix. We will identify and cultivate new foundation and governance sources and strengthen our relationship with the Champlin Foundations.

As the United Way continues to change, our community care fund will decrease. We will to work to increase our donor designations through United Way but do not expect them to fulfill our funding requirements.

The Association will test the feasibility of embarking upon the largest capital effort in our history. Current capital maintenance and facility development needs point to a capital development program goal of $12 million, with further needs anticipated to 2005.

Strategies will be tested to ascertain what can be undertaken, probable timetables, and project sequencing in the launch phase of the plan. If determined to be feasible, a major capital program will be undertaken, with key organization activities and lead gift cultivation in 1997.

The Endowment program (Heritage Club) has not grown rapidly in recent years, with 137 members currently active and assets totaling $2,360,000. Monetary goals are hard to quantify; however, we will secure 50 members during the course of this strategic plan.

Other targets make the endowment program an ongoing campaign, assigning staff support for prospect calls and education efforts, developing an endowment committee, and linking this effort with capital and annual support efforts. The goal is to add $1,000,000 to the current fund by 2000.

The Association will continue its commitment to a comprehensive image and communications program. The program is critical to our service delivery, volunteer, and fund development.

A communications program will be developed in consultation with a public relations firm and will include an Associationwide approach to communications and public relations. The goal of this effort will be to position the YMCA of Greater Providence as the preeminent organization for family support, teen, and community development. It will dramatically increase the public perception of the YMCA's new dynamic focus and value to the community, especially in its service to the disadvantaged.

A special events program will be implemented to heighten this awareness, raise funds, stimulate enthusiasm, and help educate about the programs and mission of the YMCA.

Finance

The YMCA of Greater Providence is one of the most financially sound YMCAs in the country.

The balance sheet is strong, operations are balanced annually, and modest growth has been realized. Maintaining this positive financial position and continued unqualified audit opinions will remain paramount to ensure achievement of goals.

External factors and a New Century Vision will necessitate the evaluation of many of our policies. An era of growth and change is forecast, with major facility expansion and program development.

We will need to review many of our policy areas. New policies for asset and cash management, capital expenditures, contingencies, debt financing, depreciation, facility maintenance, financial assistance, fund development allocations, metro support fees, human resource development, and surplus/deficit will be implemented to achieve the New Century Vision.

The future vision is dependent on an Association-wide approach that maximizes our assets and controls our expenditures in a systematic way.

IMPLEMENTATION, MONITORING, AND EVALUATION OF THE PLAN

The YMCA of Greater Providence's Strategic Plan will be most effective if used and evaluated regularly.

The board and staff are committed to using the plan in operations as a framework for all activities and decisions. However, new challenges and opportunities will arise. They will be studied and measured against the parameters of the plan and acted on accordingly. Flexibility and responsiveness will be important.

The strategic plan will be used as the foundation for staff work plans and activities of the board, teams, and officers. The goals presented in this plan will serve as the basis for agenda setting, and the plan will also be integrated into performance goals and appraisals for staff and volunteers.

The board will develop expected outcomes annually. Staff will develop action steps to achieve the outcomes. Formal quarterly reviews will be conducted by staff and board. Annual retreats will assist in sustaining focus on our strategic agenda.

It is critical to communicate the New Century plan to our key constituencies. Staff will prepare appropriate communications vehicles for distribution as a part of our annual and long-term communications plans. Progress reports will be critical to develop one Association.

This plan will be implemented in January 1996. This strategic plan will be reviewed formally again in 1998. At that time, staff and board will determine if a planning process is appropriate for a new plan for 1999–2002. If deemed appropriate, a new planning process will be recommended and the cycle will continue.

GLOSSARY OF TERMS

Action Steps
Commitment to results, Association and Branch footwork on an annual and long-range basis.

Benchmarks
Indicators we use to determine whether we have met our goals.

Branch
A YMCA-owned facility that delivers four or more core program areas.

Collaboration
Two or more partners working toward a common goal, sharing resources with joint accountability.

Community

Community is defined as consistent, meaningful, and respectful interaction among constituent groups in local neighborhoods or unified body of individuals and groups sharing common interests.

Community Development

The process of empowerment, collaboration, and advocacy.

Core Program Areas

The product lines of the YMCA: Fitness, Aquatics, Recreation, Child Care, Camping, Teen/Youth Development, and Community Development.

Delivery

The point of contact, place of transaction.

Diversity

When the board, staff, membership, policies, practices, and programs reflect the community we serve.

Family

A family consists of two or more people living together or apart, related by blood, marriage, adoption, or commitment to care for one another.

Goals

Broad targets toward which we direct our efforts.

Major Development Effort

Focused, priority resources to make a lasting difference in a given area or community.

Member

Any person who makes a commitment to the YMCA by participating in the realization of the mission and vision/or through paying fees.

Mission

The purpose of our organization's existence.

Network

An interconnected system with interlinking lines resembling a net.

Program Center

A YMCA or partner facility that delivers up to three core program areas.

Strategies

Outcome-based, directive statements that provide the framework that guides the choices that determine the nature and direction of the Association. Strategies are the steps we take to achieve our benchmarks.

Support Areas/Systems

Infrastructure includes planning, governance, marketing, development, financing, and other systems that support the delivery of programs.

Team

Group of individuals who gather together to help do the work of the association. Can include volunteers and staff.

Values

Defines what is important to us as an Organization.

Vision

The difference we seek to make in the future.

Appendix 3–D

Strategic Planning at the Lucy Robbins Welles Library, Newington, Connecticut

This appendix presents key components of the strategic planning process for the Lucy Robbins Welles Library. Items included here are:

- Research Outline
- Lucy Robbins Welles Findings Report
- Retreat Agenda
- Strategic Plan
- Patron Survey

Courtesy of Lucy Robbins Welles Library, Newington, Connecticut.

RESEARCH OUTLINE FOR STRATEGIC PLANNING PROCESS

Introduction

Good planning depends on the quality of information upon which we make decisions. Our challenge is to balance too much information with not enough!

The Lucy Robbins Welles Library will put together the following kinds of information to help decision making: community needs; patron satisfaction; institutional capacity (infrastructure issues such as governance and management, facilities, technology, marketing, financing, fund development, etc.); and alliances.

There are two types of research.

- The first, secondary research, refers to information and data that already exists. We will identify them and use them during our decision making. For example: Library usage and financing, community demographics, etc.
- The second, primary research, refers to information that we must collect through focus groups, surveys, and personal interviews. This might include patron satisfaction, community needs, etc.

Secondary Research: Gathering Together That Which Already Exists in Print, Electronically

Method of gathering: Library staff will search for this information, compile as necessary, and provide to the consultant for preliminary review. Library staff should talk to the consultant as questions arise.

1. Library internal data, narrative overviews, and notes regarding trends
   - Multiyear comparisons (preferably 5-year) re: Library operations:
   - Usage patterns
   - Program activity, e.g., number and types of offerings, attendance, demographics
   - Financing, e.g., income and expense, Friends contributions, city allocations, etc.
   - Collection development
   - Technology
   - Use of Library by community groups, e.g., types and number of groups, repeat usage, attrition, and acquisition
2. Description of Library collaboration and key relationships, e.g., interface with school libraries, etc.
3. Relevant local, regional, and global trends, implications, and projections

- Demographics, e.g., population and education trends, cultural diversity, and ethnicity
- Economics, e.g., business shrinkage/growth/outlook, economic sustainability, tourism and attractions, workforce development and readiness, etc.
- Finances, e.g., tax base, tax payer groups, etc.

4. Reports, executive summaries, needs assessment results, plans from relevant community organizations and government agencies. For example:
   - United Way (recent community needs assessments, service priorities, etc.)
   - Hartford Foundation for Public Giving (community needs assessments, service priorities, studies of community giving, etc.)
   - Town of Newington (town comprehensive plan, school system plan, etc.)
   - U.S. Education Goals 2000
5. Library and information services
   - Priorities, direction, and plans from the American Library Association and CT Library Association
   - Overview data from nearby libraries in common marketplace
   - Overview data from "best/most admirable" libraries in state and nation
6. Narrative overview of federal and state laws, regulations, and other public policy issues relevant to library and information services.

Primary Research: Collecting Information That Does Not Already Exist

Method of gathering: Consultant will draft surveys for distribution and tabulation by Library. Consultant will write questions and facilitate focus groups; and consultant will write question and provide guidelines for Planning Committee members and trustees to conduct personal interviews. Library will arrange for printing, distribution, and scheduling.

1. Library patron survey
   - Information
     - Patron interests and needs
     - Patron perception of community needs and priorities, Library financing, public policy issues
     - General demographic and lifestyle questions
   - Distribution
     - At Library checkout/reception desks with box to return
     - Mailing to Friends

2. Community survey
   - Information
     - Perception of Library
     - Perceived value of library and information services
     - Level of awareness of Library and frequency of use
     - Perception of community needs
     - Demographic background
   - Distribution—Still to be determined whether this is feasible. Delivery through U.S. mail to a random sample is too expensive.
3. Focus group discussions facilitated by consultant
   - With Board of Directors of Friends. Meetings held second Wednesday monthly, 7–9 PM
   - With association of PTAs/PTOs at their regular meetings
   - With association of faith groups at their regular meetings
   - With not-for-profit organizations serving community groups, e.g., child care providers, arts groups, environmental groups, health care, etc.
   - With town department heads
   - With public and private school teachers (to be determined whether feasible)
4. Management and governance surveys
   - Directed to Library staff, addressing such issues as effectiveness of operations, community needs (Or utilize recent organizational development survey/interview results. Consultant to determine.)
   - Directed to Board of Trustees addressing effectiveness of governance
5. Personal interviews
   - Personal interviews will be conducted by members of the Planning Committee and trustees. Typically, we will conduct interviews for individuals who might not participate in a focus group.

Table of Contents

AGENDA FOR THE PLANNING RETREAT

At the Planning Retreat, Library leadership will make decisions for the future. Following the retreat, staff, consultant, and the Planning Committee will carry out subsequent activities to flesh out the strategic plan. The Board will review and take action at regular intervals in order to adopt a formal strategic plan.

Logistics

- The Planning Retreat will be held in two parts, both integral to decisionmaking.
  - Session #1: Tuesday, September 7
  - Session #2: Monday, September 27
- A light supper will be served from 5:00–5:30 PM. The retreat will begin each evening at 5:30 PM and end no later than 9:00 PM.
- There will be one break midway through each evening session.

Please note: The sessions are two parts of one whole. We will not repeat work. We will not accept new thoughts from people who have not participated in the prior session. All decisions are group decisions and will not be revisited at any future time.

Session #1: Tuesday, September 7

1. Welcome
   - Self-introductions — Everyone
   - Review of strategic planning process — Joyaux
   - Purpose and format of the retreat, sessions #1 and #2 — Joyaux
   - Discussion of values as the context for decision making — Everyone
2. General discussion regarding results of market research (*Findings Report*) — Everyone
   - What struck you as most interesting or surprising?
   - What causes you greatest concern regarding its impact on the Library?
3. Focused discussion based on the *Findings Report* — Everyone
   - Outline the lessons learned.
   - Identify the probable assumptions/scenarios for the next 3–5 years.
   - Articulate the implications of the probable assumptions/scenarios for the Library.
4. Next steps
   - Joyaux prepares summary of lessons learned, implications, and scenario 2005 for distribution and review prior to Session #2.

Session #2: Monday, September 27

1. Welcome and quick review of lessons learned, probable assumptions/scenarios, and their implications.
2. Where we want to go: vision for the future
   a. Difference between mission and vision.
   b. Vision.
      - Based on values and lessons learned.
      - Response to probable assumptions/scenarios and implications for Library.
   c. Creating the vision.
      - Create narrative statements describing the desired future in key areas such as:
        - Collection, programming, customer service
        - Target audiences
        - Desired image
        - Governance (e.g., Board recruitment, committees, performance) and management
        - Physical plant
        - Financing, e.g., tax allocation, fee for service, charitable contributions, Friends, etc.
        - Collaboration, planning, and operations
      - Further interpret the narrative vision statements.
        - Define terms as necessary.
        - Identify benchmarks to signal when the vision is achieved. (*Staff following the Planning Retreat sessions.*)
        - Outline general direction/questions/issues that arise when considering the vision statement and the process to attain it. Identify management and governance processes necessary to achieve the vision. (*At session #2 of the Planning Retreat.*)
        - Identify Board and staff skills required to do this work.
3. Next steps — Joyaux
   - With this vision, decide whether you still belong on the Library Board. Can you support this vision? Are you prepared to do the work necessary to accomplish this vision?
   - Joyaux drafts vision, goals, and some strategies.
   - Staff and Board review and adopt vision and goals.
   - Joyaux conducts session with staff about next steps in developing the plan.
   - Outline benchmarks for review by Planning Committee and subsequent action by Board.
   - Outline strategies, time frames, and costs for review by Planning Committee.
   - Draft plan for review and adoption by Planning Committee, then recommendation to the Board. Board reviews and adopts.
   - Library communicates plan to key constituents and begins implementation.

STRATEGIC PLAN: OUR VISION FOR THE FUTURE AND HOW WE WILL GET THERE: JANUARY 2000–JUNE 30, 2003

Table of Contents

Overview of the Strategic Planning Process

In early 1999, the Lucy Robbins Welles Library of Newington, Connecticut embarked on a strategic planning process to determine its direction for the 21st century. The Library committed to a process that included stakeholders and was based on quality information.

The planning process began with a Kick-Off to discuss components of the plan and issues facing the Library. Library staff, Board, Friends, and others identified many important issues facing the Library as it approaches the 21st century.

Following the Kick-Off, the Library initiated a market research process to gather quality information to inform decision making. The market research was designed to further explore the issues identified at the Planning Kick-Off. The market research process and results are detailed in the Findings Report, which serves as a resource for implementing this plan.

In the fall of 1999, the staff, board, Friends, and others gathered together at two retreats to make decisions for the future. First, retreat attendees reviewed the information presented in the Findings Report and discussed the potential implications for the Library. Attendees then created a desired vision for the future.

Following the decision-making retreats, staff worked with the planning consultant to draft strategies to attain the goals and achieve the vision. The Board reviewed and adopted the plan for implementation.

Who We Are: Values, Mission, and Vision

Introduction

Our mission states what we want to accomplish. Our values state how we want to accomplish our mission. And our vision describes what we aspire to become.

Our Mission

The Lucy Robbins Welles Library provides information, education, and cultural enrichment for the Newington community through a commitment to excellence in Library resources.

Our Values

These values guide our actions and judgments. We, the staff, the Board of Trustees, and the Friends believe in . . . .

Service

- We are here to serve the community. We exist because of its support, and our future success depends on its continuing support.
- Our commitment to service is foremost in our minds, no matter what job we hold. We deliver our service in a way that exceeds expectations. We will know the preferences of the community and meet its needs.

Respect

- All people have worth and value. The way we work—with individuals and organizations inside and outside the Library—demonstrates our own trustworthiness and honors the contributions of others.
- We treat each other with respect, fairness, and good faith. We welcome different opinions and agree to disagree. We respect the group and honor decisions made by the group.
- We reach out to our diverse community, regardless of race, religion, creed, age, gender, income, physical challenge, ability, sexual orientation, social or political views.

Pursuit of Excellence

- We pursue excellence in every area of operation and continually assess and improve ourselves.
- We strive for excellence in the business of libraries and information services by maintaining and enhancing our professional knowledge and skills, and by encouraging the professional development of co-workers and volunteers. We make a difference by

generating ideas, fostering learning, contributing knowledge, and offering solutions.

Accessibility and Intellectual Freedom

- Free and convenient access to the world of ideas, to information, and to the creative experience is of vital importance to all people. We uphold the principles of intellectual freedom and accessibility, and resist all efforts to censor materials and limit access.
- Materials will not be excluded because of the origin, background, or views of those contributing to their creation. Materials will not be proscribed or removed because of partisan or doctrinal disapproval. We will challenge censorship and limits to access, and we will foster free expression, free access, and enlightenment.
- We protect each individual's right to privacy and confidentiality with respect to information sought or received and resources consulted, borrowed, acquired, or transmitted.

Teamwork and Collaboration

- The Library's greatest results come from the combined efforts of staff and volunteers, and the Library itself, partnering with other organizations and groups. Just as we have much to teach, we have much to learn—from our colleagues, from our community, and from our patrons and supporters.
- We believe in and encourage cooperation and collaboration through the use of partnerships with other organizations and groups, with task forces, and with committees.
- We are always ready to work cooperatively with others who share our commitment to quality, service, accessibility, and intellectual freedom. We expect all staff and volunteers to contribute to an atmosphere of teamwork and cooperation.
- We believe that camaraderie and a sense of humor contribute positively to the Library.

Innovation and Risk Taking

- We bring innovative solutions to both the commonplace and to challenges. While we honor tradition, we also explore new opportunities. We encourage thoughtful risk taking and recognize that intelligent change keeps the Library vital, alive, and relevant.

Fiscal Integrity

- We operate in a fiscally sound manner, providing optimum value for reasonable cost. We believe in

government support of the Library because we believe that information services are the right of every community member. We are good stewards of the Library's assets and strive for sufficient tax support, enhanced with charitable contributions.

Our Vision for the 21st Century

The Lucy Robbins Welles Library makes significant contributions to the quality of life in our community. We do so by operating in accordance with our values of service, respect, excellence, accessibility, and intellectual freedom, teamwork and collaboration, innovation and risk taking, and fiscal integrity.

Our Library is the showroom of the knowledge society and the one-stop place for information. We are recognized as "the best" and are known for being on the cutting edge. Our quality service and pursuit of excellence consistently exceed standards and the expectations of those we serve. Our satisfied patrons are our best advertisement.

As the community's primary information resource, we reach out beyond our walls and traditional patrons to ensure that community members understand what services are available and perceive their Library as accessible, inclusive, and responsive to their needs.

We provide access to information for everyone in the community when and where the individual needs it. We take the Library to those who cannot visit or access us electronically.

The state's universal Library card helps community members link to all libraries. There are many ways to take items out of the Library, and patrons use them all, including downloading from off-site and self-checkout.

We are a recognized leader in collaborative efforts, both locally and regionally. We have taken on the role of changing traditional boundaries.

We collaborate with other information service providers, emphasizing access over ownership. We can neither own nor specialize in all areas, so we coordinate, collaborate, and network extensively. We collaborate with for-profit, not-for-profit, and government agencies to identify and meet the needs of the community.

We create and maintain an exemplary collection of print and non-print resources that meet the needs of our diverse and ever-changing community. The collection and services are accessible, inclusive, and affordable, 24 hours per day, 7 days per week, and are delivered through a variety of options, in various formats, and at diverse sites in order to meet patron needs.

We recognize that technology increases the patron's ability to manage his/her own information future. We continually redefine our role in this ever-changing environment, keeping abreast of technological trends that help our patrons, adapting quickly through in-house or outsourced experts, and enhancing Library staff capacity to serve.

We exploit technology in all its forms, whenever this resource can help meet the needs of our community, patrons, and staff. We offer training to ensure that patrons can access our services and collection.

Even as we respect and use technology, we honor the human desire for building community. The Library is a community center and gathering place for both scheduled and chance meetings. Our facilities and staff create a warm and friendly atmosphere that reaches out and welcomes the entire community. With our homey atmosphere, comfortable reading spaces, light refreshments, and professional work stations, people visit us for entertainment, work, research and study, and to meet friends and colleagues.

We provide access to cultural programs and other activities that meet the interests and needs of our diverse community. We may develop these programs and activities within the Library, and we also collaborate with other organizations to plan and deliver programs both on and off site.

We organize our work and service in ways that best achieve our vision, without being bound by traditional Library formats and roles. As information facilitators, our staff help access and organize, compile, and present information, as well as offering instructions and advice.

The Lucy Robbins Welles Library is the best Library in which to work and volunteer. We offer challenging experiences and support innovation, teamwork, and learning. We provide opportunities for personal and professional development. We anticipate new training needs and ensure skill development in a timely fashion. We develop and maintain compensation and recognition systems that recruit, retain, appraise, and reward the best human resources, whether employee or volunteer. We look outside the Library profession to meet our professional needs, including outsourcing, technical skills, marketing, and fund development expertise.

Our Board of Trustees reflects the diversity of our community and is recognized and respected for its leadership and commitment. Our Board and individual Board members understand their legal and moral accountability, including that of fund development. We regularly evaluate Board and Board member performance in order to ensure that we are carrying out our governance function.

Continued interaction between the Board, the Friends, and Library staff ensures that we operate effectively in order to carry out the strategic plan and achieve our vision.

We are expert communicators, not only in the services we provide but also in the marketing of our services. Our comprehensive marketing and communications program, designed and implemented with professional expertise, helps us maintain a strong marketplace position. A comprehensive marketing and communications plan clearly articulates our short- and long-range goals and benchmarks for success, identifies our competitors, and outlines diverse strategies to reach diverse audiences. We regularly monitor progress and evaluate performance.

A diversified funding base ensures the health, vitality, and stability of the Library. The Town recognizes the Library's value as a lead collaborator, facilitator, and information center. Effective advocacy by the Library Board, Friends, and patrons ensures the Town's continued financial support. The state plays a larger role in funding for the dissemination of information.

The Library institutes a philanthropic fund development program, designed and implemented with professional expertise, to build community understanding of and charitable support for the Library. Activities of the Friends continue as a vital part of this philanthropic fund development program. A comprehensive fund development plan clearly articulates our short- and long-range goals, benchmarks, and strategies. We regularly monitor progress and evaluate performance.

Continuous feedback from the community, coupled with our own enhanced capabilities, allows us to respond in a timely and innovative fashion to meet changing needs and interests. The services we provide today may well be delivered in a different way tomorrow; we may change or abandon some services and may develop alternatives.

Planning and evaluation, both short- and long-term, is a standing function of the Library. We regularly acquire quality information to make strategic decisions. We have evaluation and feedback systems for internal and community needs assessment.

We have a plan and process for determining the data we need and for collecting and analyzing the data. We constantly evaluate emerging trends in information services, customer service and technology, not-for-profit management and governance, fund development, and other relevant areas. We establish standards and benchmarks, by which we measure our performance, cost-effectiveness, and accountability.

The Context for Our Vision

The Library articulated its vision for the future, based on lessons learned and implications of those lessons. This context reminds us of where we come from and what we anticipate in the marketplace.

Lessons Learned

Along with our values, these lessons learned provide the foundation for the decisions made about the Library's future. These lessons learned were articulated at the decision-making retreat after a discussion of the research results presented in the *Findings Report*.

1. Demographics are changing and will continue to change dramatically. Newington is diverse now and will likely be more diverse in the future.
2. The world is getting smaller and smaller. We live in a global society, and there is more awareness of international issues.
3. Constituents have diverse needs—sometimes complementary and sometimes contradictory. The Library can never be all things to all people.
4. The community's interests and needs change. Continuous feedback from constituents, coupled with the ability to respond in a timely and innovative fashion, are essential if the Library is to retain its good marketplace position.
5. Ongoing planning and flexibility and timely decision making are also critical to retain the Library's marketplace position.
6. The economy goes up and down. No government will have enough money to meet the wants and needs of its community based on what its taxpayers are willing to pay. Citizens complain more and more about taxes. Governments regularly cut allocations to services, including libraries.
   * The Library will probably never have enough dollars to meet all the library information needs of its constituents.
7. Technology is ever-changing. Technology has increased and will continue to increase a user's ability to manage his/her own information future.
   * Library must define its technology role in this ever-changing environment, keep abreast of technological trends that will help Library users, and enhance Library staff capacity.
8. Traditional organizational and governmental boundaries are changing. Others may now take on roles that once belonged to a particular organization or government entity.
   * People use different libraries and bookstores to meet their information and entertainment needs.
9. Constant communication and creative partnerships are essential. Increased collaboration and even regionalization may be necessary.
10. There is a decline in people's sense of community and sense of belonging. More and more, people seek ways to bring people together and build community.
11. Bookstores are more like libraries, and people use both bookstores and libraries as entertainment and information centers, as well as places to gather together.

How the World We Anticipate in 2005 Will Affect the Library

1. Changing demographics/diversity
   * Need for:
     a) Multilingual and multicultural programs and materials and ESL classes.
     b) Bilingual Library staff.
     c) For the elderly: security, social services, day programs, and alternatives to reading books (sight problems).
2. Financing
   * Limited funding for services, materials, and programs will affect Library services, outreach, staff retention, and recruitment.
   * Need for:
     – Raising money beyond tax dollars.
     – Developing alternative revenue streams, e.g., possibility of Library fees, fund raising.
     – More collaboration to better spend resources and eliminate duplication.
     – More advocacy to retain tax allocation.
3. Audience
   * More outreach to targeted audiences is necessary.
   * Less foot traffic but more and different demands on staff.
4. Services
   * Change in ways the Library provides information to homes, e.g., more training for staff and public, more on-line services.
   * Change in nature of services.
   * New focus for collection development.
   * Change in the way programming is provided for families.
   * Development of homework centers.
   * Increasing pressure for multimedia delivery.
   * Even higher expectations for quality and scope of Library service. People want more services for fewer dollars.
   * Life experiences outside the Library create expectations that are difficult to meet.
5. Staffing issues
   * Ability to communicate in languages other than English.

- Technology skills.
- Assignments to different locations.
- Training.
- More staff, fewer staff, different types of staff.

6. Management
   - Change the structure or organization of Library services, Library staffing, etc.
   - Discipline problems with teens and, hence, need for staff training, space allocation, intragency coordination, and cooperation to serve teen needs.
   - Policies and procedures
     - To protect the Library from lawsuits.
     - Regarding children left in the Library.
   - Find and eliminate duplicative services.
   - Despite high satisfaction levels, there are areas that need improvement at the Library.
   - The data we collect and the way we evaluate the Library will probably have to change.
   - More significant partnership between school system and public library. Library is major resource for Newington schools.
   - CT State Library has a long-range plan that will reach out to libraries and help direct the future for Connecticut libraries.

7. Level of visibility and presence in the community
   - Presence on the Web and on public access TV.
   - Scope of marketing to build awareness.
   - Strategies (audience reasons/needs) to draw people into the Library as more people use the Library from the home.
   - Issues related to non-patrons:
     - What is the issue regarding non-patrons?
       a) Lack of awareness of the Library, its services, etc. (communications issue on the part of the Library).
       b) Perception that the Library is not available, accessible, and inclusive?
       c) Library does not meet their needs (communications issue on the part of the Library).
       d) People choose not to use the Library (people's choice).
     - To what degree is the Lucy Robbins Welles Library available, accessible, and inclusive to the diverse constituencies of Newington?

- To what degree are diverse constituencies aware of the availability, accessibility, and inclusiveness of the Library?
  a) How does a government-supported library adequately reach out to and communicate its availability and accessibility—without diverting excessive or unreasonable resources to those who do not use or may not wish to use the library?

8. Facility issues
   - Redistribution of services and resources.
   - Adequacy of security.
   - Adequacy of space.
   - Need to anticipate space needs and develop expansion/adjustment plans as an ongoing Library activity rather than an every-decade occurrence.

Summary of Goals To Achieve Our Vision

Our strategic plan describes the steps we will take to move from our current reality (described in October 1999) to achieve our vision for the 21st century. As this strategic plan draws to a close, we will devise another plan directed at achieving this vision. If we have achieved this vision, our next strategic plan will help us achieve our new vision.

Goals

1. Cultivate the Library as a center of this changing and growing community by enhancing collections, programming, and delivery to meet its diverse needs and interests.
2. Strengthen marketing and communications to enhance community awareness and marketplace position.
3. Improve our planning and evaluation in order to support strategic decision making.
4. Launch a comprehensive philanthropic fund development program to ensure financial stability.
5. Strengthen management and staffing of the Library to meet the needs of the 21st century.
6. Strengthen governance to meet the needs of the 21st century.

Strategies To Achieve Our Goals

General strategies are outlined in this section, along with target time frames, assignments of responsibility, costs as possible, and financing sources.

Goal 1:

Cultivate the Library as a center of this changing and growing community by enhancing collections, programming, and delivery to meet its diverse needs and interests.

Collections

a. Develop and implement ways to assess our current collection of materials.

Planning start date:	FY1999-III
Report date to the Board:	Ongoing
Implementation date:	Ongoing
Cost:	Request from Town appropriations
Responsibility:	All appropriate personnel

b. Develop and implement methods to determine needs of the community.

Planning start date:	FY1999-III
Report date to the Board:	Ongoing
Implementation date:	Ongoing
Cost:	Request from Town appropriations
Responsibility:	All appropriate personnel

c. Keep informed of trends in new collection formats.

Planning start date:	FY1999-III
Report date to the Board:	Ongoing
Implementation date:	Ongoing
Cost:	Request from Town appropriations
Responsibility:	All appropriate personnel

d. Develop test marketing for new formats.

Planning start date:	FY1999-III
Report date to the Board:	FY2000-II
Implementation date:	FY2000-III
Cost:	Request from Friends
Responsibility:	All appropriate personnel

e. Undergo a space and security needs assessment for current facility and develop a plan and financing to implement results.

Planning start date:	FY2002-I
Report date to the Board:	FY2002-III
Implementation date:	To be determined
Cost:	To be determined
Responsibility:	Library Director, House Committee

Programming

a. Use demographic statistics to determine changing populations.

Planning start date:	Annually
Report date to the Board:	Annually
Implementation date:	Ongoing

Cost:	No cost
Responsibility:	All appropriate personnel

b. Continue to develop and implement programming for targeted audiences.

Planning date:	Ongoing
Report date to the Board:	Ongoing
Implementation date:	Ongoing
Cost:	Request from town appropriations and Friends.
Responsibility:	All appropriate personnel

c. Explore, develop, and implement as appropriate, programming possibilities in different and innovative venues, i.e., cable TV, Internet, other places in the community.

Planning start date:	FY1999-III
Report date to the Board:	Ongoing
Implementation date:	Ongoing
Cost:	To be determined
Responsibility:	All appropriate personnel

d. Develop and implement ways for constant evaluation and improvement of programs.

Planning start date:	FY2000-I
Report date to the Board:	FY2000-II
Implementation date:	Ongoing
Cost:	To be determined
Responsibility:	All appropriate personnel

Delivery

a. Enhance existing Web presence, making remote delivery of information and services a routine task deliverable as a 24-hour/day 7-day/week operation.

Planning start date:	Ongoing
Report date to the Board:	Ongoing
Implementation date:	Ongoing
Cost:	To be determined
Responsibility:	Community Services and Children's staff

b. Increase hours of operation at current Library site.

Planning start date:	FY1999-III
Report date to the Board:	FY1999-IV
Implementation date:	FY2000-II
Cost:	Request from Town appropriations
Responsibility:	Library Director

c. Explore and, as appropriate, develop and implement alternative convenient delivery of materials, i.e., self checkout, mail delivery.

Planning start date:	FY2001-I
Report date to the Board:	FY2001-III
Implementation date:	FY2001-IV
Cost:	Request from Town appropriations
Responsibility:	Library Director, Collection Management staff and consultant

d. Focus on presentation and display of materials in a retail-oriented manner—easy to find, easy to use.

Planning start date:	Ongoing
Report date to the Board:	Ongoing
Implementation date:	Ongoing

Cost:	To be determined
Responsibility:	Staff Marketing Team

e. Develop a plan for redesign of existing spaces to better utilize physical plant and to allow easier access to collections.

Planning start date:	FY1999-III
Report date to the Board:	FY1999-IV
Implementation date:	To be determined
Cost:	To be determined
Responsibility:	Consultant and appropriate staff units

f. Continue to build an information infrastructure that provides electronic access to the public.

Planning start date:	Ongoing
Report date to the Board:	Ongoing
Implementation date:	Ongoing
Cost:	Request from Town appropriations and Friends
Responsibility:	Technology Team

Goal 2:

Strengthen marketing and communications to enhance community awareness and marketplace position.

a. Develop and implement a comprehensive marketing and communications plan for the Library and the Friends that includes measurable goals, activities, and supporting materials.

Planning start date:	FY2001-I
Report date to the Board:	FY2001-III
Implementation date:	FY2001-IV
Cost:	Cost to develop plan is estimated at $5,000. Cost to copywrite, design, and print support materials to be determined.
Responsibility:	Consultant and Staff Marketing Team

b. Continue to enhance presence on the Web by constant work on Library's home page.

Planning start date:	Ongoing
Report date to the Board:	Ongoing
Implementation date:	Ongoing
Cost:	Request from Town appropriations
Responsibility:	New position, Staff Marketing Team

c. Continue to foster strong relationships with local and regional media representatives.

Planning start date:	Ongoing
Report date to the Board:	Ongoing
Implementation date:	Ongoing
Cost:	No cost
Responsibility:	Staff Marketing Team

d. Improve signage for the existing building. Monitor trends of local competition, i.e., bookstores, in order to determine marketing strategies.

Planning start date:	FY2001-II
Report date to the Board:	FY2001-III
Implementation date:	FY2002-I
Cost:	Cost and financing to be determined
Responsibility:	Consultant and Staff Marketing Team

e. Personalize messages and communications strategies to new target markets.

Planning start date:	FY2000-I
Report date to the Board:	FY2000-II
Implementation date:	FY2000-III
Cost:	Part of marketing consultancy to devise. Cost for implementation to be requested from Town appropriations
Responsibility:	Community Services

Goal 3:

Improve our planning and evaluation in order to support strategic decision making.

a. Integrate short- and long-term planning, evaluation, and revision of policies and plans, as a standing function within Library operations. This includes monitoring progress of this current plan, evaluating performance, and extending the plan beyond 2003.

Planning start date:	Ongoing
Report date to the Board:	Ongoing
Implementation date:	Ongoing
Cost:	There will be costs—to be determined—associated with extending the plan beyond 2003.
Responsibility:	Library Director and Staff and Board task forces as necessary

b. Engage the Board, through its due diligence function, in ongoing planning and evaluation.

Planning start date:	Ongoing
Report date to the Board:	Ongoing
Implementation date:	Ongoing
Cost:	No cost
Responsibility:	Library Director and Board President

c. Establish procedures to measure effectiveness in all relevant areas of the plan. These areas include fiscal, governance, customer service, technology, library and information services, not-for-profit management, fun developing, and marketing/communications.

Planning start date:	FY2000-I
Report date to the Board:	FY2000-III
Implementation date:	FY2000-IV
Cost:	Cost and financing to be determined
Responsibility:	Library Administrative staff and PEP Committee

d. Build a cost-benefit analysis structure as a measurement tool in order to continually measure costs and evaluate benefits of new, existing, and proposed library services and materials.

Planning start date:	Ongoing
Report date to the Board:	Ongoing
Implementation date:	Ongoing
Cost:	No cost
Responsibility:	Library Administrative staff

Goal 4:

Launch a comprehensive philanthropic fund development program to ensure financial stability.

a. Articulate the role and relationship of the Board of Trustees, Friends, and staff as they relate to fund development.

Planning start date:	FY2001-II
Report date to the Board:	FY2001-IV

Implementation date: FY2002-III

Cost: If it is decided to secure consulting assistance, cost estimate of $5,000 will support this entire goal.

Responsibility: Fund Development Committee, Board, Friends, consultant

b. Based on an evaluation of the philanthropic marketplace and the Library itself, design, develop, and implement a fund development program that brings together and coordinates fundraising activities for the Library.

Planning start date: FY2001-II
Report date to the Board: FY2001-IV
Implementation date: FY2002-III
Cost: Part of Fund development consultancy
Responsibility: Fund Development Committee, Board, Friends, consultant

c. Clearly articulate the case for support.

Planning start date: FY2001-II
Report date to the Board: FY2001-IV
Implementation date: FY2002-III
Cost: Articulation is part of fund development consultancy. Cost to be determined for copywriting and designing a communications piece.

Responsibility: Fund Development Committee, Board, Friends, consultant

d. Orient and train staff, trustees, and others regarding best practice and the body of knowledge in fund development.

Planning start date: FY2001-II
Report date to the Board: FY2001-IV
Implementation date: FY2002-III
Cost: Part of fund development consultancy.
Responsibility: Fund Development Committee, consultant

e. Monitor progress of development plan and evaluate performance.

Planning start date: FY2002-III, then ongoing
Report date to the Board: Ongoing
Implementation date: Ongoing
Cost: No cost
Responsibility: Fund Development Committee and Board

f. Continue to build the endowment fund to support the Library.

Planning start date: Ongoing
Report date to the Board: Ongoing
Implementation date: Ongoing

FY 2003. Consider initiating a formal fundraising program to build endowment after the fund development consultancy has built capacity.

Cost: Costs associated with fund development; to be determined.
Responsibility: Fund Development Committee and every Board member

Goal 5:

Strengthen management and staffing of the Library to meet the needs of the 21st century.

Staffing

a. Determine core competencies for the new vision. Develop, implement, and evaluate a structured professional development program for staff based on these competencies.

Planning start date:	FY1999-III
Report date to the Board:	FY1999-IV
Implementation date:	FY1999-IV, then ongoing
Cost:	Request from town appropriations
Responsibility:	All supervisory personnel

b. Work within existing Town and bargaining unit structures in order to provide the best salary and benefits packages available in order to attract and retain highly qualified staff. Review and improve recognition and retention activity for staff and volunteers.

Planning start date:	FY2000-II
Report date to the Board:	FY2000-II
Implementation date:	FY2000-IV
Cost:	Request from Town appropriations, Friends
Responsibility:	Bargaining unit staff members, administrative staff

c. Look at current internal organizational structure with an eye toward redesign and reassignments where necessary. Determine changing nature of each function and the changing needs of patrons.

Planning start date:	FY2001-I
Report date to the Board:	FY2001-III
Implementation date:	To be determined
Cost:	If there is additional cost, request from town appropriations.
Responsibility:	Staff Personnel Task Force and Board Finance Committee

d. Continue to cultivate talents and interests of existing staff.

Planning start date:	Ongoing
Report date to the Board:	Ongoing
Implementation date:	Ongoing
Cost:	No cost
Responsibility:	All supervisory personnel

e. Continue to enhance automation systems that support staff functions, including staff training in those functions.

Planning start date:	Ongoing
Report date to the Board:	Ongoing
Implementation date:	Ongoing
Cost:	Cost and financing to be determined
Responsibility:	Staff Technology Team

Collaboration

a. Evaluate existing partnerships with Newington schools and libraries in surrounding towns, with an eye toward alternative management arrangements. As appropriate, develop and implement plans.

Planning start date:	FY2002-I
Report date to the Board:	FY2002-III
Implementation date:	To be determined
Cost:	Cost and financing to be determined
Responsibility:	Library Director

b. Identify duplication of town services as they pertain to the Library and negotiate changes.

Planning start date:	FY1999-III
Report date to the Board:	Ongoing

Implementation date:	FY2000-II
Cost:	Cost and financing to be determined
Responsibility:	All appropriate personnel

c. Continue to work with existing Library consortia and the CT State Library on partnering and outsourcing ventures that will improve access for patrons and be cost-effective.

Planning start date:	Ongoing
Report date to the Board:	Ongoing
Implementation date:	Ongoing
Cost:	Request Town appropriation
Responsibility:	All appropriate personnel

Goal 6:

Strengthen governance to meet the needs of the 21st century.

a. Develop policies and procedures for identifying, cultivating, and screening candidates for trusteeship.

Planning start date:	FY2000-II
Report date to the Board:	FY2000-III
Implementation date:	FY2000-IV
Cost:	No cost unless consulting assistance is necessary
Responsibility:	Committee on Trusteeship and Board

b. Develop and implement a Board orientation and training program to help trustees develop skills in fund development, governance, and other areas of responsibility.

Planning start date:	FY2000-III
Report date to the Board:	FY2000-IV
Implementation Date:	FY2001-II
Cost:	No cost unless consulting assistance is necessary
Responsibility:	Committee on Trusteeship, Library Director

c. Clarify the legal and moral accountabilities of the Board and articulate the performance expectations of each individual as a trustee. Communicate these to appointing bodies, appointees, and those who are nominated and elected. Regularly assess the performance of the Board and Board members.

Planning start date:	FY2001-II
Report date to the Board:	FY2001-III
Implementation date:	FY2001-IV
Cost:	No cost unless consulting assistance is necessary
Responsibility:	Committee on Trusteeship and Board

d. Redesign Board structures as necessary to incorporate more ad hoc task forces, committees, and specialized assignment groups.

Planning start date:	Ongoing
Report date to the Board:	Ongoing
Implementation date:	Ongoing
Cost:	No cost
Responsibility:	Library Board

e. Set up investment policies and procedures for the Endowment Fund.

Planning start date:	FY2002-II
Report date to the Board:	FY2002-IV
Implementation date:	FY 2003-II
Cost:	No cost
Responsibility:	Fund Development and Finance Committees

Plan of Work, 2000–2001

Listed below is the plan of work that the Library will follow through fiscal year 2000–2001. During the month of March, after formal adoption of the Strategic Plan, library department heads met with the library director for evaluation and planning meetings. This plan of work is the result of those meetings. It will be adjusted as needed. The Library Board and Friends will work on their own strategies outlined in the Strategic Plan.

Goal 1, Collections:

- Complete a weeding project (Adult and Children's) to dispose of old and out-of-date books and to provide shelf space for new books.
- Run periodic, informal patron surveys targeted to specific areas of the collection. Magazine collection is the first area to be targeted. Adult fiction will follow.
- Increase magazine holdings.
- Begin to build circulating DVD and books on CD collections.
- Develop policies, procedures, and test marketing for e-book readers.

Goal 1, Programming:

- Implement a summer reading program for adults.
- Expand services, programs, and collections for young adults.
- Assist in the production of a local cable access news show.
- Review computer class offerings for senior citizens and seek grant monies to implement more innovative outreach in this area.

Goal 1, Delivery:

- Continue to increase Sunday hours through May.
- Initiate a homework center.
- Target library service to home-based businesses.
- Seek funding in order to implement redesign plan of popular materials areas.
- Migrate to a new on-line bibliographic database system.
- Introduce newly designed, more durable library cards.
- Explore and implement, if appropriate, the use of wireless technology.
- Offer more and better training for staff and public on the use of electronic resources.

Goal 2, Marketing:

- Devise an in-house plan to coordinate existing marketing efforts. Review, delete, and change current procedures as necessary.

Goal 5, Staffing:

- Redesign existing staff workspaces.
- Create a staff development clearinghouse that will provide opportunities and coordination of efforts.

Goal 5, Collaboration:

- Spearhead the effort to create a shared business database with appropriate Town departments.

Implementation

Together, the Board of Trustees and the staff are accountable to the community to ensure the achievement of the Library's vision. The Board is legally and morally accountable to the community and aggressively carries out its due diligence function.

Staff is responsible for implementing the strategic plan. Staff provides guidance and leadership to the Board of Trustees, its committees and task forces, and the Friends, enabling these groups to help the Library achieve its vision. As the chief executive officer of the organization, the Library Director is held accountable for leading the Library to its vision.

The Board sets policy and direction. The Board and its individual Board members are responsible for ensuring financial integrity and acquiring the necessary resources to carry out the plan.

Standing committees of the Board help the Board carry out its work. Ad-hoc task forces work on a time-limited basis to carry out specific projects or activities, then go out of business. Committees and Board task forces report to the Board and are accountable to the Board.

In addition to Board committees and task forces, staff may establish management task forces to work on particular activities. These staff task forces report to management.

Library staff, Board, and committees/task forces use this strategic plan to direct their work. Under the guidance of staff, committees and task forces create work plans to carry out strategies and define benchmarks to measure achievement. The plan is used to outline employee job expectations and to appraise employee performance.

Recommended Board Committees and Task Forces for This Strategic Plan

Note: All committees are responsible for engaging the Board in strategic discussion regarding issues. All committees recommend policy to Board, relevant to committee scope.

Budget Committee
General role

- Reviews the budget proposed by staff and recommends it to the Board for action.
- Reviews the year-end financials (library budget) and presents results and trends to the Board.
- At least quarterly, analyzes financial trends and their implications and discusses with the Board.

Investment Committee
General role

- Helps the Board fulfill its due diligence function regarding Library financial affairs.
- Recommends policies to the Board concerning investment and distribution of funds.
- Provides general oversight in the management of invested funds.
- Recommends policy regarding financial management.

Committee on Trusteeship
(Formerly the Nominating Committee; expanded responsibilities)
General role

- Annually identifies the skills and qualifications required of Board members and reviews with the Board. Conducts an inventory of skills, determines gaps, and identifies candidates who fill these gaps.
- Works with Town Council to explain the performance expectations and role of all Board members and recommends candidates for Town appointees.
- Annually conducts an appraisal of the performance of all Board members, discusses performance with each Board member, and recommends action for improvement.
- Every other year, conducts assessment of Board performance, discusses results, and helps the Board determine action for improvement.
- Works with staff to develop and conduct annual Board orientation and to develop additional training opportunities throughout the year.

Nominating Subcommittee (members to be appointed from Committee on Trusteeship)

–Conducts screening interviews with candidates for Board membership and for officers to determine appropriateness of nomination.
–Presents a slate of nominees for Board and officer positions.

Planning, Evaluation, and Policy (PEP) Committee
(Formerly the Operations Committee)
General role

- Works with staff to continually assess community needs and to evaluate Library programs, policies, and services.

House Committee
General role

- Provides general oversight for facility planning, improvements, and maintenance.

Fund Development Committee
General role

- Responsible for institutionalizing the process of philanthropy and fund development within the Board as a whole.
- Works with staff to develop the annual fundraising plan and monitor progress.
- Analyzes fundraising results and discusses trends, implications, and interventions with the Board.
- Provides personalized follow-up to each Board member to engage each individual in the fund development process.

Monitoring Progress of the Plan and Institutional Health

Monitoring progress and institutional health is a primary due diligence function of both Board and staff. The Library will enhance its due diligence by focusing on the following types of evaluation:

- Regular review of monthly financials and annual fiscal year compilation and analysis of what this means for achieving the strategic plan.
- Regular review of progress of strategic plan, including an annual goal-setting process that directs budgeting.
- Periodic self-assessment of the Board's governance performance.
- Annual assessment of individual Board member performance.
- Periodic assessment of the Library's adherence to its own values.

To monitor progress of this plan, the Library will carry out the following activities:

Board activities

- The Board will discuss progress of the strategic plan at every Board meeting.
- Committees and task forces will use the strategic plan to help establish their work plan for each year.
- The Board will use progress on the strategic plan as a performance appraisal element of the Library Director.

Staff activities

- Staff will discuss progress of the strategic plan at all appropriate Library meetings.
- Staff and Library management personnel will use the strategic plan to direct their work.
- Progress on the strategic plan will be used as criteria in the performance appraisal of all staff.

- The Library Director will provide a brief written progress report, on a quarterly basis, for discussion with the Board.

Annual evaluation and planning process
- As noted in the strategic plan (goal #3), the Library will enhance its evaluation processes to provide improved information for decisionmaking.
- Annually, Board and staff will meet at a planning retreat to accomplish the following:
  - Review progress of the strategic plan.
  - Discuss new information gathered through the Library's enhanced evaluation program.
  - Determine lessons learned and implications for the Library's future and its strategic plan.
  - Target direction and goals for the next fiscal year.
  - Develop the budget to support the direction and goals for the next fiscal year.

Calendar

The Library's fiscal year runs from July 1 through June 30. The quarters are:

Quarter I   July, August, September
Quarter II   October, November, December
Quarter III   January, February, March
Quarter IV   April, May, June

Ongoing, not a specific date

Goal #1, Collections, a.	Assess current collections.
Goal #1, Collections, b.	Determine needs of community.
Goal #1, Collections, c.	Keep informed of trends in new formats.
Goal #1, Programming, b.	Carry out programming for targeted audiences.
Goal #1, Programming, c.	Explore programming possibilities in innovative venues.
Goal #1, Delivery, a.	Remote delivery of services.
Goal #1, Delivery, d.	Improve display of materials in Library.
Goal #1, Delivery, f.	Build information infrastructure.
Goal #2, b.	Enhance Web presence.
Goal #2, c.	Foster strong relationships with media.
Goal #3, a.	Integrate short- and long-term planning into Library.
Goal #3, b.	Engage board in planning.
Goal #3, d.	Build a cost-benefit analysis structure.
Goal #4, e.	Monitor progress of development plan.
Goal #4, f.	Continue to build Endowment Fund.
Goal #5, Staffing, d.	Cultivate talents of staff.
Goal #5, Staffing, e.	Enhance automation systems that support staff functions.
Goal #5, Collaboration, c.	Work with library consortia on partnering and outsourcing.
Goal #6, d.	Incorporate ad-hoc task forces into operations.

Annually

Goal #1, a.	Use demographics to determine changing populations.

Fiscal Year 1999/2000: January–June 30, 2000

Quarter III

Goal #1, Collections, a.	Initiate planning.	Assess current collections.
Goal #1, Collections, b.	Initiate planning.	Determine needs of community.
Goal #1, Collections, c.	Initiate planning.	Keep informed of trends in new formats.
Goal #1, Collections, d.	Initiate planning.	Develop test marketing.
Goal #1, Programming, c.	Initiate planning.	Explore programming possibilities in innovative venues.
Goal #1, Delivery, b.	Initiate planning.	Increase hours of operation.
Goal #1, Delivery, e.	Initiate planning.	Plan for redesign of existing spaces.
Goal #5, Staffing, a.	Initiate planning.	Determine core competencies.
Goal #5, Collaboration, b.	Initiate planning.	Identify duplication of town services.

Quarter IV

Goal #1, Delivery, b.	Report to Board.	Increase hours of operation.
Goal #1, Delivery, e.	Report to Board.	Plan for redesign of existing spaces.
Goal #5, Staffing, a.	Report to Board.	Determine core competencies.

Fiscal Year 2000/2001: July 1, 2000–June 30, 2001

Quarter I

Goal #1, Programming, d.	Initiate planning.	Develop evaluation methods.
Goal#2, e.	Initiate planning.	Personalize messages to new markets.
Goal #3, c.	Initiate planning.	Establish procedures to measure effectiveness.

Quarter II

Goal#1, Collections, d.	Report to Board.	Develop test marketing.
Goal #1, Programming, d.	Report to Board.	Develop evaluation methods.
Goal #1, Delivery, b.	Implement.	Increase hours of operation.
Goal #2, e.	Report to Board.	Personalize messages to new markets.
Goal #5, Staffing, b.	Initiate planning.	Provide best salary and benefits packages.
Goal #5, Collaboration, b.	Implement.	Identify duplication of town services.
Goal #6, b.	Initiate planning.	Policies and procedures for trustee candidates.

Quarter III

Goal #1, Collections, d.	Implement.	Develop test marketing.
Goal, #2, e.	Implement.	Personalize messages to new markets.
Goal #3, c.	Report to Board.	Establish procedures to measure effectiveness.
Goal #5, Staffing, b.	Report to Board.	Provide best salary and benefits packages.
Goal #6, a.	Report to Board.	Policies and procedures for trustee candidates.
Goal #6, b.	Initiate planning.	Board orientation and training program.

Quarter IV

Goal #3, c.	Implement.	Establish procedures to measure effectiveness.
Goal #5, Staffing, b.	Implement.	Provide best salary and benefits package.
Goal #6, a.	Implement.	Policies and procedures for trustee candidates.
Goal #6, b.	Report to Board.	Board orientation and training program.

Fiscal Year 2001/2002: July 1, 2001–June 30, 2002

Quarter I

Goal #1, Delivery, c.	Initiate planning.	Alternative delivery options.
Goal #2, a.	Initiate planning.	Comprehensive marketing plan.
Goal #5, Staffing, c.	Initiate planning.	Redesign organizational structure.

Quarter II

Goal #2, d.	Initiate planning.	Improve signage.
Goal #4, a.	Initiate planning.	Articulate development roles.
Goal #4, b.	Initiate planning.	Fund development program.
Goal #4, c.	Initiate planning.	Articulate case for support.
Goal #4, d.	Initiate planning.	Orient and train.

Goal #6, a.	Initiate planning.	Clarify role of Board and members.
Goal #6, c.	Implement.	Board orientation and training program.
Quarter III		
Goal #1, Delivery, c.	Report to Board.	Alternative delivery options.
Goal #2, a.	Report to Board.	Comprehensive marketing plan.
Goal #2, d.	Report to Board.	Improve signage.
Goal #5, Staffing, c.	Report to Board.	Redesign organizational structure.
Goal #6, c.	Report to Board.	Clarify role of Board and members.
Quarter IV		
Goal #1, Delivery, c.	Implement.	Alternative delivery options.
Goal #2, a.	Implement.	Comprehensive marketing plan.
Goal #4, a.	Report to Board.	Articulate development roles.
Goal #4, b.	Report to Board.	Fund development program.
Goal #4, c.	Report to Board.	Articulate case for support.
Goal #4, d.	Report to Board.	Orient and train.
Goal #6, a.	Implement.	Clarify role of Board and members.

Fiscal Year 2002/2003: July 1, 2002–June 30, 2003

Quarter I		
Goal #1, Collections, e.	Initiate planning.	Space needs assessment.
Goal #2, d.	Implement.	Improve signage.
Goal #5, Collaboration, a.	Initiate planning.	Evaluate existing partnerships.
Quarter II		
Goal #5, Collaboration, b.	Implement.	Duplication of town services.
Goal #6, e.	Initiate planning.	Procedures for Endowment.
Quarter III		
Goal #1, Collections, e.	Report to Board.	Space needs assessment.
Goal #4, a.	Implement.	Articulate development roles.
Goal #4, b.	Implement.	Fund development plan.
Goal #4, c.	Implement.	Articulate case for support.
Goal #4, d.	Implement.	Orient and train.
Goal #4, e.	Initiate planning.	Monitor progress of development plan.
Goal #5, Collaboration, a.	Report to Board.	Evaluate existing partnerships.
Quarter IV		
Goal #6.d.	Report to Board.	Procedures for Endowment.

Financing

Current Financing

Historically, the Town fully funds the Library's operating budget. For FY 2000 (July 1, 1999–June 30, 2000), this totals $1,338,594.

The Town has been very responsive to requests for increased appropriations. However, this strategic plan recognizes that Town government will be confronted with challenging financial choices in the near future. These challenges may well affect financing of the Library.

The Library Board contributes on an as-needed basis to special projects in the Library that are not funded by the Town appropriation.

The Friends of the Lucy Robbins Welles Library also contribute annually to the Library to support projects requested by the Library. The Friends have earmarked approximately $20,000 for FY2000.

The Friends organization is an important and valued part of the Library. The Friends organization exists to support the Library, its vision, and the priorities established in its strategic plan.

Financing the Library for the Future

To finance the Library's strategic vision, more dollars are necessary. Financing will come from the Town and an improved philanthropic fund development program that incorporates the Friends.

It is clear from the strategic planning process that the Library must develop a stronger philanthropic and fund development program. To be effective, this comprehensive program must coordinate the efforts of the Friends and the Library staff and Board as they work toward one common goal.

Financial Planning

From a planning perspective, the Library develops its budget for submission to the Town in January of each year, for the fiscal year starting the following July. Budget reflects goals, and budget requires a comprehensive financing plan.

This means that the Library Board must review the multiyear strategic plan and adopt annual goals in the fall of each year. Then the staff develops the budget to support these goals, the Board approves the budget, and a request for appropriation is made to the Town. At the same time, the Library presents its goals and financial requests to the Friends. The Friends shall select their funding priorities within the Library's annual goals.

Based on these goals set in the fall, the Library's Development Committee develops the integrated comprehensive fundraising plan for the next fiscal year. Activities, roles, and calendar clearly articulate the responsibilities for the Library Board and the Friends.

Financial Calendar

September	Library establishes goals for the fiscal year beginning July 1.
	Friends' fiscal year begins.
November	Library drafts budget based on its goals for the fiscal year. The budget includes the Town appropriations and charitable contributions resulting from a comprehensive, integrated fund development program that includes the Friends.
	Library presents request for funding to the Friends for the new fiscal year. Friends plan accordingly.
	Library (with Friends) prepares fund development plan to support budget.
	Library receives budget packet from Town in November.
December	Library Board adopts budget and the fund development plan.
January	Library submits appropriation request to Town on January 1.
	Library and Town Manager negotiate budget request.
February	Library adjusts its operating budget as necessary, based on negotiations with Town Manager.
March	Town Manager presents budget to Town Council in mid-March.
April	Town Council adopts budget in mid-April.
	Friends confirm financial contribution targeted to specific projects requested by the Library.
July 1	Fiscal year begins.
August	Friends planning begins for new fiscal year.

PATRON SURVEY

Help us plan the Library's future . . . .
Complete this questionnaire and make your opinion count!

Lucy Robbins Welles Library • Newington CT

1. **How satisfied are you with the following aspects of the Lucy Robbins Welles Library?**

	VERY SATISFIED	SATISFIED	DISSATISFIED	VERY DISSATISFIED	NO EXPERIENCE
a Library hours	☐	☐	☐	☐	☐
b. Finding what you want	☐	☐	☐	☐	☐
c. Computer technology	☐	☐	☐	☐	☐
d. Programs in general	☐	☐	☐	☐	☐
e. Parking	☐	☐	☐	☐	☐
f. Library building	☐	☐	☐	☐	☐
g. In comparison with other libraries	☐	☐	☐	☐	☐
h. In comparison to bookstores	☐	☐	☐	☐	☐

2. **What is your opinion of the Library's staff in the following respects?**

	EXCELLENT	GOOD	FAIR	POOR	DON'T KNOW
a. Helpfulness	☐	☐	☐	☐	☐
b. Friendliness	☐	☐	☐	☐	☐
c. Knowledge of technology	☐	☐	☐	☐	☐

3. **What is the single most important reason why you use this library? Please check one response only.**

☐ Business/professional   ☐ Leisure/Personal   ☐ School work

4. **How many people in your household use the Library?**

☐ One   ☐ Two   ☐ Three   ☐ Four or more

5. **During the average month, about how many times do you or a member of your household attend programs at the Lucy Robbins Welles Library?**

☐ Once   ☐ Twice   ☐ Three times or more   ☐ Do not attend

6. **What do you think of the Library's collection?**

	EXCELLENT	ADEQUATE	NEEDS IMPROVEMENT	DON'T KNOW
a. Adult fiction books	☐	☐	☐	☐
b. Adult non-fiction books	☐	☐	☐	☐
c. Young adult books	☐	☐	☐	☐
d. Children's fiction books	☐	☐	☐	☐
e. Children's non-fiction books	☐	☐	☐	☐
f. Large-print books	☐	☐	☐	☐
g. Music cassettes	☐	☐	☐	☐
h. CDs	☐	☐	☐	☐
i. Videos	☐	☐	☐	☐
j. Magazines	☐	☐	☐	☐
k. Audio books	☐	☐	☐	☐

7. **During the average month, about how many times do you or a member of your household visit the following?**

AVERAGE VISITS PER MONTH

a. Lucy Robbins Welles Library .... _____
b. Other libraries .... _____
c. Local bookstores .... _____

8. **Do you have a computer at home?**
☐ Yes ☐ No (Please go to question #11.)

9. **Do you or others in your household use the home computer to access the Internet?**

☐ Yes, often (Go to question # 12.)
☐ Yes, sometimes (Go to question #12.)
☐ No

10. **Why don't you use your computer to access the Internet?**

a. Don't have access to the Internet. ....☐
b. Don't know how to use the Internet. ......☐
c. Don't want to use the Internet. ....☐

11. **Do you plan to acquire a home computer in the next year or so?**

☐ Yes ☐ No ☐ Not sure

12. **Do you use the computers at the Lucy Robbins Welles Library?**

☐ Yes ☐ No (Go to question #14.)

13. **For what purpose do you use the Library's computers?**

a. To access the Internet ....☐
b. For business resources ....☐
c. For telephone directories ....☐
d. For news and magazines ....☐
e. For encyclopedias and research ....☐
f. For word processing ....☐
g. To find a book ....☐

14. **Are you a member of the Friends of the Lucy Robbins Welles Library?**

a. Yes. (Please go to question #16.) ....☐
b. Formerly but not currently ....☐
c. No ....☐

15. **Why are you not a member of the Friends of the Library?**

a. I've never been asked. ....☐
b. I'm not familiar with Friends of the Library. ....☐
c. I prefer to support other causes. ....☐

16. **Where do you live?**
a. Newington–East of the Berlin Turnpike ....☐
b. Newington–West of the Berlin Turnpike ....☐
c. West Hartford ....☐
d. Hartford ....☐
e. Wethersfield ....☐
f. Rocky Hill ....☐
g. Berlin ....☐
h. New Britain ....☐
i. Other ....☐

17. **What is your age?**

☐ Less than 20 ☐ 20s ☐ 30s ☐ 40s
☐ 50s ☐ 60s ☐ 70s ☐ 80s +

18. **Please use this space for any comments you might have. Thank you!**

Chapter 4

The Third Relationship—With Your Constituents

Developing Connections So Constituents Are Ready To Be Asked

What could marketing be if it isn't selling? . . . finding needs and filling them . . . produces positive value for both parties. The contrast between marketing and selling is whether you start with customers, or consumers, or groups you want to serve well—that's marketing. If you start with a set of products you have, and want to push them out into any market you can find, that's selling.

Peter F. Drucker

Adopting a customer orientation does not mean . . . that the organization must cater to every consumer whim and fancy . . . customer orientation truly means . . . that marketing planning must start with customer perceptions, needs, and wants. It means that, even if an organization can't or ought not change certain aspects of its offering, the highest volume of exchange will always be generated if the way the organization's offering is described, "priced," "packaged," and delivered is fully responsive to what is referred to in the current jargon as "where the customer is coming from."

Philip Kotler and Alan R. Andreason

Marketing can persuade, it can encourage, and it can lead; but it cannot compel people to buy. Many of marketing's most severe critics give it more credit than it deserves. Marketing is not manipulation; it cannot make people buy things they do not desire . . . . As the legendary impresario, Sol Hurok, is reputed to have said,

"If the people do not want to come, there is nothing you can do to stop them."

Michael P. Mokwa, William M. Dawson, and E. Arthur Prieve

TOPICS DISCUSSED IN THIS SECTION

- why constituency development is critical to your organization
- how your fund development function will benefit
- components of constituency development
- volunteer and staff roles in the constituency development process
- moving a constituent through the steps to build a relationship
- finding new constituents
- securing information from your constituents
- maintaining contact and communicating with your constituents
- cultivating relationships with your constituents
- evaluating your constituent's readiness to be asked
- preparing to ask
- using a written constituency development plan
- challenges to the constituency development process

YOUR RELATIONS WITH CONSTITUENTS

Developing stronger relationships with your constituents is critical to effective and productive fund development. Your constituents are at the center of this relationship, not your organization.

Constituency development benefits your organization by:

- bringing people closer to you so they are ready to be asked for something
- bringing your constituents so close that you can ask them for more
- helping you know what to ask your constituents for
- retaining donors and reducing attrition
- continuing and upgrading their gifts
- acquiring new constituents and moving them through the system of relationships with your organization

For some fundraisers, constituency development is not new. For others, this may help you focus outwardly, rather than inwardly. Maybe your fund development program is technically proficient but has lost some of its soul.

Even advanced fundraising executives admit that constituency development is the right thing to do, but they don't do it enough. Less experienced fundraising executives and volunteers say these concepts make fund development seem less crass, more user-friendly, and less mechanical.

Timing the Ask

Your organization wants constituents who move closer, becoming, in turn:

- sufficiently aware and respectful to talk favorably about your organization out in the community
- more aware so they refer and bring others to you and your services
- interested enough to be receptive to a request
- concerned enough to say yes to the right request
- sufficiently involved to renew their participation when asked again
- sufficiently engaged to say yes to a larger or more complex request
- ultimately so engaged that they seek participation at ever higher levels

Often, we ask too early. We ask before the prospect is ready to be asked. For example: The nominating committee invites a business leader to join the board, but she is only vaguely aware of your mission. Your organization asks me for a first gift, yet I barely know about your service. You ask a donor for an increase, but he is not yet sufficiently interested or involved.

Repairing the damage of a premature ask requires great effort. Trying to overturn an answer of "no" demands extraordinary cultivation.

Instead, prepare the constituent. The purpose of constituency development is to get the constituent ready to be asked, whether to give money or time, serve as a board member, purchase a service, or lobby on your behalf. Constituent relations mean more than money. Constituency development is about participation in your organization. By enhancing and extending constituent relations, your organization can generate more clients. You can effectively advocate for public policy and develop a stronger board. You can secure more volunteers, particularly for fund development. And you can also raise more money.

> *To survive, your organization must have lots of constituents involved in many supportive and constructive ways.*

Helping You Build All Your Relationships

The success of your organization depends on your ability to build relationships. Four steps are required to build relationships. First, respect and understand the needs and motivations of your constituents. Second, meet those needs if they are in keeping with your values, mission, and vision. Third, communicate your programs and activities and their value to the constituents. Fourth, follow up to maintain the relationship.

When confronted with the concept of benefiting a constituent, charities usually think about the services provided to clients. Certainly, you must benefit your clients or your organization is irrelevant. However, when you seek charitable gifts, you must focus on the benefits to the prospective donor. Often, donors of time and money do not use your services. These donors experience no direct benefit from your services. Instead, you must identify how the prospect might benefit from giving a charitable contribution. You consider the heart and mind of the prospective giver. This is more complex than determining the benefit of services to clients.

To successfully secure gifts, your organization must find the common bond between the needs and interests of your constituents and the needs of your organization. You create a link between the constituent's motivation for giving and your organization's vision. Then you can produce positive value for the donor and your institution. You create a mutually beneficial exchange. Now your organization is well positioned to ask and will more likely receive.

Strong relationships with your constituents require both a philosophical commitment and an adequate infrastructure—just like the other relationships that are critical to fund development. First, you commit to respect the diverse interests, needs, and opinions of your constituents. You genuinely want to understand them better. Then your organization establishes the structures and systems to carry out the process of constituency development.

The biggest challenge is fulfillment—doing what you promised as an organization. And that means maintaining relationships.

In the case of fund development, you acquired me as a donor. This automatically constitutes a relationship between me and your organization.

I know what a relationship is. It's two-way, mutually beneficial, and rewarding *to me!* This relationship is *not* just about you asking me for money and me giving it.

But all too often, you fail your end of the bargain. You're in the fulfillment business but you don't do it. I notice. And I may leave.

Think about your lapsed donors. Consider these relationships that have been lost—or perhaps were never fully or adequately developed in the first place. And that's your responsibility.

Identifying Your Constituents

The *NSFRE Fund-Raising Dictionary* defines a *constituency* as "people who have a reason to relate to or care about an organization" (Levy and Cherry 1996, 39). In this book, synonyms include users, followers, publics, markets, consumers, customers, and audiences.

A true constituent feels some level of association with your organization. The constituent feels part of you in some way. Being a constituent is about how I feel about you, not how you want me to feel. Don't presume that someone is your constituent because you want them to be. No organization has "everyone" or "the general public" as its constituency.

Neither should you presume that someone who is predisposed to your cause is your constituent. If someone is predisposed, he or she feels an affiliation with the cause, not yet an affiliation with your organization.

> *They are constituents because they want to be, not because you want them to be.*

A constituent can be a single entity, for example, a person, family, business or corporation, service group, congregation, or foundation. Constituency refers to a group of like persons or families, businesses or corporations, religious congregations, and so forth. The single entities within a constituency (or constituent group) share common characteristics that your organization defines. To manage a constituency easily, the group must be fairly homogeneous.

Your organization's constituencies include:

- users of your service
- donors
- volunteers
- vendors

Other constituents might include:

- families or associates of your users and donors
- neighbors of your organization
- local media and politicians
- other community decision makers

You seek some exchange of value with these constituents. This is a basic marketing transaction. For example, you want more people to attend your theatre's productions, and they want entertainment. Can there be an exchange of value? You want new board members, and some people seek positions of influence in a highly respected organization. Others want to develop their resumes. Can there be an exchange of value between your organization and any of these candidates for board membership? You want a contribution, and the donor wants recognition. Still others have benefited from your service and want to ensure your continuation. Can you and the constituent both benefit?

Your constituents may be prospects for many different requests. Your constituents can progress through a continuum of engagement with your organization. A client might become a volunteer or donor. A donor might become a volunteer. A volunteer might also give money.

There are others who are not yet constituents of your organization, so they are not donor prospects, either. In fund development, these individuals or groups are often called *suspects*. Your organization suspects (and hopes) that these people or groups might become constituents. The *NSFRE Fund-Raising Dictionary* (Levy and Cherry, 1996) defines a *suspect* as "a possible source of support whose philanthropic interests appear to match those of a particular organization but whose linkages, giving ability, and interests have not yet been confirmed" (page 162).

A word of caution. The term *suspect* may be uncomfortable and even insulting to your volunteers. This book uses the term *predisposed*.

In the process of constituency development, you focus on one single individual or entity, for example, a specific corporation or foundation. You also target relatively homogeneous groups of individuals, corporations, and so forth. No matter which, the constituency development concept and process outlined here can be useful.

IT'S NOT WHAT YOU'RE SELLING THAT COUNTS

What might you want from a constituent? Your organization might seek new clients and repeat use by other clients. You might need more volunteers and new board members. You might want new donors and increased gifts from current donors. There is much that your organization wants from its constituents.

More importantly, what do your constituents want from you? Your constituents have particular interests, whether the constituent is a business, family, individual, or any other (Exhibit 4–1).

Remember, it's not what you are selling that matters. It's what the constituent is buying that counts. Furthermore, people don't want to be told what they need. They expect to be shown what they want. Your goal is to get the constituents to see that your organization can help them fulfill their aspirations.

This marketing principle is critically important for constituency development. Effective organizations understand this. Effective organizations don't focus on themselves, proclaiming their good works and expecting someone to give time and money. These organizations know they will not survive by selling the good of the community. Instead, effective organizations focus on the constituents' needs and interests.

> *Your goal is to get the constituents to see that your organization can help them fulfill their aspirations.*

Do you think this way?

- "Our community wants a children's museum. Our organization has the skills and resources to help solve the problem or meet the community need. To do the good work that the community wants, our organization needs charitable contributions."
- "There are prospects out there in the community. Our organization targets those who seem to be interested in this issue or opportunity. All our organization has to do is tell the prospect about the community need or opportunity. Then explain how good our organization is at meeting that need or opportunity. Certainly, the prospect will understand and then give."

Not good. This approach misses the point. You are selling the community want or need and your organization's ability to respond. You have yet to consider the prospect. What is she or he buying?

Consider this.

- The local manufacturing company wants employees who don't miss much work, get to work on time, and are focused on work when they are there. Your counseling organization teaches people how to manage their finances, solve family crises, and overcome drug and alcohol abuse. Can you convince the local manufacturing company that your services help employees fulfill the company's needs?
- A prospect wants to enhance her position with community leaders by volunteering for a worthy cause. Will affiliation with your recognized and respected organization help the prospect achieve her desire?
- Your AIDS organization knows a particularly affluent individual who has had friends die from the disease. Yet, the prospect has never volunteered or given to HIV/AIDS. Perhaps the prospect has never been asked. Or maybe he fears the stigma and would never associate himself with this issue. Perhaps you can seek an anonymous gift. If the prospect refuses, you may need to leave him be.
- Consider your relationship to a board member, one of your most important constituents. You want her to help fundraise. You want her to see how easy fundraising is, so you provide useful tips, support materials, and training.

Unfortunately, she doesn't make her calls. You remind her, but still no action. Why not? Why isn't she performing when you gave her all the tools? Perhaps it is because you decided what she needed. You tried selling her easy fundraising. Maybe she wasn't buying that. So the exchange didn't work. What was she buying? Who knows. Ask her. Perhaps she was buying companionship, and a fundraising partner would help. Perhaps she was buying time, and you could have scheduled the appointments for her.

Your organization needs to know what the prospect is buying. You'd best figure it out before you try to sell the wrong thing. Don't waste the prospect's time. Don't waste your organization's time.

What's in It for Me?

Think about your own giving. Why do you give to one organization and not another? Ask yourself why you give a larger gift to one institution than to another. Which of your needs is met by the organization you give to? Don't just say, "I believe in the cause." There is more to it than that. Think about why you give.

Now focus on your organization and its various constituencies. Ask yourself why each of your constituents participates in your organization. Usually, it is easy to figure out what your clients want. (But be careful. Your

Exhibit 4–1 Meeting the Needs of Your Constituents

"'I want to be remembered.' These words represent a common wish that's shared by all of us . . . We wish to register our presence here in some imperishable way.

"I am a signer [of the Endowment Book of Life] . . . I cannot overstate the gratification I feel every time I realize that the names of my parents and of their parents can be preserved for centuries to come, along with the names of the family my wife and I have created. And to know that, along with these names, something of our story will be recorded. Not just who we were, but where we came from, what we accomplished and what we believed in and stood for. All this will be set down and saved for our descendants. That is very satisfying to me." (Saul Tobin, quoted in *Promise*, newsletter of the Jewish Community Foundation of Southern Arizona.)

For hundreds of Jews in Southern Arizona, a simple signature bears witness to one's birthright. The signature honors the values and achievements of the signer, of his or her parents and grandparents, and the legacy of their culture.

Here's what happened:

In the Jewish community there were many stories to tell. These were told when people came together to socialize, work, and volunteer. Proud of their heritage as individuals, families, and Jews, they wanted to keep the stories alive forever.

The Jewish Community Foundation made all this possible with the Endowment Book of Life. On permanent display, this living document commemorates the history and continuity of the Jewish community in Southern Arizona.

The Book of Life records the names of individuals, families, and their histories. Each signer writes a brief personal statement about himself or herself, the family, and their philosophy. This statement is entered into the Book of Life for posterity, as a gift for future generations. In addition to this paragraph, each signer is encouraged to write a page or more, which is kept on file as a record of his or her generation.

Everyone can sign the Book. There is no minimum gift because that could exclude people. Carol Karsch, Executive Director of the Jewish Community Foundation, explains: "In Judaism, giving of tzedakah (which translates into righteousness, not charity) is a mandate or law. And it is forbidden to exclude anyone from the privilege of fulfilling the law. Consequently, in Jewish tradition, even those whose sole support comes from the community are expected to take a portion of what they receive and donate it for others."

People from every walk of life and all economic means sign the Book of Life. Individuals and families, small business owners, and retired people. Together they celebrate the Jewish tradition of "Chai," the Hebrew word for "life," a commitment to one's legacy and to the future.

When you sign the Book of Life, you promise that you intend to provide some portion of your estate for the continuation of the Jewish community. Your signature indicates your future intent.

Annually, the Foundation hosts a Signers Night for the Book of Life. A special ceremony recognizes new signers and each receives a certificate, suitable for framing. This designated night allows prospective donors to look forward to a set time each year when they can see themselves as signers.

At some point in time, each signer takes action. You, the signer, arrange for your gift, choosing the giving method best for you. Volunteers from the Foundation can offer advice and meet with you and your own financial and legal advisors. Signers can direct their gifts to the Foundation's unrestricted fund or to any one or more Jewish charities in Southern Arizona.

Once a signer has taken the legal step to give, his or her name is added to the roster of the Chayamim, those who believe in the tradition of "Chai," and inscribed on a plaque that is displayed with the Book of Life. The donor also receives a sterling silver replica of the "Chai," in the form of a lapel pin, charm, or pendant, handcrafted in Israel. Wearing this memento raises the consciousness of others by showing one's personal commitment.

Karsch notes that the real recognition is intrinsic: the invitation to tell one's own story. Karsch says "the opportunity to make a heartfelt personal statement is testimony to the 'why' of the legacy gift, whereas the endowment is the 'what.'"

The Foundation regularly communicates with its constituents about the Book of Life. For example:

- printed materials describe the program
- newsletter articles and features in the *Arizona Jewish Post* honor signers and tell their stories
- volunteers invite people to participate in Signing Week
- special recognition events commemorate signers and honor them when they make their gift
- an Archive Committee helps signers record their family histories and narratives
- donors are also invited to place with the Foundation, posthumous messages to loved ones or friends.

In addition to these special activities, the Book of Life is an integral part of other events and milestones for the Foundation and the Jewish community.

The Jewish Community Foundation understands its constituents well. The Book of Life commemorates the strength and vitality of hundreds of individuals and families. Each year, more people sign.

Think how each of those signers feels. They tell their own stories. They honor their birthright. Together, they build a legacy for future generations and challenge those who follow. In this way, the Book of Life ensures the tradition of each individual, the family, and the Jewish people. Think how you would feel if your own favorite philanthropy offered you an opportunity that so well reflected your interests and aspirations.

Source: Developed by the Jewish Community Foundation of Southern Arizona, Tucson, Arizona.

assumptions may not be as on target as you think.) It is harder to determine why a particular donor gives to another organization but not to yours or why a donor gives a modest gift to you when she or he gives more to others.

> *Marketing is a way to harmonize the needs and wants of the outside world with the purposes and the resources and objectives of the institution.*
> *Philip Kotler*

As fundraisers hurry to the campaign goal, they often need to know more than they do about their donors. This is true of both small organizations and large ones. Operating on experience and instinct, fundraisers may not understand interests and motivations well enough. Examining data, fundraisers must also think about personal relationships. Intent on their organization's cause, fundraisers must also think from the donor's perspective.

Think about friend raising first. Focus on your constituents, their interests, and disinterests. Pay attention to the basic human motivations, as well as changing demographics and lifestyle patterns. Inform yourself about philanthropic trends.

Tips To Learn about Changing Demographics and Lifestyles

There's lots of information available about demographics and lifestyles, and more is released every year. Some of it is free. Here are a few ideas you can pursue.

- Read *Global Demographics: Fund Raising for a New World* (Nichols, 1995).
- Take a look at all those e-publications on trends.
- Check out *American Demographics*, Dow Jones & Company, Inc., Ithaca, NY. Locate other demographic publications that pertain to your country and your marketplace.
- Consider the personality types described in *The Seven Faces of Philanthropy*, Prince and File, 1994, Jossey Bass Publishers, San Francisco.
- Review the results of studies published in newspapers such as *The Chronicle of Philanthropy* and *The Nonprofit Times*. If you don't subscribe to these publications, your public library may. Or borrow them from a development colleague who does subscribe.
- Visit your local Chamber of Commerce to find out about population trends and needs. Check out broad-based community organizations such as the

United Way and independent funds that may conduct research.
- Contact a marketing/advertising firm in your community because they often have lifestyle information and may share it with you as a contribution.
- Ask governmental agencies for demographic information and contact the agency that gathers census information in your country, state, or province.
- Tap into the Internet and World Wide Web to identify resources and gather information. If you don't have access through your own computer system, try these contact points:
  - your local library
  - the development office of a larger community institution (some collegial organizations will let you borrow their computers)
  - the computer system of one of your board members
- Attend workshops that discuss changing demographics and lifestyles.

Speaking of the Internet, there's no way that any book can keep up with that ever-changing source. Any tips or favorite sites today may be eclipsed tomorrow. But here goes. Visit http://www.refdesk.com. Try a google search there. The information is astounding, including demographic data.

Learn about Constituent Motivations

Take a look at your donors, prospects, and volunteers. Ask yourself why some give and others don't, why some give large gifts and others don't.

Better yet, ask them! Discuss giving and volunteering with your board members, donors, and lapsed donors. Ask them why they give. Ask why they don't like to ask. Ask your lapsed donors what your organization may have done to discourage their continued giving. Then work to overcome the barriers and capitalize on the opportunities.

In its 1990 edition of *Giving and Volunteering in the U.S.* (Hodgkinson and Weitzman, 1990), the Independent Sector (IS) outlines reasons why people give and don't give their time and money. IS findings are noted in Exhibit 4–2. Barbara H. Marion, CFRE, and the author have augmented this list and included a new category, "Why people don't like to ask."

These reasons—and some variation thereof—likely remain true across the years and across demographic and lifestyle groups. As times change, new reasons or different angles will also arise. The key is: You are expected to ask the question and find out what holds true within your constituencies.

Exhibit 4–2 Why Your Constituents Give and Volunteer

Why people give (time or money)

- Feeling of obligation to those who have less
- Sense of personal satisfaction
- Religious beliefs or commitments
- Belief in institution and desire to see it continue its activities
- Serve as example to others
- Being asked by the right person
- Fulfill a business or community obligation
- Create a remembrance of family or self
- Encouragement by employer
- Tax considerations and deductions
- They are asked (Generally recognized as the first reason people give!)
- Want to be an agent for change
- Develop own skills and knowledge
- Enhance resume
- Receive(d) a benefit from the organization
- Desire for prestige, peer recognition, visibility
- To be distinct
- Feel happy and have fun
- Need to be liked or feel part of a group
- Return a favor to the individual asking for the gift
- Set size of another's gift
- Guilt or fear
- Fill some personal void
- Expect a future benefit or favor from the organization or from the asker
- Continue a family tradition
- Repair or enhance public image by affiliation with the cause or the organization
- Demonstrate power
- Credibility of the organization and its case

Why people don't give (time or money)

- Not asked
- Didn't get around to it
- Prospect's needs, interests, readiness to give not understood
- Absence of [organization's] future plans for stability
- Inadequate communication and cultivation

- Wrong solicitors
- Not asked for a specific amount commensurate with need and prospect's capacity to give
- Not involving people who could influence or participate in gift
- Have no habit of giving
- Angry at the organization
- Angry at the person asking
- Little or no interest in the organization or cause
- Do not wish to be publicly affiliated with the organization or cause
- Timing is wrong
- Not interested in the particular project presented by the organization
- Organization is not credible
- No available funds to make a gift
- Give time, not money
- Not yet ready to be asked
- Project scope too large
- Does not feel that gift will make a difference in solving the problem or addressing the issue
- Tax considerations

Why people don't like to ask (for time or money)

- Shy
- Uncomfortable in new situations
- Fear of being told "no"
- Anxious that they will be unsuccessful
- Inadequately prepared for what to do and how to do it
- Not sufficiently knowledgeable about the organization and cause
- No time to do the job
- Don't want to be asked for something by those they ask
- Feel they are trespassing on friendship and collegiality
- Embarrassed by their own level of giving
- Don't want to ask people they know
- Don't want to ask people they don't know
- No experience asking for gifts
- Believe that it is impolite to talk about money
- Feel like they are begging

Source: Data from Virginia A. Hodgkinson and Murray S. Weitzman, *Giving and Volunteering in the U.S.*, Washington D.C., *Independent Sector*, 121, and Barbara H. Marion, CFRE, Hayes Briscoe Associates, San Francisco.

Talk about Benefits, Not Features

Don't keep talking about features in your brochures and case statements. Features describe only what you do. Features don't focus on the constituents' needs or interests. Features don't explain how the constituent will be better off. And features are lifeless; benefits add the life.

Talk about benefits. Benefits explain why the features provide something useful to the person participating. As Kotler and Andreason (1987) note, "People—at least those who are mentally competent—behave in ways that they perceive will leave them better off than if they behaved in some other fashion. Since every action implies perceived costs (if only some anxiety about not taking an alternative action), it follows that people act in certain

The Third Relationship—With Your Constituents   159

ways because they perceive the ratio of the benefits to costs to be better than for any alternative" (page 69).

Features tell, benefits sell. Always translate features into benefits (see Exhibit 4–3). The translation is easy. Pretend you are the constituent, and ask yourself, "What's in it for me?" Remember, "What's in it for me" is always a heart issue for the constituent.

> *A feature is a descriptive fact about a product or service. A benefit is what the user of the product or service gains as a result of the feature.*
> *Robert W. Bly*

Most often, organizations describe themselves and their activities in terms of features. A literacy center talks about teaching women to read and write. The homeless shelter describes its food and overnight program. The independent school describes its art curriculum for students in kindergarten through high school.

The benefits for clients are relatively easy. If the feature of the literacy center is teaching women to read and write, one benefit might be that the women can find job opportunities by reading want ads. Another benefit might be that the women can spend meaningful time with their children by reading a story together. The benefit of a shelter's food and overnight program is saving people from starving and freezing.

The benefits to a prospective donor are harder to determine and depend on the prospect's interests and motivations.

- If your business gives to a literacy center, perhaps the benefit is more job applicants who can read and write. As an avid reader yourself, you may want everyone to experience the joy of reading.
- As a parent, you give to your child's school because the K–12 arts curriculum teaches your child to solve problems better through creativity and self-discipline. As an artist, you give to the school because you want future audiences for the arts. You believe the school's arts program will help young children grow up loving the arts.

Effective organizations communicate their features as benefits to a specific constituency. The constituent buys benefits, not features. You must learn to communicate benefits. To sharpen your skills, use a common object and translate its features into benefits for the user. For example, differentiate between the features and benefits of a car.

Next, describe the benefits of serving as a board member. Remember, this means the benefits to the board member, not to your organization. First, list the features of serving as a board member. Then ask your board members what the benefits are for each of the features.

Exhibit 4–3 Features and Benefits

Features and benefits of a workshop on fundraising

Features	Benefits (Answer the question: "What's in it for me?")
Cost is $25 per person or $40 for 2 people from the same agency.	Reduced price makes it easy to bring more than one person from from your agency.
Located at the Holiday Inn.	Location is easily accessible off major highways, just 15 minutes from anywhere in the metro area.
Workshop content includes basic principles of fundraising.	Key tips to help you fundraise better.

Other features and benefits

Features	Benefits
Learn to read.	Read your child a bedtime story.
Attention welfare recipients: Enroll in a one-year computer training class.	Attention welfare recipients: One phone call could earn you $30,000 a year!
Enjoy the benefits of your own private library. Join the athenaeum now.	Tired of the chaos at home? Enjoy your own quiet, private reading room. Join the athenaeum now.

Now look at fund development. You must identify the benefits to donors and donor prospects. The best way is to ask them. Call a few on the telephone. Meet them for breakfast or lunch. Conduct a focus group with targeted donors. Do the same with volunteers. Hold a similar discussion with the development committee and board.

Understand Marketing

What is constituency development but marketing? What is fund development except marketing? To paraphrase Drucker (1990), marketing is the process that brings the needs and wants and values of your constituents into harmony with the service and values of your organization.

Marketing is strategic. This is the why, the context, the meaning. All the rest are marketing tools. Public relations. Advertising. Communications. These are the techniques. Without the strategic understanding, fundraisers are merely technicians.

"Marketing is the voluntary and purposive process of developing, facilitating, and executing exchanges to satisfy human wants and desires" (Mokwa, Dawson, and Prieve 1980, 15). Marketing relies on the concept of mutually beneficial exchange. Clients, donors, and volunteers are involved in an exchange with your organization. You and they receive something from the exchange. This concept is the foundation of any relationship. The marketing exchange process contains four conditions.

- There are at least two parties.
- Each can offer something that the other perceives to be a benefit.
- Each party is capable of communication and delivery.
- Each is free to accept or reject the offer.

The four relationships presented in this book depend on marketing. Marketing principles help your organization strengthen its internal relations. Marketing helps your organization remain relevant, given community needs and interests. Through marketing, you develop strong relationships with your various constituents, including clients, donors, volunteers, and employees.

Marketing is an essential part of effective organizational infrastructure, part of your corporate culture and systems. Capable organizations articulate marketing as a value and see marketing as a management activity. As a value, marketing means your constituents are at the center of your organization. You are sensitive to their needs, interests, and aspirations. You learn and understand "what I am buying," rather than relying on

"what you are selling." Marketing mandates a sensitivity to and understanding of others. As a management activity, marketing forms the basis for other activities, such as strategic planning, board recruitment, client service, fund development, constituent relations, and volunteer enabling. You incorporate marketing into all the management activities of your organization.

Marketing begins with your constituent, not with your organization. You start with your client, your donor and volunteer, your staff member. These are your customers. In a customer-focused organization, you focus on their perceptions, needs, and wants. Then you make every effort to satisfy those wants and needs within the boundaries of your organization's values, vision, and resources.

> *Market segmentation is a clinical name for one of the richest opportunities that new technology has afforded us. We are able to gather information on customers and actually determine more about what they want. This allows us increasingly to delight the customer, and it also gives employees opportunities to target offers that are relevant, thereby increasing the feeling of service and reducing the sense of selling.*
>
> *Pottruck and Pearce*

Effective marketing segments your constituencies into manageable, distinct subgroups, each of which has something in common. Then you target those you want to reach. Marketing positions your organization to meet the target group's needs and helps you communicate in ways that reach your target audiences. To do this work, you need systems that can:

- determine the target group's interests and commonalities
- decide how they will best receive information and devise responsive communications activities
- anticipate the role they want with your organization
- evaluate when and who should make the request for participation

There are eight marketing elements: products, publics, research, price, production and distribution, communication, cultivation, and documentation (see Exhibit 4–4). Fundraisers use every one of these marketing elements, often by accident. Recognize them. Use them on purpose.

Just like good fundraisers, good marketers provide opportunities to participate for those who want to do so. There is no crass selling of undesired products or programs. There is an exchange of value.

Relationships Rule

"The wealth embedded in customer relationships is now more important than the capital contained in land, plant, buildings, and even bank accounts. Relationships are now assets" (Tapscott, Ticoll, and Lowy, 2000). This certainly holds true for not-for-profit organizations that rely on such customers as donors, board members, and other volunteers.

> *The Internet will serve as a super tool to apply the established rules, and a penalizer for those who don't practice with discipline or who fail to build the culture and infrastructure to assure they can meet the expectations created by the cleverly crafted mass messages of their marketing staffs and consultants.*
>
> *Pottruck and Pearce*

Tapscott et al discuss how and why electronic commerce changes marketing, reiterating the *Clicks and Mortar* (Pottruck and Pearce, 2000) perspective of immediacy, interaction, transparency, and the required alignment between promises and action. "Products are now mass customized, service intensive, and infused with the knowledge and the individual tastes of customers" (page 307). What does this describe but constituency development?

Tapscott et al stipulate eight new marketing imperatives that would certainly benefit not-for-profit organizations. A few are presented here for application to your not-for-profit:

Exhibit 4–4 Eight Elements of Marketing

1. **Product** refers to what your organization offers. Your offerings include programs and services to clients *and* the opportunity to give money and to volunteer. Remember that these products need to be communicated in terms of benefits, rather than features.
2. **Public** is another word for *constituency, market, audience, customer*. You want your publics to participate in your organization through your products. Your publics include donors, volunteers, service users, board members, staff, and so forth. Each of them has different—and sometimes competing—needs and interests.
3. To understand your publics, your organization conducts **research**. Through research, you identify the needs and interests of your constituents. You figure out how to create meaningful, mutually beneficial exchanges with your constituents.
4. **Price** defines how much you charge for your product. In fund development, price means how much you ask for, whether it is money or volunteer time. The right amount—your price—is tailor-made for each public or prospect and is neither too high nor too low.
5. **Production and distribution** is also called the *delivery system*. This refers to how well you can meet the demand and where you make the product available. Fundraisers consider the kinds of volunteer opportunities, the scope of fundable projects, and so forth.
6. **Communication** refers to what you do to motivate people to respond and participate. Your organization positions itself by clarifying its distinct niche. You use communications and public relations to gain the attention of and to educate target constituencies.
7. **Cultivation** brings the constituents closer to your organization, increasing participation and engagement. You create strategies to maintain and expand the constituent's commitment to your organization, its vision, mission, and programs.
8. **Documentation** refers to the process of developing and recording your strategies, writing, and implementing your plans, monitoring your progress, and evaluating your performance.

---

1. Plan a communications strategy for your constituents who use the Internet. With the advent of the Internet, it's like Pottruck and Pearce (2000) say, we have a "worldwide switchboard." People can talk to each other one-on-one. "The Internet offers a route back to intimacy and customization. Ironic, isn't it, that the technology that can beget isolation can also lead us back to personal relationships with customers?" (page 225) But a caution. Not everyone is on the Net. Some of your constituents are not, whether they are clients, donors, or volunteers. Find out and reach out in a way that is personalized to your constituent.
2. Honesty is still the best policy. You want loyalty from your donors, then be candid. And remember that, with Internet immediacy and transparency, constituents can find out whether you are trustworthy.
3. Manage attention because it's a scare resource. Take a look at the sections about communications later in this chapter. Remember that inertia is your biggest challenge. People are bombarded. Everyone is fighting for people's attention and trying to overcome their inertia.
4. Engage customers in many roles. Ask their opinion. Invite them to help you evaluate services and define the value-added to relationships. Help your

constituents personalize your services to their needs and interests.

5. Engage the Net generation because they are the biggest spenders of all. The children of the baby boomers are the biggest generation ever. These kids have lots of spending money, influence their parents' spending choices, and use the Internet a whole lot!

Target the Net generation by understanding their interests and motivations. Demographers tell us that this generation likes choice, wants to try out things before committing, and expects personalization. How will this affect your constituency development program and your fund development activities? Remember that these people are your future donors and volunteers.

> *The chant of the Industrial Revolution was that of the manufacturer who said, "This is what I make, won't you please buy it?" The call of the Information Age is the consumer asking, "This is what I want, won't you please make it?"*
>
> *Lester Wunderman*

Marketing should always be about your customers, whether they are clients, donors, or volunteers. Sadly, in the Industrial Age, organizations changed their focus from customers to products. Pottruck and Pearce (2000) note that, in earlier times, there was much more attention to the customer. But with the advent of mass production, organizations turned from "intimate customization" to mass standardization, mass production, and mass marketing.

Since the 1960s, marketing has begun its return to a customer focus. And with the free flow of information and the interconnectedness of the Internet, relationships certainly rule.

Marketing isn't about making and pushing product. It's about satisfying customer needs. It's about what I'm buying, not what you're selling. As noted by Pottruck and Pearce (2000) in *Clicks and Mortar*, "one requires only efficiency, the other requires relationship skills" (page 224). Consider the terms *customer focus* and *customer-driven*. Think about the customer's values and the customer's experience. Think about donor-focused fund development strategies and donor-focused cultivation activities.

Remember the earlier comments about fulfillment? You are in the business of fulfillment. In marketing, this is called *delivering on the offer*. When you consistently deliver on the offer, you build your reputation. Pottruck and Pearce term this "building reputation one experience at a time" and note that an organization can eventually "convert that reputation into a promise that is broader than any one offer. It is the brand, the family name" (page 241).

Pottruck and Pearce (2000) go on to say that this reputation—or "broad guarantee of character"—is not made just to the customer but is also made within the organization, to the self and to the others. This fulfillment is both external, as in constituency development, the third relationship in an effective organization. And, this fulfillment is internal, as in the first relationship within the organization. Pottruck and Pearce conclude by noting that the way an organization delivers on its offer—fulfilling its internal and external promise—is the organization's legacy.

Branding is about your values. Your values help create your brand; you must be true to these values and, hence, to your brand. Take a look at Exhibit 4–5.

Imagine branding your organization as "the best place to give money" or "the greatest place to volunteer" or "the place where my gift makes the biggest difference." What brand image do you want?

Pottruck and Pearce (2000) stress that the "volume of message and name recognition is not enough to assure success. The key is brand building. A company's brand is the symbol of promises and expectations" (page 243). For Pottruck and Pearce (2000), there is a big difference between "shouting" and "building brand through providing service over time consistent with the company's promises" (page 243). There is a vital and essential difference between name recognition, a result of media positioning, and brand building. To paraphrase the authors, brand building is grounded in the daily activities of individuals who care deeply, who share values and value relationships. Brand building is a "moment-by-moment process of service" (page 247).

> *When a company confuses brand attributes with company products, it misses the essence of brand. It fails to identify the substance and instead promotes the symbol.*
>
> *Pottruck and Pearce*

"The ultimate goal of marketing is to make sales through compelling offers, but when specific offers are wrapped in a brand, their success is not dependent only on a single transaction. The brand is a tangible trust that transcends and often outlives any particular product.... Brand assures some level of consistency...a shorthand statement of expectation and promise" (page 249).

Surely this is what you want for your organization as it reaches out to serve clients, as it develops donor relationships, and as it seeks volunteers. Imagine being so well branded that people and businesses initiate contact

Exhibit 4–5 Branding: Chrysler and Bruce Springsteen

This is a story about the branding of Chrysler and the brand identity of Bruce Springsteen. It's a story about consistency in values and reputation management.

Years ago, Chrysler asked for permission to use Springsteen's "Born in the USA" as the theme song for their massive advertising campaign. Chrysler had identified its values as passionate, hard-working, every man, stubborn, open-hearted, American, brave, down to earth, battered but not broken, home grown and proud.

For Chrysler, "Born in the USA" captured this spirit and would link the company with a strong image and reputation consistent with its desired brand identity.

And what did Bruce say? No. Why? Because Bruce Springsteen has a brand identity himself. His brand identity is reflected in his core values, which include independence, integrity, and "it's not about money."

Sure, the values of Springsteen and Chrysler matched when it came to independence and perhaps even integrity. But aligning his song with making money for the car manufacturer did not match Bruce's value of "it's not about money." To remain true to his own integrity—one of his core values—Springsteen could not allow his brand to be identified with the Chrysler brand.

Just remember, part of branding is managing your brand identity, which is your reputation. Always be true to who you are as a brand.

Source: From a presentation by Lee Gustafson, Holland Mark Edmund Ingalls, Boston, MA, at the April 1999 conference of the Yankee Chapter of the International Association of Business Communicators.

---

with you. They self-identify, desirous of affiliating with your organization. Now that's branding.

Get Your Constituents Ready To Be Asked

Constituency development prepares your constituents to be asked for something. With further cultivation, you engage constituents so they will say yes to the request and say yes to more and more requests.

Let's call this the *engagement process*, which is essential when you try to construct any mutually beneficial exchange, whether with a donor, volunteer, or client. All fund development depends on this process, whether consciously or unconsciously used.

Although there are a number of different engagement processes, they all include a phase of gaining attention and building awareness, and end with a call to action. Gaining attention and building interest involve a mix of emotion and intellect. Nothing happens at this time. No action is taken by the prospect. Next, you stimulate desire and request action. This is the pivotal step—and 99 percent of this is emotion.

Consider these two traditional engagement processes, AIDA and ACCA:

- AIDA (Attention, Interest, Desire, and Action): First you gain the constituent's attention and create (or capitalize upon) an interest in the product your organization offers. Next, turn that interest into a strong desire for the product. Once there is desire, you ask the constituent to act. Remember, acting may mean buying the service or giving money or time.
- ACCA (Awareness, Comprehension, Conviction, and Action): Make the constituent aware of the product. Develop the constituent's understanding (comprehension) of what the product is and how it will benefit him or her. Remember, the product might be giving money, and the benefit to the prospective donor might be visibility within the community. Your activities must move the constituent from an understanding of the product to conviction about the product's value to the constituent. The final step is when the constituent acts, for example, giving money or volunteering time.

Bly (1985) introduces another asking process: Get attention. Satisfy the need. Prove your superiority and reliability. Ask for the order. Bly describes these as: Get the constituent's attention by focusing on the single most important benefit to that constituent. Show the constituent that she needs the product by explaining how it will help her. Satisfy the constituent's need by explaining how the product will help her. Prove your superiority and reliability by telling your own success stories. Ask for the order by requesting that the constituent participate.

In turn, Dunlop (1986) proposed a six-step fund development sequence, adapted from G.T. Smith and H.J. Seymour. Dunlop's steps are: Information. Awareness. Knowledge. Caring. Involvement. Commitment.

Use these engagement processes to focus your constituency development (and to find more clients). Decide which sequence (or combination thereof) best describes how you will get your constituents ready to be asked.

Remember that the engagement process is most easily understood when your constituents use your service. The process can be more difficult with prospective donors and volunteers.

For prospective donors and volunteers, assume that they may not use your service. Don't think they simply want to meet a community need or solve a community problem. These constituents are not interested only in the benefits that your clients receive. You have to dig deeper. Focus on how giving and volunteering meets the interests and fulfills the aspirations of your constituents.

Devise strategies for each phase in your engagement process. Use the process to help explain constituency development to your staff and volunteers. Make sure they understand that each step is essential. Figure 4–1 compares the engagement process with fundraising solicitation.

MAKING THE PROCESS WORK

Even when you and your organization value the philosophy, the process of constituency development has numerous challenges. Together, staff and volunteers overcome these by asking themselves:

- "How can we make the constituency development process practical and manageable?"
- "How will we allocate resources?"

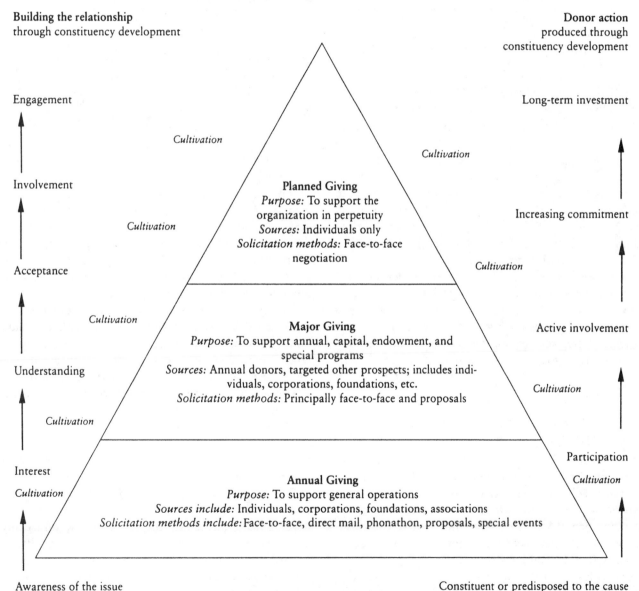

Aligning the Engagement Process with Solicitation Activities and Donor Action

Ask for the charitable gift via solicitation activities

Building the relationship
through constituency development

Donor action
produced through
constituency development

Engagement

Cultivation

Involvement

Cultivation

Acceptance

Cultivation

Understanding

Cultivation

Interest

Cultivation

Long-term investment

Cultivation

Planned Giving
Purpose: To support the organization in perpetuity
Sources: Individuals only
Solicitation methods: Face-to-face negotiation

Increasing commitment

Cultivation

Major Giving
Purpose: To support annual, capital, endowment, and special programs
Sources: Annual donors, targeted other prospects; includes individuals, corporations, foundations, etc.
Solicitation methods: Principally face-to-face and proposals

Active involvement

Cultivation

Participation

Cultivation

Annual Giving
Purpose: To support general operations
Sources include: Individuals, corporations, foundations, associations
Solicitation methods include: Face-to-face, direct mail, phonathon, proposals, special events

Awareness of the issue

Constituent or predisposed to the cause

Figure 4–1 Fund Development and the Engagement Process. *Source:* Adapted from J.M. Greenfield, ACFRE, FAHP, *Fund-Raising: Managing and Evaluating the Development Function*, p. 15, © 1991. Reprinted by permission of John Wiley & Sons, Inc.

- "What is a good return on investment?"
- "When will we actually ask?"
- "How do we set priorities?"

Challenges to Constituency Development

Challenge 1: Finding the Time

You think there is not enough time to do constituency development. Staff and volunteers are already overworked. Your organization needs money fast. In this case, identify your best prospects who are the most ready to be asked, then ask.

This doesn't stop you from doing constituency development. There is enough time. Examine how your staff and volunteers currently use their time. What is really important? Choose your priorities. Make constituency development a priority if you want your organization to survive into the next millennium. Allocate your time differently. Change the way you do business.

Challenge 2: Conducting Research without Spending Lots of Money

Research seems overwhelming, but you can accomplish it at low cost. Recruit marketing students from colleges and universities. They receive an education and a grade. You get a motivated worker who often uses the resources of his or her professors. Select employees to share research functions throughout the organization. Involve someone from your program and fund development areas. If you have the resources, hire a prospect researcher or contract with a service.

Remember that research for constituency development does not focus on assets and giving histories. Constituency development is as much about friend raising as fundraising. You seek interests and concerns of your constituents. Don't restrict research to the development operation. Make your research cross-organizational functions, addressing client needs, your strategic planning, and fund development.

Challenge 3: Getting Everyone To Value Constituency Development

The process of constituency development belongs to everyone in your organization, not just the fundraising staff and volunteers. Make constituency development part of your corporate culture. Adopt a customer orientation as one of your organizational values. Your leaders must help constituency development become part of group and individual behavior.

Challenge 4: Implementing the Process

Make constituency development part of your ongoing operations by creating the necessary management sys-

tems and using them. Use the systems and procedures in this section or modify them to meet your needs better. Regularly evaluate the effectiveness of your systems and alter them as necessary. Your shared values will support your management systems.

Challenge 5: Treating Major Donors Differently

Fundraisers usually direct the majority of their time and effort to major donors, giving proportionately less attention to smaller donors. This attitude reflects the 90/10 rule: 90 percent of your gifts generally come from 10 percent of your donors. It used to be the 80/10 rule, but now 90/10 seems closer to the truth.

> *A customer orientation holds that the main task of the organization is to determine the perceptions, needs, and wants of target markets and to satisfy them through the design, communication, pricing, and delivery of appropriate and competitively viable offerings.*
> *Philip Kotler and Alan R. Andreason*

This is all fine and good, up to a point. Be careful. Too much of this attitude and you will almost certainly overlook (or lose) some of those very constituents who might become the most stalwart and most generous. Organizations that received $10 gifts for years are sometimes the recipients of unexpected major bequests. Donors who once gave $100 a year may steadily increase their contribution to $1,000.

Anyway, what does "major donor" mean? Most define "major" according to organization standards. A small grassroots organization might define a major donor as one who gives $100. A hospital probably defines a major donor as someone who gives more than $10,000. For a recent capital campaign, an Ivy League university defined its major donors as those who gave $100,000 or more.

This approach focuses on the institution and its wants and needs, with little sensitivity to the donor's perspective. Certainly, you need some mechanism to allocate organization resources. However, the donor defines what a major gift is based on his or her own circumstance. If you forget this, you are likely to harm the relationship.

Try a different approach to allocating your resources. Focus on the outcome(s) you want from constituency development. The dollar level is only one dimension. Consider other outcomes, such as: first-time gift; increased gift; multiple gifts in one year; help fundraise, as well as give money. Then evaluate the likelihood of achieving your desired outcome. Allocate your resources based on the combination of desired outcome and likelihood of achievement.

Challenge 6: Contacting Your Constituents a Lot but Not Too Much

Find the balance between too little contact and too much. Don't overwhelm your constituents with too much contact. On the other hand, make sure you contact them enough so they remember and learn more about you.

So what's enough but not too much? This is a judgment call that you must make for each constituent or constituent group. Here are some tips: Marketers estimate that it takes 7–10 reinforcements before someone is ready to act. Some fundraisers say it takes nine cultivation activities before you can ask for a major gift.

Will these estimates still hold true in the twenty-first century? It seems likely that more cultivation—or at least more personalized cultivation—will be required to get the prospect ready for a request. And more cultivation will probably be necessary for a major gift request.

You must identify which activities will most effectively move the constituent along the continuum. Don't just consider frequency. Also, consider content, scope, and style of contact. Think about the contacts from the constituent's perspective. When will the constituent feel inundated by your contacts and become frustrated? What is so infrequent that the constituent will never notice? Decide how many resources you can afford to allocate to achieve which results.

Challenge 7: Asking for Money without Developing Relationships

Without constituency development, you have only vague knowledge about and little relationship with those you want to approach. But the truth is, sometimes you solicit a gift without adequate constituency development. Given your resources, this may be appropriate—but only rarely.

For example, many organizations conduct acquisition campaigns by mail or telephone. Interested recipients give, then you cultivate relationships. You have raised some money while introducing yourself.

Just remember: Most of the letters are thrown away or the calls refused. There is no substitute for constituency development. The ideal fund development program would use constituency development 100 percent of the time.

Challenge 8: Welcoming Diversity

Constituency development works only if it is sensitive and tailor-made to the targeted constituencies. In our pluralistic world, this means your constituency development must be sensitive to diversity, which, at the least, includes gender, generation, culture and ethnicity, socio-economics, sexual orientation, and physical challenge.

Our world is full of glass ceilings that limit the access of people of color, women, gays and lesbians, those who are poor, and those who experience some form of physical challenge. Although we make some strides, we have not overcome prejudice nor broken through all the ceilings.

Ironically, changing demographics increases the numbers of women and people of color. Economists say that, early in the twenty-first century, there may be no more middle class in the United States, only the wealthy and the poor. Is it the same in other countries?

To survive, your organization must be respected by diverse people. To be morally viable, your organization will have to embrace pluralism and welcome diversity. Effective organizations will seek, not just embrace, diversity. Successful constituency development tactics will reflect different cultural traditions, languages, and lifestyles.

Challenge 9: Compromising Organizational Values

Sometimes, organizations worry that focusing on benefits to the donor will compromise mission. Organizations see themselves following donor desires, rather than the organization's own vision and strategic plan.

Don't do it. Constituency development does not mean compromising your organization's values or vision. Don't cater to a donor's whim if it conflicts with your organization. But don't push your organization's needs with no consideration for the donor's interests. Once you understand what will benefit the donor, find the intersection with your organization's needs. If that is not possible, explain why to the donor. Based on what you understand about the donor and his or her wants and needs, try to change the donor's mind. If that is not possible, don't make the ask. Don't accept the gift.

Values are discussed more fully in Chapter 2, regarding your organization's internal relations.

> *Make sure your organization is chosen rather than abandoned.*

Challenge 10: Misrepresenting Intentions

Make sure your staff, volunteers, and constituents clearly understand that this is a professional relationship with the organization. Don't let constituents misinterpret your intentions. Volunteers are sometimes concerned about this. They worry that constituents may think that the organization's representatives are offering personal friendship. Sometimes, staff cross the line into friendship.

Take care and don't confuse the relationships. When you speak personally with a constituent, make sure the context is that of the organization. Focus on the constituent's relationship to the organization, not to any single individual.

Use the systems and procedures of your constituency development system to set boundaries and define relationships.

> *Marketing is not a peripheral activity of modern organizations but one that grows out of the essential quest of modern organizations to effectively serve some area of human need. To survive and succeed, organizations must know their markets; attract sufficient resources; convert these resources into appropriate products, services, and ideas; and effectively distribute them to various consuming publics. These tasks are carried on in a framework of voluntary action by all the parties.*
>
> *Philip Kotler and Alan R. Andreason*

Challenge 11: Competing with Other Organizations

Competition for philanthropic gifts is a myth fostered by organizations that do not know how to develop the four relationships that are critical to fund development. Competition suggests that there are limited dollars instead of donors who would give more and people who might give but have not been asked. Yet experience and studies show that more people give each year, people give more, and many have yet to be asked to give.

Certainly, there is congestion in the marketplace. There are lots of fundraising messages out there. But effective organizations distinguish themselves to their targeted constituents. These organizations ensure their relevance to the community. Then they focus on constituency development. If you develop relationships well, your constituents will give to you. They will give again and again. Many will give more and more.

Not-for-profit organizations must remember: The philanthropic process is more than a process by which money and time are given by donors to organizations so that those organizations can deliver services for the public good. Philanthropy is a process to meet the needs of and to fulfill the vision of the donor. The charity is the means. Fund development helps individuals (businesses, etc.) understand a cause enough so that they want to become involved and give.

An organization cannot take donors away from another organization. Donors choose to go away. Donors always have a choice. They leave an organization because of what the organization does—or doesn't do. Donors leave because organizations fail to develop strong relationships.

Many donors and prospects are swiftly outpacing not-for-profit organizations. These constituents expect their needs to be understood and met. (They expect a lot of other things, such as meeting community need and quality and collaboration. Organizations need to pay attention to all these expectations.)

Not-for-profit organizations and their fundraisers had best catch up and get ahead or risk that donors will go elsewhere. There's choice—on the part of donors about who they do business with and on the part of organizations about how they do business. There is no real competition. There's only congestion, which not-for-profit organizations can overcome.

Challenge 12: Universalizing Your Own Passion

You are convinced that your cause is worthy and that your organization is essential. That's great. But not everyone else *is* convinced, and lots of people are *not interested in being convinced.*

That's right. As a donor, I'm simply not interested in lots of causes. Remember my dad's fund? I appreciate the fact that the American Cancer Society exists. I respect its work and am pleased that there are many who give to this cause. However, I'm not interested. Nope. Not interested. Period. Not at all. And please don't waste your breath trying to convince me.

Beware. Is your organization universalizing its own passion by pursuing those who are not predisposed or those who appeared to be predisposed but, on further interaction, keep displaying a distinct lack of interest? Are you one of those fundraisers who keeps saying, "But if I could get her alone for 15 minutes I could convince her?"

How dare you? That's just plain arrogant and even patronizing. Don't universalize your own passion to those who do not care. It's okay not to care. We care about something else.

Challenge 13: Trespassing on Personal and Professional Relationships

Fundraisers pressure their board members and fundraising volunteers to "reach out to your friends and neighbors and colleagues." Furthermore, fundraisers exhort their board members and other volunteers to "use your personal and professional contacts to get gifts."

Stop right there. What about the match of interest between the friend or colleague and the organization and cause? This is about commitment to a cause, respect for an organization, and building relationships. This is not about robbing family piggybanks and exchanging favors to raise money.

Stop the bottom-line and short-term thinking. What should you be asking your board members and volunteers to do? Ask them to look at their personal and professional contacts and decide whether any of those contacts might be predisposed to the cause or to the organization. Ask your board members and volunteers to reach out to those who may be predisposed and explore the possibility of a mutually beneficial exchange.

Give your board members and volunteers permission to ignore the contacts who are not predisposed. Encourage them to turn to others and find out whether they are predisposed.

And what about those who are predisposed? Once your board members and volunteers have confirmed this predisposition, build a relationship. Engage your board members and volunteers in the process of building these relationships. Only then do you talk about solicitation.

Take a look at Appendix 4–A, a form that is useful to help identify the predisposed.

THE PROCESS OF CONSTITUENCY DEVELOPMENT

The purpose of constituency development is getting prospects ready to be asked. The intended outcome is engagement. You want various constituents engaged in your organization in different ways.

Every organization has constituents. You want to develop those constituents so they are prospects for some type of request. Ultimately, you'll want your constituents to see themselves as great prospects, ready to be asked. When they say yes, your prospects become givers. Now you strengthen the relationship so they are prospects for a bigger request. For definitions, see Exhibit 4–6.

Just imagine. Your organization successfully designs and implements ongoing systems and activities that actually enable the predisposed to notice your organization, then to reach out to it.

> So what is constituency development really about? Creating a process whereby people (and businesses, civic groups, etc.) self-identify as predisposed to your organization.

Surely, this is the pinnacle of a successful constituency development program. And what is this but marketing that has produced branding?

Four Principal Components of Constituency Development

Constituency development is a continuum. Your job is to help constituents move along the continuum. During the process, each constituent will become engaged in different ways. A client may become a donor, a donor might

Exhibit 4–6 Constituents Are Different from Prospects—and Other Important Distinctions

Predisposed	In fundraising vocabulary, a suspect. "A possible source of support whose philanthropic interests appear to match those of a particular organization but whose linkages, giving ability, and interests have not yet been confirmed."
Constituent	Someone who relates to or cares about your organization. Can be an individual, business, service organization, mosque, etc.
Constituency	Group of constituents. "People who have a reason to relate to or care about an organization."
Prospect	Constituent who has moved along the constituency development continuum and is now a target for a request. "Any potential donor whose linkages, giving ability, and interests have been confirmed."
Donor	A person, organization, corporation, foundation, or other entity that makes a gift of time, money, or service. Also called a *contributor*.

Source: Reprinted with permission from *The NSFRE Fund-Raising Dictionary*, Barbara R. Levy and R.L. Cherry, editors, © 1996. Reprinted by permission of John Wiley & Sons, Inc.

volunteer, a volunteer might become a trustee. Eventually, your constituents are ready to be asked for more and different things. At regular intervals, you evaluate the constituent's progress and decide how to proceed.

There are four major components to the constituency development process.

1. identifying constituents and those who are predisposed ("suspects") to enter the process
2. communicating with constituents
3. cultivating relationships
4. asking

Together, these components can produce engagement and connection. And that engagement and connection produces long-term investment on the part of the donor. Long-term investment from your donors ensures your survival as an organization.

Occasionally, the constituency development process doesn't work. When this is the case, accept it and move on.

Component 1: Identifying Entities To Enter the Process

Many of your constituents are already close to you. Think about your board members, other volunteers, and those who use your service and participate in your programs. There are other constituents who may not be as close but are constituents, nonetheless. These include your vendors and neighbors.

> **A donor is more important than a donation.**

Some organizations don't have enough constituents to operate well. Often, this happens with grassroots organizations whose clients are unable to give dollars and serve on the board. These organizations must find community people who value the service, even though they don't use it.

Bear in mind, it's harder to find new constituencies than it is to enrich relationships with current constituents. You have to identify groups that may be predisposed to your cause. Then you must introduce them to your organization and clearly explain your role in the cause. If you build sufficient interest with those who are predisposed, they become your constituents. Then you move them along the continuum of relationships so they become prospects, givers, and repeat givers.

Who else might become your constituents? Who else might be predisposed to your cause? Think inclusively. Expand your view. On the other hand, don't be too expansive. Remember, there is no "general public" for your organization.

Component 2: Communicating with Constituents

Communication is a two-way street. Effective organizations reach out and listen to their constituents, as well as provide them with information. Communication transmits information from your organization to your constituents and information from your constituents to your organization. Effective communication asks for and produces action. Effective communication requires that you understand how your constituents absorb information. Communication is discussed later in this chapter.

Component 3: Cultivating Relationships

The *Funk & Wagnalls Dictionary* (1963) defines *cultivate* as "caring for in order to promote growth and abundance." The *NSFRE Fund-Raising Dictionary* (Levy and Cherry, 1996) says "to engage and maintain the interest and involvement of."

You develop and improve a relationship through research and selective cultivation techniques. You pay attention to, seek acquaintance with, and court friendship.

(This means a friendship with your organization, not a personal relationship with an individual.)

Component 4: Asking

Eventually, you have to ask. Once you consider the prospect ready, ask clearly and concisely.

You design the request so it matches the prospect's demonstrated interest and presumed capacity. You pick the right person to solicit the gift. You appeal to the donor's need to be shown the benefits of giving, not to the features of your organization.

> **A well-timed ask is key. Premature asking harms your organization.**

This book takes you up to the ask and stops. For how-to advice about solicitation techniques, numerous books and articles are available, including the other titles in this series.

How You Can Do Constituency Development

A recommended 10-step process for constituency development is summarized in Exhibit 4–7, below.

To be successful, your organization goes through each step. You may move through some steps more quickly than others. Sometimes, you will collapse some of the steps into each other.

Warning: Don't enter the process midstream. The whole point of the process is to cultivate the constituent properly before making the ask. Constituency development is not always a linear process. It is, however, a progressive process.

Move your constituents through the continuum. At each step, ask and answer the questions provided in this book. Develop additional questions specific to your organization. If your constituents are ready, move to the next step. Otherwise, remain at the same step or retreat to an earlier step. Move only when the constituent is ready to go forward.

Use the 10-step process as a management guide. Each step describes activities and suggests questions. Give this information to your volunteers and staff. They help identify constituents and answer the questions. Create teams of workers to carry out specific tasks within each step. Use staff and volunteers to carry out the strategies your organization designs.

Try the worksheets in Appendix 4–B. These may help you carry out steps 2–9 in the constituency development process. If you don't like forms, just use the questions to direct your organization's conversations and decisions.

The 10-step process and the worksheets can be used for a single constituent (such as an individual or a busi-

Exhibit 4–7 Ten-Step Constituency Development Process

The steps	The questions to answer
1. Identify the predisposed and decide whether they might become constituents.	*What makes them a good candidate?*
2. Inform constituents.	*What do they know about us?*
3. Get to know your constituents.	*What do they want?*
4. Identify potential relationship between prospect and your organization.	*Is there an intersection?*

If there is an intersection, continue the constituency development process. If not, stop the process. Do not consider the constituent a prospect.

5. Develop the relationship.	*Are they involved, committed?*

Continue building the relationship. If at a point you determine that there isn't enough interest on the part of the prospect, discontinue the attempt to develop the relationship.

6. Evaluate the prospect's interest, readiness, and capacity.	*Is the constituent ready?*
7. Design the ask.	*What is the right ask?*
8. Ask.	*Was the ask effective?*

If the prospect gives, acknowledge and recognize. If the prospect refuses, acknowledge and decide whether you should cultivate more or discontinue the process.

9. Evaluate the prospect within constituency development process.	*What next?*

Move the prospect into maintenance or upgrade tracks.

10. Enhance the relationship.	*How can you build the relationship?*

Strengthen the constituency development process by continuously moving the donor through steps 3–10.

---

ness) or a group (200 upwardly mobile professionals with young families, for instance).

Constituency Development Steps

Your first task is to strengthen relationships with your constituents so they move through the continuum: constituents becoming prospects, prospects becoming donors, and donors giving again and more.

Your second task is to identify those who may be predisposed to your cause or organization. Encourage them to become constituents. Then move them along the constituency development continuum from constituent to prospect to donor.

Remember the distinctions between the predisposed, constituent, prospect, and donor. Review Exhibit 4–6.

1. Start with Your Constituents.

The easiest and fastest route to fundraising success is to start with your constituents. They are ready to move into the constituency development process. Because they already participate in your organization, they may be at step 2 of the process. Some may already be at step 3. You may have gotten to know them and know something about their demographics, lifestyles, and general inter-

ests. But they are still "undeveloped" at this stage. They may be prospects for many different kinds of requests. You need to cultivate the relationship and define the request so they are ready to be asked.

If You Need More Constituents, Identify the Predisposed.

Goal: Identify those who are predisposed to your cause. Qualify them so they can be introduced into your constituency development process.

Once you have done all the work you can with your constituents, begin searching for those who might be predisposed to your cause or your organization. Your world is filled with many who may be predisposed to your organization or cause. Look for them. Define why they are predisposed.

Inform them about your organization and its work with the cause. Make them your constituents. Cultivate a relationship so they see themselves as prospects ready to be asked and asked again for more.

Strategies: To identify the predisposed, ask yourself:

- Whom does our organization attract?
- Which types of individuals or businesses, which foundations and other community groups are pre-

disposed to our organization's mission, vision, and scope of service? Why?

- What makes them predisposed and how does this fit in with our organization?

Where can you find those who are predisposed to your organization?

- Look at organizations that do work like yours. Check out their board members and publicly recognized donors.
- Ask your constituents to identify those they know who are or might be interested.
- Interview community leaders for their ideas.
- Read newspapers and investigate community reports and studies.
- Talk to your colleagues at other organizations.

You can use concentric circles to help (see Figure 4–2). Your cause is always in the bull's-eye. Causes most like yours are closest to you. Once you have identified the causes, look at the people and businesses that support those causes. You may want to add some of them into the constituency development process.

Use concentric circles to identify the networks your staff and volunteers have (see Figure 4–3). Put each volunteer or staff person in the bull's-eye. Look at their networks. You may find individuals and businesses that might be cultivated to support your organization. You might also find some of your own constituents!

Evaluate: Decide whether the predisposed are likely constituents through a series of qualifying questions. Consider the following and add your own.

- Do the predisposed share some common interest(s) with your organization? For example: Are they publicly listed as donors by an organization similar to yours? Do you have information that indicates they use services like those you offer?
- Are they connected to someone in your organization? Did someone within your organization refer them to you?
- Does lifestyle and demographic information suggest they might be predisposed to your type of organization?

If you can answer yes to any of these qualifying questions, introduce those who are predisposed into your

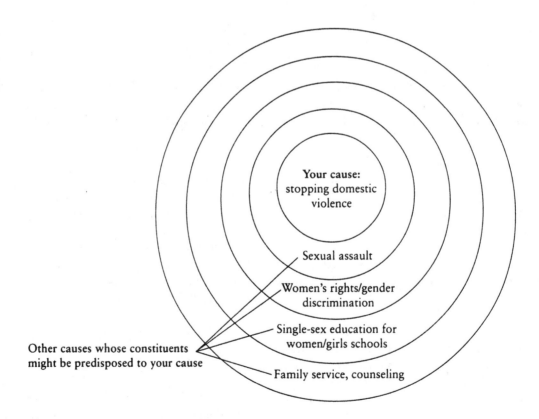

Figure 4–2 Identify Those Who Might Be Predisposed to Your Cause

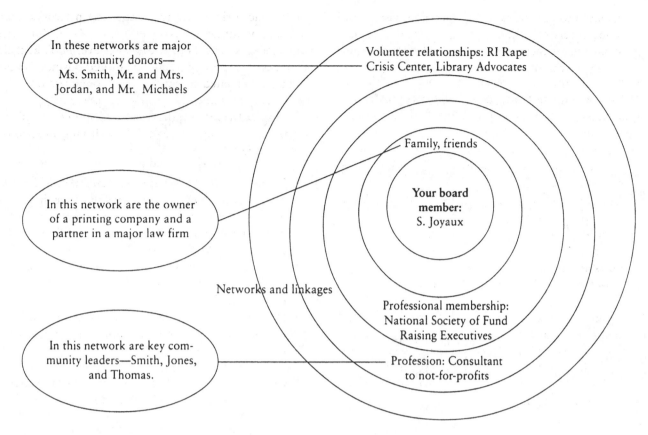

Figure 4–3 Identify Those in Your Own Networks

In the figure:

- In these networks are major community donors—Ms. Smith, Mr. and Mrs. Jordan, and Mr. Michaels
- Volunteer relationships: RI Rape Crisis Center, Library Advocates
- Family, friends
- **Your board member:** S. Joyaux
- In this network are the owner of a printing company and a partner in a major law firm
- Networks and linkages
- Professional membership: National Society of Fund Raising Executives
- In this network are key community leaders—Smith, Jones, and Thomas.
- Profession: Consultant to not-for-profits

---

constituency development process. Try to develop them into constituents. Proceed through steps 2–10.

On the other hand, if the predisposed do not qualify, do not introduce them into your process. Leave them alone and move on to others. See Appendix 4–A, a worksheet to help identify and discuss the predisposed.

2. Inform Your Constituents.

Goal: Engage the interest of your constituents by developing and increasing their awareness of your organization. (Remember, these constituents are not yet prospects, but you hope they will be soon!)

> *Your constituent could be one major corporation or 100 individuals who share certain characteristics.*

Evaluate: Think about how you inform these constituents about your organization. Consider how you are known to them and what they think of you. Ask yourself such questions as:

- What do they already know about us?

- Are their perceptions in any way different than reality?
- What do we do now to talk with each constituency?
- What don't we do that would work?
- What resources will we need to do more informing?

Strategies: Use the constituency development worksheets in Appendix 4–B. See the section entitled "Communicating with Your Constituents," later in this chapter.

Begin by providing the constituent the chance to show interest in your organization. Accomplish this through a call to action. For example:

- Invite constituents to an event and record if they do or don't attend.
- Ask if the constituents wish to continue receiving information.
- Conduct a phonathon with constituents to ask their opinion of a particular service or program.

Evaluate: Is the constituent sufficiently engaged to move into the research phase? After you have communicated for a while, evaluate how you should proceed with the constituent. Use the following kinds of questions for your evaluation:

- Is the constituent participating in some way?
- What was the response to the call to action(s)?
- Is it manageable to secure information about the constituent?

Decide whether it is worth your time to leave the constituents in the process. Are they interested enough for you to spend time getting to know them better? If yes, proceed. Now you can consider them prospects for some future request. If no, remove them from the constituency development process.

3. Get To Know Your Constituents.

Goal: Know their demographics and lifestyles. Understand constituents' interests and needs. Be familiar with relevant patterns and trends.

Research outcomes and strategies: From your research, you want to know what the constituent values and wants; what her interests and needs are; what his perception is of your mission, vision, and programs.

To gather this information, conduct focus groups and surveys. Carry on conversations. Analyze your own database and look at local and global patterns and trends. Combine research activities with a request for something. Research strategies are discussed in "Getting to Know Your Constituents." Also see Chapter 3, which discusses strategic planning.

4. Identify Potential Relationship.

Goal: Decide whether there is an intersection between the constituents' interests and needs and your organization's mission, vision, and programs. Describe the mutually beneficial exchange.

Evaluate: Think carefully about the constituents' interests and needs. Think about your organization's values and vision. Ask yourself such questions as:

- Can our organization meet the constituent's needs?
- Can we benefit the constituent without compromising our own values, vision, and mission?
- Is there a mutually beneficial exchange?

If you answer yes, consider the constituent a solid prospect. Use the research information to create a number of scenarios where your organization and the prospect might work together to achieve a shared vision. The scenarios might include such things as:

- Financial investment to support your activities. This might be a designated or unrestricted charitable contribution or a sponsorship with specific obligations.
- Volunteer opportunity. You might seek a short- or long-term commitment as a member of a committee or task force.
- Advisory opportunity. You might seek informal advice or participation.

Meet with the prospect and get his or her response to the scenarios. Find out whether the prospect has other ideas in mind. Decide whether it's the right time to ask or whether you need to cultivate more. If the prospect isn't interested at all, remove him or her from the constituency development process. If there is a spark, continue to move the prospect through the continuum.

5. Develop the Relationship.

Goal: Prepare the prospect to be asked. Cultivate more involvement and commitment.

Strategies: Using research results, enhance communications and develop cultivation strategies. See the sections on communications and cultivation in this chapter.

You spend most of your time developing relationships. This is your chance to reach out and engage people in your organization. Develop cultivation strategies that capture the attention of your constituents and prospects, and reflect the values of your organization. Some strategies are used with everyone. Other strategies are personalized for targeted groups. What you do depends on your resources.

Evaluate: Decide whether your constituents are becoming more engaged in and connected to your organization. Evaluate their relationships with your organization. Consider the following:

- What messages are your constituents and prospects sending you? Do they seem pleased with your organization? What projects or programs are of greatest interest to which prospects or constituents? Who in your organization do your prospects and constituents relate to?
- Describe how your constituents and prospects are engaged in your organization. Compare their current extent of involvement (e.g., frequency, depth, and breadth) with previous intervals.
- Do they use your services, attend special events, respond to various invitations?
- Do they volunteer? If yes, in what capacity and how often?
- Have they given financial contributions? If yes, how do these gifts compare with their prior gifts in terms of size, frequency and repetition, restriction, etc.?

6. Evaluate the Prospect's Interest, Readiness, and Capacity.

Goal: Decide whether the prospect is ready to be asked for a contribution of time or money.

Evaluate: A prospect is ready to be asked when there is an optimum intersection of interest, readiness, and capacity. See "Evaluating Readiness To Be Asked." If the prospect is not yet ready to be asked, continue building the relationship. If yes, proceed with the next steps.

7. Design the Ask.

Goal: Create an appropriate request.

Evaluate: Determine the appropriate request for the particular prospect. Personalize the request and the way of asking the prospect. Select the appropriate asker.

To design the ask, determine the following.

- How will giving benefit the prospect, given his or her interests, needs, and motivations?
- What is the appropriate focus (or project) that would be most appropriate to this prospect, given his or her interests, needs, and motivations?
- Will more than one giving option be presented to the prospect?
- Is it likely that the request will be initiated at the first meeting, with a subsequent visit required to finish?
- Who is the best solicitor or team of solicitors?
- Given the prospect's capacity and level of interest and readiness, what is the appropriate request amount?
- What is the best way to structure the ask—outright request for the amount, specific intervals within a range, costs for particular projects?
- When is the best time?
- What is the best approach—face-to-face, mail, telephone?
- What is the actual request scenario? What will be communicated, how, and by whom?

8. Ask.

Goal: Ask well and secure an answer to the request.

Evaluate: Was the ask effective? No matter what the response, assess the constituency development process. Discuss what you learned. Apply your learning to this prospect and, as appropriate, to other prospects and constituents.

Ask yourself:

- Was this the appropriate request? How responsive was the prospect?
- How well received was the person asking?

- How effectively did we anticipate and respond to questions and challenging issues?
- Was there sufficient interest, readiness, and capacity?
- How good was the quality of conversation between our organization and the prospect?
- What should we do next?

If the prospect gives, acknowledge and recognize both the donor and the gift. Then move the donor to step 9.

If the prospect refuses, acknowledge and adjust the constituency development process. Return to earlier steps. Assess the effectiveness of your strategies. If necessary, devise new ones. Examine what you know about the prospect. Get to know him or her better. Be sensitive to your prospects. Are they overwhelmed or underwhelmed by your communication and cultivation? Review the role of staff and volunteers. Strengthen their performances. Involve new cultivators.

> *Develop the best and most appropriate relationship with each prospect. Maybe this is a financial contribution or a volunteer relationship.*

9. Evaluate Prospect within Constituency Development Process.

Goal: Determine how to proceed with the prospect.

Evaluate: It is hoped that the prospect is now a donor. She or he is also a prospect for another gift, a different type of gift, perhaps a larger gift. Decide what to do next.

Consider the following questions.

- Now that the prospect is a donor of some type, how will we enhance the relationship?
- Is this donor a prospect for a different kind of gift? For an increased gift?
- Should we maintain the relationship or should we try to enhance it for more and greater asks?
- How has the prospect responded to the process? Has this been a positive experience for the prospect? Which activities did the prospect prefer?
- Has the process been worthwhile for our organization? Did we meet our goals?

10. Enhance the Relationship.

Goal: To strengthen relationships.

The constituency development continuum is also a perpetual circle, moving the donor continuously through steps 3–10. Some prospects will stay in the maintenance track. You sensitively maintain the relationship through appropriate communication and cultivation. Regularly, you ask for gifts and renew the donor's involvement.

Other donors/prospects display more interest and capacity. They are moving toward long-term investment. You enhance the relationship by moving them into the upgrade track. You hope to increase the prospect's commitment. Use more intense and personalized communication and cultivation. Ask more often. Try to upgrade involvement regularly.

ROLES IN THE CONSTITUENCY DEVELOPMENT PROCESS

Your entire institution is responsible for developing relationships. Every staff person and all volunteers must participate.

The fundraising executive leads the process of constituency development. Aware of the four key relationships, the fundraiser always reaches beyond fund development and includes the chief executive, staff, and volunteers in the process.

Together, the chief executive officer and the board of directors are responsible for the health of the organization. They ensure that there are sufficient constituents to support the organization—as clients, donors, and volunteers. The chief executive and board make sure that the organization values marketing as a philosophy and uses marketing as a management tool. These leaders ensure that there is adequate infrastructure to support constituency development.

There are many ways to integrate constituency development throughout your organization. You could establish an employee team that crosses all areas of operation. You could create a team with volunteers and staff. Or do both. Teams will support the constituency development process by:

- providing orientation and training to staff and volunteers
- setting realistic goals
- brainstorming and helping implement strategies
- monitoring progress across all organizational functions
- ensuring that constituents transition smoothly among different parts of the organization

Involve the Board, Board Members, and Others

Make sure you involve your governing board in the constituency development process. Discuss the values and systems. Ask the board to brainstorm cultivation strategies. Use the board to identify challenges and their

solutions. The board then confirms measurable goals that it has helped create and discusses the results.

Consider a board-level committee for constituency development. Establish a separate task force that reports to the development committee or make constituency development part of the development committee's responsibility.

Ask each individual board member to carry out constituency development tasks, just as each board member helps fundraise. Recruit some board members for your constituency development committee. Assign a team of trustees to implement a cultivation plan personalized to a specific prospect. Expect individual board members to carry out cultivation and communications strategies.

Reach out beyond your staff and volunteers. Involve your donors and clients. Ask them to join your constituency development committees. Donors can be your best cultivators. Clients can help tell stories.

Create Affinity Teams

Look at the targeted audiences you want to reach. Create affinity teams to support constituency development for a specific audience. From the target group, recruit a few individuals who are predisposed to your organization. Ask them to join your affinity team.

Explain your organization's values and philosophy up front, so team members understand and are supportive. Look at the discussion about values in Chapter 2 of this book. Make sure there are no value conflicts between your organization and an affinity team.

With the affinity team, set realistic goals for building relationships with the targeted constituents. Make sure your goals are not related to money alone. Remember, a donor is more important than a donation. You seek relationships. A focus on constituent needs will capture their interests; a focus on money will turn them off.

Use the affinity team to devise the constituency development plan and communications strategies. Ask these volunteers to help carry out the strategies. Use the affinity team to monitor progress and measure effectiveness.

GETTING TO KNOW YOUR CONSTITUENTS

How well do you know your constituents? Probably not as well as you should and could. Getting to know your constituents means understanding them well enough to create a mutually beneficial exchange.

Knowing your constituents requires research. Too many organizations make prospect research an information function, rather than a constituency development function. But research for research's sake can be a trap if the data are not intended to cultivate relationships. More information cannot substitute for real understanding.

Even experienced fundraising executives need to think about the process and tasks of constituency development. But they often don't, no more than their less experienced counterparts. In conversations with fundraisers around the country, even the most experienced professionals make the following comments.

- "I don't have enough time to focus on these relationship steps. I'm too busy balancing this year's budget."
- "I can't spend this kind of time or money on any but the largest donors. I just do an annual letter and a few newsletters to small donors."
- "For acquisition, my agency just sends solicitation letters to selected lists. We don't do any advance cultivation or much qualifying. There's no time or money."

You might willingly devote 12 months and lots of volunteer and staff time to understand the wants and needs of an individual from whom you seek a financial contribution that is large for your organization. You might invest lots of time to understand the wants and needs of 100 upwardly mobile young women because you hope to engage 10 in your organization as future leaders and donors.

On the other hand, you might not invest many resources getting to know 500 donors who consistently give less than $100 dollars to your organization. You just want enough information to maintain and modestly increase their participation.

> *Always keep in mind that you have to figure out how much cultivation the constituent thinks is enough to give a gift.*

Your organization makes these decisions regularly. Think carefully. Use the tools of a comprehensive constituency development process to help you decide how to spend your time with which constituents.

Figure Out What You Should Know about Your Constituents

You decide what is useful information. Find the balance between too little and too much. As Sherree Parris Nudd says, "All information gathering should lead to one thing: the process and practice of taking the donor's view in cultivating the philanthropic partnership with the organization" (Rosso 1991, 184).

Before you start researching, decide what you want to know and why. Figure out how you will use the information and why it is meaningful. Then devise your research methods and develop your research tools. Determine when and how you will involve which staff and volunteers in the research process. Decide how you will manage the resulting information, usually consisting of computer and paper files.

Ask yourself:

- What do we want to know about our constituents?
- What is the minimal information required to maintain only the most cursory relationship?
- What is necessary to cultivate the relationship further?
- What is essential to engage the constituent in our organization?

For effective constituency development, you need two kinds of information. First, you need specific information about a targeted constituent (single entity) or targeted constituency (fairly homogeneous group). Second, you need to know the general trends and patterns of your various constituencies and other audiences predisposed to your organization.

Some information must be attached to the particular constituent, as a single entity. Other information can be generalized to a homogeneous group. If you wish a closer relationship, the information must be attached to the single entity.

Generally, you seek demographic and psychographic information about your constituents. Demographics refers to the characteristics of a group, such as size, growth, and distribution; and the vital statistics of individuals such as age, gender, marital status, family size, education, income, occupation, and geographic location.

Psychographics describes the lifestyle characteristics of a group or individual, including their activities and behavioral and personal traits. Psychographic indicators cover one's interests and values, hopes and fears, aspirations and needs.

Exhibits 4–8 and 4–9 give you a taste of changing demographics and lifestyles. To get information quickly, see "Tips To Learn about Changing Demographics and Lifestyles," and "Look at Reports and Other Resources" in this chapter. These data continually evolve, so stay on top of the changes.

Pay attention to societal trends. Nichols notes there are five major ones that will significantly affect your organization's fundraising in the next century (Nichols 1995, 86).

Exhibit 4–8 A Snapshot of World Demographics in 1994

If you shrink the Earth's population to a village of 100 people using existing human ratios, the world looks like this:

57	Asians
21	Europeans
14	Western Hemispheric People (North and South Americans)
8	Africans

70	Non-white
30	White

70	Unable to read
50	Malnourished
80	Living in substandard housing

1	University graduate

50% of the entire world's wealth would be in the hands of 6 people—all citizens of the United States.

Source: Reprinted with permission from Judith Nichols, *Global Demographics: Fund Raising for a New World,* p. 86, © 1995 Bonus Books, Inc.

1. overall aging of the population and length of life
2. unique demographics and psychographics of midlife Baby Boomers, "the largest generational grouping ever seen in the developed world"
3. new life patterns because women work
4. cultural diversification of populations
5. different perspective of the young

These trends will affect not only how you ask for gifts but who you'll ask. Figure out how these trends relate to your constituents. Learn about these trends so you can develop stronger relationships.

Just consider a few of the psychographics related to the major demographic groups of the late twentieth and twenty-first centuries. Ask yourself how well you are prepared to deal with these in your constituents—whether they be donors, volunteers, or clients.

Gather This Information To Use in Your Constituency Development Process

Review the 10-step constituency development process above. You need to understand your constituents better as you proceed through the steps.

1. Mandatory information you need for step 1 in the constituency development process.
   - Correct spelling of name (first and last name of individual; any designation such as "The Reverend," "CFRE," "FAHP," "ACFRE," and "CPA;" appropriate title for business contact; proper name of the business or group)
   - Correct address
   - Criteria that justify your contact (why you think they are a constituent or are sufficiently predisposed to warrant your organization's overtures)
2. Early in step 2, secure this information.
   - For a woman, preferred designation such as "Mrs.," "Miss," or "Ms."
   - If an individual, life partner or spouse name
   - Appropriate salutation, given the constituent's relationship with your organization
   - Preferred recognition name, if the constituent has given a gift to your organization
   - Relationship with your organization, e.g., volunteering, using service, connections with individuals within your organization, etc.
3. In step 3, get to know your constituents better.
   - General demographic information that might be applicable to the single entity or group, whether individuals, businesses, or some other type of organization.

For an individual, relevant demographic information includes such things as: location of residence, estimated income, number of family members, marital/partner status, education, profession, general age range.

For a business or another organization such as a mosque or service organization, relevant demographic information might include such things as: location, number of members or employees, list of staff and board, estimated budget or profit.

   - General lifestyle information that might be applicable to the single entity or group, whether individuals, businesses, or some other type of organization.

For an individual, relevant lifestyle information might include national or local trends attributable to such things as age, education, or profession.

For a business, church, or other organization, one might consider lifestyle information to include such things as: types of participation by the organization and its leaders in the community, giving policies and history, or corporate culture.

   - How the constituent best receives or "hears" information. Some people or groups respond best

Exhibit 4–9 Compare Your Constituents to These Psychographics

Baby boomers

- have been held back 10 years economically
- are not donor or customer loyal
- grew up being told they were special, yet are over-whelmed by their own numbers
- don't trust anyone
- are very nostalgic for the "good old days"
- created networking as a way of life
- concentrate on recognition, instant gratification, and accountability
- have three key concerns: their own retirement; educating their kids; their parents' aging.

Baby busters (Generation X)

Busters are the 18- to 29-year-olds of the late 1990s. They followed boomers and the natural progression from idealists to reactives. Nichols describes them as the "throwaway children of divorce and poverty, the latchkey kids. [They] weren't trusted nor appreciated as youth and carry the scars into adulthood. They are the most right-leaning youths of the 20th century. Ignored or vilified by the media, they tend to be cautious, anti-intellectual and pessimistic; many are fearful, frustrated, angry and believe they will be exterminated in a nuclear war" (60).

They are the most diverse generation in terms of ethnicity, education, and aspirations. At the top of the list, busters describe themselves as: fun (88%); outgoing (86%); sociable (79%). At the bottom of the list, they describe themselves as: caring (49%); independent (41%), and value-conscious (39%).

Busters want a more traditional lifestyle. They focus on: home, family, and friends, rather than work; and quality, not quantity of possessions and experiences. They are less skeptical than older consumers. Busters trust advertising and the media more.

Gender differences in giving

According to the perceptions of the women in focus groups, men give for recognition and women give from the heart. When asked specifically what, if any, gender differences there were regarding motivations for giving, it appeared that lines were clearly drawn between the personal for women and the more pragmatic for men. It was noted by a number of women, however, that as women become more involved in the social and business aspects of philanthropy, these lines are beginning to blur.

Some of the gender differences identified were:

Women:
- Reasons involving a personal response to need
- Give to specific needs
- Give money and time
- Give because of personal impact
- Personal involvement in organization
- Want to make a difference

Men:
- Give for recognition
- Giving is reciprocal
- For networking
- Longer tradition of giving money
- Practical, tax-saving reasons
- Business reasons

Source: Reprinted with permission from Judith Nichols, *Global Demographics: Fund Raising for a New World,* © 1995 Bonus Books, Inc, and University of California, Los Angeles, *UCLA Women and Philanthropy Focus Groups,* 1992.

to face-to-face communication; others prefer written or telephone contact. Still others may get most of their information from the radio or television. Also pay attention to the personality styles of your constituents. Who wants more facts and figures? Who responds better to emotion? See "Communicating with Your Constituents," later in this chapter.

Know Your Constituents Well Enough To Ask for a Gift

Now get to know your constituents better. Gather more specific information about their personal interests and activities. Learn what you can to help you develop a stronger relationship.

Think about the lifestyles of your constituents. What do they do in their leisure time? How do your constitu-

ents fit in with which major societal trends? Consider what the philanthropic behaviors of your constituents say about their interests and aspirations. Find out why your constituents affiliate with your cause and your organization. Figure out which services and programs your constituents care about most. Identify the kinds of special events and volunteer opportunities your constituents prefer.

Ask the kinds of questions that the Barna Research Group and the Russ Reid Company asked in a 1994 survey of donors.

- how often they donate to faith groups
- how often they donate to other charities
- how many groups they support
- why they support particular groups

- how much they donate to charities in a particular year
- size of their typical donation
- political philosophy of groups they support
- how different actions by charities would affect the donor's relationship with the organization
- how different types of communication would affect the donor's connection with a charity
- how different donors react to different types of events

Think about information that might help you develop better solicitation materials and stronger requests. Consider asking your constituents the following kinds of questions.

- What do they consider to be the most pressing issues facing the community?
- Which charities are they familiar with? Which ones do they admire the most?
- Which of your programs and services do your donors find most important?
- How familiar are they with your special events?
- How well do they understand your mission?
- How do they want to be solicited?
- What kind of acknowledgment and recognition do they prefer?
- Do they give to charity? If yes, what kinds of groups do your donors give to?
- Do they volunteer? If yes, where do they like to volunteer and why?
- What is their image of your organization?
- Do they give to federated appeals? If yes, would they consider designating a portion of their gifts to your organization?
- If they already give to you, what would it take for them to consider an increase?

Take a look at the sample Prospect Information Worksheet in Appendix 4–C. Note the scope of information and level of detail. Consider the following questions:

- What elements would you add to make this worksheet more useful?
- How will you ensure that you have the data to complete this worksheet?
- What might be the barriers and how will you overcome them?
- How will you help your volunteers understand why this depth of information is necessary?
- How will you engage volunteers in gathering this information?

How To Conduct Your Research

The effective development function regularly uses both formal and informal means to determine opinions, identify interests, and better understand the demographics and lifestyles of its constituents. The fundraiser encourages the entire institution to reach out and get to know its constituents better and share information.

Look at Chapter 3, the strategic planning section of this book, for more information about market research methods and tools.

Ask Your Constituents

The best way to get information about your constituents is to ask them. Through formal and informal contact, you acquire lifestyle information and perspective on constituent interests and concerns. You can also gather much of the demographic data you need.

Formal contact includes written and telephone surveys, personal interviews, focus groups, and brainstorming sessions. For example:

- Enclose a survey in your newsletter or when you send out thank-you letters.
- Ask your clients to answer a few questions or complete a minisurvey when they use your service.
- Conduct focus groups with prospective donors, current donors, and lapsed donors.
- Have your volunteers conduct personal interviews during a phonathon or at private appointments.

You also obtain important information during informal conversations with constituents. You have lunch with a board member. You speak with another volunteer. You meet with committees and clients. You mingle with guests at special events.

> *Your constituents want control of the relationship. They want some uniqueness in their relationships with your organization.*

Use these informal opportunities more effectively. At special events, assign board members and staff to speak with specific constituents. The fundraiser, chief executive, and other key staff should contact different constituents regularly. For example, several times a week, have breakfast or lunch with a constituent. Daily, contact someone to get to know him or her better.

Keep in mind, it's your job to create more extensive conversation between your constituents and organization. Ask specific questions. Pursue issues your constituents bring up. Listen to what people say and don't say. Remember relevant information gleaned during conversation and record it later. Write down anecdotes and note your impressions. (But be discreet. Prospect and donor records are not all that confidential. The donor can ask to see the information. The solicitor certainly will.)

Do not misrepresent your intentions. Do not pretend to be a personal friend offering privacy and confidentiality. This is a professional exchange and should be considered so. Behave ethically and professionally, and there will be no confusion.

Both the Norman Bird Sanctuary and the Boys & Girls Club of Pawtucket used surveys to get to know their members better. See Appendix 3–B for the Norman Bird Sanctuary member survey.

In 1996, the Norman Bird Sanctuary in Rhode Island had 1,500 paying members. Some of these members also gave charitable contributions to the wildlife preserve. The Sanctuary wanted to recruit more members and increase the number of members who give. Survey questions gathered information about such things as:

- motivations for joining—which would help the Sanctuary target its recruitment materials to specific markets and interests?
- preferred special events—which would guide the design of fundraising events?
- environmental priorities—which would suggest themes for the Sanctuary's solicitation materials?
- charitable interests—which would help the Sanctuary set reasonable giving expectations?

The Boys & Girls Club of Pawtucket, Rhode Island, has more than 3,500 youth members. Yet, few of the families give to the Club. The Club used a parent survey as the first step in its constituency development strategy. The survey provided multiple opportunities.

- It reached out to parents, showing them that their opinions are important to the Club.
- It introduced the concept of charitable gifts to support the Club.
- It provided information about the importance of gifts to keep the Club open.

After the survey, the Club designed a constituency development plan targeted at parents. Components of the plan included:

- A parent newsletter written by teen members of the Club. Articles responded to misperceptions identified through the survey. Articles also talked about topics of greatest interest to survey respondents.

- A phonathon preceded by a personalized letter. The letter built on the information presented in the parent newsletter, explaining the need for charitable contributions to support the youth programs. The phonathon sought opinions about particular issues, gathered more information about the families, and asked for a charitable gift.

The Boys & Girls Club also conducted personal interviews to gather information and cultivate relationships with community leaders. The Club worried that people did not clearly understand its mission and scope of service. Furthermore, the Club suspected that people thought it was wealthy and didn't need money.

The interview asked such questions as:

- "How would you describe the Boys & Girls Club? What words and phrases would you use?"
- "What do you think are the Club's strengths and weaknesses?"
- "What do you look for when you consider giving to an organization?"
- "How important do you think youth issues are, compared with other community issues?"

The interview results confirmed the Club's fears. People were not aware of how the Club's programs met the needs of youth. Interviewees thought the Club had enough powerful fundraising volunteers and lots of money from its endowments and the United Way.

The bottom line was, community leaders didn't think the Club needed charitable contributions or fundraising help. To change this perception, the Club took several steps.

- Wrote a new case statement, which featured misperceptions, then stated the reality. (See copy in Appendix 4–D.)
- Used the annual report to help change misperceptions.
- Prepared face-to-face solicitation materials to communicate reality.

Look at Reports and Other Resources

Lots of information is readily available in your community. Local marketing/advertising firms can give you their research on the lifestyles of specific audiences. Foundations publish their own studies on philanthropy. Fundraising organizations that administer federated appeals (such as the United Way) study community and donor trends. Academic institutions and government agencies often publish useful reports.

Don't stick with just your local community. Search the global marketplace, too. Try these sources for information:

- Many national and international service organizations, funding sources, governments, consultants, and academic institutions conduct research and publish their results.
- Read the publications of the not-for-profit sector and the fundraising field.
- Ask the reference librarians at your public library. See whether you can visit the nearest academic library.
- Search the Internet and World Wide Web. If you don't have your own computer access, borrow someone else's. Try one of your board members, the local library, or another development office.
- Contact the numerous professional organizations that serve the for-profit and not-for-profit sectors.
- Approach the centers on philanthropy and academic institutions.
- Ask your not-for-profit colleagues where they get their information about global trends.

Doing Research Cultivates Relationships

The process of getting to know your constituents actually cultivates relationships with them. Much of your research includes direct contact with constituents. By asking their opinions and involving them in focus groups, you build their interest in and respect for your organization. You meet and talk about mutual interests and aspirations. This is a marvelous cultivation strategy. The following are some examples—and there are so many more.

Magazines sometimes ask their subscribers to identify which topics would be of interest to them. For the magazine, subscriber opinion would help produce a more desirable publication by meeting the needs of the buyer. For the subscriber, the list of feature stories stimulates reader interest. You could do the same with your newsletter. Convene a group of donors and ask them what they want to read about.

You want to invent a new fundraising event. Bring in constituents from your target audience and ask them what they like to do, what they would attend and why.

COMMUNICATING WITH YOUR CONSTITUENTS

Communication is central to developing relationships. Communication is two-way, transmitting ideas, information, and feelings between individuals and groups. You transmit your ideas, information, and feelings to others. You encourage them to share the same with you. You seek information and perspective from others, valuing their input.

> *Action is always the goal of communications.*
> *Tom Ahern, ABC*

Effective communication translates information into knowledge and knowledge into learning. Communication implies understanding on the part of the person you are communicating with.

Through communication, you invite people into your organization. You invite them to use your service, to give you time or money. You position your organization by communicating your distinct niche within the community.

Communication is information received and, hopefully, acted upon. The effectiveness of communication can be evaluated only after the fact. If the recipient of the communication acts in the way you wanted, there was communication. If not, there was only information.

Communication is more than a fundraising brochure, your newsletter, the annual report, or posters for an event. Communication includes

- your dialogue at board meetings
- the structure and content of formal meetings and informal gatherings
- casual conversations you conduct with co-workers, board members, clients, and donors
- gossip and official memoranda, policies, and procedures

Fund Development Must Communicate Better

Fund development produces lots of poor communications. Information is passed on but no action results, so communication did not happen.

Look at the solicitation letters and fundraising brochures that cross your desk. Review your own fund development plan and support materials for fundraising volunteers. Listen to the information given to leadership so they can make critical decisions. The communication is often complicated, and the desired action unclear. The result is confusion, frustration, and wrong (or no) action. Information was passed, but communication did not result.

Fundraisers don't talk much about communication. They talk about marketing (sometimes reluctantly, as though it conflicts with the higher values of philanthropy). Fundraisers talk lots about public relations.

Fundraising books discuss marketing and public relations. Workshops teach the content of successful proposals and case statements.

But there's little talk of communications. Few fundraising texts explain the basics of good writing techniques. Workshops don't develop communications skills. Fundraisers seek the best solicitation techniques, only to fall behind in basic communications.

> *Image and reputation are important to fund development, but they are not the solution to securing community support. Neither is media visibility.*

How ironic, because fund development is all about communication. Fund development is the epitome of communication. Fundraising asks. And the response to that ask is the test of effective communication.

Beware of the Public Relations Mistake

Organizations assume good public relations will make them famous and lead people to give. The exact opposite is true. Good public relations require immense effort and may lead to no gifts at all.

Let's define public relations as building your organization's image and reputation. Image and reputation are important to fund development. To achieve this goal, commonly used public relations strategies include media coverage and special events. You release information to the media, and you do special events. You put these out into the community and hope. You hope the media will present the information. You hope people will notice, think well of you, and remember you.

But you have almost no control. There is no call to action in public relations. You cannot guide the response or measure the effectiveness. (By the way, the same holds true of advertising. The greatest ad agencies in the world tell you that they cannot measure the effectiveness of advertising.)

You cannot control media coverage unless you buy it. The standard media releases written by organizations are notoriously poor communications, often overlooked by editors and reporters. (What works better is a personalized, well-written letter explaining the newsworthiness of your story to the particular media outlet. Better yet, first have a personal conversation with the media representative. Follow up with a letter, fact sheet, and release.)

Special events require even more effort and, often, a significant financial investment. But these events are not as important as the accumulation of printed material and dialogue that you use in fund development.

Avoid Another Mistake . . . The Focus on Media Visibility

Increased media coverage and community visibility do not produce more charitable contributions. But tailor-made communication directed at targeted audiences does produce more charitable gifts.

Just because your organization receives lots of media attention doesn't mean that anyone will pay attention. Those who aren't interested in your organization or your cause won't read the article about you. They won't listen to the broadcast about you.

Target your audiences instead. Then develop your own communications directed to the target audiences. You'll get a better return on your investment of resources.

Sure, media coverage has value. It's great when someone says something nice about you. You can use it as testimony in your own communication. You can copy a news article and distribute it to the targeted audiences you want to read it. Your volunteers like media coverage. It makes them feel secure. Media coverage gives an external seal of approval. But spend most of your time on the communication you can control.

What Can You Do?

Focus most of your effort on communications directed at your targeted constituents. Remember, communications is information received and acted on. Communications are targeted, controlled, and measurable.

Because effective communications are essential to effective fund development, each fundraiser needs to know the basics. Even if you hire professional copy and speech writers, improve your own communications skills. Every leader—especially fundraisers—needs to communicate well.

In practice, communicating well often means learning to write more persuasively because 98 percent of the content of your organization is conveyed in written form. Read Bly's *The Copywriter's Handbook* (1985). Follow his directions, and you will improve both your oral and written communications. Review the concepts and tips outlined in this book, and use them. Take a look at Appendixes 4–D and 4–E for case statements that follow the rules presented here. Have an expert critique your work repeatedly. And practice, practice, practice. (By the way, writers say there is no such thing as writer's block. Just keep writing.)

Successful Communications

Successful communications depend upon your organization's understanding of the group with which you wish to communicate. Communications should always be tailored for the audience you're addressing. You need to know their interests, and you need to understand how they best receive communication.

To penetrate your target audience, your communications message must:

- clearly state benefits to the audience
- translate information into language and images that the audience will recognize
- deliver information through means used by the target audience
- reflect the values of your organization

> *First, there is no such thing as the general public. Second, effective organizations target specific audiences rather than the general public.*

You will not, in many cases, know the actual recipient of your communications. But you should know enough about him or her to create a picture in your mind. Communicate with that picture of a real person. When you are communicating, review the following checklist:

- Will the recipient of my communication understand what I am saying (or writing or showing)?
- Will she or he understand the insider language or examples or images that I might use?
- Am I personalizing my communication to the recipient's interests?
- Have I clearly explained benefits to the recipient?
- Is my communication clear and to the point?
- If I were the recipient of this communication, would I be interested?

Reconsider features and benefits. Reflect on marketing. Repeat your mantra, "It's not what I'm selling, it's what they're buying." To paraphrase Bly (1985): successful cultivators empathize with their constituents.

Beware the onset of the institutional voice. It drives people off. Do you begin your case statements and direct mail letters by talking about your organization and all the great things it has done? The "we do this" style is the single best indication that an organization is not oriented toward the constituent.

Effective cultivators do not launch into some pitch that talks about the organization and its activities. Instead, effective cultivators try to understand the constituent's needs, mood, personality, and prejudices. By mirroring the constituent's thoughts and feelings, effective cultivators "break down resistance . . . establish trust and

credibility, and highlight only those benefits that are of interest" to the constituent (Bly 1985, 67).

Make Sure Your Constituents Hear You

You must overcome barriers so your constituents will actually hear what you have to say. The first, inadequate understanding of your constituents, has already been discussed. Three more are presented below. These are: volume of information received by your constituents, the force inertia exerts on your constituents, and the way personality types receive information.

1. Recognize the Volume of Information Your Constituents Receive

Information is being generated—and thrown at people—at a rate that defies comprehension. Ninety percent of the information now in the world was created in just the last 30 years. And the amount of information doubles again every six months.

In 1971, it was estimated that Americans were exposed to an average of 560 messages per day. In the first edition of this book (1997), it was estimated that people were exposed to somewhere between 560 and 1,800 separate communications messages daily. "Do this." "Buy that." "Give to us." Recent data indicate that Americans are exposed to some 3,000 messages per day, or more than 1 million per year.

Just think about it. When your solicitation letter or newsletter or board update reaches me, it's competing with 2,999 other items—all directed at getting my attention (see Exhibit 4–10).

Exhibit 4–10 Information about Information

Number of days it takes the contents of the World Wide Web to double	53
Amount of information stored in print everywhere in the world, in bytes	200 quadrillion
Amount of junk mail the average American family receives per year, in trees	1
Number of meetings the average manager attends per month	60
Percentage of those meetings that attendees say are unproductive	33
Percentage of people who regularly ask recipients how they want to receive information	14

Source: Data from A. Wylie, The Editors Worksheet...Wylie on Writing, May 1999, Kansas City, MO.

In self-defense, people avoid information in many areas of their lives. They tune out, ignore, block, and screen. Even when someone does read your stuff, they are less likely to remember it.

Your messages are fighting for attention and compensating for overload. However, your message can still get through—and could be remembered—if you follow the communication facts of life. See the section entitled "Communicating with Your Constituents."

2. Overcome Your Constituents' Inertia

Inertia is your biggest challenge, says Tom Ahern, marketing and communications consultant. Stand in awe of inertia! People do things quite reluctantly and often have trouble committing. That's human nature, and it is a very powerful obstacle. You have to overcome people's tendency to do nothing. Even self-interest alone may not be enough to yank people from their inertia.

Kurt Lewin (1890–1947) addresses inertia in his concept of force field analysis (Brassard and Ritter, 2000, 72). To move someone from inertia to action, change must occur. Lewin views change as the result of a struggle between forces that seek to upset the status quo and forces that want to maintain the status quo.

"Driving forces" move a situation toward change. Think about driving forces as the motivation someone has to take a particular action. On the other side, "restraining forces" block the change. These are the barriers that stop someone from taking a particular action. Remember, if the restraining forces are stronger than the driving forces, change will not happen.

You can practice by identifying the driving and restraining forces in simpler situations than fundraising. For example, think about someone who is trying to learn to read. Ask yourself: What are the reasons this person would like to read? What are the individual's personal motivations? What might stop the individual from learning? Take a look at the ideas below.

Driving forces	Restraining forces
Embarrassment	Embarrassment
Negative self-image	Negative self-image
Can't complete an employment application	No child care during scheduled classes
Can't use road signs to get to a destination	Expense of classes
Read a bedtime story to child to the classroom	No transportation

How does this apply to fund development? Force field analysis tells you to identify the reasons why people will not respond to your face-to-face solicitation, your telephone call, or your letter. Identify the restraining forces and attack them directly. Respond to the objections before they are raised by the prospect. And remember: Different people will experience different driving and restraining forces.

Attack the restraining force! Diminish and eliminate as many as possible. If a driving force is "end world hunger," a restraining force might be the fear that "my own few dollars won't do much good." Remember inertia. In force field analysis, the prospect is always ready to do nothing. If you don't make a case against the restraining forces, the prospect will choose inertia.

Then identify the driving forces. Use them. But be careful about reinforcing the driving forces. Studies indicate that strengthening the driving forces may actually increase resistance!

Different constituents will experience different driving and restraining forces. Focus on your targeted constituents and their respective needs.

3. Target the Personality Types

Not everyone hears and learns in the same way. In fact, everyone has a preference for how they like to take in information. Psychologists have identified four distinct learning styles. Personalize your communications to these styles (see Exhibit 4–11).

1. The expressive loves new stuff and is easily bored. Tell him and her about your new and exciting activities. Use bold statements and keep it lively.
2. The analytical craves facts and more facts and has trouble deciding. She or he expects documentation and statistical evidence, such as charts and lots of data.
3. The bottom-liners want you to jump to the chase, and they'll decide instantly. They appreciate summaries and want brevity.
4. The amiable values relationships above all and wants you to be a friend. Use "you" a lot and create warm-hearted pictures. Talk about an ongoing relationship by asking them to "stay in touch."

These personality types are evenly distributed among all target audiences. In a random sampling of any group, 25 percent of the group belongs to each of the four styles. Your communications must have something for everyone. Just imagine sending a dry, lengthy memo full of facts and figures. Only the analytical type would read it, and you would miss 75 percent of the audience. Worse yet, you would have reached the 25 percent who have trouble deciding.

> *The Amiable:* I'll be around lots of people I like and respect. I'll get to exchange stories and ideas with them. Maybe even make some new friends.
>
> *The Expressive:* I'll learn a bunch of new insights and skills. Who knows what will happen? Could be great! I don't want to miss something that could be important.
>
> *The Analytical:* I'm not sure. But maybe this guy has something to say. He sounds qualified. I have my doubts, but you never know.
>
> *The Bottom-Liner:* I want to do my job right the first time. Tell me how.
>
> *Source:* Copyright © Tom Ahern, ABC, Ahern Communications, Ink.

Some portion of your communication must respond to each of the personality types. Reach these different audiences through different facts and stories presented by your face-to-face solicitors. Make sure articles in your newsletters capture the attention of each learning style. When you make a presentation, pay equal attention to the expressives, analyticals, bottom-liners, and the amiables.

More Tips To Help You Communicate Better

Here are a few more tips to help you communicate with greater impact.

- Use the inverted pyramid style. Journalists are taught to structure their stories using inverted pyramids. In an inverted pyramid, the result is described first, the reasons for the result are described next, and the context or background from which the result emerged is described last. This approach lets the reader get to the point of the story immediately. That's why good news writing seems so vivid and filled with significance. This writing style works well, whether you are speaking, writing any letter, creating a fundraising case statement, or developing a foundation or corporate proposal. See Exhibit 4–12 for an example.
- Use statistics sparingly. Generally, numbers are not very persuasive because intellectual arguments are the weakest, and emotional arguments are the strongest.
- Use "you" a lot. "You" is the most powerful word in any language. Avoid the institutional "we." Do not fall back on:

- "We at the theatre company offer the best acting."
- "Our programs protect hundreds of women from domestic violence."
- "Please give us a contribution to help our good work."

Do you use "you" often enough? Examine the way you talk during a fundraising solicitation. Do you describe the community problem and your organization's solution? Does your letter or conversation eloquently explain how you benefit those served?

Well, that's not enough. What about me, the listener? Fundraisers persist in talking about the organization's need, the organization's services, and the needs of the clients. You keep forgetting me. How do I feel as your potential donor? How will giving to your organization match my interests and fulfill my needs?

Write To Communicate

Much of your communication is written. If you communicate well, your writing will produce the action you wish. Do not compose a scholarly paper. You need not follow grammatical rules. Don't show that you are

Exhibit 4–12 Visit the Pyramids . . . and Get to the Point

> Here's the story of the Three Little Pigs, as told in inverted pyramid style:
>
> "A wooden home in Fayetteville was reduced to matchsticks last night when a long-standing feud between a wolf and a family of bachelor pigs erupted into violence. Experts say feuds of this kind are 'predictable occurrences between natural enemies' and that the pigs should have built out of brick."
>
> The inverted pyramid always works the same way: first, there's the outcome ("home reduced to matchsticks"); then there are the reasons behind the outcome ("a long-standing feud"); finally, there's the background behind the reasons ("natural enemies.")
>
> It's called an *inverted pyramid* because it makes its point first, then builds toward the base.
>
> Which is exactly the opposite of how most people learn to write. In school, we're taught to build our case from the ground up.
>
> Don't do it! You'll lose the reader. Put the key points first. Put the background in the background.
>
> Courtesy of Tom Ahern, Ahern Communications, Ink. Rhode Island.

sophisticated or erudite. You want to communicate so that action results. See Exhibits 4–12, 4–13, 4–14, and 4–15.

> **The most powerful word in the world is "you."**

Avoid complexity in your writing. Sure, communicate complex thoughts, but do so simply.

Stick to active, not passive, sentences. Active does and passive is done to. As David Fryxell, author of *How to Write Fast (While Writing Well)*, notes: "Remember that the Bible opens, 'In the beginning, God created the heavens and the earth.'—not 'In the beginning, the heavens and the earth were created by God.' Active sentences seem clear, direct, and forceful. Tangled, weak and confused are what passive sentences (like this one in which you are trapped) tend to be thought of" (Fryxell 1992, 136).

> *Remember to write about benefits, not features. Benefits directly address the reader's self-interest. It is by expressing features as benefits that you speak most powerfully to specific target audiences.*
>
> Tom Ahern, ABC

Be vivid and bold. Use powerful words. Consider what Roy H. Williams, author of *Secret Formulas of the Wizard of Ads* (Williams, 1999), wrote: "Words are electric; they should be chosen for the emotional voltage they carry. Weak and predictable words cause grand ideas to appear so dull that they fade into the darkness of oblivion. But powerful words in unusual combinations brightly illuminate the mind. If a sentence does not shock a little, it carries no emotional voltage. When the hearer is not jolted, you can be sure he is not involved" (page 12).

News reporters write at an eighth-grade level, and so should you. It's easier for your readers to quickly scan and comprehend. They need not expend undue effort at understanding. The harder it is to read (above the eighth-grade level), the more effort it requires. This is true for even the most sophisticated and intelligent reader. When the reader spends too much time figuring out the communication, there is no time to act. If understanding requires too much effort, the reader may delay reading until later, perhaps too late. Or the reader may simply throw away the communication. In an oral presentation, the listener just tunes out.

Many popular word processing programs contain grammar checkers that will automatically evaluate grade level of readability and point out stylistic weaknesses, such as the passive voice. Use this just like you use spell-check programs. Then adjust accordingly. For oral presentations, check your effectiveness by talking it through with someone.

Put the important stuff first in your communication. Make it easy for the reader to find the important stuff. People won't read everything, so make sure that they read what's most important. Background belongs in the background, not at the start. Remember the three little pigs and the pyramid style of writing.

> *Exploit "communication opportunity zones." Covers, envelopes, captions, headlines: places where the eye falls almost involuntarily and where you can stick your message.*
>
> Tom Ahern, ABC

Headlines are critical. Readers use the headlines to determine whether they want to read the story. (And most of the time, people read only the headlines and never read the story!)

"Real headlines work for a living, and their job is to explain the story clearly. Cute, vague or lazy headlines leave readers cold. *Literally!!* A good headline warms up readers, easing them into the story in small, incremental steps." So says Tom Ahern (1999).

Exhibit 4–13 Write at the Eighth Grade Level To Guarantee Understanding

> Eight-grade level writing is not writing *down*; it's writing *simple*. Use short sentences; short paragraphs; clear, jargon-free language. Newspapers write at the 8th-grade level. You can write about anything—including atomic physics—at the 8th grade level. (Incidentally, popular word-processing software packages like Microsoft Word come with built-in ways to check grade level. In Word, it's a selection called *Grammar*, found on the Tools menu.)
>
> Eighth-grade-level writing is transparent to most people. They understand the author's meaning immediately, at a glance.
>
> Check out the grade levels of *your* favorite authors. You might find that today's most popular novelists are writing at the 4th- and 5th-grade level. Fund raisers are storytellers, too. Learn from the best-selling storytellers in the culture: Write for quick and easy comprehension.
>
> FYI: you've just read three paragraphs written at the 7th-grade level.
>
> *Source:* Copyright © Tom Ahern, ABC, Ahern Communications, Ink.

Exhibit 4–14 You Can Write Better Copy

Use these tips whether you're writing a letter, advertisement, brochure, or some other copy. Keep in mind that most of these hints are applicable to speaking also.

1. The reader (or listener) is most important. Focus on the benefits to that person. Use "you" lots.
2. Hit hard right away. Create interest and drama immediately when you write or speak.
3. Catchy phrases without a call to action won't motivate anyone.
4. Don't bury the important stuff. Target what is most important to the particular audience. Repeat it. As copywriters say: "Tell them what you're going to tell them. Tell them again. And then tell them what you told them."
5. Keep it simple.
   - Write and tell in small, manageable bits.
   - Avoid long paragraphs. One-sentence paragraphs are okay.
   - Avoid compound sentences. Stick to 16–20 words or less.
   - Vary sentence and paragraph length so reading isn't dull.
   - Don't use extra words that waste the reader's time and use up space you could use for something else.
   - Use simple words like "building," rather than "edifice" and "words," rather than "vocabulary."
   - Don't use technical jargon unless absolutely necessary. Make sure there is no easier way to say it. Don't use a technical term unless at least 95 percent of your audience will get it.
6. Use facts as well as emotion.
7. Don't use sexist language. There is no excuse.
8. Write in a conversational tone.
   - Use colloquial expressions.
   - Use action verbs whenever possible.
   - Start your sentences with conjunctions to help your writing flow. Just like you would talk.
   - And end your sentences with a preposition. A rigid grammarian would say "no." But rigid grammarians make dull writers. You know what I'm talking about.
   - Use sentence fragments. Same reasons.
9. Pay particular attention to your headlines and subheads, whether in newsletter articles, annual reports, posters, fundraising brochures, or direct mail letters. Why? Because busy people no longer read, they scan. And what they scan are headlines, subheads, captions, opening sentences, etc.

   Studies prove that 85 percent of people read the headline only. So a good headline gets the reader's attention and tells a complete message. A good headline communicates the benefit to the reader and creates excitement. The headline also draws the reader into the copy.
10. Make your text easy to skim. Create ways for the reader's eye to move into the text. Use bullets, subheads, numbers, underlines, boldface, and boxed text. But don't go crazy.
11. Always use a P.S. in letters. Readers look at the signature right after they look at the salutation. And the P.S. is right after the signature, so it's a great spot for important info.

Ahern (1999) goes on to talk about the *Wall Street Journal*'s use of headlines, claiming that this newspaper is possibly the best written in the United States. The *Wall Street Journal* uses this "sequence of steps to warm up readers: an 'eyebrow' (a few words of teaser above the headline), the headline itself, a 'deck' (subhead) beneath the headline, and an evocative lead sentence—these four items function *as one unit* to move the reader quickly from disinterest to high interest."

Watch Your Print Layout and Design

Design and layout are essential elements of communication and should provide easy access for the viewer. Layout and design can bring the reader in or keep him or her out.

Ironically, designers are often not especially effective as communicators. Design elements that superficially look attractive may actually undermine good communication.

For example, italics, all caps, reversed type, and small type are hard to read. Make sure that your designer's work is directed by someone who is familiar with the basic rules of good communication.

> *I do not regard advertising as entertainment or an art form, but as a medium of information. When I write an advertisement, I don't want you to tell me that you find it "creative." I want you to find it so interesting that you buy the product. When Aeschines spoke, they said "How well he speaks." But when Demosthenes spoke, they said "Let us march against Philip."*
>
> *David Ogilvy*

Use *pro bono* marketing and public relations with a few reservations in mind. Certainly, these individuals or firms may donate their time because they care about your cause. For sure, they donate because they expect creative freedom. Sometimes, their creativity does not produce effective communication.

> *The whole point of marketing is to bring in customers. So no matter how pretty or clever, it ain't creative if it doesn't do that.*
> *Pottruck and Pearce*

Set the ground rules. You need effective communication. Remember that communication is the goal, not cute copywriting or glorious design.

To navigate a page quickly, the eye needs many aids and landmarks. Here are a few rules that will improve the readability of your printed material.

- Always indent paragraphs.
- Double space between paragraphs.
- Include a few bullets and underlines.
- Use ragged right margins; do not justify.
- Select serif typeface.
- Use initial capital letters; do not use all caps except for one to three words.
- Avoid colored type on colored backgrounds.
- Write short paragraphs (one to three sentences at most) and short sentences.
- Avoid small type (that usually means anything less than 12 point).

So what's the big deal? Imagine a page of all-over gray text with justified right and left margins, lengthy paragraphs, and sans serif type. You take away the landmarks. The eye gets lost. Browsing is difficult. The result? Frustration, wasted time, lower comprehension. Worse yet, your reader may throw it away without getting to your call to action!

Look at your recent publications. Which of these design no-no's did you use? Test your most important communication before using it. Invite some insiders and outsiders to review it. Get the reaction of your targeted audiences.

By the way, this is a wonderful constituency development strategy. Your constituents are involved in a meaningful way. You get vital perspective, and they appreciate being asked.

Call Your Constituents to Action

Action is the goal, so always include a call to action in your communication. This necessary step is frequently omitted. The call to action tells people what to do. And it helps them overcome their natural inertia.

When you fundraise, the call to action is your request for a specific gift. When you recruit volunteers, the call to action is the invitation to join the committee or to take on the particular task.

But what happens before you ask? What kind of call to action do you use in the early steps? What do you want people to do when you are trying to get them to know your organization better? Consider the following ideas:

- response card or form in your newsletter that:
  - asks constituents their opinion about one or two items
  - asks constituents if they want further information about a particular project
  - tells them they have to complete the form in order to continue receiving the newsletter
  - asks them to select their areas of interest so you can send them specific information
  - asks them for demographic and lifestyle information so you can design activities targeted to their interests
- written survey that asks their opinions on various issues
- phonathon that asks their quick opinions about a few items
- invitation to give their opinions at a focus group
- invitation to a special event

The call to action is the interactive portion of your communication. The call to action tells the constituent what to do. A good call to action has all or some of the following characteristics.

- It is specific. "Saving the world" is too general. "Put food in the bellies of the kids in Momo's African village" is much better. The constituent can see how his or her money will work.
- The call to action is introduced early and repeated. Ask early and ask often.

Exhibit 4–15 Effective Communications Does Four Things

1. Grabs attention.	Is tailored to your target constituency.
2. Stirs interest.	Motivates your constituency to take the action you request.
3. Builds conviction and desire.	Promises a desired benefit to the constituency if they take the action.
4. Calls the constituent to action.	Tells the constituency what to do to act.

- A good call to action clearly states why your organization is an answer for an obvious problem or want. Your communication makes sure that the problem or want is obvious and pressing enough. Unless the constituent accepts the problem, he or she will not act.
- The call to action explains why the constituent will feel better by acting. You want the constituent to respond to your communication by thinking "Oh, this is awful (or wonderful)! What can I do to help?" Think about the biggest emotional issue associated with the problem or opportunity. For instance, if your organization provides volunteer caregivers to visit the elderly, the emotional issue might be "ending the fear and loneliness that are caused by isolation."
- Your call to action envisions a better future as a direct result of obeying the call to action. The constituent receives his or her reward and experiences a benefit just by acting.
- The call to action conveys urgency. "Act now before it's too late. Act now before another day goes by."
- You must clearly communicate to the constituent that she is the right person to act. There should be no doubt in her mind that you mean her.
- Finally, make the call to action fun or satisfying to participate in. Your reply device is as important as anything else in the communications. In fact, many professional direct mail creators feel that the reply card may be the most important piece in the communications package.

CULTIVATING RELATIONSHIPS WITH YOUR CONSTITUENTS

Cultivation moves people from interest to engagement. Engagement is a mutual state, shared between the organization and its constituent. When engaged, a constituent is ready to be asked. When engaged enough, a constituent is more likely to respond well to your request.

Cultivation means more than an invitation to a party, membership in a gift club, or participation on an advisory board. Cultivating relationships requires a careful blend of activities that are tailored to the interests and needs of the targeted constituent.

Together, cultivation and communications get your constituent ready to be asked. And asked again for more.

Cultivation is an ongoing necessity because relationships just tend to run down. This entropy is the natural tendency of relationships, says Richard A. Edwards (1989, 85). Without adequate care, your constituents become inactive and passive. Consider how similar this is to inertia, discussed in the communications section. Effective communications and cultivation overcome both inertia and entropy. Then you will have more donors and raise more money.

> *Personalize the cultivation process to your prospect(s) and your organization.*

There are many different cultivation strategies. Your institution decides what is most appropriate. What you choose to do depends on two things: the interests and needs of your constituents and the values, vision, and resources of your organization.

The central question is, Will your return on investment be sufficient? You must decide how much time and money you can spend cultivating which prospects to justify the resources you allocate. To answer this, consider the following:

- What are your cultivation goals for the particular prospect or group of prospects? What are the measurable outcomes you desire?
- Is this a good use of your organization's resources? Can you justify the commitment of volunteer and staff time and financial resources? Will you achieve the benefits for your organization in the short, mid, or long term?
- How long can you cultivate and how much can you invest before you must realize benefits to the organization?
- Do you have sufficient volunteers and staff to carry out your strategies?
- Is your organizational infrastructure (values and systems) adequate to support the cultivation strategies without hurting the institution?
- Will you be able to sustain the cultivation process, providing appropriate follow-up with prospect(s) so they are not abandoned?

Design an Infrastructure To Manage the Process

Infrastructure will help you do this work. You need core systems and procedures, and the values to support them.

Develop the best systems and procedures for your organization without creating a bureaucracy. Include things such as:

- an organized way to think about the constituency development process
- specific tools to implement the process
- board and staff committees and teams to help guide and do the work

- job descriptions and task assignments for individuals, committees, and teams
- written constituency development plan with measurable goals, strategies, time frames, and assignments
- recordkeeping to track communications and cultivation activities and record constituent response
- specific steps to monitor progress and evaluate change

Try the systems and procedures suggested throughout this book. Look back at Chapter 2, which discusses your internal relations. Look at Chapter 3, which describes systems and procedures for strategic planning. Get ideas from the sample surveys and interview questions. Try the 10-step constituency development process (Exhibit 4–7) and the constituency development worksheets in Appendix 4–B.

Moves Management

Some fundraisers use moves management as the infrastructure to coordinate the cultivation process. G.T. (Buck) Smith developed the concept to measure the progress of major gift fundraising. Smith recognized that a series of activities (which he called *initiatives* or *moves*) is necessary to build a relationship with a donor. Each move involves six steps (Dunlop 1986, 330):

1. reviewing the prospect's relationship with your organization
2. planning the right initiative to strengthen the prospect's awareness, knowledge, interest, caring, involvement, and commitment
3. coordinating the planned initiative with volunteer and staff leaders (called *primes* and *secondaries*)
4. carrying out the initiative
5. evaluating the initiative
6. documenting and discussing the results of the initiative

The initiatives are carried out by volunteers and staff. They meet regularly to discuss strategy, plot next steps, and discuss progress. Staff maintain comprehensive records of each initiative. Records document the prospect's reaction and progress of the cultivation.

Specific people, called *primes* and *secondaries*, are responsible and accountable for the cultivation process. Each prospect has one prime who is charged with managing the moves related to that prospect. The prime develops, coordinates, implements, documents, monitors progress, and evaluates the fundraising initiatives with a specific prospect. Additional individuals, the secondaries, help plot strategy, develop and carry out the initiatives, and monitor progress.

Building and maintaining any relationship requires frequency, continuity, and personalization. Moves management maintains that each major gift prospect requires at least one initiative per month. This management strategy has calculated the optimum number of initiatives, and hence prospects, that any single staff person can handle per year. (According to Dunlop [1986], each major gift staff person can manage approximately 70–80 prospects per year.)

As in all fundraising, some of the moves are personalized to the particular prospect. Other moves are common to all prospects within the organization.

Moves management may give you ideas for managing cultivation. But make sure you focus on your constituents, not your organization and its moves. If the donor or prospective donor is at the center of the process, then the question is, Is one initiative per month too much, too little, or just right to strengthen the relationship with a particular prospect? Make sure the actual initiatives focus on the prospect, rather than on your organization. Personalize your activities to the needs and interests of your prospects.

Set Realistic Goals for Each Cultivation Activity

Successful cultivation is easy to measure. It produces a "yes" to your organization's request.

Because it takes many cultivation activities to get to the "yes," what are your interim goals? What do you want to happen by the end of each separate cultivation activity?

Establish a realistic, measurable, and meaningful goal for each cultivation activity. Think about what you want your constituent to do at the end of the cultivation activity. Do this by focusing on the constituent.

William T. Sturtevant, director of Planned Giving and Trust Relations, University of Illinois Foundation, suggests you establish an optimum and minimum outcome. First describe the best outcome, what you really want to happen. Then decide what would be an acceptable, although lesser, outcome. Aim for the optimum outcome. But if the constituent is not moving toward that, negotiate to achieve the minimum (Sturtevant, 1996).

Define time frames to accomplish your goals. Estimate the amount of time it will require to carry out each cultivation activity. Anticipate the time span to carry out each step in the constituency development process for a particular constituent group. Establish target dates to evaluate progress on a span of activities or step(s) in constituency development.

Standard Business Operations Cultivate Relationships

The cultivation process includes two distinct—and equally important—parallel tracks. The first track is carrying out your standard business operations that support ongoing effective relationships. The second track is conducting special activities designed to enhance relationships. You cannot have one track without the other.

Your standard business activities initiate and sustain effective relationships with your constituents. Do business well and you develop and strengthen relationships. Do business poorly and all your relationships are threatened.

Every contact a constituent has with your organization affects the relationship. Consider how these situations would affect your constituents' relationship with your organization:

- Clients are pleased with the quality of your programs.
- A volunteer slips on your icy sidewalk.
- A caller is stuck on telephone hold too long.
- A prospective donor receives useful information in a timely and friendly manner.
- My thank-you letter says "Dear Ms. Joyaux," when I know the signer well.

Look at your standard business activities. Talk about how these activities help you enhance or hinder relationships. Consider every area of operation, including strategic planning (described as your relationship with your community) and the internal functioning of your organization (described as your internal relations). Both are critical to effective fund development. Also critical is communications, presented here as a strategy to strengthen relationships.

Consider other areas of operation. For example, providing quality service is your most important business activity. Continuous quality improvement helps you sustain and build relationships. Remember that quality is in the eye of the beholder. "It's not what you're selling that counts. It's what I'm buying that matters." Whether I am a client, donor, or volunteer, meet my expectations and I'll compliment your quality.

Direct exposure to your organization is critical for building relationships. As part of your business, you regularly interact with various constituents. Some use your service, and others provide you with service. Constituents visit your offices and attend special events. Your constituents interact with your staff and volunteers by telephone and in person, at your agency, and elsewhere in the community.

Enabling volunteers is another standard business activity that helps you cultivate relationships. This book describes enabling as the fourth relationship that is critical to effective fund development. Enabling is discussed in Chapter 5.

> *The way you do business cultivates (or harms) relationships.*

Your standard business activities lay the foundation for all your relationships. Keep the foundation solid, then develop activities especially for cultivation.

Design Cultivation Activities

Actually, cultivation is lots of fun for staff and volunteers. For many, cultivation is much more enjoyable than asking for the gift.

Group your specific cultivation activities into three categories:

1. activities directed to all your constituents
2. activities designed for targeted groups of like constituents
3. activities personalized for a single constituent

First, design cultivation activities for use with all your constituents. Don't segment your publics or target particular audiences. Devise generic cultivation activities. Make sure these activities reach your diverse constituents by following the guidelines for effective communications.

Second, add to your generic cultivation activities by focusing on specific groups of constituents. Segment your constituents into subgroups that share specific commonalties. Target specific subgroups and design cultivation activities to match the interests and needs of the subgroup. Dunlop (1986) calls these *background activities*. Although they affect individual prospects, the activities are actually designed for groups.

Proceed with constituency development and you will identify single entities that warrant more personalized attention. Perhaps you wish to cultivate further an individual or family, a business, or service group members.

Now launch the third category of cultivation activities. Develop a personal cultivation plan for each individual constituent. Design initiatives that supplement the generic activities. Dunlop calls these *foreground activities*.

Here are some ideas for cultivation. Use these as generic cultivation activities directed to all your constituents. Personalize some for targeted constituencies. Then personalize some strategies even more for a single constituent with whom you wish to build a relationship.

1. Ask Advice of Your Constituents. Get Their Opinion and Perspective.

- Use research strategies as cultivation strategies. Asking people's opinions creates interest, builds ownership, enhances relationships, and strengthens support. See "Getting to Know Your Constituents." Conduct written and telephone surveys and convene focus groups. Do this as part of your annual development work.

- Brainstorm ideas with individuals and groups. Probe for their interests, motivations, and aspirations. For example, meet with individuals to get their ideas about how they want to be recognized. Convene a group of donors and brainstorm recognition ideas. Ask individuals and groups why they give or ask people why they give to your organization.
- Test-market a specific idea or offering with selected constituents. Invite constituents to attend a focus group and get their reaction to something. For example, present the key messages from your draft case statement. Find out what works and doesn't work about these messages. (See Appendix F for guidelines about how to test your case.) Review your new recognition program and get their reactions. Thinking about a new special event? Put together a focus group and test the idea.
- Include a "non-giving call to action" in your newsletter and even your acknowledgment letters.

Enclose a quick-response card with one to three easy checkoff questions. For example, ask what they think of the newsletter. Ask them to rate particular articles. Get their reaction about gift club names. Ask their reaction to your new cultivation ideas.

2. Involve Constituents in Your Organization. Create Opportunities That Benefit the Constituent and Your Organization.

- Chat informally with constituents. Do this a lot! Set yourself a goal—perhaps two different people each day. Give them a piece of news. Share an idea with them. Thank them for something. Certainly, call your board members, fundraising volunteers, and donors regularly. Reach out to new people, too. Take this opportunity to increase their understanding and awareness, as well as your own.
- Every day, eat breakfast or lunch with someone you need to cultivate—perhaps a staff colleague or a board member, maybe a donor or prospective donor, or possibly a colleague in another not-for-profit organization.
- Create ad-hoc task forces. Set up task forces that meet two to three times to brainstorm a particular topic or identify ways to address a specific issue. Then the task force ends.
- Use committees (or teams) well. Make sure your committees and teams include people who do not

serve on the board. Make them large enough to encourage diversity and welcome many constituents. Change membership often enough to produce vitality while maintaining continuity.

- Go to every board and committee meeting early enough to mingle. Some of your constituents will arrive early, and you can take this opportunity to talk informally.
- Create short-term as well as long-term volunteer projects. Volunteer needs are changing. Find out what people want by convening a brainstorming session. Talk to people informally about their interests and disinterests. Identify tasks for groups and individuals. Then test-market your ideas with a focus group.
- Create affinity programs or special clubs for targeted constituents. Which constituencies? Consider professions or cultural background. Look at demographics and lifestyles. Perhaps you want an affinity program for women in philanthropy. Perhaps you want to build relationships with Generation X or e-commerce workers.

Affinity programs are not gift clubs, which focus on philanthropy. Neither are these the affinity teams recruited to help you develop relationships. Affinity programs (also called clubs) sponsor activities that revolve around the interests of the targeted constituency. Participation in the program may well include a financial contribution at a particular level. However, the program focuses on the constituent's interests.

See Exhibit 4–16 for a description of an affinity program and Exhibit 4–17 for tips about how to start your own. See also Hall's article in the *Chronicle of Philanthropy* (1991).

3. Communicate To Strengthen Relationships.

- Make sure your newsletter and regular correspondence follow the guidelines for effective communication. Include a call to action as often as possible. And that doesn't always mean asking for money.
- Write personal letters about their particular interests to a targeted constituency or constituent.
- Provide insider updates to targeted constituents.
- Host information gatherings and tours at your agency.

4. Acknowledge and Recognize Your Donors of Money and Time.

- Conduct a thank-you phonathon. Don't ask for a gift! Instead, thank donors for past gifts. Add a few questions to help you get to know them better. For example, ask why they give. Ask how satisfied

Exhibit 4–16 Cultivating Relationships through Affinity Programs

The Jewish Federation of Southern Arizona has a long history of constituency development. The Federation continually seeks ways to bring people closer to the Jewish community, rather than looking for increased contributions.

With this in mind, the Federation created a special club for local physicians. The Maimonides Club focuses on the doctors' professional interests, not philanthropy. Members of the Club set their own goals and design the program to meet member needs. There are other significant characteristics.

- Club activities and educational programs are not available elsewhere.
- Spouses and families of Club members are invited to Club activities.
- Club activities do not focus on fundraising, and members are not asked for gifts at Club meetings.
- Jewish professionals who are not yet members of the club are often invited to participate in Club activities.

The Federation began the affinity program by inviting a group of physician donors to informal gatherings in private homes. The gatherings featured presentations about medical practices in Israel. Guests and representatives of the Federation talked informally, identifying possible topics for subsequent presentations. Guests expressed interest in joining a formal program that revolved around their concerns as physicians and Jews.

With this endorsement, the Federation established a physicians' steering committee to design and lead the new club. The steering committee, supported by staff, decides the Club's focus and establishes the minimum contribution to join. The committee establishes operating guidelines and marketing plans, helps recruit members, and selects programs. The Club's own newsletter reflects member interests and projects a distinct identity.

For Tucson's Jewish physicians, the Federation's affinity program provides many benefits. Physicians and their spouses enjoy the camaraderie of Club meetings and the opportunity to learn more about topics of interest. Members appreciate the invitation to comment on the Federation's activities.

In turn, Club members and their families give back to the Federation as donors of time and money. The affinity program also helps the Federation learn about the interests, disinterests, and frustrations of their constituents. With constituent input, the Federation enhances the way it does business and builds stronger relationships.

Club membership increases because physicians value the benefits provided. And word about the Club has spawned like-minded groups in other Jewish communities across the country.

Courtesy of the Jewish Federation of Southern Arizona.

---

they were with their most recent contact with your organization. Find out what kind of special events they like. Ask whether they want more information about something. (Add "getting to know you" questions to your fundraising phonathon, too.)

- Make all your thank-you letters more personal. Review the guidelines for effective communication. Talk about specific programs. Tell your donor how the money will be used.
- Create special thank-you letters. The Boys & Girls Club of Pawtucket put together an album of notes and drawings from youth who received camp scholarships from a major foundation. The foundation executive was very touched and actually read each note.
- Send more than one thank-you letter. Send the official one from the organization. Ask the volunteer solicitor to send a personal note. If it's a major gift (and not anonymous), ask several board members to send personal notes.
- Host donor and volunteer recognition parties. Find a local restaurant that likes your organization. Ask the restaurant to donate the food and service. Offer a cash bar with receipts going to the restaurant.

- Develop a standardized recognition program for different gift levels. But first, brainstorm ideas with your donors. What do they value as recognition? Outline program components and test them with a focus group of donors before implementation.
- Create interesting recognition plaques. For each major donor, frame a drawing by one of your youth clients. Include the name of your organization, the donor, and the artist. For a capital campaign, feature a photograph or rendering of your facility. Give a piece of original art.

5. Other Ideas.

- At your events, use hosts. Charge them with getting to know your constituents. Make sure board members and staff are cultivating relationships, rather than socializing with friends. Assign board members and staff to cultivate specific individuals at events.
- Keep postcards or note cards on hand. Jot a quick note when someone spends time with you on the telephone. Send out a quick thought or just a "hello."

Exhibit 4–17 Tips for Creating Your Own Affinity Program

Ideally, you should develop an affinity program for each of your primary constituent groups. In reality, devise only as many as you can manage well. Start with one. Before you establish a second affinity program, evaluate the success and effectiveness of the first.

Try the following steps:

1. Identify a constituent group that you want to cultivate.
2. Examine the group's demographics and psychographics. Identify various interests of the group that your organization might be able to support through an affinity program.
3. Compare these interests to your organization's values and vision. Proceed only if there is a good match between the constituents' interests and aspirations and your organization's values and vision. Identify any areas of possible conflict and decide how you will address these.
4. Consider the resources of your organization. Decide how you will support an affinity program and outline any general guidelines or boundaries.
5. Identify a handful of individuals from the constituent group who might serve as an initial brainstorming group. Meet with them to find out whether they might be interested in an affinity program and what they think might be its focus. Share the values of your organization. Make sure you communicate any guidelines or boundaries that are necessary, based on your organization. (Do this well, without alienating people you are trying to cultivate.)
6. If response is positive, identify a handful of individuals from the constituent group (brainstorming group) who

will serve as an initial steering committee. With them, design a series of informal meetings to bring together members of their constituent group. Present a program that the steering committee has selected. Talk informally with guests to determine the extent of their interest in such a program.

7. Based on response from the initial meetings, determine whether it is appropriate to develop the affinity program. If yes, outline your next steps.
8. Make sure that the steering committee has enough key people to sustain the affinity program.
9. Use the information from the initial meetings. Help the steering committee decide the focus of the affinity program and how the new group should operate. Make sure the decisions are in keeping with your organization's values and any guidelines or boundaries. Consider the timing and frequency of the group's meetings, minimum donations to join, and so forth.
10. Plan the first formal program. Develop the invitation list and invitation plan.
11. After the first formal meeting, evaluate. Make sure that each attendee is invited to offer his or her opinions and suggestions.
12. Consider expanding the steering committee to include several new people from the first formal meeting.
13. Plan the second formal meeting.
14. Establish a marketing plan. Include communications strategies to reach your targeted constituents.
15. Launch your new affinity program for the targeted constituent group.

- Clip and send interesting articles. Perhaps something about your organization. Perhaps a topic of interest to the constituent.
- Send new year cards to your board members, key volunteers, and key donors. Include handwritten notes, or write the entire thing by hand.

Use good judgment. Be discreet. Carefully balance organization cultivation with personal relationships. For example, is a birthday card from your organization a good idea or a presumption of familiarity that may be resented?

6. Ask for a Gift.

Asking for a gift is one of the best cultivation strategies, as long as you don't ask prematurely. Don't focus on the request. Focus on the prospect. Remember this is constituent-focused and donor-centered philanthropy. Your organization is not at the center.

Create a dialogue, not a monologue. Don't just talk about your organization. Listen to what the constituent says. Watch how he or she reacts. Use this opportunity to create meaningful conversation. Don't be forced or artificial, just talk. Get to know the person even better. Create a bond, one of respect and trust.

Pick the Right People To Do Your Cultivating

Many of your cultivation activities do not involve any single person (called a *cultivator*) to do the work. Rather, the generic activities are carried out by the institution, through mailings, events, and so forth. Through standard business operations, all employees and volunteers make sure they do business in a quality manner and behave in ways that are warm, welcoming, and supportive.

In other situations, a specific individual or multiple individuals are assigned to carry out specific cultivation activities with the constituent or prospect. At this point, you must pick the right cultivator(s) for each constituent and prospect. Sometimes, this person may be a board member or fellow donor, a staff person, or user of your service. Often, you use a combination of many people. If you need help, start with the concentric circles that identify staff and volunteer networks (Figure 4–3).

To pick the right cultivator(s), ask yourself:

- Does this particular cultivation activity require someone who knows the prospect well?
- What kind of person will the prospect feel most comfortable with?
- Which constituents and prospect(s) will our cultivators feel most comfortable with?
- What advantage or disadvantage is there to involving someone new, not well known, or unknown to the prospect?

You will find someone who knows your constituent or prospect. This is the concept of six degrees of separation. It has been statistically proven that two individuals will be connected by no more than six different individuals. That means that, in a nation of 200 million people, it will only take you six calls to reach the President of the United States. Yes, it's true. Carefully track relationships and you will find someone who knows your constituent or prospect. Moreover, during the "getting to know them" phase, you will develop more contacts.

And if you must, do cold calls during the early phases of the constituency development process. If you are unable to find someone who will introduce you or make the connection, do it yourself. Invite the constituent to a meeting, even if no one knows her well. Recruit the constituent to participate in an activity, even if you don't know him. Just introduce yourself. The constituent will respond if she or he is interested in getting to know your organization better.

> *When you get a "yes" to your request, make sure you really understand why. Ask the donor and listen carefully. Learn from the "yes." Do the same with a "no."*

Keep Track of Your Cultivation Activities and Assess Their Success

Keep track of what happens when you cultivate the constituent. Record how she reacted. Jot down comments about his interests. Conduct formal debriefing sessions with volunteers and staff. You will use all this information when you design the ask.

Make sure you regularly assess your cultivation activities. Find out whether your constituents appreciate the activities. Compare the results of the cultivation with your established goals.

Many fundraising books and publications offer useful tips about managing information and keeping track of constituency development activities. Also, check with other development professionals to see how they do it.

YOUR CONSTITUENCY DEVELOPMENT PLAN

Develop a written plan to guide your activities. The plan helps you focus. To develop the plan, involve your key constituents. This is a joint effort! Talk to your board members, fundraising volunteers, donors, and staff. Ask them to help create the constituency development plan. Board and staff set the goals and identify the target constituent groups. Board and staff help carry out the plan, monitor progress, and evaluate overall performance.

Generally, the process and components of planning are the same, whether it is your institution's strategic plan, your fund development and marketing plans, or your constituency development plan. Look at the plans your organization already has. Review Chapter 3, which discusses planning in detail.

For your constituency development plan, consider the components below. Tailor the format and content to meet your organization's needs.

- measurable goals and strategies to achieve
- benchmarks to evaluate success
- targeted constituents
- description of research components to get to know constituents
- description of constituency development techniques, including communication and cultivation
- process to monitor progress, evaluate performance, and extend the plan for the next year
- role assignments
- time frames for activities
- expense budget

See the section "Set Realistic Goals." Also, you can use the 10 steps of the constituency development process as a way to organize your plan.

The Boys & Girls Club of Pawtucket knew constituency development was an issue when the Club designed its first comprehensive fund development program. The Club's fund development plan includes a section on constituency development (Appendix 4–F). See also similar sections in the fund development plans presented in Chapter 6.

Cultivation gatherings are now part of the Club's constituency development. Each quarter, selected trustees bring from one to two people to the Club for a tour, presentation, and conversation. The gatherings are small, 7–10 people total, including guests and trustee hosts. The 30-minute presentation describes the Club's response to the problems facing the community's youth. Guests observe programs in action and talk with youth. Hosts explore areas of interest with guests.

After each gathering, the Club follows up with a thank-you letter to the guests. Guests then begin receiving the Club's newsletter and special updates. Board members also keep in touch with guests. When the time is right, the individuals are invited to work on a project and to consider a financial contribution.

PREPARING TO ASK

The process of constituency development has, as its end result, the request. The request might be to join a committee or to serve on the board, to purchase the organization's service, or to cast a certain vote on public policy. You also ask for a charitable contribution, the focus of this section.

When you believe the prospect is ready to be asked, you still have two steps to complete before asking: first, evaluate the readiness to be asked; second, design the ask.

Evaluating Readiness To Be Asked

The prospect is ready when there is an optimum intersection of interest, readiness, and capacity. No one likes to be asked at a level so far beyond his means that he feels awkward. Also, it is foolish for your organization to ask a prospect for less than her capacity, interest, and readiness suggest. Fundraising is most effective when interest, readiness, and capacity all line up.

Sometimes, a particular situation arises that suggests that you may not be able to wait until interest, readiness, and capacity are fully aligned. Perhaps the prospect's financial situation indicates that a request should be made earlier. Your organization must judge each situation on its own merit.

> *Every fundraiser knows that fundraising is most successful when the right person is asked by the right person for the right project and the right amount at the right time and in the right manner.*

Interest refers to a feeling of curiosity or attentiveness. Interested people are involved and concerned. In constituency development, interest means that the prospect is attentive to, involved in, and concerned about your cause and your organization's response. Interest also signifies something that is of advantage, profit, or benefit to the interested individual. For fundraising, this means that the prospect sees how her gift will benefit her. This applies at the readiness stage.

Readiness refers to being prepared for action, likely, or liable to act in a particular manner. For constituency development, readiness means that the prospect is prepared in mind and heart, and likely to act in the manner you seek. The prospect also sees how her gift will benefit her by meeting her needs and fulfilling her aspirations.

Capacity refers to the ability or aptitude to do something. Capacity also means the maximum output or production. From a constituency development perspective, capacity refers to the prospect's wherewithal to do what you ask. This could be time, money, or something else.

Keep in mind: A prospect can be interested in your cause but not engaged enough in your organization to be asked for something. A prospect may be ready to be asked but not have the capacity currently to give. A prospect may have the capacity to give $10,000 but not enough interest now (or ever).

Another example: I may be interested in the cause and your organization. I willingly learn more about your activities. With your organization's help, I begin to see how my interests and needs can be fulfilled by participating in your organization. I begin to see ways that I could volunteer time or give money to a project. But I am not yet ready to be asked. Perhaps I do not have the capacity at this time. Maybe I must finish other commitments first. Perhaps you have not offered me the right project.

Managing the Evaluation Process

To evaluate whether or not you should ask yet, conduct a confidential screening session. Some fundraisers call this a rating session. (For your constituents, "rating" may be an uncomfortable word.)

Gather together the people who know the most about the prospects you plan to evaluate. Evaluate interest first, then evaluate readiness. If the combined rating for interest and readiness is sufficiently high, discuss capacity. Then review the results of interest, readiness, and capacity. Decide whether it is time to ask. If your answer is "yes," design the ask. If the answer is "not yet," identify additional cultivation strategies that will move the prospect into the "asking" mode.

To help you evaluate, consider the prospect's relationships with your organization. Use the questions in the 10-step constituency development process and worksheets. Develop screening scales to standardize your evaluation. Make sure you document your deliberations and keep the information on file.

You may evaluate single prospects (perhaps an individual or family or business) or a group of like prospects (possibly 100 young families who share common demographic and lifestyle characteristics).

Although it's easier to evaluate a single entity, it's also important to evaluate the interest, readiness, and capacity of a group of similar prospects. To do this, prescreen all the individuals within the group. Decide whether all members of the group continue to share the same characteristics and remain at the same approximate stage in the constituency development process. Pull out those who do not meet these two criteria. Put them in a more appropriate group or treat them individually. Now return to the remaining homogeneous group and evaluate the group's interest, readiness, and capacity.

Using Scales To Evaluate Interest and Readiness

Three versions of scales are presented here, each more complex but more useful than the prior one. Your organization may choose to start by using the simpler versions. After practice, try the third and most effective version. As necessary, modify the scales to meet your needs best.

Version 1

Use a 10-point scale with "1" being "low" and "10" being "high." Define what you mean by "low" and "high," as well as a midpoint. This helps staff and volunteers assign points to each prospect.

First, evaluate interest using the 10-point scale, then evaluate readiness. The best rating is a combined 20 points. If the rating is 15 points or less, cultivate more. Talk a lot about those prospects who receive 17–19 points. Maybe some of these prospects need more cultivation. Perhaps others could actually be asked. Together, staff and volunteers decide what to do, when, and how.

Version 2

Create a point scale with descriptive statements. Descriptive phrases help evaluators assign points to each constituent or prospect. For example, the model below uses five points as the optimum number to indicate interest.

1. Not very interested in your organization but interested in the cause.
2. Interested in the cause and somewhat interested in your organization.
3. Interested in the cause and increasingly interested in your organization.

4. Very interested in both the cause and your organization.
5. Extremely interested in the cause and your organization.

You can use a similar model to evaluate readiness.

1. Not at all ready to be solicited.
2. Somewhat ready to be solicited.
3. More ready than not.
4. Moderately ready.
5. Very ready to be solicited.

The scales in version 2 likely provide more clarity than the simple point system described in version 1. However, the descriptions are not particularly distinctive. Attendees at your screening session will still have to define what "somewhat ready to be solicited" actually means.

Version 3

Although more complex, it is more effective to combine a point system with substantive descriptions. You develop statements that describe degrees of interest within your organization. In the scenario presented here, the optimum points for interest and readiness are 8 each, for a total of 16.

The first scale describes the prospect's interest.

1. Predisposed to your organization: knows someone in the organization or is familiar with the organization.
2. Predisposed to the cause: has given time or money to similar causes.
3. Client of your organization or has family member who is client.
4. Minimally involved in your organization: is/has used the organization's services; has given a modest gift once or twice. (You establish a range to define "modest" for your organization.)
5. Moderately involved in your organization: regularly gives a modest gift to the organization. (You define "modest" as well as "regularly," e.g., annually for five years.)
6. Regularly involved in your organization: has given steadily over a consistent period of time; periodically increases contributions and may give to special projects, as well as annual operations.
7. Very involved in your organization: periodically increases contributions and gives to special projects, as well as annual operations.
8. Highly engaged in your organization: has given steadily over a consistent period of time, periodi-

cally increasing and diversifying gifts; volunteers advice, counsel, and/or time.

Using this model, a scale to describe readiness might look like this:

1. is familiar with the cause
2. is regularly informed about your organization's activities, mission, and vision through newsletters and other communications vehicles
3. has attended a special event and/or responded to a modest call to action in your newsletter or some other communications vehicle
4. has offered advice and opinion, formally through a survey, focus group, brainstorming session, and/or personal meeting
5. serves on a committee, team, or task force
6. regularly offers advice and opinion, and participates in organization activities
7. talks with you about her capacity and level of interest
8. talks with your organization about how and what he wants to give

Assessing Capacity

Once you have finished evaluating interest and readiness, review the total points for each prospect. Begin discussing capacity for prospects whose combined interest and readiness totals 75–80 percent of the maximum possible points. For prospects whose combined rating is less than 75 percent, continue cultivation. Decide what specific steps need to be taken to move the prospect forward.

For capacity, create actual request levels or ranges. Devise different capacity scenarios for different targeted groups. For one group, you might create a capacity table for gifts of $50–$500. You have decided that this range best fits their available resources. For another group, your gift requests might start at $1,000 or $100,000.

> There is no valid mathematical way to measure fair and reasonable gift size for a prospect.

Depending on your organization's relationships, some of your financial scenarios might look like this:

Capacity Code	Sample Request Amounts	
A	$ 50–99	$1,000–1,999
B	$100–199	$2,000–2,999
C	$200–299	$3,000–3,999
D	$300–399	$4,000–4,999
E	$400–500	$5,000–6,000

If you seek a volunteer commitment, your scenario might look like this:

Capacity Code	Request
A	work alone on a single, short-term task
B	work on an ad-hoc task force
C	serve on a committee (1–2 year term)
D	serve on the board

A Caveat about Capacity

Evaluating a prospect's capacity to give does not depend solely on his or her financial resources. Commitments are equally important. And you may not be able to identify all the commitments that a prospect has.

Commitments can include such things as:

- payment of pledges to other not-for-profit organizations
- education or health care commitments for family members
- gifts and loans to family and friends

Even more important are the fundamental characteristics of the philanthropic process. It is these fundamentals that produce large gifts from people with modest incomes and limited assets. These same characteristics of philanthropy produce small gifts from affluent individuals who give annual gifts.

Some propose that if you examine the income statistics of a population, you can estimate the fair share that your organization should get in philanthropic gifts. Some say that you can estimate how much a cultivated, motivated, and effectively solicited prospect will give, based on annual income and net worth.

But neither of these suppositions seems to consider the fundamental characteristics of the philanthropic process:

- the other commitments of the audience
- their specific interests (and disinterests)
- how well you develop relationships
- how relevant your particular organization is to community need
- how well you communicate with those predisposed to your organization

Designing the Ask

Use all the information you have. Look at what you know about the prospect. Examine the answers to the questions asked at each step of the constituency development process. Consider the results of your cultivation strategies. Review the debriefing notes from each cultivation activity. Talk to your cultivators. Talk with staff and volunteers.

Gather together all the right people—but not too many. After all, this is a confidential discussion. These individuals may include key cultivators (who are also potential solicitors for the request).

Focus on step 7 in the 10-step constituency development process. Keep the donor or prospective donor at the center. Devise your request around his or her interests, motivations and aspirations, readiness, and capacity. Answer the questions from step 7:

- How will giving benefit the prospect, given his or her interests, needs, and motivations?
- What is the appropriate focus (or project) that would be most appropriate to this prospect, given his or her interests, needs, and motivations?
- Who is the best solicitor or team of solicitors?
- Given the prospect's capacity and level of interest and readiness, what is the appropriate request amount?
- What is the best way to structure the ask—outright request for the amount, specific intervals within a range, costs for particular projects?
- When is the best time?
- What is the best approach, face-to-face, mail, telephone?
- What is the actual request scenario? What will be communicated and how?

Finalize what you will ask the prospect for and at what level. Outline content for your conversation with the prospect. Pinpoint the key points of your discussion. Include questions you will ask the prospect. Create silent spaces so the prospect can talk. And make sure you listen.

Anticipate potential barriers that the prospect might raise. Figure out how you will answer. Decide who will say what in the conversation. Practice. Create a natural flow. Figure out how to close the conversation.

SUMMARY

Constituency development is the third of four relationships that are critical to effective and productive fund development. Only by developing strong and effective long-term relationships will you have sufficient constituents to survive well into the next millennium.

You need many diverse constituents who will: use your services, speak well of you, serve on your board and committees, help you fundraise, give charitable contributions, and open doors to new donors. To develop these relationships, your organization has to benefit the constituent in a way that matters to the constituent. Then she or he may be willing to help you.

Unfortunately, constituency development receives little time and attention in many organizations, particularly those "fighting" for survival. Too frequently, we ask people for money before they are ready to give. We ask current donors to increase their gifts before these donors are ready to give more. We invite people to join our boards before they are comfortable with our institutions. We even set the future direction of our organizations without engaging constituents in the dialogue.

And what is the result in each of these situations? The organization does not meet the needs of the constituent, and the constituent does not meet the organization's needs. There is no mutually beneficial exchange.

Successful organizations focus first on the constituent. They create a process to develop relationships. These organizations get to know their constituents, understand their interests and disinterests, and recognize their needs and aspirations.

Effective organizations use constituency development to become more personal. They develop carefully crafted cultivation strategies that are tailored to the particular constituency. These organizations describe their activities in terms of benefit to the constituent. They communicate in ways that make it easy for the constituent to receive the message. These organizations "throw away the cookie cutter and start monogramming" (Murphy and Vaclavik 1996).

Always remember: Different people care about different causes. Your challenge is to find them and develop a meaningful relationship with them—meaningful to the constituent, as well as to your organization.

REFERENCES

Ahern, T. 1999. Ahern Communications, Ink. Foster, RI. Personal communication.

Bly, R. 1985. *The Copywriter's Handbook: A Step-by-Step Guide to Writing Copy That Sells.* New York: Henry Holt and Co.

Brassard, M., and D. Ritter. 2000. *The Memory Jogger: A Pocket Guide of Tools for Continuous Improvement.* Salem, NH: GOAL/QPC.

Drucker, P. 1990. *Managing the Nonprofit Organization: Principles and Practices.* New York: HarperCollins Publishers.

Dunlop, D. 1986. Special Concerns of Major Gift Fund-Raising. *The Handbook of Institutional Advancement,* 2nd ed. San Francisco: Jossey-Bass, Publishers.

Edwards, R. April 1989. Education: Our Legacy to the Profession. *Fund Raising Management.* Garden City, NJ: Hope Communications.

Fryxell, D. 1992. *How to Write Fast (While Writing Well).* Cincinnati: Writer's Digest Books.

Funk and Wagnalls Company. *Funk & Wagnalls Dictionary.* 1963. New York: Funk & Wagnalls Company.

Hall, H. March 26, 1991. Getting Doctors To Give. *The Chronicle of Philanthropy.* Washington, DC.

Hodgkinson, V., and M. Weitzman. 1990. *Giving and Volunteering in the U.S.* Washington, DC: Independent Sector, 121.

Kotler, P., and A. Andreason. 1987. *Strategic Marketing for Nonprofit Organizations,* 3rd ed. Englewood Cliffs, NJ: Prentice Hall.

Levy, B., and R. Cherry. 1996. *NSFRE Fund-Raising Dictionary.* New York: John Wiley & Sons.

Mokwa, M., W. Dawson, and E. Prieve, eds. 1980. *Marketing the Arts.* New York: Praeger Publishers.

Murphy, M.A., and Vaclavik, L.A. 1996. *The Dini Partners.* Houston, TX.

Nichols, J. 1995. *Global Demographics: Fund Raising for a New World.* Chicago: Bonus Books.

Ogilvy, D. 1985. *Ogilvy on Advertising.* New York: Random House.

Pottruck, D., and T. Pearce. 2000. *Clicks and Mortar.* New York: Random House.

Rosso, H. 1991. *Achieving Excellence in Fund Raising.* San Francisco: Jossey-Bass, Publishers.

Sturtevant, W. April 1996. The Artful Journey: Seeking the Major Gift. *Fund Raising Management.* Garden City, NJ: Hoke Communications.

Tapscott, D., D. Ticoll, and A. Lowy. 2000. Relationships Rule. *Business 2.0.* Brisbane, CA: Imagine Media, Inc.

Williams, R.H. 1999. *Secret Formulas of the Wizard of Ads.* Canada: Webcom Limited

Wunderman, L. 1996. *Being Direct: Making Advertisement Pay.* New York: Random House.

Appendix 4–A

Identifying the Predisposed for Your Organization

Date _____

Name of individual completing this form _____

Telephone # _____ Fax # _____

****

Name of the predisposed _____

Type, please check one:

☐ Individual   ☐ Business   ☐ Religious organization   ☐ Other _____

If the predisposed is some type of organization, please note the following:

Contact name and title _____

Address (City, Zip) _____

Telephone # _____ Fax # _____

If the predisposed is an individual, please note the following:

Spouse/partner name _____

Home address (City, Zip) _____

Telephone # _____ Fax # _____

Employer _____ City _____

Your relationship with the predisposed

☐ Friend
☐ Business colleague. What business _____
☐ Board members together. What board(s) _____
☐ Other _____

Briefly list what you know about the predisposed.

1. Connections to your programs and activities (e.g., as donor, volunteer, attendee, etc.).

2. Connections to other agency board members or staff.

3. If an individual, board(s) s/he serve on. If a group, board(s) that key contact serves on.

4. Participation in other volunteer activities (as individual or as a group, e.g., as a business).

5. Professional affiliations and interests (for the individual and for the group).

6. Personal, leisure interests, lifestyle (for the individual).

7. Briefly describe why you think this individual or group might be interested in a particular agency program or the agency in general.

Appendix 4–B

Constituency Development Worksheets: How We Can Build Relationships That Support Our Organization

1. Name all the constituent groups we can think of. What do we know about them? What don't we know? What do we want to ask for?

Constituent group	What do we know about them? What do we think are their interests and needs?	What don't we know? How will we find out?	What might we ask them for? Money, time, lobbying, what?

TIP: Don't feel you have to use this form. Answer the questions any way you like.

2. Get to know our constituents. Build relationships by understanding the needs, interests, and motivations of those we are trying to reach.

Constituent group	List the activities our organization does. These are our features.	List how each activity benefits the specific constituency.

TIP: Do this and you can use the information in your fundraising letters and in brochures to recruit new clients.

3. Build relationships through communications. We probably do more communications than we realize. The trick is coordination. We need to eliminate the weak and wasteful.

Constituent group	What do we do now to talk with each constituency?	What don't we do that would work?

TIP: Want a thumbnail communications plan? Answer the two questions posed on this worksheet. Then rank your constituencies by their importance to your fundraising. Focus your attention only on the communications do's and wanna do's that are directed at your top-ranking constituents.

4. Build relationships through cultivation. Our constituents need more than communications. Those that we get more involved will be more responsive to our requests.

Constituent group	What kinds of cultivation strategies can we use to bring our constituents closer to our organization?	Who will carry out each cultivation strategy?

5. Evaluate readiness after we have cultivated relationships. Then ask!

Constituent group	What will we ask for?	Why have we decided they are ready to be asked?	How do we propose to ask? Include names of individuals who will do the asking.

TIP: If you had unlimited time, people, and resources, how would you ask? Set this as your goal and move at least one step closer to it with every solicitation.

6. Now that we're ready to implement, make a task list so we can track our progress.

List the tasks that need to be done.	Who is responsible?	What are the key dates?

7. Evaluate and adjust.

List the activities to be evaluated.	Specify the measures of success.	Outline how we will evaluate and who is responsible.	Target dates for review.

TIP: Post-game analysis is the secret to success. Building relationships is always a work in progress. Expect that some things will work and some won't. Your real job is to draw correct conclusions from both.

Appendix 4–C

Prospect Worksheet

Evaluating readiness and interest, determining capacity, designing the ask

Individual(s) completing worksheet and dates

Prospect Name (Include First, Middle Initial, Last, Nickname for both individuals)

Person's Name _____

Spouse/Partner Name _____

Address and Telephone (Include city, state, ZIP and area codes)

Home _____ City _____ State _____ ZIP _____

Telephone ( ) _____ Fax ( ) _____ E-mail _____

Vacation _____ City _____ State _____ ZIP _____

Telephone ( ) _____ Fax ( ) _____ E-mail _____

Relationship to your organization

Person's Name _____	Spouse/Partner _____
Board of Trustees (List years) Officer (Specify office and year)	Board of Trustees (List years) Officer (Specify office and year)
Board Committee Service (List committee, year)	Board Committee Service (List committee, year)
Auxiliary, Advisory Committee Service (List group and year)	Auxiliary, Advisory Committee Service (List group and year)
Other service and year	Other service and year

Personal and family background (Note anything you think is helpful.)

Person's Name _____	Spouse/Partner _____
Clubs, affiliations	Clubs, affiliations
Hobbies, interests	Hobbies, interests
Relevant family ties and friendships	Relevant family ties and friendships
Other	Other

Pertinent information regarding any children:

Employment Information

Person's Name _____	Spouse/Partner_____
Title _____	Title _____
Employer Name	Employer Name
Address (Street, City, State, ZIP)	Address (Street, City, State, ZIP)
Area Code/Telephone/Extension	Area Code/Telephone/Extension
Area Code/Fax	Area Code/Fax
Web site address	Web site address
Associate/Secretary's Name, Title	Associate/Secretary's Name, Title
Key information about the employer (general purpose; donor to organization; reference to other relevant files)	Key information about the employer (general purpose; donor to organization; reference to other relevant files)

Community volunteering

Person's Name _____	Spouse/Partner _____
Charitable organization boards	Charitable organization boards
Other leadership work, with which charities	Other leadership work, with which charities
For-profit corporate boards	For-profit corporate boards

Major charitable gifts by either or both partners

Charity	Project/Area/Topic	Amount/Range

Demographics and lifestyle

General notes regarding relevant demographic and lifestyle trends and patterns.

Specific interests, comments, observations based on experience with this prospect.

EVALUATING

The optimum combination of interest, readiness, and capacity produces the best ask. The best ask is the right project, right amount, right time, right solicitor, and right manner of asking.

Try using a 10-point scale, with 10 being the best.

Begin with interest. Determine the point rating for the prospect. Make anecdotal remarks about why you have selected that rating. Indicate what has to be done to improve the rating.

Proceed with readiness and do the same.

Interest + readiness = 20. Great! Design the right ask and go for it.

Interest + readiness ≤ 15. You need to cultivate more.

Interest + readiness = 16–18. Talk a lot. Would more cultivation be better?

Interest

Refers to the prospect's feeling of curiosity or attentiveness. Interested people are involved and concerned about your cause and your organization's response to the cause.

Interest also signifies that something is of advantage or benefit to the interested individual. (It's not what your organization is selling, it's what the prospect is buying that counts.)

> Estimate level of interest and note date as this may change over time. Add remarks.

Readiness

Means beings prepared for action, likely or liable to act in a particular manner. Readiness means that the prospect is prepared in his or her mind and heart, and likely to act in the manner that you seek. The prospect sees how giving will benefit him- or herself by meeting his or her needs and fulfilling his or her aspirations.

> Estimate level of readiness and note date because this may change over time. Add remarks.

Total interest + readiness = _____ out of 20 possible points. Specify date _____

If interest and readiness are not sufficiently solid, what will you do to move the prospect along the relationship continuum to be more interested and/or more ready to be asked? Add pages to this Prospect Worksheet, describing your cultivation strategy.

Capacity

Refers to the ability or aptitude to do something. Also means the maximum output or production, as in the prospect's wherewithal to do what you ask.

If useful, develop a gift table to help focus on potential capacity.

Discuss what kind of resources might be available for the prospect to give. Consider the following:

1. To what extent does the prospect have personal, family, and other obligations that affect his/her giving capacity?
2. Does the prospect have sufficient cash to give and to what extent?
3. Might securities be an option?
4. Is there some other tangible property the prospect has that your organization would want?
5. Would the prospect benefit from life income? If yes, what might you want to offer to the prospect as giving strategies? Consider life insurance, pooled income fund, and various trusts.
6. Would a combination of giving strategies be helpful to the prospect? For example, a combination of life insurance and cash; or bequest and cash; or bequest and pooled income fund, etc. How would you suggest this?

DESIGNING THE ASK

With all above evaluation information in hand, plus all you know about the prospect, begin designing the ask. Consider the following questions—*from the prospect's perspective.*

1. What would be the most appropriate focus/project/theme for the ask, given the prospect's interests and aspirations? Why? How will you build the connection through the asking process?
2. What would be the most appropriate request amount/range, given all you know?
3. When would be the best time to ask and why? Is anything happening in the prospect's life that will affect the time to solicit?
4. Who would be the best solicitors? Why? (Some of the best solicitors for a particular prospect should be helping you do the prospect evaluation and designing the ask.) If a team would be best, who would be the members? Who would cover which points in the ask?
5. Would the prospect welcome a memorial opportunity or personal/family recognition? If yes, what will you propose or how will you introduce this concept to the prospect?
6. How will you prepare the solicitors for the ask? Consider the following:
   - Outlining the relevant points to cover?
   - Identifying which team member says what.
   - Figuring out beforehand how the team will decide whether the prospect is ready to "close" the sale or whether it is best to return for a follow-up discussion.
   - Who will actually ask?
   - If the prospect wishes to think about it, who will do the follow-up to get the answer?
   - How will you address recognition and memorial opportunities to the prospect?

Appendix 4–D

Case Statement—
Boys & Girls Club of Pawtucket

Courtesy of the Boys & Girls Club of Pawtucket.

What gets into a kid at the Boys & Girls Club of Pawtucket?

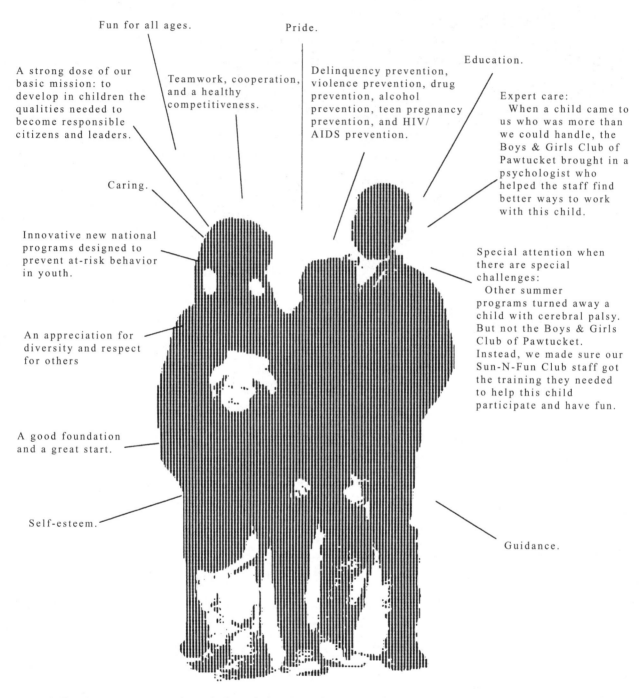

Fun for all ages.

Pride.

Education.

A strong dose of our basic mission: to develop in children the qualities needed to become responsible citizens and leaders.

Teamwork, cooperation, and a healthy competitiveness.

Delinquency prevention, violence prevention, drug prevention, alcohol prevention, teen pregnancy prevention, and HIV/AIDS prevention.

Expert care:
When a child came to us who was more than we could handle, the Boys & Girls Club of Pawtucket brought in a psychologist who helped the staff find better ways to work with this child.

Caring.

Innovative new national programs designed to prevent at-risk behavior in youth.

Special attention when there are special challenges:
Other summer programs turned away a child with cerebral palsy. But not the Boys & Girls Club of Pawtucket. Instead, we made sure our Sun-N-Fun Club staff got the training they needed to help this child participate and have fun.

An appreciation for diversity and respect for others

A good foundation and a great start.

Self-esteem.

Guidance.

The Boys & Girls Club of Pawtucket is open to ALL boys and girls between the ages of six and seventeen.
There are no restrictions.
In 94 years, we have served more than a half million youth.

Maybe we can change your mind about the Boys & Girls Club of Pawtucket.

PERCEPTION	REALITY
• The programs pay for themselves.	• Actually, the programs HALF pay for themselves. Fees, memberships, incidentals such as rentals and the sale of food provide just 50% of our annual income. Because we serve many disadvantaged children, we keep our fees low and never turn anyone away who needs our help. We need to raise at least $600,000 in contributions annually.
• The United Way makes up the difference.	• The Boys & Girls Club of Pawtucket currently receives about 5% of its annual income from the United Way. It used to be more. But the increasing emphasis on donor designation has had a significant impact on our total United Way gift. Donor-designated dollars are harder to raise, requiring a great deal of promotion. At the same time, the United Way has been steadily reducing allocations. The result? In 1994, the Boys & Girls Club of Pawtucket received 52% less from the United Way than we'd received in 1989.
• The Club's endowment generates significant income. The Club will always be there.	• In recent years, shortfalls in contributions have forced trustees to spend not just interest from the Club's endowment and reserves, but principal, reducing our safety net. The Boys & Girls Club always requires additional support, and without that support, they will close.
	• The Boys & Girls Club is unique. Yes, like other agencies, it offers a full schedule of supervised activities. But, unlike the others, it also offers a safe environment where kids can hang out, feel comfortable, study, get advice, make friends . . . and escape the stress, threats, and temptations of the streets.

Your help <u>will</u> make the difference.

1995 Income = $1,336,546

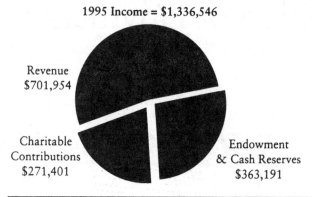

Revenue
$701,954

Charitable
Contributions
$271,401

Endowment
& Cash Reserves
$363,191

1995 Expenses = $1,336,546

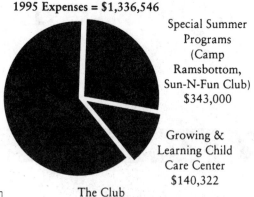

Special Summer
Programs
(Camp
Ramsbottom,
Sun-N-Fun Club)
$343,000

Growing &
Learning Child
Care Center
$140,322

The Club
$853,224

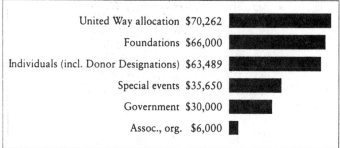

United Way allocation	$70,262
Foundations	$66,000
Individuals (incl. Donor Designations)	$63,489
Special events	$35,650
Government	$30,000
Assoc., org.	$6,000

The fiscal year is January–December.

PEOPLE SERVED

More need, more service every year
In 1994, the Boys & Girls Club of Pawtucket served 15,611 people through programs and memberships, a 10% increase from the previous year. In fact, we have seen increases in use every year for the past decade.

The Club
5,925 served
2 locations offering programs, after-school daycare, and open hours:
- Alfred Elson Jr. branch for boys and girls 6–12 years of age
- East Avenue branch for boys and girls 13–18 years of age

Special summer programs
2,025 served
- Camp Ramsbottom, 170-acre day camp in Rehoboth
- Sun-N-Fun Club at Alfred Elson Jr. branch

The Growing and Learning Preschool Child Care Center
75 served

WHO THEY ARE

Serving those who need it most
Over half our youth come from homes whose income is less than $37,500 per year. One out of every five of our youth comes from a household whose annual income level is below $13,400.

Focused on the community
90% of the people we serve come from Blackstone Valley; 5% come from Greater Providence and East Bay. An additional 5% come from nearby Massachusetts and other parts of R.I.

And helping adults, too
In addition to youth, the Boys & Girls Club of Pawtucket served 700 adults in 1994 through our cardiac rehabilitation program and our recreation facilities. 6,886 more people used our facilities through rental.

THE FUTURE

We can't cut services, and we can't afford to increase fees
Every year more people use our services, and our costs go up. But increasing our fees isn't the answer; that only excludes people who need our help.

But we CAN build contributions
The Boys & Girls Club of Pawtucket is strengthening its fundraising. We have launched a comprehensive fund development program that will:
- increase designations from donors to United Way and the state and federal campaigns
- find new donors
- increase gifts from current donors
- reach out to foundations
- start our first face-to-face solicitation campaign
- expand our direct mail program
- initiate "Homers for Kids," a new fundraising event with the Pawtucket Red Sox

Please help take care of our community's kids.

See for yourself what goes on inside the Boys & Girls Club of Pawtucket.

ALFRED ELSON JR. BRANCH

PHOTO NOT REPRODUCED

- Club branch for boys and girls, ages 6–12
- a full schedule of athletics, including swimming, baseball, indoor soccer, fitness, basketball
- supper every night, free for those who qualify
- educational activities, including arts and crafts and computer and babysitting skills classes
- resource center for study and homework
- home for the summer Sun-N-Fun Club
- preschool Growing and Learning Center

EAST AVENUE BRANCH

PHOTO NOT REPRODUCED

- Club branch for boys and girls, ages 13–18
- a full schedule of games and athletics, including swimming, soccer, basketball, fitness
- a positive—and safe—social environment for teen-agers
- an afterschool haven for supervised activities, high-quality programs, and study
- all our facilities are managed by a well-trained, superbly motivated professional staff

CAMP RAMSBOTTOM

PHOTO NOT REPRODUCED

- summer day camp
- for boys and girls, ages 6–13
- a wide choice of supervised activities, including sports, hiking, cooking, nature studies, horseback riding, swimming, model rocketry, art, mountain biking, archery, crafts . . . and more!
- lunch, transportation, supplies are provided
- founded as a youth camp in 1966, in 1995 Camp Ramsbottom celebrates its 29th season as a Boys & Girls Club of Pawtucket facility
- we think it's the best day camp in New England

"THE POSITIVE PLACE FOR KIDS"

Boys & Girls Club of Pawtucket
Gregg A. Pappas, Executive Vice President
One Moeller Place
Pawtucket, RI 02860
(401) 722-8840

Appendix 4–E

Case Statement—
Children's Aid and Family Services

Courtesy of Children's Aid and Family Services, Paramus, New Jersey.

THE ENDOWMENT FUND

THE LASTING GIFT

we believe

in happy endings

CHILDREN'S AID
AND FAMILY SERVICES, INC.

CHILDREN'S AID AND FAMILY SERVICES

Mission Statement

The mission of Children's Aid and Family Services, Inc. is to help individuals of all ages live and thrive in families and communities. This mission is based upon a belief that human beings have the capacity to heal, to learn, and to grow.

We believe that interdependent relationships that practice and teach mutual respect, responsibility, honesty, and permanency play an integral and powerful role in a person's growth and development.

We believe that self-sufficiency is intrinsic to human dignity and to society's prosperity.

These beliefs are the foundation upon which our mission is built and upon which we pledge the resources and talents of a caring, accountable organization dedicated to serving individuals, families, and the community.

we believe in human dignity

we believe in **family** and **community**

Building a better future one gift at a time.

A gift to the Endowment Fund is a permanent gift, producing income in perpetuity, doing good for generations to come. Your endowment gift will help:

Underwrite research and development.
Children's Aid and Family Services wins high marks for its innovative responses to emerging problems. But forging new programs is costly.

Diversify and stabilize the agency's funding mix.
The Endowment Fund provides Children's Aid and Family Services with a major new source of annual income...a source safe from the uncertainties that affect government contracts.

Accommodate change.
The Endowment Fund acts as our strategic reserve, giving Children's Aid and Family Services the flexibility to adjust rapidly to a changing environment.

Manage emergency shortfalls.
Income from the Endowment Fund can provide a safety net when government or foundation support for essential programs suddenly fails.

Subsidize fees.
We can offer financial aid to families who might otherwise be unable to afford fee-based programs.

Make capital improvements.
Income from undesignated endowment gifts can help fund renovations, construction, and the acquisition/upgrading of major equipment and technology.

Attract and train qualified professionals committed to serving families and children.
Good people are hard to find. The Endowment Fund supplies Children's Aid and Family Services with the means to invest in its "intellectual capital" and attract and keep the best staff.

In 1999, Children's Aid and Family Services entered its second century of innovation and service to the children, families and communities of northern New Jersey.

Even if you already give to Children's Aid and Family Services on an annual basis, please consider a separate gift to the Endowment Fund. We need your help...to build a legacy of caring.

4

Building independence.

A well-funded endowment will help balance the agency's funding mix and reduce our dependence on the taxpayer. The following pie chart shows our current funding situation.

Current Typical Funding Mix (without Endowment)

75%   Government Contracts[1]
15%   Other Revenues[2]
10%   Annual Charitable Contributions[3]

(1) Virtually all of this derives from the State of New Jersey Department of Youth and Family Services.
(2) Fees, interest, etc.
(3) Individuals, corporations, foundations, United Way.

The table below shows how an endowment can offset the program's dependence on government funding.

AMOUNT OF ENDOWMENT	ANNUAL INCOME @ 5% YIELD	% ENDOWMENT CONTRIBUTES TO A TYPICAL ANNUAL BUDGET
$5 million	$250,000	3%
$10 million	$500,000	6%
$15 million	$750,000	8%

You are investing in a well-managed agency that focuses on stronger families and stronger communities.

Today, the annual operating budget for Children's Aid and Family Services is approximately $9 million. This budget underwrites 20 different programs: adoption, clinical counseling, crisis prevention and intervention, and more. Each year these programs directly touch the lives of thousands of individuals and families living in northeastern New Jersey.

Children's Aid and Family Services: Expenses

87%   Programs & Services[1]
12%   General & Administrative
1%   Fund Raising

(1) Children's Aid and Family Services directs an unusually high percentage of its budget into programs and services. Other well-regarded human service agencies routinely expect to spend 20% of their annual budgets on administrative costs.

5

Your gift grows over time.

The Children's Aid and Family Services Endowment Fund has two fundamental financial objectives:

(1) to give the agency a reliable new source of revenue (interest income);

(2) to self-fund the endowment's growth through the steady reinvestment of a portion of its income.

What money can buy.

The table below demonstrates the relationship between endowment dollars and services.

SERVICE	COST	ENDOWMENT PRINCIPAL NECESSARY
Day Care	$7,000/child/year	$150,000/child
Counseling	$700/treatment (averaged)	$15,000/person
Adoption	$10,000/adoption	$200,000 covers one adoption annually
Group Home Social Worker	$30,000 annual salary	$600,000/employee

we believe in self-sufficiency

6

CHILDREN'S AID AND FAMILY SERVICES

A century of service and innovation.

In 1995, two well-established community agencies with complementary missions agreed to join forces.

Merging 20 programs under one umbrella, they formed a new, integrated agency — Children's Aid and Family Services — that now delivers a comprehensive choice of child development and adoption services, as well as many kinds of individual and family counseling.

The Children's Aid and Family Services team includes —

- licensed clinical social workers
- certified alcoholism counselors
- child psychiatrists
- family-life educators
- geriatric specialists
- licensed marriage and family counselors
- certified school social workers
- early-childhood educators
- school psychologists
- paralegals specializing in adoption
- more than 800 skilled and compassionate volunteers, providing everything from fund raising to mentoring to community outreach

established
1899

7

Scope of services.

Children's Aid and Family Services provides assistance to those residing in the five counties of northeastern New Jersey (Morris, Essex, Bergen, Passaic, Hudson). Three million people live in our service area.

Children's Aid and Family Services welcomes anyone who could benefit from our help. We offer help without discrimination of any kind and without regard for the person's ability to pay.

serving anyone in the
5 counties of **northeastern**
New Jersey

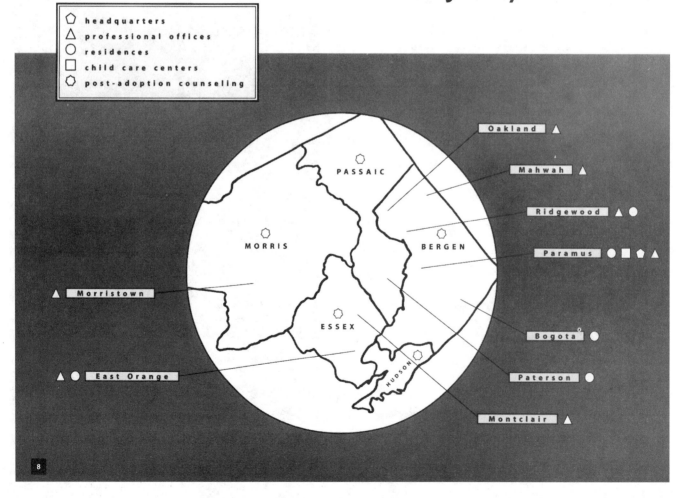

Permanency services for children.

Pre-Adoption Treatment Homes
(PATH I in Paramus, PATH II in Bogota) Helping severely damaged children ages 4–12 regain their capacity to trust and love, so that they are ready for adoption into permanent homes.

Adoption
Placing children of all ages in loving and caring homes.

Adoptive and Foster Family Recruitment
Recruiting suitable families for the harder-to-place child, including older, special needs, and minority children.

Adolescent Group Homes
(Children's Haven in Paterson, Eastlea in East Orange, Woodlea in Ridgewood) Care, treatment, and nurturing for adolescents ages 13 to 18, with 24-hour professional supervision.

Treatment Foster Homes
Trained foster parents helping children of all ages, as well as unwed teenage mothers, cope with their emotional and behavioral problems.

Permanency for Boarder Babies
Finding permanent homes for infants (often abandoned, or at-risk) who are languishing in area hospitals.

Mentoring Adolescents (Visions)
Carefully matched adults providing life skills and a six-month internship for adolescents who are leaving foster or group homes.

Paralegal Support Services
More than three dozen CAFS paralegals specializing in adoption help the state and adopting parents navigate the paperwork.

Dependent care prevention services.

Child Development Center
(Paramus) Affordable, therapeutic, curriculum-based child care in a state-licensed facility.

Warm Line Telephone Counseling (201.445.8281)
Confidential professional assistance for parents.

Elder Care
Services include in-house assessments, specialized counseling, and referrals; Medicaid-approved.

Family and Schools Together (F.A.S.T.)
An intervention and follow-up program for families whose children are having problems in school and are at high risk for substance abuse.

Family Life Education
Low- or no-cost public seminars on vital issues such as substance abuse, divorce, parenting, elder care and stress management.

Early intervention counseling services.

Family Counseling Service
Family and group therapy, individual psychotherapy, marital counseling.

Child Custody Mediation
Objective third-party when divorced parents encounter custody and visitation conflicts.

Substance Abuse Recovery Program
For children and adults with drug and alcohol problems; includes clinical treatment and support programs.

Child and Adolescent Treatment Service
Professional help for children and teens.

Work Place Services
Short-term intervention for employees.

Adoption Counseling
Pre- and post-placement, for birth and adoptive parents.

Post-Adoption Counseling
Therapeutic intervention programs.

we believe in

growing

healthy adults,

stabilizing

families, and

enriching

lives

1899
Children's Aid and Protective Society of the Oranges established. First official meeting of the board of directors held February 9, 1899, at 65 Essex Avenue, Orange, NJ.

1945
Name changed to Children's Aid and Adoption Society (CAAS).

1952
CAAS and the New Jersey Children's Home Society decide to divide coverage within the state, with CAAS focusing exclusively on northern New Jersey.

1956
Family Counseling Services of Ridgewood and Vicinity, Inc. founded.

1965
The Depot established to raise funds to benefit Family Counseling Services.

1973
Woodlea group home established. The Child Development Center opens January 3.

1974
CAAS merges with the Sister Mary Eugene Foundation, Inc., effective April 26. Sister Mary Eugene's Bogota facility becomes CAAS main office. Eastlea group home for girls established at old main office in East Orange. Treatment Home program established.

1976
Renaissance House group home for adolescent boys opens.

1979
Southeast Asian Refugee Youth program created.

1983
Mother/Child Treatment Home program created.

1984
Post-Adoption Counseling Services begin.

1986
Independent Living program created. Morristown branch office opens.

1987
PATH I opens for boys and girls, ages 6-12. Program provides post-adoptive therapy for children. Mahwah office opens.

1990
CAAS headquarters moves from Bogota to larger facilities, the Turrell Program Services Center at 575 Main Street, Hackensack.

1992
PATH II opens for girls, ages 5-12. PATH I becomes boys' home.

1993
Children's Haven group home, Paterson, merges with CAAS.

1995
Children's Aid and Family Services founded, merging CAAS and Family Counseling Services of Ridgewood and Vicinity, Inc.

1996
Boarder Babies program begins. Endowment Fund receives $500,000 anonymous challenge gift.

1997
Endowment Fund grows to $1 million in gifts and commitments.

1998
New Child Development Center and Turrell Program Services Center opens at 200 Robin Road in Paramus. Second Century Circle Endowment Fund grows by another $1 million in gifts and commitments.

1999
Centennial anniversary of Children's Aid and Family Services. Endowment Fund grows by another $3 million in gifts and commitments, reaching its first-phase target of $5 million. Recognition of founding members of Children's Aid and Family Services Legacy Society.

Why my yearly check for $50 grew into a $500,000 endowment gift.

I'm a doctor.

But, until that night, I never really thought a heart could break.

The night the police rang our doorbell to tell me that Michael, my husband for fifteen rich and interesting years, had skidded to his death on an icy road.

Megan was upstairs doing her homework. I knocked and walked in, "Megan, honey, your daddy's had an accident." She looked up, under control, a doctor's daughter, "What kind of accident? Where is he?"

I knelt by her chair and looked into her eyes, our special treasure, our only child. The girl Michael could almost cup in his hands the day she was born. "Megan, I'm sorry. Daddy didn't survive."

Beginning a change in Megan that turned my adorable, gentle, studious child into a danger-loving, self-destructive stranger who lied automatically, and stole money from me and visitors to our home, to buy herself drugs, and to finance rides into New York City instead of attending school.

The help I got — the family counseling I received through Children's Aid and Family Services — stopped the corrosion. In time — and I mean that literally — counseling reversed the direction. Brought Megan home, back to school, under control, happy.

That was three years ago. Now Megan's in her first year of college. It's not too much to say that Children's Aid and Family Services saved my family.

I know, from my personal experience, that what the agency does, works. I feel far too strongly for just a $50 or $100 check each year. I want to make sure that Children's Aid and Family Services is around for good, for any family who needs it, no matter who they are or whether they can afford to pay.

So why did I give so much to Children's Aid and Family Service's endowment? Because my daughter is beyond price. Ask yourself: What is it worth to save a family?

we believe

human beings

(have the capacity to)

heal

> "I've been interested in health issues for years. And like a lot of people, I want to see some of my estate go for a purpose I select. I believe in the work of Children's Aid and Family Services. It's an agency with a lot of ideas and a talented staff. They have a role to perform, and they do it well."
> — endowment donors, **Ethel & Arthur Toan**

> "If people in New Jersey knew all the things that Children's Aid and Family Services does for orphans, AIDS babies, homeless and abused boys and girls, and family after family in deep psychological trouble, I know they'd be touched and want to give. And giving to the Endowment makes a contribution that will last."
> — **Robin Willis**, Children's Haven advisory committee member, a volunteer involved for 25 years with Children's Aid and Family Services

KEN LENTH*

The bequest from a thousand miles away.

A city firefighter until his retirement and a devoted beekeeper all his life, Ken Lenth taught his children — and now his grandchildren — to read the "honey clock," to track the seasons by the bees' nectar sources. Red maples in the spring. Then dandelions, apple trees, clover, sumac, and weeds throughout the summer. Finally, until the hard frosts, goldenrod and aster.

"It's aster time for this bee," Ken laughed over the phone. Ken is 83. "Time to put the finishing touches on our will." Which is why he was calling: to verify the agency's current name and address.

Back in the sixties, when he and his wife, Cynthia, lived in New Jersey, they adopted two infants from the agency that later merged to form Children's Aid and Family Services.

Time flies. Infants Carl and Laura grew up, went to college, began careers, got married. Carl now teaches college biology, and Laura is a successful businesswoman, operating a natural bakery in Vermont. And Ken and Cynthia, proud grandparents several times over, have retired to a lakeside cottage in Wisconsin.

But they never forgot the agency that helped them build a family, or the thoughtful way they'd been treated. As part of a legacy to others who wish to adopt, the Lenths have included in their will a bequest for the Children's Aid and Family Services endowment.

* Some minor details in these stories have been changed to protect anonymity.

13

we believe

in **mutual**

respect

14

Choosing the right kind
of endowment gift.

Endowment gifts like yours guarantee that Children's Aid and Family Services will continue to build strong families for the foreseeable — and unforeseeable — future.

Endowment gifts can also offer you, your family, and your estate significant financial or tax advantages.

Your gift need not be cash. You can give stocks, bonds, an insurance policy, even real property.

You may wish to give immediately. Many donors view an annual gift to the endowment as part of an overall strategy for reducing taxable income.

You may also wish to give a "planned gift"...as part of your estate, or as part of your long-term financial strategies. Some of the more popular planned giving options are described on the following pages.

Planned endowment gifts.

Bequests

Your bequest (a gift through your will) may take a number of forms, including a percentage of your estate, a specific dollar amount, stock, real estate (or other property), or the residue or "remainder" of your estate after all other bequests are made. Typically, the largest gifts result from this so-called "remainderman" option. (See side-bar for suggested language in stating your bequest.)

Life Insurance

A life insurance policy naming Children's Aid and Family Services as a beneficiary is a simple and cost-effective way for you to make a substantial gift.

Special advantage: if you make Children's Aid and Family Services the owner and sole beneficiary of your policy, you can report the annual premiums, or the cash value of a paid-up policy, as a charitable deduction in the year of the gift.

We encourage you to consult with your insurance agent or financial advisor to learn how a small investment in life insurance now can yield a very large payoff for Children's Aid and Family Services in the future.

Gifts that produce lifetime income for you or your designee.

Your endowment gift to Children's Aid and Family Services can also be structured to provide you (or someone else, such as your spouse or child) with income, either immediately or when you retire.

The basic concept is simple: in exchange for your asset — cash, stock, or property — you receive a fixed or variable income for life (or a specified term of years).

Advantages

• Even though your gift produces income, a portion of the gift — often a generous portion — can still be claimed as an itemized income tax deduction on this year's tax return.

• You (or a beneficiary) receive income from the gift for a term of years or life (some restrictions regarding the recipient's minimum age may apply).

• Often, you can avoid paying capital gains tax if a gift is funded with appreciated property, such as stock or real estate.

The most common life-income gift plans are summarized on the next page. All are available through Children's Aid and Family Services.

How to state your bequest.

If you wish to make a bequest, ask your attorney to consider the following suggested language:

I give and bequeath to Children's Aid and Family Services, Inc., of Hackensack, New Jersey, _____ percent; or the sum of _____ from my estate; or all the rest, residue or remainder of my estate. This bequest is designated for the Endowment Fund, to be used by Children's Aid and Family Services wherever the need is greatest.

Most endowment gifts are unrestricted. If you choose, however, to name a specific purpose for your gift, please consider adding the following language:

If, as a result of changed conditions in the future, my gift shall not be needed for the specific purpose set forth here, the Trustees of Children's Aid and Family Services are authorized to use the gift for other purposes that advance the agency's mission.

Language like this will allow Children's Aid and Family Services a degree of flexibility as the future unfolds.

15

we believe in **preparing**

for the **future**

Common life-income gift plans.

Charitable Gift Annuities
In exchange for your gift of cash or stock, Children's Aid and Family Services will establish an annuity that guarantees you or a beneficiary a fixed income for life.

Donors can also defer income, if they wish. Deferred payment gift annuities often appeal to younger donors who would like an immediate tax deduction, while at the same time adding to their retirement income.

Special advantage: a portion of the gift annuity is tax-free for the life expectancy of the annuitant.

Pooled Income Fund
Similar to a mutual fund (in that gifts from many donors are commingled for investment purposes), the Pooled Income Fund (PIF) provides the

beneficiary with fluctuating income for life. The PIF is managed by a highly qualified investment committee. Note: real property cannot be used for PIF gifts.

Special advantage: if you fund your PIF gift with long-term appreciated stock, you completely avoid paying capital gains tax.

Charitable Remainder Trusts
A Charitable Remainder Trust (CRT) is an irrevocable trust you create, with or without contacting Children's Aid and Family Services (we can take fiduciary responsibility of the trust, if you desire). The trust produces either a fixed or fluctuating income for life or for a term of years.

Special advantage: if you fund your CRT with long-term appreciated stock, you will avoid paying the capital gains tax.

Who manages the Endowment Fund?

A specially appointed Investment Committee manages the Children's Aid and Family Services endowment. The Investment Committee reports regularly to the agency's Board of Trustees.

Members of the Investment Committee are hand-selected for their significant expertise in investment and financial matters. Our proximity to New York City offers Children's Aid and Family Services the important advantage of recruiting key Investment Committee members from one of the world's great pools of financial management talent.

The Investment Committee is guided by certain general policies regarding rate of growth relative to inflation, preservation of principal, acceptable levels of risk, portfolio mix, and diversification.

The manner in which the agency invests and employs its endowment is also examined as part of the annual audit. A copy of our annual audit is available upon request.

16

This brochure is not intended as legal or financial advice.

Please contact your own attorney and financial advisor regarding your personal questions and circumstances.

Materials describing all these giving options in greater detail are available by contacting Robert B. Jones, Ph.D., President and CEO of Children's Aid and Family Services, at 201.261.2800.

A representative from the agency can meet with you personally and confidentially to discuss such things as:
• your interests and aspirations;
• the qualifications of our Investment Committee;
• the mission and plans of Children's Aid and Family Services.

Recognition of your endowment gift.

Donors to the Endowment Fund can be specially recognized in a number of ways. All Endowment Fund donors are featured in Children's Aid and Family Services publications. Donors also receive a handsome certificate, suitable for framing and display in home or office.

The Endowment Fund was established as a "fund for the future," to ensure that Children's Aid and Family Services is here to help generations to come. Your recognition as a donor to the Endowment Fund is permanent.

Gift Categories

All gifts to the Endowment Fund are listed alphabetically by gift category. The categories are:

Ambassador	$1 million and above
Founder	$500,000 – 999,999
Angel	$250,000 – 499,999
Champion	$100,000 – 249,999
Guardian	$50,000 – 99,999
Sustainer	$20,000 – 49,999
Sponsor	$10,000 – 19,999
Patron	$5,000 – 9,999
Benefactor	$2,500 – 4,999
Friend	$1,000 – 2,499
Grandparent	$500 – 999
Parent	$250 – 499
Sibling	$100 – 249
Cousin	up to $99

Named Funds

If you'd like to honor or remember someone special, you can create your own specially named fund within the Endowment Fund, with a gift of $10,000 or more.

The named fund can include the donor's name as well, for example: "the Philip Arthur George Fund, established in his memory by his sister, Marion Winston."

Second Century Circle

All donors making a planned gift by will, life insurance or other means receive lifetime membership in the Second Century Circle and a recognition listing in a variety of Children's Aid and Family Services publications.

In addition, Second Century Circle members receive a handsome certificate suitable for framing.

As a Second Century Circle member, you will receive an invitation (for you and a guest) to all Circle gatherings. At least one event is held each year.

Founding Members

If you join the Second Century Circle before December 31, 1999, you will receive a special Founding Member certificate, suitable for framing and display.

Anonymity

While Children's Aid and Family Services welcomes the opportunity to honor publicly those who partner with us, we also carefully protect the identity of any donor who wishes to remain anonymous.

17

we believe

in happy

endings.

For More Information

Children's Aid and Family Services

President and Chief Executive Officer
Robert B. Jones, Ph.D.

Headquarters
The Turrell Program Services Center
200 Robin Road
Paramus, NJ 07652

Phone
201.261.2800

FAX
201.261.6013

Accreditation and Regulating Authorities
Council on Accreditation of Services to Families and Children, Inc.
NJ Division of Youth and Family Services
Medicaid Approved

Affiliations
Child Welfare League of America
Commerce and Industry Association of Bergen County
Consortium of Family Agencies of Bergen County
Family Service America
Family Service Association of New Jersey
Human Service Advisory Council of Bergen County
New Jersey Association of Children's Residential Facilities
New Jersey State Adoption Advisory Council
Northern New Jersey Maternal and Child Health Consortium
United Way of Bergen and Morris Counties

18

Appendix 4–F

Excerpt from Boys & Girls Club of Pawtucket Fund Development Plan for Fiscal Year 1996

SECTION 5. CULTIVATION ACTIVITIES

This cultivation outline was originally developed and approved in March 1995, to support the Fiscal Year 1995 Fund Development Plan. These activities are essential to our short- and long-term fundraising success. We will improve implementation of cultivation activities in fiscal year 1996. We will set up a task force to oversee implementation.

The *purpose of cultivation* is to:

- prepare prospective donors to be solicited
- encourage current donors to give more
- involve more people in fundraising

Cultivation means building relationships. This is a very personal activity and does not happen solely through printed material or requests for money. *The Club must get to know its donors and prospects in order to:*

- understand their particular interests—and hence which project(s) might interest the prospect
- recognize their readiness to give—and hence when it might be most appropriate to ask
- evaluate capacity to give—and hence determine an appropriate request amount

Our target audiences for cultivation are:

- Current donors (trustees, individuals who designate through workplace giving, and others)
- Service beneficiaries who do not currently give (e.g., parents of members)
- Individuals and businesses identified through the fund development process

Courtesy of the Boys & Girls Club of Pawtucket, Rhode Island.

MAJOR COMPONENTS OF OUR CULTIVATION PROGRAM

1. Education and Communication Strategies

- Club updates to trustees (periodic letter from president regarding activities)
- feature articles in *News & Views*
- insiders information letter to targeted prospects
- donor option on appropriate information throughout the year
- for fiscal year 1996, introduce new newsletter directed to parents

**NEW: All donors, Club trustees, and Club volunteers will receive *News & Views*. Businesses and individuals identified as cultivation prospects (e.g., invited to President's Gatherings, etc.) will receive *News & Views*.

**NEW: In the fall of 1995, staff and consultants developed a communications plan for fiscal year 1996 and 1997. This plan has as its goal the creation of sufficient awareness within targeted prospects to secure more charitable contributions and fundraising volunteers for the Club.

2. Cultivation Activities

This means personal contact and dialogue between a prospect and representative of the Club. This is an ongoing process. Generally, more than one contact is necessary before a solicitation is made. Once someone has given, cultivation continues. Cultivation never ends.

Sometimes there are formal activities (e.g., meetings, events, etc.). Sometimes there are informal encounters or telephone calls. For example:

- *Information meetings and tours*
  Identify individuals to be cultivated. Have a trustee bring the prospect(s) to an informational tour of the Club, then follow up afterward. Requires approximately 1 hour of the prospect's time. This can be done for just one individual or for a group of individuals.
- *Special events* (for "hot" prospects with key resources)
  Includes such events as Awards Dinner, Camp Ramsbottom Tour, and/or Vespers.
  Requires more time on the part of the prospect—approximately 2–3 hours—hence the prospect needs to have demonstrated some level of interest before being invited to such an event. Identify individuals to be cultivated. Have a trustee bring the prospect(s) to the event, and then follow up afterward.
- *Major donor cultivation* (may include items #1 and #2 above)
  As necessary, we will actually develop a specific cultivation outline/strategy for selected prospects. For example, we recently had a small meeting with a handful of individuals and outlined a strategy and made assignments to cultivate a relationship with a local corporation that had not previously given to the Club.
- *Engaging trustees in the Club*
  Buddy Program for trustees: Members of the Executive and Fund Development Committees periodically call trustees to engage them in the fund development process. We strive to find different ways for trustees to be more involved in non-fundraising activities.

INFORMATION MEETING/TOUR

1. Trustees may call the executive director or development officer at any time to arrange a personal tour and info session for one individual at a convenient time.
2. In addition, the Club will conduct at least four President's Gatherings in fiscal year 1996.

   General description of the President's Gathering
   Small group (approximately 10 total) that lasts no more than one hour. Selected trustees will bring invited guests that have been identified as prospects for cultivation. Trustees will be responsible to do follow-up cultivation after the President's Gathering.

   Scheduling
   The four President's Gatherings will be held during February, April, and Christmas vacations and during July or August so that the attendees see youth in the Club. Gatherings will be presented at East Avenue and Elson branches at 8:00 AM, 12 noon, and 5:00 PM.

   Hosts and presenters
   Staff will recruit 3–4 trustees who can act as presenters, depending on schedule availability.

   Invitation
   Executive and Fund Development Committees will ask 2–3 trustees (or other community leaders) to each bring two people to a specific President's Gathering.

   Agenda
   1. Refreshments and mingling (Trustees will talk and cultivate, one on one with prospects.)
   2. Tour of facility
   3. 15-minute "dog and pony" show covering the following key points
      - History and experience/expertise of the Club
      - Mission and audience
      - Personal stories of youth
      - Operations and financing
   4. We will make every attempt to have a youth talk briefly
   5. Minimal handouts will be provided, e.g., case statement, annual report
   6. The closing will include an "ask." The ask will *not be for money*. It is premature. The ask will be something like:
      - Please think about us after you leave here today.
      - Tell one other person about the Club.
      - Complete this evaluation card. Possible questions would be:
        – Did you find the President's Gathering interesting, useful? How might we improve it?
        – Do you have suggestions about who we might invite in the future?
        – Do you now feel more knowledgeable about the Boys & Girls Club?
        – Would you like to get involved in a project/activity with the club?

SECTION 6. ACKNOWLEDGMENT AND RECOGNITION

Acknowledgment refers to the thank-you letter that we provide each donor, no matter the gift amount. Recognition refers to listing in a publication or some other special "public" credit.

Acknowledgment Letters

All gifts, no matter the amount, receive a personal thank-you letter from the office. This letter complies with the IRS regulations, as provided in the special handout from Joyaux Associates, and any new changes!

The letter is personalized. Both salutation and signature reflect the donor's relationship with the Club.

As appropriate, more than one letter may be sent. For example, staff and volunteer may send letters, etc.

As we secure larger and larger gifts, we will create additional thank-you letters. Youth members may write them and draw pictures.

Recognition

We always provide our donors the opportunity to maintain the anonymity of gifts. For those who do not wish to remain anonymous, we will continue to develop recognition opportunities. For example:

1. Create gift clubs/levels of giving, with various names.
2. For major gifts from foundations and other donor sources that have display areas, we will consider framed pictures created by our youth members. We will also consider memento albums and other special strategies. These recognition opportunities are generally reserved for significant gifts (in 4 and 5 figures).
3. In our annual report, we will list major donors. Each year, depending on the number of donors, we will determine what level of gift to list. Generally, our benchmark will be $500 and higher.
4. We will recognize donors and volunteers in our *News & Views*.

Chapter 5

The Fourth Relationship—With Your Volunteers

Enabling Them To Take Meaningful Action on Behalf of Your Organization

Hoarding power produces a powerless organization. Stripped of power, people look for ways to fight back: sabotage, passive resistance, withdrawal, or angry militancy. Giving power liberates energy for more productive use. When people feel a sense of efficacy and an ability to influence their world, they seek to be productive. They direct their energy and intelligence toward making a contribution rather than obstructing progress.

Lee G. Bolman and Terrence E. Deal

To what extent are the professionals in the independent sector becoming alienated from the volunteers? . . . I worry most about the growing lack of mutual understanding and deep sense of common values between . . . professionals and . . . volunteers.

A volunteer who works at a botanical garden says that she resents being given the scut work, relegated to it by paid staff. "That isn't what I volunteered for," she says.

More ominous, of course, are the comments that denigrate the competence, dedication, and value of the volunteers. "If it weren't for the alumni, I'd love alumni work." A certain

amount of that kind of talk . . . is exasperation and not cynicism, and shouldn't be taken seriously. But all of us have also detected at times a different and more troubling tone of contempt in such remarks.

Robert L. Payton

TOPICS DISCUSSED IN THIS SECTION

- what enabling means and how it benefits your organization
- enabling as a preventive measure and an intervention
- carrying out the 16 enabling functions
- developing the attitude, skills, and knowledge of an enabler
- coping with the challenges of enabling
- action steps to strengthen enabling in your organization
- enabling volunteers in appropriate and meaningful ways
- assessing your own capacity to enable

ENABLING YOUR VOLUNTEERS

Enabling volunteers is the final of the four relationships critical to a healthy organization and effective fund development. It is definitely "last, but not least." Your relationship with volunteers enables them to take meaningful action on behalf of your organization.

There are several predictable benefits if you enable your volunteers well: If you enable your volunteers (or staff, for that matter) well, your organization will achieve its goals. When you enable, your volunteers do what

Source: Portions of this chapter were adapted with permission from S.P. Joyaux, ACFRE, Voluntary Association and Volunteer Leadership, *Nonprofit Oganizational Culture: What Fundraisers Need to Know*, R.C. Hedgepeth, CFRE, Editor, No. 5, Fall 1994, pp. 17–32, Copyright © 1994, Jossey-Bass, a subsidiary of John Wiley & Sons, Inc.

is necessary to help your organization. And when you enable well, you will likely raise more money.

Volunteers are critically important to not-for-profit organizations. Whether the individuals serve as board members, do clerical work, solicit gifts, or provide direct service, they make a difference in your organization. Volunteers contribute the "voluntary action for the common good," which is the hallmark of philanthropy. Volunteers justify your organization as philanthropy and extend your reach, capacity, and capability.

Fundraisers know this is true for effective fund development. No matter how many fundraising staff your organization has, they cannot substitute for volunteers. Nevertheless, fundraisers get frustrated by their volunteers. How often have you heard (or said) these phrases?

- "My board members just don't understand fundraising."
- "My volunteer solicitors procrastinate. Why won't they just finish their calls?"
- "My volunteers will do anything but fundraise."

Get a group of fundraising professionals together, and they talk about their volunteers. Fundraisers complain about their boards and talk about how to get fundraising volunteers to do their jobs.

We fundraisers expect our volunteers to understand their roles, respect staff authority and competence, and perform appropriately. We urge our volunteers to use their skills on behalf of our organizations.

And it's not just the fundraisers who wrestle with volunteers. Just watch chief executive officers (CEOs) struggle as volunteers cross the line into management, or listen to the gasp from the marketing office when a volunteer speaks to the media.

Volunteerism is a hot topic in most not-for-profit organizations. It's a continued focus for research and writing in the field. Certainly, volunteerism is a hallmark of philanthropy. Volunteerism is also a challenging function within an organization, raising as many questions as opportunities. See Exhibit 5–1, questions of meaning about volunteerism. Do you talk about this at your organization?

One of the most significant questions about volunteerism is, What are we as staff doing to help our volunteers? Are we doing enough? Are we doing the right thing? For example, do we honor their roles and recognize their rights? Do we respect their interests and seek out their abilities?

Consider this: If your volunteers are not as effective as you want them to be, examine yourself first. Usually, volunteers are only as effective as we enable them to be. Their failure is too frequently ours.

By the way, staff need to be enabled, too. Although this book focuses on enabling volunteers, the concepts and functions can be applied to staff, as well.

CONCEPT OF ENABLING

Enabling is the process of empowering others. Enabling means giving people the wherewithal, opportunity, and adequate power to act. Synonyms for *enable* include invest, endow, and authorize. Synonyms for power include ability, influence, capability, and authority.

When you empower someone, you distribute and share your own power. Power shared is power multiplied. If someone has power, she or he has the authority to make decisions. Equally important, she or he has the right (and safety) to voice opinions, even if these opinions conflict with those of the "boss."

Enabling depends on reciprocity, relating, and connecting. Enabling encourages participation, shares responsibility and authority, enhances the self-worth of others, and energizes everyone in the organization. Exhibit 5–2 demonstrates the positive results of enabling.

Enabling produces the optimum performance from individuals or groups. And there's another result: Enabling allows your volunteers to succeed, using their own power. The advantage? They may well volunteer for you again.

> *Enabling helps others exercise their potential and power.*

Usually, staff (i.e., both employees and consultants) want volunteers to perform a specific task competently, efficiently, and in a timely fashion. Fundraisers, for instance, may want their volunteers to plan a special event and sell tickets to it, cultivate relationships, and solicit major gifts.

Tasks are important. But they are only part of the system. The best staff also want their volunteers to participate in process, ask challenging questions, think critically, and help make key decisions. Effective staff want their volunteers to be so invested that they insist on discussion and dialogue. These volunteers may disagree and argue about complex issues. And the best staff are pleased.

Enabling Is Good

Some people mistake enabling for caretaking or suspect that it will end up being patriarchal and patronizing. Enabling is even considered manipulative. In social service circles, the word *enabling* can be a pejorative term, meaning coconspirator or codependent.

Exhibit 5–1 Questions of Meaning about Volunteerism

1. How do we build community and enhance the capacity of our community to identify and address its issues (called *civic capacity of a community*? What role does volunteerism play in building community and enhancing civic capacity, and how do we use this resource?
   - What role does "growing the Third Sector" play in building community and enhancing civic capacity, and how do we go about this "growing"?
2. To what degree does volunteerism result from excess capacity (e.g., time and money available in a community, within individuals), and how do we maintain volunteerism during times of scarcity (e.g., economic downturn, change in the nature of family and work commitments, etc.)?
3. How does volunteerism add value to this organization? How do we measure the "net" benefit or "return on investment" of volunteers?
4. What benefit is there to professionalizing volunteerism, and how do we achieve these benefits without compromising the value of voluntary action?
5. How do we encourage colleagues in our organization to value volunteers?
6. What are the major challenges that staff encounter working with volunteers, and how do we prepare for, manage, and overcome these challenges?
7. How do we create opportunities for volunteers to feel engaged, successful, and effective?
   - To what degree do staff understand why volunteers volunteer?
   - How do we ensure that we understand what volunteers value—and where their interests intersect with our organization—in order to create a mutually benefit exchange?
   - To what degree can our organization—and our interaction with volunteers—fulfill their needs?
8. What is the difference between paid staff jobs and volunteer positions? What are the commonalities? How do we manage and balance these differences and commonalities?
9. How do we help the leadership of our organization understand and value that paid staff are often volunteers within the organization?
10. How do we create processes and opportunities for people to self-identify as volunteers for our organizations?
11. What is the process for finding the right volunteers, recruiting, placing and retaining them, orienting and training them, ensuring their satisfaction and that of the organization, and promoting and releasing them as necessary?
12. How do we value volunteers who may not share our values but wish to volunteer?
13. How do we help volunteers distinguish between acting as a board member or acting in a different volunteer capacity?
14. How do we enable volunteers to educate staff so that staff listen and learn from the wisdom of volunteers?
15. How do we engage new generations and different cultures in volunteerism?
16. When is it appropriate to translate oral tradition into written policy and procedure, and how do we accomplish this so as to add value to the organization and its volunteers?
17. Why do we accept/tolerate behaviors from our own board members and other volunteers that we (and they) would not accept in an employment relationship? What effect does this acceptance and tolerance have on the organization, other volunteers and staff, those we serve, and achievement of our mission?
    - Why do we expect a certain level of performance, and more quickly take action to correct performance below that level, with financially compensated people but not with volunteers?
18. What attitude, skills, and knowledge are necessary within our volunteers and staff in order for organizations to succeed in an ever-changing networked world that requires innovation, collaboration, and continual learning?

About Conversation and Questioning

19. When communication breaks down between volunteers and management—or between volunteers, e.g., within the board—whose responsibility is it to restart the conversation and facilitate resolution? How does this happen?
20. How do we create the organizational culture—reinforced through systems and processes—to encourage ongoing conversations?
21. How do we develop a more disciplined process of asking essential questions, questioning the assumptions and answers, and creating the optimum answers for our organization at this time?
22. How do we create ongoing and meaningful conversations between staff and volunteers (e.g., fund development volunteers, the board, etc.) about issues related to volunteerism without moving into management?
23. How do we decide in which situations to engage which volunteers in what levels of dialogue and decision making?
24. How do we take the "parking lot" conversations (those that happen outside the authorized group, e.g., the board) and form alliances to effect positive change without forming cliques that cause damage within the organization?
25. How can we enable people to participate in larger community/organization conversations, as well as small group conversations?

Source: Copyright © Simone P. Joyaux, ACFRE and the Divine 9 (Cohort 9, Master's Program in Philanthropy and Fund Development, St. Mary's University of Minnesota).

Exhibit 5–2 This Could Have Been a Tale of Conflict and Dissatisfaction

---

"Invite the actors," said one volunteer at the theatre. "They'll have fun, and our guests will be thrilled!"

"We could use the theatre's props and costumes to help decorate the space," suggested another.

"Let's use the stage for the event," added the next volunteer.

Whenever I sat down with special event volunteers at the theatre, I worried. I enjoyed their enthusiasm but I feared their desires.

I understood the expectations of our volunteers. But meeting all their expectations simply wasn't possible.

Most of the actors did not enjoy being on parade. Usually, they were rehearsing and/or performing anyway. Props and costumes were precious and expensive. A set was always on stage, filling the space. Or we were taking one down or putting another up.

But what could I say to the volunteers? My alternatives were to say "no" or to be a good enabler.

"No" made volunteers feel unsupported and unappreciated. The theatre looked bad, and volunteers quit in frustration. So I had to meet the needs of the volunteers and the theatre.

The most important thing I learned was to anticipate. I knew what the volunteers would ask. I even understood why. All I had to do was explain first. Set the context and build understanding so they would rarely ask for what the theatre could not give.

No rules. No bold statement of procedures. Instead, orchestrate a friendly dialogue about what it was like to operate a theatre. Give volunteers insight before they made demands. Share with our volunteers the needs of actors, the stress of technical crew, and union restrictions. Talk about what we could do.

And I had to do all this before the volunteers asked for something that required a "no" response.

I had to make the volunteers part of the inner circle, with special information and knowledge. Then the volunteers understood what was possible and what was not. Soon our volunteers were explaining theatre operations and realistic expectations to newcomers!

Enabling worked. I did not wait until they asked. I did not withhold information. I did not say "no." I enabled. We were all happier and more successful.

True enabling is none of these. Rather, enabling is a value-driven philosophy that invests influence and responsibility in all parties. Enabling empowers individuals, groups, and the organization itself.

Enabling Depends on Two Other Relationships

Successful enabling relies directly on two of the relationships discussed earlier in this book: the relationship within your organization and the relationship with your constituents. These two relationships are particularly entwined with enabling.

First, look at your organization's internal relations, described in Chapter 2. To strengthen your organization's internal relations, focus on these seven components.

1. shared values
2. art of leadership
3. learning organization
4. ongoing conversation
5. participatory decision making
6. well-managed change
7. culture of philanthropy

Leadership is a prerequisite for enabling. Review the discussion of leadership—its skills and functions—in Chapter 2. Enabling uses many of these.

Enabling requires that you, the enabler, respect and be sensitive to the diverse opinions and experiences of others. Sharing values with those you enable can also enhance the process. When individuals who work together share values, these individuals are working within a common framework. Certainly, your board—a particularly critical group—must share the values of the organization, as should those you hire on staff.

However, not everyone will share your values—and such an expectation is unreasonable. You will likely have the opportunity to work with volunteers who do not necessarily share the values of your organization (and donors who give but for motivations that may not exactly match your values).

Nonetheless, these individuals may offer you valuable service and support. Neither their values, motivations, nor behaviors harm your organization. Undoubtedly, you welcome many of these volunteers and donors now.

Look back at the seven components of your organization's internal relationship. Enabling is a prerequisite for five components. The learning organization, ongoing conversation, participatory decision making, well-managed change, and culture of philanthropy need enabling to work well.

Now consider your relationship with constituents, described in Chapter 4. Look back at the constituency development steps. Think about getting to know your constituents so you understand and meet their needs. Consider how you engage your constituents in meaningful ways.

The constituency development process creates a mutually beneficial exchange. The final exchange happens when a constituent gives to your organization because your organization is the mechanism to fulfill the constituent's aspirations. The gift can be many things, for example, money, service on the board or a committee, advice, or political advocacy on your behalf.

In many ways, enabling is the same process. You get to know your volunteers, understanding their interests and concerns. You help volunteers overcome their concerns by eliminating barriers and providing support. The ultimate exchange happens when the volunteer successfully carries out activities on behalf of your organization because you have enabled him or her to do so. The process of enabling creates a successful use of volunteer resources for your organization.

Enabling Means Stewardship and Partnership

The enabler helps people and groups to work together so your organization is more likely to achieve its goals. Enablers make sure people have the resources and authority to influence the system. The enabler helps develop the capacity of others.

To be successful, everyone needs to feel responsible. Everyone in the group (or organization) has to own the goals and strategies to achieve the goals. The enabler helps build this ownership.

Peter Block's concept of stewardship helps explain enabling. Block (1993) describes stewardship as "operating in service, rather than in control, of those around us."

Block goes on to say that authentic service requires four elements.

1. Power is shared and balanced.
2. People are, first, committed to the larger community.
3. Everyone helps define purpose and decides organizational culture.
4. Rewards are balanced and distributed equitably.

Note how well these elements fit with the seven components that strengthen your organization's internal relationship.

Stewardship includes partnership. Block observes that partners are connected in a way that the power between them is "roughly balanced." He describes four requirements for partnership, also reminiscent of the infrastructure that enhances the relationship within your organization. These requirements are:

- exchange of purpose
- right to say no
- joint accountability
- absolute honesty

First, partners define purpose and values together. People at all levels talk to each other, sharing conversa-

tions and decision making. They may disagree at times but, together, they learn for the good of the organization and themselves.

Second, each partner can say no. As Block (1993) observes, "If we cannot say no, then saying yes has no meaning." There may be someone who has higher authority when you say no. Even though this individual may be able to tell you what to do, you can still say no. Block reminds us that partnership doesn't necessarily mean you get what you want.

But you never lose your right to speak. Enablers create a safe environment so people can disagree and even say no.

> *Partnership does not do away with hierarchy and we still need bosses. Stewardship is the willingness to hold power, without using reward and punishment and directive authority, to get things done.*
>
> *Peter Block*

Third, everyone is responsible. Partners have joint accountability for outcomes. Partners know that, together, they created the current situation and can change it. Enablers help people see their roles, capabilities, and influence.

Fourth, absolute honesty is essential. Block describes not telling the truth as an act of betrayal. An omission is equally unacceptable. Enablers tell the truth and make sure that there is no retribution when others speak honestly, too.

BENEFITS OF ENABLING

Enabling may be the single most important contributor to improving your organization's fundraising performance. Enabling certainly is the primary factor in a healthy relationship between governance and management.

The thing is, people are loyal to your organization's mission, not to fund development. So it can take lots of work to get them to help fundraise. Enabling does this.

Enabling holds multiple benefits for your organization. First, enable your volunteers, and they will do tasks well, including fund development activities. Second, enable your volunteers, and they will feel successful and important to your organization. Third, enable your volunteers, and they will stick with you longer.

If your volunteers have good experiences, they are more likely to continue volunteering and to volunteer more. They will likely give you money and even increase their gifts. Equally important, satisfied volunteers will tell others about how great your organization is, thus encouraging more gifts of time and money.

Enabling can do more. It will:

- engage volunteers in the meaning of your organization, rather than the tasks and mechanics alone
- develop stronger relationships between your organization and its volunteers
- enhance the quality of your organization's decision making

Preventive Measure

Enabling is *the* strategy to enhance volunteer performance. When incorporated into the way you do business, enabling anticipates potential problems and prevents them from occurring. Effective enabling makes the system work.

Intervention Strategy

Enabling is an excellent intervention strategy. Once there is a mess—big or small—turn the situation around by using the enabling functions. Enabling can solve the mess that resulted because enabling wasn't used in the first place. It's a neat little circle. Enabling is both an anticipatory/preventive strategy and a reactive/intervention strategy.

When you use the enabling functions as an intervention strategy, consider the following steps:

- Carefully examine the situation, its full scope, and all its dimensions.
- Analyze what happened and is happening. Identify what caused the problem and continues to cause the problem. Describe how the situation got to this point. Make sure that you clarify your own assumptions, then question them. Do the same with the assumptions of others involved.
- Focus on the barriers that arose. Consider process and task issues.
- As appropriate, engage others in a discussion about the situation. Learn together.
- Then, using the enabling functions, outline how you would now intervene.

Take a look at Appendix 5–A, a real-life situation with an intervention based on enabling functions.

Sometimes—despite every effort—enabling will not solve the problem. Perhaps the individual or group is too dysfunctional. Perhaps individual egos will not tolerate enabling and so will not change, even for the good of the organization.

In this situation, you can use the enabling functions to co-opt the individual or group. If that doesn't work, use the enabling functions to contain and neutralize them.

Enable others in the organization to help you contain and neutralize—but only through appropriate use of the enabling functions. Remember that the end never justifies the means. You still must act ethically.

> *Once you understand the barriers, enabling will get you beyond them.*
> *Divine 9, Cohort 9, Masters Program in Philanthropy and Fund Development, St. Mary's University of Minnesota.)*

Finally, what if containment doesn't work? What if the volunteer is harming the organization? What would you do if a staff person were harming the organization and the person refused to change, despite your great enabling?

Hopefully you would pick the good of the organization, the good of the group over the individual. You would fire the person.

So what do you do with a volunteer who is harming the organization and will not change? Enhance his or her attrition. Take a look at enabling function 15 (see below), the final act of a consummate enabler.

Raising More Money

Enable volunteers, and you will likely raise more money. Enabling makes the entire fund development process work better.

Think about it.

- Does your fundraising goal result from the difference between expenses and revenue without considering the available prospects?
- Do your volunteers propose fundraising activities without understanding the costs and benefits?
- Is your organization cultivating too few donors and soliciting only a handful of prospects?

Enabling can fix these problems. With enabling, volunteers can establish a viable fund development plan that reflects the resources of your organization. How?

Staff communicate appropriate information, both qualitative and quantitative, about fundraising productivity and solicitation strategies. Staff talk with volunteers about the implications of the information, the trends, possible choices, and consequences. Then, together, volunteers and staff establish realistic goals and determine the best mix of effective solicitation and cultivation techniques.

The process of enabling ensures that you have more volunteers asking. And the more people asking, the greater will be the possibility of gifts. Enabling helps volunteers feel comfortable with asking and provides them with the tools to ask better. When staff provide formal and informal training and demonstrate tactics, volunteers gain confidence in their own knowledge and strengthen their skills.

The Right Thing To Do

There is another reason to enable. It's the right thing to do. It's good for your volunteers, staff, and the organization. The concept of enabling volunteers is inextricably entwined with voluntary association and volunteer leadership. Even if there were no tangible benefits, enabling would be worthwhile because it links organizations more closely to their volunteers.

ENABLING FUNCTIONS

Enabling is much more than managing volunteers. It is a leadership concept. Enablers, like leaders, carry out very specific functions. Indeed, many of the leadership functions (and attitude and skills), described in Chapter 2, lay the foundation for enabling. Furthermore, enabling is one of the major responsibilities of a leader.

Exhibit 5–3 What You Do As an Enabler: the Principal Functions of Enabling*

---

1. Transmit the organization's values.
2. Engage volunteers in the meaning of your organization.
3. Respect and use the skills, expertise, experience, and insights of volunteers.
4. Provide direction and resources, remove barriers, and help develop skills.
5. Articulate expectations and clarify roles and relationships.
6. Communicate (which includes helping people transform information into knowledge and learning).
7. Encourage people to question organizational assumptions and ask strategic questions.
8. Ensure quality decision making.
9. Anticipate conflicts and facilitate resolution.
10. Engage volunteers in process, as well as tasks.
11. Encourage volunteers to use their power, practice their authority, and accept their responsibility.
12. Model behavior.
13. Coach people to succeed.
14. Manage.
15. Enhance attrition.
16. Monitor, evaluate, and enhance enabling.

(*Compare these functions with the leadership functions described in Chapter 2.)

Enabling has many facets. Sixteen functions are proposed here, each related to the others. Without one, the others will not work (see Exhibit 5–3).

1. Transmit the Organization's Values.

If an organization honors enabling, this will be reflected in its core values and, hence, its corporate culture. Values describe an organization's philosophical approach to its work, the way the organization relates to its various constituencies, and how it carries out its work. Values and values clarification are described in Chapter 2.

Enablers make sure that volunteers understand the organization's values and how these values affect programs and operations. Enablers help synchronize volunteer behavior with organizational values—but only to the degree necessary.

Remember: Not all volunteers will share your organization's values, and that's okay. Synchronicity is necessary only to the degree that there is no apparent conflict. Alignment is not required except in certain situations, as previously discussed.

If an organization has not yet articulated its values, enablers make sure this happens. As organizational development specialists, enablers respect the importance of values clarification, particularly within the board and staff, and within the fund development function.

2. Engage Volunteers in the Meaning of Your Organization.

Volunteer understanding of and personal experience with your mission and program validate the time and energy spent with the complex issues and endless tasks of your organization. Engaging volunteers in the heart and soul of the institution helps maintain interest in governance and fund development.

Keep the following two points in mind. First, the tasks and mechanics of one organization look pretty much like any other. So does their fund development. It's the meaning that is different. Enabling shows (and explains) the meaning unique to your organization.

Second, your volunteers (and staff) may feel that fund development is taking over the organization. Sometimes, it seems that the board and its members do nothing but fundraise. This is an unhappy state of affairs. Stuck in fund development, volunteers get increasingly frustrated and disinterested.

It's very easy to focus on fund development and the tasks and mechanics of an organization. Sometimes, the link to meaning is forgotten or assumed without adequate conversation.

Do you find yourself in these situations?

- A board discusses finances instead of their effect on programs and constituents.
- Individual board members pore over the giving history of prospects, rather than explore prospect interests and aspirations.
- Staff report the results of fundraising solicitations without discussing the trends and explaining the implications for future solicitation activities.

It's up to staff to make sure the organization avoids this disconnect between meaning and activities. Staff show volunteers how fund development fits into the organizational and community system. Staff—remember, that's both employees and consultants—help volunteers understand the meaning behind tasks and mechanics. Through enabling, staff link these operations to the meaning of the organization and the strategic nature of its choices.

> *Enabling engages your board and its members in the meaning of the organization so its fate belongs to them.*

You use the enabling functions to help your volunteers feel more connected to your organization. When volunteers understand and participate in the meaning of the organization, they feel a sense of ownership. Then they work better, give more time, and may give more money.

3. Respect and Use the Skills, Expertise, Experience, and Insights of Volunteers.

The experienced enabler personally cares about the success and satisfaction of his or her volunteers and is committed to fulfilling their needs as fully as possible. The accomplished enabler makes volunteers into heroes.

People give their time and money to meet their personal needs and fulfill their own visions. They want to feel comfortable while contributing. They want to perform well and make a valuable contribution.

Enablers know that successful volunteer placement appropriately balances the volunteer's interests, knowledge, and skills with the organization's needs and the nature of the volunteer activity. Enablers ensure this successful placement by understanding the interests, skills, expectations, and concerns of their volunteers.

Enablers figure out what their volunteers know. Enablers recognize the scope of knowledge and the degree of skills possessed by their volunteers. With this perspective in hand, enablers work with the volunteers to identify the appropriate activity or role. Then enablers are ready to carry out the fourth enabling function, providing direction, resources, and skill development.

Enablers explore the interests, motivations, and skills of their volunteers without making value judgments.

Sometimes, the volunteer's motivations may not be aligned with the organization. Yet, the volunteer wants to participate. The consummate enabler will try his or her best to negotiate a mutually beneficial exchange between the organization and the volunteer. And if this match is not possible, the enabler will help the volunteer understand why, while maintaining the volunteer's integrity and sense of pride.

4. Provide Direction and Resources, Remove Barriers, and Help Develop Skills.

Enablers provide direction and describe the specific tasks necessary to complete the work. Also, enablers provide appropriate and adequate resources, be it clerical support, telephone numbers, answers to questions, and so forth.

Equally important is to ensure that volunteers understand why something is being done, as well as what is being done. The enabler translates the big picture into action steps and manageable tasks. The enabler also describes tasks in terms of the big picture.

Enablers remove the barriers that can stop volunteers from succeeding. Enablers cannot always make the work easy. But they do make it interesting, challenging, and dynamic.

Many tasks require special skills. Your volunteers may need training to develop these skills. Acting as a teacher, the enabler provides the training, both formally and informally.

5. Articulate Expectations and Clarify Roles and Relationships.

The enabler clearly differentiates between staff and volunteer roles. Equally important, the enabler helps volunteers and staff to create a shared vision of roles and expectations.

This function means more than writing and distributing job descriptions. Certainly, a written job description is essential in most situations. But what precedes the written document?

- The enabler must have the knowledge to differentiate clearly between staff and volunteer roles, and the skill to negotiate these potentially treacherous waters.
- The enabler must value the process of articulating roles and expectations, rather than merely announcing them.
- The enabler must garner volunteer support for the process of clarifying roles and relationships, and the benefit of such work.

- The enabler must determine when negotiation of roles and expectations is acceptable and when it is not.

Naturally, the big question is, which roles belong to whom? Both for-profit and not-for-profit practice and literature offer good guidelines. The enabler works with volunteers and staff to adapt these guidelines for his or her own organization and each specific circumstance. For example, see Appendix 5–B for a brief overview of roles in fund development.

To ensure that volunteers are exercising their authority, an enabler must understand the difference between governance and management. The enabler knows that the distinction is not always clear-cut. She can judge when a decision is hers to make or whether it belongs to the volunteers. But the enabler also knows when and how to negotiate these judgments with volunteers.

This enabling function helps set boundaries. Boundaries are an important element in both the social and work context. Boundaries provide guideposts to help people make judgments. Often, boundaries help people feel more comfortable. The challenge, of course, is to ensure that boundaries are neither too limiting nor overly bureaucratic. Boundaries should facilitate roles and relationships, not inhibit question, creativity, and participation.

Articulating expectations and clarifying roles and relationships helps get the work done. Each individual focuses on his or her task; each group carries out its responsibility. All see how their respective roles fit into the overall picture, working together for the common good.

But this enabling function does more than help get the work done. Ragan D. Royal, Director of Development for the School of Business at Wayne State University in Detroit, observed that a job description conveys how important the person is. Extend this thought to the function of articulating expectations and clarifying roles and relationships. Through this enabling function, you convey how important the volunteer is to the organization's efforts.

6. Communicate (Which Includes Helping People Transform Information into Knowledge and Learning).

Communication is essential to effective enabling. DePree (1989) notes that good communication has a number of obligations. "We must understand that access to pertinent information is essential to getting a job done. The right to know is basic. Moreover, it is better to err on the side of sharing too much information rather than risk leaving someone in the dark. Information is power, but it is pointless power if hoarded. Power must be shared for an organization or a relationship to work" (page 104).

An enabler is a good communicator, using the basics described in Chapter 4. The enabler transmits information and helps people transform that information into knowledge and learning. The enabler also seeks information, asking for opinion, listening to interests and concerns, and hearing that which is hard to discern.

Martha Golensky describes five properties that contribute to effective communication (1990, 177–189).

1. frequency: how often communication is received
2. timeliness: when it is transmitted
3. comprehensiveness: how complete it is
4. specificity: how detailed it is
5. directional flow: who originates it

The competent enabler knows what information volunteers need—from whom—in order to make which decisions. The enabler provides information appropriate to the situation, to the individuals and involved, to the roles and responsibilities, and based on the boundaries.

The enabler figures out which things key people have to hear immediately, which items are just an FYI, and which items are of no interest. The enabler does not censor information; neither does she or he waste people's time with items of no interest.

> *People must take responsibility for informing their bosses and colleagues, and above all, for educating them. And then all members of the non-profit institution—paid staff and volunteers—need to take the responsibility for making themselves understood.*
>
> *Peter Drucker*

Good enablers pay lots of attention to *how* they communicate. These enablers ensure that the receiver actually hears and understands the communication. Effective enablers recognize that the means of communication is as important as the content. They know that different people hear best in different ways. Effective enablers also respect the power of words and take special care with language and its meaning.

Drucker (1990) notes the importance of building your organization around information and communication, rather than hierarchy. He observes that every individual within the organization is responsible for information. Better yet, every individual is responsible for providing information and helping others translate the information into knowledge and learning.

To paraphrase and expand on Drucker, you assume this responsibility by continually asking yourself:

- What information do I need to do my job—from whom, in what detail, when and how often, and in what manner?
- What information do I owe others so that they can do their jobs, in what form and detail, when and how often?
- What do I need to do (with what help from whom) to understand the information given to me?
- How can I ensure that the information I communicate is understandable and useful, and results in learning?

Enablers know that people need knowledge, not information. Enablers take three critical steps.

1. Disclose all necessary information.
2. Translate information.
3. Help transform information into knowledge and learning.

> *What at one time would have been termed "manipulating" to me is now more appropriately viewed as utilizing the principal functions of enabling. With the best of intentions and with a clear understanding of my organization's purposes and values, this can be a positive thing.*
> *Stacey Vanden Heuvel*

With good enabling, individuals in the organization can then exercise their own curiosity, judgment, and authority, and make responsible and informed decisions.

First, the enabler discloses all the necessary information. Because knowledge is power, full disclosure is critical if you want to enable well. But this doesn't always happen. Staff (and volunteers) think carefully about who they will tell about what. Sometimes, this is done to retain power. Sometimes, this is done to protect people. But the result is the same—disempowerment.

Block (1993) observes that full disclosure is a basic difference between partnership and patriarchy. He goes on to say that, when we don't tell a partner the truth, we are betraying him or her. And volunteers are partners in the not-for-profit organization.

For people to contribute effectively to their organization, they need to know the truth about what is happening. Clearly, this does require some discretion. Not

everyone needs to know everything. But err on the side of inclusion and fuller disclosure, rather than exclusion and limited information.

Regina Herzlinger (1999) of the Harvard Business School talks about full disclosure as a strategy for enhancing performance. She describes how not-for-profits can "boost public confidence in vital institutions and thereby broaden their financial base" (page 373).

Disclosure can also increase confidence internally and bring more wisdom to tackle tough issues. Consider how you would use Herzlinger's (1999) four questions (page 376) to enable increased knowledge and learning within your organization:

- "Are the organization's goals consistent with its financial resources?"
- "Is the organization practicing intergenerational equity?"
- "Are the sources and uses of funds appropriately matched?" Herzlinger notes that "variable revenues," such as grants, should not fund ongoing expenses, such as salaries.
- "Is the organization sustainable?"

After disclosure, the enabler translates the information, explaining its meaning and implications. Information is just raw data, useless without its current and potential meanings. Keep in mind, however, that translating information does not mean controlling the receiver's interpretation.

As Chatterjee (1998) notes: "Whereas knowledge is the gathering of information, learning is the development of creative intelligence to transform this information into action. Knowledge deals with the *what* of reality; learning deals with the *how* of it. Knowledge is merely classification of information; learning is the ability to draw the energy out of this information into the arena of action. Leaders integrate the what of knowledge with the how of learning. There is total integration between knowledge and action" (page 94).

Lorsch (1995) describes the need to transform information when he writes about the chief executive officer (CEO) and board. "Directors may obtain any data they want, but such information must be converted into useful knowledge through the prism of a broader understanding of the company and its markets and operations—information that inevitably must come from management at board meetings. . . . Superior knowledge about such matters provides even the most well-intentioned CEO with a real power advantage over . . . directors" (page 111).

Third, the enabler helps transform information into knowledge and learning. The enabler does this by encouraging dialogue that investigates the information and its meanings. As the authors of *Framebreak: The Radical Redesign of American Business*, note, "the right information conveyed at the right time to the right people is what enables effective decision-making in an organization" (Mitroff, Mason, and Pearson, 1994, 44).

7. Encourage People To Question Organizational Assumptions and Ask Strategic Questions.

Enablers encourage people to ask questions and challenge the "way things are always done." The enabler creates an environment where this is accepted and expected practice.

The confident enabler accepts questions as part of healthy dialogue. She or he does not consider questions to be criticisms or accusations. The consummate enabler welcomes this challenge on the part of volunteers and believes that the best solutions, plans, and outcomes result from this curiosity and interest.

But more than accepting questions, the enabler encourages them. The enabler actually instigates questioning at every opportunity.

The enabler knows that the functions of communications and questioning work to produce good decision making and quality decisions. The enabler uses ongoing conversation to help people question.

See Chapter 2 for a detailed discussion of ongoing conversation and asking the right questions. See also Exhibit 5–1 for stimulating questions related to volunteerism.

8. Ensure Quality Decision Making.

Quality decision making, discussed in Chapter 2, is critical to organizational health and effective fund development. Enabling ensures effective group decision making. Enablers help volunteers use their expertise to add value to the decision-making process. The enabler fosters open debate so that the best decisions result.

Enablers set the context for decision making and shape discussion. At different levels within the organization, volunteers make tactical and strategic decisions. To make these decisions well, volunteers need the following from staff:

- context of this issue, relative to mission, direction, and past decisions
- appropriate and sufficient information, possible and likely implications of the information
- possible choices and consequences of those choices
- why this falls within the volunteer, rather than staff purview

When setting the context, the enabler encourages dialogue. Volunteers are repeatedly asked to add their own observations, suggest more implications, and identify other choices and consequences.

9. Anticipate Conflicts and Facilitate Resolution.

Inevitably, conflict happens. But conflict is valuable when the process of its resolution builds understanding and mutual respect (see Chapter 2).

Enablers recognize the benefits of disagreement and conflict and use them. Rather than avoid conflict, enablers anticipate the situation. They help clarify the nature of the conflict, then they facilitate resolution.

As Drucker (1990) observes, important decisions are risky and, hence, should be controversial. The dissent and disagreement found in controversy can resolve conflict. "Because it is essential in an effective discussion to understand what it is really about, there has to be dissent and disagreement" (page 126).

Enablers create a safe and risk-free environment. In this environment, conflict and its resolution are not threatening.

10. Engage Volunteers in Process, As Well As Tasks.

Fund development involves more than tasks, it requires process. Volunteers need to be involved in both, and enablers make sure that involvement happens.

Think of a task as a defined activity with a beginning, middle, and end. Think of process as a course or method of operation, a series of continuous actions that bring about a particular result.

Process is nonlinear, sometimes cumbersome, always time-consuming, and usually messy. Just take a look at Chapters 2–4, all of which involve process and mess.

Process involves a lot of thinking and talking and exploring. To be effective, process involves lots of different people, all stakeholders in the outcome and owners of how to get there.

Joline Godfrey (1992), in *Our Wildest Dreams: Women Entrepreneurs Making Money, Having Fun, Doing Good*, notes that "comfort with complexity often extends to comfort with process." Naturally, the reverse is true. Those who are not comfortable with complexity are not comfortable with process. They feel out of control—and feeling out of control for some feels like losing power. For others, feeling out of control is empowering. Godfrey observes, "To relate, to be connected, one must pay attention, and paying attention is what process is all about. If comfort with complexity is the ability to hold and deal with conflicting problems all at once, comfort with process is a tolerance for the gradual unfolding of surprise" (page 17).

Enablers engage volunteers in all three forms of process, described by Godfrey (1992) as creative, group, and operational.

- The creative process means brainstorming, getting input and reactions from stakeholders, encouraging questioning and dialogue, and welcoming heated discussion. "This is the difference between wanting a slick new brochure and understanding that the way you get that brochure will affect everything from employee relationships, vendor success and motivation, the quality of the finished product, and customer satisfaction" (page 18).
- Group process empowers others to participate in decision making. This is the difference between "a staff meeting in which the leader talks, gives orders, and sticks strictly to the agenda, and one in which there is time and room to explore issues that are new, troubling, or confusing—or just time to share, brainstorm, or laugh" (page 19).
- Operational process means taking care of the systems, policies, and procedures that make things happen in a reliable, efficient, and quality manner. This dimension of process also balances the needs of the system and the needs of the system's people.

Enablers know which process and which tasks are appropriate for volunteers in general and which volunteer (or group of volunteers) in particular. Enablers understand that volunteers are not merely extra bodies to carry out assigned tasks.

Talking about and carrying out tasks may not keep the most experienced and talented volunteers involved for long.

These individuals need to understand why, not just how. They want to discuss strategy and help make critical decisions. If you relegate these volunteers to tasks alone, they may lose interest in your organization. Sure, they may continue giving a financial contribution. But a limited or poor volunteer experience will probably not produce increased gifts, repeat volunteering, or good referrals.

Here are some tips for involving volunteers in process:

- At a board meeting, spend 15 minutes brainstorming the case for support. See Appendix F, "Thoughts about Creating a Case for Support."
- In the appropriate setting with the appropriate volunteers, brainstorm any of the questions in Exhibit 2–12, regarding building an effective board, and

in Exhibit 5–1, on the questions of meaning about volunteerism. Continue asking the questions in various groups.
- Conduct the complain and whine session described in Chapter 2. Do it with the board. Do it with the development committee. Conduct a session with some fundraising volunteers.
- With the development committee, brainstorm reasons why donors lack recognition. Test these ideas in focus groups with donors. Or convene a focus group of donors to brainstorm how to improve your donor recognition program.

Before you initiate process, review how to make it effective. Take a look at Chapter 2, the internal relationship. Take a look at Chapter 3, strategic planning. Remember that good process demands outcome. Don't be a process abuser, one who uses process to placate people, to delay decision making, and to avoid outcome.

When you use process, you owe people the following:

- Explain the purpose of the process, the desired outcome, and how you plan to use the information.
- Describe how the process will work, how the session will be managed, and the ground rules for making the process work.
- Summarize the results of the process and outline the next steps.
- Use the resulting information and validate people's participation.

11. Encourage Volunteers To Use Their Power, Practice Their Authority, and Accept Their Responsibility.

This is the enabling function most often resisted by staff. Many believe that only the select few should exercise power. These individuals insist that power is territorial and has boundaries. This narrow view fails to recognize that sharing power causes a dramatic increase in power for all concerned.

The enabler encourages volunteers to use their power and authority and to accept their responsibility. An enabler makes it possible and practicable for individuals and groups to carry out their rights, authorities, and responsibilities.

When operating in groups, volunteers need cohesion. As noted in Chapter 2 of this book, effective groups depend on sufficient (but not too much) cohesion. The enabler helps the group build this solidarity by doing the following:

- encouraging free communication between volunteers when they are together as a group or talking one on one
- making sure all members of the group have the same translated information
- remaining loyal to the group, rather than to its individual members

Psychologist Robert Coles (1994) advises board members, fundraising volunteers, and other volunteers to be "stubbornly curious." Coles says, "We [volunteers] must watch for signs of conformity, a behavior that limits the possibilities of our own independence and personal initiative as philanthropists." He observes that it's easy for volunteers to avoid asking questions and hard for volunteers to suggest something new. Yet, as Coles notes, a key role of volunteers is to "shake up the organization."

Accountability is a big part of this enabling function. As an enabler, your job is to encourage volunteers to accept their responsibility. And that is one of the biggest challenges working with individuals or groups. How do you ensure that an individual—whether volunteer or staff—is accountable? How do you ensure that the group—whether it is the development committee or the board—is accountable?

Sure, you can enable all you want. You can carry out these various functions. But accountability is a reciprocal act. The other—individual or group—must accept the responsibility and act accountably.

When was the last time your board discussed *how* it would hold its individual members accountable for their performance expectations? Does your board regularly discuss *how* it holds itself accountable for carrying out due diligence, for executing governance? The board is legally and morally accountable for the health of the organization. But what does this mean in practical terms? As an enabler, you are responsible for helping individuals and groups to hold themselves accountable. You are responsible for facilitating conversations about accountability and helping to design and implement systems, policies, and procedures for ensuring accountability. Then, as an enabler, you help determine and implement the consequences when people and groups do not act accountably.

12. Model Behavior.

One of the best ways to enable others is through one's own acts and behaviors. As leaders know, one's own behavior begets the behavior in others. The enabler's own behavior shows volunteers how to communicate well, how to help make decisions, and how to carry out specific tasks well. By sharing information, knowledge, and power, the enabler encourages others to do so.

For enablers, teaching other staff how to enable is a critical aspect of modeling behavior. As an enabler, you want other staff to enable well, thus producing benefit to the organization. In addition to transmitting information about enabling and helping others learn the functions, you regularly demonstrate appropriate enabling behavior.

13. Coach People To Succeed.

Enablers don't abandon volunteers to their own devices. Once an assignment is made, staff members stay in touch. Volunteers receive ongoing contact and support. Sometimes, staff members offer advice to help volunteers complete tasks successfully. Sometimes staff help volunteers brainstorm solutions to situations. Other times, staff join volunteers in a task or process. Staff may just call to say hello, thanking volunteers for their efforts.

No matter what, enablers help their volunteers succeed. Mary Whelan, development director at All Saints Catholic observed: An important part of enabling is to uphold a volunteer's integrity and self-respect whenever possible.

Faced with a difficult volunteer, the enabler strives for a respectful resolution. Confronted with harmful volunteer actions, the enabler tries to protect the volunteer.

And what happens if the situation between the volunteer and the organization becomes dysfunctional? So dysfunctional that the volunteer is harming your organization? Then the enabler enhances attrition, with the volunteer's integrity and self-respect still intact.

14. Manage.

Enabling requires efficient administrative skills, an attention to detail, the ability to balance competing demands, and a thorough knowledge of the particular topic (for example, fund development) for which you are providing the enabling.

Enablers coordinate and integrate many tasks and processes with lots of volunteers. Enablers make sure that volunteers don't step on each other's toes, but rather complement each other's activities.

The dictionary defines *managing* as "directing, arranging, and administering." Management texts frequently define *management* as the process of getting work done through people. These texts define distinct but interrelated activities, such as coordinating, planning, organizing, and controlling (and yes, some texts include leading as part of managing).

Many thinkers distinguish between managing and leading. For example, Charles Handy (1996), former professor at the London Business School, says that "leadership focuses on doing the right things; management focuses on doing things right. Leadership makes sure the ladders we are climbing are leaning against the right wall; management makes sure we are climbing the ladders in the most efficient ways possible" (page 154).

Is managing the same as leading? Not in this description of enabling functions. However, effective enablers—and effective leaders—manage. Enablers and leaders do not absolve themselves of the skills required of managers and the responsibility for managing.

15. Enhance Attrition.

Enablers enhance attrition. They don't fire. They enhance attrition, and the volunteer leaves with his or her integrity and self-respect intact.

Let's face it. The fact is, sometimes nothing works. You're a great enabler. You enable as a preventive measure. You use enabling as an intervention strategy, too. You continually monitor your performance as an enabler, and you tweak and tweak. You successfully enable any number of individual volunteers and groups.

But there is that one individual. No matter what you do, it doesn't work. The individual is harming the organization. Others realize this, too. (And if it were a staff person, she or he would be fired. But this is a volunteer, perhaps even a board member. People complain but the organization tolerates the behavior because "he is a volunteer.")

When no other enabling is successful, the best enablers turn to this fifteenth enabling function—enhance attrition. The best enablers figure out how to encourage the volunteer to step away from the activity or even from the organization.

> *Enablers are strategists, not technicians. That's the toughest thing about enabling. There aren't any technical tools to help. All you have are attitude, skills, and functions.*

Is this hard to do? Sure. Is it impossible? No way. Over and over, effective enablers enhance the attrition of volunteers. It may take months or even years. The only question is: How long can your organization bear the harm that is being done? And the sub question is: How quickly can we enhance attrition—coping with the harm—or do we actually have to revert to firing? (Firing is confrontational. Firing rarely allows the volunteer to leave with integrity and self-respect.)

Review all the enabling functions. Use them to help the volunteer realize that he or she does not have the resources (whether it be skills, time, or whatever) to do the job at hand. Use the enabling functions to help the volunteer realize that his or her skills would be put to better use in another situation.

Try any ethical strategy that you can. Your job is to get the volunteer to opt out, to choose to move on and even to save face.

You may be surprised at how easy this often is. Sometimes, volunteers already feel uncomfortable or awkward. They are waiting for an excuse or the opportunity to depart gracefully without looking like a failure, without appearing to "cop out." As an enabler, you help them to do so.

And if the volunteer does not accept the excuse or take the opportunity? Use enabling as an intervention strategy. Enable others within the organization to help you co-opt the individual, discouraging him or her from staying.

Shocking? Hardly. What's best for your organization? You are accountable. As a staff person, you are morally liable for the health of the organization. (And the board is both morally and legally liable.) Are you actually going to allow a volunteer to harm the organization? What does this say to the community, to your clients and donors, to the other volunteers?

16. Monitor, Evaluate, and Enhance Enabling.

Enabling is a fluid process that benefits from continuous monitoring, regular evaluation, and ongoing enhancement. As a tool of leadership, organizational development, and change, enabling is constantly examined and refined.

Enablers know this. They incorporate both internal and external monitoring, evaluation, and enhancement. Enablers monitor and evaluate their own performance of the enabling functions, then adjust. Enablers invite colleagues to provide feedback. Enablers also engage in conversation those whom they are enabling. Part of enabling is talking with volunteers about "How is it going?" "Are you satisfied with your experience?" "How might we better meet your needs?" These are questions that monitor, evaluate, and enhance enabling.

ATTITUDE, SKILLS, AND KNOWLEDGE OF AN ENABLER

So how do you carry out these functions? An effective enabler is a person with the willingness and ability to lead and influence others and the knowledge, skills, and assets to do so. The enabler helps others be the best they can be. The enabler empowers others so that power is shared, tasks are accomplished, and the philanthropic need is met.

The enabler understands all four relationships that are critical to effective organizations and productive fund development. The enabler pays particular attention to the relationship with constituents and within the organization, because these two are central to effective enabling.

The enabler uses constituency development to understand his or her volunteers better. This awareness helps the enabler make sure that enabling functions are sensitive to diversity, particularly those of universal concern—gender, generation, and ethnicity. Then enablers use the seven core components that contribute to the organization's effective internal relations.

1. shared values
2. art of leadership
3. learning organization
4. ongoing conversation
5. participatory decision making
6. well-managed change
7. culture of philanthropy

The enabler leads, facilitates, guides, and manages. As a leader, the enabler influences conduct, takes initiative, and sets an example. As a facilitator, the enabler works with others to determine direction, set standards, identify issues, and encourage resolution. As a guide, the enabler goes ahead to show the way. As a manager, the enabler coordinates activities, explains and gives instructions, and makes tasks easier and more convenient for others to do.

Individuals who enable possess three assets.

1. the right attitude
2. the necessary skills
3. adequate knowledge

Combined, these help the enabler to move the institution forward.

The Enabler's Attitude

Attitude refers to a state of mind, behavior, or conduct that reflects a person's values and opinions. Like values, attitude cannot be acquired through training. People choose their attitude and values through self-examination, personal experience, and thought.

A true enabler believes that enabling is the consummate artistry of the philanthropic process. The enabler is committed to ensuring that his or her institution embraces enabling as an essential aspect of corporate culture and organizational systems.

The enabler believes that enabling will work. She or he is patient, helpful, encouraging, and hopeful. The enabler is upbeat and acts as a cheerleader. Despite periodic setbacks and frustration, enablers have confidence in their volunteers.

Typically, enablers are generous in attitude and behavior, sharing responsibility for success and balancing their personal egos with those of others. They are trustworthy and respect and trust others. Enablers, like leaders, value process, as well as outcome. They welcome different opinions and differences of opinion. Both enablers and leaders acknowledge failure and still persevere. They are open and flexible.

The Enabler's Skills

Skill means proficiency or technical ability and is demonstrated by ease or expertise in performance and application. Skills help a person translate his or her attitude into behavior. The professional acquires skills through self-assessment, experiential learning, training, and study.

First and foremost, enablers are organizational development specialists. They know what organizational development is, and they can do it! Enablers are leaders and managers and learners.

Enablers are good communicators and effective teachers. They adeptly resolve conflict by sharing power. Enablers anticipate potential problems and identify possible solutions. Enablers are good at focusing and, if need be, redirecting volunteer energies. Great people managers, enablers also manage systems, processes, and tasks well.

Effective enablers possess the executive competencies and knowledge described in Chapter 1. These are summarized as commitment to results, business savvy, leading change, and motivating.

Compare the enabler's attitude and skills in Exhibit 5–4 to the essentials of good people management, quoted here from Kay Sprinkel Grace in *Achieving Excellence in Fund Raising* (Rosso, 1991, 141).

1. respect for one's self and others
2. open communication
3. confidence in one's own abilities to manage and lead
4. personal and professional goals that are clear and achievable
5. belief in the organization's goals and the importance of seeing them accomplished
6. trust in others
7. ability to delegate, reward, and provide feedback
8. a belief that "systems liberate"—that people function best in a structure that systematizes routine tasks and encourages creative approaches to tasks that are new and unusual

Exhibit 5–4 Attitude and Skills of Enablers

Attitude of enablers

They:

- respect and trust others
- are trustworthy themselves
- are comfortable with diversity and complexity
- welcome divergent opinions
- question their own assumptions
- are flexible and comfortable with change
- commit to process, as well as outcome
- appreciate conversation and disagreement
- share responsibility for success
- acknowledge responsibility for failure
- balance personal ego with egos of others
- persevere
- are patient

Skills of enablers

They are:

- organizational development specialists
- proficient teachers and learners
- effective communicators (listening, informing, and helping to transform information into knowledge and learning)
- critical thinkers (anticipating problems, identifying solutions, and redirecting volunteer energies)
- strategists (analyzing situations, identifying barriers and opportunities, capitalizing on strengths, and ensuring action and results)
- comfortable with conflict and resolve conflict through shared power with as many individuals as possible
- effective motivators and can focus and manage people well

---

9. consistency, including standards and expectations that are broadly communicated and understood
10. accessibility

The Enabler's Knowledge

Knowledge refers to a deep and extensive learning, a certainty, and conviction. Knowledge is more than the accumulation of facts. Knowledge means understanding the information, perceiving relationships, elaborating concepts, and translating information to application. Knowledge means formulating principles and evaluating. Knowledge is acquired through experience, practical ability, and skill.

The enabler acquires knowledge and uses it to carry out the enabling functions. The best enablers learn key management theories to improve enabling. The following are of particular benefit to enablers:

- organizational development theory, including process, facilitation, and group dynamics
- marketing and constituency development
- systems thinking and learning organization theory
- leadership theory
- conversation and decision-making processes
- change management

To enable fund development volunteers successfully, the enabler also knows the following:

- role of volunteers and staff in fund development
- difference and similarities between governance and management
- philanthropic theory
- fund development practice
- fundraising strategy and techniques
- process and task opportunities for fund development volunteers

THE CHALLENGE OF ENABLING

Leadership requires major expenditures of effort and energy—more than most people care to make." So says John Gardner, in his book *On Leadership* (1990). Enabling requires this same level of effort and energy.

Good enabling can produce immediate, albeit somewhat limited, results. However, the most dramatic and protracted benefits require the cumulative effect of long-term effort and energy.

Enabling is one of the most critical functions within a philanthropic organization. This holds true for all philanthropic organizations of any size or type. As such, enabling is an essential role of the chief executive and development officer. Through enabling, the staff/volunteer relationship works. Without enabling, there is dysfunction.

For professionals in the philanthropic sector, the challenge is to create an organizational culture in which volunteers are enabled well. If there are no professional employees, volunteers perform the staff function of enabling.

Sometimes, we professionals succeed in creating this culture. But often, we don't. Fundraisers and chief executives still complain about their volunteers, particularly boards and fundraising volunteers. Many volunteers seem only modestly pleased with their own efforts and experiences with not-for-profit organizations.

Why is it so difficult to create the culture of enabling? There are five principal factors.

1. interdependence of volunteer and staff
2. organizational life cycles
3. corporate culture
4. staff capability
5. staff conflict

Interdependence of Volunteer and Staff

Take a look at any philanthropic organization. Immediately, you see the paradoxical position of volunteers. The volunteer serves at the top and bottom of the organization. Also, the volunteer is neither paid nor made to work for the organization.

One moment, the volunteer is the authority; at another time, staff are. For example:

- The board of directors hires the CEO, evaluating his or her performance and, if necessary, firing him or her. Yet, the CEO is the principal enabler of the board.
- The development officer must lead, guide, and facilitate the efforts of fundraising volunteers. However, the development officer has no structural authority over these volunteers.
- The staff direct and supervise the clerical and service volunteers but have difficulty dismissing them.

Often, the question arises, Who is boss? Rarely is there a definitive answer. It depends on situation and circumstance. And generally, if there is effective enabling by staff, the question does not arise.

This is the complex and intrinsically conflicted relationship at the core of philanthropic organizations. This relationship demands effective enabling—but also makes enabling difficult.

Using Rules and Judgment

To address this inherent conflict, both volunteers and staff seek rules. We find industry standards that describe volunteer and staff roles and relationships.

We write policies and procedures. We rationally define responsibilities for the chief executive, boards, officers, and committees. We clearly outline the reporting structure.

All of this helps. But it's not the complete answer.

Judgment is as important as rules. Despite role delineation and defined lines of authority, all organizations face changing circumstances. These situations demand judgment, rather than rules. The best rules, the clearest roles, and the tightest policies and procedures cannot respond to every issue. Judgment is necessary, and good enablers have it.

Enablers know when to involve volunteers more, despite conventional standards. Enablers know that roles may change, depending on the particular situation or its possible implications.

Recognizing Authority

Authority is spread throughout your organization between staff and volunteers. Different degrees of preroga-

tive are exercised in different situations, depending on different circumstances.

The fact is, the board is legally and morally accountable to the community—those who are served, those who give, and those who regulate and legislate. Volunteers are the acknowledged stewards of the public trust. By virtue of position, theirs is the inherent and inherited authority.

Staff receive their authority from the volunteers. The board confers authority on staff through acts of hiring and delegation. Staff also possess moral authority. As philanthropic professionals, staff, too, act as stewards.

Staff exercise the most control. As day-to-day implementers of mission and program, staff act as the institution's gatekeepers. Staff hold the information and regulate access. Staff set context and manage activities.

Enabling the Most Responsible Volunteers

Enabling is most difficult with volunteers who have the most responsibility (and authority) in an organization. Generally, this includes board members, committee members, and fund development volunteers.

Some of these volunteers possess legal and/or moral responsibility because of their position within your organization. Others, because of their capability, give significant input and hold major responsibility.

You choose to bring these individuals into your organization because of their expertise, experience, and insights. With their attributes, knowledge, and skills, these volunteers can be particularly beneficial to your organization. Because of their capability, these volunteers can also be difficult to enable.

> Staff must be convinced of the value of empowered volunteers. If staff resist, they don't enable and the organization doesn't progress.

Most staff want experienced and insightful volunteers who will do the work well, using their contacts and knowledge on the organization's behalf. These volunteers usually exercise initiative and critical thinking, professionally and personally. They expect to do the same when volunteering. This can cause confusion, toe stepping, and conflict. (But actually, all this experience and expertise—of both staff and volunteers—is wildly exciting, deeply rewarding, and extremely beneficial to your organization.)

In response to this situation, some staff try to limit volunteer access and input. This frustrates the volunteers and they will ultimately abandon your organization.

On the other hand, if staff welcome volunteers into the organization and enable them well, volunteers add value. Competently enabled volunteers will carry out the specific tasks you want done, do them well, and in a timely fashion. In addition, well-enabled volunteers will help your organization to remain relevant and healthy. These volunteers will ask strategic questions, challenge the status quo, and consider things critically.

Organizational Life Cycles

Organizations evolve through life cycles. These can be summarized as:

- emerging
- maturing
- institutionalizing

Different organizations spend different lengths of time in each cycle. Organizations may return to an earlier cycle, then move forward again.

When an organization is emerging, it usually has few staff. Traditional distinctions between governance and management do not adequately reflect practical reality. Volunteers often serve as governors, administrators, service providers, and fundraisers. Some volunteers do more than one of these functions at the same time.

Lines of demarcation blur. Wearing so many hats, volunteers often confuse their roles. For example, when a board member volunteers professional advice about renovations, she is not acting in a governance capacity. If a board member reviews brochure copy, he is a volunteer reporting to the staff person responsible.

As an organization matures, professional staff increase. The organization begins to differentiate between the roles of its volunteers and staff. A formalized structure typically results.

Further maturation often produces more staff. As the organization moves into the institutionalizing cycle, volunteer roles are more clearly delineated. Distinctions between governance and management are more clear. As boards try to focus on governance, they sometimes lose close contact with the mission and program of the organization. The same may happen as committees move from implementation to policy and as staff encourage volunteers to focus more on fundraising.

Moving through the life cycles causes lots of change for staff and volunteers. Each group may need to adjust attitude and develop new skills as the organization evolves. Sometimes, the staff and volunteers for one life cycle are neither comfortable nor skilled for another cycle. If they cannot change their attitude and learn new skills, effective organizations encourage these staff and volunteers to move into more appropriate positions or to move on. Then the organizations recruit the appropriate volunteers and staff.

Organizations seem to be most vulnerable during the emerging and institutionalizing years. For emerging or-

ganizations, the concept of enabling is rarely understood. Practical matters usually supersede strategic thinking about organizational development. At this time, staff may not understand the theory nor possess the skills, knowledge, or experience to operate as enablers.

Even in more established institutions, people often don't pay enough attention to enabling. During the institutionalizing phase, staff absorb more responsibility, sometimes leaving volunteers behind. For example:

- The development officer writes the fund development plan with no input from volunteers and gives the committee a draft to review, edit, and approve.
- The chief executive avoids in-depth discussion of strategic issues with volunteers and merely encourages them to do tasks.

Now a great danger arises—one that is inexcusable. Some staff abandon enabling. Some volunteers accept this. Both staff and volunteers are responsible.

Whether staff cease enabling willfully or unknowingly, the harm is equal and the action unconscionable. What is the harm? When a board does not adequately exercise its governance function, those trustees may be legally and morally vulnerable. If poorly enabled, volunteers lose interest and move away, taking their gifts of time and money with them. Without voluntary action, access to constituent insights decreases, community credibility lessens, and charitable contributions shrink.

Corporate Culture

Corporate culture, discussed in Chapter 2, describes the way that an organization arranges the interaction of its participants. This "arrangement" may be intentional—designed and documented through values, systems, and procedures. Or this arrangement may be unwritten and unnegotiated by tradition. It's "just the way we do things."

Concepts of voluntary leadership, moral accountability, philanthropic stewardship, and interrelationship with community help to define corporate culture in not-for-profits. So does the relationship of volunteers and staff, which is unique to not-for-profits.

> *Make enabling a value of your organization and a responsibility of management.*

In effective not-for-profits, enabling is a central element of corporate culture. When your organization respects the volunteer role, you have the attitude necessary to comprehend enabling. Then your staff can develop the competencies and carry out the functions to enable volunteers.

The individuals and groups in your organization make the corporate culture. Either they value enabling and this attitude then pervades your organization—or they don't and it doesn't. Either they try to modify behavior accordingly and you see it in the interchanges of staff with staff, staff with volunteer, and volunteer with volunteer—or you don't.

Staff Capability To Enable

Capability includes willingness and commitment, as well as ability. Staff who are enablers possess the right attitude, skills, and knowledge.

Staff capability to enable volunteers is likely the most critical factor affecting overall institutional health and fundraising productivity and, thus, your organization's capacity to serve. If there are no capable enablers within your organization, you will make very little progress.

Unfortunately, many professionals—both staff and consultants—don't understand this responsibility or they avoid it. To improve fund development, they seek better solicitation strategies, rather than enabling volunteers.

Not surprisingly, these same professionals complain that their fellow employees don't always understand fund development. Of greatest concern to fundraisers are the chief executive and financial officers. It is essential that these individuals understand fund development. To achieve this end, some fundraisers suggest that the fundraising profession develop training materials and resources directed to these staff. But this is a very, very small part of the solution. More appropriately, the organization's fundraiser has to enable the staff. That's how the best learning will happen. It is the fundraiser's responsibility to enable the chief executive and other staff, as well as volunteers.

Initially, enabling may be compared to the personnel function of a supervisor, a theory familiar to not-for-profit professionals. The effective supervisor develops the effectiveness of his or her employee through such activities as: encouraging; supporting; motivating; appraising; directing; and facilitating problem solving, decision making, and independence.

> *We know, intellectually and empirically, that partnership and participation are the . . . strategies that create high-performance [organizations].*
>
> *Peter Block*

Unfortunately, this function is more complex when one is enabling volunteers. There is only a moral imperative—no authority—on the part of staff. This paradoxical relationship between staff and volunteer demands an accomplished enabler.

Staff and Power

Abuse of power is the major barrier that limits enabling. When staff act as power holders, they are neither enablers nor leaders. For some, this abuse is intentional. For others, it is unintentional. Unfortunately, the result is the same: poorly enabled volunteers, a less-than-effective organization, and ineffective fund development.

Some staff don't enable their volunteers because staff don't want to share power. Instead of enabling, they focus on their own vision, their own goals, and their own authority. These individuals are busy exercising control to ensure the outcomes they wish and to prohibit those they do not wish. These individuals will likely never accept enabling.

Other staff don't understand empowerment. The concept of enabling is foreign to them. These professionals hold power loosely and get by as best they can. They will likely consider enabling if it is explained to them.

There is a third group. These individuals know that things aren't working well, even if they aren't sure why. These individuals are ready to explore enabling.

Staff Conflict

What happens if you want to enable but your boss doesn't? Can you enable without the boss's permission?

The first answer is yes. You do lots of work without your boss's direct permission. As Nike says, "Just do it." For example, start talking about enabling with the development committee as one of the key strategies in a good fund development program. Get the buy-in of the development committee chair and committee members. Start an advocacy campaign with other staff, one person at a time.

The second answer is, enable your boss to understand how beneficial enabling is. Remember that it's not what you're selling but what your boss is buying that counts. Figure out what your boss is buying. Use the enabling functions to convince your boss that enabling volunteers will meet his or her needs.

But what happens if your boss actually prohibits your use of certain enabling functions? It could happen. So, if you've already starting enabling, talk about results. Tell your boss what enabling has produced and why it is beneficial. That may reassure him or her.

If you've already started enabling your volunteers, they will expect you to continue doing so. (Even if they don't say this out loud, they will actually *feel* different if you stop enabling. They will likely express frustration or discomfort, even if they cannot define why.) Once enabled, volunteers balk when they no longer experience the same level and type of interchange with you. You can report this volunteer dissatisfaction to your boss and help him or her see the value of "reverting to the old way," and that's enabling!

You can back down somewhat on the degree within a particular enabling function. Your boss may feel more comfortable and learn to value the results.

Try to enable others in the organization—staff and volunteers—to get your boss to see the light. Be very careful doing this. You are trying to co-opt your boss without behaving inappropriately. You cannot criticize your boss. You cannot pit yourself or your volunteers against your boss. But it might be possible to engage others sufficiently in enabling that they actually help convert or co-opt your boss.

What if none of this works? Your boss does not believe in the enabling functions, and you cannot enable him or her to value this way of doing business. Face it. Your boss is abdicating his or her responsibility, and you don't like it.

Remember enabling function 15? Perhaps it's time to enhance your own attrition. You face the ultimate dilemma: Do you want to continue working somewhere that does not share your values, that does not work to its optimum capacity? Do you want to work with people who do not share your beliefs in leadership and management? Now it's your decision.

Also consider the opposite. You don't want to enable. It's too much work and too frustrating. It's easier to do it yourself. Your boss keeps encouraging you to enable but you simply don't devote adequate time and attention. Now your boss is faced with enhancing your attrition.

The Biggest Challenge Facing Not-for-Profits

Engaging volunteers in appropriate and meaningful ways may be the biggest challenge faced by not-for-profit organizations. Enabling is the way to answer the challenge.

The big question is, what are the meaningful and appropriate activities volunteers can do? Philanthropic organizations continually wrestle with this. Often, staff and volunteers disagree about what is meaningful and appropriate involvement. Through enabling, your volunteers and staff decide together.

Keep in mind that meaningful involvement depends on the individual's needs and interests. Now we're back to the process of constituency development. But, of course, the involvement also has to be useful to the organization. This need for a mutually beneficial exchange confronts the organization as it develops relationships with its constituents. Balancing constituent and organization needs is part of the challenge of constituency development.

Appropriate involvement also has multiple dimensions. Aside from the legal requirements for the appropriate involvement of boards (which staff and volunteers sometimes interpret differently), the rest is up for grabs. Sure, there are industry standards that describe best practice, but best practice is situational. Staff and volunteers translate the standards for their own organization.

Appropriate involvement often depends on the number of professional staff available to carry out key organization functions. Staff capability often affects how involved volunteers get and in what areas. Appropriate involvement also depends on the organization's culture and its maturation.

The more professional staff you have, the more the volunteer jobs change. Volunteers no longer do management. Indeed, they may rarely hear discussion of management functions, such as marketing, public relations, and program development. Staff even identify strategic issues and forecast trends and their implications, while volunteers are left to focus on results and overall institutional health.

> *Enabling your volunteers helps engage them in meaningful and appropriate ways.*

Sometimes, this changed focus causes volunteers to move further and further away from the organization. Boards seem to do more routine business with less strategic dialogue. There are fewer committees, and those that operate may step on staff toes. In lots of organizations, staff just want volunteers to fundraise.

So now there's potential for trouble. We weaken the philanthropic sector if our volunteers become disengaged or are relegated to limited mechanical tasks, routine activities, or one single area of endeavor, such as fund development. On the other hand, we thwart staff if volunteers intrude inappropriately.

The only solution is for staff, in partnership with board, to figure out how to engage volunteers appropriately. There's lots of material available. Don't just look at resources in the philanthropic sector. Look at evolving business theory in the for-profit sector.

For example, consider how you can focus your board members on policy and institutional health and results, rather than on operations. What kinds of board committees would you establish to help the board do this work? How would you manage board meetings to keep discussion within these boundaries?

Consider the new business functions and organizational structures proposed in management theory. For example, how might you apply the following ideas from *Framebreak: The Radical Redesign of American Business* (Mitroff, Mason, and Pearson, 1994) to your governance and management, volunteers, and staff?

- Four dimensions of new organizational structure
  –World service and spirituality: how our organization helps develop a healthy outside world

–Knowledge and learning: what we need to know to produce and deliver quality programs and services (think of this as information and learning organization theory)

–Recovery and development: how we develop a healthy organization, employees, and volunteers

–World-class operations: how we ensure quality infrastructure, e.g., culture, systems, and operations

- Six new functions for business

–Issues management: tracking and anticipating long-term societal trends so they don't become crises

–Crisis management: managing major internal and external forces that threaten organizational health

–Total quality management: designing and using processes that produce top-quality products and services

–Environmentalism: assessing how our organization's activities affect the environment and our local community

–Globalism: paying attention to and operating as part of the larger world

–Ethics: examining the ethical and moral dimensions of your organization's culture, systems, and behaviors, and making sure they contribute to a healthy local and global community

In summary, keep asking yourself how to engage volunteers in meaningful and appropriate ways. Get the opinions of your volunteers and staff. Talk to colleagues in other organizations. Test your ideas, then improve them.

Also, make sure you enable your volunteers well. Carry out the 16 enabling functions described in this chapter and you will engage your volunteers meaningfully and appropriately.

STRENGTHENING ENABLING

Unfortunately, there are all too few accomplished enablers. Instead, organizations employ very good technicians who do not carry out the enabling functions.

The thing is, it's easier to do the work yourself than to enable others. Enabling requires enormous amounts of energy, unlimited patience, and deeply held values that buoy you when the hassles are huge.

> *Chief executive officers and fundraisers must be good enablers.*

Furthermore, the not-for-profit sector does not appear to focus on enabling. The philosophy and functions are not found on workshop and conference agendas for fundraisers. The required skills and knowledge aren't discussed much by chief executives and other leaders. It is difficult to find documented models of success or analyses of failures. There is little evidence that professionals gather together to analyze enabling functions, explore the skills and knowledge, and discuss successful and unsuccessful experiences. This must change, and it can.

Action Steps for Your Organization

It's time that institutions demand proficient enablers. Institutions should include an understanding of and capability to enable as part of job descriptions, hiring decisions, and performance appraisals. This is particularly important for the chief executive and development officers, as well as most consulting relationships.

Your organization can incorporate enabling into its operation and immediately see some improvement. Try these ideas.

1. Adopt enabling as an organizational value. Talk with staff and volunteers about what enabling means and how it affects individual and group behavior, and organizational systems. Remember that enabling is a natural outgrowth of such values as respect for and sensitivity to others, understanding the needs and interests of volunteers, and honoring marketing and the basic premise of constituency development.

2. Make enabling a hiring criteria. Acknowledge that enabling is one of the competencies required by your CEO and fundraiser, at least. Start with your CEO. If he or she doesn't know how to enable, get help fast. Make sure that he or she selects fundraisers who are good enablers. Your interview process should ask questions that help you discern competence in this area. When you check references, ask how well the applicant carries out the enabling functions.

3. Make enabling a performance expectation. Incorporate enabling as a function in staff job description. Use the performance appraisal process to assess an employee's effectiveness at enabling. Make sure that the board evaluates the CEO's effectiveness as an enabler and that the CEO evaluates the fundraiser's enabling performance.

4. Expect your leaders to help employees develop and enhance their enabling skills. Make sure that your leaders model and coach proper enabling behavior among staff. Provide written materials about enabling and associated topics, such as constituency

development, marketing, servant-leader, and stewardship theories.

5. Make enabling a focus of management dialogue. Design formal and informal opportunities for staff to explore enabling and to problem solve. For example, staff may:
   - analyze specific situations, identifying why enabling did or did not work and how it might be improved
   - discuss the enabling functions and brainstorm specific ways to carry out the functions
   - consider particular individuals and their interests and barriers, and decide how staff might better enable these volunteers
   - observe each other's enabling behavior and coach one another to strengthen performance
   - develop benchmarks to appraise performance
   - identify resources (e.g., printed materials, workshops, etc.) that can help staff to develop their enabling skills

6. Include enabling in your governance dialogues. Talk about the philosophy and practice. Get volunteer input about enabling effectiveness.

Challenge to the Professional and the Profession

Most importantly, we professionals must direct our attention to enabling. We can help develop enablers, just as leaders develop leaders.

First, we develop our own individual proficiency. We model this behavior to others and pass along the values and philosophy. We make sure that volunteers, organizations, and other professionals understand the benefits of enabling.

Second, working through the profession, we insist that enabling be developed as a core competence. Then we help the profession figure out how to develop this competence in its leaders.

We make sure that the profession studies, talks, and writes about enabling. We teach those skills that are teachable and help develop the attitude and behaviors that are not teachable. We help people develop enabling skills by doing such things as:

- defining the functions of enabling
- describing the attitude that an enabler has
- identifying skills that support enabling
- stimulating the professional's thinking
- encouraging self-examination
- creating opportunities for practice
- modeling appropriate behavior

- observing the professional's behavior, coaching, and providing feedback

Personal Action Steps for You

As a professional, you can enhance your own capacity for enabling by taking the following steps.

1. Evaluate your own understanding of enabling, its functions, attitude, and skills.
2. Assess your own effectiveness as an enabler. Then ask someone you trust and respect to evaluate your enabling. See Appendix 5–C.
3. Talk about enabling with colleagues and learn together. Discuss situations and help each other use the enabling functions as a preventive and intervention.
4. Recruit a personal observer, someone who works closely with you. Ask this individual to watch your actions and comment on your enabling performance.

As a professional, you can enhance your organization's capacity for enabling. For example, discuss enabling with the volunteers and staff in your organization. Create a shared vision and benchmarks for strengthening enabling. Identify situations that would benefit from enabling as an intervention. Within your organization, teach others about enabling. Model behavior and coach others to succeed as enablers.

Finally, as a professional, you can enhance the profession. Talk about enabling with your colleagues, particularly those in fund development or CEOs. Help them to see the meaning, value, and benefit to their organizations. Outline ways that you can help each other to develop this competence. Insist that professional associations talk about enabling, organizational development, and leadership. Demand continuing education opportunities that go beyond training in fund development.

Be Patient during the Transition and Stick to It

With a little bit of effort, you'll see some immediate gain. But long-term significant improvement requires lots of effort, more time, and infinite patience.

If enabling is not yet part of your organization's culture and behavior, this will mean a new way of doing business. When you start something new, there are always some rough spots, even a little chaos.

That's to be expected. You'll stumble along the way, but just be patient and persevere. Change is tough. People will be tempted to return to the old way of doing things. Look back at Chapter 2, your organization's internal relations. Review the section about well-managed change, one of the key components for an effective infrastructure.

Remember the benefits of enabling. This is a new way of relating to each other. Talk about the philosophy and practice the functions. Give each other feedback.

SUMMARY

We don't need new ideas in philanthropy or fund development. We need to understand and embrace the fundamentals and do the basics better. And enabling is one of the basics.

What happens if you don't enable? Here are just a few results.

- There is too much work for staff, particularly in fund development.
- Without enabling, you create disenfranchised volunteers who may reduce (or not increase) their monetary contributions.
- There are fewer knowledgeable people out in the community advocating for your constituents, your programs, and your support.
- If you don't enable, there is less information and perspective (and thus, diversity) coming into your organization.

Lack of enabling produces role confusion. Without enabling, the lines between governance and management blur, and the door opens for micromanaging by the board. Lack of enabling reduces your organization's capacity to make sound judgments and good decisions.

On the other hand, lots of wonderful things happen if you do enable your volunteers. For example:

- More people know about your organization and advocate on its behalf.
- Volunteers engage in the meaning and processes of your organization, as well as its activities.
- The best volunteers stay with your organization and add value to your activities.
- You make better decisions with diverse input.
- More volunteers make more fundraising solicitation calls, so more donors and gifts result.

Through enabling, you provide adequate power, means, and opportunity to ensure an effective organization, which helps to build a healthy community. Enabling enhances the volunteer experience and makes the organization more attractive. Enabling especially helps to fund development.

Enabling is leadership and management. Enablers are philosophers and strategists. They possess assets and skills that they hone to carry out functions that they can define.

Consider this: If you are not a good enabler, should you be a chief executive or fundraiser?

REFERENCES

Block, P. 1993. *Stewardship: Choosing Service over Self-Interest.* San Francisco: Berrett-Koehler Publishers.

Bolman, L.G., and T. Deal. 1995. *Leading with Soul: An Uncommom Journey of Spirit.* San Francisco: Jossey-Bass Publishers.

Chatterjee, D. 1998. *Leading Consciously: A Pilgrimage Toward Self-Mastery.* Boston: Butterworth-Heinemann.

Coles, R. 1994. Doing Well by Doing Good: Why We Volunteer. *Advancing Philanthropy,* 2(1).

DePree, M. 1989. *Leadership Is an Art.* New York: Dell Publishing.

Divine 9. Cohort 9, Masters Program in Philanthropy and Fund Development, St. Mary's University of Minnesota.

Drucker, P. 1990. *Managing the Nonprofit Organization: Principles and Practices.* New York: HarperCollins Publishers.

Gardner, J. 1990. *On Leadership.* New York: Free Press.

Godfrey, J. 1992. *Our Wildest Dreams: Women Entrepreneurs Making Money, Having Fun, Doing Good.* New York: HarperCollins Publishers.

Golensky, M. 1990. The Board-Executive Relationship in Nonprofit Organizations: Partnership or Power Struggle. *Nonprofit Management and Leadership,* 4:2. San Francisco: Jossey-Bass, Publishers.

Handy, C. 1996. *The New Language of Organizing and Its Implications for Leaders. Leader to Leader.* New York: The Peter F. Drucker Foundation for Nonprofit Management.

Herzlinger, R. 1999. *Full Disclosure: A Strategy for Performance. Leader to Leader.* New York: The Peter F. Drucker Foundation for Nonprofit Management.

Lorsch, J. January–February 1995. Empowering the Board. *Harvard Business Review.* Boston: Harvard Business School.

Mitroff, I., R. Mason, and C. Pearson. 1994. *Framebreak: the Radical Redesign of American Business,* xiv. San Francisco: Jossey-Bass, Publishers.

Payton, R. 1988. *Philanthropy: Voluntary Action for the Public Good.* New York: American Council on Education/Macmillan Publishing Co.; London: Collier Macmillan Publishers.

Rosso, H. 1991. *Achieving Excellence in Fund Raising.* San Francisco: Jossey-Bass, Publishers.

Vanden Heuvel, S. August 2000. Personal communication. Executive Director, CommunityNet, Rochester, MN.

Appendix 5–A

Passionate Board Member Running Wild: A Real-Life Story with an Enabling Response

A colleague contacted me with the following story. She was frustrated and worried about a particular volunteer. She had read my book chapter about enabling volunteers. We talked about the enabling functions and how they might be a strategy to help in her situation. Some weeks later, she provided me with the update that follows her first story. I call this "before" and "after." These are her words.

BEFORE ENABLING

Mary is a devoted board member and volunteer in California. She is a founding board member of the agency and is still on the board, despite term limits listed in the bylaws. The board overlooks term limits in Mary's case because the board thinks Mary is so valuable to the agency's progress. Mary is willing to continue to serve and just completed a two-year term as president.

Mary is a computer expert and vice president in a major technology company. She is wildly passionate about nonprofits using technology to achieve their missions, and she has a strong interest in human service agencies such as ours. Mary is a natural to chair our technology committee. She gets support from her company when asked to do so or when she thinks it is necessary. Mary takes the initiative to do whatever she thinks is great for the agency.

Mary has leveraged a great deal of in-kind support from her company, amounting to $10,000 or more per year. Our agency boasts the finest and latest in computer equipment, printers, software, and, most recently, a network to serve up to eight workstations in our office. (However, we don't have a fax machine in our office. As board president, Mary deemed a fax unnecessary because "we should be encouraging the use of e-mail,

not faxes"—even though many small nonprofits still cannot afford computers or Internet access but are able to receive a fax. So our agency shares a fax with multiple other agencies in our building. As the new executive director, I plan to buy a fax. Management is my responsibility, not Mary's or any other board member's.)

As chair of the technology committee, Mary often directs our agency's technology staff. She directs staff to focus on her pet projects, rather than agency priorities, spending money we do not have. Now the agency risks going over budget.

No one on the board knew what Mary was doing when she was president. No one questioned Mary because she knows "everything" about technology and the board "trusts" her. But the technology stuff is only the tip of the iceberg. As the new executive director, I'm just finding out what has been going on and sharing this information with our new board president.

For example: Mary has been making promises to other agencies, including our funders. There's one funder who is angry at our agency because of promises made that the agency cannot deliver on. Mary even submitted proposals that the board had not approved. In a recent conversation with a funder, the director said to me: "Apparently, I shouldn't accept Mary's word as being good for speaking on behalf of the board. Doesn't she know her role?"

Furthermore, Mary goes around me as executive director and asks staff members to do things that are not in the scope of their work. She makes deals with agencies and businesses. The Lone Ranger rides again, and no one knows what she is doing. Board and staff are increasingly frustrated with Mary but afraid to do much about her because she works hard and gets us so much in-kind support from her company.

Despite the problems that Mary causes, she is very committed to the agency. She does help us get resources

Source: Anonymous

from her company. She contributes more time to the agency than other board members. She rarely says "no" when asked to do something. Bottom line: She provides energy that, if properly channeled, could be very helpful to the agency.

What do we do to rein in Mary? How can we channel her energy and passion? How can we enforce term limits without alienating her? And if Mary has to leave, how do we make sure that we do not lose the support from her company?

As the new executive director—bequeathed this mess—my first reaction was to remove Mary from the board. But despite term limits, the board and nominating committee have chosen to ignore this situation and continue to re-elect Mary because of her connections and commitment. If I encouraged the release of Mary, it would be radical and could cause further problems.

So what's my solution? How can I use the enabling functions to fix this mess?

AND AFTER . . . USING THE ENABLING FUNCTIONS

I have to be proactive with board members, including the nominating committee. I cannot wait to convene a meeting when the committee chair suggests one. Also, I have to prepare better for committee meetings.

With the nominating committee, I will familiarize myself with the bylaws so I can anticipate questions and problems. I will prepare an overview of the trustee participation, committee assignments, attendance record, and their contributions to the agency in terms of time, talents, and financial resources. I will note term limits on this overview.

Already, I'm enlisting the understanding and support of the new board president and some of the experienced trustees who understand the damage that Mary causes. I'm not bad-mouthing Mary but I am keeping leadership informed of the problems. Volunteers need to help me manage Mary. I'm trying to fence Mary in gently—another one of the enabling functions—without making her feel bad.

I'm using the managing and coaching enabling functions with Mary. For example: A few years ago, I became "franklinized," and now I use the Franklin Planner to manage my time and hold people accountable. When I speak to people and they agree to do something, I write it down in my Franklin Planner, right in front of them. Then they know I have a record of what we agreed to and that I will hold them accountable. This may be helpful in keeping Mary on task, doing the things she promises and does well. I hope this will help keep her focused, rather than involved in inappropriate areas.

Mary is a big advocate of e-mail. When I communicate with her, I also send a copy to the board president and to the relevant committee chair. The board chair (and two other committee chairs) have agreed to send confirming notes back to Mary. These volunteer leaders will also follow up with Mary by telephone or in person whenever she crosses over into their areas of responsibility. The board president will talk with Mary when she operates outside the collective board decision.

I'm enabling other volunteers to help me enable Mary. The board president and I are very concerned that Mary thinks she has the "power" to go off on her own, making promises and representing the agency without the direction of the board. Also, she encroaches on the work and authority of the executive director. Certainly, Mary covets information, which, in my estimation, is often an immense abuse of power.

But on second thought, I wonder if it isn't so much an issue of "power," but rather an issue of "insecurity." Perhaps Mary lacks the fortitude or courage to speak clearly the decisions made by the board, particularly when they may not be popular. Mary seems to find it difficult to say "no" to others and likes to be seen as "Ms. Nice Gal." Perhaps this insight will help me enable Mary in different ways.

Regrettably, Mary's actions demonstrate that she is not committed to the collective that is our board. She may not even realize this. And, unfortunately, there has been no process whereby the agency articulated its shared mission, defined its purpose, and collectively decided what we mean to the community and how we will function. So Mary just invents and communicates her own views.

The new board president recognizes that the agency must create a shared view of mission purpose, and way to work. He understands the concept of the board as a collective. If he and I together begin to reinforce the group, rather than single individuals, we can help change the dynamic of the agency. This is bigger than Mary but also about Mary. This planning process will help me particularly with the enabling function of transmitting organization values—because the collective board will have worked on this together.

I will have to build a relationship with Mary's company to ensure that the company is committed to our agency and mission, not just committed to Mary. The company's support in terms of in-kind gifts and technological expertise has been critical to building our agency's technological infrastructure. Without it, we would certainly suffer. However, Mary is not the only active volunteer who works for this company. I must strengthen the other relationships. We cannot rely overly on one individual in any situation within the agency.

My board and I will have to mend the community relationships that have been damaged by Mary's actions. I am meeting with funders and rebuilding our credibility without insulting Mary. This will take a long time, and I will involve other board members as appropriate.

I am learning to use my "newness" as the executive director (a briefly opened window!) to ask the right questions of the right people at the right time so that Mary's antics can be "exposed" innocently enough. This is certainly part of the communications function of enabling.

With Mary, I'm using the enabling functions as an intervention to solve existing problems. But I'm also using the enabling functions to prevent a recurrence with Mary—and to bring us all together as a stronger agency.

I particularly value the enabling function that talks about identifying barriers. It's my job to identify the barriers that exist, thereby understanding the content of the problem. Then I develop short-term and long-term strategies to overcome the problem. I have learned that I must identify and understand the barriers—because the practice of enabling cannot occur and make a positive difference unless I do.

Within the context of limited time resources, this all seems a daunting prospect. I have some impatience to deal with, and I will struggle with this.

But I recognize that the enabling functions have already been very useful to me. I consider each enabling function as I examine the challenges with Mary. And although enabling Mary may not be the entire solution to the agency's problem with Mary, it can be the solution to the greater problems she and others have created if I work to enable the entire board effectively.

Appendix 5–B

Key Roles in Fund Development: Board, Board Member, Committee, Staff

ROLE OF THE BOARD

1. Review results; discuss progress, trends, and implications.
2. Identify and discuss internal strengths and weaknesses, and external opportunities and threats.
3. Endorse goals and directions throughout the year (while implementing current plan) to include in subsequent year's plan.
4. Adopt plan (with board member names in it for specific activities) when budget is adopted.

ROLE OF THE INDIVIDUAL BOARD MEMBER

1. Commit to and carry out specific activities in the fund development plan—and be accountable for what you said you would do.
2. Identify and cultivate the predisposed.
3. Cultivate donors and real prospects. Help solicit as appropriate.
4. Watch what is happening at your organization and in the community. Share your observations, ask questions, help the organization wrestle with issues, and make good decisions.
5. Give your own personal gift at the start of each year's fund development.

ROLE OF THE DEVELOPMENT COMMITTEE

1. Review results; discuss progress, trends, and implications.
2. Identify strategic issues for board discussion and action. Facilitate board discussion and decision making.
3. Identify and discuss internal strengths and weaknesses, and external opportunities and threats.

4. As appropriate, recommend action for board adoption. Or present well-thought-out alternatives for board discussion and action.
5. Propose goals and directions throughout the year (while implementing current plan) to include in subsequent year's plan.
6. Through the fund development planning process, test proposed goals, adjust, and refer to Finance Committee.
7. Review staff-drafted plan. Discuss and adjust. Recruit every board member to participate in the plan in some way.
8. Recommend the plan to the board for adoption.

ROLE OF THE STAFF

(See Joyaux handout on components of fund development, as well as job description of chief development officer.) In summary:

1. Lead and enable the volunteers.
2. Be familiar with and understand the body of knowledge and best practice in fund development. Educate and guide the board accordingly.
3. Manage and coordinate all activities. So is there enough staff to do this?
4. Maintain gift management systems and acknowledgment and recognition programs.
5. Develop progress reports and analyze trends and implications.
6. Draft materials and provide resources.
7. Review results; discuss progress, trends, and implications.

8. Identify strategic issues for board discussion and action. Facilitate board discussion and decision making.
9. Identify and discuss internal strengths and weaknesses, and external opportunities and threats.
10. As appropriate, recommend action for board adoption. Or present well-thought-out alternatives for board discussion and action.
11. Propose goals and directions throughout the year (while implementing current plan) to include in subsequent year's plan.
12. Through the fund development planning process, test proposed goals, adjust, and refer to Finance Committee.
13. Draft plans for review by appropriate individuals and groups.

Appendix 5–C

Assess Your Performance as an Enabler

Use this tool to assess your own performance as an enabler. First, answer the questions yourself. Second, ask someone you trust and respect to evaluate your behavior. Make sure this individual works closely enough with you to observe your behavior with volunteers.

Use the scale to evaluate your performance. For each question, rate yourself according to the scale. Add up the points and divide by the total number of questions. Compare your average to the scale.

Once your evaluator has done the same, compare the two averages. How close is your perspective to that of your evaluator? Discuss the discrepancies. Ask for specific examples from your evaluator and offer the same. Examples will help you understand your strengths and weaknesses better.

Based on the assessment results, outline specific steps you will take to improve your performance. Use the enabling functions to help you outline your action steps.

ASSESSMENT SCALE

"I" is used when you assess yourself. Substitute your own name or "she" or "he" when the evaluator assesses you. Include "staff" along with "volunteers" in each of these questions, and you will know whether or not you enable your staff well. Also use this tool for regular staff performance appraisals.

5 Yes, I almost always behave this way. I need to help develop this capacity in others.

4 In general, I behave this way. I need to capitalize on appropriate behaviors to improve my other behaviors.

3 My behavior is inconsistent. I need to improve significantly. I could likely use some assistance.

2 Sometimes I behave this way, but most often not. Dramatic improvement is necessary, but first I have to commit to the philosophy of enabling before I can make any progress.

1 Rarely do I behave this way. I need to rethink the way I do business.

ASSESSMENT QUESTION RATING

1. Do you have good relationships with colleagues, both staff and volunteers? _____

2. Do you trust and respect volunteers and other staff? _____

3. Are you trusted and respected by others? _____

4. Do you have confidence in many (or most of) the volunteers with whom you work? _____

5. Are you comfortable with process, tolerating surprise? _____

6. Are you comfortable with diversity, complexity, and disagreement? _____

7. Do you mind being questioned by others, both volunteers and staff? _____

8. Do you understand and respect the interests, disinterests, concerns, and needs of your volunteers? _____

9. Do you create a rewarding and challenging experience for volunteers? _____

10. Do your volunteers seem interested and content working with your organization? _____

11. Do you encourage others to ask questions, experiment, and explore? _____

12. Do you ask lots of questions yourself and look for the new, unusual, and original? _____

13. Do you help volunteers identify their barriers to success and help them overcome the barriers? _____

14. Are you enthusiastic? _____

15. Can you laugh at yourself and awkward situations and help others do the same? _____

16. Do you consistently try to master the functions of enabling and enhance your own behavior? _____

17. Are you constantly learning new things? _____

18. Do your actions effectively model the attitude and behavior you ask of others? _____

19. Do you encourage conversation (interchange of ideas that stimulates learning) among staff and volunteers and between them? _____

20. Are you a good teacher? _____

21. Are you an effective communicator, translating information into knowledge, setting the context for dialogue, and listening well to others? _____

22. Do you enjoy sharing power, helping others take on authority and responsibility? _____

23. Are you able to delegate without breathing down people's necks? _____

24. Do you motivate others? _____

25. Do you constantly devise meaningful ways for volunteers to be engaged in your organization? _____

26. Do you reward volunteers in ways that are meaningful to them? _____

27. Do you create opportunities for quick success to help volunteers build their self-confidence? _____

28. Can you sort out what is a serious trespass by a volunteer and what is no big deal? _____

29. When other staff are frustrated by volunteers and ready to "do it themselves," do you try again? _____

Chapter 6

Creating the Most Effective Fund Development Plan for Your Organization

Leaders who engage their groups...may enjoy higher levels of morale, employee motivation, and loyalty...involvement, attention, and a willingness to listen, to reflect, and to be moved are all indications of respect.

Joline Godfrey

It is our deepest desires that provide us with the strength and the willingness to attend to the tedium of process when we otherwise would turn off the light, close down the meeting, or just lose interest. When people follow their hearts, they equip themselves to grapple with process.

Ibid

Most leaders and managers are task proficient to one degree or another. Organizational cultures emphasize task and results, and base most rewards and promotions on them. In the last 25 years, there has been an increasing interest in examining the processes by which results are obtained. ...What has been largely missing is any focus on relationship and its importance in producing quality results. Even the current emphasis on process is not about human process, the dynamics of how we work and communicate with one another. ...This presents a dilemma because, in actuality, nothing gets done except in relationship. Task, process, and results depend on it. Action does not occur in a vacuum. ...Ignoring relationship and its dynamics is ostrich behavior of the most dangerous kind.

Ellinor and Gerard

TOPICS DISCUSSED IN THIS SECTION

- Linking fund development planning to the four relationships
- Benefits to the fund development planning process
- Creating a fund development plan that produces ownership and results
- Roles in the planning process
- Components of the fund development plan
- Planning for the future while you operate today
- Setting benchmarks
- Measuring results
- Interfacing with the budgeting process
- Challenges to the process

THE MOST EFFECTIVE FUND DEVELOPMENT PROGRAM

Fund development is not a separate and independent activity that can be pulled out whenever there is need, focused on by only a few, and ignored the rest of the time. Instead, fund development is an ongoing, rewarding (but invasive) process that engages all staff and every board member in some way.

Fund development affects everything your organization does, from board and staff recruitment to patron service to communications. (However, this does not mean that the only qualification for board membership is the ability to raise money!)

Fund development depends on the four relationships described in this book. Your fund development program relies on your organization's ability to develop and nurture these relationships.

Effective fund development produces more than money. Effective organizations understand that fund development goals include more than money. Goals include things such as creating a culture of philanthropy, building stronger relationships, helping board members feel comfortable with fund development, understanding the interests of patrons so the organization can ask for a gift, and so forth.

No matter what you want to raise money for, you must pay attention to process. Process means addressing fund development and organizational development issues together in one system. The process requires a commitment of time and energy on the part of the organization's staff and volunteers. Direct participation (asking questions, discussing, deciding) of key leadership is essential to build understanding and ownership.

What do you think about as you create an effective fund development program? First, you think about philanthropy and community. Always, you think about the four relationships described here.

> **The fund development plan provides the framework for your development program.**

Then what? Take a look at Appendix A, the key components of fund development. All those components belong in your fund development program.

How does this all hang together? What's the framework for managing and implementing the development program? It is your organization's fund development plan.

What is a fund development plan? It's almost identical to the institutional strategic plan (and planning process) described in Chapter 3. You use the four relationships to create and implement your fund development plan and your fund development program. And creating your fund development plan is a major way to nurture the four relationships.

The development planning process produces the optimum development program. If you already operate a development program (and most organizations do in some manner), the ongoing development planning process strengthens your development program.

Who is responsible for all this? The development operation. The development operation is accountable for creating a development program that is based on the four relationships *and* reflects the components of fund development.

WHAT IS FUND DEVELOPMENT PLANNING AND HOW WILL IT BENEFIT YOUR ORGANIZATION?

Sound familiar? Reread the section entitled "What Is Strategic Planning and How Will It Benefit Your Organization?" in Chapter 3. Indeed, reread all of Chapter

3. Just substitute "fund development planning" for "institutional strategic planning." It's pretty much the same process.

> **Fund development planning is very similar to institutional strategic planning.**

Good development planning is a process that builds organizationwide understanding of and ownership for philanthropy and fund development. Like the process of institutional planning, the process of development planning should produce a shared sense of accountability.

Just like institutional strategic planning, good development planning also produces results. No matter what kind of planning, both process and results are important.

In summary, the fund development planning process accomplishes the following (Exhibit 6–1):

- Engages key constituencies in order to gather quality information, build understanding, and enhance ownership.
- Assesses the productivity and effectiveness of current and prior fundraising activities.
- Assesses the internal and external environments, addresses the challenges, and capitalizes on the opportunities therein.
- Ensures volunteer (board members and other fundraising volunteers) understanding of the basic principles of philanthropy and fund development.
- Ensures volunteer acceptance of best practice.
- Identifies the case for support and fundraising themes.
- Enhances the organization's position in the philanthropic marketplace.

Exhibit 6–1 Benefits of Fund Development Planning

The process typically produces the following benefits, when done well:

- More money
- More volunteers to help raise money
- Better use of volunteers to help raise money
- Growing understanding of what works and why, and what doesn't work and why
- Criteria to measure success
- Specific fundraising activities that specific volunteers have agreed to implement
- Institutionalization of development within the board

- Develops volunteer skills.
- Reaffirms values, vision, and direction.
- Sets goals and benchmarks to measure performance.
- Tests the feasibility of goals and benchmarks.

AVOIDING OR COMPROMISING FUND DEVELOPMENT PLANNING

Despite its obvious benefits, the process is not always embraced. Some people want to jump to the bottom line: "forget process just write a plan!" Don't go there. Remember that the end does not justify the means. Process is as important as outcome.

Often, development staff don't want to do process. "There isn't enough time!" you cry. Or, "Volunteers don't understand and I'll just draft it myself."

> *Development planning depends on enabling.*

If that's you, take a look at Chapter 5, which describes enabling. Ask yourself why you do not choose to enable your board, other volunteers, and staff. The first three relationships depend on your ability to enable. Effective and productive fund development requires your enabling. And creating a fund development plan that produces ownership and results requires enabling. So get over it. Value it, learn it, and do it.

Maybe it's your volunteers and your chief executive officer (CEO) who don't want to do process. Enable them to see the benefit. Or start the process yourself. You don't need their permission to plan. Simply begin the process, and they will likely follow along.

Perhaps people in your organization think that a fund development plan is a few pages listing solicitation activities and a timetable. Wrong! You know better than that. Look back at those fund development functions in Appendix A. Convince your colleagues that fund development is more than just asking for money.

Maybe your organization will have trouble with development planning because the internal relationship is not strong. Take a look at Chapter 2. Work on group process and dialogue. Encourage conversation and participatory decision making.

Do what it takes. Don't avoid or compromise your planning.

PLANNING FOR THE FUTURE WHILE YOU OPERATE TODAY

Planning for the future occurs in tandem with current operations. While you plan, you also carry out your current business.

You have a fund development plan right now. Maybe it's written and maybe it's only in your head—but you're doing something. So carry out your current plan while you devise your new plan.

As you implement your current activities, evaluate results. Evaluate results for each activity in order to make decisions for the next year and the new plan.

For example: Compare results with goals and current results with those of prior years. Analyze return on investment and productivity. Compare cost with dollars raised. Contrast your results with standards in the industry. See Exhibits 6–2 and 6–3. See also *Fund-Raising Cost Effectiveness: A Self-Assessment Workbook*, by James M. Greenfield, FAHP, ACFRE (1996).

With your evaluation results in hand, analyze the trends and discuss the implications. What do these results mean for your organization? What should you do differently next year? What do you recommend for the next plan?

Make sure that you conduct this evaluation—and the ensuing strategic discussion—with key constituents. Debrief and evaluate with staff and the development committee, with the CEO, and with the board.

This evaluation and discussion develops volunteer and staff understanding and promotes best practice. This process makes sure that you hear their perspective and valuable input. You learn about their concerns and identify their barriers. Together, you make decisions for next year's plan.

Keep a record of the results, trends, and implications. Document the discussion and recommendations. Record the decisions made. Then file it all for use later when you create the new fund development plan.

YOUR FUND DEVELOPMENT PLANNING PROCESS

It's up to you. You must design a process that accomplishes the outcomes listed earlier. You also have to produce a written plan!

In addition to this chapter, review Chapter 3 for ideas to consider in your planning process. Also review Chapter 4 for ideas to include in the plan.

In some way, your planning *process*—and the resulting plan—should address each of the issues presented in Exhibit 6–4. Naturally, your fund development *program* should address these issues, too.

The Written Development Plan

This is a written document, used regularly by staff, the development committee, and the board. Like the

Exhibit 6–2 Measuring Fund Development Performance

BASIC DATA TO COLLECT ABOUT EACH SOLICITATION STRATEGY

For example, face-to-face, direct mail, etc.

Solicitations = Total number of solicitations made

Participation = Total number of donors responding with gifts to the solicitation

Income = Gross contributions

Expense = Fundraising costs for this solicitation

MEASURING PERFORMANCE OF THE PARTICULAR SOLICITATION STRATEGY

Compare all measures to prior years in the organization. Maintain spreadsheets of comparative data.

1. Examine participation rates.
   - Acquisition (percentage of new donors)
   - Attrition (percentage of donors who did not renew)
   - Retention (percentage of donors who gave again)
2. Calculate net income (subtract expenses from income received).
3. Determine average gift size (divide income received by number of participants).
4. Calculate average cost per gift (divide expenses by number of participants).
5. Examine upgrading.
   - Percentage of donors who increased their gifts from the prior year
   - Average size of upgrade
6. Examine effectiveness of rating (intersection of interest, readiness, and capacity).
   - Percentage who gave the requested gift amount
7. Compare performance with pre-established goals (set goals prior to launching activity).
8. Compare performance with standards in the industry.
9. Calculate cost of fundraising (divide expenses by income received; multiply by 100 for percentage).
10. Evaluate performance of volunteer solicitors.
    - Number of solicitations made compared with number assigned
    - Number of gifts received compared with number of solicitations made
    - Match between amount asked for and gift made
    - Number of donors who increased their gift compared with gifts made

---

organization's strategic plan, the development plan sets direction and boundaries, and guides action.

The plan is reviewed regularly. Staff and development committee monitor progress, report on achievements, and develop interventions as necessary.

You decide the content areas and organization of your fund development plan. Begin by brainstorming general content areas with the development committee. This helps them accept the complexity, scope, and length of the resulting plan. Engage staff colleagues. Also talk briefly with the board about the scope and content of the plan.

You decide the format of the plan. Typically, plans include narrative sections, as well as bulleted lists, financial data, and even graphs.

Typical components of the fund development plan are listed below (Exhibit 6–5). This is neither an all-inclusive nor a requisite list. However, experience shows that components 3–6 and 10–13 are most essential.

1. *Organization mission and values.* What a great way to start your fund development plan—reiterate your mission. Consider also reprinting your values and even your vision, if it's short enough.
2. *Mission, vision, and values for fund development.* How about creating a mission, vision, and values for your fund development operation? Remember that your values might include the *Donor Bill of Rights* and a code of ethics and standards of professional practice. And, naturally, you follow the organization's mission and values.
3. *Strategic goals.* These goals do not reference money. Rather, these goals may address such issues as: improving board recruitment so that everyone understands his or her obligation to fund development, ensuring quality information for decision making by enhanced fundraising reports or a new database, strengthening board understanding of the body of knowledge and best practice through training, and so forth.
4. *Financial goals.* This is the place to summarize the charitable revenue goals presented in your budget. Also, it is useful to present financial goals for each solicitation strategy.
5. *Communication and cultivation strategies.* See Chapter 4 for details about developing your relationships with constituents. Within the cultivation section, some plans include acknowledgment and recognition activities. You can organize this section by target audience or by activity.
6. *Solicitation strategies.* All too often, this is the only element included in fund development plans. This section outlines how you will ask for money, for example, face-to-face solicitation, direct mail, a special event, foundation proposals, and so forth. Usually, each solicitation strategy is targeted to a particular audience.

Exhibit 6–3 Standards in the Industry

Current level of achievement for a solicitation activity that has been in active use for a minimum of 3 years.

Solicitation Activity	Reasonable Cost Guidelines
Direct mail (acquisition)	$1.25–$1.50 per $1.00 raised
Direct mail (renewal)	20¢–25¢ per $1.00 raised
Membership association	20¢–30¢ per $1.00 raised
Activities, benefits, and special events	50¢ per $1.00 raised (gross revenue and direct costs only)*
Donor clubs and support group organizations	20¢–30¢ per $1.00 raised
Volunteer–led personal solicitation	10¢–20¢ per $1.00 raised
Corporations	20¢ per $1.00 raised
Foundations	20¢ per $1.00 raised
Special projects	10¢–20¢ per $1.00 raised
Capital campaigns	10¢–20¢ per $1.00 raised
Planned giving	20¢–30¢ per $1.00 raised
Overall fundraising program	**18¢–20¢ (not to exceed 30¢)**

* To calculate the bottom-line costs and net proceeds of events, calculate and add the indirect and overhead support costs to direct costs incurred, and subtract from gross revenue.

GENERAL COMMENTS

- Quality of the list (your prospects) is the most critical factor.
- While it may be less expensive to raise money from corporations and foundations, their gifts often represent the smallest percentage of dollars given in any community and do represent the smallest percentage of dollars given in the United States annually.
- Direct mail is estimated to be 16 times less effective than face-to-face solicitation.
- In direct mail, the letter must capture the readers' attention within 15 seconds; some experts say within 4 seconds. A four-page letter achieves a higher rate of response and a larger average gift than the more common single-page letter. (True!)
- Pledge payment rate for phonathons averages 70–80%, less than the payment rate for pledges in personal solicitation.

Response Rates for Acquisition and Renewal Strategies

New Donor Acquisition	Moderately Qualified	Highly Qualified
• Direct mail	0.5–2%	10–15%
• Telephone	2–5%	15–25%
• Personal solicitation		30–50%
Donor Renewal		
• After 1 year	20%	50–60%
• After 3 years	40%	60–70%
• After 5 years	60%	80–90%
Donor Upgrade	15%	15–20%
Overall fundraising program for renewal		80–85%

Source: Data from J.M. Greenfield, FAHP, ACFRE, *Fund-Raising Cost Effectiveness: A Self-Assessment Workbook*, Direct Mail Marketing Association, American Association of Fund Raising Counsel, *The Costs and Benefits of Deferred Giving*, by N.S. Fink and H.C. Metzler, Karla A. Williams, ACFRE, *Donor-Focused Strategies for Annual Giving*, S.P. Joyaux, ACFRE.

7. *Retention, acquisition, and upgrading strategies.* Some plans include a separate section to describe these activities. In other cases, solicitation strategies can be described as retention, acquisition, or upgrading activities.
8. *Case for support.* You might choose to present key components of your case for support in your plan. Sometimes, fundraising themes are targeted to certain audiences or noted for use with specific solicitation strategies.
9. *Benchmarks.* Benchmarks, or measures of success—no matter what you call them—are how you evaluate results. And evaluating results is more than the overall financial goals. Measuring

Exhibit 6–4 Key Issues in the Fund Development Planning Process

1. Fostering a culture of philanthropy within the organization
   - Ensuring that everyone throughout the organization values philanthropy and donors
   - Using systems thinking
   - Understanding that most fund development problems are not fund development programs but actually are organizational development challenges
2. Identifying potential funding sources
   - Examining the charitable contributions marketplace in order to address such issues as:
     - level of congestion in fund development
     - issues and organizations receiving donor focus
     - strategies that have been effective in reaching donors
     - opportunities for networking with other philanthropic organizations and donors
   - Identifying current constituents (e.g., volunteers, referral sources, clients, etc.) and getting to know them well enough to evaluate whether they are potential donors
   - Identifying those who might be predisposed to your cause and getting to know them well enough to determine whether they might be cultivated into constituents and then donors
3. Developing the relationship with potential funders/donors
   - Developing an ongoing process to get to know prospects
   - Understanding their giving interests, disinterests, motivations, and aspirations
   - Identifying the value match between your organization and the prospect
   - Developing communications and cultivation strategies to build the relationship
   - Building mutual understanding and commitment
   - Providing adequate and appropriate acknowledgment and recognition for donors
4. Positioning your organization within the philanthropic marketplace
   - Determining what constituents, community leaders, and those predisposed to your cause think of your organization (Much of this can be done through the institutional strategic planning process and maintained through development planning.)
   - Identifying interests, disinterests, motivations, and aspirations of prospective donors and determining whether there is a value match with your organization
   - Identifying optimum ways to communicate and cultivate relationships
5. Organizing to do the fund development work
   - Outlining the values, ethics, and standards for fund development at your organization
   - Defining the fund development functions, competencies, and skills necessary to carry out fund development and the appropriate structure for optimum performance
   - Defining roles of your organization staff, the board as a group and its individual members, and other possible volunteers
   - Identifying training needs for volunteers and staff, and developing appropriate materials
   - Developing the fund development plan
6. Maximizing the return on investment through the best use of solicitation strategies
   - Determining the appropriate solicitation process, request, and solicitor for each prospect
   - Evaluating interest, readiness, and capacity of prospective donors
   - Estimating the dollars that might be generated and the cost to do so, and preparing the budget
   - Using the skills and contacts of board members and staff
7. Implementing
   - Developing solicitation materials, e.g., case statement, gift transmittal mechanism
   - Asking for the gift and securing the answer
   - Monitoring progress, identifying challenges, and intervening
   - Evaluating productivity and return on investment
8. Evaluating
   - Compiling participation rates, e.g., acquisition, attrition, retention; calculating gift upgrades and average gift size. Determining cost to raise a dollar, cost-effectiveness, and return on investment.
   - Determining trends and analyzing implications

---

results might include such things as: recruiting two new volunteers to participate in the face-to-face campaign, producing four issues of the newsletter, hosting two cultivation events, increasing the number of donors by 10 percent, increasing gifts from 15 percent of current donors, retaining 80 percent of current donors, and so forth.

10. *Assignments of responsibility*. Make sure that you distinguish between the responsibilities of staff and volunteers. Get each board member to take on a particular responsibility, and stipulate his or her name in the appropriate section of the plan.
11. *Timetable*. Decide whether your plan is for the fiscal year or for multiple fiscal years. Outline

the general time frames for the major activities. Remember that this is a strategic plan, not your complete operational plan.

12. *Resources.* Describe the resources required to do the work. This would include your budget. You might also list materials and equipment. You might describe the hiring of a new staff person or use of a consultant.

   Sometimes, organizations include key job descriptions in this section to clarify the roles of the board, development committee, development officer, and individual board member.

13. *Monitoring progress and evaluating performance.* Describe how you will monitor performance. What will staff do, when, and how? What is the role of the development committee and the board? You might describe the key types of reports that you will provide for strategic discussion and decision making.

Remember, monitor and evaluate the plan as you implement it. Staff prepare assorted fundraising reports, trend analyses, and overviews of implications. The quality of information that you prepare is critical to help volunteers talk strategically and make appropriate decisions. Engage your development committee in the discussion. Make sure that the board also participates in the process of monitoring and evaluating. Reserve major decisions for the board.

Take a look at the sample fund development plans included in the appendices of this chapter. Each organization selected content and format based on its own needs.

Exhibit 6–5 Key Components of the Fund Development Plan

1. Organization mission and values
2. Mission, vision, and values for fund development
3. Strategic goals
4. Financial goals
5. Communications and cultivation strategies
6. Solicitation strategies
7. Retention, acquisition, and upgrading strategies
8. Case for support
9. Benchmarks
10. Assignments of responsibility
11. Timetable
12. Resources
13. Monitoring progress and evaluating performance

The Women's Foundation of Southern Arizona (WFSA) serves the unique needs of women and girls through grant making, enhancing philanthropy by and for women, and focusing community attention on the status of women and girls. The fund development plan is a direct result of the organization's six-month strategic planning process. See Chapter 3 for remarks about the WFSA strategic planning process. Take a look at the WFSA vision as it relates to philanthropy and fund development (Appendix 6–A). See also the goals on page 284.

Once the board adopted the vision, goals, and strategic plan, the development officer worked with the Strategic Fund Development Team to create the development plan. The board discussed the plan in depth and adopted it for implementation.

A key element of the WFSA plan is the statement of assumptions. Located at the start of the plan, this section sets the context for the plan and clearly states what must happen for success. This plan includes substantial financial data. See Appendix 6–A.

Rhode Island's Fund for Community Progress supports 23 grassroots organizations that work for social justice. The Fund is one of the nation's oldest independent funds. The Fund primarily solicits gifts through workplaces. The Fund also uses direct mail, special events, and face-to-face solicitation to secure gifts.

The Fund's plan organizes its goals and activities into the following areas:

- General management, strategic discussion, and decision making
- Member agencies
- Building relationships
- Telling our story better
- Workplace solicitation
- Personal solicitation
- Direct mail
- Proposal development

See Appendix 6–B for the complete plan.

The Tockwotton Home provides assisted living and nursing home services to those requiring long-term care or short-term residential care. As a health care institution, the Home is financed primarily through government and insurance reimbursement.

Nonetheless, Tockwotton Home recognized the value of a stronger philanthropic orientation. Charitable contributions provide the venture capital to institute value-added services that are not reimbursed by third parties. With this focus in mind, Tockwotton Home set up a Fund Development Committee and launched a development planning process.

The resulting development plan extends over two fiscal years. A significant portion of the plan describes how to strengthen the board's understanding of and support for philanthropy. Another section describes how the Home will educate its residents and their families about philanthropy and its benefits.

The Tockwotton Home development plan is presented in Appendix 6–C.

In New Jersey, Children's Aid and Family Services had a long history of annual giving, generated primarily through direct mail. When the agency decided to launch an endowment program in 1996, the planning process examined all areas of fund development.

The resulting development plan—shown in Appendix 6–D—focused on both endowment and annual giving. The agency accepted face-to-face solicitation as the strategy to invite endowment gifts, then introduced face-to-face solicitation as part of the annual solicitation program. The agency devised a comprehensive, integrated recognition program, embracing annual, endowment, and other forms of giving. Staff and volunteers spent some time analyzing agency constituencies. In subsequent years, Children's Aid and Family Services continued to devise an annual development plan.

INTERFACING YOUR FUND DEVELOPMENT PLAN WITH THE BUDGETING PROCESS

Your fund development plan should coincide with your fiscal year and your budget. You may create an annual development plan or a multiyear plan.

Your board should approve the fiscal year budget *and* the fund development plan *at the same time*. The fund development plan describes how the organization will secure the charitable contributions depicted in the budget.

> *The optimum fund development planning process tests the proposed budget figures for charitable contributions.*

Staff and finance committee typically draft the budget. The development portion of the budget usually reflects *what the organization must raise in order to do what it wants to do*. Sometimes, the development portion of the budget also reflects prior year trends in fundraising.

But rarely has the development portion of the budget actually *tested* the likelihood of raising the money. Testing means that, once the budget is drafted, the development staff and committee go through the planning process to verify whether that goal is reachable.

The testing process *is* the fund development planning process. The testing process takes the proposed budget figure and does the following:

1. Conducts a SWOT analysis (strengths and weaknesses [SW] and external opportunities and threats [OT]) for the organization and the fund development program, examining internal strengths and weaknesses and external opportunities and threats. Outlines ways to address the SWOT results and talks with the board about its willingness to address the results.
2. Reviews the evaluation results of current-year fundraising activities and examines the recommendations and decisions for the new year. What improvements were agreed to by staff and board? Are these still likely, and what will it take to accomplish them?
3. Analyzes all donors (individually or by some form of segmentation) and determines the likely changes, for example, retention, gift increases or decreases and how this might happen, and attrition.
4. Evaluates the predisposed and prospects to determine readiness for solicitation and potential new gifts for the new fiscal year and its plan.
5. Figures out what has to be done to build relationships with diverse constituencies.
6. Explores new fundraising activities and decides what resources are necessary to carry these out and what level of dollars might result.
7. Outlines the staff and volunteer resources necessary to enhance current-year activities and launch new activities.
8. Estimates financial costs to do the work outlined.
9. Synthesizes everything. Adds up the money, both income and expense. Adds up the human resources, volunteer, and staff.
10. Compares the resulting "likely dollars to be raised in charitable contributions" to the proposed budget.
11. Shares planning results with the board and determines organization readiness to do what it takes.
12. Secures individual board member support to take on specific activities within the plan.
13. Recommends final budget figure for charitable contributions for the new year.

Staff and development committee engage the board in the discussions of items 1–9 above. Staff and development committee remind the board of its previous discussions and decisions throughout the year.

Typically, staff are actually drafting a preliminary written plan during the testing process. Once items 1–9 are completed, the staff and development committee compare the resulting "likely dollars to be raised in charitable contributions" to the proposed budget.

> *Your fundraising goal depends on the availability of donors and prospects, and the capacity of your organization to do the work.*

The development committee presents the test results to the finance committee and board. What happens if the test results show that the "likely dollars" are less than the proposed budget? The smart finance committee reduces the proposed budget to match the development committee's findings. Why? Because the finance committee trusts that the development committee and staff have undertaken a rigorous process that has produced the best possible results based on available donors, prospects, and organization resources, and capacity.

The bottom line is: Your fundraising goal does *not* depend on how much money you want. Your fundraising goal depends on the availability of donors and prospects, and the capacity of your organization to do the work.

And what about the capacity of your organization? That depends on the strength of your four relationships. Your organization's capacity also depends on the willingness of each individual board member to take on specific tasks. Get their commitment before the budget is finalized and before the plan is adopted. Put their individual names into the written plan. Then adopt the plan when you adopt the budget.

ROLES IN THE FUND DEVELOPMENT PLANNING PROCESS

There are four groups or individuals that are critical to produce an effective planning process for development—and they are the same as those for the institutional planning process.

1. planning committee (this is your development committee)
2. board
3. process manager
4. staff

Take a look at Exhibit 6–3, key issues in the fund development planning process. Figure out which of the groups or individuals you will involve in which of these issues. See Exhibit 6–6, which outlines the interrelationship between the board, its fund development committee, and staff.

Your planning committee is the development committee. This is the place where discussion starts and gathers momentum. Staff bring issues to this group. Staff present trends and preliminary implications here. The committee probes, explores, and may come to some conclusions. Sometimes, the committee makes recommendations to the board. But most importantly, the committee presents strategic issues to the board and engages the board in meaningful discussion and decision making.

If you don't have a development committee, establish one now. Let it start its work with the fund development planning process.

The board is the final decision maker. Your fund development plan belongs to the organization, not to the development operation or to the development staff. Just like the institutional strategic plan and the budget, the fund development plan is a board policy.

Make sure that the board participates in strategic discussion and decision making regarding fund development. The board should help evaluate current fundraising activities, discuss strategic issues, and make decisions.

Translate board work into individual board member action. The board functions as a collective. But the development operation requires that each individual board member do specific work. Secure commitment from each board member to carry out a portion of the development plan.

> *Every board member must take on a fundraising activity. Put their names in the plan and, together, they can hold themselves accountable.*

For fund development, the process manager is the chief development officer. If you don't have development staff, then it's the CEO, if he or she serves as chief development officer. The process manager designs and manages the fund development planning process. The process manager actually writes the plan. (But for heaven's sake, don't draft something for committee review without prior committee discussion!)

You're building a culture of philanthropy, so you need to engage staff within the organization. Involve development staff in the planning process. Involve other staff, as well, but in lesser ways. (Remember, they do have their own jobs.) Staff have ideas. They have concerns that you must overcome. And the program staff live the stories that you tell in fund development.

Great planning processes also engage other fundraising volunteers, not just those who serve on the board. And a really great development planning process engages donors, prospects, and even the predisposed. Review the chapter on constituency development. You'll find

Exhibit 6–6 Interrelationship among Board, Development Committee, and Staff in the Fund Development Planning Process

Activity	Responsibility
Set organizational goals and policies for fund development. ▼	Board
Develop committee tasks and procedures that relate to development and advance the organizational goals and policies. ▼	Staff, Development Committee
Develop strategic fund development plan(s) to support institution's mission, vision, and programs. ▼	Staff, Development Committee
Outline action steps to accomplish activities and identify any policy recommendations necessary to accomplish the plans. ▼	Staff, Development Committee
Review and adopt working plans and activities. ▼	Development Committee
Review and approve plans, activities, policy recommendations. ▼	Board
Carry out activities. ▼	Board and Development Committee members, Staff, other fundraising Volunteers.
Monitor progress. ▼	Staff, Development Committee, Board
Evaluate progress and performance toward meeting goals. ▼	Staff, Development Committee, Board
Evaluate the committee's role in helping to achieve organizational goals and begin the fund development process again.	Staff, Development Committee, Board

Source: Copyright © Sarah C. Coviello and Simone Joyaux.

lots of tips about engaging donors, prospects, and the predisposed. Some of that work affects the development planning process.

Things to keep in mind as you execute the planning process for fund development:

1. The fund development plan belongs to the organization. This is an organizationwide strategic plan and is adopted by the board. From this plan, staff will develop operational plans for specific activities. These operational plans do not require the approval (or even the review) of the board. The operational plans belong to the development operation and to specific fundraising task forces that take on particular activities.

2. Be very careful about drafting anything. Talk first. Engage staff and volunteers in conversation. Capture some of their perspective and concerns first. Consider their thinking. Only then should you draft elements of a *very preliminary* plan. Forget the theory of drafting for review. It doesn't build ownership or understanding. And you might step on some pretty big toes because you don't have the benefit of advance conversations.

3. Creating the development plan actually happens throughout the 12 months of the fiscal year while you're implementing the current plan. A more intense effort—testing the proposed organization budget and actually drafting the plan—occurs about 3–4 months before the start of the new fiscal year. The actual time frame depends on your organization's budgeting calendar.

4. The plan is not written to meet a budget or to reach a goal. Instead, this is a process that tests the feasibility of a goal or budget and negotiates that goal or budget.

5. Clearly distinguish between sources of charitable contributions and solicitation strategies. Sources in-

clude individuals, foundations, corporations, civic groups, faith groups, and government. Often, special events are considered a source of income, too. Your organization's budget, monthly financial reports, and year-end audit should present charitable contributions by source. Solicitation strategies include face-to-face, direct mail, telephone, e-mail, proposal development, and, yes, special events. Your fund development plan should present information both by source and by solicitation strategy.

SUMMARY

The fund development plan provides the framework for your development program. Develop a plan effectively and work that plan well—and you'll see a difference in attitude, accountability, and productivity.

The process of creating the development plan is as important as the resulting plan. A good process produces ownership of the plan, ensures shared accountability, and achieves your targeted results.

The challenge, of course, is the process itself. Good process depends on the four relationships described in this book. In particular, good process requires highly effective enabling by the process manager, typically the development officer.

Each of the prior chapters in this book contains ideas that are helpful to the development planning process. For example, see Chapter 2 for a review of values clarification, group process, conversation, and participatory decision making. Take another look at managing change and leadership. See Chapter 3 for a detailed description of strategic planning. You can apply most—if not all—of this to your fund development planning. In Chapter 4, review the ways to engage constituents in the development process. Use some of these ideas for your planning. Finally, Chapter 5 describes your role as the principal enabler. The proverbial ball is in your court. Take it!

REFERENCES

Ellinor, L., and G. Gerard. 1998. *Dialogue: Rediscovering the Transforming Power of Conversation*. New York: John Wiley & Sons, Inc.

Godfrey, J. 1992. *Our Wildest Dreams: Women Entrepreneurs Making Money, Having Fun, Doing Good*. New York: HarperCollins Publishers.

Greenfield, J.M. 1996. *Fund-Raising Cost Effectiveness: A Self-Assessment Workbook*. New York: John Wiley & Sons, Inc.

Appendix 6–A

Women's Foundation of Southern Arizona

Fund Development Plan for Fiscal Year 2000–2001

I. MISSION & VISION

The Women's Foundation of Southern Arizona changes the lives of women and girls by securing the financial resources to fund programs that promote the empowerment, advancement, and full participation in society of women and girls.

The Women's Foundation of Southern Arizona is part of a strong Women's Funding Movement across the world that focuses educational and grantmaking efforts explicitly on the needs of women and girls. The Women's Foundation envisions a world where women occupy positions of strength, power, and leadership, and are active philanthropists. In our vision, women and girls have equal opportunities in society—economically, socially, culturally, and politically.

The Women's Foundation has a vision of a southern Arizona in which women and girls

- Live with dignity.
- Live in an environment safe from physical violence and violence to the spirit.
- Are respected regardless of their circumstances.
- Make their own choices, including choices regarding pregnancy and birth.
- Are empowered as full participants in their communities.
- Have access to, and voice in, their communities' centers of decision making.
- Are recognized for their unique strengths and talents.
- Reach their full potential.

II. OVERVIEW & ASSUMPTIONS

A. The Women's foundation consistently falls short of its fundraising goals and has never raised enough

Courtesy of Women's Foundation of Southern Arizona, Tucson, AZ.

money in one year to cover grantmaking and operating expenses. We have covered operating expenses by dipping into our "carry forward," otherwise known as our reserve. This must change this year.

B. The Women's Foundation must increase its fundraising goal to $400,000 during FY 2000–2001 in order to support grantmaking, operating expenses, and the implementation of the newly adopted strategic plan. This represents a 20 percent increase over FY 1999–2000.

C. If we are to reach our fundraising goals for the coming year, it is essential that the Board as a group, and each individual Board member, participate in fundraising and give according to her own personal ability. Participating in fundraising means asking people for gifts in support of the Women's Foundation.

D. It is also essential that we increase the number of people we are soliciting, both in person and by mail. One of the only ways for us to do this is for Board members to share names with the development office and to recruit supporters for the organization.

E. One of the goals of the strategic plan is to increase the endowment to $3.5 million by 2005. In order to be institutionally ready for an endowment campaign, we must demonstrate our ability to raise grantmaking and operating funds on an annual basis.

F. The 2000–2001 Fund Development Plan will rely upon six strategies:
  1. Conducting a face-to-face solicitation campaign.
  2. Utilizing the Tribute Book as a face-to-face solicitation strategy.
  3. Hosting the *Numbers Too Big To Ignore* Special Events—the 8th Annual Luncheon and the Community Forum.
  4. Acquiring more and larger corporate partnerships.
  5. Retaining and acquiring donors through direct mail.

6. Securing foundation grants.

G. Stewardship and Cultivation is an essential component of any fund development plan and will be incorporated into our fund development work.

H. A new structure has been adopted to enable us to carry out our fund development work. The structure will include a Strategic Development Committee, a Stewardship and Cultivation Committee, committees for each of the two events, and a pool of Volunteer Solicitors.

III. GOALS

A. To raise $300,000 from individuals, including $21,000 from Board members and $80,000 from the Advisory Council.

B. To raise $100,000 from businesses and corporations, primarily through corporate support of the *Numbers Too Big To Ignore* events.

C. To engage each Board member in the process of philanthropy and fund development.

D. To ensure that each Board member actively participates in one of the fund development teams or task forces.

E. To ensure that each Board member gives a financial contribution to the best of her personal ability, securing 100 percent Board participation in giving.

F. To develop an effective corps of at least 30 face-to-face solicitors.

IV. STRATEGIES

A. Face-to-Face Solicitation

1. Board

Board members will be asked to make a philanthropic commitment to the Women's Foundation within the first two months of the fiscal year. The commitment will be based on the Board member's self-determined giving capacity. Staff will meet with each Board member to discuss the amount, schedule, and designation of gifts. The goal for Board giving is based on the giving history of current Board members and includes annual gifts as well as endowment, special events, and the tribute book. See Attachment *Board Member Pledge Form*.

> Goal: $12,000
> Timeline: July–August

2. Advisory Council

Advisory Council members will be asked to make a philanthropic commitment to the Women's Foundation within the first two months of the fiscal year. The commitment will be based on the Advisory Council member's self-determined giving capacity. Staff will meet with each Advisory Council member to discuss the amount, schedule, and designation of gifts. The goal for Advisory Council giving is based on the giving history of current Advisory Council members and includes annual gifts as well as endowment, special events, and the tribute book. See Attachment *Advisory Council Pledge Form*.

> Goal: $60,370
> Timeline: July–August

3. Major Donors

a. Prospects

Major donor prospects are defined as people whom we can ask for $1,000 or more, or whom we believe can eventually reach that level of giving. We currently have about 41 donors and 52 prospects in the $1,000-$30,000 range. We will ask these people for money in person. We need to have over 225 donors and prospects (not all will result in a face-to-face meeting or a gift) in order to safely reach our goal this year. All Board members will be asked to provide names of prospects for the annual campaign and the tribute book campaign. The Development Officer will research additional prospects in the community and periodically will bring lists of names to Board members for contacts and information. We need to build up to 225 prospects by the end of summer 2000. See attached *Gift Chart 2000–2001* and *Gifts Needed to Meet Fundraising Goals*.

> Goal: $46,320
> Cost: $2,600
> Timeline: Sept–October

b. Solicitation Strategy

A small group of the volunteer solicitors will meet to: identify prospects, judge their level of interest and ability to give and their readiness to be asked, choose an apppropriate solicitor, and devise a solicitation strategy for each prospect.

Each solicitor will be assigned 2–5 donors and will be provided a Donor Prospect worksheet for each donor (information will include interests in the foundation, involvement in the community, giving history, gift amount to request, etc.).

Each solicitor will receive a packet of information from the Development Officer and will be accompanied by staff (the Development Officer or Executive Director) on their solicitation call. Packets will include the following:

- Fact sheet about the Women's Foundation
- Talking Points sheet with standard questions and answers
- Financial summary
- Most recent newsletter
- Tribute book
- Prospect sheets
- Thank you cards
- Instruction sheet for the solicitor
- Articles/handouts with tips for effective face-to-face solicitation

Solicitors will receive introductory letters to each of their prospects that they can sign and send before contacting their prospect by phone. All prospects must be contacted and appointments set up by September 30, 2000. Progress reports will be presented to the Board at each meeting for review of volunteer solicitor participation and possible intervention when solicitors are not completing their asks.

All asks should be completed by October 31, 2000. The Development Officer will call solicitors to check on their progress and find out their needs. Solicitors are encouraged to host the donor or prospect for a meal, but may submit expenses for reimbursement to the Women's Foundation if needed.

c. Cost Benefit Analysis and Goals

	99–00	00–01
# Solicitations Assigned	89	225
# Solicitations Completed	36	100
# Donors Participating	21	75
Total Cost	$495.33	$2,600
Total Income	$30,675	$50,000
Cost per Solicitation	$ 13.76	$26
Cost per Response	$ 23.59	$34.60
Cost per $ Raised	.02	.05
Average Gift Size	$1,460	$750
Average Gift Upgrade	300%	15%
Acquisition Rate (% of new donors)	14%	25%
Retention Rate (% of renewing donors)	86%	75%

d. Accountability

The Strategic Development Team will be responsible for review of campaign progress and monthly reporting to the Board of Trustees. All Board members are responsible for contributing names to the prospect list for possible solicitation. Volunteer Solicitors are responsible for

meeting with their assigned prospects, asking for gifts, and reporting back to the development office about their solicitation activities.

B. The Tribute Book

1. Overview

This year's tribute book will be called *In Celebration of Women: Everyday Heroes*. In addition to raising over $50,000, our goal for this year's book is to make it more meaningful by enriching the content of the book. A new two-page tribute size, called a "Herstory" tribute, will be added this year to give people an opportunity to tell a fuller story about the person they are tributing. We will also add quotes by inspirational women throughout the book. The essential look and feel of the book will remain predominantly the same.

> *Goal: $58,000*
> *Cost: $15,000*
> *Timeline: July–Nov*

2. Tribute Gift Sizes

Sizes and gift categories for tribute pages will be changed this year in order to meet the goal of raising $53,500. Goals are based on the history of tribute book success.

Tribute Size	Gift Size	Number	Total
2-page Herstory	$1,500	20	$30,000
Full Page	$1,000	20	$20,000
Partial Page	$350	10	$3,500

As has been done in the past, corporate partners will receive tributes as part of their recognition package. In addition to the above tributes, we are also anticipating 13–15 corporate tributes, making the total number of tributes 65 (a 25 percent increase over last year).

3. Solicitation Strategy

This year the tribute book campaign will occur simultaneous to our face-to-face solicitation campaign and should be viewed as a face-to-face solicitation strategy. All Volunteer Solicitors will be trained to solicit face-to-face and tribute book gifts (sometimes both to the same donor at the same meeting). See section VI, Volunteer Training and Recognition. Solicitation materials, such as tribute book samples and a Tribute Form Sheet, will be available for volunteers to use when making solicitation calls. The deadline for all tribute submissions this year will be November 15, 2000.

4. Accountability

All volunteer solicitors are accountable for meeting with their assigned prospects, acquiring tribute gifts, and reporting back to the development office about their solicitation activities.

C. The *Numbers Too Big To Ignore* Special Events

For the purposes of corporate partnership, our special events for this year have been combined into one package for corporate solicitation and recognition. See section D, Corporate Partnership for details.

1. Community Forum on the Status of Women in Arizona

a. Overview

The *Community Forum on the Status of Women in Arizona* will be a sneak preview of the forthcoming *Status of Women in Arizona Report* and will feature keynote speaker Heidi Hartmann, Executive Director of the National Institute for Women's Policy Research. Following the keynote speaker, there will be a "town hall" forum, which will be a dialogue between the audience and a statewide panel of experts. Lupita Murillo of KVOA-TV has agreed to moderate the forum. The panel will include Heidi Hartmann, along with no more than five people from around the state who can speak to the status of women in Arizona and the implications of the report. Panelists currently invited include Attorney General Janet Napolitano, Senator Elaine Richardson, and Representative Debra Norris. Other panelists are still being identified.

The goal is to create a dialogue between the panel and the audience on the current status of women in our state, from which we may draw implications for public policy, funding, and activism. Ultimately, the Community Forum should help us develop a statewide agenda for improving the lives of women and girls in Arizona.

> *Goal: 500 attendees & $20,000*
> *Cost: $12,135*
> *Date: Oct 24, 2000*
> *Location: Doubletree*

Participants will be invited to an opening reception, the Heidi Hartmann talk, and the panel/forum. They will also receive a copy of the report in the mail as soon as it is released.

b. Fundraising

The *Community Forum* will derive most of its fundraising capacity from corporate sponsorships. However, tickets will be sold at $20 each. The $20 ticket includes the reception, the talk, the forum, and a copy of the *Status of Women in Arizona Report*. We are hoping to have between 300 and 500 guests.

Status of Women Income Allocation
Corporate Sponsorships

1 @ $15,000	5,000
2 @ $5,000	4,000
4 @ $2,500	4,000
6 @ $1,000	1,800
Tickets/Tables	10,000

Program Ads

Full Page - 8 @ $150	400
Half Page - 19 @ $75	475
Quarter Page - 25 @ $35	375
Total	$26,050

Corporate sponsorship and program ads for the *Community Forum* and *The Luncheon* were negotiated as a single package with donors. One third of the sponsorship and income is allocated to the *Community Forum* and two thirds is allocated to *The Luncheon*.

c. Publicity Plan

The *Community Forum* will have an Honorary Committee of recognizable individuals from across the state to lend credibility and notoriety to the event. Jane Amari, Editor of the Arizona Daily Star, has already agreed to co-chair the Honorary Committee. Linda Ronstadt will be invited to serve as her co-chair. Special letterhead has already been designed for this event that will include the names of the Honorary Committee members. The co-chairs will sign letters to other potential committee members and corporate sponsors.

Community Sponsors willll also be sought for this event. Community sponsors will include organizations that serve women and girls such as the YWCA, Planned Parenthood, and many others. These organizations will be asked to assist us in getting their constituents to the event by sharing their mailing lists, posting flyers, and using their existing communications to advertise the event.

The Community Forum will be heavily advertised in the Daily Star, which has agreed to be the presenting media sponsor for this event. Other advertising, press releases, and news coverage will be sought in the Arizona Wildcat, the Tucson Weekly, the Desert Leaf, and other media. In addition, there will be a poster and invitations printed and sent to supporters of the Women's Foundation and the other community partners for this event.

d. Accountability

The Development Officer is planning this event with the help of the Community Forum Committee. The committee is chaired by Marcia Klipsch and includes Mary Jo Fox, Jan Monk, Jennifer Nye, Barbara Ratner, Lory Warren, and Teresa Welborn. All volunteers are responsible for selling tickets and acquiring corporate partnerships.

2. 8th Annual Luncheon

a. Overview

This year's luncheon will be similar in format and content to last year's luncheon.

b. Fundraising

The Luncheon will also derive its fundraising capacity from corporate partnerships (see D). However, tickets will be $30 this year, and tables will cost $300, a modest increase over last year's cost. The Luncheon also serves as a great forum for a group gift solicitation, which will be planned closer to the event. We are hoping to match gifts received at last year's event, which totaled $18,000.

> *Goal: 1,000 attendees* & *$73,700*
> *Cost: $35,750*
> *Date: April 12, 2001*
> *Location: Westin*

Luncheon Income

Corporate Sponsorships	Allocation
1 @ $15,000	10,000
2 @ $5,000	6,000
4 @ $2,500	6,000
6 @ $1,000	4,200
Tickets/Tables	30,000
Donations (at the event)	15,000
Center Piece Sales	500

Program Ads	
Full Page - 8 @ $150	800
Half Page -19 @ $75	950
Quarter Page - 25 @ $35	500
Total	$73,950

Corporate sponsorship and program ads for the *Community Forum* and *The Luncheon* were negotiated as a single package with donors. One third of the sponsorship and income is allocated to the *Community Forum* and two thirds is allocated to *The Luncheon*.

c. Publicity Plan

Invitations to the luncheon will be sent out in January, as has happened in the past. No further publicity is planned, although many tables and tickets are sold to donors one-on-one.

d. Accountability

The Luncheon is being planned by the Development Officer along with a Luncheon Committee. The committee will be co-chaired by MJ Jensen and Mary Rowley. Other committee members are still being identified. Volunteers are responsible for selling tickets and tables, and acquiring corporate partnerships.

D. Corporate Partnership

1. Overview

This year, corporate partnerships will be aggressively sought. The *Numbers Too Big To Ignore* theme and events will be used to acquire new partners and increase past support. Corporate partners will receive recognition at both events and in the tribute book, as well as public exposure through advertising.

> *Goal:* See *Numbers Too Big To Ignore* Goal
> *Timeline: July–Sept*

This year we will have a Program Ad Booklet at both events that will include the same ads and interchangeable information about the Women's Foundation and the appropriate event. We are hoping to procure around 50 ads and make about $5,000. We will obtain outside service assistance with this project.

2. Solicitation Strategy

Prospects have been identified by staff as indicated in section 3 below. The volunteers for the event committees and the Development Officer will be responsible for all corporate and business solicitations, and will ask board members and/or the Executive Director to assist in meetings with potential donors as appropriate.

3. Prospects

Sponsorship Level	Amount	# Needed	# Prospects
I am Invincible	$15,000	2	2
I am Strong	$5,000	2	5
I am Wise	$2,500	4	5
I am Brave	$1,000	6	20
Table + Program Ad	$450	10	13
Program Ad	$35–300	50	500

4. Accountability

Volunteers on the event committees, as well as volunteer solicitors, will be responsible for identifying and contacting corporate prospects and asking them to participate as corporate partners. Progress will be reported to the Board on a monthly basis.

E. Direct Mail

1. Overview

Two direct mails will be sent this year, one in November and one in April. These letters will each have a set theme, to be established throughout the year. Each mailing will be sent to the same group of 1600–2000 donors. Mail will be sent to new donors and to grass roots level donors only—not face-to-face prospects. All previous donors will receive a personalized, hand-addressed letter and will be asked for a specific amount. Only new donors will receive automated mail. Board members will again be asked to make personal notes on the letters of donors whom they know.

> *Goal: $40,000*
> *Cost: $4,140*
> *Timeline: Nov 2000 and Apr 2001*

An effort will be made this year to strengthen our response mechanism to include actual benefits of certain size gifts, i.e., $1,000 provides X for grantees, etc.

2. Acquiring New Donors

New donor acquisition will be a goal during this fiscal year. The Development Officer will research donor lists in town and periodically bring lists of people to be identified by board members as potential new donors. New board members will be asked to provide names of at least 10 people to whom they would be willing to write letters of introduction. The Development Officer will also research purchasing targeted lists of potential new donors, and using professional services to research and provide data on current and potential donors.

3. Cost Benefit Analysis and Goals

	99–00 Actual	00–01 Projected
# Solicitations	1,700	2,125
# Donors Participating	227	425
Total Cost	$3,485	$4,140
Total Income	$33,685	$40,000
Cost per Solicitation	$2.05	$1.95
Cost per Response	$15.35	$9.74
Cost per $ Raised	$.10	$.10
Average Gift Size	$148.39	$94.11
Average Size of Gift Upgrade	14%	15%
Acquisition Rate (% of new donors)	33%	25%
Retention Rate (% of renewing donors)	67%	75%

F. Securing Foundation Grants

Foundation grants will be sought throughout the year for FY 2000–2001 and 2001–2002. The goal indicated here includes only grants that will apply toward FY 2000–2001. In order to increase the Women's Foundation's income to the desired goal, acquisition of grant dollars must be an integral part of our development plan.

1. Grants Secured

The Women's Foundation has fulfilled its challenge by the Diamond and Pitt families and will receive $50,000 for FY 2000–2001. In addition, each year the Women's Foundation receives approximately $12,000 in unsolicited foundation grants. We will also apply for grants this year to supplement our income.

> *Goal: $79,200*
> *Cost: Staff time and minimal operating*
> *Timeline: Ongoing*

2. Grants Applied For

Foundation	Amount	Notification	Purpose
Stocker Foundation	$7,845	Fall 2000	Status of Women
Changemakers	$25,000	November	Change Management

3. Research

The Development Officer will prioritize grant research this year, and may seek outside service assistance for this task. The goal is to apply for 7–10 grants during FY 2000–2001.

V. STEWARDSHIP & CULTIVATION

A. Overview

Stewardship and Cultivation will be driven and overseen by the new Stewardship and Cultivation Team, to be convened in summer 2000. The first task of that committee will be to develop a Stewardship & Cultivation Plan. What follows is a rough outline of the year's Stewardship & Cultivation activities.

B. Strategies

1. Annual Report to be published when audit is complete.
2. Site-Seeing Tour series planned for January 2001.
3. Grantee Evaluation meeting in May 2001

4. Recognition
   a. Recognition wall (portable)—currently being researched for possible implementation in March 2001
   b. Logo pins—May be given for recognition by staff throughout the year
   c. Luncheon activities (i.e., slide show, announcements, program)
   d. Newsletter—listing of donors, articles highlighting donors
5. Communication
   a. See attached *Donor Contact Grid* for periodic communications with donors throughout the year, including newsletters, RFPs, grant announcements
6. Face-to-Face meetings—not to ask for money, just for cultivation

C. Accountability

The Stewardship & Cultivation Team will create a specific Stewardship & Cultivation Plan and will be responsible for implementation and monitoring of the plan.

VI. VOLUNTEER TRAINING AND RECOGNITION

A. Training

Volunteer Solicitors will be recruited over the summer for the Face-to-Face and Tribute Book Campaign in the fall. Volunteers may include Board and Advisory Council, as well as community volunteers. Training sessions for Volunteer Solicitors will be developed and presented for volunteers in August and September of 2000. Several sessions will be presented to give volunteers flexibility in attendance.

There will be an official Kick-Off for the Face-to-Face and Tribute Book Campaign on September 7, 2000. At that time we will announce a contest for all solicitors, with prizes for achieving certain benchmarks. Solicitors will receive solicitation packets and letters at that time.

Solicitation Packets will include:

- Overview Instruction Sheet
- Tribute Book Marketing Sheet
- Sample Tributes for donors to look at

- Forms for donors to return to the Women's Foundation
- 1999 Tribute Book
- Marketing Materials
- Tracking Sheets: For solicitors to keep track of their prospects and communicate with the office.

B. Motivation and Recognition

1. Contest

There will be a contest to help motivate volunteers to solicit donors for gifts and tributes. The contest parameters and prizes will be for:

- Most face-to-face visits accomplished
- Most money raised
- Largest gift
- Most tributes sold
- Most money raised through tributes
- Most successful "Friends Of" campaign
- Honorable mention gifts will be given to everyone who makes their appointments and follows through, regardless of whether or not the donor said yes.

2. Volunteer Recognition Event and Campaign Celebration

There will be an event in December or January to recognize and thank all volunteers and to celebrate the success of the FTF/TB Campaign. Prizes will be distributed at that time. Staff are working on getting the event donated.

VII. ATTACHMENTS

A. Advisory Council Pledge Form
B. Board Member Pledge Form
C. Development Calendar
D. Donor Contact Grid
E. Gifts Needed To Meet Fundraising Goals in FY 2000–2001
F. Corporate Philanthropy Opportunities for the 2000–2001 Season (attachment not included)
G. Program Ad Booklet for the 2000–2001 Event Season
H. Corrected Income Statement for Budget 00–01 (attachment not included)

Women's Foundation of Southern Arizona
Advisory Council Pledge

In consideration of the ongoing operational needs of the Women's Foundation, I pledge $_____ during the 2000–2001 fiscal year.

I designate my gift as follows:

Annual Giving $_____ Unrestricted (where the need is greatest)

Designated $_____ Grant Making
$_____ Community Forum Tickets/Underwriting
$_____ Luncheon Tickets/Table/Underwriting
$_____ Tribute Book
$_____ Endowment
$_____ Other

Total Pledge $_____

I understand that payment for this pledge is due by June 30, 2001. I will fulfill my gift in the following way:

❑ Check included $ _____.
❑ Please charge my Visa/Mastercard $_____
  Card number _____ Exp. _____
❑ I intend to donate stock.
❑ Please send payment notices.
    ❑ Semi-annually
    ❑ Quarterly
    ❑ Or as follows: _____
❑ My gift will come through _____
  Foundation by _____ (date)
❑ My company will match my gift
    ❑ Company _____
    ❑ Phone_____
❑ I would like my/our names listed as donors to WFSA as follows:
  _____
❑ I/We do not wish to have any public recognition regarding this gift.

Date:_____   Signature: _____

                Name (print): _____

A copy of this completed pledge form will be returned to you for your files.

Women's Foundation of Southern Arizona
Board Member Pledge

In consideration of the ongoing operational needs of the Women's Foundation, I pledge $_____ during the 2000–2001 fiscal year.

I designate my gift as follows:

Annual Giving $_____ Unrestricted (where the need is greatest)

Designated $_____ Grant Making
$_____ Community Forum Tickets/Underwriting
$_____ Luncheon Tickets/Table/Underwriting
$_____ Tribute Book
$_____ Endowment
$_____ Other

Total Pledge $_____

I understand that payment for this pledge is due by June 30, 2001. I will fulfill my gift in the following way:

❑ Check included $ _____.
❑ Please charge my Visa/Mastercard $_____.
  Card number_____ Exp. _____
❑ I intend to donate stock.
❑ Please send payment notices.
  ❑ Semi-annually
  ❑ Quarterly
  ❑ Or as follows:_____
❑ My gift will come through _____ Foundation by
  _____ (date)
❑ My company will match my gift
  ❑ Company _____
  ❑ Phone_____
❑ I would like my/our names listed as donors to WFSA as follows:
  _____
❑ I/We do not wish to have any public recognition regarding this gift.

Date:_____   Signature: _____

     Name (print): _____

DEVELOPMENT CALENDAR 2000–2001

July 2000	August 2000	September 2000	October 2000	November 2000	December 2000
Corporate Campaign Begins Tribute Book (TB) Campaign Begins	Corporate Campaign Ongoing Newsletter Published	Corporate Campaign Ongoing Official Face-to-Face (FTF) TB Campaign Ongoing Community Forum Invites Out 9/7 FTF/TB Campaign Kick-Off 9/15 Deadline for Program Ads	FTF/TB Campaign Finishing 10/24 Community Forum at Doubletree	Newsletter published	Winter Direct Mail Sent Volunteer Recognition Event and Campaign Celebration

January 2001	February 2001	March 2001	April 2001	May 2001	June 2001
Site-seeing Tours Luncheon Invitations Out 1/12 TB Deadline		Tribute Book Printed Newsletter Published	Newsletter Published Spring Direct Mail Sent April 12 Luncheon and TB Premiere	Public Grantee Evaluation Meeting (all donors invited)	

Development Activity	Goal	Jul-00	Aug-00	Sep-00	Oct-00	Nov-00	Dec-00	1-Jan	1-Feb	1-Mar	1-Apr	1-May	1-Jun
FTF Solicitation—Community	$ 46,320				$10,000	$10,000	$16,320				$5,000	$3,000	$2,000
FTF—Board	12,000				2,000	2,000	4,000				2,000	1,000	1,000
FTF—Advisory Council	60,370				8,000	10,000	20,000				20,000	1,370	1,000
Foundation Grant Seeking	79,200	50,000					29,200						
Luncheon (incl BD/AC)	73,700		2,700	4,000	4,000	5,000	6,000	6,000	6,000	15,000	22,000	2,000	1,000
Tribute Book (incl BD/AC)	58,000			3,000	3,000	10,000	10,000	8,000	20,000	4,000			
Community Forum	20,000		1,000	2,000	4,000	13,000							
Direct Mail	40,000						13,000	9,000	4,000		7,000	6,000	1,000
Total	$389,590	$50,000	$3,700	$9,000	$31,000	$50,000	$98,520	$23,000	$30,000	$19,000	$56,000	$14,370	$11,000

DONOR CONTACT GRID 2000–2001

	June 00	Jul 00	Aug 00	Sep 00	Oct 00	Nov 00	Dec 00
Major Donors ($1,000 +)	#'s Too Big To Ignore Save the Date Card	Thank you Postcard for D/P Challenge	Newsletter RFP	Comm Forum Invite FTF Visits	Comm Forum FTF Visits	Newsletter	
High Level Donors ($250–1,000)	#'s Too Big To Ignore Save the Date Card	Thank you Postcard for D/P Challenge	Newsletter RFP	Comm Forum Invite	Comm Forum	Newsletter	Direct Mail
Grass Roots Donors (under $250 or prospect)	#'s Too Big To Ignore Save the Date Card	Thank you Postcard for D/P Challenge	Newsletter RFP	Comm Forum Invite	Comm Forum	Newsletter	Direct Mail
Corporate Partners	#'s Too Big To Ignore Save the Date Card	Corporate Package	Newsletter	Comm Forum Invite	Comm Forum	Newsletter	

	Jan 01	Feb 01	Mar 01	Apr 01	May 01	Jun 01
Major Donors ($1,000 +)	RFP Site Tour Invites	Lunch Invitations Site Tours	Newsletter	Luncheon	Thank You Postcard Public Grantee Eval Mtg	RFP
High Level Donors ($250–1,000)	RFP Site Tour Invites	Lunch Invitations Site Tours	Newsletter	Luncheon Direct Mail	Thank You Postcard Public Grantee Eval Mtg	RFP
Grass Roots Donors (under $250 or prospect)	RFP Site Tour Invites	Lunch Invitations Site Tours	Newsletter	Luncheon Direct Mail	Thank You Postcard Public Grantee Eval Mtg	RFP
Corporate Partners	RFP Site Tour Invites	Lunch Invitations Site Tours	Newsletter	Luncheon	Thank You Postcard Public Grantee Eval Mtg	RFP

Women's Foundation of Southern Arizona

Gifts Needed To Meet Fundraising Goals in FY 2000–2001

Rank	# of Gifts	# Prospects/ Ratio	Prospects Needed	Current Prospects	Range of Gift	Total of Gifts	% of Total
A	25	3:1	75	8	$10,000–30,000	$150,000	50%
B	50	3:1	150	45	$1,000–9,999	$90,000	30%
C	425	5:1	2125	1400	$999 and under	$60,000	20%
					Total	$300,000	

Appendix 6–B

The Fund for Community Progress

Fund Development Plan for Fiscal Year 1999

Member agencies, Board members, staff, and volunteers are committed to The Fund's mission and vision, actively build relationships on behalf of The Fund, and carry out activities to achieve The Fund's mission and vision.

MISSION OF THE FUND FOR COMMUNITY PROGRESS

To build a better community by raising funds for nonprofit grassroots agencies committed to a vision of social change necessary to guarantee fairness and opportunity for all Rhode Islanders.

OUR VISION FOR THE FUND'S FUTURE (FROM THE STRATEGIC PLAN ADOPTED 01–99)

The Fund for Community Progress is passionate about equality and opportunity, and the way we work is reflective of the work we do. The Fund is recognized as promoting progressive, inclusive philanthropy in Rhode Island.

The Fund carries out its mission by:

- raising funds, primarily through workplace giving, and allocating charitable contributions to its member agencies;
- advocating for and encouraging philanthropy through workplace and direct solicitation and public relations activities;
- advocating for and encouraging the health and well-being of its member agencies by enhancing their capacity to carry out their own missions.

Courtesy of the Fund for Community Progress, Rhode Island, N.Y.

The Fund increases charitable contributions for its members by:

- building strong relationships between The Fund and the community;
- steadily gaining access to diverse Rhode Island workplaces and presenting the case for support in a clear and personal way to employees;
- identifying, cultivating, and soliciting other prospects through direct solicitation; and,
- enhancing the capacity of member agencies as effective not-for-profit philanthropic organizations.

Member agencies are committed to a vision of social change that guarantees fairness and opportunity for all Rhode Islanders. The Fund's members are carefully recruited and nurtured to be active participants in the work of The Fund.

The Fund operates effectively and efficiently, demonstrating models of creativity, leadership, and collaboration. The Fund recruits and nurtures Board members and other volunteers who represent the richness of the Rhode Island community, including representatives from member agencies and diverse individuals committed to The Fund's vision and mission. The Fund recruits and retains sufficient professional and support staff to provide leadership, enabling and implementation to work in partnership with Board, member agencies, and other volunteers to achieve The Fund's mission and vision.

ASSUMPTIONS UPON WHICH THIS FUND DEVELOPMENT PLAN IS BASED

This Fund Development Plan can be successful only if The Fund for Community Progress effectively pursues the vision and direction articulated in its strategic plan.

Specifically, this Fund Development Plan is based on the following assumptions:

- The Board of Directors, Fund Development Team, and Executive Director provide leadership to the fund development process.
- Increased professional staffing ensures adequate leadership, management, support, and enabling for fund development.
- Membership in The Fund is expected to add value to the member agency *and* add value to The Fund itself. Each member agency is expected to commit to and behave in accordance with clearly articulated guidelines and expectations.
  - It is the responsibility of the Executive Director and Board President of each member agency to ensure that the member agency carries out its responsibilities. The Fund staff, board, and teams/committees are a resource to assist member agencies. The Fund provides ongoing feedback to member agencies regarding their participation and performance.
  - According to the strategic plan, member agencies are expected to:
    1. Pledge to actively participate in The Fund for Community Progress. (Both Board members and staff must so pledge when they are recruited to work for the member agency.)
    2. Regularly evaluate their own service quality and effectiveness of their infrastructure (e.g., governance, management, fund development) and take steps to enhance service and infrastructure.
    3. Think and behave strategically so that all community activity and involvement reinforces the mission, vision, and activities of The Fund.
    4. Proactively engage in marketing (and counter demarketing) of The Fund.
    5. Remain in regular contact with The Fund and alert The Fund to actions and activities that affect the community and might affect The Fund.
    6. Adhere to the articulated member agency rights and responsibilities, including participation in strengthening The Fund for Community Progress and participation in fund development.
    7. Regularly identify and cultivate relationships to better support the member agency itself and The Fund for Community Progress.
    8. Participate in the fund development activities of The Fund.
- Member agencies build strong community relationships to support marketing and fund development, including workplace access and direct solicitation.
- Member agencies are expected to enhance their own fund development in order to help the FCP.
- The FCP and its member agencies support and adhere to the *Donor Bill of Rights* and the *Association of Fundraising Professionals Code of Ethical Principles and Standards of Professional Practice*.
- Allocations to member agencies are based on effort *and* results.

KEY GOALS AND ACTIVITIES FOR THIS PLAN

General Management, Strategic Discussion, and Decision Making

1. To ensure a consistently professional and personalized fund development program, coordinate all fund development efforts through the FCP office. (*Executive Director and staff*)
2. Identify, recruit, and train qualified individuals from member agencies, the FCP Board of Directors, and other community people to carry out specific tasks. Ensure an equitable distribution of these tasks among all member agencies. (*Executive Director and Fund Development Team*)
   - Provide appropriate coordination, leadership, enabling, and support.
   - Measure volunteer satisfaction through conversation, surveys, focus groups. Make changes as necessary for the next Fund Development Plan or activity.
3. Improve communications regarding fund development to Fund Development Team, Board, and member agencies in order to enhance awareness, understanding, and decision making. (*Executive Director*)
   - Improve flow of information, progress updates, and examples of solicitation and support materials.
   - Improve strategic reporting of efforts and results, effectiveness, and productivity. For example:
     - Track and analyze participation rates, including overall response, acquisition, retention, and attrition.
     - Track and analyze gift increases and decreases.
     - Track cost to raise a dollar by solicitation strategy and cumulatively.
     - Evaluate volunteer satisfaction and performance in fund development.
   - Facilitate strategic discussion and decision making.

Member Agencies

1. With the Member Relations Team, develop services that help member agencies to enhance their own fund development capacity.
   - Ensure that all member agencies are on the AFP RI Chapter mailing list for announcements of monthly training programs and annual fundraising conference (now the Association of Fundraising Professionals). (*Executive Director*)
   - Ensure that all member agencies are on the mailing list of Nonprofit Resources for announcements about training and other opportunities. (*Executive Director*)
   - Provide scholarship dollars to attend fund development training.
   - Host at least one workshop annually—for FCP members only—on fund development. (*Fund Development Team/Member Relations Team*)
   - Provide resource materials regarding fund development to member agencies at least twice per year. (*Executive Director*)
2. Improve communications with member agencies regarding fund development. See #3, above. (*Executive Director*)
3. Provide information about marketing and communications to help member agencies. See #5, Telling our story better, on subsequent pages of this plan. (*Executive Director*)
4. Encourage member agencies to create meaningful alliances for creating community solutions and opportunities. (*Executive Director, Board of Directors, Fund Development Team*)
   - Provide information about available funding opportunities.
   - Convene member agencies to discuss alliances.
   - As appropriate, help devise funding proposals.

Building Relationships

1. Institute a comprehensive relationship building program in order to: retain current donors and encourage them to give more; prepare prospects for the ask; and identify and recruit fundraising volunteers.
   - Identify five major gift prospects (who are currently donors) and devise strategies personalized to those prospects in order to increase their gifts dramatically. (*Fund Development Team*)
   - Use annual "Roast" as a cultivation activity with FCP representatives assigned as hosts and cultivators to targeted prospects. (*Roast Committee*)
   - Distribute quarterly Chair's Letter as update to communicate with all donors of $250 + (giving through workplace and other means), and to targeted prospects. (*Executive Director*)
   - Get to know our donors and prospects better. What are their interests, disinterests, and aspirations? How can the FCP help them to meet their aspirations?
     - FCP Board members and staff and volunteers from member agencies do this informally and provide the information to the FCP.
     - FCP does this at events and other occasions with donors and prospects.
     - Conduct a written survey in 1999, directed at all donors, both workplace and other. (*Fund Development Team and Executive Director*)
   - Design recognition program for donors. (*Fund Development Team for Board approval in March 1999.*)
   - Have volunteers call and thank selected donors personally.
2. Conduct annual Roast/Workplace Kick-Off in September. (*Roast Committee*)
   - Purpose: Cultivate and produce net profit of $10,000. (Gross income = $20,000 and expenses = $10,000.)
   - Target audience: Invitees of individual being roasted; FCP member agencies; FCP donors and prospects.
   - Concept: Recognize someone who has helped the community.
   - Secure sponsor(s) to cover expenses.
   - Make sure cultivation tasks are assigned and carried out by FCP board members and member agency Board members.
3. Introduce new Awards Event. (*Awards Committee, April or May 1999*)
   - Purpose: Recognize corporations that have both FCP and United Way campaigns. Also recognize major donors and volunteers to the FCP. Break even.
   - Target audience: All FCP workplaces; workplaces where FCP is trying to gain access; targeted prospects; community leaders; and leadership individuals and foundation donors to the FCP.
   - Secure a corporate sponsor.
   - Recruit corporate Planning/Sales Committee.
   - Executive Director drafts concept paper and pursues corporate sponsorship. (*Board to discuss at March meeting.*)
   - Have an important guest speaker to encourage corporate attendance.

- Make sure cultivation tasks are assigned and carried out by FCP Board members and member agency Board members.
4. Participate in National Philanthropy Day. (*Fund Development Team, November 1999*)
   - FCP recognizes one person at the event. Leaders from the FCP attend to be seen and to cultivate.
   - FCP encourages each member agency to recognize one person and to attend National Philanthropy Day celebration.
   - FCP and member agencies attend, sit together until conclusion of the event at the FCP, and cultivate relationships.

Telling Our Story Better

1. Devise, implement, and evaluate a marketing program (*Executive Director*), whose goals are to:
   - Demonstrate the impact of gifts to the FCP through measurable outcomes and results told through personal interest stories.
   - Enhance the visibility of the FCP—within targeted predisposed markets—particularly during the fall workplace solicitation period.
   - Increase charitable giving to the FCP.
2. Ensure that the printed solicitation materials, both for workplace and other solicitations, clearly tell the story of the FCP. (*Executive Director*)
3. Seek regular articles in the *Providence Journal* and *Providence Business News*. Aim for four articles in 1999, between the two publications. (*Executive Director*)
4. Require that member agencies support telling the story (*Member Relations Team*) by:
   - Providing quality, inclusive services with demonstrable results.
     - Regularly secure data and personal interest stories from member agencies to use in telling the FCP story.
   - Recognizing the FCP, in accordance with clearly articulated guidelines, in appropriate printed materials, on letterhead, in articles.
5. Develop and provide to member agencies a resource manual about marketing and communications, including: how to get your story in the newspaper; how to write better letters and brochures; examples of press releases, media fact sheets, and letters requesting coverage; how to recognize the FCP in member agency materials; and so forth. (*Executive Director*)

Workplace Solicitation (Workplace Committee)

1. Standardize workplace management, materials, and presentations into a consistent, professional, user-friendly program.

- Make donor materials easy to use. Measure user satisfaction.
  - Review and ensure ease of use of pledge forms and other materials, particularly in comparison to the United Way materials.
  - Conduct focus groups or interviews with donors regarding use of materials.
- Make management of workplace solicitation easy for corporations, particularly in comparison with United Way. Measure user satisfaction by interviewing corporate campaign managers.
- Enhance workplace presentations by identifying and developing a corps of qualified and experienced presenters to carry out these assignments. (*September–December 1999*)
- Increase cultivation activities at workplaces through personal contacts, articles for in-house newsletters, and so forth.
2. Ensure sufficient workplace access to increase number of donors and promote inclusive philanthropy. (*Fund Development Team*)
   - Retain all (100 percent) of current workplaces for solicitation.
   - Approach 10 new workplaces through a professional, personal approach and gain access to at least five for campaign 1999. (*January–June 1999*)
     - Target high potential markets with a minimum of 25 employees, e.g., not-for-profit human service agencies; municipalities; independent schools; colleges and universities; and entrepreneurial companies.
     - Recruit qualified access contact to solicit each worksite.
3. Cultivate relationships with workplace donors ($250+) through quarterly Chair's Letter and invitation to roast and other activities, as appropriate. (*Executive Director*)
4. Send advance announcement letter to all workplace givers just before start of workplace solicitation. (*Executive Director*)
5. Retain at least 50 percent of 1998 workplace donors in 1999. As expected for workplace solicitation, this is a lower retention rate than more direct fund development.

Personal Solicitation (Fund Development Team)

1. Design and launch an annual personal solicitation campaign targeted at key donors and prospects.
   - Review donors of $500 and above, and select those who should be personally solicited. Identify additional prospects who are ready to be asked for a gift of $750 or more.

- Identify and recruit solicitors.
- Match the right solicitor with the right prospect and determine the appropriate gift request amount.
- Conduct a solicitor training in early March. Solicit gifts in March and April 1999. Secure pledges for payment by December 1, 1999.
- In 1999, solicit at least 30 prospects personally, with at least 6 volunteer solicitors. Increase gift from at least 20 percent of these prospects, 5 percent more than the industry standard of 15 percent.

2. Monitor progress, evaluate performance, and expand for FY 2000.

Direct Mail (Executive Director)

1. Expand current direct mail program by:
   - expanding number of recipients of the letter
     –identifying all current donors who should be solicited through mail;
     –identifying prospects (referrals from member agencies, FCP Board members and volunteers, other FCP friends; and through list brokering).
   - soliciting three times per year, as outlined below.
2. Solicit three times per year from the same prospect base.
   - Mail first letter to all prospects in February 1999, including those who gave and did not give to the December 1998 solicitation. Select one theme or story. Do *not* refer to "annual fund" or "annual operations."
   - Mail second letter in mid-November to all those who gave and to those who did not give to December 1998 and February 1999 letters. Select a different theme. For those who gave before, acknowledge their gift, then move into the second solicitation.
   - Mail the second letter again, to all non-respondents, in the middle of December.
3. Strengthen the solicitation letters by doing the following:
   - Personalize.
   - Request consideration of a specific amount (always more than the prior year).
   - Ask someone who knows the prospect to add a personal postscript and, as possible, to actually sign the letter.

Proposal Development (Executive Director)

1. Staff will devise and submit proposals to support the strategic plan and budget of The Fund for Community Progress.

2. Possible themes
   - Technical assistance and training for member agencies: scholarship dollars, and designing and developing FCP-specific workshops.
   - Positioning the FCP through communications and media coverage.
   - Supporting strategic plan/operations of the FCP.
   - Granting dollars for allocation to FCP members.

MONITORING PROGRESS OF THIS PLAN AND EVALUATING PERFORMANCE

Together, the Board of Directors and the Executive Director of The Fund are responsible for changing The Fund into its desired vision of the future. This plan serves as the blueprint for staff, Board, and the Fund Development Team.

We will carefully monitor progress and evaluate performance, compared with the goals and activities outlined in this plan. At the conclusion of each fund development activity, the staff and team will evaluate effectiveness and productivity, analyze trends and implications, and consider any recommendations for the future. The Fund Development Team will then facilitate a strategic discussion with the Board of Directors and engage the Board in decision making.

The Fund Development Team will meet at least six times per year to discuss progress, review reports and analysis of effectiveness and productivity, and identify next steps. At each of its meetings, the Fund Development Team will consider the following:

- Progress on the Fund Development Plan: trends, implications, interventions
- Involvement of the Board of Directors and individual Board members
- Involvement of member agencies

The Executive Director will maintain ongoing communications with member agencies and the Board of Directors regarding fund development.

The Fund Development Plan is an outgrowth of the multiyear strategic plan and the annual goal-setting (November) and budgeting (December) process. The proposed budget is tested by the Fund Development Team to determine whether charitable contribution goals are realistic. The budget and detailed Fund Development Plan are reviewed, discussed, and adopted together, at the January Board meeting.

Summary of Financial Goals

1. Raise $289,165 in charitable contributions, a decrease from both fiscal year 1997 and fiscal year

1998, due to the following: elimination of Shona Event; change in foundation grants.
- Retain FY 98 level through workplace.
- Produce two events: Roast that produces $10,000 net; new awards event that breaks even but positions The Fund.
- Increase direct mail from $6,970 in FY 98 to $10,000 in FY 99.
- Increase contributions from individuals personally solicited from $2,855 to $5,000.
2. Retain 100 percent of 1998 workplaces and acquire five new workplaces.
3. Increase the cumulative number of donors to the FCP from 1,105 (1998) to 1,300.
4. Increase the overall average gift size from $100 to $125.

5. Secure gift increases from at least 20 percent of those who are personally solicited and from at least 15 percent of all donors.
6. Involve at least six volunteers in personal solicitation.

See attachments that support this plan

- *Donor Bill of Rights, NSFRE Code of Ethical Principles and Standards of Professional Practice*
- FCP budget and comparisons with actual results and FY 1998 gift table
- List of workplace sites and participation
- Reasonable cost guidelines

CALENDAR

Month	Activity
January 1999	Member agency meeting to update on: • Progress of strategic plan and annual goals and direction for year. • Calendar of trainings for the year. • Report on prior year's fund development and presentation of new year's plan. • Quarterly Chair's Letter to donors (of $250+) and prospects (copy to member agencies). Drop just before direct mail #1.
January–December	Access workplaces.
February	Direct mail #1.
March–April	Personal solicitation campaign.
March	Quarterly Chair's Letter (drop just before personal solicitation begins). Board approves Fund Development Plan and new awards event concept.
May	Awards Event. Board approves donor recognition program.
June–July	Prepare for workplace solicitation.
June	Quarterly Chair's Letter.
September	Advance letter to donors in workplaces.
September	Roast and Workplace Solicitation Kick-Off.
September–December	Workplace solicitation.
October	Quarterly Chair's Letter.
November	Early November: Board annual planning retreat. Adopt annual goals. By mid-November: Direct Mail #2. National Philanthropy Day Celebration.
January 2000	Adopt budget and fund development plan.

Appendix 6-C

Tockwotton Home

Two-Year Fund Development Plan

January 1, 2000–December 31, 2001

This is the institution's plan and was adopted by the Board in April 2000. The Board and its members are accountable for implementation and results.

TABLE OF CONTENTS

THE CONTEXT FOR FUND DEVELOPMENT AT TOCKWOTTON

Our fund development program is based on the values, mission, and vision of Tockwotton Home. Specifically:

Courtesy of Tockwotton Home, Providence, Rhode Island.

Mission and Vision of Tockwotton Home

Tockwotton Home is dedicated to helping older adults and their families meet the challenges of their changing lives. Our goal is to enable older adults to live their lives with a sense of fulfillment in warm and comfortable surroundings. We achieve this goal through a variety of services, including nursing home care, assisted living residence, and home and community services. Toward that end, we collaborate with others who share our vision.

We strive to foster the personal growth and development of all those who are associated with the Home. We serve a broad spectrum of the community, including those whose financial resources are limited.

We continually seek to expand our capacity to create a better future for those we serve. We commit ourselves to continuous improvement in quality.

Values of Tockwotton: Nourish the Seeds of Independence

- Service: Serve each individual with compassion.
- Excellence: Value every task—each deserves our best.
- Empowerment: Offer the potential for fulfillment to each individual who journeys with us.
- Dignity: Seek and honor the worth of every human being.
- Stewardship: Manage wisely the time, talent, and treasure entrusted to us.

Mission and Vision of Philanthropy and Fund Development at Tockwotton

As a not-for-profit organization, Tockwotton Home depends on philanthropy—voluntary action for the common good—to achieve its mission and vision. Gifts of time and money are vital to provide our extended services.

We continually seek to enhance our philanthropy and fund development program, recognizing that the catalyst of philanthropy is asking through the fund development process. Our board and staff value the culture of philanthropy and strive for quality in this special area of operations.

Operating Principles for Fund Development at Tockwotton Home

Fund development is a growing profession throughout the world. As a profession, fund development relies on a documented body of knowledge and best practice.

Moreover, qualified fund development programs and professionals assert a code of ethics and standards to protect the public.

Tockwotton Home subscribes to the *Donor Bill of Rights* and the *National Society of Fund Raising Executives Code of Ethics and Standards of Professional Practice* (now the Association of Fundraising Professionals, AFP). Tockwotton operates its development program in accordance with these two documents.

Integration of the Fund Development Plan with Tockwotton Home Plans

The fund development plan supports Tockwotton's strategic plan and annual goals. The fund development plan is carefully integrated with marketing and communications plans, and board recruitment and enhancement plans.

Fund development goals and solicitation themes (e.g., what we're raising the dollars for) are decided by the board during the annual budgeting process.

See Resources, Roles in fund development.

PHILANTHROPY AND FUND DEVELOPMENT GOALS, FY 2000 AND FY 2001

1. Develop a culture of philanthropy within Tockwotton Home and its key constituencies, including board members (current and previous), staff, volunteers, residents, and their families.
2. Strengthen operations of the philanthropy and fund development program.
3. Carry out an ongoing constituency development program to support philanthropy and fund development.
4. Increase charitable giving from targeted audiences.
5. Launch a planned giving program.
6. Based on board action, design and launch a capital campaign.

7. Determine the appropriate resources to support fund development and marketing/public relations at Tockwotton. See the Resources for Roles and the notes about development resources at Tockwotton.

Strategies To Achieve the Goals

General Strategies

1. Learn best practice, diversify skills, and foster the culture of philanthropy.
   * Participate in the fund development consultation with Joyaux Associates. (1999 and 2000)
   * Join the Association of Fundraising Professionals, Rhode Island Chapter, and attend monthly programs and annual conference. (2000 and thereafter)
   * Provide periodic training sessions for volunteers through local conferences and meetings, and special sessions at Tockwotton. (1999 and thereafter)
2. Strengthen the board recruitment and development program—based on recommendations and resources provided by Joyaux—to enhance the board and board member participation in fund development. (responsibility of the Nominating Committee)
   * Clarify role and expectations of the board, and the individual as a board member. (completed in 1999)
   * Expand the process for identifying and cultivating candidates for board and committee membership. (2000)
   * Develop a board member assessment process and conduct annually.
   * Institute a governance assessment process. Conduct biannually; develop plan for improvement. (2001)
   * Revise the board orientation and training program. (2000)
   * Launch a plan for succession within officers and committee chairs, and continuity within committees. (in process)
3. Devote a portion of each board meeting to report on and discuss philanthropy and fund development, an essential part of due diligence and governance. (1999 and thereafter)

To strengthen operations of the philanthropy and fund development program

1. Make good decisions based on quality information.

- Enhance data collection for donor and prospect histories, cultivation, and participation rates. (2000 and thereafter)
- Provide enhanced information (e.g., analysis of trends and implications) for decision making by developing the appropriate reports about fundraising productivity and performance. (2000 and thereafter)

To *carry out an ongoing constituency development program*

1. Design and launch a program that includes targeting audiences, getting to know their interests, communicating, and cultivating. (Detailed in this plan. Expand in 2001.)
   - Devise activities that can be carried out by the organization itself.
   - Devise personalized plans for targeted individuals, to be carried out by volunteers and development staff.

To *increase charitable giving from targeted audiences*

1. Carry out the constituency development program. (2000 and thereafter)
2. Increase the average gift size by: (2000 and thereafter)
   - asking all prospects—whether in writing or personally—to consider a specific amount and ask for an increase each year; and
   - increasing the number of solicitation mailings per year and merge/purge the mailing list, as appropriate.
3. Improve solicitation strategies by: (2000 and thereafter)
   - carrying out face-to-face solicitation with an increased number of prospects each year;
   - recruiting additional face-to-face solicitors, both board and non-board members; and
   - providing training in face-to-face solicitation.
   - strengthening direct mail solicitation through improved letters, specific themes, and an improved response mechanism.
   - encouraging people to give memorial gifts.
4. Increase the number of donors by identifying those who may be predisposed to the cause, cultivating the relationship, and asking them to give. (2000 and thereafter)

To *launch a planned giving program*

1. Devise a plan in 2001, for launch as determined, based on available resources and enhanced capacity of the organization.

Preliminary Benchmarks To Measure Success

Benchmarks will be established annually, when the fund development plan is revised during the annual budgeting process.

1. Improved fundraising reports support quality decision making. (Immediate and ongoing)
2. Stronger board through activities of the Nominating Committee.
   a) Board member assessment launched in 2001.
   b) Revised orientation program in summer 2000.
   c) Succession and continuity plans in place by third quarter 2000.
   d) Governance self-assessment conducted no later than first quarter 2001, with plan to address issues launched by second quarter 2001.
   e) Each board member:
      - makes at least one fundraising solicitation.
      - participates in cultivation of donors and prospects.
      - identifies and cultivates at least two predisposed and gets them ready to be asked
3. Constituency development activities carried out, as noted in calendar.
4. Participation rates in giving.
   a) 100 percent giving from all board and committee members
   b) Increase from 58.6 percent to 65 percent of employees giving
   c) Increase from 28.9 percent to 40 percent of vendors giving
   d) Increase from 21.6 percent to 30 percent of families/friends of residents giving
   e) Return average gift size to 1998 level of $150 from 1999 level of $133
   f) Retain 60 percent of all donors from 1999, compared with 50.7 percent in the prior year.
   g) Acquire 100 new donors (individuals, businesses, etc.), compared with 86 in 1999.
   h) 25 percent of small donors give to both solicitation letters
8. Face-to-face solicitation
   - Solicit board members + an additional 10 prospects in 2000.
   - Solicit board members + an additional 25 prospects in 2001.

Monitoring Progress and Evaluating Performance

Staff, Fund Development Committee, and the board share the responsibility for monitoring progress and evaluating performance in fund development.

1. Staff prepares appropriate reports at the end of each fund development activity, including constituency development. Reports include prospect and

donor participation rates, volunteer performance, and analysis of trends and implications.

2. Fund Development Committee reviews reports and discusses implications, and recommends improvements and next steps.

3. Fund Development Committee designs strategic discussion with the board after each activity to determine the following: effectiveness of the activity; worthiness of repeating this fiscal year or the next (e.g., add to next year's fund development plan); strengths and weaknesses of board participation; and next steps.

4. Staff and Fund Development Committee monitor dollars raised, compared with goals/benchmarks, and devise interventions as necessary, to ensure achievement of goals and benchmarks.

5. Staff and Fund Development Committee devise activities and review performance compared with standards in the profession, Tockwotton performance, and the operating principles accepted by Tockwotton.

The fund development plan is formally evaluated annually, revised for the new fiscal year, and approved by the board. The Fund Development Committee and staff establish benchmarks annually. Each board member helps carry out fund development activities.

The fund development plan is adopted by the board simultaneously with budget adoption each year. The plan is adopted with board member names assigned to specific activities.

Target Audiences

Target audiences for the year 2000 are:

1. Current donors
2. Former board members
3. Committee members who are not board members
4. Families and friends of residents who are not donors
5. Employees of Tockwotton Home
6. Vendors
7. Individuals, businesses, foundations, and civic groups that have been qualified as prospects for giving.
8. Individuals, businesses, foundations, and civic groups that have been identified as predisposed to the cause, but it is as yet unclear whether they are qualified prospects.

All of these audiences will be targeted in the constituency development program described below.

Audiences #1–7 will be solicited during the year. Audience #8 will be solicited only if it is determined that they have moved from predisposed to prospect.

For the purposes of solicitation and cultivation, Tockwotton segments its donors and prospects as follows:

• Smaller givers, both donors and prospects: Less than $100. Typically solicited through the mail and by mail.
• Major givers, both donors and prospects: $100 +. All solicited face-to-face eventually.

Constituency Development Program

Constituency development is the process of: getting to know an organization's constituents; understanding their interests, disinterests, aspirations, and motivations; cultivating a relationship; and getting them ready to be asked for a contribution. Constituency development also includes the process of donor acknowledgment (the thank-you letter) and recognition (public recognition of gifts).

In 2000, **to get to know prospects and donors,** Tockwotton will:

• Conduct customer satisfaction research that asks questions about services and philanthropy. (Activities survey by mid-2000 and an overall customer satisfaction survey in 2001.) Customer satisfaction research will then be integrated into Tockwotton operations on a biennial basis.
• Engage the Residents Council in talking about interests.
• Regularly call donors to thank them for their gifts and ask about their interests.
• Schmooze at gatherings.
• In 2001, Tockwotton will continue all these getting-to-know activities and add in focus group discussions.

In 2000, to cultivate relationships, Tockwotton will:

• Launch a *Family Ambassadors Program* to help get to know prospects and donors, to help plan and execute fundraising and cultivation activities, and to promote customer satisfaction.
  –Recruit at least 15 family ambassadors from residents and their family members, former board members, and other Tockwotton friends.
  –Job description for the Family Ambassadors
      Reach out to families on behalf of residents.
      Help plan limited resident activities.
      Plan the Tockwotton Gathering.

Assist with marketing, e.g., Speakers Bureau, etc.

Participate in customer satisfaction process, e.g., identifying some of the questions, making follow-up telephone calls, etc.

Help plan fundraising activities, sign solicitation letters, identify prospects, and cultivate relationships.

- Launch the *Tockwotton Gathering*, an opportunity to mingle and share vital information.
  - –Audience: Invited guests (selected by board members and staff) we wish to cultivate; residents and families, and two invitations to each resident.
  - –RSVP required because seating is limited.
  - –Mingling with refreshments and entertainment (and schmoozing by board members!).
  - –Tockwotton sharing vital information about activities, developments, etc.
  - –Q & A opportunity for guests.
  - –Possibly guest speaker, tours.
- Send personal *acknowledgment letters* within 48 hours of receipt of a financial contribution or a single volunteer activity. For regular volunteers, send an annual thank-you letter.
- Recognize gifts according to the new *Recognition Program* devised by the end of the second quarter 2000.
- Annual *holiday celebration* (Hanukkah, New Year's, Christmas, Kwanza) instead of the current bazaar. (Responsibility of activities staff, not development staff or committee.)
  - –Audience: Invited guests, community neighbors, donors, etc.
- Each board member will get to know and cultivate a relationship with at least two predisposed to determine whether they are prospects, then move them into asking.
- In 2001, Tockwotton will continue all these cultivation activities and Tockwotton will: increase the number of Tockwotton Gatherings; incorporate personal cultivation plans for selected individuals or businesses; and launch breakfast cultivation meetings.

In 2000, to communicate, Tockwotton will:

- Consider discontinuing the newsletter and launching a "newsy" letter, which will be distributed at least three times in 2000 and at least four times in 2001.
- Introduce an annual report that includes financial reports for the fiscal year, summarizes numbers served, recognizes major donors, highlights services,

and positions the organization for philanthropy and fund development.

- Prepare fundraising materials to support face-to-face solicitation, gift transmittal, and philanthropic inquiries.

Solicitation Strategies

Face-to-Face Solicitation

Face-to-face solicitation is the most effective and least expensive solicitation strategy. Tockwotton will focus on this strategy to build it over the next several years.

In 2000, we will solicit board members + 10 additional prospects face to face. We will need approximately seven solicitors to do this work. In 2001, we will solicit board members + 25 additional prospects face to face. For that, we will need approximately 10 solicitors. We will recruit board members and other Tockwotton friends to serve as solicitors.

Our goal is to move our face-to-face campaign up to January–March in 2001. In 2000, we will solicit face to face in the spring, with pledge payments due by December 31.

Direct Mail

We will increase our direct mail letters to two in 2000 and perhaps three in 2001. These letters will focus on particular themes, e.g., year-end tax benefits of giving, financing activities for residents, and so forth.

We will develop a stronger response mechanism to direct mail. Board members will write personal notes for those they know. In 2001, we will begin annual telephone follow-up for one of the direct mail solicitation letters.

Fundraising Event

In 2001, Tockwotton will launch an annual special event to raise money. This event will be developed and planned in 2000. The event will be designed to generate a net profit, secure business sponsorships to cover expenses, and provide another cultivation opportunity for donors and prospects.

In keeping with industry standards, the event should net at least 50 percent of gross. This is intended as a major event and, to justify the time that will be required, the event should net at least $5,000 in year one, with substantive growth thereafter. Within three years, the event should be netting at least $12,000.

Foundation Research and Proposal Development

Staff are responsible for identifying and researching foundations and developing proposals. Staff will review foundation prospects with board to determine whether anyone has contacts.

Memorial Gifts

Tockwotton will develop a plan to foster memorial giving.

Timetable

Time Frame	Activity	Entity Responsible
March 2000	Publish newsletter.	Staff
April 2000	Adopt FY 2000 fund development plan and Recognition Program.	Board
April 2000	Drop direct mail solicitation letter (#1).	Staff with board members signing
May 2000	Outline Philanthropic Recognition Program (includes donors of money and volunteers).	Fund Development Committee
May 2000	Produce annual report.	Staff
May 2000	Tockwotton Gathering.	Fund Development Committee
Summer 2000	Design and launch Family Ambassadors Program.	Task force from Fund Development + some non-board members
Summer 2000	Convene Fundraising Task Force. Decide event, sales plan, and budget.	Selected individuals; some from Fund Development Committee, board, non-board members
August 2000	Publish newsletter or newsy letter.	Staff
August 2000	Prepare year-end direct mail solicitation letter (#2).	Staff with board members signing
Fall 2000	Solicit board and major gift prospects face to face for FY 2000. Pledges to be paid by 12-31-00.	Solicitors
Fall 2000	Solicit Tockwotton employees through United Way campaign.	Staff
Fall 2000	Prepare resource materials for face-to-face solicitation campaign.	Staff
Fall 2000	Convene task force to plan and carry out Holiday Celebration.	Holiday Celebration Task Force comprised of Family Ambassadors and 1-2 Development Committee members
Fall 2000	Approve 2001 Special Event Plan.	Board
Fall 2000	Finalize fund development plan for 2001, integrated with budget. Recruit board members for activities.	Staff, Fund Development Committee
September 2000	Tockwotton Gathering.	Fund Development Committee
September 2000	Newsy letter.	Staff
October 2000	Drop direct mail solicitation letter #2.	Staff
November–December 2000	Approve FY 2001 budget and fund development plan.	Board
December 2000	Holiday Celebration.	Holiday Celebration Task Force
Early January 2001	Kick-off and orientation for face-to-face campaign.	Fund Development Committee, all board members for training purposes, solicitors
January 2001	Newsy letter.	Staff
January–March 2001	Face-to-face solicitation.	Solicitors
February 2001	Prepare April direct mail solicitation letter #1.	Staff with board members signing

Time Frame	Activity	Entity Responsible
January–February	Recruit special event sponsors.	Fundraising Event Task Force
March 2001	Publish annual report.	Staff
March 2001	Print event materials. Drop invitation approximately six weeks in advance.	Staff, Special Event Task Force
April 2001	Drop direct mail solicitation letter #2.	Staff
April 2001	Sell tickets to fundraising event.	Staff
April–June 2001	Recruit new committee members for Fund Development Committee.	Committee, chair, Board President, staff
May 2001	Newsy letter.	Staff
May 2001	Special event (fundraising event).	Fundraising Event Task Force
June 2001	Solicit board for their gift for FY 2001, thereby shifting the calendar for the year.	Development Committee
Summer 2001	Prepare for fall activities.	Staff, Fund Development Committee
Fall 2001	Solicit Tockwotton employees as part of United Way campaign.	Staff
2001	Design planned giving program for launch in 2002.	Consultant and Fund Development Committee
September 2001	Newsy letter.	Staff
September 2001	Tockwotton Gathering.	Fund Development Committee
October 2001	Drop year-end direct mail solicitation (#2).	Staff with board members signing
November 2001	Telephone follow-up to year-end direct mail solicitation.	Board members and other volunteers
November 2001	Finalize FY 2001 development plan.	Fund Development Committee and staff
December 2001	Adopt FY 2001 budget and fund development plan.	Board

RESOURCES

Roles in Fund Development

Role of the Board

- Review results; discuss progress, trends, and implications.
- Identify and discuss internal strengths and weaknesses and external opportunities and threats.
- Endorse goals and directions throughout the year (while implementing current plan) to include in subsequent year's plan.
- Adopt plan (with board member names in it for specific activities) when budget is adopted.

Role of the Individual Board Member

- Commit to and carry out specific activities in the fund development plan—and be accountable for what you said you would do.
- Identify and cultivate the predisposed.
- Cultivate donors and real prospects. Help solicit as appropriate.
- Watch what is happening at your organization and in the community. Share your observations, ask questions, and help the organization wrestle with issues and make good decisions.
- Give your own personal gift at the start of each year's fund development.

Role of the Development Committee

- Institutionalize the process of fund development within the full board.
- Review results; discuss progress, trends, and implications.
- Identify strategic issues for board discussion and action. Facilitate board discussion and decision making.

- Identify and discuss internal strengths and weaknesses and external opportunities and threats.
- As appropriate, recommend action for board adoption. Or present well-thought-out alternatives for board discussion and action.
- Propose goals and directions throughout the year (while implementing current plan) to include in subsequent year's plan.
- Through the fund development planning process, test proposed goals, adjust, and refer to Finance Committee.
- Review staff-drafted plan. Discuss and adjust. Recruit every board member to participate in the plan in some way.
- Recommend the plan to the board for adoption.

Role of the Staff (See Joyaux handout on components of fund development, as well as job description of chief development officer.) In summary:

1. Lead and enable the volunteers. (See Joyaux book for description of enabling.)
2. Be familiar with and understand the body of knowledge and best practice in fund development. Educate and guide the board accordingly.
3. Manage and coordinate all activities. So is there enough staff to do this?
4. Maintain gift management systems, acknowledgment, and recognition programs.
5. Develop progress reports and analyze trends and implications.

6. Draft materials and provide resources, including solicitation materials, direct mail letters, proposals, etc.
7. Review results; discuss progress, trends, and implications.
8. Identify strategic issues for board discussion and action. Facilitate board discussion and decision-making.
9. Identify and discuss internal strengths and weaknesses and external opportunities and threats.
10. As appropriate, recommend action for board adoption. Or present well-thought-out alternatives for board discussion and action.
11. Propose goals and directions throughout the year (while implementing current plan) to include in subsequent year's plan.
12. Through the fund development planning process, test proposed goals, adjust, and refer to Finance Committee.
13. Draft plans for review by appropriate individuals and groups.

At Tockwotton, the development officer is also in charge of marketing and public relations. Although it is not uncommon to group these functions together, one individual cannot handle both without support staff. Indeed, a development office should have one professional and at least one or two administrative/clerical support persons just to do development work.

The other resources stipulated in this plan are *not* included here because they are included elsewhere in this book.

Appendix 6–D

Children's Aid and Family Services Development Plan for Endowment and Annual Support

January 1997–December 1998

Our emphasis is on the relationship between the constituent and Children's Aid and Family Service. We believe that donors are more important than gifts.

We will try our best to genuinely find out what people value and how we can create together a sharing of values between people and CAFS.

> "Finding needs and filling them . . . produces positive value for both parties. The contrast between marketing and selling is whether you start with customers, or consumers, or groups you want to serve well—that's marketing. If you start with a set of products you have, and want to push them out into any market you can find, that's selling."
>
> (Peter F. Drucker, *Managing the Nonprofit Organization*)

INTRODUCTION

The primary reason anyone gives is because they are asked. An individual might be asked to give money or to serve on the board. A business might be asked to print an annual report or give a grant. No matter. The primary reason anyone gives is because they are asked.

So Children's Aid and Family Services (CAFS) is in the business of asking. That is part of the culture of philanthropy. The better we ask, the more likely we will get "yes" as an answer. In order to get a "yes" answer, we need to have the right person ask the right prospect for the right thing for the right amount at the right time.

To create this "best request," we need to know what the prospect is interested in and how we can create an exchange of value between CAFS and the prospect.

_____

Courtesy of Children's Aid and Family Services, Paramus, New Jersey.

This is the fundamental concept of marketing. A mutually beneficial exchange. It's not what CAFS is selling but what the prospective donor is buying that matters.

Goals of This Plan

1. Strengthen the understanding of and participation in a culture of philanthropy at CAFS.
   - Carry out all our development activities in keeping with our values.
   - Involve every trustee in the development process and ensure that all trustees help cultivate relationships on behalf of CAFS.
   - Establish a comprehensive program to build stronger relationships between CAFS and its constituents so our constituents are ready to be asked to participate in some way.
   - Refine the way we design our requests and strengthen the way we ask.
2. Secure gifts and pledges to the endowment fund.
   - Build constituent understanding of the importance of endowment to the future of CAFS service to the community.
   - Create an endowment program that is inclusive, allowing anyone who wants to give to participate, whatever his or her financial capacity.
   - Our financial targets are:
     - $2 million in gifts and pledges by January 1998; and
     - $3–5 million by the CAFS Centennial in 1999.
3. Mature the annual appeal and develop a major gifts capacity.
   - Launch our first annual face-to-face solicitation campaign in fall 1997 and expand thereafter.
   - Expand our direct mail program and try a direct mail acquisition program in 1998.

Key Dates

February 1997	Finalize development plan and secure Board adoption.
March	Finalize communications materials and giving mechanisms for new Endowment Program.
May–June	Solicit all Board members and President/CEO, and finalize pledges.
July–October	Solicit first group of prospects for Endowment Program.
August	Plan annual fund campaign with identification of face-to-face prospects and solicitors. Develop solicitation materials.
September	Conduct face-to-face solicitation of targeted prospects for annual fund.
Early November 1997	Mail direct mail letter for annual fund.
January 1998	Mail announcement of Endowment Program to selected prospects.
January–March	Solicit second group of prospects for Endowment Program.
Fall 1998	Mail acquisition letter.

For its own use, management will develop an integrated monthly calendar that includes all activities, e.g., cultivation, communications, preparation, solicitation, etc.

Designing and Implementing the Best Development Program

In order to ask well, CAFS carefully organizes its activities. We create a written plan to support all our development activities. We know that development includes various functions, such as:

- communications and cultivation (together, this is called *constituency development*);
- volunteer recruitment, training, and support;
- goal setting, monitoring progress, and evaluating performance;
- solicitation strategies; and
- acknowledgment and recognition

We design our development plan with the help of committees, Board, and staff. The Board formally adopts the development plan, thereby committing their personal resources, contacts, and skills to carry out the plan.

Roles in Development

Board members and other fundraising volunteers help carry out the plans with the assistance of staff. CAFS auxiliaries and advisory committees play a critical role in the process of building relationships on behalf of the agency. Execution of all activities is carefully coordinated and managed by staff.

The Board establishes the overall goals, both financial and strategic, based on advice from development committees and staff. Staff prepare reports and identify trends during implementation of the plan. With staff, the development committees and board help monitor progress and evaluate performance. Specific strategies include:

- Discussion about philanthropy and development (constituency development and fundraising) at every Board meeting.
- Management analysis of results and trends of all development activities and discussion by Development Committee and Board.
- Annual Board self-assessment about performance in the development area.
- Annual review of overall development performance by staff, Development Committee, and board and establishment of new goals and plans.

Management will develop standardized protocols and reporting mechanisms as necessary.

Development leadership (staff and volunteer) will meet on a regular basis (every two weeks) to review progress, identify areas requiring intervention, and outline assignments. One of these meetings occurs in conjunction with the visit by fundraising counsel. The CEO ensures that the Chair of the CAFS Board is kept closely involved with development activities.

Key Definitions

Constituent: Someone who relates to or cares about our organization. Can be an individual, business, mosque, etc. The key is, they choose us; we do not choose them.

Constituency development: The process of building relationships with constituents in order to get them ready to be asked for something.

Constituency development continuum: Constituents increasing their involvement in and commitment to

CAFS. For example, volunteers becoming donors; prospects becoming donors; and donors giving again.

Donor: A person, organization, corporation, foundation, or other entity that makes a gift of time, money, or service. Also called a contributor.

Predisposed: An individual, business, or other organization whose contacts or interests might help develop a connection with our organization. In fund development vocabulary, "A possible source of support whose philanthropic interests appear to match those of a particular organization but whose linkages, giving ability, and interests have not yet been confirmed." (*NSFRE Fund-Raising Dictionary*)

Prospect: Constituent who cares enough that they are now ready to be asked. "Any potential donor whose linkages, giving ability, and interests have been confirmed." (*NSFRE Fund-Raising Dictionary*)

CAFS CONSTITUENT ANALYSIS

Overview of Current CAFS Constituency

- Approximately 11,000 names in the database who have had some relationship with CAFS or its two premerger agencies.
- Approximately 500 of these names are businesses and foundations, and the balance are individuals.
- For purposes of constituency development (building relationships), these constituents are segmented in two ways:
  –Relationships of constituent to CAFS/Type of constituent
  –Lifestyle/demographics
- CAFS uses segmentation to enhance our ability to build relationships.

Segmentation #1: Relationship of Constituent to CAFS/Type of Constituent

Many of these constituents have multiple relationships with CAFS. For example, an individual could be a donor, client, and volunteer. These relationships are coded within the CAFS database.

Type

- Businesses/corporations
- Civic organizations
- Corporate foundations
- Foundations
- Government (elected and appointed)—in priority order
  –State
  –County, Bergen
  –Municipal
  –Federal
- Individuals
- Religious organizations

Relationship with CAFS

- Client (current and past)
- Community ally (defined as individuals and organizations with which CAFS communicates and collaborates)
- Donor (donors of time are called *volunteers* and defined as a separate segment)
  –By gift size (major donors, donors)
  –By solicitation method (e.g., direct mail, face-to-face, special event)
  –By gift intent (e.g., annual operations, endowment, awards dinner)
  –By gift mechanism (e.g., cash, stock/securities, in-kind)
- Staff (management, professional and support)
- Vendor
- Volunteer (donors of time)
  –Adoption Auxiliary
  –CAFS Board of Trustees and committee members
  –Child Development Center Advisory Committee
  –Children's Haven Advisory Committee
  –The Depot
  –Eastlea Advisory Committee
  –FCS Auxiliary
  –PATH II Advisory Committee
  –Woodlea/Path I Advisory Committee

Segmentation #2: Psychographics and Demographics

It is important to know how our constituents relate to us (are they donors or volunteers or both?) and what type of constituent they are (are they business, state government, church, individual?).

However, it is equally important—perhaps more important—to understand the interests, motivations, and aspirations of our constituents. Constituents make decisions based on their interests, motivations, and aspirations. This personal context goes far beyond "helping others." That is far too simplistic.

First, CAFS will get to know its constituents well enough to understand their interests, motivations, and aspirations. Then our goal is to get our constituents to see that CAFS can help them fulfill their aspirations and meet their needs.

To best understand constituent interests, motivations, and aspirations, CAFS will look at psychographics and demographics. Psychographics refers to "the activities, lifestyle, interests, and behavioral and personal traits"

(*NSFRE Fund-Raising Dictionary*) of constituents. Demographics refers to such characteristics as age, sex, marital status, family size, education, income, and occupation.

How We Will Gather Lifestyle/Demographic Information about our Constituents

This is the heart of our constituency development process: learning about the interests, motivations, and aspirations of our constituents. CAFS will gather information to know its constituents better, thereby enabling us to find out what our constituents value and whether we can fulfill those values.

We will seek two types of information:

- that which can be generalized to relatively homogenous groupings of people (or businesses, etc.); and
- that which is unique to the particular individual (business, etc.).

General information, patterns, and trends

- Data from existing market research and studies in global demographics, reasons donors and volunteers give, etc.
- Results from CAFS anonymous surveys and focus groups with donors and volunteers.

Focus groups will be conducted as part of our annual development activities, for example, to do the following:

- Test an idea for a special event
- Get opinions about a new service
- Find out why people give and volunteer
- Test themes for direct mail letters
- Test cultivation ideas
- Evaluate a special event
- Brainstorm ideas for a new event

A donor survey will be conducted every other year. Mini-surveys (or bounce-back cards) will be used regularly to test such things as:

- Satisfaction with a special event
- Reactions to and ideas for the newsletter
- Request for further information
- Interest in estate-planning seminars and other cultivation activities

Information unique to the particular individual (business, etc.):

- Formal and informal conversations

- Public information from others who know the constituent(s)

How We Will Use Lifestyle/Demographic Information about Our Constituents

Again, this is the heart of our constituency development program. CAFS will use the information to:

- design activities (e.g., special events and cultivation gatherings) that might be of interest to the constituent group;
- personalize acknowledgment and recognition;
- develop communications that focus on constituent interests; and
- develop solicitation requests based on the interests, motivations, and aspirations of the constituents.

Current CAFS Lifestyle Groupings (to be completed at next Development Committee meeting)

- The Annes
- Young grandparents
- Grandparents
- Mid-cycle families

CAFS CONSTITUENCY DEVELOPMENT PROCESS

Constituency development means communications and cultivation. Both are based on our understanding of the constituent's interests, motivations, and aspirations.

Communications and cultivation are divided into three general categories:

- activities directed to all constituents;
- activities designed for targeted groups of like constituents; and
- activities personalized for a single constituent.

Communications

The goal of communications is to get people to act.

CAFS communications occurs through writing and conversation, both formal and informal. Communication is two-way. CAFS seeks information and opinions from and provides information to its constituents.

Specific Strategies To Improve Our Communications

- Focus on benefits to the constituent, their interests, motivations, and aspirations.

- Target the four personality types: expressive, analytical, bottom-liner, amiable.
- Tell stories, don't just relay information.
- Use inverted pyramid style (journalism—punch the point first). Don't tell the three little pigs version of a story.
- Make sure print design and layout support, rather than hinder, communication. Make text easy to skim with bullets, indented paragraphs (always!), underlines, boldface, etc.
- Write at the eighth grade level so the reader doesn't have to work hard to understand.
- Always include a call to action.
- Keep it simple:
  - Use short paragraphs, even one sentence only.
  - Avoid compound sentences. Stick to 16–20 words or less.
  - Vary sentence and paragraph length to introduce drama. Use sentence fragments.
  - Use simple words such as "car" rather than "automobile." Don't use technical jargon unless absolutely necessary.
  - Use facts as well as emotion.
  - Don't use sexist language.
  - Talk and write in a conversational tone. Use colloquial expressions and action verbs. Start sentences with conjunctions and end with prepositions.
- Make sure headlines get the reader's attention, tell a complete message, and state a benefit.

Cultivation

Cultivation works with communications to strengthen the relationship between CAFS and its constituents. Cultivation includes such activities as: getting to know our constituents; involving them in CAFS mission and values; and acknowledging and recognizing constituent contributions.

Goal Setting, Evaluation, and Management

Every communications and cultivation activity is designed based on a rigorous management process. Specific steps include:

- Identifying the target constituent(s) and clearly understanding their interests.
- Advance market testing of the activity with representatives of the constituency before finalizing the activity.
- Setting clear and measurable goals for the activity and its contribution to constituency development, followed by debriefing and evaluation of the activity and its results.
- Determining role of volunteer and staff cultivators and communicators and ensuring availability.
- Ensuring that cultivators and communicators report information and perspective from constituents to office.
- Follow-up plan for constituents so that the communications/cultivation activity is not an isolated incident.

Volunteers play the most critical role in the process of constituency development.

- Development committees and Board brainstorm constituency development activities and adopt the plans.
- Every Board member and each member of the development committees use their contacts with CAFS constituents to help cultivate relationships.
- Every Board member and other volunteers help identify those who might be predisposed to CAFS and help bring them into the CAFS constituency development process.

SUMMARY OF CONSTITUENCY DEVELOPMENT ACTIVITIES

For all activities:

- Based on interests, motivations, and aspirations of constituents.
- Follow the guidelines for effective communications outlined above.
- Designed based on rigorous management process outlined above.

Activity	*Constituent Group*
Building culture of philanthropy within CAFS leadership (ongoing conversation at meetings and one on one; carrying out activities, etc.)	• Board of Trustees • Auxiliaries and advisory committees • Staff
Ongoing conversation through formal and informal meetings (e.g., interviews to test the case for support; regular lunches, breakfasts, and other conversations; etc.)	• Targeted constituents
Special events sponsored by auxiliaries and advisory committees	• Targeted constituent groups determined by volunteers and staff together • Outreach to families with young children and mid-career young families with both partners working
Service on Board of Trustees, board committees, auxiliaries, and advisory committees	• Targeted individuals determined by volunteers and staff together • Outreach to families with young children and mid-career young families with both partners working
Agency tours (hosted by key staff and corps of volunteer guides)	• Every trustee, board committee member, and member of an auxiliary and advisory committee • Targeted constituents invited by volunteers and staff • General announcement to constituents
Cultivation gathering (quarterly gathering of 5–10 people with brief presentation and tour)	• Targeted constituents invited by volunteers and staff
CAFS program events (e.g., awards event, dinner at an agency home, etc.)	• Targeted constituents invited by volunteers and staff
Orientation and training opportunities about development	• Board of Trustees • Development committees • Other fund development volunteers
Estate-planning seminars (providing a service not talking about CAFS)	• Donors • Volunteers • Selected clients

Communications Activities	Constituent Group
Annual community seminar on topic of interest to families	• Donors • Volunteers • Clients • Civic organizations • Community invitation also
Interview and recruitment process for board and committee membership	• Candidates for all leadership positions
Recognition program for volunteers and donors • Invitation to annual donor/volunteer thank-you party • Listing in annual report • Listing in special issue of newsletter • Naming of endowment funds	• Personalized and targeted to donors and volunteers, depending on gift level and type of gift
Quarterly newsletter	• Volunteers • Individual donors
Special issue of the newsletter (at least once annually)	• Foundation, corporate, and government funders • Service consumers
Targeted insider update (at least twice a year)	• Major donors • Prospects for giving to endowment
Targeted insider update (at least twice a year)	• Foundation, corporate, and government funders • Service consumers
Annual report with letter targeted to specific constituents	• Donors (all types) • Volunteers • Service consumers
Case statement communications materials (e.g., describing Endowment Program, ways to give, etc.)	• Modified as necessary for targeted constituents
Acknowledgment to donors and volunteers • Annual thank-you letter to volunteers serving on year-long or multiyear projects • Thank-you letter for project volunteers upon completion of activity • Thank-you letter(s) to donors within 48 hours of receipt of gift	• Personalized to volunteers and donors

RECOGNIZING AND CREDITING GIFTS

Background

1. Recognition

Introduction

Children's Aid and Family Services (CAFS) will offer a unified recognition program to those donors who wish to be publicly recognized. At this time, the four critical elements of the recognition program are the Annual Fund, the Endowment Program, Special Projects (e.g., giving a restricted gift to a specific path home or for construction of the new child development center), and Planned Gifts.

Role of Recognition

Recognizing donors is an important part of philanthropy. Recognition refers to public acknowledgment.

Although some donors might object to donor recognition, research indicates that 99 percent are genuinely motivated by the recognition. Still others respect the value of recognition but wish to remain anonymous.

It is important that organizations offer donors the opportunity to be recognized or to remain anonymous. No assumptions should be made. The recipient organization must ask the donor about his or her desires. This should be secured in writing.

Difference between Recognition and Acknowledgment and Cultivation

Recognition refers to *public* acknowledgment, acknowledgment seen by others. This should not be confused with the means of acknowledgment and cultivation personalized to the individual donor. Acknowledgment and cultivation are not outlined as a public program. Strategies are personalized. For example, acknowledgment and cultivation might include:

* personalizing a thank-you letter to focus on the donor's interests and to acknowledge his or her role in a particular activity;
* having a CAFS Path Home child create a thank-you letter or drawing for a donor who is interested in that issue;
* inviting a donor for lunch to give an update about how his or her gift made a difference in a specific program; and
* inviting selected donors to attend the children's awards ceremony.

What Is Recognized

Generally, organizations recognize donors who give to support annual activities (e.g., the annual fund, also called budget-supporting gifts), special activities, including capital programs, endowment giving, and planned giving.

Sample recognition categories might include:

* by gift amount, in groupings by gift range. Sometimes, these groupings are named.
* by cumulative gifts given over a period of time. Sometimes, these are in groupings by range of dollars given, and sometimes they are designated with an asterisk (or some other designation) by the donor's name in a listing by gift amount.
* membership in a gift club of some sort. Gift clubs are frequently established with a minimum gift requirement. Sometimes, organizations establish a legacy or heritage society to recognize all donors of planned/deferred gifts.

Using Premiums or Mementos

Some organizations find that premiums or mementos are useful when fundraising. Public radio and television often use this strategy. However, with the new IRS rules, the fair market value of benefits must be deducted, so this strategy is often not practical.

Mementos must be carefully selected to interest donors. Before selecting a memento, CAFS will talk to donors to test market ideas. The most effective mementos are one of a kind and relate directly to the not-for-profit's work. However, this uniqueness is not always possible.

Recognition Devices

Recognition devices come in many forms. The devices may be summarized into the following areas:

* Informational benefits/access to privileged information. For example: newsletters, annual reports, special "insider" updates
* Prestige benefits. For example: certificates and plaques, photos, and mementos
* Cultivation benefits. For example: invitation to special events, donor recognition events, access to leadership through informal gatherings and meetings
* Public acknowledgment benefits. For example: listed as donor in annual report or on wall in the organization; named fund

Together, these recognition devices are intended to do such things as:

* with sensitivity and genuine consideration, thank the donor for giving;

- encourage the donor to remain an active supporter;
- offer information to help build donor understanding;
- provide incentives for the donor to increase the level of participation; and
- provide opportunities for the donor to affiliate further with the organization.

2. Crediting Gifts

Where We Are Now

CAFS needs to decide how it will credit gifts and how or whether this affects recognition. Staff will develop a policy for review by the Finance and Development Committees and action by the Board.

What's Happening in the Field

Each organization makes its own decision about how it will credit gifts. Without advance decision making, organizations can get caught up in conflict and controversy. Some of this controversy and conflict has become public and has alienated donors.

Many problems seem to arise when organizations are trying hard to reach a monetary goal and begin to include gifts that do not actually qualify within the initially defined objectives and time frames of the campaign or activity. Also, organizations need to consider their own business practices, the recommendations of their accountant, and the accounting standards.

General Standards

Typically, good fund development practice says that gifts should not be credited toward a campaign, goal, or activity and should not be recognized unless the donor has provided some form of written commitment. Accounting rules and standards also guide the reporting of gifts and pledges.

Some organizations recognize and credit a total pledge when made. Other organizations recognize and credit only the paid amount.

Many organizations will recognize a donor of a planned gift through a legacy or heritage society but will not credit the gift toward a goal or fundraising activity without a signed commitment form. On this form, the donor estimates the gift value. The donor also provides appropriate substantiation, for example, a copy of the pertinent portion of the donor's will. *Please note:* Signing a commitment form does not make a planned gift irrevocable if it is a revocable gift, e.g., a bequest in a will.

Planned gifts are difficult to credit. For example, how do we recognize a 50-year-old donor who has made a bequest in her will giving CAFS 5 percent of her estate? How do we count her commitment toward our desired $5 million endowment fund?

Some organizations credit planned gifts (for example, life insurance or a bequest in a will) based on actuarial tables and an inflation factor. Other organizations credit planned gifts—when a commitment form is provided—at the face value.

Proposed Recognition Program for CAFS

1. Overview of Giving, Recognizing, and Crediting

Type of Gift	Recognition	Credited toward Fundraising
Annual support Cash pledge/gift or transfer of securities made to support operations and paid by the end of the fiscal year	Donor is listed by gift category (by size) during the fiscal year the gift is given.	All cash, pledges, and securities transfers are credited, at fair market value, toward the fund total on the date the gift is received by CAFS.
In honor/memory of Cash pledge/gift or transfer of securities in memory/honor of someone	Donor is listed by gift category (by size) during the fiscal year the gift is given. Honoree's name is listed in alphabetical order under the heading called "In Honor Of" or "In Memory Of" during fiscal year gift is given.	All cash, pledges, and securities transfers are credited, at fair market value, toward the fund total on the date the gift is received by CAFS.
Special project Cash pledge/gift or transfer of securities made to support a special project	Donor is listed by gift category under project heading for duration of fundraising appeal for the project.	All cash, pledges, and securities transfers are credited, at fair market value, toward the fund total on the date the gift is received by CAFS.
Donated service or product (in-kind)	Donor is listed in alphabetical order under heading Gifts In-Kind during fiscal year gift is given.	Generally not credited toward fundraising goals unless expense is also credited.
Endowment Program Cash pledge/gift or transfer of securities made to the Endowment Program with final payment paid no later than 12–99 for first cycle of solicitation	Donor is listed by gift category (by size) for duration of Endowment Program.	All cash, pledges, and securities transfers are credited, at fair market value, toward the fund total on the date the gift is received by CAFS.
Planned gift (e.g., bequest in will, life insurance policy, lifetime income gift, etc.)	Membership in legacy/heritage society and listed as member of society.	These intentions are credited toward a fundraising activity and are reported in the total dollars raised according to face value—when a commitment form is completed and signed.

2. General Principles of Recognition for All Programs

A. CAFS Recognizes Pledges and Gifts
- Children's Aid and Family Services accepts gifts and pledges of cash, securities, and planned gifts.
- In order for a pledge to be credited and recognized, CAFS needs some form of written intention from the donor. This intention can be in the form of a letter from the donor or completion of a CAFS commitment form. This is the donor's choice.
- CAFS recognizes pledges at total value.

B. Timing and Duration of Recognition
- Recognition begins once CAFS receives an actual gift of cash or securities or a pledge, through written

intent or completion of the CAFS commitment form from the donor.
- A donor is recognized with a special note during the fiscal year that she or he dies. At the end of the fiscal year in which the donor dies, a deceased donor is no longer listed.

C. Employee Matching Gifts
- Corporate matching gifts are credited to the employee, and the employee is recognized at the appropriate gift level.
- Corporations providing the matching gift are listed alphabetically under the heading "Corporate Matching Gifts" during the fiscal year that the gift is given.

D. Informing Prospective Donors about Our Policies

- When a prospect has indicated that she or he wishes to make a gift, a commitment and recognition information is provided. For example: Provide Commitment Form and a one-page summary of Recognition Program.
- This printed information explains CAFS's policies regarding recognizing and crediting gifts.

3. Information Related to Specific Giving Programs

A. Endowment Program

1. Payment of pledges to the Endowment Program
   - In 1996, Children's Aid and Family Services formally launched its new Endowment Program. Fundraising for the program officially began in 1997.
   - For this first fundraising initiative, cash pledges may be paid over three years, beginning in 1997 and ending in December 1999. CAFS requests that all cash pledges be paid by December 31, 1999. To remain in the donor listing, cash pledges must be fully paid by December 31, 1999.
   - Subsequent solicitations will also provide for a three-year pledge payment period. Final payment would be due by the end of the fiscal year three years from the pledge date.

2. Named gift opportunities for the Endowment Program
   - A donor may establish a named Endowment Fund with a minimum contribution of $10,000 in cash and/or securities.
   - The donor of the named endowment fund will be recognized in accordance with the CAFS recognition program. If the donor assigns the naming opportunity to someone other than him/herself, the donor is also recognized.

B. Planned Giving Program

- Donors who make a planned gift to CAFS are invited to join the legacy society, the Second Century Circle, and enjoy the benefits of this society.
- Founding or charter members of the legacy society will be designated in the membership listing.
- Gift intentions must be received by CAFS by December 31, 1997 to be considered a founding member of the legacy society.

4. Gift Recognition Categories

A. General Guidelines

- All donors (individuals, businesses, organizations, foundations, etc.) to annual operations and the Endowment Fund will be recognized by gift amount.
- CAFS will introduce gift categories with higher dollar amounts. See suggestions below. CAFS will not change any of its current categories (amounts or names). Donors may have a particular affinity to where they fit.

B. Gift Categories

Cousin	(up to $99)
Sibling	($100–$250)
Parent	($250–$499)
Grandparent	($500–$999)
Angel	($1,000–$2,499)
Benefactor	($2,500–$4,999)
Patron	($5,000–$9,999)
Sponsor	($10,000–$19,999)
Sustainer	($20,000–$49,999)
Ambassador	($50,000 and above)

RECOGNITION BENEFITS

All donors who so wish are recognized as follows:

- Friends of CAFS—Donors who have contributed budget-supporting gifts during the fiscal year: Recognize by gift category according to the following list, then list the categories, including the non-specific amount category.
- Special projects—Donors who have contributed to non-budgeted or capital purposes: alphabetical listing.
- Endowment Fund—Donors contributing a designated gift to ensure the agency's financial future: by gift category, as described above.
- Second Century Circle—Donors making a planned gift by will, life insurance, or other means: lifetime membership in the Society and alphabetical listing.
- Life member—Donors who have contributed budget-supporting gifts for 10 consecutive years, whose cumulative outright gifts total $10,000, or whose irrevocable planned gift commitments have reached $50,000: symbol by name within other donor listing.
- Honorary and memorial gifts—Donors are listed by gift category in the Friends section, and the honoree is recognized in the specially titled section.
- Donated (in kind) service or product—Donors are listed alphabetically in the specially titled section.

Donors are identified by the following symbols in printed lists:

- ◆ Annual budget-supporting donors during the current fiscal year.
- ✳ Life Member. Life Membership is reserved for individuals who have given for 10 consecutive years, whose cumulative outright gifts total $10,000 or whose irrevocable planned gift commitments have reached $50,000.
- ✚ or ☆ Person passed away in fiscal year.
- ♥ Founder and charter member of the Legacy Society.
- * Additional gift to the Legacy Society.

Boldface signifies a new donor to the Legacy Society.

Donors who wish, receive the following benefits:

All donors

- All donors are recognized in the annual CAFS Honor Roll, according to the guidelines above.
- Each issue of the quarterly newsletter recognizes donors who have given since the previous issue.
- All donors receive the quarterly newsletter and the CAFS annual report providing you with important information as well as recognizing donors and volunteers.

Additional benefits for donors

- All donors to the Endowment Program receive a commemorative pen that signals your commitment to the future when others see it.

Major donors are recognized in the annual report as follows:

- Friends of CAFS and donors to Special Projects: Donors of $500 or more are recognized by gift category.
- All members of the Second Century Circle are listed alphabetically.
- Life Members are noted with the symbol ✳ within their other donor listing.
- Donors of $1,000 or more to the Endowment Program are listed by gift category.

Donors who contribute $1,000 or more to any program, who are lifetime members, and/or who are members of the Legacy Society receive:

- Handsome certificate suitable for framing
- Insider Reports on developments in family services and child welfare

- Commemorative memento symbolic of your support to children and families, presented at the annual philanthropy awards ceremony.

Donors who contribute $500 or more to any program, who are lifetime members, and/or who are members of the Second Century Circle are invited to attend the CAFS annual meeting and philanthropy awards ceremony.

Members of the *Second Century Circle*

- Founding or charter members will make their intentions known to CAFS no later than December 31, 1997. Founders receive a special charter member certificate, suitable for framing.
- Members of the Second Century Circle are listed in the CAFS Honor Roll and annual report. As new members join, they are recognized in the quarterly issue of the CAFS newsletter.
- Founders are noted with a special designation of ♥ in all recognition listings.
- New members are designated in **boldface** in the Second Century Circle listing. Persons who have given an additional gift are recognized with an asterisk within the Second Century Circle listing.
- Members receive an invitation to all Second Century Circle gatherings, at least one to be held each year, with the opportunity to bring guests.

Sample Donor Listing

Children's Aid and Family Services Honor Roll of Donors, 1997

Contributions received from ___ to ____.

This honor roll expresses our thanks to those who have made contributions to Children's Aid and Family Services in 1997.

Your charitable gifts are essential to the agency's ability to preserve, protect, and provide families to our communities.

Donors are identified by the following symbols throughout this honor roll:

- ◆ Annual budget-supporting donors during the current fiscal year.
- ✳ Life Member. Life Membership is reserved for individuals who have given for 10 consecutive years, whose cumulative outright gifts total $10,000 or whose irrevocable planned gift commitments have reached $50,000.
- ✚ or ☆ Person passed away in 1997.
- ♥ Founder and charter member of the Second Century Circle.
- *Additional gift to the Second Century Circle.

We have honored the request of those donors who wish to remain anonymous.

Every effort has been made to ensure that this list is accurate and complete. Please direct any errors or omissions to the Development Office and accept our sincerest regret.

Friends of Children's Aid and Family Services

We acknowledge here donors who have contributed budget-supporting gifts in 1997.

Individuals and Family Foundations

Ambassador	($50,000 and above)
Sustainer	($20,000–$49,999)
Sponsor	($10,000–$19,999)
Patron	($5,000–$9,999)
Benefactor	($2,500–$4,999)
Angel	($1,000–$2,499)
Grandparent	($500–$999)
Parent	($250–$499)
Sibling	($100–$250)
Cousin	(up to $99)

Corporations, Foundations, and Organizations

Ambassador	($50,000 and above)
Sustainer	($20,000–$49,999)
Sponsor	($10,000–$19,999)
Patron	($5,000–$9,999)
Benefactor	($2,500–$4,999)
Angel	($1,000–$2,499)
Grandparent	($500–$999)
Parent	($250–$499)
Sibling	($100–$250)
Cousin	(up to $99)

In Memory Of (an alphabetical list of the honorees; donor is in appropriate gift category)

In Honor Of (an alphabetical list of the honorees; donor is in appropriate gift category)

Gifts In-Kind (an alphabetical list)

Special Projects

We acknowledge here donors who have contributed restricted gifts for non-budgeted or capital purposes, such as facilities.

Endowment Fund

The Endowment Fund was established as the "fund for the future" for Children's Aid and Family Services. Donors to this fund help ensure that Children's Aid and Family Services is here to help generations to come. Donors contributing $10,000 or more may establish a named fund within the endowment.

Ambassador	($50,000 and above)
Sustainer	($20,000–$49,999)
Sponsor	($10,000–$19,999)
Patron	($5,000–$9,999)
Benefactor	($2,500–$4,999)
Angel	($1,000–$2,499)

Legacy Society

The Second Century Circle was established to honor individuals who make planned gifts to Children's Aid and Family Services. Examples of such gifts are those made through a charitable bequest in a will or charitable gift of life insurance.

These donors play an important role in securing the financial future of Children's Aid and Family Services, thereby ensuring that our care is available for generations to come.

Persons whose names are printed with a (♥) are founding members of the society. Persons whose names are printed in **boldface** type are new members of the Society this year. Persons whose names are marked with an asterisk (✳) made an additional planned gift this year.

ACTIVITY SUMMARY BY CONSTITUENT GROUP

Constituent Group	Activity
All constituents	• Receive at least one communication per year, providing an update and opportunity to get involved in some manner. Include a call to action.
Current donors and those who gave within the past 24 months	• Ongoing constituency development (two-way communications and cultivation) activities to strengthen the relationship. • Receive at least one solicitation during the year to support general programs.
Volunteers	• Ongoing constituency development (two-way communications and cultivation) activities to strengthen the relationship. • Receive at least one solicitation during the year to support general programs.
Board members, advisory and auxiliary volunteers, and selected donors	• Ongoing constituency development (two-way communications and cultivation) activities to strengthen the relationship. • Receive at least one solicitation during year to support general programs. • Receive an invitation to participate in the Endowment Program.
New residents Families with young children Mid-career young families	• Within the next 18 months, some outreach to determine whether they might wish to become involved in CAFS in some manner.

SUMMARY OF CONTRIBUTIONS PROGRAM, SOLICITATION STRATEGY, AND TIME FRAME

Contributions Program	Solicitation Strategy	Time Frame
General programs (annual fund)	• Face-to-face of major prospects • Direct mail to prior donors* • Special events sponsored by auxiliaries and advisory committees • Direct mail acquisition**	September–October 1997 Early November 1997, May 1998, November 1998 Ongoing Fall 1998
Endowment Program	• Face-to-face solicitation of Board of Trustees • Face-to-face solicitation of selected prospects • Face-to-face solicitation of selected prospects • Mail announcement of Endowment Program to selected prospects	Spring 1997. Finish by June. Summer–Fall 1997 January–March 1998 January 1998

In 1997, CAFS will strengthen its annual fund development through constituency development actions *and* by adding face-to-face solicitation. We will solicit selected prospects personally rather than through the mail.

In 1998, CAFS will continue to strengthen its annual fund development by:

- Expanding the face-to-face campaign to include more prospects
- Expanding and diversifying the direct mail program

*Direct Mail to Prior Donors

- Targeted audiences: Anyone who has given within the prior 5 years. Letters would be modified slightly to distinguish between current and lapsed donors.
- 2 letters mailed to the same group of constituents during a 12-month period. Each letter will have a different service theme. Donors to the first letter will also receive the second letter. Their prior gift will be acknowledged even as the new giving opportunity is presented.

- Targeted schedule: Early November 1997, May 1998, November 1998.
- Evaluate response and adjust accordingly.

Direct mail acquisition (Possible exploration for CAFS. Consider for Fall 1998.)

- Targeted audiences: Purchased and donated lists of appropriate market segments within the five counties served by CAFS.
- Professionally written letter and response mechanism to test whether this is a cost-effective way to acquire new donors. Response rate estimated at 0.5–2 percent. Thousands of names necessary. Goal is to at least break even, cost versus income.

REACHING OUT TO THOSE WHO ARE NOT YET CONSTITUENTS

Overview

Our first priority is to build strong relationships with current constituents. Our second priority is to reach out to those who are predisposed to CAFS, its services and work.

Our Endowment Program focuses on constituents who are donors. Our annual fund development, including special events, reaches out to all constituents, whether or not they are donors. Also, we may reach out to predisposed market segments as an expansion strategy for our annual fund development and special events.

Developing New Constituents: Market Segments for Outreach

In addition to strengthening relationships with our constituents, CAFS needs to find new constituents. We reach out to people, organizations, and businesses. These are not yet constituents because they have no relationship with CAFS. Some may be predisposed to CAFS and its services. Others may not. However, if they respond to our outreach, they may then be considered a constituent and enter into the process of constituency development.

First, we let people know about our services. We do this through various strategies:

- Sending welcome letters and service information to new residents
- Contacting businesses to determine whether we can offer EAP programs to employees
- Devising new methods as time progresses.

Second, we need to expand our volunteer and donor base. For CAFS to remain strong in the future, we need to involve more diverse audiences as volunteers and donors. Currently, our donor base is middle-aged, older, and more affluent. To be strong, we also must involve younger generations and those of more modest means.

Beginning in 1997, our annual fund development, special events, and volunteer development will reach out to include the following market segments:

- Families with young children
- Mid-career young families with both partners working

These outreach activities are principally the responsibility of our community affairs and volunteer development function. Our auxiliaries and advisory committees also play an integral role.

Chapter 7

In Conclusion

No matter how difficult, millions of donors, volunteers, and staff around the world work together to build better communities. Together, people of every culture participate in philanthropy.

The philanthropic process brings people together in acts of giving. Participating in this experience enhances one's own life significantly. The act of giving is shared between the donor, the cause, and an organization that responds to *both* the cause and the donor.

Part of philanthropy, fund development is the means for securing contributions. And effective fund development depends on four fundamental relationships.

- the organization's internal relations
- its relationship with the community
- the organization's relationship with its constituents
- its relationship with volunteers

Each of these four relationships depends on the basic principle of marketing, which says: "It's not what you're selling that matters, it's what I'm buying that counts." Or, in other words, "Don't tell me what I want. Show me you have what I need." Even more simply put, these statements mean that you must pay attention to your various constituencies, whether the "I" is a donor or volunteer, the community itself, or the individuals and groups working in your organization.

> *Donors give to people, causes, and organizations. Organizations give to donors on behalf of the cause.*

Make no mistake. The survival of your organization depends on developing these four relationships. They make a healthy institution. Together, they can produce more philanthropic dollars.

The most effective organizations recognize that each relationship is a contributor to and a beneficiary of the other relationships. These organizations know that the four relationships interrelate into one interdependent system, each relationship adding value to the others.

The most competent professionals see the entire complex system. These professionals—including the fund raisers—are leaders, managers, and enablers. This means that the most accomplished fundraisers are much more than master technicians. The best fundraisers are organizational development specialists, too. They understand, develop, and nurture the four relationships.

You want to raise more money? Then get ready for change. Your organization probably needs to change the way it does some of its fund development. Get ready for your own personal change, too. You probably need to change some of the ways *you* do the business.

The reward is survival. With the four relationships in place, an organization can do everything better, including fund development. Without these relationships, nothing will be done well enough.

In order to be a realist, you must believe in miracles.

David Ben Gurion

Appendix A

Components of Fund Development

Fund development is the process that supports philanthropy. Organizational leadership—especially development staff—is responsible for enhancing a culture of philanthropy within the organization.

Fund development is more than fundraising. Fund raising is asking for the gift. Fund development includes activities such as planning, communicating, thanking—and, of course, asking.

Both staff and volunteers play a role in carrying out these functions. If there are no staff, volunteers do everything.

Many organizations don't have staff devoted solely to fund development. In these organizations, the executive director may well carry out the development functions.

Even if your organization has development staff, the executive director and volunteers still play major roles in carrying out many of these functions.

PLANNING

1. Design the overall development program.
2. Identify strategic issues that may impact the institution's ability to fundraise; assist in resolution of these issues.
3. Establish realistic goals for charitable gifts, considering available prospects and volunteer and staff resources.
4. Evaluate interest, readiness, and capacity of donors to give.
5. Prepare fund development plans, monitor progress, and evaluate performance.
6. Evaluate cost-effectiveness and productivity of solicitation strategies. Assess return on investment.

MANAGEMENT

1. Manage the development function and its budget.

2. Develop and manage compliance and accountability standards for contributions and promote ethical standards of practice.
3. Design and maintain comprehensive gift processing, reporting, acknowledgment, and recognition systems.
4. Provide the support system required to implement the fund development program by:
   - researching and providing background information on donors and prospects;
   - keeping accurate records;
   - preparing communications and solicitation materials;
   - scheduling and coordinating activities.
5. Create a culture of philanthropy within the organization, helping volunteers and staff to understand the philosophy and operation of the fund development process.
6. Act as organizational development specialists, helping address organizational issues that affect fund development.
7. Work closely with the marketing and communications function to make sure that the organization's image, programs, and perspective are appropriately projected to targeted audiences.
8. Enable staff and volunteers so that the fund development process moves forward.

CONSTITUENCY DEVELOPMENT AND CULTIVATION

1. Represent the institution within the community.
2. Build linkages within the fund development and donor communities.
3. Work with volunteers and staff to build and strengthen relationships with key constituents.

VOLUNTEER DEVELOPMENT

1. Enable board and fundraising volunteers to carry out fund development activities. Specifically:
   - build volunteer understanding of and support for fund development within the organization;
   - keep fundraising volunteers current on all activities and results;
   - coordinate all fundraising contacts;
   - facilitate communication with volunteers;
   - participate in the board recruitment process so that fund development is understood and supported by all candidates;
   - help board members and other fundraising volunteers carry out their responsibilities by encouraging, supporting, thanking, educating, and nurturing, routinely and sincerely;
   - facilitate best use of the volunteer's time.
2. Identify, cultivate, and recruit fundraising volunteers.
3. Train, support, and evaluate fundraising volunteers.
4. Ensure proper recognition.
5. Guide, advise, and support committees and auxiliary groups whose activities support the organization.

6. Help board members and other fundraising volunteers to understand the organization, its values, mission, and services.

FUNDRAISING

1. Develop proposals and other solicitation materials.
2. Solicit contributions. (Note: Peer-to-peer solicitation by volunteers is usually the most effective solicitation. Staff may well participate in these solicitations. Staff also may solicit gifts.)
3. Plan, coordinate, and sell special events.

DONOR RELATIONS

1. Respect the motivations of donors and, as appropriate, meet their needs.
2. Ensure organizational accountability to donors.
3. Develop relationships to build stable and increased support from donors.
4. Encourage, support, thank, recognize, and nurture donors, routinely and sincerely.

Appendix B

Sample Questions for a Development Audit

These questions demonstrate the scope of issues you should consider if you want to evaluate your fund development program.

Often, a development audit is conducted by an outside evaluator. However, you can also use this survey to conduct your own internal assessment.

Ask your development staff to complete this audit. Go through the questions with your development committee. Or use this detailed audit to develop your own brief version targeted to the board's role in fund development.

Remember, these are questions to stimulate discussion. Your organization may decide that it doesn't need to subscribe to all of these statements. However, exceptions should be rare.

Use the scale below to rate your organization's fund development effectiveness.

Below Standard (1): We don't operate this way.
Standard (2): Usually we operate this way.
Above Standard (3): We regularly operate this way.

	Below (1)	Standard (2)	Above (3)

ORGANIZATION'S PURPOSE

1. Services and programs are deemed relevant by your organization's constituents and the community at large. ___ ___ ___

2. Justifiable reason, recognized by the community at large, to raise public and private contributions. ___ ___ ___

ORGANIZATIONAL PLANNING

3. Mission statement is regularly evaluated for relevance. ___ ___ ___

4. Organizational values and vision are clear and shared by all staff and key volunteers. ___ ___ ___

5. Strategic plan, based on market research, addresses internal strengths and weaknesses and external opportunities and threats, and sets corporate goals for a specific time period. ___ ___ ___

6. Ongoing review and adjustment of the plan. ___ ___ ___

	Below (1)	Standard (2)	Above (3)

7. Ongoing evaluation of program effectiveness, client satisfaction, health of infrastructure, and systems to intervene as necessary. ____ ____ ____

8. Systems for continuous quality improvement. ____ ____ ____

CONSTITUENCY DEVELOPMENT

9. Clear understanding of who current constituents are and what motivates their participation. ____ ____ ____

10. Clear vision of new markets (i.e., those predisposed to your cause) to target for relationship building. ____ ____ ____

11. Ongoing mechanisms to gather demographic and lifestyle information about constituents and the predisposed. ____ ____ ____

12. Strategies to cultivate relationships with donors and prospects. ____ ____ ____

ORGANIZATIONAL LEADERSHIP

13. Understanding and acceptance that, together, the board and CEO are responsible for the success or failure of the organization and the fulfillment of its mission. ____ ____ ____

14. Leadership that stimulates organizational learning and, when appropriate, change. ____ ____ ____

15. Effective enabling of volunteers by staff. ____ ____ ____

MARKETING AND COMMUNICATIONS

16. A positive image in the community. ____ ____ ____

17. Clear understanding of image you wish to have, image you currently have, and strategies to align the two. ____ ____ ____

18. An effective communications program to reach constituents. ____ ____ ____

ORGANIZATIONAL OPERATIONS

19. Clearly articulated role, responsibilities, and relationship between board and staff. ____ ____ ____

20. Comprehensive financial management system that includes annual budgeting and revision processes, monthly statement of revenue and expense compared with budget, and fund accounting. ____ ____ ____

21. Financial and program systems that fulfill accountability and reporting requirements to clients, donors, and regulatory agencies. ____ ____ ____

22. Board that represents the community and the organization's constituencies. ____ ____ ____

23. Board includes new and incumbent directors in order to guarantee continuity and new opinions. ____ ____ ____

24. Bylaws that limit tenure and ensure rotation of board members. ____ ____ ____

	Below (1)	Standard (2)	Above (3)

25. Conflict of interest policy and compliance by board and staff. ____ ____ ____

26. Comprehensive board recruitment process that includes identification of necessary skills, qualifications, and performance expectations. ____ ____ ____

27. Clear articulation of roles, responsibilities, and performance expectations presented to each candidate before nomination to board. ____ ____ ____

28. Annual process to assess performance of board members and to distinguish between those who should be invited to continue to serve and those who should be thanked and released on completion of (or prior to completion of) the term of appointment. ____ ____ ____

LEADERSHIP AND FUND DEVELOPMENT

29. Each board member, the CEO, and the development officer give a gift every year. Yes ____ No ____

30. During a capital campaign, all board members, the CEO, and the development officer give to both capital and annual campaigns. Yes ____ No ____

31. The board understands its role in fund development. ____ ____ ____

32. Each board member does some fundraising task each year. ____ ____ ____

33. Within the board, there are individuals who effectively solicit gifts face to face. ____ ____ ____

34. Within the board, there are individuals who effectively plan and sell tickets to special events. ____ ____ ____

35. Within the board, there are individuals who effectively use their business contacts on behalf of your fund development activities. ____ ____ ____

36. Board members attend special events. ____ ____ ____

37. The board regularly discusses the strategic issues and progress of philanthropy and fund development for the organization. ____ ____ ____

38. The chief development officer has direct access to the board to discuss fund development issues. ____ ____ ____

39. There are board-level committees/task forces that assist in the planning, implementation, and evaluation of fund development activities. ____ ____ ____

DEVELOPMENT WITHIN THE INSTITUTION

40. The organization's senior management understands and supports a culture of philanthropy. ____ ____ ____

41. Staff understand that they are each fundraisers. ____ ____ ____

42. Fund development ethics and standards have been adopted by the board, and the organization acts accordingly. ____ ____ ____

	Below (1)	Standard (2)	Above (3)
43. The organization understands the four relationships that are critical to fund development (internal relations; relationship with community, constituents, and enabling).	____	____	____

VOLUNTEERS IN FUND DEVELOPMENT

	Below (1)	Standard (2)	Above (3)
44. Fund development activities use both board and non-board members.	____	____	____
45. Fundraising volunteers also give to the organization.	____	____	____
46. Volunteer responsibilities and expectations are clearly articulated for each fundraising project.	____	____	____

THE DEVELOPMENT STAFF

	Below (1)	Standard (2)	Above (3)
47. The chief development officer reports directly to the organization's CEO.	Yes____	No ____	
48. Chief development officer participates along with other senior staff in strategic discussions regarding health, program, and markets of organization.	____	____	____
49. Development staff demonstrate an understanding of the organization's mission, programs, and goals.	____	____	____
50. The chief development officer effectively recruits and enables volunteers and staff.	____	____	____
51. Other development staff effectively recruit and enable volunteers.	____	____	____
52. Development staff (or consultants) are experienced in designing and conducting fund development programs.	____	____	____
53. Development staff (or consultants) are experienced in using different kinds of solicitation strategies.	____	____	____
54. Development staff are encouraged to enhance fund development through workshops and conferences.	____	____	____
55. Our development staff (and consultants) are members of a fundraising professional association and subscribe to a code of ethics.	____	____	____
56. Our development staff (and consultants) are certified by a national fundraising certification program.	____	____	____

FUND DEVELOPMENT MANAGEMENT

	Below (1)	Standard (2)	Above (3)
57. Clerical resources are in place to support fund development.	____	____	____
58. Space and equipment are in place to support fund development.	____	____	____
59. Records are kept of all fund development activities and their effectiveness and productivity.	____	____	____

	Below (1)	Standard (2)	Above (3)

60. Donor gift histories are maintained that include date and amount of gift, solicitor, if applicable, and response.

61. Prospect histories are maintained that include date of solicitation, method, solicitor, if applicable, and response.

62. Gift potential is evaluated, and request amounts are targeted for each prospect.

63. Standard operating procedures, gift acceptance policies, and overall fund development policies exist and are reviewed regularly.

64. Transmittal mechanisms help donors give easily.

65. Appropriate training and support materials exist for prospects and volunteers.

FUND DEVELOPMENT PLANNING AND EVALUATION

66. Our chief development officer participates in our organization's annual budgeting process and helps to establish the contributed income figure.

67. Operating budget and contributions goals are set by a thorough analysis and evaluation of current donors and available prospects, coupled with an analysis of fund development cost-effectiveness, return on invesment, and agency resources.

68. To make good decisions, the agency collects and analyzes: solicitation response rates; fundraising cost-effectiveness; return on investment; donor renewal, attrition, acquisition, and upgrade rates; average gift size; and solicitor performance.

69. The fund development program is diversified and not dependent on any one funding source or solicitation strategy.

70. Effective case statement(s) are developed with participation by the CEO and volunteer leadership.

71. A written fund development plan is developed with participation of CEO and volunteer leadership, and addresses strategic and financial goals, staff and volunteer resources, solicitation strategies, and timetable.

72. Target markets are segmented for the appropriate solicitation strategy.

73. Prospects are solicited by the right solicitor at the right time for the right project and the right amount.

74. Strategies are developed to renew and upgrade gifts of current donors and to acquire new donors.

75. Volunteer and staff leadership outline the criteria to evaluate fund development effectiveness and assess results.

	Below (1)	Standard (2)	Above (3)

76. Fund development effectiveness and success are not evaluated solely on the dollars raised. ____ ____ ____

77. Assessment results are used to develop subsequent plans. ____ ____ ____

ACKNOWLEDGMENT AND RECOGNITION

78. Gifts are acknowledged within 48 hours of receipt, and staff understand why this is important. ____ ____ ____

79. Mechanisms exist to recognize donors and their contributions. ____ ____ ____

80. Mechanisms exist to recognize fund development volunteers. ____ ____ ____

FUNDING FUND DEVELOPMENT

81. There is an adequate budget to support fund development efforts. ____ ____ ____

82. Fund development compensation is sufficient to ensure top-quality staff. ____ ____ ____

Appendix C

A Donor Bill of Rights

Philanthropy is based on voluntary action for the common good. It is a tradition of giving and sharing that is primary to the quality of life. To assure that philanthropy merits the respect and trust of the general public and that donors and prospective donors can have full confidence in the not-for-profit organizations and causes they are asked to support, we declare that all donors have these rights:

I.
To be informed of the organization's mission, of the way the organization intends to use donated resources, and of its capacity to use donations effectively for their intended purposes.

II.
To be informed of the identity of those serving on the organization's governing board and to expect the board to exercise prudent judgment in its stewardship responsibilities.

III.
To have access to the organization's most recent financial statements.

IV.
To be assured their gifts will be used for the purposes for which they were given.

V.
To receive appropriate acknowledgment and recognition.

VI.
To be assured that information about their donations is handled with respect and with confidentiality to the extent provided by law.

VII.
To expect that all relationships with individuals representing organizations of interest to the donor will be professional in nature.

VIII.
To be informed, whether those seeking donations are volunteers, employees of the organization, or hired solicitors.

IX.
To have the opportunity for their names to be deleted from mailing lists that an organization may intend to share.

X.
To feel free to ask questions when making a donation and to receive prompt, truthful, and forthright answers.

Developed by:

American Association of Fund Raising Counsel (AAFRC)

Association of Fundraising Professionals (AFP), formerly the National Society of Fund Raising Executives (NSFRE)

Association for Healthcare Philanthropy (AHP)

Council for Advancement and Support of Education (CASE)

Endorsed by:

Independent Sector

National Catholic Development Conference (NCDC)

National Committee on Planned Giving (NCPG)

National Council for Resource Development (NCRD)

United Way of America

Courtesy of the Association of Fundraising Professionals, Alexandria, Virginia.

Appendix D

NSFRE Code of Ethical Principles and Standards of Professional Practice

Amended October 1999.

STATEMENT OF ETHICAL PRINCIPLES

Adopted November 1991

The National Society of Fund Raising Executives (NSFRE) exists to foster the development and growth of fundraising professionals and the profession, to promote high ethical standards in the fundraising profession and to preserve and enhance philanthropy and volunteerism. Members of NSFRE are motivated by an inner drive to improve the quality of life through the causes they serve. They serve the ideal of philanthropy; are committed to the preservation and enhancement of volunteerism; and hold stewardship of these concepts as the overriding principle of their professional life. They recognize their responsibility to ensure that needed resources are vigorously and ethically sought and that the intent of the donor is honestly fulfilled. To these ends, members embrace certain values that they strive to uphold in performing their responsibilities for generating philanthropic support.

NSFRE members aspire to:

- practice their profession with integrity, honesty, truthfulness, and adherence to the absolute obligation to safeguard the public trust;
- act according to the highest standards and visions of their organization, profession, and conscience;
- put philanthropic mission above personal gain;
- inspire others through their own sense of dedication and high purpose;
- improve their professional knowledge and skills in order that their performance will better serve others;
- demonstrate concern for the interests and well-being of individuals affected by their actions;

Courtesy of the Association of Fundraising Professionals, Alexandria, Virginia.

- value the privacy, freedom of choice, and interests of all those affected by their actions;
- foster cultural diversity and pluralistic values, and treat all people with dignity and respect;
- affirm, through personal giving, a commitment to philanthropy and its role in society;
- adhere to the spirit as well as the letter of all applicable laws and regulations;
- advocate within their organizations, adherence to all applicable laws and regulations;
- avoid even the appearance of any criminal offense or professional misconduct;
- bring credit to the fundraising profession by their public demeanor;
- encourage colleagues to embrace and practice these ethical principles and standards of professional practice; and
- be aware of the codes of ethics promulgated by other professional organizations that serve philanthropy.

STANDARDS OF PROFESSIONAL PRACTICE

Adopted and Incorporated into the AFP Code of Ethical Principles, November 1992

Furthermore, while striving to act according to the above values, NSFRE members agree to abide by the Standards of Professional Practice, which are adopted and incorporated into the Code of Ethical Principles. Violation of the Standards may subject the member to disciplinary sanctions, including expulsion, as provided in the Ethics Enforcement Procedures.

Professional Obligations

1. Members shall not engage in activities that harm the member's organization, clients, or profession.

2. Members shall not engage in activities that conflict with their fiduciary, ethical, and legal obligations to their organizations and their clients.
3. Members shall effectively disclose all potential and actual conflicts of interest; such disclosure does not preclude or imply ethical impropriety.
4. Members shall not exploit any relationship with a donor, prospect, volunteer, or employee to the benefit of the member or the member's organization.
5. Members shall comply with all applicable local, state, provincial, federal, civil, and criminal laws.
6. Members recognize their individual boundaries of competence and are forthcoming and truthful about their professional experience and qualifications.

Solicitation and Use of Charitable Funds

7. Members shall take care to ensure that all solicitation materials are accurate, and correctly reflect the organization's mission and use of solicited funds.
8. Members shall take care to ensure that donors receive informed, accurate, and ethical advice about the value and tax implications of potential gifts.
9. Members shall take care to ensure that contributions are used in accordance with donors' intentions.
10. Members shall take care to ensure proper stewardship of charitable contributions, including timely reports on the use of management of funds.
11. Members shall obtain explicit consent by the donor before altering the conditions of a gift.

Presentation of Information

12. Members shall not disclose privileged or confidential information to unauthorized parties.
13. Members shall adhere to the principle that all donor and prospect information created by, or on behalf of, an organization is the property of that organization and shall not be transferred or utilized except on behalf of that organization.
14. Members shall give donors the opportunity to have their names removed from lists that are sold, rented to, or exchanged with other organizations.
15. Members shall, when stating fundraising results, use accurate and consistent accounting methods that conform to the appropriate guidelines adopted by the American Institute of Certified Public Accountants (AICPA)* for the type of organization involved. (*In countries outside of the United States, comparable authority should be utilized.)

Compensation

16. Members shall not accept compensation that is based on a percentage of charitable contributions; nor shall they accept finder's fees.
17. Members may accept performance-based compensation, such as bonuses, provided such bonuses are in accord with prevailing practices within the members' own organizations, and are not based on a percentage of charitable contributions.
18. Members shall not pay finder's fees, commissions or percentage compensation based on charitable contributions and shall take care to discourage their organizations from making such payments.

Appendix E

The Accountable Not-for-Profit Organization

Each not-for-profit organization holds a public trust to improve the quality of life.

The accountable organization clearly states its mission and purpose, articulates the needs of those being served, and explains how its programs work, how much they cost, and what benefits they produce.

The accountable organization freely and accurately shares information about its governance, finances, and operations. It is open and inclusive in its procedures, processes, and programs consistent with its mission and purpose.

The not-for-profit organization is accountable to all those it exists to serve, to all those who support it, and to society.

The accountable not-for-profit organization is responsible for mission fulfillment, leadership on behalf of the public interest, stewardship, and quality.

Mission Fulfillment

- Doing what it says it will do
- Maintaining relevance by meeting needs in a changing environment

Leadership on Behalf of the Public Interest

- Enhancing the well-being of communities and society
- Promoting inclusiveness, pluralism, and diversity within society
- Educating the public, business, not-for-profit organizations, and government, including appropriate advocacy and lobbying

Stewardship

- Maintaining effective governance and management
- Generating adequate resources, managing resources effectively, supporting and recognizing volunteers, and appropriately compensating staff

Quality

- Striving for and achieving excellence in all aspects of the organization
- Evaluating the total organization and its outcomes on an ongoing basis

Source: Accountability and Nonprofit Organizations, a Think Tank Program for National Nonprofit Sector Leaders, June 24–26, 1995, presented by the Mandel Center for Nonprofit Organizations and the National Health Council, supported by a grant from the Lilly Endowment, Inc.

Appendix F

Thoughts about Creating a Case for Support

What Is a Case for Support?

For fund development purposes, case for support refers to the written document that outlines everything anyone should know about your organization, the community need it serves, why charitable contributions are necessary, and how these gifts benefit the prospective donor.

The case for support is an *internal management document*, which is used by staff and volunteers. This document could be 10 or 15 pages long. It is your guidebook for why you are raising money.

From the case for support, you develop *external* communications materials for target audiences.

What Should Be Included in the Comprehensive Case for Support?

Think about writing a proposal to a foundation. What would you include?

1. *The problem (or opportunity) to be addressed.*
   Talk about community need. Talk about the people who need and want your service.
2. *Trends affecting the problem (or opportunity).*
   Demonstrate your knowledge and insight. What is happening in the world and your community that has produced this problem and what is happening now (and what do you anticipate happening in the future).
3. *Your response to the problem (or opportunity).*
   How does/will your organization respond to the community problem or opportunity? How will you respond to the trends?
4. *Role of the prospective donor.*
   Engage the prospective donor. Focus on target audiences and the key messages for each audi-

ence. Describe how a prospective donor might participate in addressing the community problem or opportunity. Talk about how you can help the prospective donor achieve his or her own goals and dreams. Describe donor acknowledgment and recognition opportunities.
5. *Your mission.*
   Now is the time to weave in your mission. You exist (your mission) because you wish to respond to community situations. Explain how your response to this particular community situation fits in with your overall mission.
6. *Your history, track record, and marketplace position.*
   Explain why you are the right organization to respond to this community situation. Talk about your track record. Demonstrate why the prospective donor should believe that giving money to your organization is a sound investment. Make sure you position your organization within the marketplace. How are you different from other organizations doing the same or similar work? Talk about cooperation and collaboration.
7. *Goals, strategies, and objectives.*
   Provide detail about how you will respond to the community situation. What, specifically, are you going to do? Why? When?
8. *Organizational resources.*
   Demonstrate that you have the resources necessary to address this situation. Describe your staff, professional expertise, volunteer structure, operations, and so forth. Talk about money: how you currently finance your organization and how you propose to finance this new activity; what kind of money is necessary; how you will raise the money; and who is helping you raise it.
9. *Accountability and evaluation.*

You must assure the prospective donor that you comply with all relevant regulations and laws and that you are good managers of the organization, its programs, and finances. Also describe how you evaluate program and institutional health.

10. *Future organization plans.*

Present your organization's goals and activities that will continue to help the community address the situation in the future.

How Do You Translate This Detailed Case into an Effective Public Communications Vehicle?

You write a case statement. You probably write multiple case statements.

This public communications vehicle expresses the magic of your vision. The case statement informs, inspires, and motivates people and groups to act.

A case statement is a message directed to a particular audience. The message is designed to stimulate a monetary response. How? By engaging the prospect and articulating benefits to him or her. By establishing your community's needs and your organization's ability to respond.

The case statement is your "brochure." However, you needn't produce an expensive brochure. Your case statement could be printed on your letterhead.

What Should Be Included in the Case Statement?

Include everything in the detailed case for support, but *much* briefer.

The case statement must be compelling. Create short and powerful messages. Use short, action-oriented statements. Use emotion and facts. The case statement uses copywriting. The comprehensive case for support does not.

The case statement describes how the donor's personal gift will fulfill his or her aspirations and help solve a specific problem. The case statement translates the community problem and your organization's response into compelling benefits to the prospective donor.

Different messages work for different audiences. You must personalize the message to the audience.

You must consider "packaging." What will the case statement actually look like? (The detailed, comprehensive case for support is simply typed on 8 1/2″ by 11″ pieces of paper.) Your case statement might be designed into a brochure. Or it might be more appropriate for you to use regular paper or your standard letterhead.

Make sure that the packaging reflects your values. Just because a designer and printer will donate their services, don't get too glitzy, even if the brochure says "donated"

all over it. Glitzy might conflict with your values and what you want to transmit to your prospective donors.

How Do You Develop the Case for Support and the Case Statement?

1. Gather together your existing organizational information. Things such as:
   - values and vision statements
   - mission statement
   - strategic plan
   - descriptions about your various services
   - service statistics and growth patterns
   - articles and community information about the problem or opportunity
   - organization budget and operational descriptions
   - your favorite proposals
   - media articles about your organization

2. Look for powerful quotations about your organization and the community problem or situation. Find those testimonials from clients. Look at the newspaper articles about your organization.

3. Conduct brainstorming sessions with staff, board, and fund development leadership. This is a great way to develop understanding, ownership, and support. Use the sample questions below or invent your own.

4. Write. Write. Write the detailed case for support.

5. Review the general content of the comprehensive case for support with the board. Do not wordsmith. Secure formal board approval.

6. From the comprehensive case for support, pull out the key points for the case statement. Test this information with targeted prospects. (Use focus groups and personal meetings. This is a wonderful cultivation strategy.) Adjust as necessary.

7. Draft the case statement "brochure." You may wish to use a professional copywriter. The executive director approves the case statement. (She or he may find it useful to show the final copy to the campaign chair(s) and board president prior to final approval.) The case statement is then provided as a finished/printed document to the fund development leadership, staff, and board.

Suggested Questions for Brainstorming Sessions with Staff and Board

Remember, for questions 1 and 2 below, you have already made these decisions. You are not doing strategic planning. You are not brainstorming new ways to respond. You are articulating what you have already decided.

You work from your organization's strategic plan. You state what you have already decided—clearly, concisely, and with substantiation.

Now ask your board and staff these questions:

1. How would you describe the community problem/ opportunity that our organization wants to address? Describe the facts. Describe the trends affecting the problem. Provide actual figures. Use brief, powerful phrases. Use emotion.
2. Based on our strategic plan (what we have decided we will do), how would you describe how our organization will address this community problem?
3. Describe—with facts and emotions—why we are the best organization to do this work.
4. Briefly and concisely, what are the top five messages we want to convey in this fundraising program? Who are our target audiences for each message?
5. Given our targeted audiences, are there additional messages some of those audiences might want to hear?

6. What are the most powerful personal stories we can tell about our successes?

Suggested Questions for Brainstorming Sessions with Fund Development Leadership, Donors, Prospects, and Clients

Take a look at the results of the staff and board brainstorming sessions.

Decide what should be the top five messages and the targeted audiences. Now test these messages:

1. Are these the appropriate messages we need to convey to our target audiences? Do these messages adequately and appropriately represent the organization and what we are trying to achieve? Are there any modifications to general content?
2. Given our target audiences, are there any additional messages that are necessary?
3. What are the most powerful personal stories we can tell about our successes?

You can also ask participants to comment on the key points gathered together for the case for support.

Selected Bibliography—To Help You Be a Better Fundraiser and Organizational Development Specialist

Argyris, Chris. "Good Communication That Blocks Learning," *Harvard Business Review*, July–August 1994.

Block, Peter. *Stewardship: Choosing Service Over Self-Interest.* San Francisco: Berrett-Koehler Publishers, 1993.

Bolman, Lee G. and Terrence E. Deal. *Leading with Soul: An Uncommon Journey of Spirit.* San Francisco: Jossey-Bass, Publishers, 1995.

Bridges, William. *Managing Transitions: Making the Most of Change.* New York: Addison-Wesley Publishing, 1991.

Carver, John. *Boards That Make A Difference: A New Design for Leadership on Nonprofit and Public Organizations.* San Francisco: Jossey-Bass, Publishers, 1991. See also *The Policy Governance Fieldbook*, Caroline Oliver, General Editor. San Francisco: Jossey-Bass, Publishers, 1999.

Collins, James C. and Jerry I. Porras. *Built to Last.* New York: HarperCollins Publishers, 1994.

Conger, Jay A., David Finegold, and Edward E. Lawler III. "Appraising Boardroom Performance," *Harvard Business Review*, January–February 1998.

Dayton, Kenneth N. "Governance Is Governance," Occasional paper from the Independent Sector, Washington, DC, (202) 223-8100.

De Geus, Arie. "Planning as Learning," *Harvard Business Review*, March–April 1988.

De Geus, Arie. "The Living Company," *Harvard Business Review*, March–April 1997.

DePree, Max. *Leadership Is an Art.* New York: Dell Publishing, 1989.

Donaldson, Thomas. "Values in Tension: Ethics Away from Home," *Harvard Business Review*, September–October 1996.

Eisenhardt, Kathleen M., Jean L. Kahwajy, and L.J. Bourgeois III. "How Management Teams Can Have a Good Fight," *Harvard Business Review*, July–August 1997.

Ellinor, Linda and Glenna Gerard. *Dialogue: Rediscover the Transforming Power of Conversation.* New York: John Wiley & Sons, 1998.

Fast Company, a regular magazine about how smart business works. PO Box 52760, Boulder, CO 80321–2760. (800) 688-1545.

Gardner, John W. *Building Community.* Independent Sector, Washington, DC, September 1991.

Gardner, John W. *On Leadership.* New York: Free Press, 1990.

Godfrey, Joline. *Our Wildest Dreams: Women Entrepreneurs Making Money, Having Fun, Doing Good: A Whole New Definition of Success and an Entirely New Paradigm of Working Life.* New York: HarperCollins Publishers, 1992.

Hamel, Gary. "Strategy as Revolution," *Harvard Business Review*, July–August 1996.

Herzlinger, Regina E. "Effective Oversight: A Guide for Nonprofit Directors," *Harvard Business Review*, July–August 1994.

Katzenbach, Jon R. and Douglas K. Smith. *The Wisdom of Teams: Creating the High-Performance Organization.* New York: HarperCollins Publishers, 1993.

Keshavan, Nair. *A Higher Standard of Leadership: Lessons from the Life of Gandhi.* San Francisco: Berrett-Koehler Publishers, 1994.

Leader to Leader. Quarterly publication of the Peter F. Drucker Foundation for Nonprofit Management and Jossey-Bass, Publishers. (888) 378-2537.

McFarlan, F. Warren, "Working on Nonprofit Boards: Don't Assume the Shoe Fits," *Harvard Business Review*, November–December 1999.

Perdido: Leadership with a Conscience. Homewood, IL: Trinity Foundation/High Tide Press, (708) 206-2054.

Pottruck, David S. and Terry Pearce. *Clicks and Mortar: Passion Driven Growth in an Internet Driven World.* San Francisco: Jossey-Bass, Publishers.

Pound, John. "The Promise of the Governed Corporation," *Harvard Business Review*, March–April 1995.

Senge, Peter M. *The Fifth Discipline: The Art and Practice of a Learning Organization.* New York: Doubleday, 1990.

Senge, Peter M., Art Kleiner, Charlotte Roberts, Richard B. Ross, and Bryan J. Smith. *The Fifth Discipline Fieldbook: Strategies and Tools for Building a Learning Organization.* New York: Doubleday, 1994.

Systems Thinker, a newsletter published ten times per year by Pegasus Communications, Inc. Waltham, MA. (781) 398-9700.

Taylor, Barbara E., Richard P. Chait, Thomas P. Holland. "The New Work of the Nonprofit Board," *Harvard Business Review*, September–October 1996.

Index

Not-for-profit organization
  accountable organization, 338
  creating value, 2
  effective, 1
  entitlement, 4
  as human-change agents, 13
  increased scrutiny, 4–5

O

Obsolescence, 6
Organization
  relevance, 5
  traditional, 1–2
Organizational culture, xi, 14–15. *See also* Corporate
  culture
  defined, 14
Organizational development, 54–55
  culture of philanthropy, 54
Organizational life cycle
  emerging, 261
  enabling, 261
  institutionalizing, 261
  maturing, 261
Organizational relationship, enabling, 247

P

Pacesetting leader, 30, 31
Participatory decision making, 46–49
  advantages, 46
Partnership, 262
  enabling, 248
  requirements, 248
Personal engagement, 12
Philanthropy
  basic marketing exchange, 11–12
  community needs and wants, 3
  defined, xi, 2
Planning. *See also* Specific type
  defined, 59
  fund development, 327
Planning committee, strategic planning,
  65–66
Planning process manager
  consultant, 68–69
  strategic planning, 67–69
    as analyst, 67
    attributes, 67–68
    as catalyst, 67
    responsibilities, 68
    as strategy finder, 67

Planning retreat, 97–98
  strategic planning, 63, 77
    format, 78, 79, 132
Political climate, 4
Predisposed, 171–173
  defined, 155, 169
  identifying, 171–173, 202
Process, 41, 169–176, 172
Prospect
  defined, 155, 169
  designing the ask, 216
  determining capacity, 215
  evaluating readiness and interest, 215
  evaluation, 175
  worksheet, 212–216
Public relations, pitfalls, 183

Q

Quality improvement, 118
Question
  change, 42–43
  conversation, 42–46

R

Readiness, 215
Reflective practitioner, 31–32
Relationship, ix
  community relationship, 2
  constituent relationship, 2
  development, personal and organizational attributes,
    8
  four key relationships, 2
  internal relationship, 2
  volunteer relationship, 2
Reputation, marketing, 163
Research. *See also* Market research
  constituency development, 166, 176–179
  formal and informal contact, 180–181
  methods, 180–182
  report, 181–182
  resources, 181–182
Risk, decision making, 46

S

Self-awareness, 29
Self-interest, 12
Self-management, 29

About the Author

Simone P. Joyaux, ACFRE, provides consulting services in fund development, board and organizational development, planning, and personnel. Clients include all types and sizes of not-for-profit organizations in the United States and other countries. Joyaux works with health and human service organizations, arts, cultural and educational institutions, environmental and advocacy groups, and other philanthropic organizations. Ms. Joyaux also provides services to government agencies and foundations. She has helped for-profit corporations develop their volunteer programs and outline long-range direction.

Ms. Joyaux is a recognized international speaker, talking about fund development, planning, and organizational development issues. She serves as a faculty member for the Master of Arts Program in Philanthropy and Fund Development at St. Mary's University of Minnesota.

Ms. Joyaux is one of the few individuals who hold advanced certification in the fundraising profession. In 1994, she achieved the credential of Advanced Certified Fund Raising Executive (ACFRE), based on a rigorous peer review process, demonstrating an advanced level of fundraising knowledge and professional competency.

Ms. Joyaux has more than 25 years of experience working in the not-for-profit sector. As staff, she has served as an executive director and chief development officer. As a volunteer, she has served on numerous boards of directors, in the capacity of president, development and nominating committee chairs, and director-at-large.

Nationally, Ms. Joyaux has served as the chair of the CFRE Professional Certification Board, the international baseline credential for fundraisers, and the State Arts Advocacy League of America. She has served as an officer of the Association of Fundraising Professionals (AFP), formerly the National Society of Fund Raising Executives (NSFRE), and as a board member of the Family Foundation of North America and the Alumni Board of the Michigan State University College of Arts and Letters.

Locally, she was the founding president of RI Arts Advocates and has been a board member of the Sexual Assault and Trauma Resource Center, RI Coalition of Library Advocates, and Looking Glass Theatre. Currently, she is starting a women's fund for Rhode Island, to be held at the Rhode Island Foundation.

Ms. Joyaux lives in Rhode Island (and in France) with her husband, Tom Ahern, a marketing and communications consultant.